# ABSOLUTE BSD
## The Ultimate Guide to FreeBSD

# ABSOLUTE BSD

# The Ultimate Guide to FreeBSD

## Michael Lucas

**NO STARCH
PRESS**

San Francisco

Printed in the United States of America

2 3 4 5 6 7 8 9 10–05  04  03

BSD Daemon Copyright ©1988 by Marshall Kirk McKusick. All rights reserved. Reprinted with permission.

Publisher: William Pollock
Editorial Director: Karol Jurado
Cover and Interior Design: Octopod Studios
Composition: 1106 Design, LLC
Copyeditor: Andy Carroll
Proofreader: Robyn Brode
Indexer: Kevin Broccoli

Distributed to the book trade in the United States by Publishers Group West, 1700 Fourth Street, Berkeley, CA 94710; phone: 800-788-3123; fax: 510-658-1834.

Distributed to the book trade in Canada by Jacqueline Gross & Associates, Inc., One Atlantic Avenue, Suite 105, Toronto, Ontario M6K 3E7 Canada; phone: 416-531-6737; fax 416-531-4259.

For information on translations or book distributors outside the United States, please contact No Starch Press, Inc. directly:

No Starch Press, Inc.
555 De Haro Street, Suite 250, San Francisco, CA 94107
phone: 415-863-9900; fax: 415-863-9950; info@nostarch.com; http://www.nostarch.com

*Library of Congress Cataloguing-in-Publication Data*

```
Lucas, Michael, 1967-
      Absolute BSD : the ultimate guide to FreeBSD / Michael Lucas.
              p. cm.
      Includes index.
      ISBN 1-886411-74-3 (pbk.)
        1. FreeBSD.  2. UNIX (Computer file) 3. Internet service
providers--Computer programs. 4. Web servers--Computer programs. 5.
Client/server computing.  I. Title.
QA76.76.063 L83 2002
005.4'4769--dc21
```

                                                                    2002001428

As always, for Liz

# ACKNOWLEDGMENTS

I would like to thank all the members of the FreeBSD community for their hard work, dedication, and friendship. FreeBSD has saved my hide on numerous occasions, and has taught me immense amounts about how computers and the Internet really work. I have yet to speak with the president of a software company, whereas I've spent many hours discussing FreeBSD with project leaders.

Having said that, there are a few people in that community who deserve my particular thanks for reviewing the book in your hands. They are, in order, Szilvester Adam, John Baldwin, Wilko Bulte, Chris Dillon, Giorgos Keramidas, Chris Knight, and Joel Wilsson. Any errors in this book were introduced by myself, despite their best efforts.

The folks at No Starch Press also deserve my heartfelt thanks for actually bringing this to print. My original manuscript needed a lot of work to become something that looks decent on the printed page. Thanks, guys, and I'll make it easier next time. I would also like to thank Chris Coleman, my editor at OnLamp.com, who brought No Starch Press and I together in the first place.

Most of all I want to thank my wife, Liz, for her patience and support while I sat in the corner and muttered under my breath for months at a time while writing this book.

**Michael Lucas**
**St. Clair Shores, Michigan**

# BRIEF CONTENTS

# CONTENTS IN DETAIL

## INTRODUCTION

# 1

## INSTALLATION

# 2
## GETTING MORE HELP

# 3
## READ THIS BEFORE YOU BREAK SOMETHING ELSE!
## (BACKUP AND RECOVERY)

# 4

## KERNEL GAMES

# 5

## NETWORKING

# 6

## UPGRADING FREEBSD

# 7
## SECURING YOUR SYSTEM

# 8
## ADVANCED SECURITY FEATURES

# 9

## TOO MUCH INFORMATION ABOUT /ETC

# 10
# MAKING YOUR SYSTEM USEFUL

# 11

## ADVANCED SOFTWARE MANAGEMENT

# 12

## FINDING HOSTS WITH DNS

# 13

## MANAGING SMALL NETWORK SERVICES

# 14

## EMAIL SERVICES

# 15

## WEB AND FTP SERVICES

# 16

## FILESYSTEMS AND DISKS

# 17

## RAID

# 18

## SYSTEM PERFORMANCE

# 19

## NOW WHAT'S IT DOING?

# 20

## SYSTEM CRASHES AND PANICS

# 21
## DESKTOP FREEBSD

## AFTERWORD

# FOREWORD

Twenty five years. My god, has it really been that long? In 1976, the first BSD release was produced by U.C. Berkeley's CSRG, it and subsequent releases of BSD having either spawned or substantially influenced every Unix operating system to come after, including Linux and AT&T's System V, through a commitment to innovation and to adding all the "missing pieces" that Unix was lacking. Features like Virtual Memory, TCP/IP networking, job control, and even the venerable vi screen editor (before which there was simply ed(1)) all came out of BSD. Not just operating systems, but a number of POSIX and X/Open standards also owe their existence to it—an influential "little project" indeed!

We started FreeBSD in 1992, a project that you'll read quite a bit about in this book, as a means of carrying this work forward after the CSRG was disbanded and it looked like the BSD project, for all its history and promise, might be coming to an end. This was not a state of affairs that BSD's many fans were willing to settle for, and I'm happy to say that they rallied magnificently to the cause.

Far from being the end of BSD, the last 10 years have seen an almost explosive amount growth in the BSD community, with FreeBSD operating systems powering some of the most significant companies and sites on the Internet, setting new bandwidth and "uptime" records and making the acronym BSD almost synonymous with high performance, security, and reliability for those in the Internet service industry.

FreeBSD's success has also hardly been limited to servers. With Apple's adoption of FreeBSD as a key open-source technology for its Mac OS X operating system, it has since been introduced to a whole new generation of enthusiastic users, many of whom would never have considered themselves Unix users before but are now enjoying the benefits of a powerful operating system combined with Apple's legendary user interface technology and a world-class suite of applications. Even the most jaded Unix experts have been impressed at what BSD has grown into, and I suspect that, at this point, it has surpassed even the wildest dreams of its creators.

Whether you're a Unix expert or someone who has never touched Unix before, you'll find this book to be an excellent introduction to the unique and impressive world that is BSD. If you enjoy it even half as much as I have, you're in for a great time!

**Jordan Hubbard**
**Co-Founder, The FreeBSD Project**

# INTRODUCTION

Welcome to *Absolute BSD*! This book is a one-stop shop for new UNIX administrators who want to build, configure, and manage dedicated FreeBSD servers. It will also be useful for those folks who want to run FreeBSD on their desktop or combined desktop/ server systems.

By the time you finish this book, you should be able to use FreeBSD to provide network services. You should also understand how to manage, patch, and maintain your FreeBSD systems, and have a basic understanding of networking, system security, and software management. We will discuss FreeBSD version 4, which is the version recommended for production use as this book is being released. Most of this book will be applicable to earlier and later versions, as well. Much of this book is also applicable to NetBSD and OpenBSD.

## What Is FreeBSD?

FreeBSD is a UNIX-like operating system,[1] available freely over the Internet, that is used extensively in the ISP (Internet service provider) world, embedded devices, and anywhere reliability is paramount. It's based directly on the original UNIX produced by AT&T in the 1970s.

Many years ago AT&T needed a lot of computer software to run their business. They were not allowed to compete in the computer business, however. As a result, they licensed various pieces of software, and the source code for it, to universities at low, low prices. University students with access to this nifty technology could read the source code to learn how it worked. In return, AT&T got free exposure, some pocket change, and a generation of computer scientists who cut their teeth on their equipment. Everyone was happy. The best-known software distributed under this licensing plan was UNIX.

## How Did FreeBSD Get Here?

Compared with modern operating systems, the original UNIX wasn't very good. But, since so many students had the source code for UNIX, and so many teachers needed projects for their students, UNIX was quickly improved by their efforts. Gradually, useful commands were built. The ability to control running programs (also known as *job control*) was added. A filesystem appeared that supported features we take for granted now. Over many years, entire chunks of the original UNIX operating system were extracted and replaced.

The various universities that worked on UNIX shared their improvements and enhancements, with the Computer Systems Research Group (CSRG) at the University of California, Berkeley, acting as a central clearinghouse for UNIX code improvements. The CSRG distributed this code for free to anyone with a valid AT&T UNIX license.

The resulting collection of patches for UNIX came to be known as the Berkeley Software Distribution, or BSD UNIX. (It didn't hurt Berkeley's status any that the Defense Advanced Research Projects Agency (DARPA) contributed funding to the CSRG to implement TCP/IP in UNIX.)

This development process continued for a long, long time. In fact, if you look at the copyright statement on FreeBSD, you'll see this:

```
Copyright 1979, 1980, 1983, 1986, 1988, 1989, 1991, 1992, 1993, 1994
         The Regents of the University of California. All rights reserved.
```

[1] Why UNIX-like? Well, the word UNIX is a trademark that belongs to The Open Group. For an operating system to be certified "UNIX," someone must pay The Open Group large chunks of money. Since FreeBSD is developed in a not-for-profit manner, this isn't likely.

Yep, 15 years of work—a lifetime in software development. In fact, so much development went into the original UNIX that the CSRG found that over the years they had replaced almost all of UNIX with code created by the CSRG and their contributors. What remained of AT&T's work was actually pretty small.

## The BSD License: BSD Goes Public

Eventually, the CSRG's funding started running out. After some political wrangling within the University of California, in 1992 the code was released to the general public under what became known as the BSD license. Today, the BSD license has three clauses that can be summarized as follows:

- Don't claim you wrote this.
- Don't blame us if it breaks.
- Don't use our name to promote your product.

(The original license required that every time someone used the software, they had to include a notice that it included software copyrighted by the University of California. This requirement was dropped a few years later. Today, people can use BSD code without having to announce it or notify anyone.)

The BSD license may be the most liberal software license ever used. People are free to take BSD and include it in proprietary products, free products, and open-source products, or print it out on punch cards and cover the lawn with it.

Instead of "copyright," the BSD license is sometimes referred to as "copycenter," as in "take this down to the copy center and run off a few for yourself." Not surprisingly, companies such as Sun Microsystems jumped right on it because, well, it was free.

## The Birth of Modern FreeBSD

During the CSRG's heyday, however, UNIX work proceeded apace at AT&T. AT&T took parts of the BSD UNIX distribution and integrated them with their UNIX, then turned around and relicensed the result.

This worked well for AT&T until the grand breakup, when the mother of all telephone companies suddenly was permitted to compete in the software business. They had one particularly valuable property: a high-end operating system that had been extensively debugged by thousands of people all over the world. They happily started selling UNIX to enterprises and charging very high fees for it, all the while maintaining the university relationships that had given them such an advanced operating system.

Berkeley's 1992 release of the BSD code met with great displeasure from AT&T's subsidiary USL (UNIX System Laboratories). Almost immediately they took some of the software users, and the university, to court. USL claimed that Berkeley had given away their intellectual property. The University of California said that it was their intellectual property. In the meantime, various people picked up on the code released by Berkeley and began building commercial and free products out of it. One of these products was 386BSD, which would eventually be used as the core of FreeBSD 1.0.

In 1994, after two years of legal wrangling, the case was settled out of court once it was proved that a great deal of the code in AT&T UNIX was actually taken in its entirety from BSD, rather than the other way around! A half-dozen files were the only sources of contention, and to resolve these outstanding issues some of the files were donated and others were kept proprietary. Unfortunately, FreeBSD 1.X contained some of these files, so various BSD users worked frantically to rebuild these missing components.

Once the dust settled, this new version of UNIX was released to the world as BSD4.4-Lite. A subsequent update, BSD4.4-Lite2, is the grandfather of the current FreeBSD source, as well as the ancestor of many other operating systems, such as NetBSD, OpenBSD, and Mac OS X.

Today FreeBSD is used throughout the Internet by some of the most vital and visible Internet-oriented companies. For example, at this writing, Yahoo! is run almost entirely on FreeBSD. The "baby Bell" US West uses FreeBSD to power its Internet operations. IBM, Nokia, and many other hardware companies use FreeBSD in embedded systems where you'd never even know it's there.

The fact is, if a company needs to pump some serious Internet bandwidth, it's probably running FreeBSD. FreeBSD is all around you; you just may not see it because it rarely crashes.

## FreeBSD Development

There's an old saying that managing programmers is like herding cats. However, despite what you might think, for the most part these FreeBSD developers work well together as members of the FreeBSD team. And, unlike some other projects, all FreeBSD development happens openly. Two groups of people develop FreeBSD: contributors and committers.

### Committers

Today, FreeBSD has almost 300 developers, or *committers*. Committers have read-and-write access to the FreeBSD master source-code repository and can develop, debug, or enhance any piece they deem necessary.

To plug yourself in to the beehive of FreeBSD development, consider subscribing to the mailing list FreeBSD-hackers@FreeBSD.org, which contains most of the technical discussion. Some of the technical talk is broken out into more specific mailing lists—for example, the networking development is discussed on FreeBSD-net@FreeBSD.org. There are also a few IRC channels where the FreeBSD crew hangs out and discusses things. Visitors and eavesdroppers are welcome, so long as they don't interfere. (Yes, Internet chat can be used for a variety of useful technical purposes!) The committers are responsible for keeping FreeBSD working, adding new features, and evaluating patches from contributors. Most of these developers are volunteers; only a handful are actually paid to do this painstaking work.

### Contributors

In addition to the committer team, FreeBSD has thousands of contributors. Contributors don't have to worry about breaking the main operating system repository; they just submit patches for consideration by committers. Committers evaluate submissions and decide what to accept and what to reject. A contributor who submits consistently acceptable code will frequently be asked by the committers he works with to become a committer himself.

For example, I spent several years as a contributor. Any time I feel that I've wasted my life, I can go look at the FreeBSD Web page and see where my work has been accepted by the committers and used by thousands of users. (It helps. Sort of.) Between submitting this book and getting it back from the editor, however, I had some spare time. I spent a while submitting patches to the FreeBSD FAQ. Eventually, some members of the FreeBSD Project approached me and asked me to become a committer. I initially refused, but finally allowed a few developers to persuade me.[2]

### Users

Finally, FreeBSD has a mob of users, though it's impossible to realistically estimate their number. After all, you can download the whole of FreeBSD for free, and never register, upgrade, or mail to a mailing list.

Estimates are that somewhere between 5 and 10 percent of the machines on the Internet are BSD-based. That's 5–10 percent of all the systems connected to the Internet, including the countless Windows systems sitting on office desks. If you remove those systems from the count and only count Internet servers, the percentage rises.

Since FreeBSD is by far the most popular open-source BSD, that's not an inconsiderable number of machines. And since one FreeBSD server can handle hundreds or thousands of Internet domains, a disproportionate number of sites uses FreeBSD compared to the number of servers.

## Other BSDs

FreeBSD is the most popular BSD, but it's not the only one. BSD 4.4-Lite spawned several different projects, each with its own focus and purpose.

### NetBSD

NetBSD is similar to FreeBSD in many ways, and the teams share developers and code. NetBSD's main purpose is to provide an operating system that can be ported to any hardware platform.

As such, NetBSD runs on VAXes, PocketPC devices, and high-end Alpha servers, as well as the Compaq iPaq. It even runs on hardware that doesn't exist yet—as I write this, the AMD Sledgehammer is fully supported even though you can't get sample chips. Now *that's* portable.

---

[2] And some day I might forgive Will, Wilko, and Bruce for that. But I'll *never* let them live it down.

The NetBSD code is specifically licensed to be freely reusable, just like the original BSD 4.4-Lite code it's based on.

### OpenBSD

OpenBSD branched off from NetBSD in 1996 with the goal of becoming the most secure BSD. OpenBSD was the first to support hardware-accelerated cryptography (allowing it to encrypt and decrypt information at a remarkable rate), and the developers are rather proud of the fact that their default install hasn't been hacked remotely for over four years.

The OpenBSD people have audited the entire BSD code base, fixing most (but not all) potential security holes before they can be exploited. OpenBSD is not as friendly or as easy to use as FreeBSD, however.

### BSD/OS

BSD/OS, produced by Wind River Systems, is a commercial, closed-source operating system that greatly resembles FreeBSD. Some hardware manufacturers will not release hardware specifications without nondisclosure agreements, and developers for a freely available operating system cannot develop device drivers for such proprietary hardware. BSD/OS supports much of this hardware.

A great deal of the BSD/OS code is available to FreeBSD committers, and FreeBSD absorbs BSD/OS enhancements that don't break nondisclosure agreements.

### Mac OS X

Mac OS X? That's right. Large chunks of FreeBSD were incorporated into Apple's Mac OS X. If you're looking for a stable operating system with a friendly face and a powerful core, Mac OS X is unquestionably for you. While FreeBSD makes an excellent desktop for a computer professional, I wouldn't put it in front of grandma. I would put Mac OS X in front of grandma without a second thought, and even feel that I was doing the right thing.

Mac OS X includes a lot of things that aren't at all necessary for an Internet server, however, and it only runs on Apple hardware, so I don't recommend it for an inexpensive, high-powered server.

While you cannot get the user interface source code for Mac OS X, you can view the operating system's BSD core and Mach kernel; Apple has released them under the code name Darwin.

## Other UNIXes

There are several other UNIX operating systems out there, some of which have even rented the trademark UNIX so they can label themselves as such. This list is by no means exhaustive, but we'll touch the high points.

### Solaris

The best-known UNIX is Sun Microsystems' Solaris. Solaris runs on high-end hardware that supports dozens of processors and gobs of disks. (Yes, "gobs" is a technical term.) It's used by many enterprise-level applications, such as Oracle.

Solaris runs mainly on the SPARC hardware platform, which is manufactured by Sun. Since Sun controls both the hardware and software, they can make their systems support many interesting features, such as hot-swappable memory and main boards.

### AIX

Another UNIX contender is IBM's AIX. AIX's main claim to fame is the journaling filesystem, which records all disk transactions as they happen. It allows you to recover from system crashes without much trouble, providing great reliability. AIX includes a great deal of BSD code.

### Linux

Linux is a clone of UNIX, written from the ground up in the last decade or so. Linux is similar to BSD in many ways, though BSD has a much longer heritage, and is more friendly to commercial use than Linux. Linux includes a requirement that a commercial user contribute all changes back to Linux, while BSD has no such restriction.

Among many UNIX users, there's a perception of conflict between the BSD and Linux camps. If you dig a little deeper, however, you'll find that most of the developers of these platforms communicate and cooperate in a friendly and open manner. It's just a hard fringe of users and a very few developers that generate friction.

### IRIX, HPUX, etc.

Other UNIXes include Silicon Graphics' IRIX, a solid UNIX for graphics applications, and Hewlett-Packard's HP-UX, popular in large enterprises. Many high-end software packages, such as Informix, are specially designed for HP-UX.

If you look around you'll also find smaller contenders, such as SCO and UnixWare. They aren't unimportant, they just aren't as popular. You'll also find old castoffs, such as Apple's A/UX and Microsoft's Xenix. (Yes, Microsoft was a licensed UNIX vendor, very, very long ago.) Xenix was eventually sold to SCO and became SCO UNIX.

## FreeBSD's Strengths

So, after all this, how can we summarize FreeBSD?

### Portability

FreeBSD's goal is to provide a freely redistributable operating system that runs on popular hardware. While system security is a vital concern, FreeBSD's main goal is to run on the hardware people are most likely to have. Today, this means the Intel x86-compatible systems (386, 486, Pentium I through IV, Celeron, and AMD). FreeBSD also supports the Alpha processor, and work is underway to support Intel's new IA64, AMD's new 64-bit chips, and Motorola's PowerPC, as well as Sun's SPARC. (These platforms aren't afterthoughts; the hardware is just now coming out, or only now becoming popular enough to port to.)

### Power

Since FreeBSD runs adequately on 386 hardware, it runs quite well on modern computers. It's rather nice to have an operating system that doesn't demand a Pentium III and a half-gig of RAM just to power the user interface. As a result, you can actually use all that computing power to do the work you want, rather than to run tasks you don't care about. If you choose to run a pretty graphical interface with all sorts of spinning geegaws and fancy whistles, FreeBSD will support you, it just won't require you to do so.

### Simplified Software Management

FreeBSD also simplifies software management through its ports collection. Traditionally, tuning software for a UNIX system has required considerable expertise. The ports collection simplifies this considerably by automating and documenting the install, uninstall, and configuration process for thousands of software packages. (Several other BSD operating systems have built their own packaging systems based on the ports collection.)

### Optimized Upgrade Process

Unlike operating systems that require painful and risky upgrade procedures, such as Windows, FreeBSD's simple upgrade process builds an operating system that is optimized for your hardware and application. This lets FreeBSD use every feature your hardware supports, instead of just the lowest common denominator. If you change hardware, you can rebuild your system for that particular hardware. Vendors such as Sun and Apple do exactly this, since they create both the hardware and the operating system, but FreeBSD doesn't lock you in to a particular hardware platform.

### Filesystem

A *filesystem* is how information is stored on the physical disk—it is what maps "My Web Page" to a series of zeros and ones on the metal disk in your hard drive. FreeBSD includes very sophisticated filesystems. It can support files up to a petabyte (one thousand thousand gigabytes) in size, it is highly damage-resistant, and it reads and writes files extremely quickly. The BSD filesystem is so advanced that it has been adopted by many commercial UNIX vendors, such as Sun and HP.

## Who Should Use FreeBSD

While FreeBSD can be used as a very powerful desktop or development machine, its history shows a strong bias toward Web, mail, file, and support services. In fact, FreeBSD's main strength is on Internet servers, and it is an excellent choice for any Internet service.

If you're thinking of running FreeBSD (or any UNIX) on your desktop, you'll need to understand how your computer works. FreeBSD is not your best choice if you're looking for point-and-click simplicity. If that's your goal, get a Macintosh computer and use Mac OS X, which has a BSD core, so you can access the power of UNIX when you want it and not worry about it the rest of the time. Or, if you want to use the lowest common denominator, there's always the various iterations of Microsoft Windows. You won't have to understand your computer, but Windows is easy.

## FreeBSD as Your Desktop

You can, of course, use FreeBSD as a powerful desktop OS.

There's a concept in computing called "eating your own dog food." If you ran a dog food company, you'd want to make a product that your own dog would eat. If your dog turns up his nose at your latest recipe, your company has a problem. The point here is that if you work with a product, you should actually use it.

This total immersion method provides the fastest possible training and is the approach I took to learn UNIX. By running FreeBSD exclusively on my desktop, I learned how to make a UNIX system do anything I needed, and I became a much more powerful server administrator as a result.

In fact, I even wrote this book on my FreeBSD laptop, using an open-source word processor (Emacs) and a business suite called StarOffice. I also use FreeBSD to watch MPEG video from unencrypted video CDs and DVDs, burn MP3s from my own CDs, and listen to the MP3s when I should be working. This is a fairly exhaustive sample of desktop tasks.

Desktop operating systems also allow you to do all sorts of silly things. At the moment, I have a small animated BSD daemon sleeping under my mouse pointer. When I move the mouse, the daemon awakens, chases down the pointer, and stabs it with his pitchfork. If this doesn't count as a Stupid Desktop Trick, I don't know what does.

## Who Should Run Another BSD

NetBSD is FreeBSD's closest competitor. However, unlike competitors in the commercial world, this competition is mostly friendly. NetBSD and FreeBSD share code and developers freely; some people even maintain the same subsystem in both operating systems. For example, NetBSD and FreeBSD share their USB support. In fact, as I write this, work is actively underway to integrate the FTP server used in both operating systems.

NetBSD's main advantage is that it runs on anything. For example, I have an ancient Silicon Graphics workstation running NetBSD that I use as an NFS (Network File System) and DNS (Domain Name System) server. It does the job. If you have old or weird hardware, NetBSD is a good choice for you.

OpenBSD seems to stand apart from the rest of the BSD projects. While its code is available for general use, the developers appear to be more interested in security than in making their system approachable. OpenBSD has features that make it easy to do tasks such as bridging firewalls, however, so if you find you can't do some security work in FreeBSD, check out OpenBSD.

## Who Should Run a Proprietary Operating System

Proprietary operating systems like Sun's Solaris, Microsoft's Windows NT, IBM's AIX, and their ilk are still quite popular despite the BSDs and Linux gnawing at their market share. Solaris, in particular, holds a great deal of the UNIX market.

High-end enterprises (the Fortune 500) are fairly closely shackled to Solaris and Windows NT. While this is slowly changing, it is true for now, and in such environments you're probably stuck with those operating systems. But slipping in an occasional FreeBSD machine to handle basic services such as DNS and file serving can make your life much easier at a much lower cost.

Of course, if your software will only run on a proprietary UNIX, your choice of operating system is probably clear. Still, always ask a vendor if a FreeBSD version is available; you may be pleasantly surprised.

## How to Read This Book

Many computer books are thick enough to stun an ox, if you can lift them high enough without an athletic supporter and a back brace. Plus, they're either encyclopedic in scope or so painfully detailed that they're difficult to read. Do you really need a screenshot when you're told to "click OK" or "accept the license agreement"? And when was the last time you actually sat down and read the encyclopedia?

*Absolute BSD* is a little different. It's designed to be read once, from front to back. You can skip around if you want to, but each chapter builds on what comes before. It's also short enough to be digestible. After you've read it once, you can easily use it as a reference.

(If you're a frequent buyer of computer books, please feel free to insert all the usual stuff about "read a chapter at a time for best learning" and so on. I'm not going to coddle you—if you picked up a book on computing, you probably have two brain cells to rub together. Follow the examples, and you'll learn.)

## What Must You Know?

This book is aimed at the new UNIX administrator. Several years ago the new UNIX administrator was already a skilled UNIX user with real programming skills and a degree in computer science, or at least most of one. Today, UNIX-like operating systems are freely available from the Internet and even 12-year-old children can run UNIX, read the source code, and learn enough to intimidate us older folks. As such, I don't expect you to know a huge amount about UNIX before firing it up.

To use this book to its full potential, you should be familiar with some of the basic UNIX commands, such as how to change directories (cd), list files in a directory (ls), and log in with a username and password. If you're not familiar with basic commands and running UNIX from the shell, I recommend you begin with a book like *UNIX System Administration Handbook* by Evi Nemeth, Garth Snyder, Scott Seebass, and Trent R. Hein (Prentice Hall PTR).

You'll also need to know something about PC hardware. (Not a huge amount, mind you, but some.) For example, it will help to know what an IRQ (interrupt request) is and how to differentiate between a SCSI and IDE hard drive. Your need for hardware knowledge will, of course, depend on the hardware you're using, but if you're interested enough to pick up this book and read this far, you probably have the hardware knowledge that you need. We'll make this a little easier by assuming you're dedicating a system to FreeBSD; very few network servers dual-boot Windows and FreeBSD, after all!

**NOTE**  *Absolute BSD is about how to administer FreeBSD, not about how to redirect output from a shell command. To make it easier for newer administrators, however, I include the exact shell commands needed to produce the desired results. If you learn best by example, you should find everything you need right here.*

*Many new system administrators these days come from a Windows background. They learn that "ls" is like "dir", and "cd" is the same on both platforms. You can learn the commands by rote, reading, and experience. What you cannot learn, coming from this background, is how a UNIX machine thinks. It will not adjust to you; you must accommodate it. With that in mind, we're going to spend a little time discussing how you must think about your FreeBSD system.*

## How to Think About UNIX

If you'll be working with FreeBSD, you should understand some of the UNIX ways of thinking. Users from a Windows background might very well go into shock during their first attempts to administer a FreeBSD system if they don't understand how UNIX behaves, and how it expects you to behave.

People who are used to GUI environments, such as Windows and Macintosh, are probably unfamiliar with how UNIX handles input and output. If you are new to UNIX, you may be used to clicking something and seeing either an "OK" message, an error, nothing, or (all too often) a pretty blue screen with nifty high-tech letters explaining exactly where the system crashed. UNIX does things a little differently.

### Channels of Communication

UNIX programs have three "channels" of communication: standard input, standard output, and standard error. Once you understand how each of these channels work, you're a good way along to understanding how a computer works.

*Standard input* is the source of information. When you're at the console typing a command, the standard input is the keyboard. If your program is listening to the network, the standard input is the network. Many programs can rearrange standard input to accept data from the network, a file, the keyboard, or any other source.

The *standard output* is where the program's output is displayed. This is frequently the console (screen). Network programs usually return the output to the network.

Finally, *standard error* is where error messages are sent. Frequently, console programs return errors to the console; others log errors to a file.

### Working with Channels

The channels just described can be arbitrarily arranged, a concept that is perhaps the biggest hurdle for new UNIX users and admins. While it seems simple enough, it's slightly more difficult to grow accustomed to than you might think.

For example, if you don't like the error messages appearing on the terminal, you can redirect them to a file. If you don't want to type a list of information into a command, you can put the information in a file (so you can reuse it), and dump the file into the standard input of your command. Or better still, run a command to generate that information and put it in a file, or just pipe (send) it directly to your second command.

### The Command Line

Taken to its logical extreme, these input/output channels can overwhelm a new user. The first time I saw someone type something like the following on a command line during my UNIX admin training, I wanted to change careers.

```
# tail -f /var/log/messages | grep -v sudo | grep -v named &
```

Lines of incomprehensible text began spilling across the screen. And worse still, my trainer kept typing as this output poured out!

If you're coming from a point-and-click environment, a long string of commands like this is definitely intimidating. What do all those funky words mean, let alone the symbols?

Think of learning to use the command line as learning a language. When learning a language, we start with simple words. As we increase our vocabulary, we also learn how to string words together. Learning to use the UNIX command line is like learning a language. You begin with simple single commands and only later string them together into monstrosities like the one shown earlier.

Another difficulty people have is with the general UNIX program function philosophy. Most consumer operating systems have monolithic software packages that try to be all things to all people. UNIX programs are small, simple tools. That's in part because of the redirectable input/output channels, and in part because of UNIX's heritage. Remember, at one time you needed to be a programmer to run a UNIX system. Programmers don't mind building their own tools. Assembling a tool on the command line is fairly easy compared to compiling a whole software package.

These smaller programs also provide unparalleled flexibility. Have you ever wished you could use a function from one program in another program? By using a variety of smaller programs and arranging the inputs and outputs as you like, you can make the system behave in any manner that amuses you. Many modern platforms have only started catching up with this idea of small, reusable tools in the last few years.

# Contents of This Book

Absolute BSD contains the following chapters.

Chapter 1, "Installation," gives an overview of installing FreeBSD on a dedicated machine and advice on an optimal install.

Chapter 2, "Getting More Help," covers the additional information resources the FreeBSD Project provides for users because no one book can possibly cover everything. Knowing how to use the many available FreeBSD resources will help you fill any gaps in the information you find here.

Chapter 3, "Read This Before You Break Something Else! (Backup and Recovery)," discusses how to back up your data on both a systemwide and a file-by-file level, and how to make changes that can be easily undone.

Chapter 4, "Kernel Games," describes configuring the FreeBSD kernel. Unlike some other operating systems, you are expected to tune FreeBSD's kernel to best suit your purposes. This gives you tremendous flexibility and lets you maximize your hardware's potential.

Chapter 5, "Networking," discusses TCP/IP and how it works in FreeBSD.

Chapter 6, "Upgrading FreeBSD," teaches you how to use FreeBSD's incredible upgrade process. The upgrade system is one of the most remarkable, and smoothest, of any operating system.

Chapter 7, "Securing Your System," teaches you how to make your system resist attackers and intruders.

Chapter 8, "Advanced Security Features," describes some of FreeBSD's more interesting security features, such as packet filtering and virtual machines.

Chapter 9, "Too Much Information About /etc," describes FreeBSD's main configuration files and how they are used.

Chapter 10, "Making Your System Useful," describes the ports and packages system that FreeBSD uses to manage add-on software.

Chapter 11, "Advanced Software Management," discusses managing some of FreeBSD's system-level software.

Chapter 12, "Finding Hosts with DNS," describes the Domain Name Service and teaches you how to troubleshoot and install nameservice.

Chapter 13, "Managing Small Network Services," discusses some of FreeBSD's supporting infrastructure for network services and some smaller network programs.

Chapter 14, "Email Services," teaches you how to install, use, and manage serving email for both servers and clients.

Chapter 15, "Web and FTP Services," discusses how to run these very popular Internet servers.

Chapter 16, "Filesystems and Disks," discusses some details of FreeBSD's filesystems, support for other filesystems, and the Soft Updates system that makes FreeBSD so reliable.

Chapter 17, "RAID," covers FreeBSD's built-in software-based hard-drive array tools.

Chapter 18, "System Performance," describes some of FreeBSD's performance-testing and troubleshooting tools.

Chapter 19, "Now What's It Doing?," teaches you how to monitor your system through a variety of tools.

Chapter 20, "System Crashes and Panics," teaches you how to deal with those rare occasions when your FreeBSD system fails, how to debug problems, and how to prepare a problem report.

Chapter 21, "Desktop FreeBSD," gives pointers to a variety of programs that make FreeBSD a solid and reliable workstation platform.

The afterword wraps it all up.

Finally we have an Appendix, *Some Useful sysctl MIBs*, that describes some of the more interesting and useful kernel-tuning options.

Okay, enough with the introductory stuff. On to the install!

# 1

# INSTALLATION

Before you can learn to run FreeBSD, you need to install it. A successful installation requires both the software (FreeBSD) and supported hardware. You can get FreeBSD easily enough by visiting http://www.FreeBSD.org/ and clicking the link that says "Getting FreeBSD," or by ordering it from any of several vendors, such as FreeBSD Mall (http://www.FreeBSDmall.com) or Daemon News (http://www.daemon-news.org). [1]

Hardware is another issue entirely.

## FreeBSD Hardware

FreeBSD runs on several different hardware platforms, the most popular of which are Intel-compatible systems 80386 and better. It also runs on the late and lamented Compaq Alpha, and ports are in process to the SPARC, StrongARM, and PowerPC as well.

[1] I recommend these vendors in particular, since they both contribute a portion of their proceeds back to the FreeBSD community. You will find cheaper distributors, but they keep all the money for themselves.

This book discusses the Intel platform (aka X86 or i386) because they're the most common and best supported, and you probably have one around. In fact, even your old systems can run FreeBSD; you probably have something in storage that would do nicely. Since our focus is on network servers, the instructions given here discuss installing FreeBSD on a dedicated machine. To learn how to make FreeBSD coexist with other operating systems, see the FreeBSD online documentation.

Still, FreeBSD will run best with certain minimum configurations. Here are some basic recommendations.

### Processor

Your brand of processor is really irrelevant to FreeBSD; FreeBSD won't care if you're running an Intel, AMD, IBM, or Cyrix CPU. It probes the CPU on booting, and uses whatever chip features it recognizes. I've run effective servers on 486 machines before—in fact, I've filled a T1 Internet circuit with a 486. However, I would still recommend that you get a Pentium or faster CPU. Some of the demonstrations in this book take less than an hour on my twin 1 GHz Pentium system, but take almost three days on my ancient 25 MHz 486.

### Memory (RAM)

First, memory (as in RAM) is good, and the more memory, the better. In fact, adding RAM will do more than anything else to accelerate your system. You should have at least 16MB of RAM at a bare minimum.

### Hard Drives

Hard drives can be a big performance bottleneck. While IDE drives are dirt cheap, they don't perform as well as SCSI drives. A SCSI system can transfer data to and from each and every drive at the full speed of the SCSI controller, while an IDE controller splits its available speed between the drives. Also, a SCSI controller can have up to 15 drives, while an IDE controller can have no more than 2. Having 15 drives, each running at full speed, versus 2 drives averaging half speed makes a big difference in the amount of data throughput!

Still, if all you use are IDE drives, put multiple hard disks on separate controllers. Many systems now have a hard drive on one IDE controller and a CD-ROM on the other. When you add a second hard drive, put it on the second controller. (You won't be using the CD-ROM nearly as often as you use the hard drive, after all.)

You'll be happiest with at least 1GB of disk on your system, though I'm assuming for purposes of this book that you have at least 10GB.

## Downloading FreeBSD

If you choose to download FreeBSD via FTP instead of buying it on CD, you'll find a comprehensive mirror list at www.FreeBSD.org, though you can pick out mirrors easily enough without the mirror list. Each mirror server has a name following this pattern:

```
ftp<number>.<country>.FreeBSD.org
```

The trailing country code is optional; if there is no country code, it's usually assumed to be in the continental United States. For example, you can have ftp3.FreeBSD.org, ftp2.uk.FreeBSD.org, ftp.ru.FreeBSD.org, and so on, and so on.

As a rule, the FTP mirrors with the lower numbers are more heavily loaded than those with higher numbers. Try a site down around ftp5.FreeBSD.org,[2] or some high-numbered server under your country code, and see if you can get a nice fast connection.

Many FreeBSD mirrors also mirror other software, and they store all the FreeBSD content under /pub/FreeBSD. Let's take a look there:

```
..
.message
.notar
CERT
CTM
CVSup
FreeBSD-current
FreeBSD-stable
README.TXT
branches
development
dir.sizes
distfiles
doc
index.html
ls-lR.gz
ports
releases
snapshots
tools
updates
```

That's a lot of stuff! Fortunately, you don't have to worry about what most of it does. For your initial install, the important directory is releases/i386. There you'll find a complete listing of all current FreeBSD releases that the mirror carries, as well as a directory of ISO images for burning your own bootable CD-ROM. (See your CD recorder documentation for help in doing so.)

[2] Since I've now mentioned a particular FTP server by name, it's going to be overloaded by those folks who follow instructions to the absolute letter. Pick a server. Pick any server. Poke around until you find one that works well for you.

## Installing by FTP

Downloading an entire ISO image is a waste for many people, because that ISO will include things you really don't need, such as dozens of packages you probably won't install. A better bet, if you have a reasonable amount of bandwidth—meaning a cable modem, corporate LAN, or reliable 56K line and a lot of time—is to install FreeBSD via FTP.

If you choose to install by FTP you'll need to download two floppy disk images first and make the floppies. Why floppies? Well, booting from floppy can take a while—floppy drives are slow by modern standards—but most systems have them and they usually work without a hitch. These floppy images are like old-fashioned DOS boot disks; they contain just enough information to boot FreeBSD, run the installation program, read information from a CD or an FTP server, and write to disk.

You'll find the floppy disk images in the directory for the release you want (that is, 4.5-RELEASE) in the floppies subdirectory. In there, you'll see the following:

- **boot.flp**   This is a disk image for 2.88MB disks. If you don't have a 2.88MB floppy drive or a CD burner, it's useless to you.
- **fixit.flp**   This disk holds some basic commands that you can use for system recovery. See Chapter 3 for more information.
- **kern.flp**   This is the boot disk image. It contains the basic kernel and will actually talk to your hardware during the installation process.
- **mfsroot.flp**   This is the second boot disk image. It contains the programs that will be used to install FreeBSD on a compressed memory-based filesystem.

Of the preceding floppy images, all you need to get are the kern.flp and mfsroot.flp files. Once you have these files, you'll need to copy them onto floppy disks. The catch is, you cannot use basic filesystem-level copying, like the typical Windows drag and drop. These are image files and must be copied onto the disk in a particular way.

If you're already running a UNIX system, the dd command will do everything you need. But first, you'll need your floppy drive's device name, which is probably /dev/fd0, /dev/floppy, or /dev/rfd0.

If the device name was /dev/fd0, you'd enter

```
# dd if=kern.flp of=/dev/fd0
```

to write the kern.flp floppy image to disk.

Repeat the preceding process to copy mfsroot.flp to a second floppy disk, substituting mfsroot.flp for kern.flp.

If you're running Microsoft Windows, you'll need a special utility that will copy disk images for you. Microsoft doesn't provide one, but FreeBSD does, and you'll find it in the "tools" subdirectory of the main directory for your release—it is called fdimage.exe.

Fdimage.exe is a free program that you can run under Windows to copy disk images, and it's quite easy to use. For example, to copy the floppy image kern.flp to the floppy in your a: drive, enter the following at a DOS prompt:

```
c:> fdimage kern.flp a:
```

Once the floppy drive finishes churning (which may take a while), repeat the process for mfsroot.flp using a second floppy disk.

### Other FTP Install Information

If your local network uses DHCP (Dynamic Host Configuration Protocol) to assign IP addresses and other network information, things should Just Work. If your network administrators assign IP addresses by hand, however, you will need to get the following information from your network administrator:

- IP address for your FreeBSD system
- IP addresses of nameservers used by your network
- Your network's default gateway

# Hardware Setup

In order to continue with your hardware setup, you'll need to make a quick trip to the BIOS. Most computers let you enter the BIOS setup screen immediately after booting, usually by pressing F2 or the DELETE key.

Once you're in the setup screen, set the computer to boot from your chosen media, either floppy disk or CD. Floppy disks are shown either as "floppy" or "A:". CD-ROMs are usually listed as "CDROM".

**NOTE** *If you need help using your BIOS, see your manual or visit the BIOS publisher's site online.*

While you're in the system BIOS, set the "Plug and Play OS" option to "no." This tells the BIOS to do some basic hardware setup, rather than relying on the operating system to do everything. Modern versions of Microsoft Windows expect the hardware to do as it is told, and hence expect full access to the hardware. FreeBSD, on the other hand, expects a system to perform as the hardware standards and specifications demand, and hence can take advantage of some setup work that is most easily done in the BIOS.

**NOTE** *Many devices (particularly network cards) will behave poorly if you don't change this option.*

## Actually Installing FreeBSD

When you have either a bootable CD-ROM or your two floppy disks, it's time to reboot your machine using one or the other. When you reboot, you should see a message offering you a chance to continue with the install, to configure your kernel in a visual menu, or to configure your kernel in a text menu, as shown in Figure 1.1.

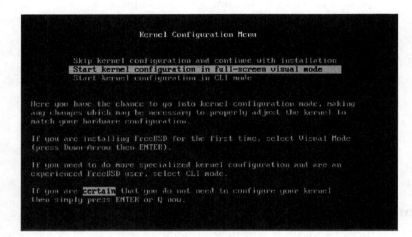

*Figure 1.1: First boot menu*

If you have old hardware, you might have to configure the kernel, which means telling the kernel about your hardware. For example, FreeBSD supports ISA network cards from the early 1990s but requires a very particular configuration to work properly. (This is a limitation of the hardware, not of FreeBSD.)

If you don't have any ISA cards, you can just continue with the install, but if you're using ISA cards, you'll need to configure your kernel to use them. Personally, I recommend replacing ISA cards with PCI whenever possible; they're easier to manage and have much better throughput. If you're running FreeBSD on a very old system, however, that might not be an option.

**NOTE**  *If you have problems, check the FreeBSD Handbook (online at http://www.FreeBSD.org) for help. If your hardware is less than a few years old, you should be able to continue with installation without configuring the kernel.*

### Configuring the Kernel for ISA Cards

If you have any ISA cards, you'll need to know how to identify and adjust their hard-jumpered IRQs (interrupt requests) and memory port addresses. (If not, you'll need to learn, or better yet upgrade, your ISA cards.) Once you tell FreeBSD the card's proper IRQ and memory address, it should work.

At the initial boot menu (shown in Figure 1.1), choose the option to configure the kernel in full-screen visual mode. That will bring up a menu like the one shown in Figure 1.2.

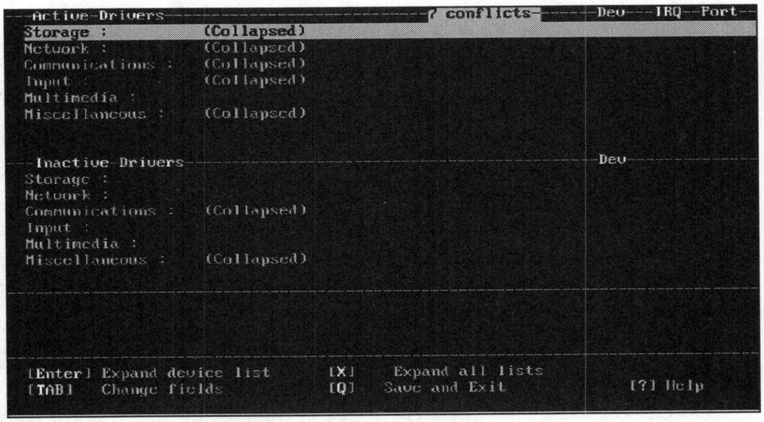

Figure 1.2: ISA card configuration

Devices are grouped into rough categories: storage, network, and so on. Select the category your ISA card belongs to, and press ENTER to expand it. If your device is listed, FreeBSD supports it. If your device is not listed, it either does not require configuration or FreeBSD does not support it. Select your device, and enter your card's IRQ, port number, and memory address in the spaces provided.

Once you finish telling the FreeBSD kernel about your card, type **Q**. You will be asked if you want to save your configuration and exit. Type **Y** to continue. This will bring you to sysinstall.

### Sysinstall: The Ugly FreeBSD Installer

The FreeBSD installer (shown in Figure 1.3) is a notoriously ugly, menu-driven system called sysinstall. While other operating systems have pretty graphical installers with mouse-driven menus and multicolor pie charts, FreeBSD's looks

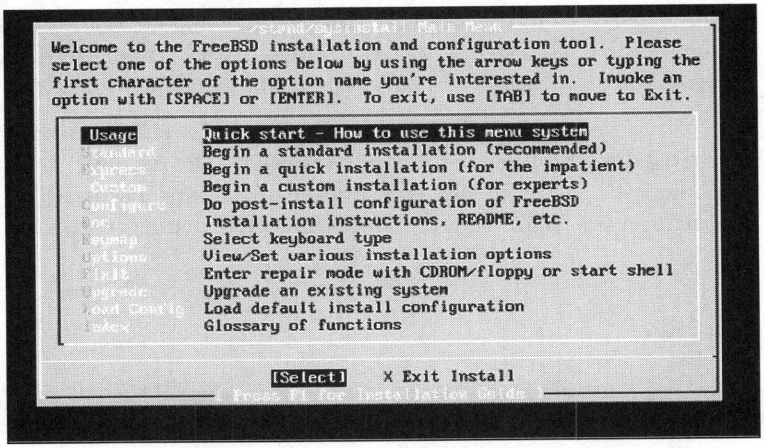

Figure 1.3: Sysinstall main menu

like an old DOS program. Even the system's author has referred to the underlying library as "genuinely evil." (While a replacement is in the works, as I write this it looks like sysinstall will be with FreeBSD for some time.)

Despite its looks, sysinstall is fairly simple to use, and it works well. While I won't present a step-by-step walkthrough of the interface (that shouldn't be necessary), I will discuss the various options presented during installation so you can make sensible choices.

You will need one very important instruction when dealing with sysinstall: *Use the space bar to select.* The funny thing is, even though this simple bit of information is displayed on several screens in sysinstall, in the help file, and in the instructions, people keep missing it. Then, once it's pointed out, they spend the rest of their days wondering how they missed it. If you don't use the space bar to select what you want, the install will fail.

Oh yes: The first time through, choose Standard install. Arrow down one line, and press **ENTER**.

### Disk Usage

Many people have a computer that boots multiple operating systems. They divide their hard disk into sections by OS, using one chunk for Windows and another for their other operating systems. FreeBSD works well in such a setup. However, since we're building Internet servers, you should use the entire disk for FreeBSD. Internet servers have to be up all the time, and you won't be shutting down the company mail server to, say, play Civilization on a Windows partition!

The standard FreeBSD install leaves tiny partitions at the beginning and end of the disk, marked "unused." This blank space is present when a disk is formatted for use with any operating system; FreeBSD just shows you it's there. (As usual, the FreeBSD-hackers mailing list archive contains a painful amount of detail on just why things work this way.)

**NOTE** *If you're installing FreeBSD 3.X or earlier, you might see an option for "dangerously dedicated" mode. This eliminates the tiny partitions and the beginning and end of the drive. Some very, very old hard drives perform best in dangerously dedicated mode. Don't use it unless you've researched the issues involved and are ready to deal with the consequences. The FreeBSD-hackers mailing list archives at http://www.FreeBSD.org/ search are a good source of information on this topic (see Chapter 2).*

The installer will first display a list of all the partitions on your hard drive. Arrow down and delete them by pressing **D**. The example shown in Figure 1.4 shows four partitions: the two "unused" partitions discussed previously, one FAT partition (for Windows), and one Windows Extended partition.

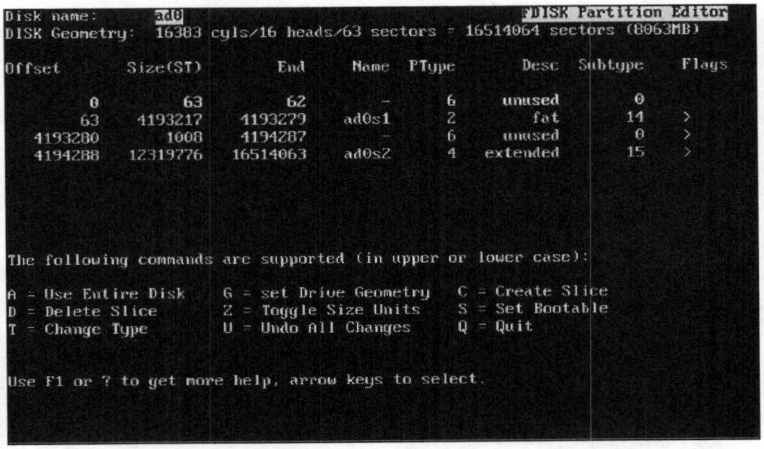

```
Disk name:       ad0                                    FDISK Partition Editor
DISK Geometry:  16383 cyls/16 heads/63 sectors = 16514064 sectors (8063MB)

Offset       Size(ST)        End       Name  PType      Desc  Subtype     Flags

       0           63         62        -      6     unused       0
      63      4193217    4193279     ad0s1     2        fat      14        >
 4193280         1008    4194287       -       6     unused       0        >
 4194288     12319776   16514063    ad0s2     4   extended      15        >




The following commands are supported (in upper or lower case):

A = Use Entire Disk    G = set Drive Geometry   C = Create Slice
D = Delete Slice       Z = Toggle Size Units    S = Set Bootable
T = Change Type        U = Undo All Changes     Q = Quit

Use F1 or ? to get more help, arrow keys to select.
```

Figure 1.4: Fdisk with Windows partitions

Once you've deleted all of the old partitions, use the **A** key to assign the entire disk to FreeBSD. The resulting screen will look something like Figure 1.5.

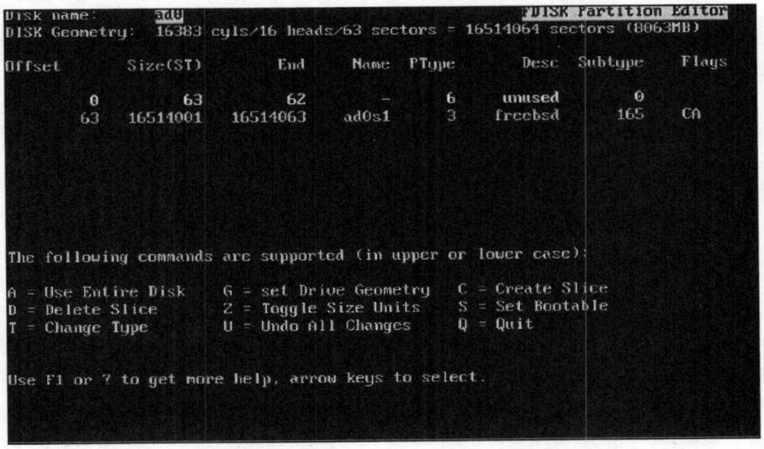

```
Disk name:       ad0                                    FDISK Partition Editor
DISK Geometry:  16383 cyls/16 heads/63 sectors = 16514064 sectors (8063MB)

Offset       Size(ST)        End       Name  PType      Desc  Subtype     Flags

       0           63         62        -      6     unused       0
      63     16511001   16514063    ad0s1     3    freebsd     165       CA




The following commands are supported (in upper or lower case):

A = Use Entire Disk    G = set Drive Geometry   C = Create Slice
D = Delete Slice       Z = Toggle Size Units    S = Set Bootable
T = Change Type        U = Undo All Changes     Q = Quit

Use F1 or ? to get more help, arrow keys to select.
```

Figure 1.5: Fdisk with one FreeBSD partition

Type **Q** to finish. The installer will drop you into the Boot Manager screen, shown in Figure 1.6. Install a standard master boot record (MBR), which removes any existing boot manager that your computer would use if you booted into multiple operating systems. (We're building Internet servers and won't be sharing the hard drive with, say, Windows Me.) Just arrow down to "Standard", press the space bar, and press **ENTER** to leave the screen.

Once you do this, the installer will take you to the Disklabel menu.

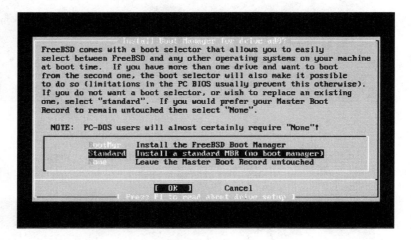

Figure 1.6: Boot Manager selection

## Partitioning

Now we come to the first tricky part: how to partition the hard drive. Unlike other operating systems that just hack up the drive in various sections, FreeBSD allows you to control where each partition lies on the hard drive. This is important for a variety of reasons.

Each partition is accessible to the user as a *mount point*. In Windows, each partition has a mount point of a letter, (such as C: or D:). In UNIX, all partitions and disks are part of a single directory tree. A partition is assigned a directory and is said to be "mounted" at that directory. You can have one partition for the root of your directory tree (/), and can assign others arbitrarily. For example, if you're building a large-capacity Web server, you might have a hard drive partition dedicated to Web sites, and mount it as /www. We'll discuss how to assign mount points and partition your drive.

FreeBSD normally uses four different basic partitions: / (or root), swap space, /var, and /usr. If you're already familiar with UNIX, you might wish to create additional partitions and assign them mount points of your choosing. We'll discuss each of the main partitions, as well as some considerations for their size and placement.

**NOTE** *Here and there we'll mention another possible partition you might create. If you're not familiar with that partition, just skip over it; more experienced administrators can take or ignore that advice as they choose.*

The first thing to note is that the outer edge of the disk moves more quickly; thus, the closer a file is to the edge of the disk, the faster it can be accessed or altered. Place your most important files close to the edge so you can read and write to them more quickly, and put your more static data closer to the center. (Data access on a spinning hard drive is much like a merry-go-round; you can sit in the middle and hardly feel anything, but lie with your head dangling over the edge, and in a few minutes you won't be able to stand up.[3])

You edit partitions on a drive with the Disklabel menu (shown in Figure 1.7).

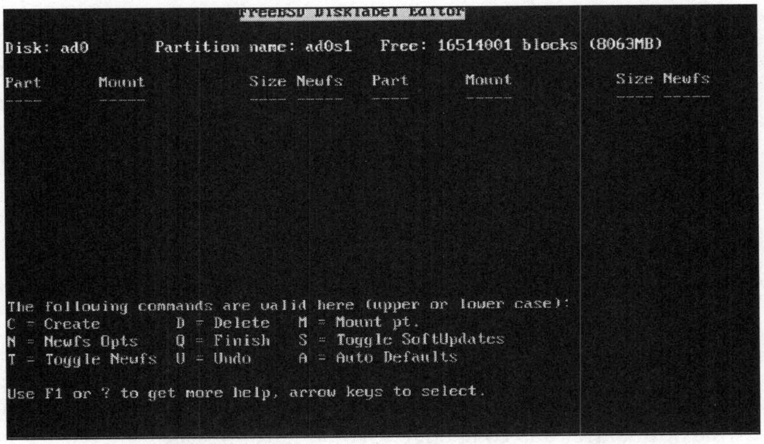

Figure 1.7: The Disklabel menu

*In the disk partitioning menu, partitions that appear closer to the top are closer to the edge of the disk. If you're partitioning multiple disks, do them one at a time to help keep the order straight in your mind.*

We'll discuss each of the standard partitions in turn. You cannot change the partitions on a running system, so it's important to get them correct the first time.

## Root

Your system should have fast access to its root filesystem (/), which contains the kernel and just enough utilities and programs to boot the computer into its most basic running status, single-user mode (explained in Chapter 3). Therefore, place the root at the outer edge of the disk, and make it at least 128MB in size, no matter how big your disk is.

Some other UNIX-like operating systems, such as some distributions of Linux, use a large root partition that contains more of the operating system or, worse, use nothing but a single large root partition for all files on the disk. This is a bad idea for a variety of reasons. First, you can't control which files are put

[3] Okay, a lot of that dizzy feeling has to do with centrifugal force, but the outside edge does move more feet per minute than the inside edge. Now quit picking on my analogies.

where in a partition. This hurts performance. Second, in the event of disk damage, you're most likely to have a bootable system if you have a small root partition. This gives you a fighting chance to recover any surviving data.

Your root partition should be about 128MB. Press **C** to create the partition, type in 128M, and press **ENTER**. The installer will ask you if you're creating a filesystem or swap space. Select "filesystem", and it will ask you for a mount point. Type / and press **ENTER**.

# Swap Space

Next, create your swap space, the disk space used by virtual memory. When your computer fills its physical memory, it will start to put information that hasn't been used for a while into swap. Putting swap toward the outer edge of the disk measurably improves performance.

So, how much swap space do you need? This is a matter of long debates between sysadmins. The short answer is, "it depends on the system." General wisdom says that you should have at least twice as much swap as you have physical memory. This isn't a bad rule, so long as you understand that it's very general. More won't hurt. Less might, if your system runs out of RAM. FreeBSD's virtual memory system assumes that you have at least twice your physical memory in swap space, and makes certain choices and optimizations based on that assumption.

It's difficult to add swap space when you add memory because this is a disk partition, after all. To change it you'd have to resize the partition—always a bit risky! As a general rule, try to create at least twice as much swap as you think you will have memory. If your system currently has 128MB of RAM, but you expect to increase it to 1GB, use 2GB of swap space.

### Swap Splitting

If you have multiple disks, you can vastly improve the efficiency of your swap space by splitting it among multiple drives. Put the first swap on the second-outermost partition of your boot drive (the one with the root partition), and other swaps on the outermost partition of the other drives. (This works well for up to four partitions on four drives; if you create more than four swap partitions, the partitions after the first four will be used as optimally as the first four.)

For swap-space splitting to work best, however, the disks must be SCSI. If you have IDE drives, the drives need to be on different IDE controllers. Remember, each IDE controller splits its total data throughput among all the connected hard drives. If you have two hard drives on the same IDE controller, and you're accessing both simultaneously, each disk will only be half as fast. The major bottleneck in using swap space is data throughput speed, so you won't gain anything.

If you split your swap space among multiple drives, create partitions that are roughly the same size. FreeBSD has some optimizations for four swap partitions.

Four swap partitions leads to a conflicting problem, however. Upon a system crash, FreeBSD can write a copy of its physical memory image to a swap partition. This allows a developer to try to debug and fix whatever caused the crash.

To dump a memory image, however, at least one swap partition must be at least the same size as the system's physical memory. If you have four swap partitions, each as large as the system's physical memory, you'll wind up with four times as much swap as physical memory. That's a lot of swap, especially on modern systems. That's even twice the standard "twice-physical-memory" rule of thumb. Extra swap won't hurt, mind you, and disk space is very cheap these days. If you *really* need your swap, you'll have it. If you find you're continually using swap, you'll want to buy more RAM anyway.

Once you decide how much swap space to allocate, create a partition by pressing C. Enter the size you want—for example, for a 1,000MB swap partition you would enter 1000m. When the installer asks if you want to create a swap partition or a filesystem, choose "Swap".

## /var, /usr, and /home

The next step is to create the /var partition, which holds rapidly changing data, such as log files, databases, mail spools, and the like. If your system will have a lot of logs or mail files, this partition might very well need to be 1GB or more. On a small server, I'll frequently make this 20 percent of the remaining disk space. On a mail server, I'll kick that up to 70 percent or more.

The /usr partition holds the operating system programs, source code, and other little details like that. Many people use the rest of their disk for the /usr partition; it's frequently the most populated.

**NOTE** *If you're building a Web server, where each Web site has its own user and home directory, assigning the rest of the disk to /usr might not be a great idea. In such a case, using 3GB of hard drive space for /usr will more than suffice for just about any use, and you can assign the remainder to /home, the partition for users' home directories. Doing so segregates their files from the system, and file access speed is generally unimportant once it exceeds a certain acceptable minimum.*

When you finish, the Disklabel menu will look something like Figure 1.8.

```
                    FreeBSD Disklabel Editor
Disk: ad0        Partition name: ad0s1    Free: 0 blocks (0MB)

Part      Mount          Size Newfs    Part      Mount          Size Newfs

ad0s1a    /             100MB UFS Y
ad0s1b    swap          516MB SWAP
ad0s1e    /var          100MB UFS Y
ad0s1f    /usr         7347MB UFS Y




The following commands are valid here (upper or lower case):
C = Create       D = Delete     M = Mount pt.
N = Newfs Opts   Q = Finish     S = Toggle SoftUpdates
T = Toggle Newfs U = Undo       A = Auto Defaults

Use F1 or ? to get more help, arrow keys to select.
```

*Figure 1.8: Disklabel after partitioning*

## A Second Hard Drive

If you have a second hard drive of comparable quality to your main drive, you can make good use of it if you plan properly. First, use the outer edge of the drive for swap, as discussed earlier in the "Swap Splitting" section. Use the rest of the drive to segregate your data from your operating system. Do this by assigning the remainder of the drive to the partition that stores files for whatever your server is for. If it's a mail server, use the second drive for /var or /var/mail. If it's a Web server, make it /www or /home. If it's a network logging host, assign the second drive to /var/log.

In general, segregating your operating system from the data you're serving will increase system efficiency. Like all rules of thumb, this is debatable. But no sysadmin will tell you that this is an actively bad or dangerous idea, whereas they can argue endlessly about other variations on drive usage.

If you have no idea what your server will be for, make your second drive for /usr and use most of the space on your first drive for /var.

If your second drive is much slower than your main system drive, don't bother using it. Not only will its performance not be that good, chances are that it is much older than your main drive and more likely to fail.

The FreeBSD installer will detect all of your system hard drives when it boots, and it will give you the opportunity to partition each and every one.

### Soft Updates

FreeBSD includes a bunch of fancy filesystem tricks collectively known as *soft updates*. We'll learn more about soft updates in Chapter 16. For now, just accept that enabling them during the install is a good idea. If you learn about soft updates and decide that you don't like them, you can easily disable them. We'll learn about that in Chapter 16 as well.

Arrow down to select each partition, and press **S**. This will enable soft updates.

### Block Size

This section contains options that can really impair system performance. If you're new to FreeBSD, take the defaults! This is for experienced UNIX administrators who know *exactly* what they're doing.

Block size refers to the minimum size of a file. If you have a file that contains just one tiny character, it uses one whole block, even if it barely fills that block. By the same token, if your file is just over the block size, it takes up one block and a fragment of another. Each block can be divided into fragments, so that multiple, slightly oversized files can use one block to store their extra tidbits.

FreeBSD defaults to 8KB blocks. If you're creating a large partition—say, 1GB or more—use 16KB blocks. When you do this, you also need to change your fragment size. The FreeBSD file system (UFS, or UNIX File System) works best with fragments one-eighth the size of a block. This would be 16,384-byte blocks and 2,048-bit fragments.

Set the block size with the newfs program. From the Disklabel screen, press **N** while on a partition to display a pop-up dialog box containing newfs options.

To use 16KB blocks and 2KB fragments, enter

```
newfs -f 2048 -b 16384
```

### What to Install

The next menu gives you a choice of what to install. While there are quite a few options, I'll simplify them. If you're building an Internet server, choose the "Developer" option. If you're building a desktop or general-purpose experimental machine, choose the "All" option (as shown in Figure 1.9). (Remember to use the space bar to select your choice, and the **ENTER** key to proceed!)

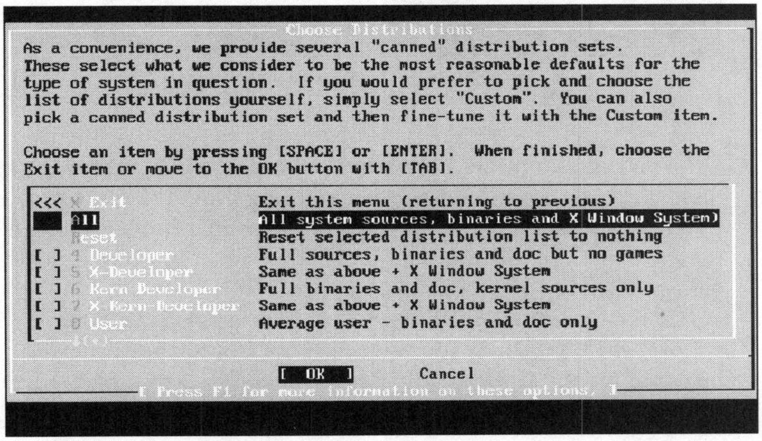

Figure 1.9: Distributions menu

Install will then ask you if you want to install the Ports Collection. You do, even if you don't know it yet. Select "Yes".

If you're installing the X Window System, or X for short, accept the options to install everything in X. (It's much simpler to add them now than to add them later.) Again, once you have a good grip on FreeBSD, you can always go back and remove pieces if you need to.

### Installation Media

You'll have a variety of options for installation media, as shown in Figure 1.10. The most popular are CD-ROM and FTP. If you have a FreeBSD CD-ROM, use it. If you don't have a CD, but you have a live network connection, you can install via FTP. This is probably the option you want if you created the floppy disks. If you're behind a firewall, choose to either install via FTP "through a firewall" or "through a http proxy." Be sure your network cable is plugged in before you choose any FTP install options.

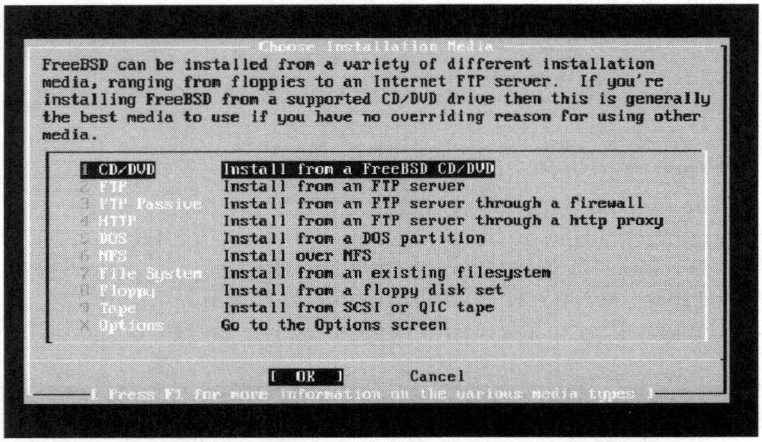

Figure 1.10: Installation media menu

You can also install FreeBSD from tape backup, NFS, several dozen floppy
disks, or a few other media. If you're using one of these, you're either already a
UNIX sysadmin (NFS, tape), or you have probably been brained by falling
masonry and are just waiting for the kind gents in white coats to cart you off to
your padded room (floppy disks).

If you are using an FTP install, the system will pop up a menu asking you to
choose which interface you want to use. Choose your Ethernet card. You'll then
be asked for the IP address information you gathered back when you started
preparing for an FTP install.

### Committing

Once you choose your installation media, sysinstall will ask you if you're sure. If
you choose "Yes", the hard drive will start to spin, your CD drive will light up, and
you can go get lunch. When you come back, most of the install will be complete.

Finally, you'll see a dialog box asking you if you want to do any post-install
setup. Choose "Yes".

## Post-Install Setup

The post-install FreeBSD Configuration menu provides some basic options for
setting up your computer (see Figure 1.11). We'll discuss how to configure everything later, but your life will be easier if you do some basic setup now.

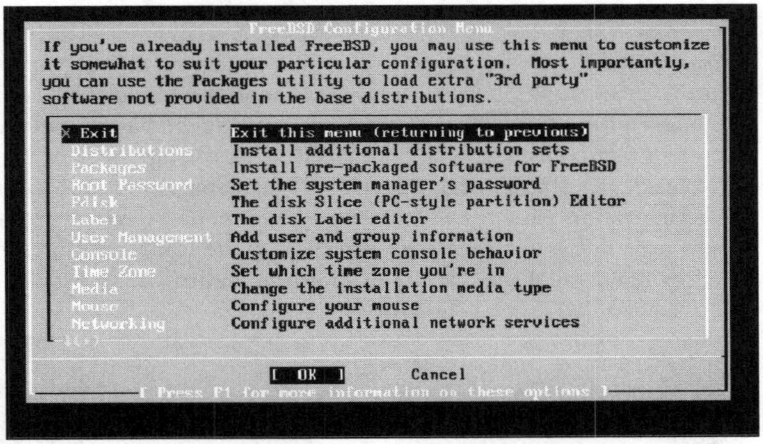

*Figure 1.11: Post-Install configuration*

### Root Password

To begin, set a root password. If you don't have one, any doofus can log into the system as root without using any password. (Since root has absolute control over your hardware and software, this would be bad.) Choose the third option in the Configuration menu, "Set the system manager's password". It will ask you to enter the root password twice (as shown in Figure 1.12). Remember your root password, as it's a bit of an annoyance to recover it if you lose it.

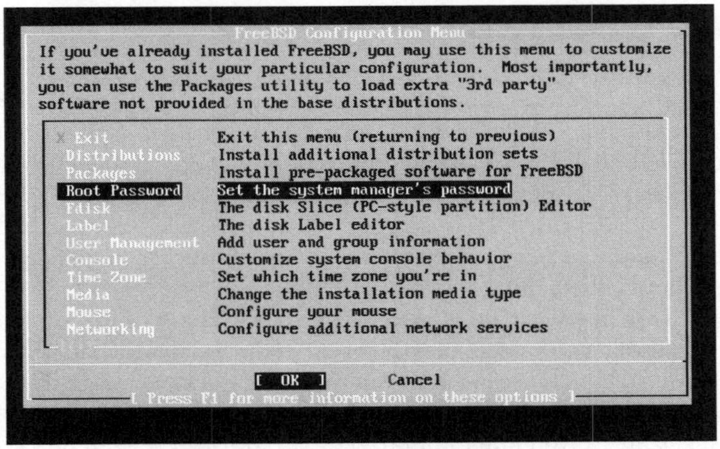

*Figure 1.12: Setting the root password*

### Adding Users

You should do everything possible while signed on as a regular user, and only use the root account when you must change the system. That will happen frequently at first, but will grow less common as time passes. Before you can sign on as a regular user, though, you need to set one up for your use.

To add a regular user, select the User Management option in the Configuration menu. It will pop up a brief menu offering you a chance to add a new user, add a new group, or exit back to the Configuration menu. Choose "User", and you'll see the screen shown in Figure 1.13.

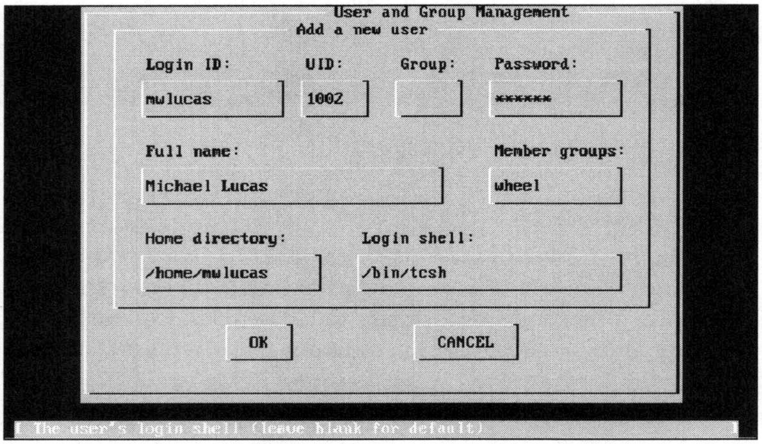

*Figure 1.13: Adding a user*

Your first selection in this screen should be the Login ID, or username. Your company might have a standard for usernames. I prefer to use first initial, middle initial, and last name (not using the middle initial creates a surprising number of conflicts).

The UID (user ID) is assigned by the system. If you're an experienced systems administrator you can alter this, but it's not recommended and there's generally not much point.

The FreeBSD default is to have the user in a "Group" of the same name as the username; for example, the user "mwlucas" is automatically in the Group "mwlucas". If you know what you're doing, you can change this.

"Full name" is, simply enough, the user's name. Other system users can see this name, so you don't want to set it arbitrarily. I've seen new systems administrators get in trouble when they gave a customer a full name of, say, "Pain in the Tuckus."

The "Home directory" is where the user's files are kept. The default is generally fine.

"Member groups" is just a list of other system groups this account is part of. If you want this user to be able to use the root password and become root, add your user to the group "wheel" under the "Member groups" space.

Administrators need to be in the wheel group, users don't. (Make sure your personal user account is in wheel!)

Finally, choose a shell for your new user. Older admins and greybeards-in-training frequently prefer /bin/sh. The examples in this book are written assuming your shell is /bin/tcsh, which is the modern BSD standard and much friendlier.

Select **OK** when you're done, and your user will be created.

### Time Zone

Set your time zone by selecting the Time Zone option from the Configuration screen (shown in Figure 1.11). You'll be asked if the system clock is set to UTC; answer "No", and walk through the menus presented. You'll be asked to choose a continent, a country (as shown in Figure 1.14), and then a time zone.

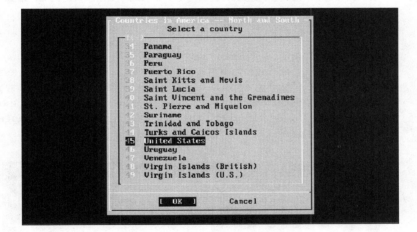

Figure 1.14: Time selection by country

### Mouse

If you have a mouse, it's easy to set it up now. If you have a dead-standard two- or three-button PS/2 mouse or trackball plugged in, just choose Mouse from the Configuration menu, and then choose Enable. You should see a mouse pointer on your screen, and it should wiggle when you move it.

If your mouse isn't dead-standard, that's okay. By using the menu shown in Figures 1.15, you can change the port your mouse runs on and the type it is.

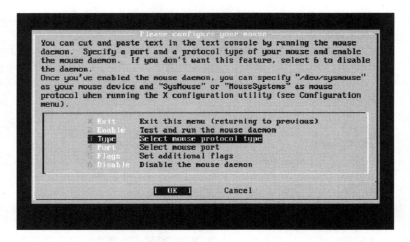

Figure 1.15: Mouse management

Once you have set the mouse type and port, choose Enable and you will get a pop-up menu asking you if the mouse is working. Wiggle your mouse, and enter "Yes" or "No" as appropriate (see Figure 1.16). If it doesn't work, your settings probably don't match your mouse. I've had more than one mouse surprise me by being something other than what I thought it was. To change your settings and try again choose "No".

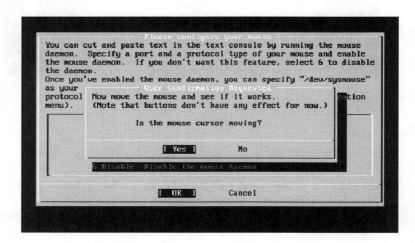

Figure 1.16: Mouse test menu

### Configuring Network Cards

If your machine has a network card, and you did a CD-ROM install, you probably want to configure your network card now. It'll save you trouble later. Be sure your card is plugged into the network, and then choose Networking from the Configuration menu, and then Interfaces from the Network Services menu shown in Figure 1.17.

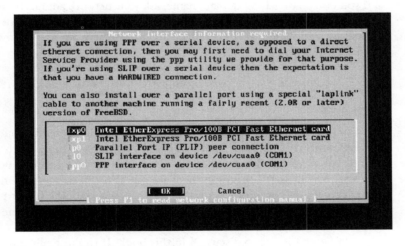

```
                    Network Services Menu
You may have already configured one network device (and the other
various hostname/gateway/name server parameters) in the process
of installing FreeBSD.  This menu allows you to configure other
aspects of your system's network configuration.

    <<<   Exit          Exit this menu (returning to previous)
    [ ]   Interfaces     Configure additional network interfaces
    [ ]   AMD            This machine wants to run the auto-mounter service
    [X]   AMD Flags      Set flags to AMD service (if enabled)
    [ ]   Anon FTP       This machine wishes to allow anonymous FTP.
    [ ]   Gateway        This machine will route packets between interfaces
    [X]   inetd          This machine wants to run the inet daemon
    [ ]   NFS client     This machine will be an NFS client
    [ ]   NFS server     This machine will be an NFS server
    [ ]   Ntpdate        Select a clock-synchronization server
    [ ]   PCNFSD         Run authentication server for clients with PC-NFS.
    [ ]   portmap        This machine wants to run the portmapper daemon

              [  OK  ]         Cancel
```

Figure 1.17: Network Services menu

You'll get a choice of network interfaces to configure. (If you're fairly new to computing, you might not have realized that your parallel port can be a network interface!) Look for an entry that includes Ethernet, and choose it. In Figure 1.18, we see an Ethernet card called fxp0.

```
              Network interface information required
If you are using PPP over a serial device, as opposed to a direct
ethernet connection, then you may first need to dial your Internet
Service Provider using the ppp utility we provide for that purpose.
If you're using SLIP over a serial device then the expectation is
that you have a HARDWIRED connection.

You can also install over a parallel port using a special "laplink"
cable to another machine running a fairly recent (2.0R or later)
version of FreeBSD.

    fxp0    Intel EtherExpress Pro/100B PCI Fast Ethernet card
    fxp1    Intel EtherExpress Pro/100B PCI Fast Ethernet card
    lp0     Parallel Port IP (PLIP) peer connection
    lo      SLIP interface on device /dev/cuaa0 (COM1)
    ppp0    PPP interface on device /dev/cuaa0 (COM1)

              [  OK  ]         Cancel
         [ Press F1 to read network configuration manual ]
```

Figure 1.18: Network interface information menu

You'll get a pop-up dialog box asking if you want to try IPv6 configuration of the interface. If you don't know what IPv6 is, don't choose it. A second pop-up will offer to try DHCP configuration of the interface. If you are on a network with DHCP, you can try it; otherwise, choose "No". You'll get a network interface configuration screen as shown in Figure 1-19.

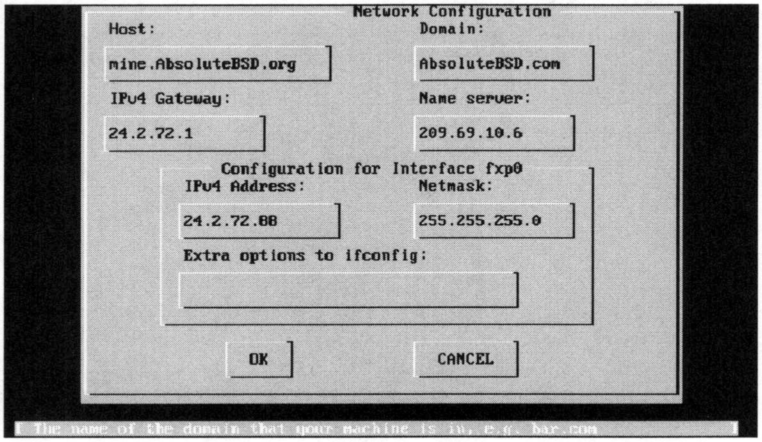

*Figure 1.19: Network Configuration menu*

Your Host name is a unique name for your computer. It might be something like "Webserver" or "test". It should be all one word.

The Domain name is the domain your computer is a part of. This computer was set up to test examples for *Absolute BSD*, so I made it part of AbsoluteBSD.com. If you don't have a local domain name, ask your network administrator.

Earlier in the install I suggested that you get an IP address, netmask, default gateway, and nameserver IP address from your network administrator. Enter this information here.

Even if DHCP configuration works, you will still need to set your Host name and Domain name. Otherwise, your system will boot calling itself "Amnesiac."

### Xfree86

If you're an experienced UNIX administrator, you'll probably notice a couple of menu items that say "Configure XFree86". XFree86 is the GUI that generates pretty pictures on your monitor. Take my advice; don't go there now. I've had several installs fail at this point because my XFree86 configuration went bad. You can always configure X after a reboot, using xf86cfg or your preferred tool. And X isn't useful on a server, in any event. All it does is consume system resources.

We aren't going to discuss X in this book. If you're really interested in X, I suggest you get *The New Xfree86*, by Bill Ball (Premier Press). X is not just a window system, like the Microsoft Windows GUI; it's an entire protocol.

### Software

If you're an experienced UNIX hand, you probably know what software you want to install. One popular choice is the Emacs text editor, for example. You can choose to install these programs under the Packages option on the Configuration menu. The Packages option will bring up the Package Selection menu shown in Figure 1.20.

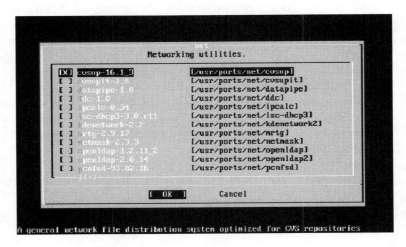

```
            Package Selection
To mark a package, move to it and press SPACE.  If the package is
already marked, it will be unmarked or deleted (if installed).
Items marked with a `D' are dependencies which will be auto-loaded.
To search for a package by name, press ESC.  To select a category,
press RETURN.  NOTE:  The All category selection creates a very large
submenu!  If you select it, please be patient while it comes up.

   All            All available packages in all categories.
   afterstep      Ports to support the AfterStep window manager.
   archivers      Utilities for archiving and unarchiving data.
   astro          Applications related to astronomy.
   audio          Audio utilities - most require a supported sound card.
   benchmarks     Utilities for measuring system performance.
   biology        Software related to biology.
   cad            Computer Aided Design utilities.
   chinese        Ported software for the Chinese market.
   comms          Communications utilities.
   converters     Format conversion utilities.
   databases      Database software.

                   [ OK ]     Install
```

Figure 1.20: Package Selection menu

If you're already familiar with UNIX, you probably know the names of several packages you would like to install. One popular choice is bash, a command shell. Arrow down to "shells", press **ENTER** to open that category, arrow down to "bash", and press the space bar to select it. Then press **ENTER** to go back to the Package Selection menu.

If you're not familiar with UNIX software, there's one package you need to install to use this book properly. Select Packages from the Configuration menu, select "net" from the Package Selection menu, and then select "cvsup" (see Figure 1.21). We'll use the cvsup tool in Chapter 6.

```
                              net
                       Networking utilities.

   [X] cvsup-16.1_3              [/usr/ports/net/cvsup]
   [ ] cvsupit-3.0              [/usr/ports/net/cvsupit]
   [ ] datapipe-1.0            [/usr/ports/net/datapipe]
   [ ] dc-1.0                   [/usr/ports/net/ddc]
   [ ] ipcalc-0.34              [/usr/ports/net/ipcalc]
   [ ] isc-dhcp3-3.0.r11        [/usr/ports/net/isc-dhcp3]
   [ ] kdenetwork-2.2           [/usr/ports/net/kdenetwork2]
   [ ] mrtg-2.9.17              [/usr/ports/net/mrtg]
   [ ] netmask-2.3.3            [/usr/ports/net/netmask]
   [ ] openldap-1.2.11_2        [/usr/ports/net/openldap]
   [ ] openldap-2.0.14          [/usr/ports/net/openldap2]
   [ ] pcnfsd-93.02.16          [/usr/ports/net/pcnfsd]

                   [  OK  ]     Cancel
A general network file distribution system optimized for CVS repositories
```

Figure 1.21: Individual package listings

When you have chosen all the packages you want to install, return to the main Package Selection menu. Press **TAB** to move the cursor from **OK** to Install, then press **ENTER**. Your system will begin installing packages.

## Restart

This last step should get you up and running! Remove any CD-ROMs or floppy disks from your computer, exit the installer, and reboot. You should now have a complete FreeBSD system, configured properly for most Internet operations and for all the examples in this book.

If you find that you need to do some configuration later, you can always reenter sysinstall:

```
# /stand/sysinstall
```

Throughout the course of this book, you'll learn how to work more quickly and efficiently by avoiding sysinstall and manipulating the configuration files directly. The sysinstall program can act as a crutch to get you through the worst parts, however.

## A Note on Editors

No, I'm not talking about the fine editors of this excellent book: text editors. Which is the "best" UNIX text editor has been a matter of prolonged debate over many years. FreeBSD includes vi, as its licensing terms are the same as FreeBSD's. Vi terrifies many newcomers, however; it's from an earlier aeon of UNIX. It's a dinosaur—specifically, a velociraptor, small and deadly and very powerful if you have mastered its arcane syntax.

If vi is not your bag, try the Easy Editor, ee. It holds your hand and is much more approachable for the newcomer. The ee program is also much more limited than vi; when you're tired of those limitations, you can graduate to vi or install Emacs. (I use both, and prefer Emacs.) Vi has the unquestioned advantage of being available on all UNIX platforms, however, and is well worth knowing.

You can tell most programs to use your editor of choice by adding the following line to the .cshrc file in your home directory. Substitute your preferred editor for vi.

```
setenv EDITOR vi
```

# 2

## GETTING MORE HELP

As thick as this book is, it can't possibly cover everything you might need to know. After all, UNIX itself has a 30-year heritage, BSD UNIX is over 20 years old, and FreeBSD is pushing 10. Even if you memorize this book, it won't be enough to cover every possible situation.

The FreeBSD project maintains a wide variety of information resources, including numerous FreeBSD mailing lists, the www.FreeBSD.org Web site, the Handbook, the FAQ, man pages, and assorted user Web sites. The flood of information can be overwhelming and difficult to wade through. But before you send a question to a mailing list, make sure that the information you want isn't already available in one of these resources.

### Why Not Mail First?

The FreeBSD mailing lists are excellent resources for technical support. Many people who frequent them are very knowledgeable and can answer your questions very quickly. But remember: When you mail a question to a FreeBSD mailing list, you are requesting that one or more people take the time to help you rather than watch a favorite TV show, enjoy dinner with family, or catch up on sleep. Problems arise when these experts answer the same question 10, 50, or even 100 times, or more. They become grumpy. Some get downright cranky.

What makes matters worse is that these same people have spent a great deal of time making the answers to most of these questions available elsewhere. If you make it clear that you have accessed the various information resources the FreeBSD project makes available, and your answer really can't be found there, you will probably receive a polite, helpful answer. However, if you ask a question that has been answered several hundred times already, the expert on that topic just might snap and go bonkers on you.

Also, remember that the FreeBSD project only maintains FreeBSD. If you're having trouble with some other piece of software, a FreeBSD mailing list is not the place to ask advice. FreeBSD developers are generally proficient in a variety of software; but that doesn't mean that they want to help you, say, configure the WindowMaker X window manager—harass the folks who handle WindowMaker instead.

Do your homework, and chances are you will get an answer more quickly than the mailing list can provide.

## The FreeBSD Attitude

To use FreeBSD successfully, you'll need to do a bit of homework.

"Homework? What do you mean, *homework*? Am I back in school? What do you want, burnt offerings on bended knee?" Yes, you are back in school. With FreeBSD, even the teachers are still in school. Burnt offerings, on the other hand, are difficult to transmit digitally, and really aren't relevant today.

Commercial operating systems such as Windows 9x/NT conceal their inner workings. The only access you have to the computer are the options presented by the GUI, plus a few command-line tools that are almost an afterthought. Even if you want to learn how something works, you *can't*. When something breaks, you have little choice but to phone the vendor and grovel for help. Worse, the people paid to help you frequently know little more than you do.

FreeBSD, on the other hand, is completely open, allowing you to learn exactly how things behave, in intimate detail. As an open operating system, you can read the source code for commands, as well as the kernel. And people in the FreeBSD community overwhelmingly want to learn. The community welcomes people who want to learn, and will be delighted to help you if you're willing.

There are other parts of the FreeBSD community that you should be aware of: segments who are not as interested in learning how FreeBSD works. These include a group that doesn't care how FreeBSD works, just that it works well. For example, many ISPs don't care what serves up their Web pages; they just care that their Web pages are being served reliably. Embedded systems programmers as a group are often not as interested in FreeBSD's inner workings; for the most part, they are attracted by FreeBSD's power and its commerce-friendly license. This is not to say that there is anything wrong with these groups whatsoever, just that these people aren't likely to be found hanging around FreeBSD mailing lists answering user questions.

As a grossly overgeneralized rule, people help those like themselves. As a FreeBSD user, you should make the jump from eating what you're served to reading the cookbook and creating your own dinner. If you're willing to learn what really goes on in your computer, you will be welcomed with open arms. If you just want to know which box to click, read the Handbook and FAQ. The general FreeBSD community simply isn't motivated to help those who won't help themselves or who can't follow instructions. If you need more hand-holding than the community provides, you'd do best to invest in a commercial support contract. (Several good support vendors are available; check the FreeBSD Web site for details.)

The fact is, the number of people familiar with everything that FreeBSD offers are few enough to be counted on one hand. Just the week before I wrote this chapter, I saw one of the FreeBSD Project's founders express surprise when he learned that a program worked in a particular way. That made me feel good; even the masters are still learning.

The first part of your homework, then, will be to learn what resources the FreeBSD Project has available.

## Man Pages

*Man* pages, short for "manual," are the original UNIX documentation. While they have the reputation of being obtuse, difficult, or even impossible to read, they're quite user-friendly—for particular users. When man pages were first created, the average systems administrator was a C programmer and, as a result, they're written by programmers, for programmers. If you can think like a programmer, man pages are perfect for you. I've tried thinking like a programmer but have only achieved real success after remaining awake for two days straight. (A high fever helps, too, and lots of Coke.)

Over the last several years, the skill level required for systems administration has dropped, and you no longer need to be a programmer. Similarly, man pages have become more and more readable. As such, they should be your first line of attack in learning how something works. If you send a message to a mailing list without checking the man page, you're likely to get a terse "man whatever" in response.

### The FreeBSD Manual

The FreeBSD manual is divided into nine sections. Each man page (page of the manual) appears in only one section. Roughly speaking, these sections are:

1        General commands

2        System calls and error numbers

3        The C libraries

4        Devices and device drivers

5        File formats

6        Game instructions

7        Miscellaneous information

8        System maintenance commands

9        Kernel system interfaces

When reading man pages, you'll usually see the section number in parentheses after the command, like this: reboot(8). This represents both the name of the command (reboot) and the man page (8). When you see something in this format, you can check the man page for detailed information. (You can view a manual page with the man(1) command.)

Almost every topic has a man page. For example, to see the man page for the editor vi, enter this command:

```
#man vi
```

In response, you should see the following:

```
VI(1)                                                    VI(1)



NAME
       ex, vi, view - text editors

SYNOPSIS
       ex [-eFGRrSsv] [-c cmd] [-t tag] [-w size] [file ...]
       vi [-eFGlRrSv] [-c cmd] [-t tag] [-w size] [file ...]
       view [-eFGRrSv] [-c cmd] [-t tag] [-w size] [file ...]

LICENSE
       The vi program is freely redistributable.  You are welcome
       to copy, modify and share it with others under the  condi-
       tions  listed  in  the  LICENSE file.  If any company (not
       individual!) finds vi sufficiently useful that  you  would
       have  purchased  it,  or  if  any company wishes to redis-
       tribute it, contributions to the authors would be appreci-
       ated.

DESCRIPTION
       Vi  is  a  screen oriented text editor.  Ex is a line-ori-
:
```

The first bit of information shown on the top line gives the title of the man page and the relevant section number. (The title isn't necessarily the same as what you typed; for example, man ex would also lead you to the vi man page.)

### Man Page Headings

Man pages have a variety of headings. While just about any section name can appear in a man page, several are standard. (See mdoc(7) for a partial list and other man page standards.) Like book authors, man page authors generally arrange their content in a manner that makes sense for the program they're discussing. Still, there are standard headings you will see:

- NAME tells you the commands' various names. In this case, vi, ex, and view are all intertwined, and share a man page. (A little digging would show that they're the same program whose behavior depends on how they're activated.) The NAME also includes a brief description of the program.
- SYNOPSIS lists the possible command-line options and their arguments. Frequently, you'll find that this header is enough to spark your memory and remind you of a flag you've used before that caused the program to behave appropriately.
- DESCRIPTION contains a brief synopsis of the item described by the man page. The contents of this section vary depending on what the man page covers—programs, files, and kernel interfaces all have very disparate requirements.
- OPTIONS describes a program's various command-line options and their effects.

Further discussion of the program generally follows these basic headings. Two sections that commonly follow are BUGS and SEE ALSO.

The BUGS section describes known problems with the code and can frequently save a lot of headaches. How many times have you wrestled with a computer problem, only to find out that it doesn't work the way one would expect from the happy, cheerful documentation? The goal of the BUGS section is to describe known errors and other weird behavior. [1]

SEE ALSO is traditionally the last section. Remember, UNIX is like a language, and the system is an interrelated whole. Like the Force from Star Wars, or duct tape, the SEE ALSO links will show you how everything holds together.

Sometimes, too, one name will appear in multiple sections of the manual. For example, there's a man page for amd, the AMD SCSI driver, in section 4 of the manual, and a man page for amd(8), a program that automatically mounts file systems. To read a page from a particular section of the manual, put the number between the man command and the name of the page, like this: man 4 amd. (This is the first thing to look for when you get a page that seems completely irrelevant.)

To see all man pages related to a particular subject, use man -k to do a keyword search on all the man page titles. You can also use the apropos(1) command to do the same thing, which may be easier to remember if you already know what "apropos" means.

To search a man page for a word, type / followed by the word. You'll jump down to the first appearance of that word in the page. Typing **n** subsequently will jump you to the next occurrence of that word.

---

[1] It's called "honesty" as opposed to the "marketing" included in many other software products.

## The FreeBSD Documentation

If you installed the FreeBSD documentation, you'll find it under /usr/share/doc. You'll find several directories there, including one for each language that FreeBSD's documentation has been translated to. If your language of choice is English, you'll probably want the "en" directory.

The FreeBSD documentation is divided into *articles* and *books*. The difference between the two is highly arbitrary: As a rule, books are longer than articles, and cover broader topics; articles are short and focus on one topic. The two books that should most interest new users are the Handbook and the FAQ, both of which are available online at http://www.FreeBSD.org.

The Handbook is the FreeBSD Project's continually changing guidebook. It describes how to perform basic system tasks and is a good reference when you're starting on a project. The FAQ (Frequently Asked Questions), like the Handbook, is divided by topics, but also contains answers to mailing list questions. Some of the FAQ's information is duplicated in the Handbook, but most is not.

If you think you know what you're doing and have a particular question about an error you're encountering, check the FAQ. If you don't have a clue about what you're doing, check the Handbook. If the Handbook doesn't help, search for an article about what you're trying to accomplish. (You can search the entirety of the FreeBSD documentation set at http://www.FreeBSD.org/search/. If that doesn't help, you can use that same page to check the mailing list archives.)

## The Mailing List Archives

Unless you're really on the bleeding edge, someone has probably struggled with your problem before, and likely posted to the mailing lists about it. After all, the archives go back to 1994 and contain about a million messages. Of course, the challenge of having a million messages is finding what you want.

When you're stumped, take your error message and copy it into the mailing list archive search box at http://www.FreeBSD.org/search/. Remove common words such as "and," "or," "but," and so on, and hit the search button. (This page defaults to searching the FreeBSD-questions mailing list.) If you don't get a result right away, try entering another message or phrase the computer is giving you during your troubleshooting. I usually get an answer within two or three searches.

If you can't find anything useful in the FreeBSD-questions archives, try another mailing list that seems appropriate. Some good ones include FreeBSD-hackers, FreeBSD-stable, and FreeBSD-current. If you're having a problem with a particular subsystem, check for a mailing list devoted to it.

**NOTE** *The entry fields for searching the documentation and the mailing list archives are on the same page! More than once, I've searched the documentation when meaning to search the mailing list archives.*

## Other Web Sites

If you haven't found your answer by this point, there are a variety of other Web sites you might try.

**FreeBSD Diary (http://www.FreeBSDdiary.org)**   This site details users' experiences with FreeBSD. The articles include detailed descriptions of how they make everything work.

**Google (http://www.google.com)**   This site archives Usenet news on many topics, including FreeBSD. Try a power search on mailing.FreeBSD.* or comp.unix.bsd.FreeBSD.*, which will give you both the mailing lists and the newsgroups. (Google also hosts a BSD-specific search engine at http://www.google.com/bsd.)

**Daemonnews (http://www.daemonnews.org)**   This is a popular BSD news site. Their monthly issue contains a variety of articles on various BSD topics.

**The FreeBSD 'zine (http://www.FreeBSDzine.org)**   This is a bimonthly FreeBSD article site, and includes many useful articles.

**Defcon1 (http://www.defcon1.org)**   Another FreeBSD article site.

**BSD Today (http://www.bsdtoday.com)**   This Internet.com site hosts BSD articles and news links.

**O'Reilly Network BSD Developer Center (http://www.onlamp.com/bsd)**   This site hosts a variety of BSD articles, including the column "Big Scary Daemons" by yours truly.

## Using FreeBSD Problem-Solving Resources

Okay, now let's pick a common problem and use the FreeBSD resources to solve it. We'll use several different methods to find an answer. Take this typical message sent to FreeBSD-questions@FreeBSD.org.

"I've just installed FreeBSD and my network isn't working. When I try to ping, the console shows the message ed0: device timeout. What's wrong?"

### Checking the Handbook/FAQ

A scan of the handbook shows nothing related to the problem. In the FAQ, however, there's an entry under Troubleshooting:

```
I keep seeing messages like ed1: device timeout
```

That's close enough. Read that entry, and try the solution presented.

### Checking the Man Pages

As we go on, you'll learn that the numbers after device names are simply instances of a particular device. ed0 is simply device ed, unit number 0. So, type **man ed**. You will see the following:

```
.................................................................................................
ED(1)                   FreeBSD General Commands Manual                   ED(1)


NAME
     ed, red - text editor

SYNOPSIS
     ed [-] [-sx] [-p string] [file]

DESCRIPTION
     Ed is a line-oriented text editor.  It is used to create, display, modify
     and otherwise manipulate text files.

     If invoked with a file argument, then a copy of file is read into the
     editor's buffer.  Changes are made to this copy and not directly to file
     itself.  Upon quitting ed, any changes not explicitly saved  with a w
     command are lost.

     Editing is done in two distinct modes: command and input.  When first
     invoked, ed is in command mode.  In this mode commands are read from the
     standard input and executed to manipulate the contents of the editor
     buffer.  A typical command might look like:

     ,s/old/new/g
:
.................................................................................................
```

What the heck? Something's obviously amiss here. Every device driver has a man page. Run **man -k ed** to get a complete list of all the man pages related to ed. You'll get a whole list of functions, in slightly skewed alphabetical order. (Capital letters come before lowercase ones.) Scroll down to the e's, and you'll see this:

```
.................................................................................................
...
ed(1), -(1)              - ed text editor
ed(4)                    - high performance ethernet device driver
...
.................................................................................................
```

Aha! There are two different eds, in different sections, each with their own man page. Type **man 4 ed** and you'll see what you want:

```
ED(4)                    FreeBSD Kernel Interfaces Manual                    ED(4)


NAME
     ed - ethernet device driver

SYNOPSIS
     device ed

DESCRIPTION
     The ed driver provides support for 8 and 16bit ethernet cards that are
     based on the National Semiconductor DS8390 and similar NICs manufactured
     by other companies.

     It supports all 80x3 series ethernet cards manufactured by Western Digi-
     tal and SMC, the SMC Ultra, the 3Com 3c503, the Novell NE1000/NE2000 and
     compatible cards, and the HP PC Lan+.  ISA, PCI and PC Card devices are
     supported.

     The ed driver uses a unique multi-buffering mechanism to achieve high
     transmit performance.  When using 16bit ISA cards, as high as 97% of the
     theoretical maximum performance of the IEEE 802.3 CSMA ethernet is possi-
     ble.


:
```

This is what you're looking for. Looking at the error message, you can guess that timeout is a good keyword. Type **/timeout** and press **ENTER**.

```
ed%d: device timeout Indicates that an expected transmitter interrupt
     didn't occur. Usually caused by an interrupt conflict with another card
     on the ISA bus.
```

Voila! Here we have a terse explanation of the problem, and a probable cause (interrupt conflict). We have a good old-fashioned IRQ problem.

### Checking the Mailing List Archives

Searching for "ed0: device timeout" spit out quite a few results from the mailing list archives. On the day I did the search, the first response gave the solution.

### Using Your Answer

Any answer you get for our "ed0 timeout" example assumes that you know what an IRQ is, and how to adjust one on your hardware. This is fairly typical of the level of expertise required for basic problems. If you get an answer that is beyond your comprehension, you need to do the research to understand it.

While an experienced developer or systems administrator is probably not going to be interested in explaining IRQs to you, he or she might be willing to point you to a Web page that explains IRQs.

### Mailing for Help

If the archives, FAQ, Handbook, tutorials, and other assorted resources cannot help you, ask for help. When you do, be sure that you include all the information you have at your disposal, as discussed shortly. There's a lot of suggested information to include, and you can choose to skip it all. But if you do, one of two things will happen:

- Your question will be ignored.
- You will receive a barrage of email asking you to gather this information.

If, on the other hand, you actually want help to solve your problem, include the following in your message:

- A complete problem description. A message like "How do I make my modem work?" is going to generate a multitude of questions, like what do you want your modem to do? What kind of modem is it? What are the symptoms?
- It's much better to start with a message like, "My modem isn't dialing my ISP. The modem is a BleahCorp v.90 model 6789. My OS is version 4.6-stable, on a dual Athlon motherboard. There are no error log messages in /var/log/ppp.log." You'll shortcut a whole round of email by doing so. While I have never seen anyone flamed for offering too much information on the FreeBSD-questions mailing list, the converse is not true.
- The output from uname -a. This gives the operating system version and platform.
- If you run CVSup and "make world", give the date of the last CVSup, if you have it.

  The CVSup date, in seconds from the epoch, is the third field in the first line of your log file. (Of course, if you have upgraded your source without building "world", this is moot.) For example, on my system, CVSup records its data in /usr/sup. The first line of /usr/src/src-all/check-outs.cvs:RELENG_3/ is:

```
F 5 939160270
```

Running date -r 939160270 spits out the following:

```
Tue Oct  5 21:51:10 GMT 1999
```

- Any error output. Be as complete as possible, and include any messages from your logs, particularly /var/log/messages.

Finally, here are some tips for getting your best results out of a FreeBSD mailing list:

- Be polite. Remember, this list is staffed by volunteers who are answering your message out of sheer kindness. Before you hit that send key, ask yourself, "Would I be late for my date with the hot twins down the hall to answer a message from someone like this?"[2]

- Use plain text. Many FreeBSD developers read their email in a command-line environment, and find reading raw HTML quite annoying. (To see for yourself, install /usr/ports/mail/mutt and read some HTML email with it.)

- State up front exactly what you have done to solve this problem or answer this question. Make it clear that you have done your homework.

- Be on topic. If you are having a problem with XFree86, check the XFree86 site. If your window manager isn't working, ask the people who maintain it. Asking the FreeBSD folks to help you with your Java Application Server configuration is like complaining to hardware salespeople about your fast-food lunch. They might have an extra ketchup packet, but it's not really their problem. On the other hand, if your FreeBSD system starts sendmail on every boot, and you want to turn it off, check the online resources and then ask.

- Send your message to FreeBSD-questions@FreeBSD.org. Yes, there are other FreeBSD mailing lists, some of which are probably dedicated to what you're having trouble with. As a new user, however, your question is almost certainly best suited for FreeBSD-questions. I've lurked FreeBSD-stable, -current, and -hackers for years now, and have yet to see a new user ask a question there that wouldn't have been better served in FreeBSD-questions. Generally, the questioner is referred back to -questions.

Sending a message to FreeBSD-hackers asking how to fix your dial-up connection is only going to annoy them. You might get an answer, but you won't make any friends. Conversely, the people on FreeBSD-questions are there because they are volunteering to answer questions. These people want to hear from you. Quite a few are FreeBSD developers, and some are even core members. Many of them are very skilled, and many are new users who have already dealt with your problem.

[2] Quite a few developers would accept the phone number for said twins in lieu of politeness. This isn't guaranteed, and is only supported in the bleeding-edge-current.

If those folks can't help you, they'll probably refer you to another mailing list. It's much better to go to -hackers and say, "The folks on -questions suggested I ask you about this" than to just jump straight to -hackers. If you respect the FreeBSD community, they'll respect you.

- Follow through. If you're asked for more information, provide it. If you don't know how to provide it, treat it as another problem. Go back to the beginning of this chapter and try to figure it out. If someone asks you for a debugging dump, go look at Chapter 16 and set your system up for it. The bottom line is, if you develop a reputation as someone who doesn't follow up on requests for more information, you won't even get a first reply.

- Lastly, "how can I learn this" questions are more likely to be answered than "what do I do" ones. It doesn't matter if the question is about obscure system functions or simple troubleshooting; being willing to work for your answer is a necessary part of running FreeBSD. The upside is, when you're done, you will actually understand more about your computer than you did before.

Now that you understand where to go when this book doesn't quite go far enough, let's look at how you can protect yourself from your own mistakes.

# 3

# READ THIS BEFORE YOU BREAK SOMETHING ELSE! (BACKUP AND RECOVERY)

Computers fail on many levels, and hardware, software, users, and sysadmins all can damage a system. As such, you should always be ready for the worst; in our case, that means being able to back up and restore your hard drives.

Because FreeBSD is a continually evolving system, you will inevitably need to upgrade and patch your system from time to time, and any time you do so, there's a chance you'll damage the operating environment. If that happens, you'll need to recover or rebuild your system. (Just think of how many times you've patched a Microsoft server system and found something behaving oddly afterwards.) On any computer, even small configuration changes can potentially damage data.

Worse still, if you're reading this book, you're probably just learning how to configure your FreeBSD system and you're probably not well prepared for disaster. As a new user, you'll need to test a variety of configurations and review the "history" of how your system has been configured. And, if you learn that some obscure but important system function has been broken for months, you will need to look up the changes you've made in order to go back and fix it. Will you really remember what a particular file looked like weeks or months ago? In fact, if you're experimenting hard enough, you may even utterly destroy your system, so you'll need a way to recover your important data.

This chapter begins with the large-scale approach: backing up the entire computer. However, this approach won't work well if you only want to back up individual files, so we'll go on to look at ways to handle those. If a file can change three times a day, and you take weekly backups, you can lose valuable information if you rely on your weekly backups. Finally, should you encounter a partial disaster, we'll consider ways to recover and rebuild using single-user mode and the fixit disk.

## System Backups

You only need a system backup if you care about your data. The question for you to answer is "how much would it cost to replace my data?" A low-end SCSI tape backup system, for example, can run several hundred dollars. IDE systems are less expensive than SCSI, but slower, hold much less data, and are less well supported.

The questions to ask yourself when choosing a backup solution are how much your time is worth and how long it would take to restore your system from the install media. If the most important data on your hard disk *is* your Web browser's bookmarks file, it might not be worth investing in a backup system. But if your server is your company's backbone, or part of it, you'll want to take this investment very seriously.

A complete backup and restore operation requires a tape drive and tape backups. You can also back up to files, across the network, or to removable media such as CD-ROMs or floppy disk. Since we're discussing network servers, however, I'll focus on production-grade solutions.

## Tape Devices

FreeBSD supports both SCSI and IDE tape drives. When compared with IDE drives, SCSI drives are faster and more reliable, though IDE drives are cheaper. In most cases, either format will suffice.

Once you've physically installed your tape drive, you'll need to confirm that FreeBSD recognizes it. The simplest way is to check the /var/run/dmesg.boot file, which displays the system's boottime messages and shows all the hardware on your system. This is a very long file, so I won't reproduce it here. I do suggest that you examine the dmesg on your FreeBSD system and become familiar with it, because you'll have to look at it almost every time you have to troubleshoot hardware.

When you examine this file, you'll see IDE tape drives displayed as "ast" devices, and SCSI tapes as "sa" devices. Scan this file for your tape drive; if you see it, your system kernel is probably properly configured. (FreeBSD's GENERIC kernel picks up most tape drives.)

### How to Read Dmesg.boot

The first item on each line of the example boot file shown next is the device name. This particular entry represents a DDS3 tape drive, which is fairly slow by modern standards, but is still adequate. If your system has multiple tape drives, they will have sequential numbers, such as sa0, sa1, sa2, and so on. Once you know the device name, you can access the tape drive. SCSI drives are represented by the initials sa and a trailing number; IDE tape drives show up as astX instead of saX. If you have multiple identical drives, you should label which is which. If you don't know where the tape drive is plugged into the physical bus, or the SCSI ID of the device, a bit of trial and error will identify each drive. (Every time I set up a new backup server, I mean to label the tape drives by SCSI ID as I physically assemble the machine. Every time, I wind up putting a tape in each drive and trying to access it under various tape numbers, and labeling the drive that way. Either works.)

Each line for a device contains some information about the device. For example, the tape drive shown in the following example has three descriptive lines identifying how the tape is hooked into the computer's SCSI system, the model name, and the maximum speed.

```
sa0 at ahc0 bus 0 target 6 lun 0
sa0: <ARCHIVE Python 04106-XXX 7350> Removable Sequential Access SCSI-2 device
sa0: 10.000MB/s transfers (10.000MHz, offset 15)
```

Every device on your system, from onboard clock chips to PCI busses to sound cards, will have a similar entry in dmesg.boot.

The dmesg.boot file is an invaluable source of information on what hardware is actually installed. Take a look at this file on your system; you probably never knew just how much stuff was in that little beige box.

If your tape drive doesn't appear in the /var/run/dmesg.boot file, check the release notes for the version of FreeBSD you're running to be sure it's supported. If it's listed as supported, but is not in the dmesg.boot file, ask for help (see Chapter 2). You'll probably be told to rebuild your kernel (this is covered in Chapter 4).

## Controlling Your Tape Drive

Tape drives have been around for many years, and the way FreeBSD handles them reflects that history. As with many old-fashioned UNIX devices, the way you access a tape drive controls how it behaves, and before you can use your tape drive for a backup you'll need to know how to control it. The most basic tape-control mechanism is the device node you use to access it.

### Device Nodes

Device nodes, found in the /dev directory, are files that are tied to a physical device in your computer. You can use UNIX commands on the device node to control the hardware, but you shouldn't arbitrarily run commands on device nodes; doing something like cat /dev/console might not do anything, or it might damage your hardware or data. In most cases, device nodes have the same name or one similar to what appears in dmesg.boot.

Each type of tape drive has several device nodes, but for your average SCSI tape drive, you only need to worry about three nodes: /dev/esa0, /dev/nsa0, and /dev/sa0. Similarly, if you have an IDE drive, you only need concern yourself with /dev/east0, /dev/nast0, and /dev/ast0.

If you use the node name that matches the device name, the tape will automatically rewind when you're finished. For example, our sample SCSI drive is sa0, so if you run a command using /dev/sa0 as the device node, the tape will automatically rewind when the command finishes. Depending on the operating system you're used to, this might or might not match what you expect. Different versions of UNIX, with different tape management software, handle tapes differently.

**REMEMBER** *Tapes are sequential access devices; data is stored on the tape linearly. To access a particular piece of data on a tape, you must roll the tape forward or backward. To rewind or not to rewind is an important consideration.*

To have a tape eject automatically when you've finished with it, use the node that begins with "e". For example, if all you're doing is running a full system backup, you can use the /dev/esa0 device to automatically eject the tape after the job finishes. (Some older tape drives may not support automatic ejection; they'll require you to push the physical button to work the lever that winches the tape out of the drive. The simplest way to find this out is to simply try it.)

If you don't want the tape to automatically rewind when you're finished (because you need to append a second backup from a different machine onto the tape, or something similar), stop it from rewinding by using the node name that starts with an "n". In our example, if you use /dev/nsa0 in your command, the tape drive will not rewind.

### Using the TAPE Variable

Many programs assume that your tape drive is /dev/sa0, but that choice isn't always appropriate. Even if you have only one SCSI tape drive, you might not want it to automatically rewind upon completion (/dev/nsa0), or you might want it to eject after the backup (/dev/esa0). Or, you might have an IDE drive, which uses an entirely different device node.

Many programs use the environment variable $TAPE to control which device node they use, which you can always override on the command line. Most backup programs will use the device node specified in $TAPE as a default.

You can set the $TAPE variable with the following command:

```
# setenv TAPE /dev/sa0
```

**NOTE** *Not all programs recognize $TAPE, but it's generally worth setting.*

### The mt Command

Once you know which device node you want to use to talk to your tape drive, you can make it do basic things (such as rewind, retension, erase, and so on) with mt(1). The mt command is most commonly used for checking the status of a tape drive, as follows:

```
# mt status
Mode      Density              Blocksize    bpi      Compression
Current:  0x25:DDS-3           variable     97000    DCLZ
---------available modes---------
0:        0x25:DDS-3           variable     97000    DCLZ
1:        0x25:DDS-3           variable     97000    DCLZ
2:        0x25:DDS-3           variable     97000    DCLZ
3:        0x25:DDS-3           variable     97000    DCLZ
---------------------------------
Current Driver State: at rest.
---------------------------------
File Number: 0  Record Number: 0      Residual Count 0
#
```

You won't need to worry about most of the information in this output, but if you want to go through it line-by-line, the mt(1) man page contains a good description of all the features. The first thing to note in this output is that mt can find your tape drive, which means that your system is set up properly to actually use the tape drive. (In this example, mt recognizes that the tape drive is a DDS-3.) The various "modes" shown are ways that the tape drive can run. Current Driver State tells you what the drive is doing at this moment.

The first time you run mt status, you might get something like this:

```
# mt status
mt: /dev/nsa0: Device not configured
```

This means that you don't actually have a tape device at the device node your $TAPE variable is set to. You can experiment with device nodes and mt(1) by using the -f flag to specify a device node (for example, mt -f /dev/nsa1 status), though you should get this information from dmesg.boot.

Other useful mt commands are mt rewind, mt offline, and mt retension. As you might guess, mt rewind rewinds the tape, mt offline ejects it, and mt retension tightens it by running it through its complete length, both forward and back. (Retensioning is often necessary because tapes tend to stretch on their first use; retensioning prestretches the tape before you write data to it.)

**NOTE** *Not all tape drives support all mt functions, and many older drives are quite temperamental. If you have a problem with a drive, check the FreeBSD-questions mailing list archive for messages from others who have used it. You'll probably find your answer there.*

Now that you know your tape's device name and how to control it, you're ready to back up your system.

## Backup Programs

Two popular packages for backing up systems are tar(1) and dump(8). You'll certainly hear of other backup tools besides dump when working with FreeBSD, such as Amanda, pax, and cpio. Tools like these are all well-suited for certain environments, but aren't as universally useful as tar and dump. If you have mastered dump and tar, however, any of the other programs will be easy by comparison.

Tar is designed to work on files, and tar backups can be restored on almost any operating system. Dump works on disk partitions and filesystems, and can only be restored on the same operating system that the dump was made on. If you're backing up an entire computer, use dump. If you're performing small backups, or might have to restore on a very foreign computer, use tar.

### Tar

The tar package, short for "tape archiver," can back up anything from a single file to your entire system. Tar works on the files and directories only and has no idea of the underlying filesystem (which has its advantages and disadvantages). Tar is a common standard recognized by almost every UNIX and software vendor. You can find tar programs that run on Windows, Linux, UNIX, BSD, and just about every other operating system. You can even extract tar files on a Windows machine!

Tar can back up files to tape, or to a file. A tar backup file is known as a *tarball*. Since tar works on files, it's very easy to extract just one file from your tarball and restore it.

FreeBSD uses GNU tar, which is based on an old public domain tar program. GNU tar might have problems with unusual files (such as files that are mostly empty). If you have a program that writes such unusual files, the program documentation generally says to use something other than tar for your backups. And if your filesystem is corrupt in any way, heaven knows what tar will back up.

One of tar's disadvantages is that it can be dumb; for example, it will happily restore files that were damaged during the original backup (although this rarely happens in practice).

### Tar's Modes

Tar has several common modes, set by command-line flags. (See tar(1) for a description of all the modes; we'll discuss the most common ones here.)

**-v (verbose)**   One useful option is -v, or verbose mode, which tells tar to list every file it touches. You can use verbose mode to create a complete list of all the files that are backed up or restored. If you are backing up your entire system, this will be a very long list, in which it can be difficult to see errors.

**-c (create a new archive)**   Use create mode (-c) to create a new tar archive. Unless you specify otherwise, this flag backs up everything on the tape drive specified in your $TAPE environment variable. To back up your entire system, tell tar to archive everything from the root directory down:

```
# tar -c * /
```

In response, your tape drive should light up, and, if your tape is big enough, eventually present you with a complete backup of your system.

Of course, many hard drives today are considerably larger than most tapes, often by many gigabytes. As such, it will often make sense to back up only portions of your system. For example, if all the files that change on your system are under /home, /usr/local, and /var, you could specify those directories on the command line:

```
# tar -c /home /usr/local /var
```

**-t (list all files in an archive)**  List mode (-t) lists all the files in an archive. Once the drive finishes running, you can use this flag to list the tape's contents:

```
# tar -t
COPYRIGHT
bin/
bin/cat
bin/chio
bin/chmod
bin/cp
bin/date
bin/dd
bin/df
...
```

In the output above, note that the initial slashes are missing from every filename. For example, /COPYRIGHT shows up as COPYRIGHT. This becomes important during restores, which we'll discuss under the -x flag, next.

**-x (extract all files from an archive)**  In extract mode (-x), tar retrieves files from the archive and copies them to the disk.

Tar extracts files in your current location; to overwrite the existing system /etc with the backup, go to the root directory first. For example, to restore my /etc directory under /home/mwlucas/etc, use the following commands:

```
# cd /home/mwlucas
# tar -x etc
```

Remember when I said that the missing initial slash would be important? Here's why. You might want to restore a system to some location on disk other than where it came from. I've had old servers that were backed up and shut down, their hard drives thrown in the trash or donated to charity. If the backup included the initial slashes, tar would consider the filenames to be absolute path names and would restore the files exactly where they originally were; /kernel on the backup would be restored over the current system's /kernel! This would be bad.

Without the initial slash in the backup, tar will restore the file in the current directory. If I really wanted to restore the backed-up files to their original locations, I would just have to type cd / to take me to the system's root directory and then run tar.

**-d (diff an archive)**    Finally, verify the backup with the -d (diff) flag. If everything on your tape matches everything on your system, tar -d will run silently. It will be a surprise, though, if absolutely everything matches: If nothing else, log files usually grow while a backup runs, so the backed-up ones won't compare properly. Or, if you have a system with a live database, the database files might not match.

You'll need to decide which errors you can live with, and which need fixing. For example, while you may decide that you need to shut down your database before running a backup, you might not care about log files. (If you encounter problems when verifying your backups, check the documentation for the program that is giving you trouble.)

### Other tar Flags

Tar has several other useful flags that you can add to one of the previously mentioned ones to enhance its operation.

**-z (gzip)**    The gzip flag (-z) runs the files though the gzip compression program on their way to and from the archive. (Compressed tarballs usually have the extension .tar.gz or .tgz, and on rare occasions .taz.) Compressing files can greatly reduce the size of an archive; in fact, many backups can be compressed by 50 percent or more. While all modern versions of tar support -z, older versions don't, so if you want absolutely everyone to be able to read your compressed files, don't use the -z option.

**-Z**    In contrast, all versions of tar on all versions of UNIX can shrink files with the -Z flag, which utilizes compress(1). The compress program isn't as efficient as gzip, but it does reduce file size. Tarballs compressed with -Z have the extension .tar.Z.

**-y**    FreeBSD's tar supports bzip compression, which compresses files more tightly than gzip but is only readable on a few platforms and uses more CPU time than gzip compression. If you'll only be reading your files on a FreeBSD system, use the -y flag.

**-f**    The -f flag allows you to specify another device or file as the destination for your archive. For example, in all of the preceding examples, I've set $TAPE.

If you haven't, you might need to specify the tape drive with -f:

```
# tar -cz -f /dev/east0 *
```

Instead of writing a backup to tape, you can create a tar file. Source code distributed over the Net is frequently distributed as tar files, or tarballs. Use the -f flag for this as well. For example, to back up my chapters for this book as I wrote them, I'd run the following every so often to create the tarball mybookbackup.tgz:

```
# tar -cz -f mybookbackup.tgz /home/mwlucas/absolutebsd/
```

Once complete, I'd FTP the tarball to a server elsewhere so that if my house were to burn down, my book would be safe. I could then run phone and power lines to the neighbor's house, download the tarball to my laptop, run `tar -xzf mybookbackup.tgz`, and work amidst the charred timbers while waiting for the insurance company. (It's not like I could do much else at that point!)

**-v (verbose)**   To watch tar at work, use the -v flag. Tar will then list every file it touches in verbose mode. But beware: If you're backing up your entire system, this can lead to a lot of information.

### And More

Tar has many, many other options. Some good options include -C (change directories), -p (restore permission information), and -l (don't span filesystems). Read tar(1) for the full details. This section has given you enough to start working, however.

### *Dump/Restore*

Dump(8) is a disk-block backup tool. In some ways, dump is similar to tar, with the significant difference that it's aware of the underlying disk and actually reads what is directly on the disk; the filesystem is irrelevant. We'll talk more about filesystems in Chapter 16. For now, know that a filesystem is simply the order in which zeroes and ones are arranged on the physical hard drive. Different operating systems arrange data in different ways: Windows has the NT File System (NTFS), Linux has the Second Extended File System (EXT2), and FreeBSD uses UNIX File System (UFS). A tool like dump doesn't care about whatever goofball contortions the operating system puts on the physical disk—it just backs up the ones and zeroes on the physical disk. This makes it possible to

---

[1] Some sysadmins will disagree and insist that tar(1) is better. This is a disagreement of epic proportions in the UNIX community, and any recommendation I make will undoubtedly anger the 49 percent of the sysadmin community that is devoted to the other tool. (The remaining 2 percent insists that the only way to provide proper backups is via one of a dozen other tools.)

create a more reliable backup. New sysadmins aren't as likely to be familiar with dump as with tar, but dump is more efficient and safer than tar. When you have a choice, use dump.[1]

On the downside, dump works on entire filesystems, not on individual files. Therefore, you can't dump /etc unless you want to back up the entire / partition. (Though if you do, you can restore individual files.)

On the positive side, dump uses separate programs for backup and restore (restore is discussed in "Restoring from an Archive" later in the chapter). This means you don't have to worry about confusing your flags and accidentally overwriting the file you're trying to recover from. Dump is considerably faster than tar, too.

### User Control

Perhaps dump's most significant advantage is that users have a certain amount of control over dump. For example, they can mark a file as "do not dump," and it won't be backed up. Many users have stuff that they don't care about, and they will happily agree not to back those things up if it means that the data they care about is backed up.

To set the nodump flag, use chflags(1):

```
# chflags nodump filename
```

When you set chflags on a directory, everything in or below that directory is not backed up. I use chflags to avoid backing up my downloads directory to save time and space during backups because I can always re-download those items.

### Dump Levels

Dump has a variety of options, the most common of which is the *dump level*, which ranges from 0 to 9. The default level is 0, which tells dump to copy everything on the disk not marked nodump. Higher levels of dump mean "back up any files that have changed or been created since a dump of any lower level." This sequence of levels allows you to do incremental backups—just specify the desired dump level as a command-line flag:

```
dump -0
```

This command means do a level 0 dump.

For example, say you start each Monday with a level 0 dump. On Tuesday you could do an incremental dump at level 1, and only files that have changed since Monday will be dumped. If you then perform a level 2 dump on Wednesday, everything changed since Tuesday will be backed up. If, however, you were to run another level 1 dump on Thursday, everything that has changed since Monday will be backed up.

Although you can run incremental backups with dump, I recommend that you run level 0 dumps only because they are far, far easier to restore from than a series of incremental backups. Level 0 dumps do take longer to run than incrementals, however, and take up more space, but in most cases, saving recovery time is more important than the cost of tape. With proper planning, you can simply run your level 0 dumps overnight.

### Other Dump Flags

You can use a variety of other flags to control exactly how dump behaves.

**-f**   Unfortunately, dump doesn't recognize $TAPE, and rather blindly defaults to /dev/sa0. If that is your tape drive, you're all set. If not, use -f to tell dump where to put the archive.

> **NOTE**   *-f can point to a file, not just a tape device. If you're experimenting with dump or if you plan to copy the archive to another machine, it's perfectly legitimate to dump to a file.*

**-a**   The -a flag is another important option. While dump tries to allocate tape space intelligently, tapes have grown considerably since dump first came out, and the math dump uses isn't really applicable to the large tapes of today. Dump tends to assume that you have an old-fashioned, and much smaller, tape, and doesn't really understand that some people have 200GB tapes. In fact, when you're using -f, you might not even have a tape.

The -a flag tells dump not to bother calculating tape requirements, and to just dump to the tape until it hits a physical end-of-tape marker. Use -a whenever you dump to a file.

**-h**   As the systems administrator, you can use the -h option to decide when to honor the nodump file flag. This option takes a dump level as an argument.

By default, files marked nodump will be backed up anyway if the sysadmin runs a level 0 dump. At dump level 1 or higher, the nodump flag is honored; the -h flag changes this behavior by specifying the minimum dump level to start obeying the nodump flag. Any dumps of levels below that given by -h will archive everything, regardless of the dump flag.

For example, I usually back up a system with a command like dump -0 /; this performs a full dump on my entire system, and even backs up items marked nodump. If my backups suddenly fill the tape, or start running over a tape, I change this to dump -0 -h0 /. The backup then obeys the nodump flag, which reduces the backup size. This gives me a bit of breathing room; the backups are manageable, and I won't lose important data. I immediately order more tapes.

**-u**   The file /etc/dumpdates records everything that you've dumped on your system. If you use -u, you'll update the file. This is most useful if you decide to do incremental backups, in which case you will need to know the date of your last full backup to successfully restore the system.

To dump the root partition onto your IDE tape drive, skip files marked nodump, update /etc/dumpdates, and eject the tape afterwards, enter:

```
# dump -0ua -h0 -f /dev/east0 /
```

Once you issue this command, several fairly self-explanatory messages will pass across your screen with information on how the dump is going. If the size of your dump exceeds the size of your tape, dump will tell you when to swap tapes.

### Volumes

Hard drives are frequently bigger than tapes, and one hard drive might need several tapes for a complete backup. When using multiple tapes to back up a hard drive, every tape has a volume number: The first tape you fill is volume 1, the second is volume 2, and so on.

Dump will tell you each tape's volume number as it finishes filling them. (I strongly recommend labeling each tape as it is finished!) When you have to restore from your dump, you will either be prompted for a particular volume or asked which volume you're loading.

## Restoring from an Archive

Archives are nice, but they're useless unless you can use them to recover your system. Dump's recovery utility, restore(8), can recover either complete filesystems or individual files. As with tar and dump, the -f flag lets you choose the device or file you wish to restore from.

### Checking the Contents of an Archive

To list the contents of an archive, use the -t flag. If you add a filename after -t, restore will check to see if that file exists, like so:

```
# restore -f /dev/ast0 -t /etc/motd
Dump   date: Thu Mar 22 13:30:39 2001
Dumped from: the epoch
Level 0 dump of / on turtledawn.blackhelicopters.org:/dev/ad0s2a
Label: none
    18935     ./etc/motd
#
```

In this example, we're using the tape drive device node of /dev/ast0 in the input, which, as we discussed in the "Device Nodes" section of this chapter, is an IDE drive. Using this device node tells the command to rewind the tape when it finishes. The –t tells restore to check for the file /etc/motd. Restore tells us when the dump took place, which system it was taken on, and which disk device was backed up.

### Extracting Data from an Archive

Once you know whether a file is in an archive, you can extract data from the archive in two ways: on a file-by-file basis or as a complete filesystem.

#### Restoring a File

If all you want is a few select pieces, use -x and the filename to extract only the named file. For example, to recover /etc/namedb from a dump archive written to a file, you'd enter the following command and see the subsequent response :

```
# restore -f /var/tmp/slashbackup -x /etc/namedb
You have not read any tapes yet.
Unless you know which volume your file(s) are on you should start
with the last volume and work towards the first.
Specify next volume #:
Specify next volume #: 1
set owner/mode for '.'? [yn] y
#
```

**NOTE**  *Notice that restore asks you for a volume number. If you're recovering from a file, this is irrelevant, but if you're restoring from a series of tapes, you'll need to enter the tape number. If you only have one tape, enter 1.*

Once the preceding command completes, the current directory should have a directory etc, containing the complete namedb directory.

### Restoring a Filesystem

Restoring an entire filesystem is rather straightforward; just bear in mind that it's best not to restore a filesystem over the existing one. If you need massive restorations, it's safer to erase the partition and start over.

In the following example, we will completely erase a partition on a second IDE disk and recover from our backup tape. We won't go into details on the disk work here (see Chapter 13 for more information), but what we're doing can be summarized like this:

1.  We build a new filesystem with fdisk.
2.  We attach that filesystem to the directory system, under /mnt.
3.  We go into that directory and run the restore from the tape device /dev/ast0.

These are the commands:

```
# newfs /dev/ad1s1g
# mount /dev/ad1s1g /mnt
# cd /mnt
# restore -rf /dev/ast0
```

### *Restoring Interactively*

One of dump's most interesting features is interactive mode, -i, which you can use to crack open a dump (either file or tape) and access it with a command-line tool, marking files that you want to restore. Interactive mode is terribly useful when a user says something like, "I accidentally erased my resume. It's somewhere in my home directory, and the name has the word resume in it—I'm not sure exactly what it's called. Can you get it back?" Obviously the −t flag won't help us; we don't know exactly what the file is called! Instead, we can wander around in restore's interactive mode until we find the file.

The following listing shows me interactively opening a dump file called root.dump. (It works just as well on a dump on tape, mind you!) Restore then presents a *restore command prompt*, which looks a lot like your regular FreeBSD command prompt but only supports commands specific to restore.

```
#restore -i -f root.dump
restore > ls
.:
.cshrc          compat@         kernel.GENERIC  modules.good/   sys@
.profile        dev/            kernel.good     modules.old/    tmp@
COPYRIGHT       dist/           kernel.old      proc/           usr/
bin/            etc/            laptop-kernel   root/           var/
boot/           home@           mnt/            sbin/
cdrom/          kernel          modules/        stand/

restore >
```

Once you've opened the dump file, as shown in the listing, you can maneuver through it using ls(1) to list the contents of a directory, and cd(1) to change directories.

Once you have found the file you want to restore, you need to actually restore it. The interactive version of restore keeps a list of files that need to be extracted from the dump. When using restore, you add each file you want to restore to the list, and then tell restore to pull the files from the dump. You can add a file to this list by entering add and the filename. For example, to restore /etc/master.passwd and /etc/passwd from the interactive dump shown in the earlier example, enter the following commands:

```
restore > cd etc
restore > add master.passwd
restore > add passwd
restore > extract
You have not read any tapes yet.
Unless you know which volume your file(s) are on you should start
with the last volume and work towards the first.
Specify next volume #: 1
set owner/mode for '.'? [yn] y
restore > quit
```

The "volume #" referred to in the preceding listing is the number of the tape you have placed in the machine. Many dumps require several tapes, and each gets a volume number during the dump. If you're restoring from a file, the volume number is 1. If you were able to fit your entire dump onto a single tape, the volume number is 1 as well.

**NOTE** *Whenever you perform a full disk restore, run another level 0 dump before another incremental dump. Restore rearranges data on the disk, so further incremental backups won't be useful without a new level 0 backup. And have I mentioned how much easier your life is when you always run full backups?*

## Recording What Happened

Script(1) is one of those rarely mentioned but quite useful tools every systems administrator should know. It records everything you type, as well as everything that appears on the screen, in a file called *typescript*. You can then use this typescript file to record errors or long output to be dissected or analyzed later. Script continues recording until you type **exit**.

For example, if you're running a program that fails at the same spot every time, you can use script to copy your keystrokes and what the screen says in response. This is particularly useful when upgrading your system or building software from source code; the last 30 or so lines of the typescript file make a nice addition to a request for help.

## Revision Control

Generally speaking, revision control is the process of tracking changes. In the UNIX world, this means changes to source code or configuration files. Revision control allows a developer to see how a piece of code looked on a specific date, or an administrator to see how the system was configured before things stopped working. Even a lowly writer can use revision control to see how a manuscript has changed over time. If you're not using revision control, you're making your work more difficult than it needs to be. [2]

While you'll encounter many revision-control systems, from UNIX's SCCS (Source Code Control System) to Microsoft's Visual SourceSafe, we'll discuss RCS (Revision Control System), included with almost all UNIX systems. Once you learn how to work with RCS, you should find it simple to work with most any other revision-control system.

When using revision control, you're essentially keeping a record of what happened to a file. First, you mark the file as *checked out*, which tells the system that you are going to change the file. You then edit the file as you like, record changes in the system, and release the file for others to edit. RCS uses three basic commands to accomplish this: ci (check-in), co (check-out), and rcs.

---

[2] Some reviewers commented that this section might scare off new sysadmins. Others said that they'd wished they'd known about revision control when they started. Don't be intimidated; it's not that difficult and it really will make life better for you.

Think of revision control as a library—an old-fashioned brick-and-mortar one. To edit a file, you must first tell RCS to keep track of it, or give it to the library. To use it you check it out, like removing a book from a library. Once checked out, nobody else can save or edit that file, though any legitimate user can view, use, copy, compile, or access that file. Once you finish with the file, you check it back in, thus releasing it for others to edit. The whole process is called RCS.

Each file in RCS has a version number. Each time you return an edited file to the system, the Revision Control System compares the returned file with what you checked out. If there is any change at all, the version number is increased by one, which is the system's way of tracking changes to the file. You can use the version number to identify specific versions of the file.

Begin the revision-control process by checking in a file with ci(1), which is much like giving a book to the library. For example, a good file to protect with RCS is /etc/rc.conf. To start the RCS process, enter **ci <path/filename>** as shown in the following listing:

```
❶ # ci /etc/rc.conf
rc.conf,v <-- rc.conf
❷ enter description, terminated with single '.' or end of file:
NOTE: This is NOT the log message!
❸ >>System configuration file
❹ >> .
initial revision: 1.1 done
#
```

When you first check in a file with ci (❶), ci creates or edits a revision-control file. You see this in the second line of the preceding output, where it creates rc.conf,v. It then asks you for a description (❷); enter a descriptive bit of text here (❸) for any RCS user to later view the file's description. (While this description isn't very important for standard system files, it can be very helpful for source code or configuration files for custom or complex programs.) Once you've finished the description, enter a single period on a line by itself (❹) to exit ci.

If you run ls immediately after checking something in, you'll notice that the file appears to have vanished. Instead you'll see a file with the same name, with a trailing ",v". This is an RCS file, where the file and its changes are stored. While it's fine for some files to disappear in this fashion, source code or Web pages can't just vanish. To solve that problem, when checking in a file you can leave a copy in the working directory with ci -u.

If a file is checked in and has vanished, and you want to put a clean copy in the working directory without editing it, use the co command. In the following example, you can see that the file test has been pulled out of the file test,v, and that it's revision 1.1.

```
# co test
test,v  --> test
revision 1.1
done
#
```

Looking closely at the directory where the file test lives, you'll see this:

```
# ls -l
total 62
-r--r--r--  1 mwlucas   mwlucas   12663 Oct  4 18:06 test
-r--r--r--  1 mwlucas   mwlucas   12867 Oct  4 17:56 test,v
#
```

I own this file, test, but the permissions have been set to read-only (-r--r--r--, as discussed in Chapter 7). I no longer have permission to edit my own files! This is because the file isn't checked out to me. I've checked it in, or handed it over to the Revision Control System librarian. I can view the file, but if I want to edit it, I have to ask the Revision Control Librarian for it—I need to check it out, and then lock it for my personal use. I use the -l flag with co.

```
# co -l test
test,v  --> test
revision 1.1 (locked)
done
```

Notice the third line of this listing (the second line of output), which specifies locked. This file is checked out and locked by me, and I am the only one who can save it until I unlock it.

Running another ls at this point will show that the permissions on the file test are now set back to read and write, allowing me to save.[3] (We'll discuss permissions in Chapter 7.) Anyone else who tries to check out this file will get a warning that the file is in use and will be told the username of the person who has locked the file.

When finished, I check in the file and, since I want other people to be able to edit the file, I use ci -u to release my lock.

[3] A warning to vi users; if you or your group owns the file, a w! will force a permission change and allow you to write to the file even without checking it out. Everything will look fine, but the next person who checks out the file will overwrite your changes! Be careful using w! anything; if vi complains that you don't have permission to save, there's a good reason. Listen to it.

```
# ci -u test
test,v <-- test
new revision: 1.2; previous revision: 1.1
❶ enter log message, terminated with single '.' or end of file:
>> enable sendmail again
>> .
done
#
```

When you check something in, you are asked for a log message (❶). Enter a brief description of your changes here. (These log messages are comparable to the CVS log messages seen on the various BSDs' commit mailing lists.)

These log messages allow others to know what changes you've made to a file without checking through all the changes—or, alternatively, to see what you were *trying* to do when your change broke something and someone has to start debugging. Your own RCS logs can also be useful for you, months later, when you stare at something and wonder just what was going on inside your head at the time.

**NOTE** *If you have lots of files in RCS, the ",v" files can quickly clutter a directory. You can hide them by creating a directory called RCS. The ci program will then put the ",v" files in that directory, keeping the working directory cleaner.*

Now that you understand the basics of checking files in and out, let's examine some of the more interesting functions of RCS. These include getting old versions of files, breaking locks, finding differences between file versions, and putting RCS identifiers in files.

### Getting Older Versions

Every file in RCS has a revision number, and each time you check in a file, the revision number increases. The system remembers what the file looked like during earlier revisions, however, so you can use the revision number to check out any previous version of a file.

For example, if you're trying to track a bug that's just appeared, you can check out earlier versions of your code to see if they also exhibit the bug by using co's -r flag. To retrieve version 1.1 of /etc/rc.conf, enter the following:

```
# co -r1.1 rc.conf
RCS/rc.conf,v --> rc.conf
revision 1.1
done
#
```

### Breaking Locks

Always check files in once you've finished with them. If you don't, and another user needs to edit your locked file, they'll have to break your lock, and any changes you've made since locking it will be lost.

To break a lock on a file, use rcs -u. RCS will ask you to enter a message about why you're breaking the lock, and this message will be mailed to the lock holder.

**NOTE** *Be careful when breaking locks: If someone is really editing a file when you force the lock, they'll be justifiably upset. If they've gone home for the day, that's another thing. Do your best to find the person before you break his or her lock!*

### Viewing Log Messages

The rlog command shows you the log messages for the file.

```
# rlog /etc/rc.conf

RCS file: /etc/RCS/rc.conf,v
Working file: /etc/rc.conf
head: 1.4
branch:
locks: strict
access list:
symbolic names:
keyword substitution: kv
total revisions: 4;     selected revisions: 4
description:
----------------------------
revision 1.4
❶date: 2000/09/08 17:45:29; ❷author: mwlucas; ❸state: Exp; ❹lines: +2 -0
minor updates
----------------------------
revision 1.3
date: 2000/09/07 19:05:30;  author: mwlucas;  state: Exp;  lines: +1 -1
❺ *** empty log message ***
----------------------------
revision 1.2
date: 2000/09/05 16:09:47;  author: mwlucas;  state: Exp;  lines: +1 -1
enable sendmail
```

```
--------------------------
revision 1.1
date: 2000/09/02 14:53:43;  author: mwlucas;  state: Exp;
Initial revision
--------------------------
========================================================================
#
```

All sorts of useful information appear here, including the date each check-in was made (❶), the author of the change (❷), the entry's state (❸), which we won't worry about here (see ci(1)), and the number of lines changed (❹).

### Reviewing a File's Revision History

Notice that in the previous section I didn't bother to leave a log message in revision 1.3 (❺). To see what changed, I use rcsdiff, which takes three arguments: two revisions and a filename, as shown here.

```
# rcsdiff -r1.2 -r1.3 /etc/rc.conf
==================================================================
RCS file: /etc/RCS/rc.conf,v
retrieving revision 1.2
retrieving revision 1.3
diff -r1.2 -r1.3
6c6
< inetd_enable="NO"
❶ > inetd_enable="YES"
#
```

Apparently I turned inetd on between the revisions (❶), which is important information (especially if yours is a production system, especially one administered by several people). We'll discuss inetd in Chapter 13.

You can also use rcsdiff between arbitrary revision numbers, allowing you to view all the changes made between any two revisions. In the preceding example, we chose the differences between two consecutive versions. I could have asked for the differences between revisions 1.1 and 1.4, however, and seen everything that had changed since the file was first checked in.

### Ident and ident Strings

Identification strings are used to make it easy for someone to see who has changed a file, and when it was changed. For example, if I have a server that has been behaving oddly for the last week, I just want to know what changed a week ago. I could go around running rlog on every system configuration file to see when things were changed, but that's a bit annoying. It would be much nicer to just look at the file and have that information presented to me. That's where identification strings come in. You can put ident strings in your system configuration files. When you check a file out, RCS will automatically update them.

RCS supports many ident strings, each with the form $string$. For example, the RCS ident string $Id$ puts information about the last change in the file. I always put #$Id$ in the first line of my systems' /etc/rc.conf and check it in. It appears as:

```
#$Id: rc.conf,v 1.5 2000/10/05 18:29:49 mwlucas Exp mwlucas $
```

*The pound sign (#) is a comment that tells /etc/rc not to try to run the line. Use whatever comment marker is appropriate for the file.*

The following are some typical ident strings.

$Id$ is the most commonly used ident string. It shows the full path to the RCS file, the revision number, the date and time of the first check-in, the author, the state, and the person who last locked it.

*RCS state is an arbitrary string that you can assign with ci(1) or rcs(1). You can set arbitrary states for a file to give a hint about what it's for or what its condition is. Many people will use this to mark a file as "experimental" or "production" or "don't change for any reason whatsoever." You don't need to worry about the file state, just accept that it defaults to* Exp, *or "experimental." RCS state is not generally used in systems administration.*

$Header$ is another common ident string. It's identical to $Id$, except that it gives the full path for the RCS file instead of just the filename.

$Log$ is an interesting ident string that adds the RCS log message to the file itself; when you view the file, you will see the log messages. While the log messages can be overwhelming on heavily edited files, they can be useful in files that change less frequently. For example, the /etc/rc.conf on my servers doesn't change at all after a month or so of production use. If I put this ident string in the file, I will see all RCS log messages in the actual file. This makes it very obvious what's changed, who has changed it, and why.

There are several more ident strings, but they're basically subsets of the three just described. See ident(1) for a complete list.

### Going Further

Revision control is a powerful tool. You can find a mostly complete tutorial at http://www.csc.calpoly.edu/~dbutler/tutorials/winter96/rcs/.

# Single-User Mode

Unlike many other operating systems, BSD-based systems can perform a minimal boot, which is important for troubleshooting and system repair.

This minimal boot, also called single-user mode, loads the kernel and finds devices, but doesn't automatically set up your disk, start the network, enable system security, or run the standard UNIX services. Single-user mode is the first point at which the system can possibly give you a command prompt, however, so you can enable any of these services from there.

When a FreeBSD box first starts to boot, it gives you a ten-second countdown and offers you a chance to pause the system. If you press a key, it drops you to an OK prompt. To boot into single-user mode from this prompt, enter the following:

```
OK> boot -s
```

You'll see the regular device-probe messages flow by, and then the system will offer you a chance to choose a shell. (You can enter any shell on the root partition; I usually just take the default, /bin/sh, but you can use /bin/tcsh if you prefer.)

You can use single-user mode to reset a lost root password by simply doing this:

```
# fsck -p
# mount -a
# passwd root
# exit
```

The mount -a command mounts the filesystems listed in /etc/fstab (see Chapter 13). If one of those filesystems is misbehaving and crashing the system, you can mount filesystems individually by specifying them on the mount command line (for example, mount /usr).

If your system is even more badly damaged, you might not be able to read /etc/fstab. In this case, you can mount the root partition by using the device name as described in Chapter 13, which is probably either /dev/ad0s1a (for IDE disks) or /dev/da0s1a (for SCSI disks). You can use this to mount the partition, specifying the mount point where you want it to be accessible. For example, to mount your first IDE disk to root, enter this command:

```
# mount /dev/ad0s1a /
#
```

Here's how this has worked for me: Once I was experimenting with FreeBSD's Linux mode. I had an experimental Linux filesystem listed in /etc/fstab. When

---

[4] Please note that none of this is recommended. One of the nice things about FreeBSD is that it doesn't forbid you to do dangerous things; instead, it lets you learn *why* they're considered dangerous.

I upgraded to a recent FreeBSD-current (see Chapter 6), that filesystem stopped working.[4] When that filesystem was mounted, the computer crashed. Worse, the computer tried to mount it every time the system booted. The computer would boot halfway, crash, and try to boot again, over and over and over again. I booted into single-user mode, manually fsck'd /usr, mounted it, and used vi to edit /etc/fstab to comment out the offending filesystem.

You can use similar techniques to enable or disable anything on your system before it finishes booting, just by editing /etc/rc.conf (see Chapter 9) or the appropriate /usr/local/etc/rc.d file (see Chapter 11). This lets you do things like alter the system's securelevel (explained in Chapter 7) before the system finishes booting.

**NOTE** *To activate the network while in single-user mode, use the script /etc/netstart to do so without starting any network services, such as inetd or httpd.*

The commands you have available to you in single-user mode will depend on which partitions you have mounted. Some basic commands are on the root partition, in /bin and /sbin. Others (such as vi and ee) live on /usr and are inaccessible until you mount that partition. Take a look in /bin and /sbin on your system to get an idea what you'll have to work with.

If you can't even boot into single-user mode, then you're left with one final option: the fixit disk.

## The Fixit Disk

The best way to learn UNIX is to play with it, and the harder you play, the more you learn. If you play hard enough, you'll break something for sure, and having to fix a badly broken system is arguably the fastest way of all to learn. If you've just rendered your system unbootable, or plan to learn quickly enough to risk doing that, this section is for you. You're going to learn a lot quickly—though mostly on your own.

One of the more interesting portions of FreeBSD is the fixit disk. You can boot off the installation media but choose to enter *fixit mode* instead of installing the OS. The choice to use fixit mode is in the first menu the installer gives you.

You *must* have some familiarity with systems administration to use the fixit system successfully! Essentially, the fixit disk gives you a command prompt and a variety of UNIX utilities. You get to use your brains and the boottime error messages to fix the problem. It's you against the computer. Of the half-dozen times I've resorted to the fixit disk, the computer won the first three. The time was well spent, however, as I'm now fairly capable of restoring a damaged system. Definitely finish reading this book before you even try.

It's impossible to outline a step-by-step fixit process; the exact process you need to follow depends on exactly what sort of damage you've done to your poor, innocent computer. If you're really desperate, however, fixit mode gives you a shot at recovery without a complete reinstall. I've had problems where I've accidentally destroyed my /etc or /dev directories, or fried the "getty" programs that display a login prompt. Careful use of fixit mode can repair these problems in a fraction of the time a reinstall would require.

To use fixit mode, you need a set of FreeBSD installation media (either the CD or the two boot floppies) and either a fixit floppy or the second CD from the FreeBSD release you're using. You can download the fixit floppy image from any FreeBSD FTP server. You can get recent FreeBSD release CDs from various vendors, such as Daemon News and the FreeBSD Mall.

It's important to use a fixit disk that's roughly equivalent to the FreeBSD version you're running. A point or two off won't make much difference, but you won't be happy trying to fix a 4.4-stable system with a 5.0-current fixit disk.

Boot off the installation media. When you reach the first menu, you'll see a choice to enter fixit mode. Select it. You'll then get a choice of using the CD or the floppy. Use the CD if you have it. The fixit floppy only contains the programs that will fit on a single floppy disk. If you have a fixit CD, you will have the full range of programs available on a default FreeBSD install. While it might not include your favorite editor or shell, it should have everything you need.

You can mount your existing hard drive under /mnt. Programs are either under /stand or /mnt2. The exact commands you get vary from one release of FreeBSD to another; run `ls /mnt2` and `ls /stand` to see what you have.

At times, all you can hope for is to get the hard drive mounted so that you can read data from it—the fixit CD contains all the tools you will need to get the system on the network. One of the good points of the FreeBSD installer is that you have the option to keep existing partitions. You can tar up existing data files while running on the fixit disk, and then reinstall. Once you have a running system, you can extract the tarballs, and have your system back.

Now that you understand how to recover your system, configuration, and files, let's go on and start customizing your operating system for your computer.

# 4

## KERNEL GAMES

The first step in optimizing FreeBSD is to configure the kernel. If you're new to UNIX administration, the word *kernel* might be intimidating. After all, the kernel is one of those secret parts of the system that mere mortals are not meant to dabble in. In fact, in some versions of UNIX, such as Solaris, going in and tampering directly with the kernel is unthinkable. In the open-source UNIX world, however, meddling with the kernel is the best way to improve your performance. (It would probably be the best way to tune other operating systems as well, if you were allowed to.)

The FreeBSD kernel can be dynamically tuned, or changed on the fly, and most aspects of system performance can be changed as needed. We'll discuss the kernel's sysctl interface, and how you can use it to alter a running kernel.

At the same time, some parts of the kernel cannot be altered while running, and some kernel features require extensive reconfiguration. Also, you might want to reduce the size of your kernel by removing unneeded components. The best way to do this is to build your own kernel, and I'll show you how.

Finally, we'll discuss loadable kernel modules—kernel subsystems that can be turned on or off as needed.

# What Is the Kernel?

You'll hear many different definitions of *kernel*. Many are just flat-out confusing. The following definition isn't complete, but it's good enough for our purposes, and it's comprehensible: *The kernel is the interface between the hardware and the software.*

The kernel allows you to write data to disk drives and the network. It handles CPU and memory operations. It translates an MP3 to a stream of zeros and ones that your sound card understands, and tells your monitor where to put the little colored dots. The kernel provides interfaces to programs that need access to the hardware.

While the kernel's job is easy to define (at least in this simplistic manner), it is difficult to actually perform. Different programs expect the kernel to provide different interfaces to the hardware, and pieces of hardware provide their resources in varying ways. The kernel has to cope with all of this. For example, your kernel controls memory usage, and if you have a program that demands that memory be allocated in a way your kernel doesn't support, you're in trouble. (Programs request memory in a variety of ways.) Too, if your kernel doesn't know how to talk to your network card, the network card won't work. The way your kernel investigates some hardware during the boot sequence defines how the hardware behaves, so you have to control that. Some network cards identify themselves in a friendly manner, while others lock up hard if sent a simple query.

The actual kernel is a file on disk: /kernel. *Kernel modules*—the kernel code that can be loaded and unloaded after boot—lives in /modules. Kernel modules are required in this day of detachable hardware, such as PC Cards and USB, and they can also provide additional functionality that you don't want to permanently add to the kernel. Every file you see outside of /kernel and /modules is not part of the kernel; these files and programs as a group are called the *userland*, meaning they're meant for users. But at the same time, these programs and data use the kernel facilities.

On a newly installed system, you'll also see a file /kernel.GENERIC, which is the generic install kernel. On systems that have been running for a while, you might also find a variety of other kernels, some of which will be old, while others are alternates for particular circumstances or experiments that didn't work out. The FreeBSD team makes configuring and installing kernels as simple as possible. Let's take a look.

# Configuring Your Kernel

FreeBSD provides two main ways to configure an existing kernel: sysctl(8) and the boot loader.

## Sysctl

The sysctl program allows you to peek at values used by the kernel, and in some cases to set them. Just to make things confusing, these values are also sometimes known as *sysctls*. Sysctl is a powerful feature because, in many cases, it will let you solve performance issues without rebuilding the kernel or reconfiguring an application. Unfortunately, this power also gives you the ability to kick the legs out from under a running program and make your users really, really unhappy.

All sysctl operations are performed with the sysctl(8) command. Throughout this book, I will be pointing out particular sysctls that change system behavior, but you should understand what they are first.

Before we begin playing with sysctl operations, take a look at the sysctls available on your system. The following command will save them to a file so you can study them easily:

```
# sysctl -A > sysctl.out
```

After running this command, the file sysctl.out will contain hundreds of sysctl variables and their values, most of which will mean absolutely nothing to you at this point, but some are easily understood:

```
kern.hostname: bigbox.blackhelicopters.org
```

This particular sysctl is named kern.hostname and has a value of "bigbox.blackhelicopters.org". The system I ran this command on happens to be called "bigbox.blackhelicopters.org". From the name of the sysctl, it's fairly easy to guess that this is the kernel's name for the computer it's running on. Easy enough to figure out, no?

Some are much more curious:

```
p1003_1b.memory_protection: 0
```

As a user, I have no idea what this value means. Still, if I'm having trouble and ask for help from a software vendor or on a mailing list, I can produce this information upon request. They might ask me to adjust it to better support their software.

The sysctls are organized in a tree format called a Management Information Base, or MIB, with several broad categories, such as net, vm, and kern. (The Management Information Base tree is used in several other parts of system administration; we'll see another example later in this book.) Each of these categories is further subdivided; for example, the net category covers all networking sysctls and is divided into categories such as IP, ICMP, TCP, and UDP. The terms sysctl MIB and sysctl are frequently used interchangeably. There are many sorts of MIB—we'll see examples of SNMP MIBs in Chapter 19—but throughout this chapter, we're only discussing sysctl MIBs.

We saw the kern.hostname MIB earlier, and if you look at the sysctls available on your machine, you'll see that a whole bunch of them begin with "kern". These are all general kernel values. If you go down a little further, you'll see a whole bunch that begin with "kern.ipc.", such as these:

```
kern.ipc.maxsockbuf: 262144
kern.ipc.sockbuf_waste_factor: 8
kern.ipc.somaxconn: 128

. . .
```

These sysctls describe the kernel's IPC[1] behavior. This branching of sysctls can go on for several layers.

You will eventually wind up with individual MIBs, such as net.inet.raw.recv-space. Each MIB has a value that represents some buffer, setting, or characteristic used by the kernel. By changing the value, you change how the kernel operates. For example, some sysctls control how much memory is used for each network connection. If your network performance is poor, you could increase the amount of system reserved for network connections. Some of the roots of the sysctl MIB tree are listed in Table 4.1.

**Table 4.1: Some roots of the sysctl MIB tree**

| Sysctl | Function |
| --- | --- |
| kern | core kernel functions |
| vm | virtual memory |
| vfs | filesystems |
| net | networking |
| debug | debugging information |
| hw | hardware information |
| machdep | platform-dependent variables (i.e., Alpha, i386, etc.) |
| user | userland interface information |
| p1003_1b | POSIX behavior[2] |

[1] IPC is an acronym for interprocess communication, and various programs need this. Your program documentation will tell you if this sysctl needs to be altered.
[2] POSIX is an international standard for UNIX program behavior and kernel features. Most of FreeBSD complies with POSIX.

Each sysctl value is either a string, integer, binary value, or opaque. *Strings* are free-format text of arbitrary length; *integers* are ordinary whole numbers; *binary values* are either 0 (off) or 1 (on); and *opaques* are in machine code and only specialized programs can interpret them.

Unfortunately, sysctls are not well documented, and rather than there being a single document listing all available sysctl MIBs and their functions, what MIB documentation there is generally appears in the man page for what it controls. For example, the original documentation for the MIB kern.securelevel (discussed more in Chapter 7) is in init(8). Many have no documentation. Appendix A includes a list of some common sysctls and their uses.

Fortunately, some MIBs are obvious. For example, if you scan your file of saved MIBs, near the top you'll see this one:

```
kern.bootfile: /kernel
```

This is an important MIB if you regularly boot different kernels. (We'll look later in this chapter at how to boot an alternate kernel.) If you're debugging a problem and have to reboot with several different kernels in succession, you can easily identify which kernel you're using by checking this MIB. More than once I've booted a test kernel, tested a problem and found it fixed, and realized that I had forgotten which kernel I'd booted.

To view a subtree of the MIBs available in a particular tree, such as kern, enter this command:

```
# sysctl kern
kern.ostype: FreeBSD
kern.osrelease: 5.0-CURRENT
kern.osrevision: 199506
...
```

This list goes on for quite some time. If you're just becoming familiar with sysctls, you might want to look and see what's available. To get the exact value of a particular sysctl, give the full MIB as an argument:

```
# sysctl kern.securelevel
kern.securelevel: -1
#
```

In this case, kern.securelevel has the integer value −1. We'll discuss exactly what this means in Chapter 7.

### Changing Sysctls

Some sysctl values are read-only. For example, take a look at the hw (hardware) and machdep (machine dependencies) MIB trees.

```
hw.machine: i386
```

Since the FreeBSD project has yet to develop the technology to change Intel-based hardware into PowerPC hardware via a software setting, this setting is read-only; all you'd accomplish by changing a MIB like this is to hose your system. FreeBSD protects you by making these sorts of MIBs read-only. Trying to change it won't hurt anything, but you'll just get a warning that the MIB cannot be changed.

On the other hand, consider the following MIB:

```
vfs.usermount: 0
```

This one, which controls whether or not users can mount media such as CD-ROMs and floppy disks, can be changed. By default it is set to 0, or off. To turn it on, use sysctl's -w flag to set it to 1.[3]

```
# sysctl -w vfs.usermount=1
vfs.usermount: 0 -> 1
#
```

Sysctl returns a nice little message showing the previous value and the change to the new value. That's all there is to changing a sysctl.

### Setting Sysctls at Boot

Sysctls you want set at boot-time should be entered in /etc/sysctl.conf. To do so, list each sysctl you want to set, and the desired value, in the sysctl.conf file.

For example, to allow users to mount filesystems by setting the vfs.usermount sysctl, add the following on a line by itself in sysctl.conf.

```
vfs.usermount=1
```

### Kernel Configuration with Loader.conf

Some kernel configuration must take place before the system starts to boot. For example, when the kernel initially probes an IDE hard drive, the device driver determines whether or not to use write caching. This decision must be made when the drive is first detected, during boot, and you can't change your mind after booting. Similarly, you might have a new network card and want to load

---

[3] In more recent versions of FreeBSD, the -w is unnecessary; just give the assignment.

the kernel module for its driver before you boot. That's where the system loader comes in.

The loader has many functions: It finds the hard drive that contains the kernel, loads the kernel into memory, triggers the booting process, and feeds information to the kernel. The most important part of the information the loader feeds to the kernel is the sysctl MIBs, which must be set at boot.

The most common way to configure the system loader is to edit a configuration file, though you can also enter configuration commands manually at the loader's ok> prompt. For long-term changes, you're better off including them in /boot/loader.conf.

There are two important loader.conf files: /boot/loader.conf and /boot/defaults/loader.conf. We'll have a look at the second of the two in Chapter 8. For now, we'll change /boot/loader.conf only. The entries in /boot/defaults/loader.conf are the system defaults; anything you put in /boot/loader.conf will override the default settings.

Loader.conf has two main functions: loading kernel modules and providing hints to device drivers. The device driver hints are generally sysctl MIBs that can only be set at boot.

When you look at /boot/defaults/loader.conf, you'll see a lot of options that you might find useful in various circumstances, such as the ability to specify a different kernel rather than the default, or the ability to specify verbose booting. Just for reference, here's a snippet of /boot/defaults/loader.conf.

```
kernel="/kernel"
kernel_options=""

userconfig_script_load="NO"
userconfig_script_name="/boot/kernel.conf"
userconfig_script_type="userconfig_script"
. . .
```

To change one of these default settings, you would copy the appropriate line from the default file to /boot/loader.conf, and make the change there.

For example, the first entry in the preceding listing is for the kernel filename, which we saw in our sysctl example earlier. Suppose you were working on a remote machine, and you wanted it to reboot the next time with a different kernel, but you didn't want to copy this other kernel to /kernel. You could change the kernel your system will use on boot by editing this one line. This is a sysctl that, obviously, can only be set at boot.

Let's look at two specific examples: passing hints to device drivers and automatically loading kernel modules.

### Passing Hints to Device Drivers

Loader.conf's first purpose is to pass hints to device drivers. (If a device driver can use these hints, they're described in the manual page.)

As discussed earlier, the IDE hard drive's device driver must know if it should ask for write caching before booting the system. (This is documented in the ata(4) man page, and we will discuss write caching in Chapter 16.) To enable write caching, set the hw.ata.wc flag to 1 by entering the following in loader.conf:

```
hw.ata.wc="1"
```

That does it.

This type of flag should look familiar; it looks suspiciously like a sysctl MIB. In fact, once the system boots, check to see if it is a sysctl:

```
# sysctl hw.ata.wc
hw.ata.wc: 1
#
```

What do you know, it is!

When the system is running, you cannot change this sysctl. (Go ahead, try it, you won't hurt anything.) You changed a write-only sysctl by setting it at boot time. While this still won't help you turn that old Pentium into an Alpha, it does give you added flexibility.

### Loading Kernel Modules Automatically

As I mentioned earlier, kernel modules are portions of a kernel that can be started (or loaded) when needed, and unloaded when unused. This feature can save system memory, and it improves system flexibility.

Loading a kernel module automatically at boot is fairly straightforward, and the default loader.conf offers many examples. To do so, copy the module name to loader.conf, cut off the trailing ".ko", and add the string _load="YES". For example, to load /module/procfs.ko automatically at boot, add the following to loader.conf:

```
procfs_load="YES"
```

The hard part, of course, is knowing which module to load. The easy ones are device drivers; if you add a new network or SCSI card, you can load the module at boot rather than rebuilding the kernel. If you're loading kernel modules to solve a particular system problem, you're probably doing this either from program documentation or someone's advice. Knowing which other modules to load comes with experience, reading documentation, and knowing what you want your system to do. I'll give specific pointers to certain kernel modules later.

### *Manually Configuring the Loader*

If you're repeatedly rebooting to experiment with modules and sysctls, you probably don't want to keep editing /boot/loader.conf because it's just too time-intensive. Instead, adjust the loader manually at boot time. Then, once you find a configuration you like, you can alter /boot/loader.conf to your taste.

As discussed earlier, when your FreeBSD system first boots, it displays a 10-second countdown. If you hit a key and interrupt the countdown, you're brought to a loader command prompt—a simple command-line system where you can control initial system setup. You'll know you're in the loader when you see the loader prompt

```
ok
```

The loader is not UNIX—it's actually a small command interpreter written in Forth.[4] While a couple of loader commands resemble their UNIX counterparts, that's more for convenience than because of any underlying similarity.

### Loader Commands

Entering a question mark (?) at the loader prompt will give you a very brief tutorial. Here are some of the most useful commands.

#### ls

The ls command lists files, just like in UNIX. It defaults to displaying the root directory; you can list another directory by giving the full path.

#### unload

Unload empties the system memory, which starts off containing the kernel and any modules specified in loader.conf.

#### load

The load command copies a file into memory. Use load to add kernel modules or even a new kernel. (You cannot load one kernel while another is still in memory though; you must unload the old one first.)

For example, you could load the Intel EtherExpress network card driver like this:

```
ok load /modules/if_fxp.ko
ok
```

#### set

The set command allows you to set the value of a variable. For example, to test IDE write caching, you need to set hw.ata.wc to 1.

```
ok set hw.ata.wc=1
ok
```

---

[4] Forth is one of the very few programming languages that can fit in the tiny amount of space available in a computer's boot record. A similar program in C would require much more space. Every so often, someone volunteers to rewrite the boot loader in C, or BASIC, or some other language. These people are never heard from again.

## Loading and Unloading Modules in Multi-User Mode

Some kernel modules don't need to be loaded in your system at boottime; they can be loaded and unloaded while the system is running. We'll look at how you can find out what modules you have in your system, then how to load and unload them.

### Viewing Loaded Modules

Once your system is fully booted, you can see which kernel modules are loaded with kldstat(8):

```
# kldstat
Id Refs Address    Size    Name
 1    5 0xc0100000 2d505c  kernel
 2    1 0xc0c6c000 13000   linux.ko
#
```

In this listing, the laptop has two modules loaded: the kernel (kernel) and the Linux compatibility module (linux.ko, discussed in Chapter 10). Each module contains submodules, which you can view using `kldstat -v`, but be ready for a couple hundred lines of output.

### Loading and Unloading Modules

Load and unload software modules with kldload(8) and kldunload(8). For example, to load the warp console-mode screen saver, enter this command:

```
# kldload /modules/warp_saver.ko
#
```

Once you've finished, you can unload the module with this command:

```
# kldunload warp_saver.ko
#
```

If all possible functions were compiled into the kernel, the kernel would be much larger than it is. This way, you can have a smaller, more efficient kernel and only load modules as you need them.

# Customizing the Kernel

You'll eventually find that you cannot tweak your kernel as much as you desire using only modules and sysctl, and your only solution will be to build your own custom kernel. But don't worry, the process is perfectly straightforward if you take it step by step.

The kernel shipped in a default install is called GENERIC. GENERIC is designed to run on a wide variety of hardware, though not necessarily to run *well* or optimally. GENERIC boots nicely on a 486 and later systems, but newer x86 systems have advanced features and optimizations that help them perform better, and GENERIC doesn't take advantage of these features because it's aiming for the lowest common denominator.

When you customize your kernel, you'll get better performance, and you can also include new functionality in it, or support for new hardware.

## Preparation

You must have the kernel source code before you can consider building a kernel. If you followed the advice in Chapter 1, you're all set. If not, you can either go back into the installer and load the kernel sources or jump ahead to Chapter 6 and use CVSup instead.

If you don't know whether you have the kernel source code installed, look for a /sys directory. If it exists, and there are a bunch of files and directories in it, you have the kernel sources.

Before building a new kernel, you must know what hardware your system has. This can be difficult to determine, because the brand name on a component doesn't necessarily have any relationship to the device's identity or abilities. After all, many different companies made an NE2000-compatible network card. Even if the box said "3com," the circuits inside the chip said "ne2000."[5] Similarly, companies such as Linksys rebrand inexpensive network cards that all have very different internals. The boxes all say "Linksys," but the chip says something else depending on the month of manufacture.

Fortunately, PCI-based systems have sophisticated hardware-recognition systems, and FreeBSD will almost certainly find these devices at boot. If yours is an older ISA system, on the other hand, you might have to dig through the component manual to learn what sort of device you have and how to set IRQs and I/O ports.

The best place to see what hardware your FreeBSD system found is the file /var/run/dmesg.boot, which contains the boottime kernel messages buffer, also known as all that garbage you saw on boot. (There's an example of dmesg.boot in Chapter 3.) If you've never looked at your dmesg.boot file, take a few moments to do so now. You probably never knew that your computer had so much stuff in it!

---

[5] Actually placing such a label on the outside of the chip would be far too convenient, so computer manufacturers generally don't bother.

When looking at the dmesg.boot file, you'll find the device names at the beginning of the dmesg lines. Each piece of hardware has a separate device name, typically a few letters followed by a unit number, such as npx0. The letters are the name of the driver (npx), and each device is numbered, starting with 0. One device might span several lines, and if you have multiple devices, they'll show up with sequential unit numbers.

### Your Backup Kernel

A bad kernel can render your system unbootable, so you absolutely must keep a good kernel around at all times. While the kernel install process retains one old kernel, it's easy to overwrite it.

If you don't keep a good, reliable kernel around, here's what can happen: You forget to put a network driver in your current kernel, so you decide to rebuild it. Your rebuilt kernel becomes the current kernel, your previous (imperfect) kernel becomes the old kernel, and your old working kernel goes off to the Land of Oz. When you discover that your new kernel won't keep running for more than a few hours, you'll really regret the loss of that reliable kernel.

A common place to keep a known good kernel is /kernel.good. Back up your working, reliable kernel to /kernel.good before tweaking your kernel, like this:

```
# mkdir modules.good
# cp kernel kernel.good
# cp -R modules/* modules.good/
#
```

**NOTE**    *Don't be afraid to keep a variety of kernels on hand. Some people even put kernels in directories named by date, so that they can have a long-running history of kernels. You can have too many kernels on hand, but only if they fill up your root partition.*

### Editing Kernel Files

You've now backed up your working kernel and are ready to build a new one. To begin, check out /sys/i386/conf, where you should find several files. The important ones for your purposes are GENERIC and LINT. GENERIC is the kernel configuration file for the standard kernel used on first install. LINT contains all kernel options and the documentation for them, including a variety of really obscure ones.

Do not edit any of the files you find in /sys/i386/conf directly. Instead, copy GENERIC to a new file and edit the copy, not the original, and name the file after your machine (the most common convention). For example, if you have a server called "webserver," you would do this:

```
# cp GENERIC WEBSERVER
```

Now open the new configuration file in your favorite text editor. Here's a snippet from the part of the GENERIC configuration that covers IDE (aka ATAPI) drives.

```
# ATA and ATAPI devices
device      ata0    at isa? port IO_WD1 irq 14
device      ata1    at isa? port IO_WD2 irq 15
device      ata
device      atadisk             # ATA disk drives
device      atapicd             # ATAPI CDROM drives
device      atapifd             # ATAPI floppy drives
device      atapist             # ATAPI tape drives
options     ATA_STATIC_ID       #Static device numbering
```

Each line in the kernel configuration file is either a comment or description of a kernel feature. The pound sign (#) marks comments and the computer ignores them; they're there for your benefit.

Some lines have comments that start in the middle of the line, describing what appears earlier on the line. Lines beginning with "device" are device drivers; in this example, you'll see entries for IDE disks, IDE CD-ROM drives, IDE floppy drives, and IDE tape drives. There are also entries for the actual IDE bus on the motherboard, and for both of its connectors.

Other lines are for software features, or "options." In this example, the option ATA_STATIC_ID enables "static device numbering"; you'll learn what that means in Chapter 16. You'll also see a few special-purpose keywords, such as "pseudo-device" and "cpu," which are either software options or descriptions of hardware.

Because the GENERIC kernel is designed to run on the greatest variety of equipment, it includes a huge array of network drivers, disk drivers, controllers, and features. As a general rule, begin customizing a kernel by commenting out unnecessary entries to shrink and simplify your kernel. Of course, when you streamline the kernel in this way, you'll have to rebuild it when you change your hardware, and if you're one of those folks who constantly swaps hardware in and out, you probably don't want to gut your kernel. On the other hand, if you have a specific server hardware setup and you mass-produce kernels, strip out anything unnecessary.

Your copied kernel configuration file (WEBSERVER, in our example) starts off with comments describing the purpose of the configuration file and containing pointers to the official FreeBSD documentation. Once you skip these comments, the new config file starts with the following:

```
machine     i386
cpu         I486_CPU
cpu         I586_CPU
cpu         I686_CPU
ident       GENERIC
maxusers    0
```

### machine

The *machine* keyword in the preceding listing describes the system architecture. You really don't want to change this, unless you're building a kernel for your Alpha on an x86.

### cpu

The *cpu* statements describe the on-chip features the kernel can expect to use and support. This is important because newer CPUs provide instructions that others don't. (For example, consider the Pentium versus the Pentium with MMX.)

You only need to include the CPU you have. If you're not sure of the CPU in your hardware, check dmesg.boot. My laptop's dmesg.boot includes the following lines:

```
CPU: Pentium III/Pentium III Xeon/Celeron (497.56-MHz 686-class CPU)
  Origin = "GenuineIntel"  Id = 0x681  Stepping = 1

Features=0x383f9ff<FPU,VME,DE,PSE,TSC,MSR,PAE,MCE,CX8,SEP,MTRR,PGE,MCA,CMOV,PAT,PSE3
6,MMX,FXSR,SSE>
```

The important part of this description is the 686-class CPU at the end of the first line. This tells me that I can remove the cpu statements I486_CPU and I586_CPU to make my kernel smaller and faster. As a result, the kernel will use 686-class CPU-specific optimizations instead of slower generic code.

### ident

The *ident* statement is the kernel's name, which is usually the same as the server name. If you build one kernel and install it on many machines, you might want to give the kernel a name that reflects its purpose, such as WEBSERVER.

### maxusers

The *maxusers* value is a rough value used to compute the size of various in-kernel tables (not the maximum number of users). These in-kernel tables control things such as the number of available network connections and the number of files that can be open at one time.

Beginning with FreeBSD 4.5, the kernel will look at a system's resources and assign a maxusers value that it believes is appropriate for most users. The maxusers 0 entry means the kernel will take the defaults, which will be entirely appropriate for most systems. (You can still hard-code a MAXUSERS value if you wish, however, as I describe below.)

On FreeBSD versions 4.4 and earlier, you needed to hard-code your maxusers value. I typically ran an X-based laptop with a maxusers value of 16, which is fine for my laptop because I'm the only user of the system; no matter how many fancy desktop widgets I fire up, or how many Web pages I'm browsing, I'm only one person and cannot possibly open more files or make more network connections than a maxusers of 16 can support. On a busy Internet server, though, I might kick this value up to 256; this is high enough that the server will prepare to handle thousands of network connections and open files.

If your maxusers value is too low, the system will start to be unable to handle all your files and network connections. The kernel will notice that it cannot handle all these requests, and will log errors. You'll start to get warnings on the console and in /var/log/messages telling you quite explicitly to increase maxusers.

Don't raise maxusers above 256, though, unless you have an insane number of files on a single partition (millions, for example) or you push multiple T1s of bandwidth.

## Basic Options

Following the maxusers value in the config file, there are a variety of basic options, including things like INET for TCP/IP support, and FFS for UNIX filesystem support. You'll also encounter rarely used ones that you can remove. We won't discuss all the kernel options, but merely some specific examples from different types of options and some of the more common options. I'll specifically mention ones that can be trimmed from an Internet server.

Consider the following options:

```
options        MATH_EMULATE
```

Older CPUS (specifically the 386 and the 486SSX) have no math co-processor. If your system lacks a math co-processor, you should leave MATH_EMULATE in so your kernel will emulate a math co-processor in software. Any modern CPU will have a math co-processor, however, and if that's true in your case, you can cut it.

```
options        INET
```

The INET option provides support for network protocols, such as TCP/IP. Keep this one.

```
options        INET6                    #IPv6 communications protocols
```

If you're using IPv6, you need INET6. If not, cut it.

```
options        FFS
```

The FFS option specifies UNIX Fast Filesystem, FreeBSD's default. Keep it.

```
options        SOFTUPDATES
```

Softupdates is a method for ensuring disk integrity with FFS. (We'll discuss softupdates at some length in Chapter 13.) Keep this line unless you specifically decide against using softupdates.

```
options        MD_ROOT
```

If you use MFS to build diskless workstations, you need the MD_ROOT option. Otherwise, give it the axe.

```
options        NFS
options        NFS_ROOT
```

These two options support the Network File System. The NFS_ROOT option allows you to boot off an NFS drive, rarely used in Internet servers. You can delete both entries if you aren't using NFS.

```
options        MSDOSFS
```

The MSDOSFS option supports MS-DOS-formatted filesystems and floppies. If you mount or unmount MS-DOS floppy disks, or if you are sharing your hard drive with a Microsoft operating system, you might want this option. You can also temporarily load this functionality with the msdos.ko module.

```
options        CD9660
```

The CD9660 option supports the standard CD-ROM filesystem. Like the MS-DOS filesystem, you can temporarily load and unload this functionality with the cd9660.ko module.

```
options        PROCFS
options        COMPAT_43
```

If you remove the preceding two lines, your system will break. Many user programs rely on BSD4.3 functions. The COMPAT_43 option provides kernel compatibility with BSD4.3. Similarly, process-monitoring programs rely on the process file system (PROCFS).

```
options        SCSI_DELAY=15000
```

The SCSI_DELAY option specifies the number of milliseconds FreeBSD waits after finding your SCSI controllers before probing the SCSI devices, giving them a chance to spin up. If you don't have any SCSI hardware, you can delete this line. If you have new SCSI hardware, you can reduce this setting to 5000 (5 seconds) or lower.

```
options         UCONSOLE
```

Some programs allow users to look at the system console in an X Windows terminal. The UCONSOLE option is the kernel support for that feature. You can
delete this line if you aren't using X, or if you don't have this system set up as a
desktop.

```
options         USERCONFIG
options         VISUAL_USERCONFIG
```

These two userconfig lines allow you to enable and disable devices before your
kernel boots. While you don't absolutely need them, when you read some
FreeBSD hardware documentation that says "set this in userconfig," you'll regret
not having them.

```
options         KTRACE
```

The KTRACE option enables kernel-level tracing. Keep it unless you know
exactly what it is and what you're doing.

```
options         SYSVSHM
options         SYSVMSG
options         SYSVSEM
```

The preceding three options support System V-style interprocess communication, and many applications expect to have them. They can also be loaded as
modules.

```
options         P1003_1B
options         _KPOSIX_PRIORITY_SCHEDULING
```

The two lines support kernel POSIX functions, and many programs expect to
find POSIX features in the kernel.

### Multiple Processors

If your system has multiple processors, you need the following kernel options:

```
options         SMP             # Symmetric MultiProcessor Kernel
options         APIC_IO         # Symmetric (APIC) I/O
```

The SMP option tells the kernel to use the appropriate code for multiple processors; APIC_IO handles input and output for SMP kernels.

When you're building an SMP kernel, remove the I386_CPU and I486_CPU
from your kernel configuration. FreeBSD only supports SMP on systems that fit

the Intel SMP specification, and this specification does not support SMP with 386 or 486 chips.

If you do not have multiple processors, leave these options commented out!

### Device Entries

After the options entries in the config file, you'll find device entries, which are grouped in fairly obvious ways.

#### Bus Entries

The first device entries are bus entries, such as `device pci` and `device isa`. Keep these, unless you truly don't have that sort of bus in your system. (You might be surprised at the number of "legacy-free" systems that have an ISA bus hidden somewhere in their innards; for example, my brand-new laptop has an old-fashioned ISA bus hidden in it.) The EISA device, however, can probably be removed on modern computers.

#### Interfaces

The IDE/ATAPI interfaces and devices are next (we saw an example of these at the beginning of the "Editing Kernel Files" section). Even if your system has no IDE devices, it's probably a good idea to keep the "device ata", especially since most motherboards have an IDE controller or two on them. You can eliminate entries for any IDE devices you don't have.

Next are the SCSI controllers and cards, used for SCSI features, including those needed by parallel port Zip disks and USB storage devices. If you don't have any of these devices, this whole section can go away. If you're using SCSI, just remove the controllers you don't have.

```
# SCSI Controllers
device          ahb           # EISA AHA1742 family
device          ahc           # AHA2940 and onboard AIC7xxx devices
. . .
```

After the SCSI section, you'll find a few lines of device drivers for such mundane things as keyboards, monitors, your PS/2 port, and so on. Don't delete these.

The network card list comes next; it is quite long and looks much like the SCSI and IDE sections. If you're not going to replace your network card any time soon, get rid of the drivers from any hardware you don't have. If your system doesn't have any ISA slots in it, you can certainly delete all of the ISA drivers.

#### Pseudo-Devices

Near the bottom of the GENERIC kernel, you'll find a list of pseudo-devices. As the name might suggest, these are created entirely of software. For example, when you telnet or SSH (see Chapter 13) into the system remotely, the system has to have a way to keep track of your terminal session, send characters to it, and read what you type. It wants to treat your remote connection just as it treats the physical monitor and keyboard attached to the system. To do so, it uses a pseudo-device called a pseudo-terminal. Because the kernel treats these much like devices, we call them pseudo-devices.

Here's one, for example:

```
pseudo-device          loop
```

This is the loopback interface, lo0, a network interface that points back to the local machine. If you remove it, many pieces of software will break in interesting ways. This can be very educational, but you don't want to do this in a production system.

```
pseudo-device          ether
```

The ether pseudo-device provides general Ethernet support. You probably want it.

```
pseudo-device          sl
```

The sl pseudo-device is for Serial Line Internet Protocol (SLIP). It is an old protocol that has been replaced by Point-to-Point Protocol (PPP). You probably don't need this unless your ISP requires it.

```
pseudo-device          ppp      1
```

The ppp pseudo-device is for kernel-based PPP. Kernel-based PPP has fallen out of favor, being supplanted by userland PPP. You probably don't need this.

If you do want to use kernel PPP, the number after "ppp" is the number of PPP devices to create.

```
pseudo-device          tun
```

The tun pseudo-device is the logical packet tunnel. Various programs use this to sneak packets in and out of the kernel. You need this for userland PPP (regular dial-up connections).

```
pseudo-device          pty
```

The pty pseudo-devices are pseudo-terminals, used for things like telnet connections, and so on. You want these.

```
pseudo-device          md
```

The md pseudo-device is for memory disks. Again, if you're not using memory disks, you don't need them. For most (but not all) Internet servers, memory disks are just a waste of RAM. However, a very few special-purpose servers (such as, anonymous CVS servers) need memory disks.

```
pseudo-device          gif
pseudo-device          faith
pseudo-device          bpf
```

The bpf pseudo-device is the Berkley Packet Filter, which allows you to examine packets on your network. It's used for packet sniffers and for the DHCP client and server. If you don't need any of those, turn this off.

### USB Devices

Finally, after the pseudo-devices you have USB devices, which can all be dynamically loaded via kldload. Many Internet servers don't use USB, so you might be able to delete them entirely from your kernel.

## Building Your Kernel

The previous sections have shown you how to gut your kernel configuration. Before you start adding other things in, I recommend trying to build and boot this minimal kernel to learn what your kernel really needs before adding customizations.

**NOTE** *Use the steps described in this section when building a kernel without upgrading. If you're upgrading (as discussed in Chapter 6), you must follow a slightly different procedure.*

Once you've selected and modified your kernel options, it's time to build your kernel. To do so, first use config(8) to assemble the necessary files and check your configuration's syntax. For example, to run config on MYKERNEL, enter the following command:

```
# config MYKERNEL
Kernel build directory is ../../compile/MYKERNEL
Don't forget to do a ''make depend''
#
```

While config cannot detect a good kernel configuration, it will find a variety of configuration mistakes if they exist. If config detects a problem, it will report an error and stop. For example, if you include a nonexistent option, config will complain, loudly. (Config always reminds you to run a *make depend*. We haven't discussed this yet, but forgetting this step is the single most common error in building a kernel.)

Some error messages are blatantly obvious—for example, you might have accidentally deleted support for the Unix File System (UFS), but included support for booting off of UFS. One requires the other, and config will tell you exactly what's wrong. Other messages are strange and obscure, and you should investigate them as discussed in Chapter 2.

Assuming that config runs correctly, config tells you which directory it has assembled your kernel pieces in. In our example, this is ../../compile/ MYKERNEL. Go to the directory shown and do this:

```
# make depend && make all install
```

The "make depend" stage of the command ties the pieces of your kernel and the kernel modules together, making sure that everything has the pieces it needs. The second command, "make all install", takes all the source code and dependencies and compiles a kernel out of source code.

Then wait. The kernel building process will take a few hours on a 25 MHz 486, or a few minutes on a dual-processor 1 GHz Pentium. You will see all sorts of cryptic compiler messages scrolling down your screen while this is happening. In the install step, your current kernel will be moved to /kernel.old, and your new kernel installed as /kernel.

Once the build is finished, reboot your server and watch your boot messages. Near the top of these messages you should see the directory where your new kernel was compiled, as shown here in bold:

```
Copyright (c) 1992-2001 The FreeBSD Project.
Copyright (c) 1979, 1980, 1983, 1986, 1988, 1989, 1991, 1992, 1993, 1994
        The Regents of the University of California. All rights reserved.
FreeBSD 5.0-CURRENT #0: Sun May 20 16:49:05 EDT 2001
    mwlucas@turtledawn.blackhelicopters.org:/usr/src/sys/compile/MYKERNEL
...
```

If you see a message like this, you have been successful. You're up on your new kernel!

### Troubleshooting Kernel Builds

If your kernel build fails, the first step in troubleshooting is to look at the last lines of the compile output. You saw the compile output after typing the make depend && make all install command. You might be able to guess at the meaning of an error, but it can be very cryptic to people who don't breathe, eat, and live kernel code.[6]

---

[6] Personally, I prefer to breathe, eat, and live air, food, and my life, in that order, but some people seem to get by living on computers.

Here's an example of something you might see in a failed kernel build:

```
===> sys/modules/xl
cc -O -pipe  -D_KERNEL -Wall -Wredundant-decls -Wnested-externs -Wstrict-prototy
pes  -Wmissing-prototypes -Wpointer-arith -Winline -Wcast-qual  -fformat-extensi
ons -ansi -DKLD_MODULE -nostdinc -I-  -I. -I@ -I@/../include  -mpreferred-stack-
boundary=2 -c /usr/src/sys/modules/xl/../../pci/if_xl.c
❶ /usr/src/sys/modules/xl/../../pci/if_xl.c:155: syntax error before`<'
cpp: output pipe has been closed
*** Error code 1

Stop in /usr/src/sys/modules/xl.
*** Error code 1

Stop in /usr/src/sys/modules.
*** Error code 1

Stop in /usr/src/sys.
*** Error code 1

Stop in /usr/src.
*** Error code 1

Stop in /usr/src.
*** Error code 1
```

At the top of this message, the compiler is in the directory sys/modules/xl and is trying to build a working kernel module out of the source code there. You see the command it's trying to run; it's on the next few lines, starting with cc –O. What appears as several lines on paper is actually one very, very long line to the computer; this particular line goes down to just above the ❶ symbol.

On the next line (❶), we see the error code (syntax error before '<'), as well as the line number and the filename. This error stops the compile, and we see a cascading series of errors. The kernel module cannot be built, so the whole range of kernel modules cannot be built, so the kernel cannot be built, so everything basically comes to a screaming, crashing halt.

Fortunately, FreeBSD will insist upon compiling a complete kernel before installing anything. You haven't damaged your system by doing this; your failed compile is still sitting in the directory created by running config.

You know the step in the kernel build where the process stopped (the bit beginning with cc), and you know what error resulted from that step (syntax error before '<'). The cascading errors that follow are really irrelevant; a failure in one step makes the whole process blow apart.

Don't be embarrassed if you don't understand these errors; most people don't. Just go through the "Getting More Help" process in Chapter 2. Your first best bet is the FreeBSD-questions mailing list archive. Take the last lines of your compile output (if_xl.c:155: syntax error before`<'), paste it into the search engine, and see who else has had the problem. If you don't find any hits on that, try the next line of the failure (cpp: output pipe has been closed).

If nothing shows up in the mailing list archive, send a message to the FreeBSD-questions@FreeBSD.org mailing list. Include the following information:

- The end of the output of the failed compile
- Your FreeBSD version number
- The contents of /var/run/dmesg/boot
- The output of uname -a
- The kernel config file

Chances are, your problem is fairly simple to fix, and if you include all of this, someone will write you back with suggestions. These sorts of errors are generally the result of an incorrect kernel configuration.

## Booting an Alternate Kernel

So, what do you do if your new kernel doesn't work? Perhaps you forgot a device driver, or cut the ppp pseudo-device and cannot dial out to the Net. Don't panic, you're not lost. You did keep your old kernel, right? Okay, here's what to do.

First, interrupt the boot, as discussed in the "Manually Configuring the Loader" section earlier in this chapter, by pressing any key. When you see the loader prompt, the kernel has already been loaded. You need to unload that kernel and any corresponding modules before you can load another kernel. To do so, run this command:

```
ok unload
ok
```

Your kernel should now be unloaded and your command prompt at the root directory. If you're not sure of the kernels you have, use ls to see everything under /.

Next, choose the kernel you want, then load it and boot. (Be sure to also load whatever kernel modules you require.)

```
ok load /kernel.good
ok load /modules/if_fxp.ko
ok boot
```

Your system should now start booting off your selected kernel.

**NOTE** *If you didn't back up a good kernel, and both your new and old kernels are bad, don't despair yet. FreeBSD installs a GENERIC kernel in /kernel.GENERIC. It should at least get you back to a command prompt, or to single-user mode in the worst case.*

## Adding to the Kernel

At this point, if everything has gone well, you should have a minimal kernel that works well. Now you can add features and tweak it.

### LINT

You'll find a list of all kernel features in the file /sys/i386/conf/LINT, including every kernel option and driver, as well as some documentation.

If you have hardware that doesn't appear to be supported in the GENERIC kernel, take a look at LINT. Some of these features are obscure, but if you have the hardware, you'll appreciate them. For example, FreeBSD supports the special features of the IBM BlueLightning CPU, which will allow both of you BlueLightning owners to use your CPU to its full extent.

Let's look at a typical entry from LINT:

```
# CPU_PPRO2CELERON enables L2 cache of Mendocino Celeron CPUs.  This option
# is useful when you use Socket 8 to Socket 370 converter, because most Pentium
# Pro BIOSs do not enable L2 cache of Mendocino Celeron CPUs.

options        CPU_PPRO2CELERON
```

We're told that if you have a Socket 8 to Socket 370 converter on your motherboard, the CPU_PPRO2CELERON option will enable your L2 cache. Since FreeBSD runs so well on older hardware, this sort of hardware setup is not uncommon. Many people have taken older hardware and installed FreeBSD on it, and use adapters to augment this older hardware. While this situation isn't common enough to warrant inclusion in the GENERIC kernel, the option is there if you look for it. Skim through LINT some time, just to get an idea of what sorts of things are available.

**NOTE** *If the LINT kernel configuration includes all possible options, why not just use it? Because some of the features in that configuration contradict each other. For example, there's the CPU_PPRO2CELERON option that tells the kernel you're running a Celeron on a Pentium Pro motherboard. Meanwhile, the kernel option CPU_RSTK_EN enables the return stack on the Cyrix 5x86 CPUs. There is no such thing as a Cyrix-made Celeron, and if it existed, it probably wouldn't use this motherboard adapter.*

### Fixing Errors with Options

You'll use certain options when you get an error. For example, a friend of mine has several Web servers built on low-end i386 hardware. When one became busy enough to start serving several hundred Web pages a second, he started getting errors on the console like this:

```
Jun  9 16:23:17 ralph/kernel: pmap_collect: collecting pv entries --
suggest increasing PMAP_SHPGPERPROC
```

When he ignored the error, the system crashed. He asked for my help.

By reading the error from the log and searching LINT, I found this:

```
# Set the number of PV entries per process.  Increasing this can
# stop panics related to heavy use of shared memory. However, that can
# (combined with large amounts of physical memory) cause panics at
# boot time due the kernel running out of VM space.
#
# If you're tweaking this, you might also want to increase the sysctls
# "vm.v_free_min", "vm.v_free_reserved", and "vm.v_free_target".
#
# The value below is the one more than the default.
#
options         PMAP_SHPGPERPROC=201
```

After reading this explanation, we set out to tackle this problem. First, we backed up the old kernel to /boot/kernel.pmap-crash. (It wasn't exactly a good kernel, but I wanted it on hand in case the new one was worse.) We then kicked PMAP_SHPGPERPROC up to 400, and increased the system's RAM to 192MB. (Yes, this cheap system was serving several hundred Web pages a second on 64MB of RAM, one IDE disk, and a Celeron 433!) After doing the config-make dance, the problem went away, and the server now has 30 days uptime.

Without the ability to tweak the kernel, we would have had no choice but to buy more hardware. Admittedly, this piece of hardware is pretty low-end. But if this hardware does the job with just a little software tweak, why not use it? If you're that desperate to spend money, send the checks to me.

## Tweaking Kernel Performance

And how about improving performance?

The biggest kernel bottleneck is network mbufs. You'll see in Chapter 5 how mbufs are the chunks of memory that the kernel uses to handle network connections. They aren't the number of network connections the server can handle, but rather the memory used to hold network connections, and one connection might consume several mbufs. (You might want to read the discussion of mbufs in Chapter 5 before you start tuning them, but since we're discussing kernel configuration here, we'll discuss the mechanics now.)

The number of mbufs scales somewhat with the MAXUSERS kernel option discussed earlier in this chapter, but you will probably want to increase the setting on a high-production server. While the auto-scaling of MAXUSERS can help, this is still a very common tweak.

The NMBCLUSTERS option controls the number of mbufs created by the kernel. (This option won't appear in the GENERIC configuration file; you'll need to add it. NMBCLUSTERS does appear in the LINT file.)

```
options          NMBCLUSTERS=1024
```

Network mbuf clusters are preallocated in kernel memory, so you can't just crank this value up to a million and forget about it, because that memory won't be available for other uses when the system gets busy. You do want your kernel to be able to open files and support your Web server, don't you?

One nmbcluster uses about 2KB of memory, so the preceding example reserves 2MB of memory for networking. (2 times 1024 is 2048, and 1MB is 1024KB.) This might not be much on a modern computer, but it is a considerable chunk on a 486s that can run FreeBSD. See why we want to customize this?

To calculate the number of mbuf clusters you need, first check how many network connections you have open at a fairly busy time. You can do this with the netstat(1) command. Netstat will show you how many network connections the system has, including TCP, UDP, loopback, and UNIX socket connections. All you need care about for mbufs clusters are TCP and UDP, so you can pull those out with grep(1). Finally, you can use the wc(1) word-counting program to count the number of lines in the output, which gives you the number of TCP and UDP connections that the system is using right now.[7] Here are the commands:

```
# netstat -na | grep tcp | wc -l
    427
# netstat -na | grep udp | wc -l
    377
#
```

NOTE  *If you want to know how many network mbufs you're using at any given time, look at* netstat -m. *We'll discuss netstat in some detail in Chapter 5.*

As you can see from the results, at this particular moment, the system has 427 running and available TCP network connections, and 377 active and available UDP network connections. This is roughly 800 total. To account for possible peaks, plan for twice the number of connections you see at a typical busy time.

[7] For those of you who are newer UNIX administrators: Remember in the Introduction where we talked about UNIX commands being a language? Here's a good example. We have combined small commands to get a final answer without any tedious counting or searching through output ourselves. You might think that UNIX admins are extremely intelligent. Many of us are just creatively lazy.

Now that you know how many connections you have to handle, you need to know how much memory each connection requires. Each TCP connection requires a send buffer and a receive buffer. You can get their current size (in bits) from the sysctls net.inet.tcp.sendspace and net.inet.tcp.recvspace.

```
# sysctl net.inet.tcp.sendspace
net.inet.tcp.sendspace: 16384
# sysctl net.inet.tcp.recvspace
net.inet.tcp.recvspace: 16384
```

Bytes are difficult to work with, so we'll convert them to kilobytes; 16384 divided by 1024 is 16, so each buffer is 16KB on this system. (The default buffer size changed between FreeBSD 4.4 and 4.5, so you will want to check this on your system!) Since each network connection needs an incoming and an outgoing buffer, each TCP connection requires 32KB.

Similarly, each incoming UDP connection requires a buffer. You can't do much tuning with UDP, but assuming each UDP connection requires as much space as a TCP connection is reasonable for what we're doing here.

So, we know that each connection requires 32KB, and we know that our "average peak" usage is 800 connections. 800 x 32KB = 25600KB, or about 25MB. (1MB is actually 1024KB, but this is close enough for our purposes.) Then, to handle peaks and surges, double this to 50MB.

One mbuf cluster is 2KB, or 1024 mbuf clusters are 2MB, and we want 50MB of mbufs, so we multiply 50MB by 1024 and divide by 2 to get a total of 25600 mbuf clusters. So set the NMBCLUSTERS option to 25600 like so:

```
options        NMBCLUSTERS=25600
```

**NOTE**   *If you're running a network server, it's a good idea to set NMBCLUSTERS to roughly a quarter of your physical RAM. 32MB of RAM set aside for mbufs, with 16KB send and receive buffers, gives you NMBCLUSTERS = 16384. This might not be adequate, or it might be too much, but it's a good place to start.*

## Sharing Kernels

If you have several identical servers, you don't need to manually build a kernel on each; you can share your custom-built kernel across them. (The kernel file is just a binary, after all.)

To share a kernel, build and install one kernel and test it in every way you can think of. Then tar up /kernel and /modules and copy the tarball to each of the other servers. Back up the current kernel on each of the other servers, and decompress your tarball to install the new /kernel and /modules. Just reboot, and you're set.

# 5

# NETWORKING

BSD is famous for its network performance. In fact, the TCP/IP network protocol itself was first developed on BSD. Many other operating systems have chosen to use the BSD network stack because of its high performance and liberal licensing.

If you're a system administrator, you must understand how networking works. If you're like most sysadmins, you're probably familiar with some of the basics, but not many people understand how all of that networking stuff hangs together. Knowing what an IP address really is, understanding how a netmask works, and comprehending the symbiotic relationship between IP and TCP is what separates a novice from a professional. We'll cover some of these issues here.

If you know what makes a /31 network mostly useless, you can skip this chapter. Otherwise, read on. There will be a test later—not in this book, but in the real world.

## Network Layers

Network layers simplify the networking process. Each layer handles a specific part of the networking process, and information is said to travel down and up through these layers. New users often have trouble understanding this, but we'll go over it in detail. The important thing to remember is that each layer only communicates with the layer directly above it and the layer directly beneath it.

The classic ISO network protocol diagram has seven layers, is exhaustively complete, and covers any situation. The Internet isn't "every situation," however, and this isn't a book about networking. Since we'll limit our discussion to the Internet world, we can simplify this diagram somewhat and divide the network into four layers: the application, the logical protocol, the physical protocol, and the physical layer.

*The descriptions in this chapter are necessarily generalizations, and very thick books have been written about this topic. My favorite is Stevens'* TCP/IP Illustrated, *volumes 1 through 3 (Addison-Wesley).*

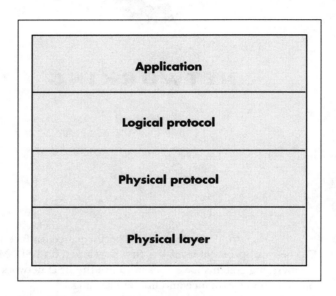

*Figure 5.1: 4-layer network diagram*

### The Physical Layer

The bottom layer is the physical one, encompassing the network card and the wire (or other connection) running out of it. This layer also includes the switch (or network hub) and the wire running to the router, as well as the fiber that carries your packets from your ISP to one of the Internet switching points (network access points, or NAPs) and on to the destination. It may even include radio waves, if you're using wireless. Without this link, you have nothing. The physical protocol is the only thing that needs to recognize how this bottom layer works.

A piece of wire—it's really that simple. If your wire is intact and meets the specifications required by the physical protocol, you're in business. If not, you're hosed.

Some physical protocols have been implemented over many different physical layers and Ethernet has been transmitted over half a dozen different sorts of cable. With minor changes in the device drivers and major changes in the network card, you can change your physical layer and not alter any other layer.

Similarly, a single connection might travel over several different types of wire. One of the functions of Internet routers is to convert one sort of physical layer into another.

The physical layer has no decision-making abilities and no intelligence; everything it does is dictated by the physical protocol.

### The Physical Protocol Layer

The physical protocol layer is where things get interesting. The physical protocol talks over the wire. It encodes transmissions in the actual ones and zeroes that are sent over the physical layer in the appropriate manner for that sort of media. For example, Ethernet uses Media Access Control (MAC) addresses and the Address Resolution Protocol (ARP); dial-up uses the Point-to-Point Protocol (PPP, usually used for home connections). The physical protocol has to understand how to speak to these addresses, and to encode and decode messages for them.

Ethernet and PPP are the main physical protocols, though FreeBSD also supports a variety of other physical protocols, such as Asynchronous Transfer Mode (ATM) and Integrated Services Digital Network (ISDN), as well as combinations such as PPP over Ethernet (used by some home-broadband vendors). Each of these protocols has special requirements, and while we'll only discuss Ethernet in some detail, you should understand that other connection protocols exist.

The physical protocol passes information to and from the physical layer and the logical protocol layer.

### The Logical Protocol Layer

Logical protocols, such as Internet Protocol (IP) and Transmission Control Protocol (TCP) handle things like IP addresses and port operations by exchanging information with the physical protocol and the application. You can use multiple logical protocols simultaneously.

There are many logical protocols. (See the /etc/protocols file for a mostly complete list.) The protocols we're most concerned with are IP and TCP (both already mentioned), Internet Control Message Protocol (ICMP), and User Datagram Protocol (UDP).

Logical protocols can work side by side, and can even depend upon one another. When a packet is transmitted, it includes a flag that identifies which protocol it belongs to.

#### Internet Protocol

The Internet Protocol (IP) is the baling wire that holds the Internet together, and every device on the Internet is expected to speak IP. IP provides very basic, core functions, such as network addresses and packet routing, as well as the fundamental infrastructure used by other logical protocols. You can live without TCP and other protocols, but if you don't have IP you don't have the Net.

**NOTE** *In this book, we only discuss IP version 4; IP version 6 is fairly new. While FreeBSD includes excellent IPv6 support, it's not yet widespread enough to cover here. Hopefully, by the time a new edition of this book comes out, IPv6 will be widespread, because it fixes many problems found in IPv4, thus eliminating the gross hacks that have been implemented to work around them.*

### IP Addresses

An IP address is a 32-bit number, generally divided into four groups of 8 bits each. Translated into English, this means that you'll see four numbers, each from 0 to 255, separated by periods. For example, 192.168.1.87 is a valid IP address, while 192.259.0.87 is not—one of the numbers exceeds 255. 607.322.843.999 is Right Out.

Every device on the Internet has a unique IP address, unless it's using Network Address Translation (NAT) or some other ugly hack.

### *The Application Layer*

Finally, we have the application layer—what the user deals with. The application might be a Web browser, a word processor, or a shell client. The application only has to worry about the user interface and the logical protocol. (You might consider the end user to be another layer, but problems with this layer are beyond the scope of this book.[1])

# The Network in Practice

Now that you understand something of each layer, let's look at some of them in detail. Let's consider how these network layers work for an office desktop connected via Ethernet.

Say you type www.absolutebsd.com into your Web browser. The Web browser needs to know how to make requests of the next layer down, so it translates the hostname into an IP address (a series of numbers like 192.168.1.84).

**NOTE** *By default, a server delivers services on network ports, or logical identifiers. We'll look more at ports in a little bit; for now, just understand that each service a computer offers runs on a unique port. Web servers usually run on TCP port 80. The browser sends a request for a connection to that IP and that port to the next layer down.*

The logical protocol layer then examines the request it has received from the application. Since the application has requested a TCP/IP connection, the logical protocol allocates the appropriate system resources for that sort of connection. The request is broken up into chunks of the correct size to be sent over Internet Protocol, called *packets*.

From here on, the logical protocol doesn't care about the application's actual request; instead, it wants to deliver these packets to the specified address. The IP layer checks its internal tables to see how to reach the requested IP address from this computer. It then bundles up the packets, adds on the IP layer routing information, and hands the packets to the physical protocol layer.

[1] No matter how desperate or annoyed you are, fsck-ing or BIOS-flashing the user layer is not a good idea. You can only reconfigure this layer through a process called "education." Don't expect too much from this.

The physical protocol layer examines the request from the logical protocol layer (it doesn't know anything about the Web browser; all it cares about is getting each packet to its destination). The physical protocol layer checks the physical protocol address (the MAC address) for the packet's destination, and adds Ethernet information to the packet. This packet-plus-physical-protocol chunk of data is called a *segment*. Finally, the physical protocol hands the whole mess down to the physical layer, which converts it to zeros and ones, and feeds it to the wire. Switches and routers echo those zeros and ones all the way to the final destination.

Your wire can go through various physical changes as your data is transferred. For example, your Ethernet will probably become a T1 line (your office router will handle that conversion for you). Then, that T1 will join a piece of optical fiber that runs across the country (the phone company will handle that transition).

When the segment reaches its destination, the computer at the other end of the transaction, it starts a return trip back up the protocol stack.

The physical layer gives each segment to the physical protocol, which does some basic sanity-checking on the segment to make sure that it hasn't been corrupted in transit. Once the physical layer is satisfied that the segment is correct, it removes the Ethernet information to create a packet, and hands it up to the logical protocol.

The logical protocol, in turn, performs its own sanity-checking. Remember how the logical protocol broke up the request into packets for easy transmission? Now it assembles the packets of the answer into a stream of information, and hands that stream off to the application. The application then has its answer and can display the Web page.

Of course, this is all expected to happen very, very quickly.

This seems like an awful lot of work, but it's an excellent example of *interface abstraction*. This means that each layer only knows what it must about the layers above and below, and makes it possible to swap out entire layers if desired. When a new physical protocol is created, the other layers don't have to care; the logical protocol just hands the request off to the new physical protocol layer, and lets it deal with things internally. When you have a new type of network card, all you need to do is write a driver for the physical protocol; the application and logical protocol layers don't care.

### Mbufs

BSD optimizes networking by using *mbufs*. An mbuf is a discrete chunk of memory set aside for networking that lives within the kernel. A packet starts off life as an mbuf. Rather than copying the contents of a packet to the next layer down, each of the OS layers hand the entire mbuf down. Copying a piece of data consumes more time and resources than handing off the data in its current location.

What's more, mbufs are carefully designed not to require changes. When the logical protocol creates an mbuf, it leaves space at the front and back for physical protocol headers, which further minimizes the amount of copying. A packet becomes a segment within a single mbuf.

Those of you who are C programmers should recognize a pointer here. The pointer to the mbuf is handed around, while the mbuf itself remains constant. The rest of us just need to have a basic idea of what an mbuf is. You'll keep tripping across mentions of mbufs throughout any BSD network stack, so it's important to at least have a vague awareness of what they are.

### What Is a Bit?

As a network administrator, you're going to start seeing terms like *32 bit* and *48 bit* more and more frequently. You should understand what these terms mean so that you can recognize an illegitimate number.

You probably already know that a computer treats all data as zeros and ones, and that a single one or a zero is a bit. When a protocol specifies a number of bits, it's talking about the number as seen by the computer—this is binary math. (You were probably introduced to binary math, or *base 2*, back in elementary school, and promptly forgot about it. It's time to dust that knowledge off. Binary numbers are just a different way of describing the numbers we work with every day.)

In decimal (meaning *base 10*) math, the math we typically use every day, digits run from 0 to 9. When you want to go above the highest digit you have, you add a digit on the left and set your current digit to 0. (This is the whole "carry the 1" thing you learned many years ago, and now probably do without conscious thought.) In binary math, digits run from 0 to 1. When you want to go above the highest digit you have, you add a digit on the left and set your current digit to 0. It's the same thing, just with fewer digits.

Here are the first few decimal numbers converted into binary as an example.

| Decimal | Binary |
| --- | --- |
| 0 | 0 |
| 1 | 1 |
| 2 | 10 |
| 3 | 11 |
| 4 | 100 |
| 5 | 101 |
| 6 | 110 |
| 7 | 111 |
| 8 | 1000 |
| 9 | 1001 |
| 10 | 1010 |
| 11 | 1011 |
| 12 | 1100 |
| 13 | 1101 |
| 14 | 1110 |
| 15 | 1111 |

When you have a 32-bit number, such as an IP address, you have a string of 32 ones and zeros. Rather than expressing that 32-bit number as a single number, however, IP addresses are broken up into four 8-bit numbers. (We'll see why in the next section.)

*Many calculators have binary-to-decimal conversions. If you don't have such a calculator, the FreeBSD port math/calctool gives you one. Even the Windows calculator app does this when you use scientific mode. Take some IP addresses, punch in each of the four numbers, and convert them to binary to see how they look.*

# Ethernet

Many devices can share an Ethernet network, and the data your system receives is not necessarily meant for your system. Systems connected with Ethernet can speak directly with each other, which gives Ethernet one great advantage over other protocols, such as PPP. However, Ethernet has physical distance limitations that make it practical only for offices, colocation facilities, and other comparatively short-range networks.

Many different physical networks have been used to run Ethernet over the years. Once upon a time, most Ethernet cables were thick chunks of coaxial cable (coax); today most are comparatively thin Category 5 (cat5) cables with eight strands of very thin wire inside them. You may also encounter Ethernet over optical fiber or, if you're unlucky, Ethernet over "dark fiber." (*Dark fiber* is optical fiber without the light. It seemed like a good idea at the time.)

For the purposes of our discussion, we'll assume that you're working with cat5 cable, which is the most popular choice today. Either way, the theory is the same for all Ethernet physical layers.

## *Broadcasting*

Ethernet is a broadcast medium,[2] which means it expects that each packet you send on the network is sent to every workstation on the network. (Today this isn't necessarily true, as we'll discuss later.) Your device driver sorts out the data intended for you from the data you don't care about.

One side effect of Ethernet's broadcast nature is that you can "sniff" other people's connections, capturing everything they send and receive. While this ability can be very useful in diagnosing problems, it's also a major security issue: Capturing passwords is trivial on an old-fashioned Ethernet.

While Ethernet started out supporting only a couple of megabits per second, it has grown beyond its original design to handle gigabit speeds. Most people use 10/100 megabit per second (Mbps) speeds, as gigabit Ethernet cards are still somewhat expensive. A sub-$100 gigabit Ethernet card came out as this was written.

---

[2] It does not go through the ether, however, or travel like radio. The physical wire is very much a requirement.

## Address Resolution

Every Ethernet network card has a unique identifier, its *MAC address*, which it uses to communicate with other hosts. A MAC address is a 48-bit number. When your system wants to transmit data to another host on the Ethernet, it sends out an Ethernet request that basically says, "Which MAC address is responsible for this IP address?" If a host responds, further data is marked for that MAC address. This process is known as the Address Resolution Protocol, or ARP.

You can view the current MAC and ARP situation with the arp command. The most common form is the `arp -a` command, which shows the MAC addresses and hostnames of all hosts on your network:

```
# arp -a
? (192.168.1.1) at 0:a0:cc:35:5b:7 [ethernet]
magpire.blackhelicopters.org (192.168.1.222) at 0:4:5a:41:a4:44 [ethernet]
#
```

Here we see that the host magpire.blackhelicopters.org has an IP address of 192.168.1.222, and a MAC address of 0:4:5a:41:a4:44. The MAC address is the Ethernet address. If a MAC address is "incomplete," the host cannot be contacted. In such a case, check your physical layer (the wire) and your system configuration.

## Hubs and Switches

An Ethernet *hub* is a central piece of hardware with physical connections to many other Ethernet devices that simply forward Ethernet-layer information to every device hooked to them. Hubs broadcast all Ethernet traffic that they receive to every attached host.

A *switch* is a more modern way of connecting Ethernets. A switch improves the speed of Ethernet by tracking the MAC addresses of each attached device and, for the most part, only forwarding packets to the device they are meant for. Since each Ethernet host has a finite amount of bandwidth (for example, a 100 Mbps card can handle 100 megabits per second), switching reduces the load on individual systems by limiting the amount of data transferred to each device. However, switches do cost more than hubs.

## Netmasks

If your company is hooking up to the Internet, your ISP will issue you a block of IP addresses. You use these addresses for your local Ethernet. Frequently, this is a small block, say, 16 or 32 IP addresses. If your system is colocated on a server farm, you might only get a few IP addresses. It all depends on your needs. The size of your IP block determines your *netmask*.

If you've done networking for any length of time, you've probably seen the netmask 255.255.255.0. You might even know that the wrong netmask will keep your system from working. In today's world, that simple netmask is becoming less and less common. To understand why, we need to look at what a netmask really is and how blocks of IP addresses are issued.

Many years ago, IP addresses were issued in blocks of three sizes: class A, class B, and class C. This terminology has been obsolete for quite some time, but we'll use it as a starting point.

Class A was very simple: The first of the four numbers in your IP address was fixed. The InterNIC might issue you a class A like 10.0.0.0. You could assign any of the last three numbers in any manner you liked. For example, you could assign 10.1.0.0 through 10.1.1.255 to your datacenter, 10.1.2.0 through 10.1.7.255 to your Boston office, and so on. Only very large companies, such as Ford and Xerox, received class A blocks, as well as influential academic computing institutions.

In a class B block, the first two of the four numbers in the IP address were fixed. Your class B block would look something like 64.29.0.0. Every IP address you used internally began with 64.29, but you could assign the last two numbers as you wanted. Many mid-sized companies got class B blocks.

Similarly, a class C block had the first three numbers fixed. This was the standard for small companies. The ISP would issue a number like 209.69.9, and let you assign the last number as needed.

This scheme wasted a lot of IP numbers. Many small companies don't need 256 IP addresses. Many medium-sized companies need more than 256, but fewer than the 65,000 in a class B block. And almost nobody needs the full 16 million addresses in a class A block. Still, those were the choices. Before the Internet boom, they were good enough.

Today, IP addresses are issued by *prefix length*, commonly called a *slash*. You will see IP blocks such as 192.168.1.128/25. While this looks confusing, it's merely a way of using classes with much greater granularity. You know that each number in an IP address is 8 bits long. By using a class, what you're saying is that a certain number of bits are "fixed"—you can't change them on your network. A class A address has 8 fixed bits, a class B has 16, and a class C has 24.

This isn't a class in binary math, so I won't make you draw it out and do the conversion. But think about an IP address as a string of binary numbers. On your network you can change the bits on the far right, but not the ones on the far left.

There's no reason that the boundary between the two must be on one of those convenient 8-bit lines. A prefix length is simply the number of fixed bits you are stuck with. A /25 means that you have 25 fixed bits, or one more fixed bit than a class C. You can play with 7 bits. In the following sample, your fixed bits are all ones, and the ones you can change are zeros:

```
11111111.11111111.11111111.10000000
```

It's childishly simple. If you think in binary, that is. You won't have to work with this every day, but if you don't understand the underlying binary concepts, the decimal conversion looks like absolute gibberish. With practice, you'll learn to recognize some bits of decimal gibberish as legitimate binary conversions.

What does this mean in practice?

First of all, blocks of IP addresses are issued in multiples of 2. If you have 4 bits to play with, you have 16 IP addresses (2*2*2*2=16). If you have 8 bits to play with, you have ($2^8$) 256 IP numbers. If someone says you have 13 IP addresses, you're either on a shared Ethernet or she's wrong.

A netmask is simply another way of specifying how many fixed bits are set. In the computing world, an 8-bit number runs from 0 to 255. If you have a /24, your netmask is 255.255.255.0. If you have a /25, you have all 8 bits set in the first three numbers and 1 bit set in the last number. In the previous example, the last number is 10000000 in binary. A bit of work with a binary-converting calculator[3] gives you 255.255.255.128.

It's not uncommon to see a host IP with its attached netmask, i.e., 192.168.3.4/26. When you see a /32, it does not represent a network, but a single host. You'll see /32 used when someone wants to make it absolutely clear that he's talking about a single host and not a network.

### Netmask Tricks

You probably don't want to have to keep converting from decimal to binary and back. Here's a trick to calculate your netmask.

Learn how many actual IP addresses you have to play with. This will be a multiple of 2. You'll almost certainly be issued an amount smaller than a /24 (the traditional class C). Subtract the number of IP addresses you have from 256. This is the last number of your netmask.

For example, if you have 64 IP addresses, the last part of your netmask is (256 – 64 =) 192. Your netmask would be 255.255.255.192.

You still need to use a bit of logic to avoid binary conversions. Figuring out legitimate addresses on your network is a bit of a pain. If your IP address is 192.168.54.187/25, you'll need to know that a /25 is 25 fixed bits, so you're using a block of 128 IP addresses. Look at the last number of your IP, 187. It certainly isn't between 0 and 127, but it is in the range of 128 to 255. The other hosts on your IP block have IP addresses ranging from 192.168.54.128 to 192.168.54.255.

### Hexadecimal Netmasks

Got all that? Good. Unfortunately, UNIX's standard method of showing netmasks is in hexadecimal (base 16), not decimal or binary. Some day soon you'll see a netmask of 0xffffff00.

A hexadecimal digit is 4 bits long, so each 8-bit portion of a netmask can be expressed as two hexadecimal numbers. (IP addresses could also be expressed this way, but they're not.) Hexadecimal numbers are always preceded with "0x", so they're easily recognizable.

At this point, the simplest thing to do is use either a calculator or a conversion table. Presented for your convenience is Table 5.1, a slash-to-hex-to-binary-to-decimal conversion for netmasks /24 and longer.

---

[3] You can also do this on paper, a few times at least. You'll learn a lot more that way. Come on, try it, be brave.

**Table 5.1: Netmask conversions**

| Prefix | Binary mask | Decimal mask | Hex mask | Available IPs |
| --- | --- | --- | --- | --- |
| /24 | 00000000 | 0 | 0x00 | 256 |
| /25 | 10000000 | 128 | 0x80 | 128 |
| /26 | 11000000 | 192 | 0xc0 | 64 |
| /27 | 11100000 | 224 | 0xe0 | 32 |
| /28 | 11110000 | 240 | 0xf0 | 16 |
| /29 | 11111000 | 248 | 0xf8 | 8 |
| /30 | 11111100 | 252 | 0xfc | 4 |
| /31 | 11111110 | 254 | 0xfe | 2 |
| /32 | 11111111 | 255 | 0xff | 1 |

### Unusable IP Addresses

You now understand that a /26 has 64 IP addresses. Unfortunately, you can't use them all. The first IP address is the *network number*. It's used for internal bookkeeping. And the last number in any group of IP addresses is the *broadcast address*. According to the IP specifications, every machine on a network is supposed to respond to a request to this address. This allows you to ping the broadcast address and quickly determine which IP addresses are in use. For example, on a typical /24 network, the broadcast address is x.y.z.255. In the late '90s, this feature was turned into an attack technique. It's now disabled by default on most operating systems. If you need it to work on your BSD systems, set the sysctl net.inet.icmp.bmcastecho to 1.

In any case, the point is that you cannot assign either the first or last IP address in a network to an interface. Go ahead, try it.

If you remember, in the first part of this chapter I mentioned that a /31 is mostly useless. A /31 has two IP addresses. You cannot use the top or the bottom addresses. This doesn't leave much room for servers, or even clients.

### Routing

So, now you have the IP addresses for your Ethernet, and every host on the local network can find every other host. You still have to tell those systems how to reach other networks. Generally, every network has a router or other exterior gateway, and this device is called the *default router*. A network should have one and only one default router. Every system on the network needs to know the IP address of this device.

Once you have the default router set, you should be able to ping anything on the Internet by IP address—and by hostname, if your resolver is configured correctly (see the discussion of /etc/resolv.conf in Chapter 11).

### UDP and TCP

Now that you have IP running, you probably want to transmit some data over it. The User Datagram Protocol (UDP) is one way programs can do this. UDP is arguably the most bare-bones protocol possible in IP. It has no error handling, no content verification, no defense whatsoever against data loss. Despite this, it can be a good protocol choice, and many vital Internet services use it. An application using UDP most often has its own error-correction requirements that don't jibe with those provided by other protocols.

When a host transmits data via UDP, it doesn't know if the data reached its destination or not. And when a host receives data via UDP, it has no way to verify where that data came from. While UDP packets include a source address, this is easily faked. UDP is called *connectionless* for this reason.

Another common IP data transport is Transmission Control Protocol (TCP). TCP includes error correction and packet recovery. Every packet sent must be acknowledged by the receiver, or it will be retransmitted. Applications that use TCP can expect reliable data transmission unless one of the lower layers fails.

Unlike UDP, TCP is a connected protocol. For data to be transmitted, the two hosts must set up a channel for data to flow over. This is known as the *three-way handshake*. The exact specifics aren't important right now, but you should know that there is a certain amount of work that must be done to establish a TCP connection. When the connection is finished, there's some work to be done to tear it down.

You can compare IP, TCP, and UDP to a family sitting at a table passing dishes back and forth. IP is like knowing where everybody's sitting and understanding that to hand the peas to Uncle Jim you pass it by Cousin Colleen. TCP is where one person hands another a dish, and the other must say "Thank you" before the first person will let go. UDP is like tossing a muffin at Aunt Jane—she might catch it, or it might get snatched in midair by the dog.

### Network Ports

Have you ever noticed that computers have too many ports? Well, we're going to add TCP and UDP ports to the list. Network ports permit one server to provide many different network services—they are ways to multiplex connections between machines.

When a packet (either TCP or UDP) arrives at a system, it requests to be delivered to a certain port. Different ports provide different services. For example, the Internet mail service is called SMTP. According to /etc/services, SMTP runs on port 25. If a TCP connection request asks for port 25, we can guess that it's for the mail server. Ports allow multiple connections between multiple machines.

The /etc/services file contains a list of those port numbers and the services that they're generally associated with. It's possible to run almost any service on an arbitrary port, but by doing so you'll confuse other Internet hosts that try to connect to your system. The format of the file is very simple: the official service name, the port number, the protocol, any aliases for that service, and finally comments, all separated by tabs. For example, one old service that could be found on UNIX hosts was Quote of the Day, or qotd. If we look in /etc/services, we'll find an entry for it:

```
qotd          17/tcp    quote     #Quote of the Day
qotd          17/udp    quote     #Quote of the Day
```

Many services have both the TCP and UDP ports of a certain number assigned to them, while others only have one of the protocols.

Many programs read /etc/services to learn what port to use (or *bind to*). Depending on the program, you may have to edit the services file to assign that protocol to that port. In that case, be sure to check out revision control (see Chapter 3) before starting. Like all standards, the lists in /etc/services can be violated. I've run sshd, which normally occupies port 22, on port 80 to bypass some firewall restrictions in very unusual circumstances. This all depends on the program you're using to provide a service.

The ports 1024 and below are called *low-numbered ports*. These are the ports reserved for core Internet infrastructure protocols, such as DNS, telnet, and HTTP. Their standard usage is basically carved in stone. The ports above 1024 are less standardized, and you'll occasionally see conflicts where multiple protocols want to use the same port. Generally, a client initiates a connection from a port above 1024 and requests a connection to a low-numbered port.

Occasionally, protocols that run over something besides TCP and UDP use /etc/services. A few protocols in the file use DDP (Datagram Delivery Protocol). Don't worry when you stumble across these; they really aren't anything to worry about. Pretty much any program expects the admin to be able to make arbitrary entries in /etc/services.

## Connecting to an Ethernet Network

Now that you understand how IP addresses work, properly connecting to your network is much simpler. You probably set up your network connection during the initial install, but if you changed something or switched networks, you need to understand how to do this manually. To configure a network interface, you need the following information:

- The network interface name
- An IP address for your server
- The netmask
- The default route

You use two separate commands to configure your network card: ifconfig(8) and route(8). Ifconfig manipulates the interface configuration—if you run it without arguments, it will display all the interfaces on the system.

```
# ifconfig
dc0: flags=8843<UP,BROADCAST,RUNNING,SIMPLEX,MULTICAST> mtu 1500
        ether 00:04:5a:41:a4:44
        media: Ethernet autoselect (100baseTX <full-duplex>)
        status: active
lp0: flags=8810<POINTOPOINT,SIMPLEX,MULTICAST> mtu 1500
lo0: flags=8049<UP,LOOPBACK,RUNNING,MULTICAST> mtu 16384
        inet 127.0.0.1 netmask 0xff000000
ppp0: flags=8010<POINTOPOINT,MULTICAST> mtu 1500
```

The interfaces are listed along the far left of the output. The system here has five interfaces: dc0 (Ethernet), lp0 (printer), lo0 (loopback), and ppp0 (point-to-point). Each interface has a device name and a number.

To learn about an interface, check section 4 of the system manual pages:

```
# man 4 dc
```

We want to configure the Ethernet interface. Use ifconfig to give the interface an IP address and netmask, like this:

```
# ifconfig dc0 inet 192.168.1.223 netmask 255.255.255.0
#
```

You can also check the configuration of a single interface with ifconfig.

```
#ifconfig dc0
dc0: flags=8843<UP,BROADCAST,RUNNING,SIMPLEX,MULTICAST> mtu 1500
        inet 192.168.1.223 netmask 0xffffff00 broadcast 192.168.1.255
        ether 00:04:5a:41:a4:44
        media: Ethernet autoselect (100baseTX <full-duplex>)
        status: active
#
```

Note that the netmask has been converted to the hexadecimal equivalent.

You can configure your Ethernet card automatically at boot with an /etc/rc.conf option (see Chapter 8). The entry has the form ifconfig_interfacename="ifconfig statement". For example, the configuration shown two paragraphs earlier appears in /etc/rc.conf like this:

```
ifconfig_dc0="inet 192.168.1.223  netmask 255.255.255.0"
```

Now that the interface is configured, try to ping the default gateway IP address. You can interrupt the ping with CONTROL-C. If you get a response back, as shown in the following listing, you are actually on the network. If you cannot ping the network, you either have a bad connection or your card is misconfigured.

```
# ping 192.168.1.1
PING 192.168.1.1 (192.168.1.1): 56 data bytes
64 bytes from 192.168.1.1: icmp_seq=0 ttl=64 time=0.631 ms
64 bytes from 192.168.1.1: icmp_seq=1 ttl=64 time=0.323 ms
^C
--- 192.168.1.1 ping statistics ---
2 packets transmitted, 2 packets received, 0% packet loss
round-trip min/avg/max/stddev = 0.323/0.477/0.631/0.154 ms
#
```

The default route has a very simple purpose—this is the address where the system sends any traffic it can't reach itself. You set this with the route command.

```
# route add default 192.168.1.1
```

That's it! You should now be able to ping any IP address on the Internet. You can set the boottime default router in /etc/rc.conf with the defaultrouter statement (see Chapter 8). Here's a good example of a defaultrouter statement:

```
defaultrouter="192.168.1.1"
```

You probably want to be able to use hostnames to ping, however. If you cannot ping by name, you need to set up your resolver. See the section on /etc/resolv.conf in Chapter 11 to do so. This was probably set during the install process, however.

### Multiple IP Addresses on One Interface

One FreeBSD system can respond to multiple IP addresses on one interface. This is a popular configuration for Internet servers, especially secure Web sites. One server might have to support hundreds or thousands of domains and need an IP address for each. You can add extra IP addresses with the ifconfig command:

```
# ifconfig dc0 alias 192.168.1.225
```

Once you run the preceding command, your interface will look like this (the primary IP address always appears first; aliases follow):

```
# ifconfig dc0
dc0: flags=8843<UP,BROADCAST,RUNNING,SIMPLEX,MULTICAST> mtu 1500
        inet 192.168.1.223 netmask 0xffffff00 broadcast 192.168.1.255
        inet 192.168.1.225 netmask 0xffffff00 broadcast 192.168.1.255
        ether 00:04:5a:41:a4:44
        media: Ethernet autoselect (100baseTX <full-duplex>)
        status: active
#
```

You can configure the additional IP addresses automatically at boot with another ifconfig statement in /etc/rc.conf:

```
ifconfig_dc0_alias0="inet 192.168.1.225"
```

The only real difference between this entry and the standard rc.conf ifconfig entry is the "alias0" chunk. Each alias set in /etc/rc.conf must have a unique number, and the numbers must be sequential. If you skip a number, aliases after the gap will not be installed at boot. This is the most common cause of misconfigured interfaces; FreeBSD needs to be rebooted so rarely that errors in /etc/rc.conf can go unnoticed for months!

All outgoing connections use the system's real IP address. You might have 2,000 IP addresses bound to one network card, but when you ssh outwards, the connection comes from the primary IP address. Keep this in mind when writing firewall rules and other access-control filters.

### Using Netstat

Netstat(1) is your window into current network conditions. You can view the state of connections, the number of network buffers your kernel is sucking up, and just about anything else you might be interested in.

One of the most important netstat flags is -n. By default, netstat shows hostnames for each connection, but hostname lookups take a lot of time. The -n option turns off IP address-to-hostname lookups. If you see an interesting connection, you can easily look up the hostname yourself.

Another vital flag is -I, which allows you to specify an interface. Some netstat flags allow or require choosing a particular interface. Remember, you have a variety of interfaces on your machine: loopback, printer, Ethernet, and so on.

The -f flag allows you to choose a protocol family. If you're only interested in IPv4 connections, use -f inet. Other valid values for -f include inet6 (IPv6), ipx (Novell IPX), atalk (AppleTalk), ng (Netgraph), and unix (UNIX sockets). For our examples, you can use -f inet unless specified otherwise.

First off, let's look at the existing connections:

```
# netstat -na
Active Internet connections (including servers)
Proto Recv-Q Send-Q  Local Address        Foreign Address       (state)
tcp4       0      0  192.168.1.222.22     192.168.1.200.1067    ESTABLISHED
tcp4       0      0  *.5999               *.*                   LISTEN
tcp4       0      0  *.80                 *.*                   LISTEN
tcp4       0      0  *.443                *.*                   LISTEN
tcp4       0      0  192.168.1.222.25     *.*                   LISTEN
tcp4       0      0  *.22                 *.*                   LISTEN
Active UNIX domain sockets
Address   Type   Recv-Q Send-Q    Inode    Conn    Refs  Nextref Addr
d5ba2200 stream      0      0        0  d5ba2240      0        0
d5ba2240 stream      0      0        0  d5ba2200      0        0
...
```

Every line in the netstat output indicates a network connection of some sort. You'll see quite a few lines of UNIX domain sockets. These are sockets that run through the kernel, not through the network. You don't need to be concerned about those right now. Next time, use the -f inet flag to eliminate them from the output.

The first entry on each line is the protocol. In our example, every connection is TCP, version 4 (tcp4).

The Recv-Q and Send-Q columns show how many bits are waiting to be handled on this connection. If you see that your system has Recv-Q numbers continually, you know that it cannot process incoming data quickly enough. Similarly, if the Send-Q keeps having entries, you know that either the network or the other system in the connection cannot accept data as quickly as you're sending it. Occasional queued packets are normal. You need to watch your own system to learn what's normal and what isn't.

The Local Address is, as you might guess, the IP address on the local system. The addresses shown all have five period-delimited numbers, though! The last number is the port number. For example, 192.168.1.222.22 is port 22 on 192.168.1.222. If the entry is an asterisk, a period, and a port number, that means that the system is listening on that port on all available IP addresses. There is no connection running, but the system is ready to accept one.

The Foreign Address column shows the remote address and port number of any connection.

Finally, the "(state)" column shows the status of the TCP handshake. You don't need to know all of the possible TCP connection states right now; just become familiar with what's normal. ESTABLISHED means that a connection is complete, and data is quite probably flowing. LAST_ACK, FIN_WAIT_1, and FIN_WAIT_2 mean that the connection is being closed. SYN_RCVD, ACK and SYN+ACK are all parts of normal connection creation. In the preceding example, one TCP connection is currently running. Five TCP ports are waiting for incoming connections.

If you want to see the number of packets passed, the number dropped, and the number of errors you have, you can use netstat's -b option. The output from this command is quite wide; if you're running in X, you'll want to stretch your display as broad as your screen permits. Some of the more interesting columns are Ierrs (input errors), Oerrs (output errors), and coll (collision). These should all be zero, or close to it. If they aren't, something isn't right and you need to investigate. Anything can generate these errors: bad cables, bad switches, bad network cards, software problems, firmware errors, whatever.

You can see how many connections the system has recognized with the -L flag, which displays the *listen queues*:

```
# netstat -Ln
Current listen queue sizes (qlen/incqlen/maxqlen)
Listen        Local Address
0/0/10        127.0.0.1.1556
0/0/10        127.0.0.1.8080
```

*(continued on next page)*

```
0/0/10          127.0.0.1.554
0/0/10          127.0.0.1.7070
0/0/10          192.168.10.6.1556
0/0/10          192.168.10.6.8080
0/0/10          192.168.10.6.554
0/0/10          192.168.10.6.7070
#
```

Each line in this output indicates a unique IP address/port pair. The first number in the Listen column is the number of unaccepted connections that the system has received. The second is the number of unaccepted, incomplete
connections. The third is the maximum number of connections that address can
have in the queue. Once a connection is complete, it moves off the queue.

netstat -m is a different sort of beast. It displays the kernel mbuf statistics.
When you run out of mbufs, you cannot handle any more network data. They're
freed as data is processed.

```
# netstat -m
211/3216/10240 mbufs in use (current/peak/max):
        44 mbufs allocated to data
        167 mbufs allocated to packet headers
41/1114/2560 mbuf clusters in use (current/peak/max)
3032 Kbytes allocated to network (39% of mb_map in use)
0 requests for memory denied
0 requests for memory delayed
0 calls to protocol drain routines
#
```

This output shows that on this system, we're using 39 percent of our available
mbufs. There's plenty left to deal with any spikes. We haven't ever been denied
memory, either. If you start to run out of mbufs, increase NMBCLUSTERS in
your kernel (see Chapter 4).

The -p flag allows you to check protocol-by-protocol statistics. The protocols
you're probably most interested in are IP, TCP, and UDP. This output is fairly
long, and unique to each system, but it is worth looking at simply to get an idea
of what's normal on your system. If something starts misbehaving, it should
leave a fingerprint there.

If you want to see the system's routing table, netstat -r is your friend:

```
# netstat -r
Routing tables

Internet:
Destination     Gateway         Flags   Refs    Use     Netif Expire
default         192.168.1.1     UGSc    10      1       wi0
localhost       localhost       UH      0       2       lo0
```

```
192.168.1        link#5            UC      2     0    wi0     794
192.168.1.1      0:a0:cc:35:5b:7   UHLW    12    0    wi0     485
magpire          0:4:5a:41:a4:44   UHLW    1     453  wi0 =>
192.168.87       link#1            UC      0     0    fxp0 =>
#
```

Each line in this table is a separate route. When FreeBSD wants to send a packet to a host, it checks the routing table. Note that this took quite a while to run—netstat tried to find a hostname for every IP address. The hosts shown by an IP address had to time out. If you want quick-and-dirty routing information, be sure to use the -n flag!

The first column in the preceding output is the Destination. This is either a host, a network, or the default route.

The Gateway is where you want to send a packet bound for this host or network.

The Flags column indicates how the routes were generated or used. You can find a full listing of all route flags in netstat(1), but some of the common ones are listed in Table 5.2. You don't need to understand what each of these flags mean at this point. Just be familiar with the flags for each route that normally appears on your system. If something looks different, start digging for more information.

**Table 5.2: Common netstat route flags**

| Flag | Description |
| --- | --- |
| U | The route is usable |
| G | This is a gateway |
| S | This route is static (i.e., not added dynamically by a routing protocol) |
| L | This route is a protocol-to-link-address translation (i.e., the MAC address used to reach an IP address) |
| H | This route is for a particular host |
| C | This route is used when you dynamically create new routes (i.e., a gateway) |
| c | This route is used for protocol-specific new routes (i.e., how to reach the gateway) |
| W | This route was cloned from another route |

The Refs column shows how many connections are using a particular route entry in netstat -nr output. The system in our example has two routes in use.

The Use field shows how many packets are being sent via this route.

The Netif column shows the system interface the route is reachable through.

The Expire column shows the number of seconds until the route goes away. At that time, the system will check for a new route. In our example, both routes with Expire values are on the local Ethernet. The system will use the standard arp process to update the route.

Finally, netstat -w shows you the current system statistics. It keeps updating the display until you press **CONTROL-C**. netstat -w takes an additional argument, the number of seconds between updates:

```
# netstat -w 5
          input          (Total)           output
   packets errs     bytes  packets errs     bytes colls
         1    0        60        1    0       186     0
         1    0        60        1    0       138     0
^C
#
```

This information can help you decide whether errors you saw elsewhere are still occurring.

# 6

## UPGRADING FREEBSD

Upgrading Internet servers can be quite a pain. While you can probably deal with a bit of unexplained behavior in your desktop computer after an upgrade, you don't want anything to go wrong when you have a whole company or hundreds of customers depending on one system.

There have been many times when I've attempted to upgrade a Windows server from NT to 2000, or 2000 to XP, and found that some portion of the server no longer worked as expected. Linux upgrades can also inflict gray hair, and other UNIXes can be even worse. Quite a few experienced UNIX system administrators habitually reinstall their operating systems rather than suffer through an upgrade. And, though a few UNIX versions have straightforward upgrade procedures, they require several hours to complete and a certain amount of luck. (The last time I upgraded an HP/UX machine and the Informix database that it held, I showed up on Friday night with a sleeping bag, an alarm clock, and a box of meal bars, and I left Monday at noon. I would run a command and set the alarm clock for an hour or two later, when the command would be finished and I could start the next step.)

One of FreeBSD's greatest strengths is its upgrade procedure. For example, I have a few servers that were installed when FreeBSD 2.2.5 was the latest and greatest. They've been successively upgraded to 2.2.8, past 3.0 to the last version 3, and are now at version 4. The only inconvenience I've suffered was when jumping major version numbers—that is, from FreeBSD 3 to 4. I spent a couple of hours making those jumps. Just try that with Solaris or HP/UX, or with Windows.

# FreeBSD Versions

Why is upgrading FreeBSD a relatively simple matter? The key lies in FreeBSD's development method. FreeBSD is a continually evolving operating system. If you download certain versions of FreeBSD in the afternoon, they're a little different than the morning's version. Developers from around the world continually add changes and improvements, which makes the traditional release numbering used by less open software impractical. At any given moment, you can get several different versions of FreeBSD: releases, -current, -stable, and snapshots.

## Release

A FreeBSD *release* has a conventional version number, like you'd see on any other software: 2.2.7, 3.3, 4.4, 5.0. If you buy FreeBSD in a store, it's a release.

A release is simply a copy of the state of the most stable version of FreeBSD at a particular moment in time. Three or four times a year, the Release Engineer asks the developers to hold off on making any major changes and resolves outstanding problems. After thorough testing, the resulting code is given a release number, after which development returns to full speed, while the BSD department of your release provider rushes the release to the CD factory.

Always install the release version in a production environment.

## FreeBSD-current

FreeBSD-current is the bleeding-edge, latest version of FreeBSD and contains code that is just making its first public appearance. FreeBSD-current is where much initial peer review takes place and, at times, -current sees radical changes of the sort that give experienced systems administrators headaches.

FreeBSD-current is made available to developers, testers, and interested parties, but is not intended for general use. Support for user questions about -current is very slim because the developers simply don't have time to help a user get a Web browser working when a thousand more critical issues are begging for attention. Users are expected to help fix these problems, or to patiently endure until someone else fixes them.

If you can't read C, shell, and Perl, or don't feel like debugging your OS, or don't like computer functions failing in a seemingly random manner, or just don't like being left hanging until someone gets around to fixing your problem, -current is not for you.

The brave are certainly welcome to try -current. So is anyone who is willing to devote a large amount of time to learning and debugging FreeBSD, or who just needs a lesson in humility. This isn't so much a matter of "you're not allowed to" as "you're on your own."

People running -current must read the FreeBSD-current@FreeBSD.org and cvs-all@FreeBSD.org mailing lists. These are high-traffic lists, with as many as a couple hundred warnings, alerts, and comments a day. Read them, especially the warnings. If someone else discovers the latest Bug of Slow Hideous Death, you might have time to benefit from his experience.

### Code Freeze

Every 12 to 18 months or so, FreeBSD-current goes through a month of "code freeze" during which no non critical changes are allowed, and all remaining problems are fixed. At the end of the code freeze (or shortly after), -current becomes the new .0 release of FreeBSD-stable.

For a short time during code freeze, -current is treated like an early release of FreeBSD-stable. This focuses developers on stability and bug fixes for problems exposed by early adopters. After a release or two, a new -current is branched off the new, mainstream -stable. For example, at this writing 5-current is expected to become 5.0-release. The -current version will remain 5.0 until some point after 5.1-release, to help focus developer attention on the new release. At some point after 5.1-release, a copy of the source code will be labeled 6.0-current and another copy will be marked 5.1-stable.

### FreeBSD-stable

FreeBSD-stable is bleeding edge for the average user—it contains some of the most recent peer-reviewed code. FreeBSD-stable is expected to be calm and reliable, requiring little user attention. Once a piece of code is thoroughly tested in -current, it might be merged into -stable in a process called MFC, or *merge from current*. The -stable version is the one that is mostly safe to upgrade to at almost any time; you might think of it as FreeBSD-beta.

As -stable ages, the differences between -stable and -current become greater and greater, to the point where it becomes necessary to branch a new -stable off of -current. The older -stable is actively maintained for several months while the new -stable is beaten into shape.

Some users will want to upgrade to this new -stable immediately, while others are more cautious. After a release or two of the new -stable, the older -stable is made obsolete and users are encouraged to upgrade to the new -stable. Finally, the older -stable receives only critical bug fixes.

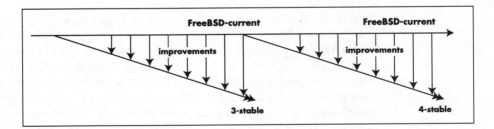

*Figure 6.1: FreeBSD development branches*

Every so often -stable is polished and tested; developers stop MFCing features and focus on testing. When everyone's happy with the quality, it's released and generally given a "point" after the main branch. (For example, the fourth release of FreeBSD 4 is FreeBSD 4.4, and you'll see references to both 4-stable and 4.4-stable—the name 4-stable includes all of the 4.x releases and -stable branches.)

The word *stable* describes the code base, not the OS itself. It doesn't guarantee that the operating system is completely stable and reliable, but that the underlying code won't suffer a radical change. For example, many people considered FreeBSD 3.5-stable more reliable than FreeBSD 4.0-stable.

**NOTE** *FreeBSD may be one of the most reliable operating systems available, but beware of any .0 release, from any company. Remember the poor folks who implemented Windows 2000 the month it came out?*

Users of FreeBSD-stable should read the FreeBSD-stable mailing list, a moderate-traffic mailing list. Important messages from developers generally have a subject beginning with "HEADS UP". Look for those messages, and take whatever action they recommend.

### Snapshots

Every so often, the FreeBSD development team releases a snapshot of -current (available via FTP, and through some vendors on CD-ROM). The snapshot does not receive the same attention to quality that -release does, but is intended as a good starting point for people interested in investigating or testing -current. Generally speaking, developers avoid adding major new features for a week or so before the snapshot is released, but the snapshot does not undergo quality analysis. Bugs exist, and while most are known, many aren't. New features are incomplete. You might call it a bleeding-edge release.

### Security Updates

With the advent of FreeBSD 4.3, the project began supporting security-update-only branches. Previously, a FreeBSD user had to upgrade to the latest -stable to get the security patches, but this caused problems, as the OS changed between releases. Why upgrade a whole server, and go through the headaches it can cause, just to get a patch for one small security problem? (Anyone who's worked through a Windows 2000 Service Pack upgrade can attest to the problems this sort of upgrade can cause.) Only actual security issues and system-damaging bugs are fixed; new features are not brought onto these branches, nor are performance enhancements. This might be considered a very timid -stable version.

The names of release security updates are the same as that of the release, with a trailing patch number—for example, 4.3-RELEASE-p6 is the sixth patch of 4.3-RELEASE.

### Which Release Should You Use?

FreeBSD uses the same release system as it does for quality control. Though it may seem like a complex system, it allows users to rest assured that a release is supported by the community, and that it has been through peer review and extensive testing. That same user knows that the nifty new features in -stable and -current are available, if she's willing to pay the price.

So which release should you use?

- **Production:** If you're using FreeBSD in a production setting, track the security branch of a -release.

- **Test:** If you're a network administrator interested in seeing how changes in FreeBSD will affect your environment, track -stable on a test system.

- **Development:** If you're an operating system developer, have too much spare time and too little excitement, or are a blind idiot, -current is for you. When -current destroys your MP3 collection, debug the problem and submit a patch to correct it.

- **Hobby:** If you're a hobbyist, you can run any version! Just keep in mind the limitations of the branch you're using. If you're just learning UNIX, -release is what you want. Once you have your feet under you, upgrade to -stable. If you have nothing better to do, and have nothing but utter contempt for your data, you're welcome to join the masochists over in -current.

## Upgrade Methods

With all of these releases, upgrading is always an issue. There are two main ways to upgrade: sysinstall and CVSup.

New and inexperienced users can upgrade with sysinstall, which only allows users to upgrade to a -release. Experienced users might wish to use CVSup and *make world*, which allows users to upgrade to the current, latest version of FreeBSD on any of the -stable, security update, or -current branches, but requires more effort to set up and use.

When upgrading from one -release to another, or to a snapshot, you can use sysinstall. If you're tracking -current, -stable, or the security update branches, you must be capable of using source code to build your system (as described in the "Upgrading via CVSup" section of this chapter).

> **NOTE** *Before upgrading, be sure you have complete backups. While sysinstall upgrade errs on the side of caution, files can still vanish if you upgrade improperly. See Chapter 3 for instructions on backups. (Of course, if you're reading this book in order, you've already been there.)*

### Upgrading via Sysinstall

The easiest way to upgrade via sysinstall is to boot off the install floppy or CD-ROM for the version of FreeBSD you are upgrading to. Then follow these steps:

1. When you reach the graphic install menu, choose the Upgrade option.

2. Sysinstall will open the upgrade notes for your version of sysinstall. (Be sure to read them carefully, because many last-minute problems will be documented there. Also check the online errata, available at http://www.FreeBSD.org. Follow the instructions carefully.)

3. You'll be asked if you want to proceed with the upgrade. If so, it will ask you about distribution sets. Here, it will be handy to know what distribution sets you originally installed on your system, because you probably want to replace all of them. At a minimum, you must replace the bin distribution. You can be greatly confused by not upgrading everything you originally installed; having the programs from 4.7-release but the documentation from 4.3-release could cause you no end of head-scratching.

4. The upgrade process continues much like the initial install until you're asked for the directory where your current /etc directory will be backed up. (Remember, /etc holds most of your system's configuration information; keep original copies of your configuration in case something goes wrong.) The default /usr/tmp/etc is generally fine.

5. Finally, sysinstall will ask you for your installation source. You can use FTP, a FreeBSD CD-ROM, or any other method available.

6. After offering you one last chance to change your mind, sysinstall will overwrite all the system binaries you chose to install. It will replace your kernel with a GENERIC kernel of the new version, and replace many files in /etc.

7. Once the upgrade completes, go through /etc and be certain that your vital system files are in the condition you want. While your password files, group file, and filesystem table will remain intact, you will want to check rc.conf, inetd.conf, shells, and any other files you've altered. (This is the most tedious part of the upgrade process.) If you have installed the source-code collection, you can ease the process with mergemaster(8). (We will discuss mergemaster in the "/etc and /dev Changes" section later in this chapter.)

After another reboot, your system will be safely upgraded.

**NOTE** *Do not use the sysinstall included in the version of FreeBSD you are currently running! If you are running FreeBSD 4.4-release, and want to upgrade to 4.5-release, use the sysinstall program included in 4.5-release. The simplest way to be sure you are doing this is to boot off the 4.5-release installation disk or CD-ROM.*

### Upgrading via CVSup

If you want a more flexible upgrade system, try upgrading your system from source with CVSup. When a developer releases improvements to FreeBSD, the changes are made available on FreeBSD servers worldwide within 66 minutes through CVS and CVSup. No non-BSD operating system in the world makes changes available so rapidly. The FreeBSD master CVS server tracks source code, all changes made to it, and who made those changes; developers can "check in" new code, and users can "check out" the latest versions.

CVS (Concurrent Versions System) is a decent tool for source-code management, but an awful tool for source-code distribution; it requires huge amounts of system resources and bandwidth, and tends to destroy the server's hard drive.

Since all of the FreeBSD Project's resources are donated, they need to be used as efficiently as possible. Thus, instead of using CVS, the FreeBSD Project uses CVSup to distribute the source code—CVSup is a combination of CVS and *sup*, the Software Update Protocol. Compared with CVS, the CVSup protocol is much faster, more efficient, easier on the servers, and generally nicer when supporting millions of users scattered across the world. The master CVS source-code repository is replicated to the worldwide CVSup servers, and users use CVSup to connect and download the source code.

Because these changes are publicly maintained through this CVS/CVSup server combination, your FreeBSD machine can connect to a CVSup server, compare its local copy of the FreeBSD source code to the version available on the server, and copy any changes to the local hard drive. As complex as this might sound, it's actually very simple. You can install CVSup on your local system and use it to efficiently download updates.

### Installing CVSup

Unlike most of FreeBSD, which is written in C, CVSup is written in Modula-3. Modula-3 is a very powerful, modern programming language well suited for applications such as CVSup. To build CVSup from pure source code, you'd need to build Modula-3 first, which takes quite a while. What's more, you'd probably never need Modula-3 again because very few programs require it. However, if you followed my suggestions in Chapter 1, you already have CVSup installed on your system.

If CVSup is not installed on your system, you can install it from a precompiled package (see Chapter 10 for details) or over FTP. To install over FTP, confirm that you have a live Internet connection and FTP connectivity to the outside world, and enter the following commands as root:

```
# cd /usr/ports/net/cvsup
# make all install clean
```

You will see lots of compiler messages go by, finally ending with a message confirming that CVSup has been installed. Once you have installed CVSup, confirm that your system has the FreeBSD source code installed—you should see something like this:

```
# ls /usr/src
COPYRIGHT          contrib        release
CVS                crypto         sbin
Makefile           etc            secure
Makefile.inc0      games          share
Makefile.inc1      gnu            sys
Makefile.upgrade   include        tools
README             kerberosIV     usr.bin
UPDATING           lib            usr.sbin
bin                libexec
#
```

This output is the FreeBSD source tree, which is all of the source code needed to build FreeBSD's programs and kernel. (We'll discuss source code at some length in Chapter 10.) Go ahead and browse through these directories if you like, to get an idea of what source code looks like.

If you find that this directory is empty, you haven't installed the source. But don't worry: You can install the source code from the installation CD by doing the following as root:

```
# mount /dev/acd0c /cdrom
# cd /cdrom/src/
# ./install.sh all
```

If you don't have an install CD, you can grab the source from a FreeBSD FTP server or, if bandwidth isn't a concern, you can simply run CVSup without a local source tree. CVSup will compare what you have to what you need, and will install the latest source code. (The CVSup mirror maintainers would prefer that you install the source from CD, however; they're donating the bandwidth and their processor time for this service, and it isn't cheap.) A full source tree uses about 300 MB of disk space.

Whatever method you use to install the source, you will initially start off with the source code for the version of FreeBSD you installed. For example, the CD-ROMs for FreeBSD 4.5 contain the source code for FreeBSD 4.5. If you install the source code when you install the system, you'll be installing the source code for version 4.5. This source code is a useful reference if you're a programmer. This source code isn't what you want to use to perform an upgrade; if you use the source code for FreeBSD 4.5 to rebuild and reinstall FreeBSD, you'll wind up reinstalling FreeBSD 4.5! CVSup compares the source code you have on disk to the source code available on the Internet, and downloads the changes between the two versions. CVSup then applies these "diffs" to the source code you have on disk, changing it to the source code of the version you want. This is much more efficient than re-downloading the entire 300 meg source tree! Even if you skip a release or two between upgrades, CVSup will only have to download a meg or two of new source code to complete the changes.

To make CVSup update your source tree, you need to tell it what to update, where to update it from, and how to perform the updates.

### Selecting Your Supfile

CVSup uses a *config* file, or *supfile*, which tells CVSup which files to update, and which version of FreeBSD you want to wind up with. (See /usr/share/examples/cvsup/ for sample supfiles.) The supfile you need will vary with the section of source code you want to upgrade. Once you've created a supfile to track -stable, -current, or a security branch, you can continue to use it forever.

A recent /usr/share/examples/cvsup should contain the following supfiles:

**cvs-supfile** This supfile allows you to download the entire FreeBSD source repository. While most users have no need for this, FreeBSD developers will think it's nifty. You need this only if you plan to roll your own releases.

**doc-supfile** The doc-supfile allows you to retrieve all FreeBSD documentation sources, including the latest FAQ and Handbook, in all available languages. Don't use this unless you intend to install /usr/ports/textproc/docproj and build the documentation from source. While building the documentation is quicker than building FreeBSD itself, building the docproj port can take quite a while.

**gnats-supfile** This supfile is for people who wish to have a local copy of the FreeBSD problem report (PR) database. Again, most users won't need this.

**ports-supfile** You can use this supfile to upgrade your ports tree to the latest version.

**stable-supfile** This supfile upgrades your source code to the latest -stable version.

**standard-supfile** This supfile upgrades your source code to the latest -current version.

**www-supfile** This supfile will download the latest version of the FreeBSD Web site.

The various components that can be updated with CVSup are called collections. For example, there is the source-code collection, the documentation collection (doc-supfile), the ports collection (port-supfile), and so on. Many collections are also broken up into subcollections: The source tree has subcollections for components such as userland programs, the compilers, the kernel, and so on. Our main concern when upgrading FreeBSD is the source collection.

**Modifying Your Supfile**

Once you've chosen your supfile, you need to modify it to fit your circumstances. To do so, first copy your sample supfile under /usr/src and open it in your preferred editor.

Any line beginning with a pound sign (#) is a comment, and all the sample supfiles have more comments than actual configuration entries. Most supfiles have at least six entries, similar to these from a recent stable-supfile:

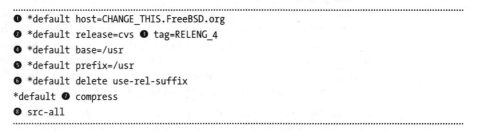

```
❶ *default host=CHANGE_THIS.FreeBSD.org
❷ *default release=cvs ❸ tag=RELENG_4
❹ *default base=/usr
❺ *default prefix=/usr
❻ *default delete use-rel-suffix
*default ❼ compress
❽ src-all
```

Your first step is to choose a CVSup server (❶). (You'll find a complete list at http://www.FreeBSD.org/handbook/mirrors-cvsup.html.) At this writing, the servers are cvsup1.FreeBSD.org through cvsup17.FreeBSD.org, but new ones are added continually, so check the mirror list. Ping each server to determine which is closest to you—a faster response time strongly hints that the server is closer. Name the closest in the default host space, where it currently lists CHANGE_THIS.FreeBSD.org.

The default release is a label for the version, or collection, you've chosen (❷). Put the label for the branch you want in the tag statement (❸). RELENG_4 is the latest 4-stable. Here are some tags you might wish to use:

| Tag | Release |
| --- | --- |
| RELENG_4 | FreeBSD 4-stable |
| RELENG_3 | FreeBSD 3-stable |
| . | FreeBSD-current |
| RELENG_4_3 | The security updates only for FreeBSD 4.3 |
| RELENG_4_4 | Security updates only for FreeBSD 4.4 |
| RELENG_4_5 | Security updates only for FreeBSD 4.5 |

The default base is where CVSup will keep its status files, including a list of updated files, which will accelerate future updates (❹).

The default prefix is where the collection you've chosen will go, and the default is almost certainly correct (❺). To install the source somewhere other than /usr/src, you can change this path.

Delete gives CVS permission to remove obsolete, unnecessary source files (❻). The use-rel-suffix entry allows CVSup to share a common base directory among several versions of the source, without confusing them.

All of the example supfiles include an instruction to compress the CVSup data (❼). If your connection is a T1 or faster, compressing the data isn't that important, and you can remove this entire line, which will reduce the CPU load while increasing the needed bandwidth. Since today's processors are usually much cheaper than bandwidth, there are very few circumstances where not using compression makes sense.

The src-all tag tells CVSup to update the entire source tree (❽). The stable-supfile has a list of commented-out subcollections, such as usr.bin, contrib, sys, and so on, which are all included in src-all. To use just one part of the source tree, you could use these subcollections. For example, to just upgrade the source code in /usr/src/usr.bin, you could specify the usr.bin subcollection. This is a spectacularly bad idea if you want to use this source code to upgrade your system. For example, installing the /usr/bin directory of a 4.5-release system on a 4.3-releasesystem will cause all sorts of unpredictable problems, and is certainly not supported.

### Specifying Multiple Collections

You can specify multiple collections in one supfile. For example, I need access to the source-code collection for the latest -stable. As a FreeBSD documentation committer, I need to have the latest documentation collection. Plus, I want the latest ports tree so I can install the very latest software on my system.

FreeBSD includes separate example supfiles for each of these collections. Since I want to get everything at once (I don't want to run CVSup three times to download all of the latest changes), I use one supfile to get the latest appropriate version of FreeBSD, the latest ports collection, and the latest documents collection, as shown here:

```
*default host=cvsup16.FreeBSD.org
*default base=/usr
*default prefix=/usr
*default delete use-rel-suffix
*default compress src-all
*default release=cvs tag=RELENG_4
src-all
❶ ports-all tag=.
doc-all tag=.
```

Everything down to the second-last line (❶) is the standard stable-supfile. We can then list whatever additional collections we want.

The last two entries are the interesting bit, where I added the ports-all and doc-all collections. Non-source collections do not have releases or branches in the same way the source code does, so if I were to ask for the RELENG_4 version of the ports tree, the server wouldn't know what the heck I was talking about and I wouldn't get my updates. By adding the tag=. keyword to the end of the collection name, we are telling CVSup to get the latest version of this collection.

We'll discuss the ports tree further is Chapter 10.

### Blocking CVSup Updates with a Refuse File

To refuse to allow updates of certain programs, create a *refuse* file. For example, I keep my ports collection up to date so I can easily grab the latest software, but the ports collection includes several categories I'm not interested in, particularly the non-English software. Looking through the /usr/ports directory, I see directories for Chinese, German, Japanese, Korean, Russian, and Vietnamese software. The chances that I will need any of these packages on my server are slim to none. To tell CVSup not to update these directories, make a file /usr/sup/refuse that looks like this:

```
ports/chinese
ports/german
ports/japanese
ports/korean
ports/russian
ports/vietnamese
```

**NOTE**   *The refuse file cannot contain comments!*

You can create a refuse file for any section of FreeBSD, though it's best not to refuse anything under /usr/src. If you refuse updates to a critical system program, that program will become incompatible with your system at some point.

This system works on pattern matching, so a refuse file line like sys would block everything that contained the string "sys", which happens to include the kernel source code available under /usr/src/sys. Be careful with refuse files; give enough context to only block what you want!

**NOTE**   *If you change the prefix in the supfile to a location other than /usr, you need to move your refuse file. (The actual location is $PREFIX/sup/refuse.) If you accept the defaults, the examples will work just fine.*

### Upgrading System Source Code

Once you've created your supfile, run CVSup by becoming root and entering this command:

```
# cvsup supfile
```

If you're running X, CVSup will open a GUI; otherwise, it will just start upgrading your source files. When CVSup finishes, you should have the very latest FreeBSD source code.

### Partial Updates

CVSup supports partial updates with the -i 'pattern' option. For example, cvsup my-supfile -i src/etc will update the /usr/src/etc directory using the default settings in my-supfile. You could also use cvsup my-supfile -i sys to just get the kernel code, or cvsup my-supfile -i ftpd to grab the latest FTP daemon.

Be careful doing this, however. FreeBSD is designed to work as a unified whole, and you cannot mix and match different versions of utilities. For example, if the latest FTP daemon expects kernel features that were only added last month, it won't work well on an older kernel.

*CVSup only takes care of the base FreeBSD operating system. If you have separate programs, such as shells, Web servers, or editors, you need to upgrade them manually. See Chapter 9 for details.*

### After Upgrading Source Code

Once you've finished upgrading your source code, take a look at the file /usr/src/UPDATING. This file lists, in reverse chronological order, any warnings and notices about source-code changes. If you need to take any special action before rebuilding your system from source code, or if any major system functionality has changed, it will be noted here.

You might also take a moment to examine the new GENERIC or LINT kernel configuration file for any new options or kernel system changes that you might be interested in.

### Building Your New FreeBSD

Once CVSup has completed the source-code update, you can rebuild your system. Different people do this in different ways, and you'll hear all sorts of anecdotal evidence that one method works better, faster, and stronger than another. The method recommended by the FreeBSD Project is both the safest and the least likely to damage your system, and also an excellent script(1) candidate (script is explained in Chapter 3).

The only recommended way to build FreeBSD is via the following commands.

```
# cd /usr/src
# make buildworld
```

The make buildworld command first uses the source code to build the tools necessary to build the system compiler, after which it builds the compiler and the associated libraries. Finally, it uses the new tools, compiler, and libraries to build all the software included in a core FreeBSD install. (It does not install these components, however, but puts them under /usr/obj for later use.)

Using make buildworld, FreeBSD literally rebuilds every single piece of itself, which may take anywhere from one to several hours, depending on your hardware. You can continue working normally as the buildworld runs; while make buildworld consumes system resources, it won't take any of your attention. Older hardware will respond quite slowly, however.

You can put optimizations in /etc/make.conf (described in Chapter 9). Some parts definitely worth considering are the CPUTYPE entry and the various NO_ flags. This can create a more efficient operating system and a faster, smoother upgrade.

*Be certain that the buildworld completes without errors! If it ends with a bunch of error-code messages like those you see during a failed kernel compile, stop immediately. Go to Chapter 2 and see how to get help. Do not attempt, under any circumstances, to install a damaged or incomplete upgrade.*

### Updating Your Kernel

When make buildworld finishes successfully, it's time to update your kernel. The catch is, the latest binaries for the tools to build your kernel are not actually installed; they're sitting off in another directory tree! The standard kernel-building config, make depend, make install routine discussed in Chapter 4 won't work well.

If you have a custom kernel configuration, set the variable KERNCONF in /etc/make.conf (this is explained in Chapter 8). Otherwise, the build process will rebuild the GENERIC kernel.

To build the kernel, stay in /usr/src and run this command:

```
# make buildkernel
```

*For maximum safety, run* make buildkernel KERNCONF=GENERIC *so that you will have an updated GENERIC kernel available.*

### Installing Your System

Once you've completed the make buildkernel, you're ready to install your newly built system. The first step is to install your new kernel and kernel modules.

The new kernel and associated modules are the easiest parts of an upgrade to test; if it's bad, you can easily fall back to your old kernel. Install the new kernel and modules by entering this command:

```
# make installkernel
```

To test the new kernel, reboot and check out your system. Do your programs still run? Is your system still receiving mail and serving up Web pages? If so, your kernel is probably all right. As you check out the system, various programs that require access to kernel structures (such as top(1)) won't work, but you can test everything else.

Once you're satisfied that your kernel works, and that everything is behaving as you expect, you can install the rest of the system. Userland installs must be performed in single-user mode. If your system is running at securelevel 1 or higher, you'll need to shut down and boot into single-user mode. Otherwise, you can just drop the running system down to single-user mode with this command:

```
# shutdown now
```

Once the system is shut down to single-user mode, you can install the userland programs by entering the following:

```
# cd /usr/src
# make installworld
```

This will install the various programs included in the FreeBSD core system. You will see numerous messages scroll up the screen, mostly including the word install. When the process finishes, you will have completed your upgrade installation, but you still have a couple more steps to complete before your FreeBSD system is truly upgraded.

### /etc and /dev Changes

As you'll recall, your system's personalized configuration lives under /etc. Because no automated process can know how your machine is supposed to run, you'll have to handle any changes to these files yourself. The make buildworld through make installworld process won't perform them for you.

The latest versions of all files and directories under /etc live under /usr/src/etc. You'll need to compare these files (particularly the "rc" files) to those in your /etc directory to see which changes you need to add. This is a tedious process that is very difficult to do by hand, so we'll use the FreeBSD utility mergemaster(8) to cut the merge time considerably.

To use mergemaster, become root and type the following command:

```
# mergemaster
```

Mergemaster will copy various configuration files from your source tree, build a temporary /etc and /dev under /var/tmp, and then compare these configuration files to those in the existing /etc. If the new file version differs from the file in /etc, mergemaster displays the differences, at which point you can decide whether to keep the old file, use the new file, or merge the two.

For example, here's the beginning of a typical mergemaster session.

```
*** Beginning comparison

❶ *** Temp ./dev/MAKEDEV.local and installed have the same $FreeBSD, deleting
❷ *** Temp ./dev/MAKEDEV and installed have the same $FreeBSD, deleting

  *** Displaying differences between ./etc/defaults/rc.conf and installed version

❸ --- /etc/defaults/rc.conf        Fri Jan 14 08:54:11 2000
+++ ./etc/defaults/rc.conf        Sun Feb 27 18:21:29 2000
@@ -9,7 +9,7 @@
 # # All arguments must be in double or single quotes.
 #
-# $FreeBSD: src/etc/defaults/rc.conf,v 1.1.2.18 1999/11/28 16:02:30 brian Exp $
```

*(continued on next page)*

```
+# $FreeBSD: src/etc/defaults/rc.conf,v 1.1.2.19 2000/02/19 13:11:28 jkh Exp $

###########################################################
### Important initial Boot-time options  ##################
@@ -193,7 +193,7 @@
 saver="NO"                 # screen saver: Uses /modules/${saver}_saver.ko
 moused_enable="NO"         # Run the mouse daemon.
 moused_type="auto"         # See man page for rc.conf(5) for available
# settings.
-moused_port="/dev/cuaa0" # Set to your mouse port.
+moused_port="/dev/psm0"  # Set to your mouse port.
 moused_flags=""            # Any additional flags to moused.
 allscreens_flags=""        # Set this vidcontrol mode for all virtual screens


  Use 'd' to delete the temporary ./etc/defaults/rc.conf
  Use 'i' to install the temporary ./etc/defaults/rc.conf
  Use 'm' to merge the old and new versions

  Default is to leave the temporary file to deal with by hand

How should I deal with this? [Leave it for later]
```

Let's look at what's happening here. The first couple of lines (❶ and ❷) indicate that the version of /dev/MAKEDEV in /dev is the same as the one in the latest source code. Mergemaster doesn't bother suggesting any changes, and instead just deleted the temporary copies it made for comparison purposes.

Then mergemaster comes to a file with some changes, /etc/defaults/rc.conf (❸). Mergemaster spits out a few lines of the file; additions are marked with leading plus signs (+) and deletions are marked with leading hyphens (-). (A few surrounding lines are provided for context.)[1]

For example, consider these lines:

```
-moused_port="/dev/cuaa0" # Set to your mouse port.
+moused_port="/dev/psm0"  # Set to your mouse port.
```

These lines tell us that the default mouse port changed between this upgrade and the previous upgrade or installation. Lines marked with a minus sign appear in the older version of the file. Lines marked with a plus sign are in the new version. The port was /dev/cuaa0 (a serial port), but it is now /dev/psm0 (a PS/2 port).

[1] This format is called a "diff," and is quite common in the UNIX world.

Mergemaster offers you three options: delete, install, and merge. The thing to do here is to install the new /etc/defaults/rc.conf file, and make any changes needed in /etc/rc.conf. Press **i** to install the file.

Some files should never be replaced via mergemaster, such as files that include system-specific configuration information, like /etc/passwd or /etc/group. Leave such files unchanged by pressing **d**.

Pressing **m** will take you through a file and let you merge the changes. This is a powerful option, and useful once you're comfortable with mergemaster, diff, and the contents of /etc, but beginners are almost certainly better off simply totally replacing or rejecting files.

You can learn all about /etc in Chapter 9.

### Device Entries

In Chapter 3 we briefly discussed device nodes, files in the /dev directory that programs can use to send data to and from devices. Then, in Chapter 4 I defined a kernel as the interface between the hardware and the software. When you run an upgrade, these two concepts intersect: The kernel might very well rearrange how it talks to devices, and the interface for how those devices are handled might change. So far in this upgrade process, we haven't changed those special files in /dev, but if you have old device nodes talking to a new kernel, you can get unpredictable behavior. These changes might not happen with every upgrade, but you have to be aware that they're possible.

FreeBSD includes a script that creates correct device nodes, /dev/MAKEDEV. The version of /dev/MAKEDEV distributed with a given kernel is expected to create the correct device nodes for that kernel. Mergemaster compares the /dev/MAKEDEV script from the updated source code with the old script still installed in /dev/MAKEDEV, and it offers to install the new one. Do it.[2] Correct device nodes are not optional. If the /dev/MAKEDEV script has changed, mergemaster will offer to run /dev/MAKEDEV for you. Do that too. Again, correct device nodes are vital.

### Last Steps

Once you have completed mergemaster, your system has every piece of the upgrade in place. Just reboot, and you will have completed a FreeBSD upgrade!

Any number of things can go wrong with a system upgrade. The `make buildworld` command might not finish, or the system might behave oddly afterwards. If something goes wrong, follow a similar process to what you do during a kernel-build failure. Search for the error in the FreeBSD mailing list archives. If the problem isn't discussed there, send the last five or six lines of your build output to FreeBSD-questions@FreeBSD.org, and include the following information:

- The end of the output of the failed compile
- Your FreeBSD version number
- The contents of /var/run/dmesg/boot
- The output of `uname -a`

[2] Unless, of course, strange behavior, weird crashes, and lost data make you happy.

### Simplifying the CVSup Upgrade Process

Now that you understand how the upgrade process works, you can simplify it somewhat by making some changes in /etc/make.conf to reduce the CVSup portion of the upgrade process to a two-word command. While I don't prefer to go this route myself, many people do, so here's what you do.

First, you'll need to set several variables in /etc/make.conf.

```
SUP_UPDATE=     yes
```

The preceding line enables the "make" front end to CVSup.

```
SUP=            /usr/local/bin/cvsup
```

The SUP setting is the default location for CVSup on your system. If you have a custom CVSup replacement, or if you need to specify the full path to the cvsup binary, set it here.

```
SUPFLAGS=       -g -L 2
```

This SUPFLAGS setting gives standard flags for your CVSup command. To run CVSup silently, change this to -g -L 0.

```
SUPHOST=        cvsup13.FreeBSD.org
```

List a reasonably close FreeBSD cvsup mirror in the SUPHOST line.

```
SUPFILE=        /usr/share/examples/cvsup/stable-supfile
```

The SUPFILE value tells CVSup which configuration file to use.

```
PORTSSUPFILE=   /usr/share/examples/cvsup/ports-supfile
```

PORTSSUPFILE specifies which supfile should be used to upgrade ports. Don't define this if you don't want to upgrade your ports collection.

```
DOCSUPFILE=     /usr/share/examples/cvsup/doc-supfile
```

Finally, DOCSUPFILE is the supfile for the source code of the documents collection. Leave this undefined if you don't want to upgrade your documentation tree (including the Handbook, FAQ, articles, and so on).

**NOTE** *DOCSUPFILE does not specify the actual documentation, but rather the source code to the documentation. If you don't have the documentation building tools, this is almost useless.*

Once you have set these values, you can replace the `cvsup stable-supfile` command with this one:

```
# make update
```

Some people find it more pleasant to simply go to /usr/src and type `make update && make buildworld && make install` than to give the full CVSup command. It's up to you.

## Building a Local CVSup Server

Many people have quite a few FreeBSD systems. During an upgrade from source, however, every single server must connect to a FreeBSD CVS server and download the latest code, which can be a pain. For one, all of the mirrors are maintained by volunteers who are donating the servers and bandwidth. Why download the same bits over and over again?

Also, each server might wind up with slightly different code if they all connect to different servers. Suppose you log in to each server and start a CVSup. In the few minutes between starting each source-code upgrade, the code on the CVSup server might change slightly. The mirrors aren't going to stop updating their code just because you're in the middle of upgrading four machines, and if you're running several production machines, you'd be best served if all the systems were absolutely identical. Even if they're running a version of -stable somewhere between 4.4-release and 4.5-release, being able to eliminate different versions of the software as a potential problem can help troubleshooting immensely. You don't want to think, "Gee, server 1 keeps dying; could it be because each server has a slightly different version of FreeBSD?" That way lies madness.

You can address this problem by running a central CVSup server (also known as a "cvsupd" server), which is essentially your own local mirror. You can control when your local mirror updates, and you can guarantee that all of your machines have exactly the same code. Doing so will not only make you popular with the mirror operators (or at least, won't make you unpopular with them), it will also eliminate a variety of possible problems resulting from having different code on each of your servers. You can still have problems if you have different settings in /etc/make.conf, but you can compare those files yourself and see what you're doing differently. It is much easier to compare two files than several thousand!

It's not particularly easy to run a CVSup server, but there's help to make it simpler. The port /usr/ports/net/cvsup-mirror handles all the tricky bits of configuring a mirror. When you install the port, cvsup-mirror asks you some questions; there are default suggestions, but you should change many of them. We'll discuss software installation in detail in Chapter 9, but installing this port is pretty straightforward.

First, make sure you have an Internet connection, and enter the following commands:

```
# cd /usr/ports/net/cvsup-mirror
# make install clean
```

You will see messages scroll up your screen, including the compiler messages you should recognize by now. (You might not know what they mean, but you should recognize compiling when you see it.)

At some point, the install process will pause and prompt you for information:

```
Master site for your updates [cvsup-master.FreeBSD.org]?
```

The default site, cvsup-master.FreeBSD.org, is reserved for official FreeBSD mirror use only; you can use it if you become an official mirror and allow the world access to your system. If not, use one of the 80-odd public CVSup servers instead. If you're setting up a CVSup mirror, you should have already identified a public mirror that's close to you. Enter the name of that mirror.

The next prompt will look like this:

```
How many hours between updates of your files [1]?
```

The script updates /etc/crontab (explained in Chapter 9) to run CVSup automatically. You can accept this default, or change it easily. If you accept the default, your system will upgrade itself once an hour via cron. This is the way the official mirrors do it. I generally enter 168, which updates the repository once a week, since I will not be upgrading servers more than weekly! Your first update will take quite a while, but later updates generally only take a few minutes.

**NOTE**    *In many cases, I only upgrade the CVSup server by hand by running the script /usr/local/etc/cvsup/update.sh. To upgrade a group of machines all to the same version of -stable, all you have to do is update your CVSup server once and upgrade all the machines from the server. I frequently upgrade one server, put it through several rounds of extensive quality-assurance testing, and upgrade the rest from the same CVSup batch, which guarantees good code and identical systems. There is no requirement for you to be more up to date than you wish; the source code is yours to do with as you see fit, after all! If you update your server manually, you will want to edit /etc/crontab to remove the automatic update! We'll discuss /etc/crontab in Chapter 9.*

```
Do you wish to mirror the main source repository [y]?
```

Most people just need the main source repository, so the default is usually fine.

```
Where would you like to put it [/home/ncvs]? /repo
```

This prompt is where you enter the path to the location on disk where you want your mirror kept. I frequently add a separate, small disk to a system to keep the mirror on, and call that disk /repo. You can put it in the default location of /home/ncvs without any problems.

Since you probably want only the main source repository, answer **n** to the next three questions:

```
Do you wish to mirror the installed World Wide Web data [y]? n
Do you wish to mirror the GNATS bug tracking database [y]? n
Do you wish to mirror the mailing list archive [y]? n
```

Of course, if you'd prefer to mirror the whole www.FreeBSD.org site, including the PR database and the mailing list archives, answer **y**. But be warned: the mailing list archives are huge. The source repository itself is well over 1GB at this writing, and growing continuously.

Use unique user and group IDs for the next series of questions. (Do not use "nobody", "nonroot", or "nogroup".) You can use the defaults, or change the usernames and group names to fit your local scheme:

```
Unique unprivileged user ID for running the client [cvsupin]?
Unique unprivileged group ID for running the client [cvsupin]?
Unique unprivileged user ID for running the server [cvsup]?
Unique unprivileged group ID for running the server [cvsup]?
```

Lastly, the maximum simultaneous client connections is easy to change later, so don't sweat it. It's fine to accept the default:

```
Maximum simultaneous client connections [8]?
```

Once you finish answering the questions, the make install process picks up where you left off, adds these usernames, sets the configuration, and generally gets you ready to go.

### Controlling Access

Just because you want to be a good systems administrator and have a private repository doesn't mean that you want every Joe Sixpack to download from your CVSup mirror. The CVSup server allows you to control which computers have access to the mirror.

The file /usr/local/etc/cvsup/cvsupd.access controls which hosts may connect to your CVSup mirror. Lines beginning with the pound symbol (#) denote a comment; a plus sign (+) means that the client can connect, and a hyphen (-) means that the client cannot. An asterisk (*) means that the client must authenticate, as discussed in the following "Authentication" section.

Each rule in cvsupd.access can refer to either a hostname or an IP address; IP addresses are preferred. You can use netmasks with IP addresses as well.

For example, to allow access from the network 192.168.0.0/16 and explicitly reject clients accessing from elsewhere, use these lines:

```
+192.168.0.0/16
-0.0.0.0/0
```

Controlling access by IP address is good for a static network. For example, an Internet service provider (ISP) knows the IP addresses of its servers and can easily keep them in cvsupd.access. You might need a more flexible system, however, if you're connecting from random IP addresses. When I was consulting, for example, I kept a mirror that accepted connections from any IP address. Users needed a username and password to connect, however. If your cvsupd.access file is empty, access is controlled entirely by username and password authentication.

### Authentication

Use authentication to allow connections to your CVSup mirror from any location on the Internet. The CVSup server uses a challenge-response system for authentication, rather than transmitting passwords in clear text. When a client connects, it combines its *shared secret* (CVSup for "password") and the system time, and runs them through a scrambler. The server does the same. In theory, both the client and the server are performing the same calculations on the same piece of secret data, and both should get the same answer. If the client's scrambled message matches what the server computed, the server assumes that the client has the secret data and permits access.

This is a very secure system. For example, if someone drops a packet sniffer on the network, she cannot grab the password. What's more, since the challenge-response system incorporates the time, a captured response cannot be used a second time.

Authentication requires a password file, /usr/local/etc/cvsup/cvsupd.passwd, which must only be readable by the CVSup user so that no one else can grab user information. (You can do this by running chown cvsup cvsupd.passwd and chmod 600 cvsupd.passwd.) If you don't have a password file, access will be controlled entirely by the cvsupd.access file.

Blank lines and comment lines (which begin with #) in cvsupd.passwd are ignored. The first code line in cvsupd.passwd is the server name and a private key, separated by a colon.

```
magpire.AbsoluteBSD.com:testkey
```

The server name is sent back to the client, and the private key is used for additional randomness. You don't have to have a private key—the CVSup password system is pretty random as is—but you must have the colon that precedes the private key. The private key cannot contain a colon.

Next in the file, you have your legitimate users. Each user appears on a separate line, in the following format:

```
user ID:shared secret:class:comment
```

CVSup IDs are email addresses, such as mwlucas@AbsoluteBSD.com. The shared secret is based upon a cryptographic hash saying you're the administrator's chosen password for that user. The class field is reserved for future use, and should be left blank. Finally, the comment field can be used by the administrator. For example, if you give someone access to your CVSup mirror, it's a good idea to put in a comment stating why they have access. (You might remember now, but will you remember in a year or two?)

The cvpasswd(1) command automates generating these cvsupd.passwd entries. Cvpasswd takes two arguments: the email address of the user and the server name. It will ask you for the password for this user twice, and spit out some instructions.

```
# cvpasswd mwlucas@AbsoluteBSD.com magpire.AbsoluteBSD.com
Enter password:
Enter same password again:

Send this line to the server administrator at magpire.AbsoluteBSD.com:
--------------------------------------------------------------------------------
❶ mwlucas@AbsoluteBSD.com:$md5$bf489b753a0a949a1c63a3f5da0d61b6::
--------------------------------------------------------------------------------
Be sure to send it using a secure channel!

Add this line to your file "$HOME/.cvsup/auth", replacing "XXX"
with the password you typed in:
--------------------------------------------------------------------------------
magpire.AbsoluteBSD.com:mwlucas@AbsoluteBSD.com:XXX:
--------------------------------------------------------------------------------
Make sure the file is readable and writable only by you!
#
```

The cryptic line in the middle of this output (❶) gives the username and the shared secret, based upon the password. Send this line to the user you want to allow to connect. The "secure channel" mentioned means that you should send this line in such a way that it cannot be captured by hostile people on the Internet. You can read the code to the other user over the phone, hand-type it into the system, copy it to a floppy disk, and hand-deliver it, or encrypt it with PGP and email it. If you send it via standard unencrypted email, anyone who captures the email en route can use this to try to access your CVSup server. However, if someone steals this information, the risk of unauthorized access is not that great; a user still needs the password to access the mirror.

Once the user has this line, he puts it in his home directory in the file .cvsup/auth. This can be copied to any system he wants to upgrade from this CVSup server. He also needs to make sure that nobody else can read this file, by running `chmod 600 .cvsup/auth`.

On the server side, copy that same line into /usr/local/etc/cvsup/cvsupd.passwd. It is formatted to be a correct, although minimal, password entry. You can add a comment at the end, if you like.

Once you have this entry on both the client and server sides, the user will be prompted for a password each time he runs CVSup and tries to connect to this server.

**NOTE** *If you have neither cvsupd.access nor cvsupd.passwd, anyone can connect to your server from any location on the Internet. The FreeBSD Project is happy to let anyone run a mirror, but you should be aware that you are doing so!*

### Combining Authentication and Access

Combining authentication and authorization by IP address can be a little tricky because you don't want hosts that are listed by IP addresses to be asked for passwords, or users with passwords to be rejected because their IP address is rejected. There is an implicit "authenticate" rule at the end of cvsupd.access. If your client hasn't been blocked out by an explicit "deny" rule based on an IP address, you'll be allowed to authenticate. No special configuration is required.

In the example cvsupd.access file shown previously, I explicitly denied access to all IP addresses that were not in the list. If you wanted to give other users a chance to authenticate, you would list IP addresses that may always connect, and explicitly reject smaller blocks that you know you will never connect from. Here's a commented example:

```
#allow anyone inside our company to connect
+192.168.0.0/16
#allow anyone from our sister company to connect
+10.10.0.0/16
# users from here can never connect
-24.0.0.0/8
```

In this example, systems with an IP address beginning with 192.168 or 10.10 could always connect. Computers with an IP address beginning with 24. could never connect, even if they had a username and password. If a computer with none of the above IP addresses tries to connect, it will be able to try a username and password.

This gives you complete control over access to your mirror.

# 7

# SECURING YOUR SYSTEM

Securing your system means ensuring that your computer's resources are used only by authorized people for authorized purposes, because even if you have no important data on your system, you still have valuable CPU time, memory, and bandwidth. In fact, many folks who thought that their systems were too unimportant to bother securing found themselves an unwitting relay for an attack that disabled a major corporation. You don't want to wake up one morning to the delightful sound of law enforcement agents kicking in your door because your insecure computer was used to break into a bank.

Sure, there are things worse than having some kid take over your servers—say, having both your legs broken. Coming in to work one day to discover that the company Web page now says, "Ha, ha, you've been r00ted!" is a pretty close second.

Sadly, over the last few years, it has become much easier to take over remote computers. Precanned point-and-click programs for subverting computers are becoming more and more common, and can be found through an underground search engine like Astalavista.com. It takes just one bright attacker to write an exploit, and several thousand bored teenagers with nothing better to do than download it and make life difficult for the rest of us. Even if you don't care about your system, you need to secure it.

Generally speaking, operating systems are not broken in to; the programs running on operating systems are. Even the most paranoically secure-by-default operating system in the world[1] cannot protect badly written programs from themselves.

Occasionally, a problem with one of these programs can interact with the operating system in such a way as to actually compromise the operating system. The most common of these are called *buffer overflows*, where an intruder's program is dumped right into the CPU's execution space and the operating system runs it. FreeBSD has undergone extensive auditing to eliminate buffer overflows, but that's no guarantee that they are totally eradicated. New functions and programs are being written all the time, and they can interact with older functions in unexpected ways.

This chapter focuses on patching and securing your systems. (Auditing your network design is a topic that fills thick books, and isn't really on topic for a book on FreeBSD.) FreeBSD gives you many tools to help you secure your system against network attackers.

## Who Is the Enemy?

First off, I'm going to arbitrarily lump potential attackers into three groups: script kiddies, disaffected users, and skilled attackers. You will find more fine-grained profiles in books dedicated to security, but that's not what you're here for. These categories are easily explained, easily understand, and include 99 percent of all the attackers you're likely to encounter.

### Script Kiddies

The most numerous attackers are *script kiddies*. Script kiddies are not sysadmins. They are not skilled. They download small attack programs that work on a point-and-click basis and go looking for people to attack. They're the equivalent of drive-by shooters looking for easy pickings. Fortunately, script kiddies are particularly easy to protect against; you simply have to keep your system and server programs' patches up to date.

### Disaffected Users

The second group causes the majority of security problems: *your own users*. The fact is, disaffected employees cause most security breaches because they're most likely to know where your security holes are. For example, you might have all your servers patched, but if you have a modem in the back closet that lets anyone who knows the password into the network behind your firewall, you're in trouble.

---

[1] That would be OpenBSD. Or any OS on a computer that's disconnected from any network, buried under 12 feet of steel-reinforced concrete and, if at all possible, crushed into a billion tiny pieces and soaked in hydrofluoric acid for several months.

The best way to stop people like these is to not be sloppy. When someone leaves the company, change all passwords, and tell all employees that the person has left and not to share information with that person. And get rid of the unsecured modem, or the undocumented telnet server, or whatever other hurried hack you put into place thinking that nobody would ever find it.

### Skilled Attackers

The last group is actually dangerous: *skilled attackers*. These are competent systems administrators, security researchers, and penetration specialists who want specific information from your company. If one of these people wants into your systems, they can probably get there.

Still, the proper security measures that will stop the first two groups of people can change the tactics that the skilled attacker must use. Rather than breaking into your computers over the network, he'll have to show up at the door dressed as a telephone company repairman lugging a packet sniffer, or dumpster-dive searching for old sticky notes with passwords scribbled on them. This raises his exposure dramatically, and can even make a break-in more trouble than it's worth.

**RANT** *You'll frequently hear the word "hacker" used to describe people who break into computers. This word has different meanings depending on the speaker. In the technical world, a hacker is someone who is interested in the inner workings of technological systems. Some hackers are interested in everything, some have a narrow area of interest—such as computers. In the FreeBSD community, "hacker" is a title of respect. The main FreeBSD technical list is called FreeBSD-hackers. In the popular media, a hacker is someone who breaks into computer systems, end of story. To them, all hackers are bad. I recommend avoiding the word entirely to avoid confusion. In this book, I call those who break into systems "intruders." [2] Technical wizards can be called by a variety of names, but they rarely object to "sir" or "madam."*

## FreeBSD Security Announcements

The best way to stop all attackers is to keep your system up to date. That means you need to know when to update your system, and what to update. An outdated system is a script kiddie's best friend.

The FreeBSD project has a team of developers who specialize in auditing source code and watching for security issues with both the base operating system and add-on software. These developers maintain a very low-volume mailing list, FreeBSD-security-notifications@FreeBSD.org, and it's a good idea to subscribe to it. While you can monitor other mailing lists (such as BugTraq and CERT) for general announcements, the security-notifications list is a handy single source for FreeBSD-specific information.

---

[2] In person, I call them much less pleasant things.

### Subscribing

To subscribe to the security-notifications mailing list, send a message to major-domo@FreeBSD.org containing the following:

```
subscribe FreeBSD-security-notifications
```

You'll receive a confirmation message, and buried somewhere in it there'll be a command string something like this:

```
auth abax55b3 subscribe FreeBSD-security-notifications        mwlucas@AbsoluteBSD.com
```

Reply to majordomo@FreeBSD.org with a message containing just that string, and you'll be subscribed.

To unsubscribe, send a similar message to majordomo@FreeBSD.org with the following body text:

```
unsubscribe FreeBSD-security-notifications
```

You'll get a message back with a confirmation string to send back to the mail server. Return it, and you'll be unsubscribed.

### What You'll Get

Two sorts of messages come across the security-notifications mailing list: *FreeBSD security advisories* and *FreeBSD ports-collection security advisories*. The two have very different purposes.

FreeBSD security advisories apply to the base operating system. When a FreeBSD component has a security hole, the security team releases a security advisory. Read the advisory carefully to determine what you need to do.

The ports collection contains literally thousands of programs that can be easily installed on FreeBSD. While it's not the definitive guide to what can work on the system, it's certainly a big chunk of it. When the security team finds a hole in one of these software packages, they notify the vendor and issue a ports-collection security advisory. These pieces of software are beyond the FreeBSD Project's control, but since they're distributed with FreeBSD, FreeBSD frequently catches the blame when one of them is broken. The security team issues these advisories in an effort to keep its users secure. If you haven't installed the software discussed by the advisory, you don't have to worry.

Both types of security advisories generally contain a description of the problem, fixes, and workarounds. Read advisories carefully, since you can be sure that some script kiddie is looking for a vulnerable machine to break into. The best thing to do is to be invulnerable to these problems.

**NOTE**   *We will discuss many security tools in this chapter. While none is sufficient, all are desirable. Treat everything you learn about in this chapter as a tool in a kit, not as the answer to all of your problems. For example, while simply raising the securelevel will not make your system secure, it can help when combined with reasonable permissions, file flags, patching your systems, password control, and all the other things that make up a good security policy.*

# Installation Security Profiles

When you first install FreeBSD (version 4.2 or later), you have the option to set a security profile, which basically enables and disables network services and sets the default system security according to some common defaults provided by the FreeBSD Project. (Everything the security profile changes is set in /etc/rc.conf.) In most cases, you should use these profiles as a starting point and edit the configuration set by the profile to meet your needs. The following sections give a rough description of the two security profiles: moderate and extreme.

### Moderate

The *moderate security profile* enables inetd, sendmail, and sshd. This way, the system can send and receive email and allow people to connect remotely via ssh. Also, if you've previously configured the system to use NFS, portmap will be running so that the system can provide NFS services. The securelevel remains at the default of -1.

### Extreme

With the *extreme security profile,* no basic system network daemons are running, except for extra software you specifically install, and the system securelevel is set to 2. The system will not receive or send email out of the box, and you cannot connect to it remotely. It's unhackable, because it's sitting there with nothing coming in or out.

While security profiles provide useful templates, you need to know how to configure each of these services yourself. Take a look at rc.conf (explained in Chapter 9) to learn how.

# Root, Groups, and Permissions

UNIX security has been considered somewhat coarse because one superuser, *root*, can do anything. Other users are lowly peons who endure the shackles root places upon them. While there is some truth to this, a decent administrator can combine groups and permissions to handle almost any security issue in a secure manner.

### The root Password

Some actions require absolute control of the system, including manipulating core system files such as the kernel, device drivers, and authentication systems. The root account is designed to perform these actions.

To use the root password, you can either log in as root at an actual login prompt or, if you are a member of the group *wheel*, use the switch user command su(1). (We'll discuss groups in the next section.) I recommend su; it logs who uses it, and it can be used on a remote system. The command is very simple to use:

```
# su
Password:
#
```

Next, check your current username with the id(1) command:

```
# id
uid=0(root) gid=0(wheel) groups=0(wheel), 2(kmem), 3(sys), 4(tty), 5(operator),
20(staff), 31(guest)
#
```

You now own the system—and I do mean *own it*. Consider every keystroke very carefully; carelessness can return your hard drive to the unformatted empty metal it shipped with. And use the root password sparingly, because anyone who has the root password can inflict unlimited damage upon the system. Do not give it to anyone who does not strictly need it!

This naturally leads to the question "Who needs root access?" Much of the configuration discussed in *Absolute BSD* requires the use of the root password. Once you have the system running the way you like it, however, you can greatly decrease or discontinue the use of the root password. One of the simplest ways to do this is with the proper use of groups.

### Groups of Users

UNIX classifies users into *groups*, each group consisting of people who perform similar administrative functions. You can have a group called "www", which includes the people who edit Web pages, and a group called "email", which includes the people who manage your mail server. You can set files and directories to be accessible to specific groups. Most group information is defined in the file /etc/group.

Each line in the group file contains four colon-delimited fields. The first is the group name. Group names are fairly arbitrary: You could call a certain group of users "xyzzy" if you wished. It's a good idea, however, to choose group names that give you some idea of what they're for; while you might remember that the group xyzzy manages your email system today, will you remember it six months from now? Choose group names that mean something.

The second field contains the group's encrypted password. Group passwords encouraged poor security practices, so most modern UNIXes don't support them. However, some old software expects to find a password field in /etc/groups, so rather than leave this field blank or remove it entirely, use an asterisk (*) as a placeholder.

The third field holds the group's unique numeric ID (GID). Many of FreeBSD's internal programs use this GID, rather than names, to identify groups.

Last is a list of all the users in that group. To add a user to a group, simply add the username to this list, separated from other names with commas.

After editing /etc/group, it's a good idea to make sure you haven't made a mistake. To double-check your work, use chkgrp(8). It will double-check your work for you; if it runs silently, you haven't shot yourself in the foot.

### Primary Group

The group file does not contain a complete list of all users in every group. When you create a new user, a group is created that contains just that user, and it has the same name as the user. This is the user's "primary group." A user is automatically a member of his or her primary group, as listed in /etc/passwd (see Chapter 9).

These primary groups do not appear in /etc/group. The only record of their existence is in the primary group field of /etc/passwd. This is arguably one of the most annoying things about primary groups, but adding a line to /etc/group for every single user can make the group file difficult to manage.

For example, when the user "pbardaville" is added, the system creates a group "pbardaville" and assigns the user pbardaville to it. This entry appears only in /etc/passwd.

This might seem complicated, but just remember that /etc/passwd trumps /etc/group, and you'll have it.

### Some Interesting Default Groups

FreeBSD ships with several default groups. Most are used by the system, and aren't of huge concern to a sysadmin. Still, rather than have them remain mysterious, I present for your amusement the most useful, interesting, and curious. Adding your own groups simplifies administration, but the groups listed here are available on every FreeBSD system.

**bin**  Group for general programs

**daemon**  Group used by various system services, such as the printing system

**dialer**  Group of users who can access serial ports

**games**  Group for games programs and files

**kmem**  Group used by programs that have to access kernel memory, such as fstat(1), netstat(1), and so on

**mail**  Group for programs that handle mail operations

**man**  Unused in modern BSD, but corresponds to the man user

**news**  Group for Usenet news programs

**nobody**  Group for user ID with no privileges

**nogroup**  Group with no privileges

**operator**  Group that can access drives, generally for backup purposes

**staff**  Group for system staff

**tty**   Group for programs that can write to terminals, such as wall(1)

**wheel**   Group for users permitted to use the root password. If a user has the root password, but is not in the wheel group, she cannot use su to become root.

### Group Permissions

You can assign particular permissions to groups, and all users in that group inherit those permissions. The permissions on a file are also called its *mode*.

The UNIX permission scheme says that every file has three sets of permissions: owner, group, and other. View the existing file permissions with the -l flag to ls(1):

```
# ls -l
total 29
-rwxr-xr--  1 mwlucas  admins    1188 Sep 14 09:35 file1
-rw-------  1 mwlucas  admins   27136 Sep 14 09:36 file2
drwxr-xr-x  2 mwlucas  admins     512 Sep 14 09:52 otherstuff
#
```

As seen in this listing, the first line ("total 29") displays the number of 512-byte disk blocks the files use. (One *block* in this case is half a KB, or about a two-thousandth of a MB.) This particular directory has two files, file1 and file2, each of which appears on its own line, with some basic information and its permissions. The permissions on these files appear at the beginning of each line, in the long lines with r's, w's, and x's, like "-rwxr-xr--".

The permissions control how each group can use the file, and they're of three types: read (r), write (w), and execute (x). The right to read means that you can view or copy the file. Permission to write means that you can alter or overwrite the file. Execute permission means that you can run the file as a program—all programs are executable files. Any entry that is a hyphen (-) means that the user does not have execute permission on that file.

The last entry, otherstuff, is a directory. You can tell it's a directory because the first entry in the permissions line is the letter "d". Directory permissions control who can use the directory in the same way file permissions control who can use the file.

Following the permissions is the number of links to the file. We will discuss links in Chapter 13. Then you'll see the file's owner and group. The number of bytes in the file comes next, followed by the date and time the file was last modified. Finally, you have the actual filename.

When combined with owners and groups, permissions are very flexible. For example, you could place a set of files in a group called www, then give the www group permission to read and write to those files, thereby allowing anyone in the www group to edit them. With this setup, you could give your webmasters control of your company Web site, not allow other users to tamper with the pages, and avoid giving root access to the www group.

The permissions string is ten characters long, the first character of which indicates whether the item is a directory. The other nine characters are broken into three groups of three that display privileges: The first group shows permissions for the file owner, the second group permissions for the group, and the third permissions for all other users.

The first character in each group represents read, the second write, and the third execute. Consider this listing:

```
-rwxr-xr--  1 mwlucas   admins    1188 Sep 14 09:35 file1
```

You can see that the first group of three characters is rwx. This tells us that the owner, mwlucas, can read, write, and execute the file. The second group of characters, r-x, tells us that people in the admins group can read and execute the file, but cannot write it. And the final group, r--, tells us that anyone on the system can read the file, but may not write or execute it.

## Changing Permissions

The permissions on a file are also called its *mode*. Chmod(1), or "change mode," lets anyone with write permission on a file change its permissions. Chmod can be used in many different ways (see the man page for a full listing), but we'll concentrate on the most common way to change permissions. Although this is not necessarily the easiest method to learn, it is the one you'll see most often and the one that all sysadmins should understand.

The modes as shown in the ls output are kind of clumsy-looking. They're difficult to say, difficult to type, and just all-around difficult to work with. UNIX professionals don't generally put up with that sort of thing for long, especially when it's easy to simplify.[3] You have to know how to read the permissions that were shown earlier, but when you use chmod you can use the short form.

In its short form, the mode is given as a three-digit number, with a range of digits from 0 to 7.[4] The first number represents the owner's permissions, the second the group permissions, and the third everyone else's permissions. (This is octal (base-8) math, much like the binary math we played with in Chapter 5 on networking.) The number 4 means "read," 2 means "write," and 1 means "execute." To set the permissions on a file, add the appropriate numbers together. Clear as mud, eh? Don't worry, we're going to go very slowly here; if you already understand modes, you might want to skip ahead a couple of paragraphs.

Assume that you want a file to be readable, writable, and executable by the owner, readable and executable by the group, and readable to others. This means that our permissions string would look like this: rwxr-xr--.

---

[3] In UNIX, "simplify" frequently means "make easier to say and faster to type, but more difficult to understand."

[4] You can have four-digit modes in special circumstances. See chmod(1) for details. You don't normally use four-digit modes except on device nodes and other special files.

The first digit of our mode is made up of the owner's permissions, the initial three-letter "rwx" chunk of the permissions string. Read is 4, write is 2, and execute is 1; 4 + 2 + 1 is 7, so the first digit of our mode is 7.

The group permissions are read and execute. Read is 4 and execute is 1; 4 + 1 is 5, so the second digit of our mode is 5.

Finally, others can only read the file. Read is 4, giving us a total of 4, so the third digit of our mode is 4. To change the mode, enter the chmod command:

```
# chmod 754 file1
# ls -l file1
-rwxr-xr--  1 mwlucas  admin   1188 Sep 14 09:35 file1
#
```

You'll most commonly see permissions documented by their mode. Once you've worked with mode for a while, it'll be second nature. Log into your FreeBSD box and play with the permissions on a test file for a while to get the hang of it.

### Changing File Ownership

Use chown(1) to change who owns a file, and use chgrp(1) to change the group. Both programs take two arguments: a username and the filename.

In the following listing, we see that file1 is owned by mwlucas, and it is in the group wheel:

```
# ls -l file1
-rwxrwxr--  1 mwlucas  wheel  1188 Sep 14 09:35 file1
#
```

You can change the group with chgrp by entering the following command:

```
# chgrp dns file1
# ls -l file1
-rwxrwxr--  1 mwlucas  dns  1188 Sep 14 09:35 file1
#
```

Now, the file is in the group dns.

You can change both owner and group with chown. To change the owner, use chown as shown here:

```
# ls -l file1
-rwxrwxr--  1 mwlucas  wheel  1188 Sep 14 09:35 file1
# chown bind file1
# ls -l file1
-rwxrwxr--  1 bind     wheel  1188 Sep 14 09:35 file1
#
```

To change both the owner and the group with chown, separate the names with a colon:

```
#chown bind:wheel file2
#
```

*Only root can give away files. If you're logged in as a regular user and want someone else to own your files, you cannot do* chown otheruser filename. *Similarly, if you're not in a group, you cannot give that group ownership of the file.*

### Assigning Permissions

So, now you know how to set permissions and change file owners and groups. What should you set or change?

Well, for one thing, many sysadmins set files needed by vital system resources, such as DNS server zone files (see Chapter 11), to be owned by root and writable only by root. Thus, regular users cannot access them.

While this approach works acceptably when you only have one administrator, it fails when delegating tasks. Some administrators work around this with add-ons like sudo(8) (in /usr/ports/security/sudo), but these programs are easily misconfigured.

In the past, I've had assistants who, while not yet competent sysadmins, needed to edit vital files, but under no circumstances could they be given the root password. My solution has been to use groups, which lets me restrict access to these files without giving out root. (I'll use DNS in this example, but this approach applies to any system where a restricted list of users needs to edit a set of files.)

First, consider what sort of access you want people to have to the files. In this DNS example, the file owner must be able to read and write the files, and people in the group need to be able to read and write the files as well. Other users must be able to view them but not edit them. Since DNS files are plain text files, not programs, nobody should be able to execute the files. (It does no harm to set executable permissions on a file that isn't a program, but it can confuse people.) So our permissions string will look like rw-rw-r--. The owner's permissions include read (4) and write (2), the group has read (4) and write (2), and others have read-only permissions (4). So, we can set the permissions on the files with chmod 664 filename.

Then you need to assign an owner to the file, bearing in mind that many system programs run as a particular user. For example, the named DNS server runs as bind, while the Apache Web server runs as nobody. While you might think that the server user is a logical owner, that's not necessarily the case, because if someone broke into your DNS server, he could execute commands as the user bind. You may not mind if someone reads these files, but you don't want anyone unauthorized to change them. The simplest solution is to create a separate user to own them.

**Creating a New User**

You can create a new user with adduser(8). (In Chapter 9, we will discuss adduser(8) and some /etc/login.conf tricks that ensure nobody can actually log in as this user.) Use vipw(8) to disable the password entirely (we will also discuss vipw(8) in Chapter 9), and then change the group on the affected file to "dns". Next, set the permissions for the owner and the group to read and write, but for others to read-only, as shown here:

```
# chown dns:dns file1
# chmod 664 file1
# ls -l file1
-rw-rw-r--  1 dns  dns  1188 Sep 14 09:35 file1
#
```

Your staff can now do their jobs without the root password, and your files are immune to tampering by the system process that uses them.

## File Flags

UNIX filesystem permissions are standard across various versions of UNIX, and BSD extends the permissions scheme with *file flags*. These flags work with permissions to increase your system's security. Some of these flags are used for non-security-related functions, but the ones we're interested in here are security related.

NOTE    *Many of the flags have different effects depending on the system securelevel, which will be covered shortly in the "Securelevels" section. For the moment, just nod and smile when you encounter a mention of securelevel; all will become clear in the next few pages.*

The following are the security-related file systems flags:

**sappnd**    The system-level append-only flag can only be set by root. Files with this flag can be added to, but cannot be removed or otherwise edited (which is particularly useful for log files). Setting sappnd on a .history file can be interesting if your system is compromised. Since a common intruder tactic is to remove .history or to symlink it to /dev/null so that the admin cannot see what was done, sappnd ensures that script kiddies cannot cover their tracks in this manner. It's almost funny to watch the record of someone trying to remove a sappnd file. You can see the attacker's frustration grow with the various things she tries. (It is better, of course, for your system not to be hacked at all!) This flag cannot be altered when the system is running at securelevel 1 or higher.

**schg**    The system-level immutable flag can only be set by root. Files with this flag set cannot be changed in any way, neither edited, moved, nor replaced. Basically, the filesystem itself will prevent all attempts to touch this file in any way. This flag cannot be altered when the system is running at securelevel 1 or higher.

**sunlnk**    The system undeletable flag can only be set by root. The file can be edited or altered, but it cannot be deleted. This is not as secure as the previous two flags because if a file can be edited, it can be emptied. It's still useful for certain circumstances, however. I've used it to solve problems when a program insisted on deleting its own log files when it crashed. It's not generally useful to set on any standard system flags. This flag cannot be altered when the system is running at securelevel 1 or higher.

**uappnd**    The user append-only flag can only be set by the file owner or root. Like the system append-only flag, sappnd, a file with this flag set can be added to but not otherwise edited or removed. This is most useful for logs from personal programs and the like, and is primarily a means to keep users from shooting themselves in the foot. The owner or root can remove this flag at any time.

**uchg**    The user immutable flag can only be set by the owner or root. Like the schg flag described earlier, the user immutable flag prevents a user from changing the file. Again, root can override this, and it can be disabled by the user at any securelevel. This flag helps to prevent mistakes, but not to secure the system.

**uunlnk**    The user undeletable flag can only be set by the owner or root. A file with this flag set cannot be deleted by the owner, though root can override that, and this flag can be turned off. This flag is mostly useless, but like the other user flags can be helpful in preventing mistakes.

### Viewing a File's Flags

You can see a file's flags with ls -lo:

```
# ls -lo important
-rw-r--r--  1 mwlucas  mwlucas  uchg 0 May 11 19:51 important
```

The uchg in the preceding listing tells us that the user immutable flag is set. In comparison, if a file has no flags set, it looks like this:

```
# ls -lo unimportant
-rw-r--r--  1 mwlucas  mwlucas  - 0 May 11 19:52 unimportant
#
```

The dash in place of the flag name tells us that no filesystem flag has been set.

An out-of-the-box FreeBSD doesn't have many files marked in this way. You can certainly mark anything you want in any way desired, however. On one system that I fully expected to be hacked, I went berserk with chflags -R schg in various system directories to prevent anyone from replacing system binaries with Trojaned versions. It might not stop an attacker from getting in, but it made me feel better to imagine how frustrated an attacker would be once he got a command prompt.

### Setting Flags

You can set flags with the chflags(1) command. For example, to be sure that your kernel isn't replaced, you could do this:

```
# chflags schg /kernel
```

This would keep anyone from replacing your kernel: both an intruder and you.

You can also recursively change the flags on a directory tree with the -R flag. For example, to make your /bin directory immutable, you could use this command:

```
# chflags -R schg /bin
```

And boom! Your basic binaries cannot be changed.

To remove a flag, use chflags and a "no" in front of the flag name. For example, to unset the schg flag we just set on your kernel, enter this command:

```
# chflags noschg /kernel
```

That said, you'd have to be running at securelevel -1 to unset this flag. So, without further ado, we'll discuss securelevels and what they mean to you.

## Securelevels

Securelevels are kernel settings that change basic system behavior to disallow certain actions. The kernel will behave slightly differently as you raise the securelevel. For example, at low securelevels the file flags we discussed can be removed. A file might be marked "do not remove," but you can remove the marker and then delete the file. When you increase the securelevel, the flag cannot be removed. Similar changes will take place in other parts of the system. Taken as a whole, the behavior changes that result from increased securelevels will either frustrate or stop an intruder. You can set the system securelevel at boot with the rc.conf options kern_securelevel_enable="YES".

Securelevels make system maintenance difficult by imposing certain restrictive conditions on system behavior. After all, many actions that you might take during normal administration are also things that intruders might do to cover their tracks. For example, when using securelevels you will need to take extra steps to patch your system. On the other hand, securelevels will frustrate the heck out of your average intruder who wishes to destroy data, plant a Trojan, or damage the system in some other way.

### Setting Securelevels

Securelevels come in five levels: -1, 0, 1, 2, and 3, with -1 being the lowest and 3 being the highest.

Once you enable securelevels with the kern_securelevel_enable="YES" rc.conf option (as discussed previously), you can set the securelevel automatically at boot with the kern_securelevel=X rc.conf variable. While you can raise the system securelevel at any time, you cannot lower it without rebooting into single-user mode. (If you could lower the securelevel without rebooting, so could an intruder.)

### Securelevel -1

Securelevel -1, the default mode, provides no additional kernel security whatsoever. If you're learning FreeBSD and are frequently changing your configuration, remain at securelevel -1 and use BSD's built-in file permissions and other UNIX safeguards as security, which should be adequate for most situations.

### Securelevel 0

The only time securelevel 0 is used is when your system is first booting, and it offers no special features. When the system reaches multi-user mode, however, the securelevel is automatically raised to 1. (Setting kern_securelevel=0 in /etc/rc.conf is effectively the same as setting kern_securelevel=1.) As such, there's really not much reason to use a securelevel of 0.

### Securelevel 1

At a securelevel of 1, things become interesting:

- You cannot load or unload kernel modules with kldload/kldunload (see Chapter 4).
- Programs cannot write directly to system memory via either the /dev/mem or /dev/kmem devices.
- Mounted disks cannot be written to directly, so you cannot format partitions. (You can write files to disk via the standard kernel interface; you just cannot format disks or address the raw devices.)
- You cannot start the X Window System.

The most obvious effect of securelevel 1 is that the BSD-specific filesystem flags cannot be altered. If a file is marked immutable and you want to replace it, you're out of luck.

### Securelevel 2

A securelevel of 2 gives you all the benefits of securelevel 1 with two additions:

- You cannot write directly to either mounted or unmounted filesystems.
- You cannot alter the system time by more than 1 second at a time.

Both of these can seem irrelevant to a new sysadmin, but they are important tricks in security. Although UNIX provides handy tools, such as text editors to write to files, it is also possible to bypass those tools and, indeed, bypass the actual filesystem to access the underlying ones and zeros encoded on the disk. If you could do this, you could change any file regardless of the permissions. The only time this happens in common use is when you are installing a new hard disk. Normally, only the root user can write directly to the disk in this manner. With this securelevel set, even root cannot do this.

Similarly, another hacker trick is to change the system time, edit a file, and change it back. That way, when the administrator looks for files that might be causing trouble, the tampered file will appear to have been untouched for months or years, and hence not seem an obvious source of concern.

### Securelevel 3

Securelevel 3 is called *network secure mode*. It behaves exactly like securelevel 2, but it prevents changes to IPFW or IPFilter rules. (We discuss these programs in Chapter 11 and Chapter 8, respectively.) If you have a system with packet filtering or bandwidth management enabled, and those rules are well tuned and unlikely to change, you can use securelevel 3.

### Which Securelevel Do You Need?

The securelevel appropriate to your environment will depend on your situation. For example, if you've just put a FreeBSD machine into production and you need to fine-tune it, you should leave the securelevel at -1. Once your system is fine-tuned, however, you can raise the securelevel, and most systems will run just fine at a securelevel of 2.

It's a good idea to use the schg and sappnd flags on selected files to help protect yourself, because the added clock-changing protection throws up still more ways to force a hacker to show herself.

If you use one of FreeBSD's packet-filtering/firewall packages, you might consider using securelevel 3. However, if you choose to use securelevel 3, be very certain of what you're doing and why, or you're liable to run into problems. For example, if you're using your FreeBSD system as a corporate firewall, securelevel 3 will disallow firewall configuration changes without interrupting your Internet connection. That said, if you're using securelevel 3 to restrict access to certain ports on your Web server, a securelevel of 3 is probably fine.

### What Won't Securelevel and File Flags Do?

Consider a case where someone compromises a CGI script on your Apache Web server, uses that to bootstrap himself into a shell, and then uses the shell to bootstrap himself into root access.

Perhaps, because you've set the securelevel accordingly, this attacker gets frustrated because he can't replace your kernel with his specially compiled one. No problem; he can still replace a variety of system binaries with Trojan-horse versions, so that the next time you log in, your new version of login will send your password to an anonymous Web-based mailbox or to an Internet newsgroup.

So, to protect your key files, you run around doing chflags schg -R /bin/*, chflags schg -R /usr/lib, and so on. Fine. If you forget one file—say, something obscure like /etc/rc.i386 or something like that—your hacker can edit that file to include chflags -R noschg /. He can then reboot your system some time late at night, when you might not notice. (How often do you sit down and exhaustively audit your /etc/rc files?)

You think that your system is safe, with every file completely protected. But what about /usr/local/etc/rc.d, the local program startup directory? The system boot process will try to execute anything it finds in this directory with a .sh extension. As such, your hypothetical hacker could do a lot of damage by placing a simple shell script there. After all, /etc/rc raises the securelevel as the last thing, after everything's started. What if he were to create a shell script that kills the running /etc/rc before it can raise the securelevel, then turns around and starts his own /var/.hidden/rc.rootkit to finish bringing up the network?

Of course, this is only one path—there are others. The thing to remember is that system security is a thorny problem, with no one easy solution. Once intruders have a command prompt, it's you against them. And if they're any good, you won't even know that they're there until it's too late. And, of course, it's always better to keep intruders out of your castle than to try to get them out of the corridors.

### Living with Securelevels

If you've been liberal with the schg flag, you might find that you can't upgrade (or even patch) your system conveniently. The fact is, the same conditions that make hackers' lives difficult can make yours a living hell, if you don't know how to work around them. So how do you work around them?

If you've protected your /etc/rc.conf with schg, you'll first have to lower the securelevel to edit your system. Of course, the securelevel setting is in that file, so you'll need to take control of the system before /etc/rc runs in order to edit that file.

To do so, follow the procedure for booting into single-user mode (explained in Chapter 3), and mount the affected filesystems. Since at that level the securelevel has not been set, you can mount your filesystems, run chflags noschg on the affected files, and continue booting. You can even edit /etc/rc.conf to disable securelevels, and let it boot normally. (You'll restore service more quickly that way, but lose the file flags' protection.)

Once you've finished maintenance, you can raise (but not lower) the system's securelevel without rebooting using the sysctl command:

```
# sysctl -w kern.securelevel=[desired securelevel]
```

Now that you can control file changes, let's take a look at controlling access to your system from the network.

## Programs That Can Be Hacked

As I mentioned at the beginning of this chapter, it's generally not the operating system that gets hacked, it's the programs running on it. Of these, network programs are the biggest target, and the question then becomes, "How do I tell which programs are running on the network?" Answer: with sockstat(1).

Sockstat(1) is a friendly FreeBSD tool that determines which sockets are open on a system and which programs are listening on those sockets. It shows both connections that are running right now and connections that are available for people to talk to.

A socket is simply a "logical device" that is listening for a connection. You can have a socket listening to the network; those are the network ports I talked about in Chapter 5. You can have sockets listening on IP version 6 networks, which are IPv6 sockets. Finally, you can have sockets listening on the local computer. Programs can create sockets to communicate with one another.

If you don't have an IPv6 network, you don't need to worry about IPv6 sockets. Similarly, UNIX sockets aren't an issue over the network; you must be logged on to the computer to talk to a UNIX socket, and you have to get through all the standard UNIX permissions to do so. If your intruder can do that, you're already in trouble. So, we'll look at the open IPv4 network sockets by running `sockstat -4` in the following snapshot taken from my laptop:

```
# sockstat -4
USER       COMMAND    PID   FD PROTO  LOCAL ADDRESS        FOREIGN ADDRESS
mwlucas    ssh        372    3 tcp4   192.168.1.200:1025   208.63.178.18:22
root       X          347    0 tcp4   *:6000              *:*
root       snmpd      296    6 udp4   *:161               *:*
root       lpd        234    6 tcp4   *:515               *:*
root       syslogd    209    4 udp4   *:514               *:*

#
```

Each line in the preceding listing represents either one open socket awaiting a connection or an established connection. (It looks a lot like `netstat -na`, doesn't it?) Most of the columns are fairly self-explanatory. USER is the user running the process, COMMAND is the command name, and PID is the process ID number of the particular process holding that socket. The command name is very helpful in securing the system. FD is the process's file descriptor—you don't have to worry about that right now. The PROTO column is the Internet protocol the connection is using. Finally, the LOCAL ADDRESS and FOREIGN ADDRESS columns show the IP addresses and port numbers on each side of the connection. If you have an IP address and port number in LOCAL ADDRESS and FOREIGN ADDRESS, you're looking at an existing connection. When the FOREIGN ADDRESS column shows two asterisks separated by a colon (*:*), that program is listening for incoming connections.

In the preceding example, I'm using ssh to connect to a remote system from the laptop. Ssh isn't actually listening for incoming connections; sockstat shows only a connection I made to another server. Four services are listening for incoming connections on the laptop: X is listening on all of the local IP addresses on port 6000/tcp; an snmp daemon is running on port 161/udp; and lpd and syslogd are listening for incoming connections.

Here's the important part. *Every network port you have open is a potential weakness and an attacker's targets. Shut down unnecessary network services and secure the ones you must offer.* Got it? Good.

**NOTE** *It's a good idea to regularly check which ports are open on your systems, because you might learn something that surprises you. For example, I installed net-snmp to get snmpwalk and related commands and completely forgot that it also installed the snmp daemon, which should be shut down and not started again at boot.[5]*

Examining sockstat output on a laptop is pretty straightforward, but the output for an Internet server is another thing entirely. A small server can have hundreds of lines of output. For example, here's a listing for a *very* small server:

| USER | COMMAND | PID | FD | PROTO | LOCAL ADDRESS | FOREIGN ADDRESS |
|------|---------|-----|----|-------|---------------|-----------------|
| root | sshd1 | 28971 | 5 | tcp | 192.168.15.18.22 | 24.2.72.241.35886 |
| ❷ nobody | httpd | 27356 | 17 | tcp | *.80 | *.* |
| nobody | httpd | 27355 | 17 | tcp | *.80 | *.* |
| nobody | httpd | 27354 | 17 | tcp | *.80 | *.* |
| nobody | httpd | 27353 | 17 | tcp | *.80 | *.* |
| nobody | httpd | 27352 | 17 | tcp | *.80 | *.* |
| nobody | httpd | 27351 | 17 | tcp | *.80 | *.* |
| root | named | 72871 | 4 | udp | *.2151 | *.* |
| root | named | 72871 | 20 | udp | 192.168.15.18.53 | *.* |
| root | named | 72871 | 21 | tcp | 192.168.15.18.53 | *.* |
| root | named | 72871 | 22 | udp | 127.0.0.1.53 | *.* |
| root | named | 72871 | 23 | tcp | 127.0.0.1.53 | *.* |
| root | httpd | 65199 | 17 | tcp | *.80 | *.* |
| ❸ root | sshd1 | 275 | 3 | tcp | *.22 | *.* |
| root | sshd1 | 269 | 3 | tcp | 192.168.15.19.80 | *.* |
| root | sendmail | 214 | 4 | tcp | *.25 | *.* |
| root | inetd | 207 | 4 | tcp | *.106 | *.* |
| ❶ root | inetd | 207 | 5 | tcp | *.110 | *.* |
| root | inetd | 207 | 6 | tcp | *.113 | *.* |

The function of some of these open ports is obvious; some are not. For example, while you'll probably recognize httpd and sendmail, what are all those open inetd ports?

To find out, "grep" the /etc/services file (see Chapter 5) for a port number, to see what service name it is using. For example, the service that's running on port 110 is curious (❶). Grep searches for lines that match a pattern, so in this case we want to find all the lines that contain the string of characters "110". Grepping for port 110 gives us this series of lines:

```
# grep 110 /etc/services
pop3           110/tcp     #Post Office Protocol - Version 3
pop3           110/udp     #Post Office Protocol - Version 3
```

*(continued on next page)*

---

[5] "What is SNMP?" I hear you cry. See Chapter 19. "And how do I shut it down?" See Chapter 11.

```
nfsd-status      1110/tcp    #Cluster status info
nfsd-keepalive   1110/udp    #Client status info
softcm           6110/tcp    #HP SoftBench CM
softcm           6110/udp    #HP SoftBench CM
#
```

The grep returns several lines that include 110, but we ignore the ones that include obvious wrong matches. For example, the third and fourth lines include the string "110", but only as a reference to port 1110. The first two lines tell us that the service is pop3, which we will discuss in Chapter 12. A quick check of the FreeBSD mailing list archives shows that pop3 delivers mail to desktop clients such as Eudora and Outlook.

**NOTE** *If you don't know what a service is, you can either search for it on the Net or shut it off and see what breaks. While I've used both techniques successfully, researching is better in the long run.*

You can use this technique to identify the other services provided by inetd. (Inetd itself is discussed in Chapter 12.) We also have several instances of httpd (❷), a Web server. There's one ssh daemon listening on port 22 (❸), and one that's listening on port 80. [6] You'll also see lots of named entries listening on port 53, and one on 2151. We'll discuss each of these programs later, as we get into discussing the various network services FreeBSD can offer. The important thing for you to realize here is that each server program listens on a network socket, and you can identify those programs with sockstat(1).

So, now that you know what's running, how do you turn things off the ones you don't need? The best way to close these ports is not to start the programs that run them. Network daemons are generally started in one of two places: either /etc/rc.conf or a startup script in /usr/local/etc/rc.d. Programs that are integrated with the main FreeBSD system, such as sendmail, ssh, and portmap, have flags in /etc/rc.conf to enable or disable them (see Chapter 9). Add-on programs, such as Web servers, start via scripts in /usr/local/etc/rc.d (see Chapter 11). The inetd program is a special case, though, since its purpose is to start smaller, rarely used programs. While inetd as a whole is enabled via an rc.conf flag, the programs within inetd must be started and stopped from within inetd. To learn how to enable and disable inetd programs, see Chapter 12.

[6] A variety of firewalls can be bypassed by sending traffic over port 80, the TCP port used for Web traffic. If you have an Internet server outside such a firewall, you can run sshd on port 80 on that server and connect from within the firewall. While a firewall that relies solely on restricting port access cannot stop you from connecting in this way, that firewall is a definite hint that you're not supposed to be using services that they've tried to block. This sort of cleverness can get you fired.

To remove unnecessary network services, run `sockstat -4`, and identify each process. Once you determine which ones you need, mark them and disable the rest; then reboot to be certain your changes will take effect. If, when you check sockstat again, you're happy with the result, you're done. Otherwise, go back to the beginning.

## Putting It All Together

Once you have only necessary network ports open, and you know which programs are using them, you know which programs you have to be concerned about securing. If the FreeBSD security team sends out an announcement of a problem with a service you don't run, you can safely ignore it. If the security team announces a hole in a program you are using, you know you have to pay attention. This will protect you against most of the script kiddies out there. Tools such as file flags and securelevels will help minimize the damage attackers can do if they do break in. Finally, using groups to restrict your own systems administrators to particular sections of the system can protect your computers from both accidental and deliberate damage.

Next, we'll look at some of the more advanced security tools FreeBSD offers.

# 8

## ADVANCED
## SECURITY FEATURES

FreeBSD includes a variety of tools for securing network traffic and users. For example, you can implement traffic controls that refuse to allow connections to or from certain parts of the Internet in a few different ways. Also, you can cage off users in a virtual machine, called a *jail*, where they have access to everything but the main server. We'll discuss these techniques in this chapter, as well as how to monitor your system's security and what to do if you are the victim of an intruder.

We'll start with the basics, network traffic control.

## Traffic Control

As a sysadmin, you must be able to control traffic to and from your systems so that you can block unwanted visitors. FreeBSD provides a variety of tools that allows you to control outside access to your systems. We'll focus on TCP wrappers and packet filtering, two access-control tools with enough overlap in functionality that they make a perfect pair.

The TCP Wrappers program controls access to particular server programs (also known as *daemons*). Connection requests are handed to the TCP Wrappers software, which evaluates them according to its configuration. TCP Wrappers is fairly simple to configure, and doesn't require much knowledge of networking, but server programs must be built to work with TCP Wrappers.

Packet filtering controls which packets the system will accept. A rejected connection request never makes it to a userland program; it is rejected in the network stack at a low layer. Packet filtering can control traffic to any program, service, or network port, but it does require more knowledge of networking.

In either case, before you can implement traffic control, you'll need to decide whether you want a default accept or a default deny traffic-control policy.

### Default Accept vs. Default Deny

One of the essential ideas in any security system is the idea of *default accept* versus *default deny*. A default accept stance means that you allow any type of connection except what you specifically disallow. A default deny stance means that you only allow connections from specified parts of the Internet, and all other connection attempts are refused. Once you have chosen your default, you can adjust your stance to protect or reveal those services you wish.

When choosing between default accept and default deny, your choice is really between whether you are offering services to the world or only to a select few, and whether anyone can access your system.

If your system acts as a corporate Web server, you may decide to make it visible only to users on your corporate network. If so, you've adopted a default deny stance, and you'll explicitly list who can talk to you. (This is my preferred approach whenever possible.) Alternatively, if you choose to keep your system open to everyone except someone you don't like, you're adopting a default accept stance.

Also, just because you choose a default does not mean that all services on your computer must obey the default. I configure Web servers on the open Internet to have a default deny stance, and specifically open the world's access to the Web server. Attempts to connect to other programs running on those machines are rejected, unless they come from one of a few IP addresses that I have specifically listed. This is a perfectly acceptable default deny stance.

We'll refer to default deny and default accept throughout the following sections.

## TCP Wrappers

Remember from Chapter 5 that network connections are made to various programs that listen for connection requests. TCP Wrappers intercepts these requests before they reach the daemon, checks the IP address that is making the request against a configuration file, and decides accordingly whether to accept, reject, or alter the request. Despite the TCP Wrappers name, it works with UDP network connections as well as TCP connections. TCP Wrappers is a long-time UNIX standard that has been incorporated into FreeBSD. Individual programs might or might not work with TCP Wrappers, though; just about everything in the base FreeBSD install does, but some third-party software won't.

Wrappers are most often used to protect inetd, the program that starts the smaller daemons. (We will discuss inetd in Chapter 12.) To start inetd with wrappers support, use the -Ww flag with `inetd_flags="-Ww"` in /etc/rc.conf, for example (see Chapter 9). The examples here will not work unless inetd is started correctly. While our examples will discuss protecting inetd programs with TCP Wrappers, you can protect any program in exactly the same way.

### Configuring Wrappers

TCP Wrappers checks each incoming connection request against the rules in /etc/hosts.allow, in order. The first matching rule is applied, and processing stops immediately. This makes rule order very important.

Each rule is on a separate line, and is made up of three parts separated by colons: a daemon name, a client list, and a list of options. Here's a simple sample line:

```
ftpd : all : deny
```

The daemon name in this example is "ftpd", and the client list is "all", meaning all hosts. Finally, the option is "deny", meaning "deny all connections." Nobody can connect to the FTP server on this host, unless an earlier rule explicitly grants access.

In our early examples, we will refer to only two options: *accept* and *deny*. They allow and reject connections, respectively. There are many more options, but we'll discuss them later.

### Daemon Name

The daemon name is the program's name as it appears on the command line. For example, inetd starts the ftpd program when it receives an incoming FTP request. The Apache Web server starts a program called httpd, so if your version of Apache supports wrappers, you would want to use "httpd" in /etc/hosts.allow. One special daemon name, ALL, matches all daemons that support wrappers.

If you have multiple IP addresses on one network card, you can specify different wrapper rules for each IP address that a daemon listens on as part of the daemon name, something like this:

```
ftpd@192.168.8.7 : ALL : deny
ftpd@192.168.8.8 : ALL : accept
```

In this example, we have two daemon names: ftpd@192.168.8.7 and ftpd@192.168.8.8. Each has a separate TCP Wrappers rule.

### The Client List

The *client list* is a list of specific IP addresses, network address blocks, hostnames, domain names, and keywords, separated by spaces. Hostnames and IP addresses are simple; just list them:

```
ALL: netmanager.AbsoluteBSD.com 192.168.4.3 : allow
```

Specify network numbers in the client list with a slash between the IP address and the netmask, as discussed in Chapter 5. For example, if some script kiddies are attacking you from a bunch of different addresses that all begin with 216.136.204, you could block them like this:

```
ALL: 216.136.204.0/255.255.255.0 : deny
```

You can also use domain names in client patterns, by prefacing them with a dot:

```
ALL : .mycompany.com : allow
```

You can reverse any of these, of course, to deny connections from just a single domain:

```
telnetd : .competitor.com : deny
```

If you have a long list of clients, you can even list them in a file and put the full path to the file in the client space in /etc/hosts.allow. I've been on networks with large numbers of widely scattered hosts, such as an ISP or corporate network environment with network management workstations scattered across the world. Each workstation shared the same TCP Wrappers rule as every other workstation, and appeared on half a dozen lines in /etc/hosts.allow. By maintaining a single file with a list of these workstations, I could centralize all changes; edit one file, and all the rules that call the file are updated.

### Client Keywords

In addition to specifically listing client addresses and names, you can also use several special client keywords to add groups of clients to your list:

**ALL**   This keyword matches every possible host.

**LOCAL**   This matches every machine whose hostname does not include a dot. Generally, this means machines in the local domain.

**UNKNOWN**   This keyword matches machines with unidentifiable hostnames, IP addresses, or usernames. As a general rule of thumb, if a machine is making an IP connection, its IP address is known. Tracing hostnames requires DNS, however, and tracking usernames requires the identd protocol. Be very careful using this option, because transitory DNS problems can make even local hostnames unresolvable, and most hosts don't run identd by default. You don't want a machine to become unreachable just because your nameserver was misconfigured—especially if that machine *is* your nameserver!

**KNOWN**   This keyword matches any host with a determinable hostname and IP address. Again, if your DNS fails, every host on the Internet will suddenly appear to have lost its hostname. If you say that all identifiable hosts can connect and your server's DNS fails, nobody will be allowed to connect.

**PARANOID**   This matches any host whose name does not match its IP address. You might get a connection from a host with an IP address of 192.168.84.3 that claims to be called mail.AbsoluteBSD.com. TCP Wrappers will then turn around and check the IP address of mail.AbsoluteBSD.com. If TCP Wrappers gets a different IP address than the source IP, the host will match this rule.

Most of the client keywords listed here require a working DNS server (see Chapter 12). If you use these keywords, you must be aware of the vital link between DNS and the rest of your programs. If your DNS server fails, daemons that use wrappers and these keywords won't be able to recognize any hosts. This means that everything will match your UNKNOWN rules. Also, broken DNS on the client end can deny remote users access to your servers, as your DNS servers won't be able to get the proper information from the client's DNS servers.

Other keywords are available, but they are not as useful or secure. For example, it's possible to allow connections based on the username on the remote machine making the request. You don't really want to permit a request based on the username at the client end, though. Any yahoo can slap together a FreeBSD or Linux box and give himself whatever username he desires. If I set up TCP Wrappers to only allow someone with a username of "mwlucas" to connect to my home system, someone who wanted in could easily add an account of that name to his FreeBSD system. Also, this relies on the same identd protocol that we mentioned earlier, and very few hosts run identd. You will find a few other obscure keywords of similar usefulness in the man page hosts_access(5).

### The ALL and ALL EXCEPT Keywords

The ALL and ALL EXCEPT keywords can be used both for daemon names and for client lists.

The ALL keyword matches absolutely everything. For example, the default /etc/hosts.allow starts with a rule that permits all connections, from all locations, to any daemon:

```
ALL   : ALL: accept
```

This matches all programs, from all clients. You can limit this by giving a specific name to either the client list or the daemon list:

```
ALL   : 192.168.1.87 : deny
```

In this example, we are rejecting all connections from the host 192.168.1.87.

Categorically blocking access to all hosts isn't that great an idea, but remember that TCP Wrappers follows rules in order and quits when it reaches the first matching rule. The ALL keyword lets you set a default deny or default accept stance quite easily. Let's consider the following ruleset:

```
ALL   : 192.168.8.3 192.168.8.4 : accept
ftpd  : ALL : accept
ALL   : ALL : deny
```

Here, we're allowing the workstations 192.168.8.3 and 192.168.8.4 to access anything they want. These are the sysadmin's desktop machines. Then we allow anyone to connect to the FTP service on this machine. Finally, we drop all other connections. This is a useful default deny stance.

Use the ALL EXCEPT keyword to compress the preceding ruleset even further. ALL EXCEPT lets you list hosts by exclusion; what isn't listed matches. Let's consider the same rules written using ALL EXCEPT:

```
ALL    : 192.168.8.3 192.168.8.4 : accept
ALL EXCEPT ftpd : ALL : deny
```

Some people will find the rules more clear when written with ALL, others with ALL EXCEPT. The important thing to remember is that the first matching rule ends the check, so you need to be careful slinging ALL around. Generally speaking, the first rule that has any combination of ALL and ALL EXCEPT in both the daemon and client lists will stop the check; every connection will match it.

### Allow Options

The *allow* option tells TCP Wrappers to accept the connection. The default hosts.allow file starts with this rule:

```
ALL : ALL : allow
```

This rule applies to all daemons and all clients, and it matches and allows all possible connections. While this rule can't be the first on the list if you want to protect your services, it's a good final rule if all you're doing is protecting particular server programs against particular network addresses.

If you're experimenting with TCP wrappers, it's a good idea to allow any connections from the local host, or you're liable to discover a number of programs that break when they can't talk to the local machine. Do so as follows:

```
ALL : localhost : allow
```

### Options for Responses

Now that you have a good grasp of the daemon and client lists, let's take a look at some of the more interesting options for responses. The concept of these options is very simple: You have an incoming connection that matches a rule, so now what do you do with it? Responses can be very simple, or very complicated and subtle.

**NOTE** *If you're using a lot of options, TCP Wrappers rules can get very long. Fortunately, the hosts.allow file uses the backslash (\) followed by a return as a line-continuation character, which helps keep the rules readable.*

The most basic options are *accept* and *deny*. If a connection attempt matches the rule, the request is either passed on to the waiting daemon or rejected. You can use additional options, however, separated by colons.

### Severity

Once you have decided to accept or reject the connection attempt, you can also *log* connection attempts. Suppose you want to block all incoming requests from a competitor; it might be nice to know if they were actually trying to connect. Logs will tell you that.[1] Similarly, you might want to know how many rejected connection attempts you're getting from people with DNS problems (especially if you're using the PARANOID client keyword).

The *severity* option sends a message to the system log, syslogd(8). You can configure syslogd to direct these messages to an arbitrary file (see Chapter 19), based on the syslogd facility and level you choose:

```
telnetd: ALL: severity auth.info : allow
```

This example will log all telnet connections.

### Twist

The *twist* option allows you to run arbitrary shell commands and scripts when someone attempts to connect to a wrapped TCP daemon, and returns the output to the user. Twist only works with TCP connections.[2] Twist takes a shell command as an argument and acts as a deny-plus-do-this rule. You must know some basic shell scripting to use twist; very complicated twists are entirely possible, but we'll stick with the simple ones. We're not demonstrating shell scripts, after all! If you're in doubt, you can always just use /bin/echo "reason" to let the remote client know why its connection has been rejected. (Note the straight double quotes around the reason, they're important!)

Twist is useful for a final rule, if you're using default deny. (If you have a restrictive security stance, end your security policy with such a catch-all deny rule.) You can use twist to return an answer to the person attempting to connect as follows:

```
ALL : ALL : twist /bin/echo "You cannot use this service."
```

---

[1] If your goal is to log all attempted connections to your system, on any port, this is more reliably done with the net.inet.tcp.log_in_vain and net.inet.udp.log_in_vain sysctls (see the Appendix). These sysctls will log all failed attempts to contact any port on your system, not just wrapped daemons.

[2] Strictly speaking, this is not true. But remember from Chapter 5 that UDP is connectionless; there is no connection to return the response over, so you have to jump through some very sophisticated and annoying hoops to make twist work with UDP. Also, programs that transmit UDP generally don't expect a response in such a manner and are not usually equipped to receive or interpret it. Twisting UDP isn't worth the trouble.

Or if you want to just deny a particular service to a particular host, you can use a more specific daemon and client listings with twist. The following example is a little too long to fit on one line, so I've split it using the backslash character:

```
sendmail : .spammer.com : twist /bin/echo \
    "You cannot use this service"
```

If you're feeling friendly, you can tell people why you're rejecting their connection attempt. The following twist rejects all connections from people whose hostnames do not match their IP addresses, and tells them why:

```
ALL : PARANOID : twist /bin/echo \
    "Your DNS is broken.  When you fix it, come back."
```

Twist will hold the network connection open until the shell command finishes. If your command takes a long time to finish, you could find that you're holding open more connections than you planned. This can reduce system performance dramatically. Twists should be simple and finish rapidly.

**NOTE** *It's tempting to put a rude message in twist output, especially when you think that nobody could have a legitimate reason for trying to access a server. But spitting back "Bite me, script kiddie!" will annoy legitimate users, and it just might peeve script kiddies enough that they try harder to get in.*

### Spawn

Like twist, the *spawn* option denies the connection and runs a specified shell command. Unlike twist, spawn does not return the results to the client. Use spawn when you want your FreeBSD system to take an action upon a connection request, but you don't want the client to know about it. Spawned commands run in the background, and their results are not returned to the client. The following example will allow the connection, but will log the client's IP address to a file:

```
ALL : PARANOID : spawn (/bin/echo %a >> /var/log/misconfigured) \
    : allow
```

If you're familiar with shell scripts, you are probably scratching your head at that %a symbol in the preceding command. TCP Wrappers supports a variety of variables for use in twist and spawn commands, which are expanded before the command is run, so that you can easily customize your responses to connection requests. This particular variable, %a, stands for client address. It expands into the client's IP address in the actual shell command before the command is run. Other variables are shown in Table 8-1.

**Table 8-1: Variables that can be used in twist and spawn commands**

| Variable | Description |
| --- | --- |
| %a | Client address |
| %A | Server IP address |
| %c | All available client information |
| %d | Daemon name |
| %h | Client hostname (if available), or IP address |
| %H | Server hostname (if available), or IP address |
| %n | Client hostname; if no hostname is found, this gives UNKNOWN. If the hostname's name and IP address don't match, this equals PARANOID |
| %N | Server hostname; if no hostname is found, returns either UNKNOWN or PARANOID |

You can use these variables anywhere you would use the information they represent in a shell script. For example, to log all available client information to a file whenever anyone connects to a wrapped program, you could use this spawn:

```
ALL : PARANOID : spawn (/bin/echo %c >> /var/log/clients) \
    : allow
```

You may have noticed that this script is the same as the earlier example, with the minor changes of the variable used and the log filename. You can do the same sort of thing with any information you want to log.

Spaces and backslashes in hostnames can give the command shell problems because they're illegal characters. While neither should appear under normal circumstances, someone might try to, say, use a hostname with a space in it just to confuse security software. To be on the safe side, TCP Wrappers replaces any character that might confuse the command shell with an underscore (_). Check for this sort of thing in your logs; they might indicate possible intrusion attempts, or just someone who likes underscores in hostnames.

### Putting It All Together

Let's take all the examples given in this chapter so far, and build a complete /etc/hosts.allow to protect a hypothetical system on a network. We must first inventory the network resources this system offers, the IP addresses we have on the network, and the users we wish to allow to connect:

- Our IP range is 192.168.0.0/16. On our network, we are running telnet, ftpd, and portmap(8).

- We have a competitor who we do not want to access our system,[3] whose IP address range is 10.5.4.0/23.

- We make the somewhat paranoid decision that hosts with incorrect information on their DNS servers might be attackers, and reject connections from them.[4]

- Hosts on our network may use the portmap daemon, but hosts on other networks cannot. Anyone on the Internet may attempt to access our FTP and telnet servers. (They will still need a username and password to get anywhere, of course!)

While these requirements are fairly complicated, they boil down to a very simple set of rules:

```
#reject all connections from our competitor, and hosts with invalid DNS
ALL : PARANOID 10.5.4.0/23 : deny
#allow our network to use portmap, but deny all others
portmap : ALL EXCEPT 192.168.0.0/16 : deny
#now that portmap is safe & competition blocked, allow telnet & FTP
ALL : ALL : allow
```

You can find many more commented-out examples in the /etc/hosts.allow file on your FreeBSD system or the hosts_allow(5) man page.

## Packet Filtering

Many add-on programs available in the FreeBSD Ports Collection (see Chapter 10) cannot use TCP Wrappers. For these programs, you can use the kernel-level packet-filtering tools IPFW or IPFilter.

When using packet filtering, every network packet that enters the system is compared to a list of rules that tells the kernel how to act on that packet. When a matching rule is found, the kernel acts based upon that rule. For example, a rule can tell the filter to allow, drop, or alter the packet. You can't use the nifty options that TCP Wrappers allows, though; instead of being able to spit a comparatively friendly "rejected" message back to the client, the connection is cut at the network level.

While the idea of packet filtering is straightforward enough, your first packet-filtering implementation will probably be an absolute pain. Be prepared to spend a few hours experimenting with packet filtering the first time you try

---

[3] Specifically blocking a competitor from using services you provide to the rest of the world is not a good idea. They can get those services easily enough by using a dial-up connection, and it just makes you look bad.

[4] This is a very careful stance. Hosts with an incorrect DNS entry are most probably on a network with neglected nameservers or incompetent/overworked administrators. But of all attacking hosts, attackers are more likely to deliberately misconfigure their DNS.

it, and don't get discouraged by failures. While you might think you know how IP works, the only way to really learn it is to work with it.

NOTE *Effective packet filtering requires a solid grounding in how IP works. Trying to filter without understanding what you're doing will be both frustrating and pointless. If you're in doubt, re-read all that apparently useless stuff in Chapter 5.*

### IPFilter

IPFilter is the traffic-filtering module we're going to discuss in detail here. It has arguably the most sophisticated packet-filtering system available in any free or proprietary software. IPFilter is developed independently of FreeBSD, but has been integrated with the main OS for a few years now. (It also runs on Solaris and the other versions of BSD.)

To use IPFilter, you must first rebuild your kernel (see Chapter 4) and include the following options:

```
options        IPFILTER
options        IPFILTER_LOG
```

The IPFILTER option adds basic IPFilter support to your kernel; IPFilter's activity is logged by IPFILTER_LOG. While the logging isn't strictly necessary to run IPFilter, the logging module is reasonably small, so you may as well include it. (If you exclude it, at some point you'll almost certainly find yourself recompiling your kernel to include it just so you can debug a problem.)

IPFilter uses a default accept stance. If you prefer a default deny stance, include the following in your kernel:

```
options        IPFILTER_DEFAULT_BLOCK
```

These options are not in the GENERIC kernel; not all people want packet filtering, and some people want to do it in a different manner.

NOTE *While you can add IPFilter rules for default deny as well, if you use this option and flush all your rules, you'll lock yourself out of remote access.*

### IPFW

IPFW is a packet-filtering tool originally created by BSDi, which may give it a wider commercial market than IPFilter and possibly more mindshare in the BSD world. With IPFW you can do nifty things, such as make different networks appear to be local to each other (Ethernet bridging), or control the bandwidth coming to or from any host (traffic throttling), as well as implement the simple access control any packet filter has. It has a sophisticated packet-state inspection system that can go toe-to-toe with anything on the open-source or proprietary market. It isn't as solid as that in IPFilter, however, which is why we're going to focus on IPFilter for packet filtering.

Fortunately, you can use both IPFW and IPFilter together, combining IPFW's nifty bridging and throttling features with IPFilter's advanced packet inspection (though not without jumping through a few hoops). We'll discuss IPFW's bandwidth-throttling feature in Chapter 13.

**NOTE** *You can use IPFW alone, though its packet-state inspection is not as sophisticated as IPFilter's. Once you understand how to configure IPFilter, you won't have any trouble with IPFW. See /etc/rc.firewall for some IPFW examples.*

### Default Accept and Default Deny in Packet Filtering

We spoke earlier about the default accept and default deny security stances, which are exceedingly important in packet filtering. If you use a default accept stance and want to protect your system or network, you will need numerous rules to block every possible attack. If you use a default deny stance, you must explicitly open holes for every little service you offer. Once you choose which you prefer, you can compile the appropriate default into your kernel.

When using a default deny stance, it is very easy to lock yourself out of remotely accessing the machine at all. After all, if you flush all your firewall rules, the rule that allows you to access the machine is deleted! I cut my own access off at least once every couple of years, generally because I'm not thinking straight while fixing some other unrelated packet-filtering problem. The only fix is to kick myself as I climb in the car, drive to the remote location, and apologize profusely to the people I've inconvenienced as I fix the problem.

Still, in almost all circumstances, a default deny stance is correct. As a new administrator, the only way you can reasonably learn packet filtering is if you have convenient access to the system console. If you're not entirely confident in your setup, do not send a packet-filtering system across the country unless you have either a competent local administrator or a serial console.

### Basic Concepts of Packet Filtering

Recall from Chapter 5 that a TCP connection can be in a variety of states, including open, opening, and so on. There's the whole three-way handshake process. When you try to open a connection, the client sends a SYN packet to request synchronization. The server responds by sending the client a packet marked as SYN-ACK, meaning, "I have received your connection request, and here is some basic information for the connection." Finally, the client responds with an ACK packet, meaning, "I have received and acknowledge your connection information." Every part of this three-way handshake must complete for a connection to actually be set up. Your packet-filtering rules must permit each part of the three-way handshake, as well as the actual data transmission. Allowing your server to receive incoming connection requests is useless if your packet-filter rules do not permit it to send back an acknowledgment.

In the 1990s, packet filters checked each packet individually. If a packet matched a rule, it was allowed to pass. The system did not record what came before, and had no idea if a packet was part of a legitimate transaction or not. For example, if a packet marked SYN-ACK, bound for an address in the inside of the packet filter, arrived at the outside of the packet filter, the packet filter would decide that the packet had to be the response to a packet it had approved earlier. Such a packet *had* to be approved to let the three-way handshake complete. As a result, intruders could forge SYN-ACK packets, and use them to circumvent seemingly secure devices. Since the packet filter didn't know who sent a SYN packet, it couldn't reject such SYN-ACK packets as illegitimate. Once intruders got packets into the network, they could usually trigger a response from some device and start to worm their way in.

State inspection, introduced with modern packet filters, arose to counteract this problem. Packet filters that use state inspection maintain a table of every connection running through the system. If an incoming packet appears to be part of an ongoing connection, but there's no matching connection, it's rejected. (While this complicates the kernel's work, it's actually easier to write packet-filter rules for stateful inspection.) For example, if a SYN-ACK packet arrives at a host with stateful packet inspection, but the host did not send out a SYN to that particular host, the SYN-ACK is dropped. The packet filter must track many, many more possible states, so this is harder than it might seem.

If you've started to think, "Hey, packet filtering sounds like a firewall," you're right, to a point. The word *firewall* is applied to a variety of devices meant to protect a network. Some are sophisticated, and scrutinize every single packet, and proxy every service they permit. Some can be out-thought by bricks. These days, the word firewall has been reduced to a marketing buzzword with very little concrete meaning. It's like the word car; do you mean a 1972 Gremlin or a 2002 Maserati? Both have their uses, but one is obviously designed for performance. While the Gremlin of firewalls might have its uses, better to buy the Maserati if you want performance.

Having said that, your FreeBSD system can be as solid a firewall as you want to make it. Packet filtering is only the beginning; if you wander through /usr/ports/net and /usr/ports/security, you'll find a variety of application proxies that can let your FreeBSD system go up against Gauntlet or Checkpoint and come out on top, for tens of thousands of dollars less.

### Implementing IPFilter

IPFilter is a rule-based filter. Packets are checked against IPFilter rules in order, using a "best fit" algorithm. This means that a packet is compared against all the rules (unless specifically told otherwise), beginning with general rules and proceeding to more specific ones. For example, you might start off by blocking everything, and then writing narrow rules to allow desired traffic.

The general form is as follows:

```
action direction options protocol source destination options
```

Every rule follows this basic format, though not all terms are mandatory. In fact, rules can be as simple as block in from any to any. (You won't be really happy with the effects, because you'd block everything, but it would work.)

Let's look at a simple rule.

```
❶ block ❷ in ❸ log ❹ quick ❺ on ed0 from ❻ any to ❻ any ❼ with short
```

The action in this case is block (❶); packets that match this rule will be stopped.

in is the direction the packet is moving in (❷), with valid word choices here being in and out (used as if you were standing inside the computer). A packet matching in is considered to be entering the system from the network.

The log and quick keywords (❸,❹) are options. The packet is logged, and if it matches a rule flagged as quick, matching stops there. Remember that IPFilter checks every packet against every rule, *unless told otherwise*. The quick keyword is what says otherwise. If a packet matches a rule with the quick keyword, no further checking will be done and the action given by the rule is taken.

on ed0 specifies an interface (❺). (All networked systems have at least two interfaces: one loopback and at least one network interface.)

The source and destination are both any to and any (❻), which say that it doesn't matter where this packet is from or where it's going.

So far, then, this rule is pretty definite: It says to block everything on this interface immediately. If ed0 is the only network interface on this system, no traffic will go in or out. (Well, at least it's secure.)

The last option is what makes this rule useful, though. The with short statement (❼) is an IPFilter keyword that means "packets are too small to be real." While tiny packets are certainly possible, they're extremely rare, and such a packet would almost certainly be part of an attack. (Normal-sized packets will not match this rule and can pass on down the rule list, to be accepted or rejected by later rules.)

### Keywords and Configurations

Now that you've seen the basic rule format, let's look at some common keywords and configurations that can be used to protect an Internet server. As shown earlier, the general form is as follows:

```
action direction options protocol source destination packet-options
```

Each of these pieces is described next.

**Action**    The two possible actions are block and pass. Blocked packets are not allowed to pass; passed packets go on down the list. (A packet can be blocked by one rule, but passed by another, more specific, rule.)

**Direction**    This has two acceptable values: in and out. Packets coming in are entering the computer from the network. Packets going out are those leaving the computer.

**Options**    The log keyword tells IPFilter to pass the packet to the logging program, ipl. (See the "IPFilter Logging" section for basic information, and Chapter 19 for details.) The quick keyword tells IPFilter to stop processing and apply this rule immediately if the packet matches. The on keyword tells the system that this rule applies only to a particular interface, such as on fxp0.

**Protocol**   This is any IP-layer protocol, such as `tcp`, `udp`, `skip`, and so on. Protocols can be specified by the name given in /etc/protocols, or by protocol number, and are preceded by the `proto` keyword, as in this example:

```
block in proto udp from any to any
```

**Source and Destination**   The `from` and `to` keywords show the direction of matching traffic. To protect your server, block incoming traffic. For example, if your server had an IP address of 192.168.1.8, and you have a default deny security stance, you'd use the following rule (be sure to use IP addresses, not hostnames):

```
block in from any to 192.168.1.8
```

**Packet-Options**   The final options describe special types of packets. The `with short` keyword describes IP packets too short to be legitimate. These are generally blocked. Similarly, the `with ipopts` keyword matches packets with IP options. In most cases, there is no legitimate reason for them to be hitting your server—you probably want to block these. The `keep state` option tells IPFilter to automatically permit connections that appear to be part of a connection in the state table. This is the part that lets you make simple rules that cover each part of the data transaction. (You'll see an example of this shortly.)

NOTE   *This is by no means a complete list of all possible IPFilter options. If you're interested in fine-tuning IPFilter, see the file /usr/src/contrib/ipfilter/BNF, which offers a full description of IPFilter configuration.*

Finally, you can filter on the packet flags. Remember the multiple states of a TCP connection discussed in Chapter 5? The initial packets had flags: SYN, ACK, and SYN-ACK. You can use these to filter based on connection state using the `with` option. The most important flags to filter on are `syn` and `syn-ack`, or S/SA.

With these basic rules and options, you can provide a reasonable layer of server protection. We'll discuss their implementation in the rest of this section, and use them to build a sample rule list that will protect a typical Internet server as we go.

### Allowing Services

Up to this point, I've recommended a default deny stance, and I've shown you how to block people from accessing your server. That's nice, but how do you allow people to access the parts of your server that you want to make available to them?

The first step in making specific services available is to find either the port number or canonical port name, and the protocol used by all network daemons you want the world to access. (See /etc/services if you're not sure of the exact names and numbers.)

For example, assume you have a Web server (HTTP), POP3 server, and mail server. The Web server runs on port 80, over TCP. Mail servers run over port 25, over TCP. Lastly, POP3 uses port 110 and TCP.

We start by blocking in all TCP connections, which catches all requests for new connections, by setting the SYN or SYN-ACK flags like so:

```
❶ block ❷ in ❸ log ❹ proto tcp ❺ all ❻ flags S/SA
```

Let's dissect this first rule. We start by blocking (❶) all connections that come into the system (❷). Then we want to log each packet (❸). The rule then narrows a bit: We only want TCP packets (❹), but from any source or destination (❺). However, we only want packets that have the SYN or SYN-ACK flag set (❻). This means that this rule is watching for incoming TCP packets with either a SYN or SYN-ACK flag, or a new connection request. Requests for connections will be denied, unless a later rule permits them.

Then, to make our Web server available, we follow up with this:

```
❶ pass ❷ in ❸ quick ❹ proto tcp ❺ from any to any ❻ port = www ❼ keep state
```

This rule allows matching traffic to pass in (❶,❷). This rule uses the quick keyword (❸), which means that a packet matching this rule will short-circuit the rest of the rules and pass immediately. A matching packet must be of protocol TCP (❹), and can be from anywhere and addressed to anywhere (❺). This is much like the earlier rule, but here's the new bit: It must come in on the port for www (❻), as listed in /etc/services. Once this packet is approved, all other packets that are part of the same connection will also be approved (❼). Packets that request access to port 80 will be accepted.

Rules for allowing pop3 and sendmail are very similar, with only the port changed:

```
pass in quick proto tcp from any to any port = pop3 keep state
pass in quick proto tcp from any to any port = smtp keep state
```

Without the use of the stateful-inspection (keep state) option, we would need to add rules that matched not only the initial incoming connection, but also our Web server's response and the following data flow, rules that would be complex and difficult to debug.

Also, when writing such rules, we couldn't be sure what random high-number port clients would use to initiate connections. Manually filling in these rules would leave security holes and block legitimate connections. By allowing IPFilter to compare each packet with its list of existing connections, we eliminate those potential holes.

## Loading IPFilter Rules

Now that you know how to create the IPFilter rules you need, how do you load them?

IPFilter is controlled by ipf(8), which you can set to read rules from a text file. (I generally put rules in /etc/ipf.conf.) The -f flag tells IPFilter to read in rules from a specific file, /etc/ipf.conf in this case:

```
# ipf -f /etc/ipf.conf
```

When you make changes to rules, you must flush the existing packet-filter rules before you load the current ones with the -F flag. Otherwise, you will have all your old rules *and* all your new rules in the packet filter. When flushing existing rules, you can also specify inbound (i), outbound (o), or all (a) rules:

```
# ipf -F a
```

Or to minimize exposure, you can do both in a single command:

```
# ipf -F a && ipf -f /etc/ipf.conf
```

**NOTE**    *You can directly manipulate the IPFilter rules table to eliminate the extremely brief period where your rules table is empty, but this requires a fair amount of experience. If you're actually learning anything from this section, you're not ready to do that yet. Once you're quite comfortable with IPFilter rules, see ipf(8) for details.*

## Rule Grouping

A rule group is a set of rules that matches a certain type of packet. For example, you will have some rules that only apply to TCP packets and some that only apply to UDP packets. Some rules will only apply to, say, requests for new connections, and others apply to every packet. It's not necessary to compare every packet against every rule. IPFilter uses rule groups to funnel packets through an optimal rule path that only evaluates that type of packet. This way, you can compare each packet against the fewest possible rules, which makes your rules easier to understand, easier to debug, and faster to actually run.

A rule that starts a rule group has a "head" statement at the very end of the rule, and members of that group have a group statement at the end of the rule. Each rule group has a group number. These group numbers are completely arbitrary. I recommend using group numbers that are at least a hundred apart from each other, so that you can add subgroups and dependent rules between them. We'll see some examples of how to do this as we go on.

For example, the following rule snippet catches all packets going out of interface ed0, and routes them into rule group 100.

```
pass out on ed0 all head 100
```

A packet that matches this rule will be processed by each rule in the rules list until it hits this rule, at which point it will only be tested against rules in group 100. What's more, a packet that doesn't match this rule will never be tested against any rule in group 100. For example:

```
block out from 127.0.0.0/8 to any group 100
```

Here, 127.0.0.0/8 is the block of addresses reserved for loopback connections, and your server should not send packets from these addresses out across the Net. This rule blocks these loopback packets. Packets from this address range are allowed over the loopback interface lo0.

You would never want to use a universal rule to block all loopback packets because they are necessary for normal operation. However, the preceding rule is in group 100, and according to the head rule for this group, the only packets that will be affected are those that are outbound on the ed0 interface. Loopback packets should never go out over a network interface, so this rule is appropriate. Thus, this rule would protect others from being damaged by a misconfiguration on your network, but wouldn't prevent someone from sending you IP packets that appeared to be from your loopback interface. After all, you're only checking outbound packets in this rule.

So, how does this all fit together? The following example rule set is for a server with one network interface, xl0, and one IP address, 192.168.1.200. This ruleset allows incoming POP3, SMTP, and Web connections, and any outgoing connections. (You can find more examples of IPFilter rules for various protocols in /usr/src/contrib/ipfilter/rules.)

```
#block garbage we never ever want to accept.
❶ block in log quick from any to any with ipopts
❷ block in log quick proto tcp from any to any with short
```

These initial rules are not in any group, and they come first, so they are applied against all packets. The first rule tells the system to reject all packets using IP Options (❶). If you don't know what IP Options are, you don't want to accept them. No standard server program will require them. The second rule tells you to reject all ultra-short TCP packets (❷). These rules are fairly standard in all IPFilter installs, and are widely recommended on any firewall or packet filter you might encounter.

The next two rules are as follows:

```
#the system loopback interface
#we can do anything we like to ourselves.
pass in quick on lo0 all
pass out quick on lo0 all
```

These two rules say that any traffic whatsoever can pass in and out on the loop-back interface. There isn't much point in using groups to optimize these rules, as they're very short and quick.

The first rule group comes after the preceding general rules:

```
#these rules control outbound traffic
❶ pass out on xl0 all head 100
❷ block out from 127.0.0.0/8 to any group 100
❸ block out from any to 127.0.0.0/8 group 100
❹ block out from any to 192.168.1.200/32 group 100
```

These rules control which traffic the server may send to the network. The first rule is very simple, and states that all traffic outbound on the xl0 interface may pass (❶). The most interesting part of this rule is the end, where we start rule group 100. (The number 100 is arbitrarily chosen.) Packets that match this rule will only be compared to rules in group 100.

The second rule is the same sort of rule we looked at earlier, blocking traffic from the loopback interface (❷). We don't need to specify an interface in this rule, as we already know that this rule group only applies to packets going out on the xl0 interface. In short, we're blocking packets going out that we should never be sending.

The next rule blocks a similar sort of illegal packet (❸). If these 127.0.0.0/8 addresses are loopback addresses, we should never try to reach them over the network.

Finally, in the last rule in the group, we block outbound packets to our own address (❹). This is another sort of problem; packets bound for our own system should not actually leave the network card.

Rule group 100 ends here. If a packet is outbound on this interface, and doesn't match any of the other rules in group 100, it will be allowed to go on its merry way. Outbound connections from this machine are running in a default accept stance.

Now, let's consider packets entering the system:

```
#these rules control inbound traffic
❶ block in on xl0 all head 200
❷ block in from 127.0.0.0/8 to any group 200
❸ block in from 192.168.1.200/32 to any group 200
❹ pass in quick proto tcp from any to any port = www keep state group 200
pass in quick proto tcp from any to any port = pop3 keep state group 200
pass in quick proto tcp from any to any port = smtp keep state group 200
#help clients close their connections when they request a service we
#don't offer. This makes our server look faster, and reduces general
#Internet load by a very, very, very small amount
❺ block return-rst in log proto tcp from any to any flags S/SA group 200
❻ block return-icmp(net-unr) in proto udp all group 200
```

The first rule in the preceding group blocks all traffic coming in from the Internet on this interface (we're using a default deny stance for inbound traffic) and it starts rule group 200, another arbitrarily-chosen number (❶). Incoming packets that have made it through the earlier rules will be diverted into this rule.

The second rule blocks anything from a loopback IP (❷). Since it is part of rule group 200, this rule will only be applied to packets that arrive over the network card. There are many possible explanations for such a packet arriving, but none of them are good.

Similarly, the next rule blocks any packet that appears to come from the server's own IP address (❸). These packets should never arrive over the network. Almost the only possible explanation for their presence is an attempted hack.

The next three rules open holes for services that this particular server provides (❹). Use of the quick keyword cuts off all further processing, and the keep state option maintains the connection throughout the request.

The final rules (❺,❻) are perhaps the most difficult to understand. Incoming network requests will remain until they time out. The first of these rules sends a "reset" notice to rejected TCP connections, telling them that their connection request is rejected rather than making the client time out (❺). The last rule does something similar for UDP connections (❻). To describe exactly how this works would require a fairly in-depth explanation of IP. These rules are not only safe, but also polite to other users, and they will reduce network traffic. I highly recommend their use when filtering incoming traffic.

Your typical incoming packet requesting a Web page will go through a total of nine rules. The first two rules will check to see if the packet is too small or contains IP options, and are obviously bogus. The next two will see if the packet is going over the loopback interface. It then checks to see if the packet is going out on the network interface. The packet is coming in, not going out, so all of the rules in group 100 are skipped. Finally, the packet is checked against the rule for incoming packets on the network interface, and drops into rule group 200. There it is checked against two rules for more obviously bogus packets, and is finally approved. Without rule grouping, the packet would go through 12 rules. A 25 percent savings might not seem like much, but it can be very important when processing millions of packets. As your rules grow more complex, the savings will increase.

### IPFilter Logging

IPFilter's ipmon(8) is a separate program that handles logging for the system. IPFilter reads packets as they pass through the kernel, and transmits them to FreeBSD's logging system as the LOCAL0 facility. (See Chapter 19 to learn how to handle this data properly.) The simplest way to use ipmon is to dump the log to syslogd(8) (see Chapter 19) with the -s flag:

```
#ipmon -s
```

# Jail

One of UNIX's oldest security mechanisms is the idea of changed root or *chroot*, which confines a user to a subsection of the filesystem, thus protecting the rest of the filesystem. Chroot is useful for small services, but isn't so helpful when you're hosting dozens (or hundreds!) of clients on a single server, because each client has special needs and each program has its own requirements for chrooting.

Clients who understand the power of UNIX frequently make requests that make an administrator's life difficult. They want to be able to install software or to reconfigure the Web server to enable the latest nifty Apache module. In short, they want root access, and under most UNIX systems you can't hand out root access willy-nilly to clients on a multi-user server.

Unless you're on FreeBSD. FreeBSD administrators faced this problem long ago, and solved it by improving the chroot process dramatically. In fact, they solved it so well that, when using FreeBSD, you can build an entire virtual machine on disk, and isolate that machine from the rest of your system. This is called a *jail*.

Think of a jail as something like a client-server environment. The main server is the host system, and each jailed system is a client. Changes made to the host can be reflected across all systems, but changes to the jail can't affect the main system, unless you allow a jail to fill up a disk drive or some such.

When in jail, clients can have root access and even install whatever nifty toys they desire without interfering with the main system. All processes that are running in the jail are restricted to the jail environment, and the kernel does not give them access to any information not in their jail. The filesystem in the jail does not know about files or filesystems outside the jail. Since no program or process in the jail knows about anything outside the jail, and cannot read or access anything outside the jail, the user is locked in. Not only can the client not break out of the jail, if the jail is hacked the intruder can't break out of the jail. This helps secure your system while meeting client needs.

On modern hardware with cheap disks and gobs of memory, a single FreeBSD system can host dozens of jailed Web servers (though you'd need to be certain that your kernel is well tweaked to allow this many Web servers to run, as discussed in Chapter 4). From a sales perspective, a jailed machine is a good intermediate step between a virtual domain on a shared server and a private colocated server.

## Configuring Your Server to Use Jail

Before you begin using jails, be sure that your server is configured properly. Jails put a number of special requirements on a server, the most annoying of which is that daemons cannot bind to all available IP addresses.

Each jail is tied to a particular IP address, and is defined by that IP address. The jail must have exclusive access to that IP address; nothing else can be using it. If your main server has a daemon that binds to all available IP addresses on the system, that daemon will prevent a jail from starting. If you look at your system's sockstat(1) output, you may notice several entries where the local address resembles "*.22". This means that the daemon is listening on all IP addresses, on that port number. If you want to use a jail, you must reconfigure these daemons to only listen on a single IP address.

Check all of the following daemons before trying to start a jail.

### Portmap

Of the standard FreeBSD daemons, portmap is the most problematic, preventing you from combining NFS and jails. (Since very few systems on the naked Internet use NFS, this usually isn't a problem.)

### Syslogd

Syslogd is another story, because the system logger opens a socket so it can send log messages to other servers. To silence syslogd entirely, set `syslogd_flags="ss"` in /etc/rc.conf, though if you do you won't be able to log remotely. We'll discuss syslogd in detail in Chapter 15.

### Named and sendmail

Other daemons, such as named and sendmail, want to attach to all available addresses. To solve this problem, you can choose to configure them to bind to only a single IP address and run them on the host system, but since you're using jails already, why not set up a "services jail" that contains these daemons? Not only is it easier, but also it allows you to provide an additional layer of security. (While named and sendmail are both quite secure today, they have a spotty history. Many older admins will feel much better if those services are jailed.)

### Inetd

Inetd also attaches to all available addresses, but it is simple enough to control with the -a flag. If your jail host has an IP address of 192.168.1.222, add `inetd_flags="-a 192.168.1.222"` to /etc/rc.conf.

### Sshd

The last problematic network service is sshd. Assume again that your jail server has the IP address of 192.168.1.222. You can tell sshd which port to listen on with the following entry in /etc/ssh/sshd_config:

```
ListenAddress 192.168.1.222
```

Since your jail host is probably not providing any network services itself, you're better off disabling every network daemon except sshd. Ideally, your sockstat output should look something like this:

```
# sockstat -4
USER     COMMAND    PID  FD PROTO  LOCAL ADDRESS       FOREIGN ADDRESS
root     sshd       248   3 tcp4   192.168.1.222:22    *:*
#
```

We have only one daemon listening to the network, sshd. It is listening on a particular IP address (192.168.1.222) and on a particular port. This daemon will not interfere with our jails.

## Configuring Your Kernel to Use Jail

The preceding section takes care of the network part of configuring jail, but we still have some kernel configuration to do. The jail system has three special sysctls:

**jail.set_hostname_allowed**   By default, the root user in a jail can set the hostname of that jail. Since the jail uses its hostname to communicate with the host, changing the hostname can easily confuse an administrator responsible for managing it. You can set this sysctl to 0 to disable changing the hostname.

**jail.socket_unixiproute_only**   A jail defaults to only communicating via IP. While it isn't that likely that a user might want to use, say, UNIX sockets or IPX, it's entirely possible. The jail system only supports IP, however, so if you allow use of these other protocols, you're allowing the user to "leak" out of the jail. They probably can't do anything with that access, but it's unwise to assume that you're smarter than every malicious hacker out there. Set this to 1 to be careful and restrain your users most tightly. Set it to 0 if you do choose to allow the use of any network or socket protocol.

**jail.sysvipc_allowed**   System V IPC is a UNIX standard for allowing interprocess communication via shared memory segments. Basically, related programs can use one chunk of memory to store shared information. By default, IPC cannot be used in a jail, as the jail system does not build separate areas of memory for each jail. Enabling IPC would allow information to leak to and from the jail. Using this weakness to compromise the system would require a skilled attacker, however. You can choose to do allow System V IPC by setting this sysctl to 1. Many database programs require System V IPC.

### Client Setup

Setting up a jail is straightforward, though you will need a FreeBSD source tree (see Chapter 6). For example, say you want to build a jail on the partition /jail1. (Jails can be in directories as well, but putting them on separate partitions gives you a quick-and-dirty method of controlling their size. Other admins will just keep an eye on their users, and raise their rates for disk hogs.) To begin, go to your FreeBSD source tree (generally under /usr/src). For your first jail, run this command:

```
# make world DESTDIR=/jail1
```

This command will build a complete copy of FreeBSD and install it in the directory /jail1.

For all subsequent jails, you don't have to build all the binaries; you can install the ones you built the first time by just running this command:

```
# make installword DESTDIR=/jail1
```

This will copy a complete set of FreeBSD userland programs into the jail.

*Many people have special methods to reduce the amount of space a jail takes up, but the preceding method is the approved one. Search the FreeBSD-security mailing list archives if you're interested in other methods.*

### The /etc Tree

Each jail has its own /etc tree. While not everything in there is functional, it's simpler to ignore the extras than trim them out. You need to grab a copy of the /etc tree from the same source code you used to build your jail, and install it properly in the jail's directory. The commands here do exactly that:

```
# cd /usr/src/etc
# make distribution DESTDIR=/jail1 NO_MAKEDEV_RUN=yes
```

Once you have the /etc directory, you'll need to create the device nodes for the jail. (Since a jail does not require all the device nodes that the full system requires, MAKEDEV has a special target for use in jails.)

```
# cd /jail1/dev
# sh MAKEDEV jail
```

Many programs expect to find a file named /kernel. Even if they don't actually do anything with this file, they're happier when the file exists. (Since you don't want people to be able to touch your actual kernel, tie this fake to a harmless point. That way hostile users can overwrite your jailed kernel all they want, but to no avail.)

```
# cd jail1
# ln -sf dev/null kernel
```

### The IP Address

Now that the directory tree is established, you need to provide an IP address for the jail, since each jail has its own IP address. We'll assume that 192.168.1.223 is our jailed IP address, and use ifconfig to attach this address to our network card.

```
# ifconfig fxp0 alias 192.168.1.223
```

You can make this attachment happen automatically on boot by adding the following to /etc/rc.conf:

```
ifconfig_fxp0_alias0="192.168.1.223"
```

### The Process Filesystem

Finally, every FreeBSD system requires its own process filesystem, or procfs. If you're not using jails, you really don't need to worry about procfs; it appears automatically when you boot the system, cannot be tuned, and programs fairly transparently access it when needed. It's a necessary bit of infrastructure, however. I create a script /usr/local/etc/rc.d/jail.sh and add all the procfs mount lines to this script.

```
# mount -t procfs proc /jail1/proc
```

Your jail is now ready.

### Entering the Jail

Once you have everything configured, use jail(8) to start a jail:

```
# jail <path to jail> <jail hostname> <jail IP> <command>
```

For example, to do basic configuration of our test jail, do this:

```
# jail /jail1 jailhost 192.168.1.223 /bin/tcsh
```

You'll see a shell prompt, at which point you're in single-user mode in your jail and your jail is up and running. You could choose any shell you like in the default install—I like tcsh for interactive use, so that's my example. There are differences between your current state and FreeBSD single-user mode, however. While the jail's startup sequence has not been run, the network is configured by jail.

Some commands are unavailable in a jail. For example, try to add an alias to your network interface, and you'll get a "permission denied" error.

Play around a little, and try to break out of the jail. Try to go to a directory you know exists on the system, but is outside of your jail directory. You're root; try to access processes you know are running on the system. When you're tired of beating your head against that brick wall, explore the jailed system. Powerful UNIX tools like perl(1) and cc(1) are fully available. You could even cvsup in a jail and rebuild world, although this is *not* a good idea. (Remember, your kernel and userland absolutely must be in sync; a jailed userland will not crash the kernel, but it certainly won't work as expected!)

#### Processes

Processes in the jail cannot see the rest of the system. Our host server is running a jail, among many other things. Here's a top snapshot from within a jail running in single-user mode. You can see that the shell process is running, and the top process, but nothing else. You cannot see the processes from the main system.

```
last pid: 10578;  load averages:  0.00,  0.00,  0.00     up 1+09:21:29  19:16:49
2 processes:   1 running, 1 sleeping
CPU states:  0.0% user,  0.0% nice,  0.4% system,  0.0% interrupt, 99.6% idle
Mem: 6708K Active, 27M Inact, 23M Wired, 36K Cache, 61M Buf, 444M Free
Swap: 1024M Total, 1024M Free
  PID USERNAME PRI NICE   SIZE    RES STATE  C   TIME   WCPU    CPU COMMAND
10574 root      20    0  1432K  1116K pause  0   0:00  0.00%  0.00% tcsh
10578 root      96    0  1956K  1136K CPU1   1   0:00  0.00%  0.00% top
```

Now that we have a jail cell, it's time to check in and decorate it a little.

## Final Jail Setup

The jail setup process is not as sophisticated as FreeBSD's installer. To prepare the environment for your jail, you must perform all of the following commands from within the jail.

1. To begin, first create a jailed /etc/rc.conf. Include the following lines:

```
❶ portmap_enable="NO"
❷ network_interfaces=""
❸ sshd_enable="YES"
```

Since portmap will not run well in a jail, we turn it off (❶). Since the jailed system startup will complain if it can't configure the interface, we tell it to ignore its interfaces (❷). And, since you'll have difficulty accessing your jail via a command line once the jail starts, it's easiest to enable sshd on the jail and access it via the network (❸).

2. FreeBSD requires an /etc/fstab file. Since the jail has no filesystem control, an empty one suffices.

```
# touch /etc/fstab
```

3. Because sendmail(8) will complain if the aliases database does not exist, we use newaliases(1) to build the proper database for it. (If you won't be running sendmail in the jail, either because you'll be running postfix, as discussed in Chapter 12, or because you just don't want a mail server here, this isn't an issue.)

```
# newaliases
```

4. Set a root password for the jailed environment. Use one that's different from the host environment—that's part of what a jail is for, after all.

```
# passwd
```

5. Your users will appreciate a correct time zone in the jail. (At least they can watch the seconds tick by in their prison.)

```
# tzsetup
```

### Starting the Jail

From this point on, your jail will resemble a default FreeBSD install in which you can configure nameservice, add packages and users, and so on. Once you exit this shell, though, the virtual machine will stop running and your jail will shut down.

*I highly recommend using packages to add software to jailed servers; building ports can take up a lot of CPU time.*

Your jail is ready to run multi-user, however. To start the jail in its full long-term, multi-user glory, just run the virtual machine's /etc/rc script from within the jail, either by hand or automatically at boot by adding the command to the end of your /usr/local/etc/rc.d/jail.sh script.

To start a jail from the host system, enter this command:

```
# jail /jail1 jailhost 192.168.1.223 /bin/sh /etc/rc
```

*You'll notice several errors on startup. Most of these are sysctls that cannot be accessed in a jailed environment.*

At this point, your jail is running. You can ssh in and configure it exactly as you would any other system.

### Managing Jails

Jails do complicate process management. If you're logged in to the actual jail server, you can see all the processes in all of your jails. Which processes are the actual ones in your server, and which belong to a jail?

Doing a ps -ax on the host system shows all running processes, even jailed ones. A STAT of J means that the process is running in a jail. If you have few jails, each with a dedicated purpose, you might be able to guess which is the process you want. For example, if you only have one nameserver, and it's jailed, it's a good bet which named process you're after.

While you might want to manage processes from outside the jail, the simplest way to manage a jail is from within. To do so, log into your jail as root and use ps -ax and all the other standard process-management tools to control running programs. If you don't want to log into the jail, you have to resort to more difficult control mechanisms.

### Procfs

To investigate individual processes to learn which jail they're part of, use the process filesystem, procfs. (This is perhaps the only time you'll ever need to manually dig around in /proc—it's normally only used by programs such as ps and top.) This procedure is most useful for identifying a jail from a process ID. If you see a database process running amok and soaking up your memory, you can check its PID under /proc to see what jail it's in and act appropriately.

/proc contains a directory for each process running on the system. (If you're bored, you can look through the various files.) To determine which jail a process is part of, first find the directory for the process ID you're interested in, and then look for a file named *status*. The last word in the status file is the host-name of the jail the process is running in. If the process is not jailed, the last word is a hyphen (-).

### Shutting Down a Jail

When you shut down the host server, the various client jails are shut down as well. Shutting down a jail without shutting down the host is only slightly more complicated.

Programs such as shutdown(8) and reboot(8) are useless for shutting down a jail because their main responsibility is to sync and unmount disks, disconnect the network, and so on. A virtual machine does not have those responsibilities.

To shut down a jail, first log in to the jail as root. If your jail is hosting programs that like a nice, safe shutdown, such as databases, you should run the shutdown script to shut them down.

```
# /bin/sh /usr/local/etc/rc.d/programname.sh stop
# /bin/sh /etc/rc.shutdown
```

Once that's done, send the jail's main process (-1) a shutdown signal, also known as signal 15.

```
# kill -15 -1
```

This will shut down all jail processes. Since a jail is only processes, the jail will be shut down at this time.

**NOTE**    *Do not do* `kill -15 -1` *on a nonjailed server. You'll shut down lots of stuff, leaving your system in a fairly useless state similar to single-user mode.*

## Monitoring System Security

So, you think your server is secure. Maybe it is, for now.

Unfortunately, there's a class of intruder with nothing better to do than to keep up on the latest security holes and try them out on systems they think might be vulnerable. Even if you read FreeBSD-security religiously and apply every single patch that comes along, you might still get hacked some day. While there is no way to be absolutely sure that you haven't been hacked, the following hints will help you be aware when something does happen:

- Be familiar with your servers. Run ps -axx on them regularly, and learn what processes normally run on them. If you see a process you don't recognize, investigate.

- Take a look at your open network ports via netstat -na and sockstat. What TCP and UDP ports should your server be listening on? If you don't recognize a port, investigate. Perhaps it's something innocent, but it might be an intruder's backdoor.

- Unexplained system problems are a hint as well. Many intruders are ham-fingered klutzes with few sysadmin skills; they use click-and-drool attacks and think that they're tough. (Truly skilled intruders can not only clean up after themselves, but also ensure that the system has no problems so that you won't be alerted.) Unexplained reboots might be a sign of a new kernel being installed. They might also be a sign of failing hardware or bad configuration, so they should be investigated anyway.

There are two security tools I particularly recommend for becoming familiar with your system. The first is lsof(8) (/usr/ports/sysutils/lsof), which lists all open files on your computer. Reading this is an education in and of itself; you probably had no idea that your Web server opened so much crud. Seeing strange files open indicates that you're either not familiar with your system or someone's doing something you probably don't want her to do.

The second tool is nessus(8) (/usr/ports/security/nessus). It's an automated vulnerability scanner. Running security audits on your own machines is an excellent way to see what an attacker might see on your systems.

## If You're Hacked

There's no easy answer for what to do if your system is hacked. Huge books are written on the subject. Here are some general suggestions, however.

First of all, a hacked system cannot be trusted. If someone has gained root access on your Internet server, she could have replaced any program on the system. Even if you close the hole she got in through, she could have installed a hacked version of login that sends your username and password to an IRC channel somewhere. Don't trust your system. An upgrade will not cleanse your system, as even sysinstall and the compiler are suspect.

Feel free to write FreeBSD-security@FreeBSD.org for some advice. Describe what you're seeing, and why you think you're hacked. Be prepared for the final answer, though: reinstall your operating system from known secure media (FTP or CD-ROM), and restore your data from backup. (You did read Chapter 3, right?)

A good security process will increase your chances of never being hacked. Good luck.

# 9

## TOO MUCH INFORMATION ABOUT /ETC

The /etc directory holds the basic configuration information needed to boot a UNIX system. Every time I encounter an unfamiliar UNIX, one of the first things I do is scope out /etc.

The fastest way to go from a junior UNIX admin to a mid-grade one is to read /etc. Yes, all of it. Yes, this is a lot of reading. But understanding /etc means that you understand how the system hangs together. As you progress as a UNIX admin you're going to pick up this information piecemeal anyway, so you might as well make it easy on yourself and assemble this portion of your toolkit at the beginning.

Many /etc files are discussed in a chapter where they're most relevant (such as /etc/services in Chapter 5. This chapter will cover the important files that don't quite fit anywhere else.

## Varieties of /etc Files

Different UNIX systems use different /etc files. In many cases, these files are simply renamed or restructured files from BSD4.3 or BSD4.4. The first time I encountered an IBM AIX box, for example, I went looking for a BSD-style /etc/fstab. It wasn't there. But a little hunting led me to /etc/filesystems, which turned out to be an IBM-specific rearranged version of /etc/fstab. Knowing that the information existed somewhere in /etc, and knowing what files it obviously wasn't in, made the search quite short.

Even radically different FreeBSD systems have almost identical /etc directories. While some add-on programs insert their own files here, you can expect certain files to be on every FreeBSD system you encounter.

*Before you touch any /etc files, review the information on RCS (Revision Control System) in Chapter 3. I strongly recommend that you create an /etc/RCS directory and use it religiously when experimenting. Changes in /etc can completely disable your system. While recovering a system's scrambled filesystem table can help turn a competent administrator into a good one, it's one of the least pleasant ways to get there.*

## Default Files

The files in FreeBSD's /etc/defaults/ directory each contain variable assignments. These files are not intended to be edited by the administrator; instead, they're designed to be overridden by a file of the same name directly under /etc.

For example, the upgrade process completely replaces the files in /etc/defaults. While every new version of FreeBSD has a slightly different default configuration, the developers go to great lengths to ensure that changes to these files are backward-compatible. This means that you won't have to go through the upgraded configuration and manually merge in your changes; at most you'll have to check out the new defaults file for nifty new configuration opportunities.

### /etc/defaults/rc.conf

One commonly used file is /etc/defaults/rc.conf. It contains dozens of lines like this:

```
"named_enable="NO"
```

To change this setting, edit /etc/rc.conf, not /etc/defaults/rc.conf. When editing /etc/rc.conf, list the variable you want to change and what you want to set it to. Your /etc/rc.conf entry will then override what's in /etc/defaults/rc.conf. (Do not just copy the default file to /etc! This causes any number of problems.)

*While the system install process creates /etc/rc.conf, it's normal to find that you need to create other override files in /etc.*

Once you understand the various default files, you can easily assess an unfamiliar FreeBSD system simply by checking the corresponding override files in /etc.

### /etc/adduser.conf

Creating new users on some UNIX systems is a pain, requiring you to manually edit /etc/passwd, rebuild the password database, edit /etc/group, create a home directory, install the various dotfiles, and so on. FreeBSD's adduser(8) program makes it much simpler to add users by running all these other programs for you. The adduser.conf file holds adduser's default settings. These variables are easily set just by putting the name, an equal sign, and the value. You can add comments just by putting a pound sign in front of them. Here's a sample entry from this file, with its related comment:

```
# verbose = [0-2]
verbose = 1
```

### Verbose

The first entry, verbose, controls how much you see when running adduser. · With verbose = 0, adduser prompts you for the new user information and nothing else. If you set verbose = 1, adduser lets you rewrite /etc/adduser.conf before adding a new user. If you set verbose = 2, adduser gives you a great many warnings, questions, and other information. (While the default is 1, you can easily set this to 0 once you're familiar with the process, and have adduser.conf set up the way you like it.)

### Defaultpasswd

The defaultpasswd entry, either yes or no, controls whether users have a password set by default. If you have a passwordless account on your system, anyone who knows the username can connect to your system. In any circumstance where you have even the mildest concern for security, set this to yes.

### Dotdir

The dotdir entry contains the path for sample user dotfiles, such as .cshrc, .login, and so on. The default directory contains reasonable defaults. If you want to create custom dotfiles for your system, it's best to make your own directory under /usr/local/share/skel so that system upgrades won't overwrite your changes (see Chapter 6).

### Send_message

If you put a full path to a file in send_message, adduser sends each new user a welcome message. If you set this to no, no message will be sent.

The adduser message uses variables; you can add your own by editing /usr/sbin/adduser. If you're familiar with Perl, this isn't difficult; if not, you're better off just using the variables offered: $username, $fullname, and $password. (Since this message is mailed to the new user, including the password is somewhat useless in addition to foolish. Too, the user has presumably used his password to retrieve this message, so he should have it.) Go ahead and create your own message instead of using the brief and generic default if you wish. I generally use an /etc/adduser.message somewhat like this, substituting the appropriate company name as needed:

```
$fullname,

Welcome to The Company.

Help is available at 800-555-1212, or online at
http://helpdesk.companyname.com.

Use of this account is governed by our acceptable use policy,
available at http://aup.companyname.com or on this system in
/usr/local/share/company/aup.

Thank you for your business. We look forward to serving you.

The Company Support Staff.
```

### Logfile
The logfile setting tells adduser where to write a log of everything it does. The default works.

### Home
If your system has unusual partitioning, you might want user directories in a different place than the usual /home. You can control this with the home setting.

### Path
If you install software in an unusual location, you might need to change the path entry. (Some systems have their additional programs stored in /opt.)

### Shellpref
The shellpref setting stores the list of available shells, in order of preference. If you add or remove a shell, you need to correct this.

### Defaultshell
The defaultshell setting contains, as you might guess, the default user shell.

### Defaultgroup
The defaultgroup entry is a little different. FreeBSD assigns a unique group to each user. For example, when you add the user mwlucas, it tries to create a group mwlucas (which allows greater flexibility when assigning permissions). To have every user be a member of a particular group, put the name of the group here; otherwise, leave this set to USER.

### Defaultclass

The defaultclass line controls what login.conf (see /etc/login.conf) class that adduser assigns by default. You can leave this empty, or assign a class from those you have previously configured in /etc/login.conf.

### Uid_start

Finally, the uid_start variable determines the user ID (UID) number that adduser will begin with; the default is 1000. You might want to change this number to match UIDs across multiple operating systems; various Linux distributions start with different UID numbers, for example. But if UID synchronization isn't important to you, don't worry about this setting.

### /etc/crontab

The crontab file controls the FreeBSD job scheduler, *cron*, which allows the administrator to have the system run a command at any time.

Each user has a separate crontab file, which can be edited with crontab -e. The /etc/crontab file is the system's file. Unlike user crontabs, /etc/crontab lets the sysadmin specify which user will run a job. For example, the sysadmin can basically say, "Run this job at 10 PM Tuesdays as root, and run this other job at 7 AM every day as nobody." Other users can only run jobs as themselves.

**NOTE**    *The /etc/crontab file is considered a FreeBSD system file. Be careful not to overwrite this file when you upgrade (see Chapter 6). One way to simplify upgrading /etc/crontab is to set your custom entries at the end of the file, marked off with a few lines of hash marks (#).*

### Environment Statements

The /etc/crontab file begins with some environment statements because cron needs to set up a shell environment for the programs it starts. If you're familiar with shell programming, you can alter these statements to fit your system, but be careful when making blanket changes because changes made at the top of /etc/crontab affect all programs run from the crontab. (You can specify environment variables on the command line for each command you run from cron.)

Here are some typical environment variables as set in /etc/crontab on a FreeBSD 4.5-STABLE system.

```
#
SHELL=/bin/sh
PATH=/etc:/bin:/sbin:/usr/bin:/usr/sbin
HOME=/
#
```

The hash marks are comments or empty lines used to separate entries and make the file somewhat easier to read.

Beneath the environment information, the crontab file is divided into eight columns, forming a table. The first five columns represent the time the command should run: minute, hour, day of the month, month of the year, and day of the week, in that order. An asterisk (*) in any column means "every one," while a number means "at this exact time."

Following the time columns is the username the job runs as, then the command. User crontab files are almost identical, lacking only the username column.

### Specifying Times

You must use a valid number for times in crontab. The rule is that minutes, hours, and days of the week start with 0, and days of the month and months begin with 1. Also, thanks to an ancient disagreement between AT&T and BSD, the day of the week uses both 7 and 0 for Sunday.

For example, to have user dbadmin run the program /usr/local/bin/db-backup.sh at 55 minutes after each hour, every day to infinity, your crontab line would look like this:

```
55      *    *    *    *       dbadmin /usr/local/bin/db-backup.sh
```

Asterisks tell cron to run this job every hour, every day of the month, every month, and every weekday.

To run this job only at 1:55 PM each day, you would use the following:

```
55      13   *    *    *       dbadmin /usr/local/bin/db-backup.sh
```

Here, 13 represents 1:00 PM on the 24-hour clock, and 55 the number of minutes past the hour.

One common mistake people make when using cron is to specify a large unit of time, but miss the small one. For example, suppose you entered the following, intending to run a job every day at 8 AM:

```
*       8    *    *    *       dbadmin /usr/local/bin/db-backup.sh
```

In this case, you'd find that the job would run at 8 AM, all right, as well as at 8:01, 8:02, 8:03, and so on, until 9:00 AM. If your job takes more than one minute to run, you'll quickly bring your system to its knees.

The correct way to specify 8 AM and only 8 AM would be to enter this:

```
0       8    *    *    *       dbadmin /usr/local/bin/db-backup.sh
```

To specify ranges of time, such as running this program once an hour, every hour, between 8 AM and 6 PM, Monday through Friday, use something like this:

```
1       8-18 *    *    1-5     dbadmin /usr/local/bin/db-backup.sh
```

To specify exact times, separate them with commas:

```
1   8,10,12,15,18   *    *    1-5     dbadmin /usr/local/bin/db-backup.sh
```

Or, more interestingly, you can specify fractions of time, or *steps*. For example, to run a program every five minutes, enter the following:

```
*/5    *    *    *    *         dbadmin /usr/local/bin/db-backup.sh
```

You can also combine ranges with steps. For example, if you want your job to run every five minutes, but want it offset by one minute from the preceding job, you could use this:

```
1-56/5  *    *    *    *         dbadmin /usr/local/bin/db-backup.sh
```

You can control the day a job runs with two fields: the day of the month and the day of the week. If you specify both a day of the month and a day of the week, the job will run whenever either condition is met. For example, you might tell cron to "Run this job on the 1st and the 15th, plus every Monday" as follows:

```
55    13    *    1,15    1      dbadmin /usr/local/bin/db-backup.sh
```

If you find that a job requires a nonstandard environment, set the environment on the command line just as you would in the shell. For example, if your db-backup.sh program requires a LD_LIBRARY_PATH environment variable, you can set it like so:

```
55  * * * *   dbadmin LD_LIBRARY_PATH=/usr/local/dblib ;/usr/local/bin/db-
backup.sh
```

### /etc/csh.*

The /etc/csh.* files contain systemwide defaults for csh and tcsh. When a user logs in with either of these shells, the shell executes any commands it finds in /etc/csh.login. Similarly, when the user logs out, /etc/csh.logout is executed. You can place general shell configuration information in /etc/csh.cshrc.

### /etc/dhclient.conf

Many operating systems give you very basic DHCP client configuration with no opportunity to fine-tune or customize it; you either use it or you don't. Any operating system that uses the Internet Software Consortium's DHCP client, including all of the BSDs, lets you fine-tune your DHCP client setup.

In most cases, an empty DHCP client file (/etc/dhclient.conf) will give you full DHCP functionality, but won't work correctly in all situations. Perhaps you're connecting to a DHCP server across the country, your local LAN is having problems, or you have multiple DHCP servers. You may be able to solve these problems by tweaking your DHCP configuration. A DHCP lease contains your network configuration information, such as the IP address you get, the default route, and the nameservers available for your use. Without a valid, correct lease, you won't have Internet connectivity.

Entries in dhclient.conf resemble C code and generally include a variable declaration, followed by a value. Each line ends in a semicolon.

### Prolonging Lease Requests

When dhclient starts, it requests the last IP address it used (leased) and, by default, spends ten seconds trying to get that address. The reboot time is the length of time the client will spend trying to get the old address re-issued. To change this waiting time, use the reboot statement. For example, I've been on large corporate networks where the DHCP server was in another state; by adjusting the reboot time upwards, I could easily get my previous network address. Just specify the reboot time in dhclient.conf, with a trailing semicolon in standard C code style.

```
reboot 20;
```

If the client cannot get its previous IP address in the reboot time, it will request a new one instead.

### Rejecting Bad DHCP Servers

One of dhclient's more interesting features is its ability to reject bad DHCP servers. For example, some networks allow just about anyone to hook just about anything to them, like the ones found on exhibition floors or at some development companies. In such situations it's quite possible for there to be a rogue DHCP server on the floor, and if your system receives a DHCP lease that just doesn't work, it might be from a rogue server.

To identify a bad DHCP server, examine the leases you have received in /var/db/dhclient.leases. This file lists all the leases you have ever received, including the bad one. Identifying a bad DHCP server is a matter of trial and error. Get the IP address of each DHCP server, and reject them one at a time until you get a working configuration. For example, if the bad server's address was 192.168.1.84, enter

```
reject 192.168.1.84
```

**NOTE**   *If you find a rogue DHCP server on one of your networks, it's much better to find and disable the rogue server than to patch around it with a reject statement. On a foreign network, however, you don't generally have the privilege to do that.*

**Announcing Host Information**

If you are on someone else's network and feel like being kind to the local network administrator, add a send statement to your dhclient.conf. The DHCP server will record the information you put in your send statement in its lease database. The local network administrator can use this information to find you if your system starts misbehaving and damaging the network. (You might not think this is a good thing, but making yourself easy to find is much better than making the administrator hunt you down.)

```
send host-name "mwlucas-laptop.bigcompany.com";
```

Of the many other options in dhclient.conf, like the ability to refuse leases that don't include information you want, most are relatively useless under normal (and most abnormal) circumstances. For truly detailed information on dhclient's more exotic options read dhclient.conf(5).

### /etc/fstab

The /etc/fstab file describes the filesystems on the system. For details on the File System Table, see Chapter 16.

### /etc/ftp.*

The /etc/ftp.* files control how the system's FTP server behaves. For details on /etc/ftpusers, /etc/ftpchroot, /etc/ftpwelcome, /etc/ftpmotd, and general FTP operations, see Chapter 15's nice little write-up on FTP.

### /etc/hosts.allow

The /etc/hosts.allow file controls who can access daemons compiled with TCP Wrappers support. It's covered in painful detail in Chapter 8.

### /etc/hosts.equiv

The /etc/hosts.equiv file allows trusted remote systems to log in or run commands on the local system without providing a password or even logging in. Hosts listed in this file are assumed to have performed user authentication on a trusted system, and hence the local system doesn't have to bother re-authenticating the user.

This file is handy and useful on friendly networks, but, unfortunately, there is no such thing as a friendly network nowadays. In fact, any one disgruntled employee can destroy a corporate network with this service. A machine running /etc/hosts.equiv on the naked Internet is pretty much dog meat for the first script kiddie who wanders by. In fact, /etc/hosts.equiv and its related services have even bitten top-notch security experts.

Still, should you decide to use this risky feature, you must have rsh or rlogin, or both, enabled in /etc/inetd.conf (see Chapter 13). The format is simple: a hostname, followed by an optional username.

For example, assume you have two UNIX boxes, "daffy" and "bugs". If bugs's /etc/hosts.equiv includes "daffy", a user on daffy can get a shell on bugs without typing a password.

```
daffy; rlogin bugs
Last login: Tue Apr  3 19:12:08 from 192.168.1.200
Copyright (c) 1980, 1983, 1986, 1988, 1990, 1991, 1993, 1994
        The Regents of the University of California.  All rights reserved.

FreeBSD 5.0-CURRENT (PETULANCE) #0: Mon Aug 21 12:27:59 EDT 2000
You have mail.
bugs;logout
rlogin: connection closed.
daffy;
```

See? No password. This works well, unless some intruder has broken into daffy. Remember, if you use this tool, a compromise on one machine means that every machine on your network is compromised. Rlogin and related tools are *really* unsuitable for any modern networked environment.

With comparatively recent modifications to rlogin and rsh, you can require a password to access another system. If you're going to do that, however, you might as well implement things properly and start using ssh (see Chapter 13).

### /etc/hosts.lpd

The /etc/hosts.lpd file is one of the simplest files in /etc. Hosts listed here, each on their own line, may print to the printer(s) controlled by this machine. While you can use hostnames, DNS problems can choke printing, so use IP addresses instead.

Unlike many other UNIX configuration files, this one does not accept network numbers or netmasks; you must list individual hostnames or IP addresses.

### /etc/inetd.conf

The inetd daemon handles incoming network connections for smaller daemons that don't run frequently. For details, see the section on inetd in Chapter 13.

### /etc/locate.rc

The locate(1) program finds all files of a given name. For example, to find locate.rc, enter the following:

```
# locate locate.rc
/etc/locate.rc
/usr/share/examples/etc/locate.rc
/usr/src/usr.bin/locate/locate/locate.rc
#
```

You'll see that locate.rc can be found in three places. One is in the main /etc directory, the second is in the system examples directory, and the third is in the system source code.

Once a week your FreeBSD system scans its disks, builds a list of everything it finds, and stores that list in a database. The list-building program uses the values shown in /etc/locate.rc as defaults (/etc/locate.rc does not affect how locate(1) itself runs). To change some of those parameters, and thereby change how your locate database is built and what it contains, consider setting the following in /etc/locate.rc:

- The file-finding program stores its temporary files in TMPDIR. If you're low on space in your system temporary directory, you can change this path.
- The location of the weekly database can be changed via the FCODES variable. This can have repercussions on other parts of the locate system, however, so be prepared for odd results.
- The SEARCHPATHS value lists every directory you want searched. This defaults to /, the whole disk; to index only a portion of your disk, set a specific value here.
- The PRUNEPATHS value lists directories you don't want to index. This defaults to excluding temporary directories that traditionally contain only short-lived files.
- The FILESYSTEMS variable controls the sort of filesystem you want to index. The default is UFS, the standard FreeBSD filesystem, but you can list other filesystem types, such as MD (memory disks) or NFS (network filesystem). If you have foreign filesystems mounted, such as an EXT2FS partition, you might want to include them as well. (By the way, indexing network filesystems is a bad idea; if all of your servers start indexing the fileserver, you will bog down the network badly.)

### /etc/login.access

Some servers have hundreds of users, each with different needs. So how do you assign different privileges to each?

FreeBSD includes a few different ways to control user access. The /etc/login.access file controls a user's ability to log in. Every time you try to open a connection to a FreeBSD system, the permissions in login.access are checked first. If login.access contains rules that forbid logins from that user, the login attempt fails immediately. This file defaults to empty, meaning there are no restrictions on anyone with a username and password.

The /etc/login.access file has three colon-delimited fields. The first either grants (+) or denies (-) the right to log in; the second is a list of users or groups; and the third is a list of connection sources.

The /etc/login.access file permits an "all" and "all except" syntax, much like /etc/hosts.allow uses for TCP Wrappers (see Chapter 8), allowing the administrator to make basic but expressive rules. The login program checks rules on a first-fit basis, rather than a best fit. When the system finds a rule where both the group and the connection source match, it immediately accepts or rejects the connection. As such, rule order is very important.

For example, to only allow members of the wheel group and the user root to log in to the system console, you might try to use:

```
+:wheel root:console
```

The problem with this rule, though, is that it doesn't actually deny users login privileges. Since the default is to accept logins, and all this entry does is explicitly grant login rights to two sets of users, this won't stop people from logging in.[1] Other rules will continue to be processed. If my username is javerage, and I try to log in to the console, this rule doesn't deny me access.

So rather than use a statement like the preceding one, try one like this, the inverse:

```
-:ALL EXCEPT wheel root:console
```

This will reject connections more quickly, and run less risk of administrator error. As a rule, it's best to build your lists by rejecting logins, rather than permitting them.

When applying this rule, we see that Joe Average matches this rule and is immediately rejected. Since rules are applied based on first fit, there's no chance that a later rule will match, so we avoid unintended access.

**Connection Source**

The last field in the /etc/login.access file, the connection source, has the greatest variety of values. You can use several different types of information here: hostnames, host addresses, network numbers, domain names, LOCAL, and ALL.

*Hostnames*

Hostnames rely upon DNS or the hosts file. If you suspect your nameserver might suffer a hack at some time, you probably don't want to use this system; intruders can give a hostname any IP address that they like, and fool your system into accepting the connection. Still, you could do this:

```
-:ALL EXCEPT wheel:fileserver.mycompany.com
```

Users in your wheel group could log in from the fileserver, but nobody else could.

```
ALL
```

ALL means always match. This is particularly useful in combination with EXCEPT, as we'll see next.

[1] Remember Chapter 8? This is a default accept security stance.

### Host Addresses and Networks

Host addresses look like hostnames, but they're immune to spoofed DNS.

```
-:ALL EXCEPT wheel:169.254.8.3
```

A network number is anything that ends in a period, like this:

```
-:ALL EXCEPT wheel:169.254.8.
```

This would allow anyone in the wheel group to log in from a machine whose IP address began with 169.254.8, and deny everyone else.

For example, if you didn't want anyone to access your firewall unless they logged in from a management workstation, you could do something like this:

```
-:ALL EXCEPT wheel:ALL EXCEPT 192.168.89.128 192.168.170.33
```

### LOCAL

The most complicated location is LOCAL, which matches any hostname without a dot in it (generally only hosts in the local domain). For example, www.AbsoluteBSD.com thinks that any host in "AbsoluteBSD.com" matches LOCAL.

This works via reverse DNS (see Chapter 12), which is the process where you look up a host's name from its IP address—this process is controlled by the owner of the IP address. Although my laptop might claim a hostname of pedicular.AbsoluteBSD.com, its IP address has reverse DNS that claims it is somewhere in the home.com network. A machine in AbsoluteBSD.com will think that my laptop has a hostname that is in the home.com domain, and hence is not local. As such, I can't use the LOCAL verification method.

So, how can we tie all this together? For one thing, we can use a one-line login.access to allow administrators to log in to the server while rejecting all other remote connections:

```
-:ALL EXCEPT wheel:ALL
```

However, this might restrict your environment too tightly if, for example, your company has staff groups. Two common groups are "dns" (people who can edit domain zone files) and "www" (people who can edit Web server configurations). Servers such as these might find this login.access appropriate:

```
-:ALL EXCEPT wheel dns www:ALL
```

A common corporate Web servers' farm login.access file looks like this:

```
-:ALL EXCEPT wheel:console
-:ALL EXCEPT wheel dns www:ALL
```

Set up this entry one time, and users cannot log in unless you add them to a permitted group.

### /etc/login.conf

If the all-or-nothing control of /etc/login.access doesn't fit your needs, you can provide more specific controls with /etc/login.conf. This file allows you to tweak the environment you present to specific users and limit the resources you allow them to have.

The login.conf system works by defining classes and assigning each user to a class. Each class has limits on its access to system resources. When you change the limits on the class, those limits affect all users in that class. You set a user's class when you create the user's account, and change it by running chsh username as root.

#### Class Definitions

Each class definition consists of a series of variable assignments. When a user logs in, login(1) checks these variables to establish the user's resource limits, accounting, and environment setup.

The default /etc/login.conf starts with the "default" class, the class used by accounts without any other class. This class gives the user basically unlimited access to system resources. If the default class fits your needs, don't adjust this file at all. (If you need to throttle users, read on.)

Each entry in the class definition begins and ends with a colon, although technically, each entry is all one line. The backslash character is a continuation character (indicating that the computer should ignore the line break), which allows the file to be arranged in a human-readable format. Here's a sample of the beginning of one class in a standard login.conf:

```
default:\
        :passwd_format=md5:\
        :copyright=/etc/COPYRIGHT:\
        :welcome=/etc/motd:\
...
```

This class is called *default*. I've shown three variables in this class (there are more, but this is enough to give you the idea). The variable passwd_format, for example, is set to md5. Each login class contains these variables and assignments. You can change a user's experience on the system by assigning her to the class that configures her environment as you desire.

Some login.conf variables don't have a value; they change account behavior just by being present. For example, the "requirehome" variable just needs to be in the class definition to have its effect.

```
        :requirehome:\
```

## Making Changes Take Effect

After you edit login.conf, you must update your login database to make the changes take effect:

```
# cap_mkdb /etc/login.conf
```

FreeBSD's default /etc/login.conf includes several classes of users. If you want an idea of what sort of restrictions to put on users for various situations, check that file. The following section will give you an idea of some of the things that can be set here.

## Resource Limits

Resource limits allow you to control how much of the system any one user can tie up at one time. If you have several hundred users logged in to one machine, and one of those users decides to compile 30MB of source code, that person can consume far more than his fair share of processor time and memory. By limiting the resources that one user can monopolize at one time, you can make the system more responsive for less needy users.

Resource limits are frequently tied to each process, so you need to consider that when assigning limits. If you give each process 20MB of RAM, and allow 20 processes per user, you might as well not be using resource limits at all, since you're assigning 400MB of RAM to each user. Each user class can have its own resource limits.

Table 9-1 describes the resource-limiting login.conf variables.

**Table 9-1: Login.conf variables for limiting resource use**

| Variable | Description |
| --- | --- |
| cputime | The maximum CPU time any process may use |
| filesize | The maximum size of any one file |
| datasize | The maximum memory size of data that can be consumed by one process |
| stacksize | The maximum amount of memory on the stack usable by a process |
| coredumpsize | The maximum size of a core dump |
| memoryuse | The maximum amount of memory a process can lock |
| maxproc | The maximum number of processes the user can have running |
| openfiles | The maximum number of open files per process |
| sbsize | The maximum socket buffer size a user's application can consume |

### Current and Maximum Resource Limits

You can specify *current* and *maximum* resource limits. Current limits (-cur) are generally advisory, and the user can override them at will. (This works well on a cooperative system, where multiple users willingly share resources.) Maximum limits (-max) are absolute, and the user cannot raise them. You can use current limits to warn the user that they are trying to exceed the standard resource allocation.

To specify a current limit, add -cur to the limit name. To make a hard limit, add -max. For example, to set a current limit on the number of processes the user can have, do this:

```
maxproc-cur: 30
maxproc-max: 60
```

If you don't specify either -cur or -max, both the current and maximum limit are set to the value you specify.

### Specifying Default Environment Settings

You can also specify default environment settings in /etc/login.conf. This can be better than setting them in a user's default .cshrc or .profile, as these settings affect all user accounts immediately upon each user's next login.

All of the environment fields recognize two special characters: the tilde (~) and the dollar sign ($). The tilde (~) is replaced by the user's home directory, the dollar sign ($) by the username. For example, in the default class, the line that sets the environment variable MAIL to /var/mail/$ becomes /var/mail, followed by the user's username. Similarly, ~bin in the path entry points to the bin directory in the user's home directory.

Table 9-2 identifies some common environment settings.

**Table 9-2: Common login.conf environment variables**

| Variable | Description |
| --- | --- |
| hushlogin | If present in class definition, no system information is given out during the initial login. |
| ignorenologin | If present in class definition, the user can log in even when a /var/run/nologin file exists. |
| manpath | The default path to search for man pages. |
| nologin | If present, the user cannot log in. This is identical to an entry in /etc/login.access (described earlier). |
| path | The default path for programs. |
| priority | The default process priority, or nice (see Chapter 18). |
| requirehome | If present in the class definition, the user must have a valid home directory in order to log in. |
| setenv | A list of default environment variables. |
| shell | The full path of a shell to be executed upon login. This overrides the shell listed in /etc/passwd. The user's $SHELL environment variable will contain the shell listed in /etc/passwd, however, resulting in an inconsistent environment. Playing games with this is an excellent way to annoy your users. |
| term | The default terminal type. Just about anything that tries to set a terminal type can override it. |

*(continued on next page)*

| timezone | The default value of the $TZ environment variable. Users can override this. |
| umask | The default umask (see builtin(1)). Users can override this. |
| welcome | The full path to a file containing a welcome message for users in this class. The default is /etc/motd. (Different welcome messages can provide instructions and messages to different sorts of users.) |

### Controlling Password and Login Options

You can control various password and login options in /etc/login.conf. Unlike the environment setup, many of these can only be set in this file. Here are some common authentication options.

**minpasswordlen**   Minpasswordlen specifies the minimum length of a password. This only takes effect the next time the user changes his or her password; it doesn't go through and check that all passwords are of this length. The following example will really, really annoy your users.

```
      :minpasswordlen=28:\
```

**passwd_format**   The passwd_format option sets the encryption hash used to encrypt passwords in /etc/passwd. This defaults to md5 for MD5 hashing. Other permissible options are des and blf (blowfish). DES is most useful when you want to share passwords between different operating systems. Blowfish might be an inherently cool algorithm, but it isn't really necessary unless you want to share password files between FreeBSD and OpenBSD systems.

**mixpasswordcase**   If mixpasswordcase is present, users cannot change their passwords to contain only lowercase letters.

**copyright**   The copyright option specifies the full path to a file containing copyright information for the system.

**host.allow**   Users in a class with this value set can use rlogin and rsh to log in to this server from the hosts specified, much like /etc/hosts.allow permits. (This does not make rlogin or rsh safe, and should be strongly discouraged.) The entry is a comma-delimited list, and can use an asterisk (*) as a wildcard to match networks or domains. A system must appear in both /etc/hosts.allow and this entry.

```
:host.allow=192.168.1.*:\
```

**host.deny**   This variable lists remote hosts that cannot log in using accounts in this class. This functionality overlaps /etc/login.access, allowing you to deny logins by particular accounts from particular IP addresses.

If host.deny conflicts with host.allow, host.deny takes precedence. As in host.allow, you can use an asterisk (*) as a wildcard to match entire networks or domains. Any host not listed in host.deny may connect as one of the users in the class.

**times.allow**   Times.allow specifies the times when the user may log in. This requires a comma-delimited field of days and times. Days are given as the first two letters of the day's name (Su, Mo, Tu, We, Th, Fr, and Sa). Time is in standard 24-hour format. For example, if a user can only log in on Wednesdays, between 8 AM and 5 PM, you would use this entry:

```
times.allow=We8-17:\
```

**times.deny**   Times.deny specifies times when the user cannot log in. Note that this does not kick a user off when he's already logged in. The format is the same as for times.allow. If times.allow and times.deny overlap, times.deny takes precedence.

### Accounting Functions

You can set a variety of accounting functions in /etc/login.conf, and these functions require system accounting to be on. Accounting isn't as important today as it was when inexpensive computers cost tens of thousands of dollars, so we won't discuss it in this book. Still, you might as well know that the capability exists.

## /etc/mail/mailer.conf

You can choose from several mail-server programs when using FreeBSD, and the mailer.conf file allows you to control which mailer you will use on your system with a minimum of fuss.

Traditionally, the only mail server program available for any UNIX was sendmail(8). As such, a lot of add-on software expects to find /usr/sbin/sendmail, and expects it to behave in a certain manner. Since programs expected to find sendmail, when replacement mail-server programs were finally created, they generally accepted the same command-line options as the original sendmail, and even were installed as /usr/sbin/sendmail, so that these packages would continue to work.

The only problem with this sendmail compatibility is that an admin on an unfamiliar system has no idea what the /usr/sbin/sendmail program really is! If someone has installed a few different mail servers to experiment with, you'll have to resort to detective work and a bit of luck just to identify your so-called sendmail.

The /etc/mail/mailer.conf file does an end-run around all this mess by eliminating /usr/sbin/sendmail as a mail program. Instead, sendmail is just a little program that checks mailer.conf and redirects the request to the mail-sending program indicated.

**NOTE**    *As yet another piece of legacy fun from the early days of UNIX, sendmail behaved differently depending on which name it was called by. The most common variant names for sendmail are send-mail, mailq, and newaliases.*

The mailer.conf file simply contains a list of program names, along with the path to the actual program to be called. For example, the Postfix mail server (described in Chapter 14) installs as /usr/local/sbin/sendmail. An appropriate mailer.conf entry looks like this.

```
sendmail        /usr/local/sbin/sendmail
send-mail       /usr/local/sbin/sendmail
mailq           /usr/local/sbin/sendmail
newaliases      /usr/local/sbin/sendmail
```

### /etc/make.conf and /etc/defaults/make.conf

To *make* a program is to build it from source code into machine language, also known as *compiling*. (We'll discuss that in some detail in Chapter 10.) The make.conf files control how that building process works. Make.conf is one of the more complex and interesting BSD features; the /etc/make.conf file controls how software is built on the local system.

Like a few other FreeBSD configuration files, make.conf is actually two files: /etc/defaults/make.conf and /etc/make.conf. As with all other files in /etc/default, /etc/default/make.conf is not designed to be edited directly. Instead, entries in /etc/make.conf override entries in /etc/defaults/make.conf. This way, an upgrade can safely overwrite /etc/default/make.conf.

By default, everything in /etc/default/make.conf is commented out. To set something, copy the relevant line from the default make.conf to /etc/make.conf, and remove the pound sign (#) to uncomment it.

In many cases, the settings in /etc/defaults/make.conf are optimizations that are not set by default, for one reason or another. Some produce bad code in certain situations; others just slow down the build process. Some settings are optional or aren't supported by FreeBSD developers. (In general, the examples given are safe; when investigating options in /etc/defaults/make.conf, be sure to pay careful attention to any notes.)

Many of the options in /etc/defaults/make.conf should only be touched by people very familiar with the FreeBSD build process. Quite a few are generally safe for anyone to use, however, and we'll look at the major safe ones here.

**NOTE**    *While the samples that follow are taken directly from a FreeBSD 4-stable system, check /etc/defaults/make.conf for any changes. This is not an area where you want surprises.*

**CPUTYPE=i686**  By default, the compiler builds programs without optimizing for the CPU on the system, though optimizing for a particular CPU can dramatically improve performance. One good example of this is OpenSSL, which FreeBSD uses to handle cryptographic functions for SSH and its related programs.

FreeBSD recognizes the CPU types for the 32-bit X86 systems listed in Table 9-3.

**Table 9-3: CPU types recognized in 32-bit X86 systems**

| CPU Type | Description |
| --- | --- |
| k7 | The AMD k7 processor |
| k6-2 | The AMD k6-2 processor |
| k6 | The original AMD k6 processor |
| k5 | The AMD k5 processor |
| p3 | The Pentium 3 |
| p2 | The Pentium 2 |
| i686 | Generic Intel Pentium 2 or better |
| i586/mmx | Original Pentium with MMX |
| i586 | Original Pentium |
| i486 | 486-class CPU |
| i386 | 386-class CPU |

**CFLAGS= -O -pipe**  This option specifies optimization settings for building non-kernel programs. The example shown in the defaults file is usable and is supported by the FreeBSD Project. Though people may recommend other settings or things to add to this setting, any options other than those shown in the example are not supported by the FreeBSD Project. If you're familiar with other free versions of UNIX, you might be familiar with some of these more obscure optimizations.

In general, FreeBSD code is expected to compile most correctly without any of these additional options, and all you can do by adding optimizations is impair your performance. If you have a problem with a program built with nonstandard flags, revert the flags to the standard form and rebuild the program.

**COPTFLAGS= -O -pipe**  The COPTFLAGS optimizations are used for building the kernel only. Again, settings other than the defaults presented can build a non-working kernel.

**INSTALL=install -C**  By default, when FreeBSD installs a built program, it copies the new binary on top of the old one. The install -C option makes the installer compare the new program to the existing one, and if they're identical, the new binary is not installed. This can accelerate upgrades and save disk writes. Saving disk writes is not usually that much of an issue, but it's there if you want it.

### System Upgrade make.conf Options

The following options might be useful when upgrading from source (explained in Chapter 6). If you're not using the component in question, setting the make options to not build those components will reduce the time you need to build the system. For example, you might choose not to build sendmail because your system doesn't need it.

These options are also useful if you've replaced part of the system. If you're running the latest version of named from the ports collection, for example, you might have replaced /usr/sbin/named with your customized version. You don't want an upgrade to clobber this, so you can tell the system not to build it.

**NOTE**  *When you set these options not to build part of the system, an upgrade will not fix security holes in the affected programs. This means that you will have older, insecure programs on your hard drive, and if you start them, you'll have system security holes. To disable building a program, it's best to dig through the system and remove the corresponding programs.*

**ENABLE_SUIDPERL=true**  Suidperl is a special version of Perl(1) that is not installed by default. Use this option if you need to install a setuid version of Perl during an upgrade from source.

**PPP_NOSUID=true**  There's a long-standing consensus that setuid programs are bad, and should be eliminated. However, the ppp program used to connect to the Internet needs to be have the setuid ability to allow multiple users to use it. If only the root user will be dialing onto the Internet, PPP_NOSUID can be set to true.

**NO_CVS=true**  CVS is the Concurrent Versions System used by advanced systems administrators. This option prevents a source upgrade from building or installing it.

**NO_BIND=true**  BIND is the default DNS server (see Chapter 12). If you have a custom nameserver installed, set this option.

**NO_FORTRAN=true**  The Fortran programming language is popular in the scientific community, not so popular in the network services community. Feel free to set this option unless you need Fortran support.

**NO_LPR=true**  LPR is the printing system. If your computer doesn't use a printer, or if you have a custom printing program installed, you can set this option. LPR has had several security holes in the past, however, so be careful.

**NO_MAILWRAPPER=true**  The mailwrapper is the mail server selection program that redirects sendmail calls to the appropriate program (see the chapter section "/etc/mail/mailer.conf"). If you're not running a mail server, or if you're using the FreeBSD defaults, you can set this option.

**NO_MODULES=true**   This option prevents the automatic building of kernel modules with the kernel. Do not set this option unless you enjoy watching your system crash on boot, or know exactly what you're doing.

**NO_OBJC=true**   This option prevents the inclusion of support for Objective C. If you and your users don't need Objective C, you can set this option. A (very) few ports will not work properly if you do this.

**NO_OPENSSH=true**   If you have a custom SSH client/server installed, set this option. Otherwise, build OpenSSH.

**NO_OPENSSL=true**   OpenSSL is the encryption package used by OpenSSH and other secure services. If you're not running any encrypted programs, you can set this option. However, it's highly recommended that you don't set this option, because it will prevent OpenSSH from building.

**NO_SENDMAIL=true**   If you have a custom mail program, or if you don't run a mail server, you can set this option. In our example in Chapter 14, we will replace sendmail with postfix. If you set this option, however, you'll have an old and possibly insecure sendmail floating around your system. You're really better off building the whole system.

**NO_SHAREDOCS=true**   FreeBSD includes documentation from the original BSD4.4 release under /usr/share/docs, as well as more recent papers describing new features. If you don't use the documentation on this system, you can save a few seconds of processor and disk time by setting this option.

**NO_TCSH=true**   This option prevents /bin/csh and /bin/tcsh being built during binary upgrades. If you have csh scripts that might be confused by an upgrade, or if you don't use csh/tcsh at all, set this option. (Programming in csh is a bad idea, anyway.)

**NOCRYPT=true**   In addition to the OpenSSL encryption code mentioned previously, FreeBSD includes code for encrypting passwords, hashing files, and so on. If you don't want to build any code for these things, set this option, though it's usually not a good idea unless you know exactly what you're doing and why.

**NO_GAMES=true**   This option prevents the building of programs under /usr/games. They don't change often, so you can probably do without them.

**NOINFO=true**   FreeBSD includes a variety of documents under /usr/share/info that don't change often. You can set this option to avoid processing these documents during an upgrade from source.

**NOLIBC_R=true**   Setting this option prevents an upgrade from source from upgrading the re-entrant version of libc. If you don't know what this is, don't set this option!

**NOPERL=true**   This option controls whether the Perl interpreter and related libraries are built. Setting this option can greatly accelerate the buildworld process, but it can also leave you with an obsolete version of Perl. After all, a FreeBSD upgrade might include a Perl upgrade some time! Some programs, such as adduser(8), are written in Perl, and those scripts might be changed to take advantage of an upgraded Perl. Not upgrading Perl might break these programs. If you're using Perl scripts that are dependent upon features in a particular version of Perl, you can set this option.

**NOPROFILE=true**   This option prevents the building of profiled libraries. Again, if you don't know what profiled libraries are, don't set this.

**NOSECURE=true**   This option eliminates anything under the src/crypto directory being built, including Kerberos, OpenSSH, OpenSSL, and assorted other encryption stuff. Don't set this option if you're running a production Internet server.

**NOSHARE=true**   This option prevents the building of anything under the src/share directory, including all the old papers, all the man pages, all the examples, and documentation in general. You can set this option if you don't care about documentation on this system.

**NOUUCP=true**   UUCP is the UNIX-to-UNIX Copy Protocol, an old standard for transferring data between machines, used before TCP/IP came into widespread use. Part of UUCP is used to handle serial consoles (see Chapter 20).

**MODULES_WITH_WORLD=true**   Whenever you build a kernel, you build the kernel modules by default. This option sets the system to only build the modules once, during upgrades instead of the kernel build. This can save a great deal of time if you experiment with a lot of different kernels between upgrades. It can also cause weird problems. Use with caution.

**NOMANCOMPRESS=true**   The upgrade install process compresses man pages to save space. When you look at a man page, the system must first uncompress the page. If you have plenty of space, and want slightly faster man-page access, you can set this option to install man pages in uncompressed format.

**COMPATxx=yes**   This option allows you to install system libraries for older versions of FreeBSD. Simply replace the xx in COMPATxx to indicate the proper library version (COMPAT1X, COMPAT20, COMPAT21, COMPAT22, COMPAT3X, or COMPAT4X). This is only necessary if you have a binary built for an older FreeBSD version, and you want to continue to use it on your newer system. You can specify multiple COMPATXX entries if desired.

**NOTE**   *The* COMPATxx=yes *option does not build the libraries from source; rather, uuencoded libraries are simply stored in the source tree. If you've upgraded from source with a compat library enabled once, you can safely remove it.*

### make.conf ports Options

The following options control the building process of add-on components. Some software will change its behavior drastically depending on these options. For example, certain pieces of add-on software are huge, and you might want to tell your system not to install them under any circumstances. Other times you will want to inform the system that a component is available.

**NO_X=true** One of the biggest ports in FreeBSD is the X Window System, and many other ports rely upon it. If you set this option to true, these ports will not attempt to build X as part of their dependencies. This means some ports cannot be built at all, but they're useless without X anyway.

Some parts of the base system (particularly doscmd) include hooks to the X Window System by default. If you do not have X on your system, and do not intend to have it, and do not want it installed as a dependency to any other program, set this option.

**NOPORTDOCS=true** Various pieces of software in the ports collection have extensive documentation that is generally installed under /usr/local/share. If you set this option, this documentation is not installed. If you have a test machine or workstation where you can install the documentation, you can set this option on your servers.

**HAVE_MOTIF=yes** Motif is a software graphics library that many ports try to use to provide various graphic widgets. Motif was very expensive for several years, but free versions are available under /usr/ports/x11-toolkits/lesstif and /usr/ports/x11-toolkits/open-motif. If you have either of these toolkits installed, set HAVE_MOTIF.

## /etc/master.passwd

This file contains usernames and passwords. When you log in, the password you type is compared with the one in this file.

The /etc/master.passwd file is important enough that there's a special program just for editing it. Vipw(8) calls up the text editor from $EDITOR, allows you to make your changes, and checks the file syntax before allowing you to save it. Vipw also updates the password databases. This prevents many of the more basic mistakes, but if you're really bent on corrupting /etc/master.passwd, vipw will make life more difficult but won't stop you.

When vipw finally allows you to save your work, it also recreates the file /etc/passwd. This file can only be read by root.

If the information in /etc/master.passwd conflicts with that in other files, programs generally assume that /etc/master.passwd is correct. For example, /etc/group sometimes doesn't list a user's primary group. The primary group that appears in /etc/passwd is correct, even when it isn't listed in /etc/group.

Many programs need access to the information in /etc/master.passwd—for example, shells and home directories must be public information. Rather than allowing anyone to read this file and try to reverse-engineer the encrypted passwords, FreeBSD provides globally readable bits of this file in /etc/passwd.

## Fields

Each line in /etc/master.passwd contains ten fields, separated by colons. These are described in the following sections.

**Username**   The first field in lines in /etc/master.passwd is the username. This is either an account created by the administrator and used by a real user, or a user created at install time to provide some system service. FreeBSD includes a variety of system accounts, such as root, toor, daemon, games, uucp, and so on. Each of these users owns some part of the system. Various programs can run as these users.

**Encrypted Password**   The second field is the encrypted password. System users don't generally have a password, so you can't log in as them. User accounts have a string of random-looking characters here.

One simple way to temporarily disable a user account is to edit the password file and put an asterisk (*) in front of the password. While the account will still be active, nobody will be able to log in to it. I've used this to great effect when a client was behind on a bill; they call quite quickly when they can't log in.

**User ID**   The third field is the user ID number, or UID. Every user has a unique UID.

**Group ID**   Similarly, the fourth field is the group ID number, or GID. This is the user's primary group, as discussed in Chapter 7. Usually, this is the same as the UID, and the group has the same name as the username.

**User's Class**   The next field is the user's class as defined in /etc/login.conf. You can change a user's class by using vipw and editing master.passwd directly, or with chsh(1).

**Password Expiration**   The sixth field is the password expiration field. If you leave this blank, or if you're not running system accounting, passwords will not expire. The expiration field is filled in as seconds since the epoch. (The epoch is midnight, January 1, 1970).

**Number of Seconds Since the Epoch**   Similarly, the seventh field is the number of seconds since the epoch until the entire account expires. If you aren't using system accounting, this is useless.

**Gecos**   The *gecos* field contains the user's real name, office number, work phone number, and home phone number, all separated by commas. Do not use colons in this field; colons are reserved specifically for separating fields in /etc/master.passwd itself.

**User's Home Directory**   The ninth field is the user's home directory. While this defaults to /home, you can move this anywhere you like. You'll just need to move the actual home directory when you change this field.

**User's Shell**   Finally, the tenth field gives the user's shell. If this field is empty, the system assumes the user gets boring old /bin/sh.

### /etc/motd

The motd, or *message of the day* file, is displayed to users when they log in. You can put system notices in this file, or other information you want shell users to see. Note that who sees this file is controlled by the welcome option in /etc/login.conf. You can have multiple message files, one for each login class.

### /etc/mtree/*

The system upgrade processes use the /etc/mtree files. They have no effect on the daily running of the system. Mtree(8) builds directory hierarchies, usually so an automated installer can put programs in them. While you don't need to edit these files, it's nice to know why they're here.

### /etc/namedb/*

The /etc/namedb files control the system nameserver. See Chapter 12 for details of how the files in /etc/namedb work.

### /etc/newsyslog.conf

This file configures the rotation and deletion of logs. See Chapter 19 for details of the system logger.

### /etc/passwd

Many programs require access to user information such as shell, real name, and so on. In older UNIX systems, this was stored in the /etc/passwd file, along with the actual encrypted passwd, and everyone could read this file. This became a problem as UNIX spread into universities. Computer science students had great fun trying to crack encrypted passwords, and regretfully succeeded on too many occasions. Hackers made /etc/passwd their target. Eventually, the encrypted passwords were moved to /etc/master.passwd. The /etc/passwd file remained as an information source for other programs.

The /etc/passwd file is generated from the /etc/master.passwd file by stripping out the class, change, and expire fields. The encrypted password is replaced with an asterisk. These are the remaining fields:

- username
- password (asterisk)
- user ID number
- group ID number
- name
- home directory
- shell

See the /etc/master.passwd section for details on these fields.

### /etc/periodic.conf and /etc/defaults/periodic.conf

The /etc/periodic.conf file is another one with a default in /etc/defaults, and overrides in /etc. Periodic(8) runs every day to handle basic daily maintenance. It's the source of the status messages mailed to root every day, and it can handle a variety of tasks, which are stored as shell scripts under /etc/periodic. (By default, periodic tries to run quite a few tasks that you might or might not need; the scripts are generally intelligent, though, and put as little load as possible on the system.) Every function available to the periodic program is enabled or disabled in periodic.conf.

Periodic runs programs either daily, weekly, or monthly. Each set of programs has its own settings; for example, programs that run daily are configured separately from programs that run monthly. These settings are controlled by entries in the /etc/periodic.conf file. Here are some standard entries from that file.

```
periodic_conf_files="/etc/periodic.conf /etc/periodic.conf.local"
```

The preceding line tells the periodic program where to look for override files, and you can choose a location other than /etc/ for your customized configuration. Many systems mount their root filesystem as read-only, so you can put your override file elsewhere if you need to.

**daily_output="root"**    This option tells periodic where to send the results of its daily checks. If you give a username, periodic will mail that user. Unless you have a user whose job it is to specifically read periodic mail, it's best to leave this at the default and forward root's email to an account you read. Alternatively, you can put a filename here and periodic will write to it like a log file. In this case, you can have newsyslog (see Chapter 19) rotate the periodic log.

**daily_show_success="YES"**    If daily_show_success is set to yes, the daily message will include information on all successful checks.

**daily_show_info="YES"**    When daily_show_info is set to yes, the daily message will include general information from the commands it runs.

**daily_show_badconfig="NO"**   The daily message will include information on periodic commands it tried to run, but couldn't. These are generally harmless, and if you set daily_show_badconfig to no, you won't miss much. If you're interested, however, you can set this to yes and get a look at everything that happens.

Each of the scripts in the daily, weekly, and monthly directories under /etc/periodic has a brief description at the top of the script. Skim through those quickly. The defaults that are enabled are sensible for most circumstances, but there's extra functionality there that you might want to enable on some systems. Each script has a tunable knob in /etc/periodic.conf to enable or disable it, and more are being added continuously. Since anything I could list here would be obsolete before I could deliver the manuscript, let alone before the book reached you, I won't go into detail about the various scripts.

### /etc/printcap

The /etc/printcap file controls printer setup. There are literally dozens and dozens of options for printers, from the cost per page to manually setting a string to feed a new sheet of paper. (We won't cover all of the options, but we will discuss the basics of printer management here.)

A UNIX printer system makes assumptions about a printer. By defining variables in /etc/printcap, you tell your printer system how your hardware differs from the classic UNIX printers of two decades ago. As you might guess, these differences can be extensive. (Fortunately, most printers understand PostScript. This greatly simplifies printer maintenance.)

If you're using FreeBSD on a network with an existing print server, you probably want to use that existing server. (See Chapter 21 for some example configurations.) When doing fine-grained printer tweaking, you might need some of the more exotic options FreeBSD provides. We'll discuss some of the ones you might need on a modern system in the following section.

#### Working with Printcap Entries

Each printer has its own /etc/printcap entry. Since all these variables let you create some very, very long lines, use a backslash character (\) to indicate that the entry hasn't finished and is continued on the next line. Use colons to separate variables. If you're using a backslash to make your entries readable, the second and subsequent lines must have a colon at both the beginning and end of the variable assignments.

The first entry in /etc/printcap is the printer name. If a printer has many names—such as "ThirdFloor", "AccountingOffice", and "BigLaserJet", list all of those names, separated by the pipe symbol ( | ).

**NOTE**   *In FreeBSD, and almost all other versions of UNIX, the default printer is named "lp". Various programs expect to find a printer named lp. It's simplest to assign this name to your preferred printer.*

After the printer's name, list the variables that define that particular printer. A comprehensive list would contain much that you'll never need, but we'll look at some of the variables that are either in more common use today or that are useful on modern networks. Let's first look at a simple sample printcap entry and see how it's set up. Then we can examine the variables that allow you to fine-tune your printer's behavior.

```
lp|SalesPS|ThirdFloorPrinter:\
        :rp=SalesPS:\
        :rm=printserver:\
        :sd=/var/spool/output/lpd:\
        :lf=/var/log/lpd-errs:
```

This printer is called lp, as well as SalesPS and ThirdFloorPrinter. The remote printer name, as the print server calls it, is SalesPS. The print server is a machine with a TCP/IP network name of printserver. Print jobs are stored in /var/spool/output/lpd while they're being processed, and printing errors are logged to /var/log/lpd-errs. (See Chapter 21 for some hints on setting up a printer.)

The following are some of the most commonly set options for printing in UNIX.

```
:ct=120:
```

This is the network connection timeout. You can use ct to control the timeout for remote network printers. If a printer does not respond, the printer service will wait ct=X seconds before returning a failure. The default is 120 seconds, which is far too high for a modern local area network. Usually, if a printer doesn't respond within 30 seconds, you have a problem. Alternatively, if you're printing to some device on another continent, you might need to increase this to as high as 240.

```
:fo=false:
```

This stands for "form feed upon open." If this is set, the system will start each printing job with a blank sheet.

```
:if=/usr/libexec/lpr/input-filter:
```

As the preceding line shows, FreeBSD can preprocess printing requests it receives over the network. This allows you to do some nifty things, such as make a boring desktop inkjet printer behave like a PostScript printer. See /usr/ports/print/apsfilter for an excellent example of how this is done.

```
:lf=/var/log/printername:
```

This lets you specify the log file for this particular printer.

```
:lp=/dev/lp:
```

These two lines identify the printer's device name. The default is correct for a device with one printer attached to the back of a system via a parallel cable. If it's a network printer, create this as a null entry, like this: `:lp=:`. If you have multiple parallel printers, you will need to specify the device name for each printer.

```
:mx=1000:
```

This specifies the maximum size of a printer job in 512-byte ($\frac{1}{2}$KB) blocks. If you do heavy graphics work, you probably want to set this to 0 for no maximum size.

```
:of=/usr/libexec/lpr/filter-program
```

This is the full path to the outbound printer filter. FreeBSD supports the ability to preprocess printer output with the output filter option, as shown here. This can be useful for, say, converting PostScript into regular output like the apsfilter package does. Many non-English languages have special output filters; FreeBSD ships with output filters for Russian-language printing, and more will be added as users contribute them.

```
:rm=printserver:
```

This entry identifies the hostname of the remote print server this printer is attached to. The printer is expected to be running lpd, and to be able to accept the job. (Most print servers, even Windows 2000, can speak lpd.)

```
:rp=printerName:
```

This gives the name the print server uses for the printer you want to use. This is only needed if you're printing to a print server.

```
:sd=/var/spool/lpd:
```

This is the spool directory, where the printing program stores files as it's processing them. Every printer needs a unique spool directory.

### /etc/profile

/etc/profile contains the default account setup information for the /bin/sh shell, much like /etc/csh.* does for csh/tcsh users. Bash and other sh derivatives also use this file; whenever sh users log in, they inherit what's in this file. However, users can override this file with their own .profile.

While csh is the standard FreeBSD shell, sh and its derivatives (particularly bash) are quite popular. Consider keeping the /etc/profile and /etc/csh.login settings synchronized. The examples in /etc/profile and the examples in /etc/csh.login are identical, so you already have a good starting point.

### /etc/protocols

In Chapter 5, we briefly discussed network protocols, and /etc/protocols lists the Internet protocols your FreeBSD system is aware of. Each protocol has an assigned number; various programs use these numbers to determine how they handle transactions.

Almost all Internet transactions happen over IP, TCP, or UDP. Most people don't realize that there are dozens of protocols, and that IP is protocol 0, TCP is protocol 6, and UDP is protocol 17. Some protocols are heavily used in specific environments, and others are so outdated you'll probably never encounter them. As a systems administrator, you don't have to be familiar with every piddly little protocol out there, but you should know that the world is bigger than TCP/IP and have some basic information about other protocols.

Each protocol has its own line in /etc/protocols. The first entry on a line is the official name, such as tlsp in the output that follows. The second line is the protocol number, 56 in this example. Following that are any aliases for the protocol, such as TLSP. Finally, comments are set off with a pound (#) sign.

Here's a snippet from /etc/protocols:

```
tlsp          56     TLSP            # Transport Layer Security Protocol
skip          57     SKIP            # SKIP
ipv6-icmp     58     IPV6-ICMP       # ICMP for IPv6
ipv6-nonxt    59     IPV6-NONXT      # no next header for ipv6
```

Raise your hand if you've ever heard of any of these protocols. Yep, that's what I thought. There's nothing to worry about, though; remember, you don't have to know everything, you just need to know where to find out about it.

**NOTE**   *The list in /etc/protocols is well maintained by the FreeBSD Project. You will probably never have to edit it unless a specific piece of software requires its own entry.*

### /etc/pwd.db

The /etc/pwd.db file is a database version of /etc/passwd, and it exists because a computer program can access /etc/pwd.db much more quickly than it can parse a text file. The /etc/pwd.db file is world-readable, and since /etc/passwd deliberately contains no secure information, this is perfectly safe.

The password database files are the reason why it's so important that you use tools such as passwd(8) and vipw(8) to edit your password file. Each of these tools automatically runs pwd_mkdb(8) when they're finishing their work. Pwd_mkdb rebuilds the password databases. If your /etc/passwd and /etc/pwd.db files are not synchronized, you will have a variety of weird user errors.

Unless you are a database hacker, under no circumstances should you use database tools to change this file. Let the password tools do their work.

### /etc/rc

Whenever your system boots to the point where it can execute userland commands, it runs the shell script /etc/rc. This script mounts all filesystems, brings up the network interfaces, configures device nodes, sets up shared libraries, and does all the other tasks required to set up a system.

There are an awful lot of tasks, and some of them aren't necessary on all systems. If your system doesn't use its serial ports, for example, you don't need to run the script to configure them. Similarly, a system that doesn't use ATM networking doesn't need to run the scripts to configure that.

Rather than having a monolithic script containing everything, some system startup tasks are broken up into smaller scripts, which keeps the scripts smaller and easier to debug. When /etc/rc needs to start the logical network, for example, it runs /etc/rc.network.

The other shell scripts used by /etc/rc include the following:

**/etc/rc.atm**  This script configures Asynchronous Transfer Mode (ATM) networking. (If you have an ATM card in your FreeBSD box, you'll know it—it probably cost more than the rest of your system combined.)

**/etc/rc.diskless1 and /etc/rc.diskless2**  If you're running a FreeBSD system without a hard disk, these scripts will be run. This is an interesting FreeBSD function that we're not going to discuss, because implementing it requires a seasoned UNIX administrator. By the time you've mastered this book, however, you'll be ready to dig into diskless operations.

**/etc/rc.firewall**  This script contains basic configuration information for ipfw. If you're using ipfw, you can use this as a sample.

**/etc/rc.firewall6**  This script contains ipfw configurations for people using IPv6.

**/etc/rc.i386**  Any FreeBSD system on the X86 architecture—the standard "Intel PC" platform—runs this script at boot.

**/etc/rc.isdn**  If you're using the built-in metered ISDN support, you'll use this script. This is moot for people with unmetered ISDN support, such as most of the United States, but it is crucial in Europe, Australia, and other areas where ISDN connection time is billed by the minute.

**/etc/rc.network**  This script is where network configuration occurs.

**/etc/rc.network6**  This script handles IPv6 network configuration.

**/etc/rc.serial**  This script sets sane defaults so that your serial ports will just work out of the box. (Serial ports are infinitely configurable, and without some setup they don't behave as you would expect.)

**/etc/rc.syscons**   This short script sets up your terminal settings, console screensaver, keyboard maps, and other console settings.

**/etc/rc.sysctl**   This script sets sysctl values from /etc/sysctl.conf (see Chapter 4).

You configure /etc/rc through /etc/rc.conf and /etc/defaults/rc.conf. Essentially, you set variables in /etc/rc.conf that control how /etc/rc behaves, what it starts, and how the system is set up on boot.

> **NOTE**   *If you ever wonder how FreeBSD configures something when it boots, /etc/rc is your friend. Find the variable in /etc/defaults/rc.conf that makes your system behave in the desired manner. Search the /etc/rc scripts for that variable—you can do this easily with* grep -i variablename /etc/rc.*. *When you find out which file the variable is used in, look at it. Reading that section of the rc script will give you the command that can be used to tweak that behavior. Then all you have to do is toddle off to the man page and read about it.*

### /etc/rc.conf and /etc/defaults/rc.conf

The /etc/defaults/rc.conf file is huge, and it contains quite a few variables, frequently called *knobs*, *tunables*, or even *tunable knobs*. We aren't going to discuss all of the variables, not only because knobs are added continually (such a list would be immediately obsolete), but also because quite a few variables aren't commonly used on servers.

Almost everything in the standard FreeBSD system can be an rc.conf tunable, from your keyboard map to your TCP/IP behavior. If you have a problem using these knobs, definitely check /etc/defaults/rc.conf or rc.conf(5) on your system to see if anything has changed.

In the next few sections, we'll examine some common entries from /etc/rc.conf. Each of these appears once in /etc/defaults/rc.conf, and can be edited by placing an override in /etc/rc.conf.

These are only the most common options. The /etc/defaults/rc.conf file contains literally hundreds of possible options. The rc.conf(5) man page is well worth a read if you're interested in fine-tuning your system.

#### Startup Options

The following few rc.conf options control how FreeBSD configures itself and starts other programs.

Once all other startup tasks are complete, /etc/rc checks the directories listed in the following variable for additional executables (generally shell scripts) and runs any it finds:

```
local_startup="/usr/local/etc/rc.d /usr/X11R6/etc/rc.d"
```

Most ports that are started at boot time install their startup scripts in /usr/local/etc/rc.d. If you're installing your programs in some other place, change this path to reflect your startup directory.

Files listed in the following variable are "additional" rc.conf files:

```
rc_conf_files="/etc/rc.conf /etc/rc.conf.local"
```

You can choose to add additional rc.conf files. For example, you might have an rc.conf file that you share among all of your servers that defines things such as network services and system behavior, and a separate rc.conf file that defines the IP address and hostname for this particular system. Such customizations can greatly simplify central administration of large server farms.

While /etc/rc.conf is traditionally the centrally maintained file, /etc/rc.conf.local is for the local system. You can even create your own rc.conf files in arbitrary locations on the system. While this probably isn't a good idea, it gives you some added flexibility if you have an odd situation.

### Network Options

These options control how FreeBSD sets up its networking features during boot.

**hostname=""**   The hostname setting specifies the full domain name of the system, such as "www.absolutebsd.org". It should have been set during the install—you must set it for programs to run properly.

**tcp_extensions="NO"**   TCP has changed over the years, with several changes and additions to the TCP protocol being lumped together as "TCP Extensions" per RFC 1323. While some applications can take advantage of TCP extensions, many can't. FreeBSD defaults to a conservative, disabled setting. Set this option to "YES" if your application requires it.

**NOTE**   *If one host is using TCP extensions and another isn't, you may see performance problems. For that reason, TCP extensions are not recommended for Web or FTP servers. Even though most modern systems use RFC 1323 extensions, you probably don't want to make life difficult for the oldest systems on the Net. Cutting off 10 percent of your potential users isn't a great idea.*

**log_in_vain="NO"**   This option logs to /var/log/messages all attempts to connect to your system on a TCP or UDP port where nothing is listening. This log shows port scans and network probes, but also picks up a lot of garbage. It's interesting to set for a time, just to see what happens, but unless you're actually going to read the log, it's just a waste of processor time and disk space. In later versions of FreeBSD, the "YES" and "NO" answers have been replaced by "0" and "1", respectively.

**tcp_drop_synfin="NO"**   To use this option, you must have TCP_DROP_SYNFIN compiled into your kernel. This option is not in GENERIC.

This option drops packets that have both the SYN and FIN flags set, and network scanners use it to identify remote operating systems. However, dropping these SYN+FIN packets violates the TCP specifications, and can cause odd network problems. If you have problems, try turning this off and seeing if your problem goes away.

**icmp_drop_redirect="NO"**   ICMP redirects are used on local networks to inform servers of additional network gateways. While there are legitimate uses for ICMP, it's also commonly used by hackers. As such, if you aren't using ICMP redirects on your network, you can set this option for a tiny measure of added security. If you're not sure if you're using them, ask your network administrator. If you *are* the network administrator, and you're not sure, then you aren't using them.

**icmp_log_redirect="NO"**   If you are using ICMP redirects on your network and want to monitor them, you can set this option to log them to /var/log/messages.

There's no limit to the number of ICMP redirects you can log, and when you're under attack or having network problems, it's pretty easy to fill up your hard disk with these messages. Use this option with care!

**network_interfaces="auto"**   This variable contains the list of network interfaces, as shown by ifconfig. If you have an unusual network interface, it's possible (but not likely) that you could have problems with interfaces not being configured on boot. In that case, try listing your interfaces manually in this variable, as in "lo0 ep0 wi0". While this probably isn't your problem, it's nice to be able to rule it out.

**ifconfig_lo0="inet 127.0.0.1"**   List each of your network interfaces in this option, on their own line, with network configuration information. Substitute the correct name of your interface for lo0. For example, to give your ep0 network card an IP address of 192.168.1.200 and a netmask of 255.255.255.0 at boot, you would use this:

```
ifconfig_ep0="inet 192.168.1.200 netmask 255.255.255.0"
```

If you're using DHCP on your network, set the interface value to dhcp.

**ifconfig_ep0_alias0="inet 192.168.1.201"**   FreeBSD allows you to assign hundreds of IP addresses to a network card. One IP address is the primary address, while the others are aliases. List each alias in this form:

```
ifconfig_interfacename_aliasnumber="inet IP address"
```

The alias numbers must be continuous, starting with 0. If there's a break in the numbering, aliases above the gap will not be installed at boot time. (This is a common problem, and if you see it, check your alias list.)

### Dial-up PPP Options

The rc.conf file has several options for handling dial-up PPP. We don't do much with PPP in this book, but you should know about these options in case you need them.

**ppp_enable="NO"** If you set this option to "YES", the system will start the ppp program automatically. (You will still need to configure it to actually do anything.)

**ppp_mode="auto"** You have four choices for this option:

- "auto" tells the system to dial out to the Internet automatically on demand.
- "dedicated" is used for systems with a dedicated connection. This isn't appropriate for a dedicated phone line—it's for serial lines into other computers.
- "direct" is for receiving dial-up calls from a modem. (See ppp(8) for details.)
- "ddial" is for dedicated phone-line access. Use this if your system is connected to the Internet by a dial-up line, and you want to automatically redial when something out in Phone Company Land disconnects you.

**ppp_nat="YES"** The ppp program has built-in Network Address Translation services. Set this option if you're using your FreeBSD box as a network gateway and connecting via dial-up.

**ppp_profile="papchap"** You can define a variety of dial-up profiles in /etc/ppp/ppp.conf; the "papchap" profile is the default.

### Miscellaneous Network Daemons

FreeBSD includes a variety of smaller daemons to handle assorted services. You can configure them from rc.conf.

**syslogd_enable="YES"** If you want to have your system log work, keep this option. I discuss syslogd in great detail in Chapter 19.

**syslogd_flags="-s"** The default for syslogd_flags means that only allowed servers (specified in syslogd_flags) can connect to yours. By default, this prevents unauthorized servers from connecting to you.

Originally, syslogd accepted log messages from any server on the Net, but if that were the case, someone would probably fill up your hard drive with their log messages. To allow a particular host to send messages to syslogd, specify them with the -a option. You can specify the host by IP address, with a netmask specified as a number of bits (see Chapter 5).

For example, to allow your host to take log messages from anything in the 192.168.0.0 to 192.168.0.255 range, you would use this:

```
syslogd_flags="-s -a 192.168.1.0/24"
```

You can also specify hostnames:

```
syslogd_flags="-s -a mail.absolutebsd.org"
```

The hostname entry relies on reverse DNS. If someone on another network changed her host's reverse DNS to match an allowed host, she could log authentic-looking messages to your server. Using IP addresses is just a better idea.

**inetd_enable="NO"**   This option disables the inetd server (see Chapter 13). If you want to run inetd, set this option to "YES".

**named_enable="NO"**   Because named requires configuration to be useful, FreeBSD ships with it disabled by default (see Chapter 13). Set this option to "YES" to run named.

**named_program="named"**   If you've built a custom named, give the full path to it here. Several customized nameservers are available in the ports collection (see Chapter 10).

**named_flags="-u bind -g bind"**   This option gives flags to named(8). The defaults are reasonable, but you can put any legitimate options you like into this field. See Chapter 12 for details on named.

**sshd_enable="NO"**   This option disables or enables the SSH daemon. Enable this if you want to connect to your system over the network securely. See Chapter 13 for details on configuring sshd.

**sshd_flags=""**   The SSH daemon can be configured via flags on the command line, but you're better off editing /etc/ssh/sshd_config to tweak your ssh service.

```
ntpdate_enable="NO"
ntpdate_flags="-b"
xntpd_enable="NO"
xntpd_flags="-p /var/run/ntpd.pid"
```

These four variables control the behavior of the network time-keeping daemons. See Chapter 13 for details on these programs.

### Network Routing Options

FreeBSD configures routing separately from the main network options.

**defaultrouter=""**   This option is where you list the IP address of your default router.

**gateway_enable="NO"** Set this option to "YES" if your system has multiple network interfaces, and you want to transmit packets from one network to another via these interfaces. The system will become a gateway, passing traffic from one interface to another.

**router_enable="NO"** If your system is a gateway, and you want it to get its routing table via the RIP protocol, set this option to "YES". Otherwise, don't go near it!

### Console Options

The console options control how the monitor and keyboard behave. You can change the language of your keyboard, the font size on your monitor, or just about anything you like.

**keymap="NO"** You can choose to use a different keyboard map with the keymap option. Quite a few keyboard maps are available under /usr/share/syscons/keymaps, with different arrangements for different countries.

I use the Dvorak keyboard layout, which is set quite easily with these lines:

```
keymap="us.dvorak.kbd"
```

**blanktime="300"** The blanktime field specifies the number of seconds the keyboard is idle before FreeBSD tells the monitor to go into power-save mode, 300 seconds in this case. If you set this to "NO", FreeBSD will not blank the screen.

**NOTE** *Some newer hardware has automatic screen-blanking features. If your monitor insists on going idle when this option is set to "NO", check your BIOS and your monitor manual.*

**moused_enable="NO"** Enable this option to use your mouse on the console. Console mouse allows you to highlight, copy, and paste.

**moused_type="auto"** Mice use a variety of different protocols to translate wheel motion into pointer actions. While FreeBSD is pretty good at automatically detecting the protocol your mouse uses, if autodetecting your mouse doesn't work, you can set this manually. See moused(8) for possible options.

**moused_port="/dev/psm0"** This option specifies the physical port your mouse is attached to. The default, /dev/psm0, is the PS/2 mouse port. If you have a serial mouse on serial 0 (com1), set this option to /dev/cuaa0. The second serial port is /dev/cuaa1.

**moused_flags=""** The mouse daemon is highly configurable to support the wide variety of mice that have been hooked up to FreeBSD machines over time. Today though, most mice are either USB or PS/2, so these options are generally useless. See moused(8) for details on how to make your ten-year-old serial trackball that demands 1350 baud work properly.

The one option still popular today is -3. Traditional UNIX mice have from three to five buttons. Many UNIX programs assume that you have a third mouse button. This flag allows you to emulate a third mouse button by pressing both buttons simultaneously.

### Other Options

Finally, we have a few options that don't fit well into any other category.

**lpd_enable="NO"**   Set this option to "YES" if you want to print from this system. See Chapter 21 for details on basic printing.

**usbd_enable="NO"**   Enable this option if you have USB devices.

**sendmail_enable="NO"**   This option allows your system to receive email from other systems. Only enable this if your system is a mail server.

**sendmail_outbound_enable="YES"**   This option allows your system to send email to other computers. You almost certainly want this on all your systems.

**dumpdev="NO"**   To save kernel images after a panic (for crash debugging), set this option to the name of a swap partition. The partition must be the same size as your physical memory, or larger. Check /etc/fstab for the name of your swap partition. On my laptop it's /dev/ad0s1b, and I set it like this:

```
dumpdev="/dev/ad0s1b"
```

See Chapter 20 for lots of detailed discussion on how the dumpdev is used during a system crash.

**ibcs2_enable="NO"**   This option enables or disables the kernel's SCO UNIX compatibility. See Chapter 11.

**linux_enable="NO"**   This option enables or disables the kernel's Linux compatibility module. See Chapter 11.

**svr4_enable="NO"**   FreeBSD has a compatibility module for UNIX System V, and this option enables or disables that module. See Chapter 11 for details.

**osf1_enable="NO"**   DEC Digital UNIX only runs on the Alpha. Since FreeBSD runs on the Alpha, a compatibility module exists, and this option enables or disables it. This option is useless on X86 hardware. We won't discuss the option except in the abstract, but it's nice to know that the option exists.

**clear_tmp_enable="NO"**   Older UNIX systems erase the contents of /tmp at boot. FreeBSD doesn't do this by default, but you can enable this behavior here.

**ldconfig_paths="/usr/lib/compat /usr/X11R6/lib /usr/local/lib"** This option lists the directories where shared libraries are stored. For most installations the default setting is adequate. If you find yourself setting LD_LIBRARY_PATH for all your users, however, you should look at adjusting this option instead. See Chapter 11 for more hints.

**kern_securelevel_enable="NO"** Set this option to "YES" to enable the FreeBSD kernel's security features at boot. See Chapter 7.

**kern_securelevel="-1"** If you've enabled kernel security, you can choose your securelevel with this option. See Chapter 7.

**start_vinum="NO"** Set this option to "YES" if you're using the Vinum software RAID machine. See Chapter 17.

### rc.shutdown

When you issue a shutdown or reboot command, the system runs rc.shutdown. This script searches through your local startup directories as specified in /etc/rc.conf, running each shell script it finds with a "stop" argument.

If you need the system to take a particular action upon shutdown, you can add the appropriate shell commands to the end of /etc/rc.shutdown. Most packaged software automatically includes the appropriate shutdown commands in its /usr/local/etc/rc.d script, so you shouldn't have to do this. You might have custom shutdown commands, however, which would be appropriate to add here. If at all possible, however, just create a script in a startup directory.

### /etc/resolv.conf

The /etc/resolv.conf file configures how the system DNS resolver works. See Chapter 12.

### /etc/security

The /etc/security file is a straightforward shell script run each day by periodic(8), and you can edit it as you like. It performs a variety of simple system-integrity checks, such as checking for changes to /etc/master.passwd, mounted filesystems, and kernel log messages, and its output is mailed to root every day. To disable it entirely, you can do so in /etc/periodic.conf with this setting:

```
daily_status_security_enable="NO"
```

Generally, the security output is worth having because it can point out a variety of system problems as well as security issues.

### /etc/services

This file lists many commonly used network ports. See Chapter 5.

### /etc/shells

/etc/shells contains a list of all legitimate user shells. Installing a shell via a port or a package adds an appropriate entry in /etc/shells, but if you compile your own shell from source, without using a port, you'll need to edit this file. Shells are listed by their complete path name.

The FTP daemon will not allow a user to log in if his shell is not listed in /etc/shells. If you're using /sbin/nologin as an FTP-only user shell, you need to add it to this file, though a better way to handle this is with login classes (see /etc/login.conf).

### /etc/spwd.db

This file resembles /etc/pwd.db, but is based on /etc/master.passwd. It contains all user account information in a database form, so other programs can quickly access it. Since it contains confidential information, only root can read it. See /etc/pwd.db and /etc/master.passwd for details.

### /etc/ssh

This file controls how your system's SSH server and client behave. See Chapter 13 for details.

### /etc/sysctl.conf

This file contains information on which kernel sysctls are set during the boot process. See Chapter 4.

### /etc/syslog.conf

This file controls which data your system logs. See Chapter 19.

# 10

## MAKING YOUR SYSTEM USEFUL

Unlike operating systems such as Microsoft Windows and Red Hat Linux, which tend to throw absolutely anything you might need into the base install, BSD systems are sparse—and that's a good thing.

For example, a Windows 2000 Professional system I'm using at a client site, with a "minimal" setup, has 1,768 items in its main system directory (C:\WINNT\system32), and just about every shared library (aka DLL, or dynamic-link library) ever. Whenever I boot the system, these DLLs are all loaded into the system memory. I don't know what each DLL is for, but I guarantee that I will never use many of them—the only software I use on that machine is SSH and Mozilla. All they do for me is soak up RAM.

This is, of course, Microsoft's approach to operating systems—give 'em everything you've got, and I mean everything. In contrast, Red Hat Linux installs a similar amount of stuff, but much of it is actual programs. You might never use most of those programs, but at least all those files aren't automatically loaded into the system memory at boottime.

A basic BSD install, however, gives you exactly enough to make the system run, plus a few extra bits that have been traditionally included with UNIX systems. You get to choose during setup whether to install additional programs or source code. However, even a complete, running BSD install takes far less disk space than the Windows 2000 system32 directory mentioned previously—the complete FreeBSD install includes far less than Windows. A Windows install that only supported SSH and Mozilla would be much smaller and simpler—in fact, it would look a lot more like a FreeBSD install.

The advantage to this sparseness is that it gives you only what you need for your system. This makes debugging a problem much simpler and helps to ensure that some shared library you've never even heard of, and would never use, won't break your system. The downside is that you may need to do a bit of thinking to determine what it is that you do need, and you'll have to install those extra, but necessary, programs. FreeBSD solves that problem by making software installation as simple as possible.

## Making Software

Building software is complicated because source code must be treated in a very specific manner to create a workable, running binary—let alone an optimized one!

While programmers could include installation instructions with each program, full of lines like "Now type `cc CPUTYPE=i686 -ohttpd -I /usr/src/crypto/kerberosIV/include -lcrypto -lkrb`," they don't. Programmers don't put up with this sort of garbage for long. If it can be automated, it will be, which is a good thing for those of us who need to install programs.

The main tool for building software is make(1). Make looks for a file called Makefile in the current directory, which is full of instructions much like that horrid example in the previous paragraph. When it finds the Makefile, make reads the instructions and carries them out. Makefiles are long and complicated creatures, and you don't really have to know their internals, so we're not going to dissect one here.

Each Makefile includes various *targets*, or types of instructions to carry out. For example, make `install` tells make to check the Makefile for a procedure called "install". If make finds such a procedure, it will execute it. Each target contains one basic step in building, installing, or configuring the software. We'll discuss various common make targets in this chapter, and when to use them.

Make can handle a huge variety of functions, some of which far outstrip the original intentions of the creators. But that's what UNIX is for, isn't it?

**NOTE**  *Be sure that you're in the same directory as the Makefile when you run make. While this isn't strictly necessary, it will make your life simpler.*

### The Pain and Pleasure of Source Code

Source code is the human-readable instructions for building the actual machine code that makes up a program. You might have already been exposed to source code in some form. If you've never seen source code, take a look at the various files under /usr/src.

While you don't have to be able to read source code, you should be able to recognize it two out of three times. Here's a snippet of source code from FreeBSD's network stack:

```
/* While we overlap succeeding segments trim them or,
* if they are completely covered, dequeue them.
*/
while (q) {
  register int i = (th->th_seq + *tlenp) - q->tqe_th->th_seq;
      if (i <= 0)
              break;
      if (i < q->tqe_len) {
              q->tqe_th->th_seq += i;
              q->tqe_len -= i;
              m_adj(q->tqe_m, i);
              break;
      }
```

Once you have the source code for a program, installing it is pretty straightforward. You build (or *compile*) the program on the system you want to run it on.[1] If the program was written for an operating system that is sufficiently similar to the platform you're building it on, it should work. If your platform is too different from the original, it will fail. Once you've built the software successfully on your platform, you can copy the resulting program (or *binary*) to other identical platforms, and it should run.

Some programs are written well enough that they can be compiled on many different platforms. A few programs specifically include support for widely divergent platforms; for example, the Apache Web server can be compiled on both Windows and UNIX just by typing **make install**. This is quite uncommon, however, and represents a truly heroic effort by the software authors.

**NOTE**   *While you can copy a compiled program to a foreign system and try to run it, this is generally doomed to fail. In most cases, one operating system cannot out-of-the-box run programs for another operating system. (FreeBSD can, with some configuration; see Chapter 11.)*

### Debugging

Generally speaking, if you can build a program from source, it will run on your UNIX; if you cannot, the program will not run. When you have the source code, however, a sufficiently experienced sysadmin can learn why a program won't build or run. In many cases, the problem is simple and can be fixed with minimal effort. (This is one reason why access to source code is important.)

---

[1] It is possible to build software on a foreign platform via something called "cross-compiling." Cross-compiling demands you know much more about building software than we want to go into here, though.

Back when every UNIX administrator was a programmer, this debugging absorbed a major portion of the admin's time. Every UNIX was slightly different, so all systems administrators had to understand the platform a program had been written for, and its differences from their platform, before they could hope to get a chunk of code to run. The duplication of effort was truly monstrous.

Slowly, tools such as autoconf and configure were created to help address these cross-platform issues. Still, not every program used these tools, and when they broke, the administrator returned to square one. Systems administrators had to edit source code and Makefiles just to have a chance of making programs work.

## The Ports and Packages System

The FreeBSD ports and packages system is a software-building system designed to simplify the configuration and installation of software. It started addressing program-building issues back in 1995.

*Ports* are instructions for compiling software on FreeBSD, and *packages* are simply precompiled ports. Packages install more quickly, and can save you time. Ports install more slowly, but will accept changes from your environment (changes you specify in /etc/make.conf).

The basic idea behind the ports and packages system is very simple: If software must be modified to run on BSD, then the modifications should be automated. If you're going to automate the changes, you might as well record what the program includes so you can easily install and uninstall it. And since you have a software-building process that produces exactly the same result each time, and you've recorded everything that the program-building process creates, you can copy the binaries and install them on any similar FreeBSD system. This is the basis of the ports and packages system.

The whole system is called the *ports collection*, the *ports tree*, or even just *ports*. When someone uses one of these terms, he's generally including the ports, the system for building ports, and packages.

### Ports

A port is a set of instructions on how to apply fixes to, or *patch*, a set of source-code files. By combining patches with installation instructions, FreeBSD can maintain a complete record of everything the software-install process has done. This frees you from struggling to install a program, and allows you to concentrate on making the program work properly instead.

If you followed the installation hints in Chapter 1, you installed the ports tree in /usr/ports, something like the following listing:

```
# ls /usr/ports/
INDEX        cad          games        misc         ukrainian
LEGAL        chinese      german       net          vietnamese
Makefile     comms        graphics     news         www
Mk           converters   hebrew       palm         x11
README       databases    irc          picobsd      x11-clocks
Templates    deskutils    japanese     print        x11-fm
```

```
Tools          devel          java          russian        x11-fonts
archivers      distfiles      korean        science        x11-servers
astro          editors        lang          security       x11-toolkits
audio          emulators      mail          shells         x11-wm
benchmarks     french         math          sysutils
biology        ftp            mbone         textproc
#
```

If you don't see something like this listing in usr/ports, you need to install the
ports to continue. To do so, visit your nearest FTP FreeBSD server, and check the
directory for the FreeBSD version you're running; you'll find a directory called
ports. Look for two files, ports.tgz and install.sh; download both and run install.sh.
When you've finished, you should see something like the previous listing.

The directories shown in the previous list are software categories. Each category contains a further layer of directories, and each directory under a category
is a port of a piece of software. Since FreeBSD has almost 6,000 ports as I write
this, this directory tree is vital to keeping them in any sort of order!

The following listing shows the contents of the "astro" ports category, where
astronomical software supported by FreeBSD is kept. (Yes, people use FreeBSD
for serious astronomical work.) This category might not be of much interest to
most people, but it has the serious advantage of being small enough to print in
a book. Some ports categories, such as "www", have hundreds of entries.

```
#ls /usr/ports/astro/
Makefile              p5-Astro-SunTime      sunclock
SETIsupport           p5-Astro-Sunrise      tkseti
dgpsip                p5-GPS                wmglobe
ephem                 p5-Geo-METAR          wmmoonclock
fooseti               pkg                   wmspaceweather
gkrellmearth          pyweather             wmsun
gkrellmoon            rmap                  x3arth
glunarclock           saoimage              xearth
jday                  sattrack              xephem
ksetiwatch            seti_applet           xglobe
luna                  setiathome            xphoon
openuniverse          sscalc                xplanet
p5-Astro-MoonPhase    stars                 xtide
#
```

### Finding Software

Some of the categories have hundreds of ports, so how can you ever find anything? For an index of ports, see /usr/ports/INDEX, which contains a list of all
the ports, in alphabetical order. Each port is described on a single line, with
fields separated by pipe symbols (|).

While this is a convenient format for the various system tools to access, it's not particularly human-readable. For you to start reading the index file, you need to know what each field means. (Some of the fields appear redundant, but they're needed for reasons we'll get to later.) Here's a sample entry, with a line break at each delimiter to make it easier to understand:

❶ fooseti-0.6.5|
❷ /usr/ports/astro/fooseti|
❸ /usr/local|
❹ GTK+ frontend to SETI@Home|
❺ /usr/ports/astro/fooseti/pkg-descr|
❻ petef@databits.net|
❼ astro|
❽ XFree86-3.3.6_9 gettext-0.10.35 glib-1.2.10_3 gtk-1.2.10_2|
❾ XFree86-3.3.6_9 gettext-0.10.35 glib-1.2.10_3 gtk-1.2.10_2|
❿ http://www-personal.engin.umich.edu/~agorski/fooseti

The first field (❶) is the name and version number of the software package—in this case, fooseti version 0.6.5. The second field (❷) is the directory where the port can be found (/usr/ports/astro/fooseti), and the next (❸) is the default installation location. The fooseti port, for example, installs under /usr/local unless the administrator chooses a separate location. Following is a short description of the software package (❹).

The fifth field (❺) gives the location of a file, with a more complete description of the software. The email address field (❻) lists the software's FreeBSD maintainer, someone who has assumed responsibility for making sure the port works properly. Next is the category (❼), the directory under /usr/ports where the port directory lives.

Field eight (❽) contains the list of ports needed to build this software. Many ports require other ports as prerequisites; for example, a piece of software might require a special version of make to build, called a *build dependency*. This example needs XFree86, gettext, glib, and gtk.

The ninth field (❾)lists the ports needed to run this software. Many ports have such *runtime dependencies* in addition to the build dependencies, meaning that when the program runs, it tries to call other programs. If the program's dependencies are not found, the program cannot run. Our example has identical buildtime and runtime dependencies, though this is not always the case.

Last is the URL of the program's home page (❿).

**NOTE** *If you forget what each field means,* make print-index *will print out a much longer, but prettier, list of everything in the index.*

### Finding by Name

Knowing what the index contains is nice, but how can it help you find a piece of software?

Well, if you know the exact name of the software package, you can use a simple grep command to pick it out. This is quick and easy, but it only works if you're comfortable with grep(1) *and* you know the exact name of the software in the FreeBSD ports tree. For example, to find staroffice you might enter this grep command:

```
# grep -i ^staroffice INDEX
staroffice-5.1a|/usr/ports/editors/staroffice5|/usr/local|Integrated
wordprocessor/dbase/spreadheet/drawing/chart/browser|/usr/ports/editors/staroffice5/
pkg-descr|mb@imp.ch|editors linux|unzip-5.42|linux_base-6.1|
staroffice-5.2|/usr/ports/editors/staroffice52|/usr/local|Integrated
wordprocessor/dbase/spreadheet/drawing/chart/browser|/usr/ports/editors/staroffice52
/pkg-descr|mb@imp.ch|editors linux|linux_base-6.1||
#
```

This output shows us that we have two different versions of staroffice available, version 5.1a and version 5.2. Both are available under /usr/ports/editors, in staroffice5 and staroffice52, respectively.

### Finding by Partial Name

If you don't know the software's exact name, try the ports collection's search feature. The make search command scans the ports index for you, searching either for the name of a port or ports where a word appears.

For example, if you're looking for the popular Midnight Commander file manager, you might try this command:

```
# make search name=midnight
#
```

Well, *that* was less than helpful.

### Finding by Keyword

If that search doesn't work, as in the preceding example, you can try a more generic search using the key option. This search scans more fields, returning more hits. (Though if you're searching for a common word, the key search can provide far too much information.)

Here's how to use the key search on the word "midnight":

```
# make search key=midnight
Port:   mc-4.5.54_2
Path: ? /usr/ports/misc/mc
Info:   Midnight Commander, a free Norton Commander Clone
Maint:  gnome@FreeBSD.org
Index:  misc
B-deps: gettext-0.10.35 glib-1.2.10_3 gmake-3.79.1
R-deps: gettext-0.10.35 glib-1.2.10_3
#
```

Aha! Midnight Commander can be found under ? /usr/ports/misc/mc.

### Other Ways to Browse the Ports Collection

If you prefer working with a Web browser, you can build an HTML index. Just go to /usr/ports and, as root, type **make readmes** to generate a file (README.html) with the contents of your ports tree. (You can click through various categories, and even view detailed descriptions of each port.)

If none of these options work, try the FreeBSD Ports Tree search service at http://www.FreeBSD.org/cgi/ports.cgi.

Between the Web and the search engine, you should be able to find a piece of software to meet your needs.

### *Legal Restrictions*

While most of the software in the ports collection is free for noncommercial use, some of it includes unusual legal restrictions. The /usr/ports/LEGAL file lists legal restrictions on various pieces of software. The most common restriction is a prohibition on redistribution; the FreeBSD Project does not include such software in its CD-ROM distributions, just instructions on how to build it. For example, for a long time FreeBSD did not have a Java license. The Project was not allowed to distribute the Java source code or compiled binaries. They could distribute instructions on how to build the source code, however. You could go to a Sun Microsystems Web page, download the Java source, and build your own version of Java on FreeBSD.

Similarly, some pieces of software prohibit commercial use or embedding in commercial products. A few cannot be exported from the United States, thanks to International Traffic in Arms Regulations (ITAR)—they contain cryptography and are classified as "munitions."[2] If you're building FreeBSD systems for redistribution, export, or commercial use, you'll definitely want to check this file.

[2] Most of this software is available from non-US sources, and can be downloaded anywhere in the world. The official FreeBSD CD-ROM's images are generated in the United States, however.

Fortunately, the software required for providing network services is free for either commercial or noncommercial use. These restricted packages are the exception, not the rule.

# Using Packages

Packages are precompiled software for a particular version of FreeBSD. We're going to discuss using packages first, as they're generally easier and faster to use than ports. Once you have a grip on packages, we'll go on to ports.

Unless a piece of software has legal restrictions against being distributed in compiled form, it's available as a package. Other software (such as Microsoft Word[3]) is only available in precompiled form. Packages are available on CD-ROM and via FTP.

Installing software as a package can save you a great deal of time because you don't have to spend your time compiling from source. To install a package, find its name by searching the ports tree, as described earlier.

### Installing from CD-ROM

If you have a FreeBSD CD-ROM set, you already have a fairly extensive collection of compiled packages. To use them, all you need to do is mount the CD and read the package file.

We'll discuss mounting and unmounting media in detail in Chapter 16, but here are the basics.

Put your CD in its drive, become root, and type this command:

```
# mount -t cd9660 /dev/acd0c /cdrom
#
```

The contents of your CD-ROM are now available under /cdrom.

**NOTE** *You won't be able to eject the CD-ROM while you're using it, or while it's mounted. If you have an idle command prompt sitting on /cdrom, you won't be able to unmount it. To unmount the CD-ROM, enter this command:*

```
# umount /cdrom
```

[3] No, Microsoft Word is not available on FreeBSD. Yet. But it's very difficult to think of a major, recognizable example of binary-only software for FreeBSD, as almost all of it is available in source form.

Once you have the CD mounted, look at the packages directory:

```
# cd /cdrom/packages/
# ls
All             deskutils       japanese        print           tk82
INDEX           devel           java            python          tk83
Latest          editors         kde             ruby            tkstep80
archivers       elisp           korean          russian         windowmaker
astro           emulators       lang            security        www
audio           french          mail            shells          x11
biology         ftp             math            sysutils        x11-fm
cad             games           mbone           tcl80           x11-fonts
chinese         german          misc            tcl82           x11-toolkits
comms           gnome           net             tcl83           x11-wm
converters      graphics        palm            textproc        zope
databases       ipv6            perl5           tk80
#
```

This should look familiar. Yep, it's the same as the ports tree listing we saw earlier in the chapter. If you go into a directory, however, you'll see something a little different. A single CD-ROM doesn't have nearly enough room to store all the FreeBSD packages, which can be quite large (up to hundreds of megs). You'll find some packages, but not all of them. Many other packages are available on other FreeBSD CD-ROMs. Second, these are files, not directories; they're tarballs containing complete software packages.

For example, in /cdrom/packages/astro we'll see two packages. Both of these are based on ports you'll find in the astro directory of the ports tree.

```
# cd astro/
# ls
openuniverse-1.0.b3.tgz xglobe-0.5.tgz
#
```

To see what a package does, check its description in /usr/ports/INDEX. Search for the package name in the index file, just as we searched for a port name in the index (in the "Finding Software" section, earlier in the chapter). In the fourth field, you'll find a description of the port:

```
# grep -i ^openuniv /usr/ports/INDEX
openuniverse-1.0.b3|/usr/ports/astro/openuniverse|/usr/X11R6|OpenGL Solar System
simulator for X Window System|/usr/ports/astro/openuniverse/pkg-
descr|trevor@FreeBSD.org|astro|Mesa-3.4.2_1 XFree86-libraries-4.1.0 freetype2-2.0.4
gettext-0.10.35 gmake-3.79.1 imake-4.1.0 jpeg-6b|Mesa-3.4.2_1 XFree86-libraries-
4.1.0 freetype2-2.0.4 imake-4.1.0 jpeg-6b|http://openuniverse.sourceforge.net/
#
```

The fourth field of this description says that openuniverse is an "OpenGL Solar System simulator for X Window System." A solar system simulator does sound kind of cool, doesn't it? Let's install it! Use pkg_add(1) to install packages:

```
# pkg_add openuniverse-1.0.b3.tgz
#
```

That's it! The software is installed and ready to use. (The installation usually runs silently, though you'll occasionally see messages during a package install. Pay attention to them, and take whatever action they recommend.)

If a package requires other packages, pkg_add(1) should automatically find those packages and install them. The CD sets are designed such that the dependencies are all on one disk whenever possible. However, if a required package is not available, pkg_add will complain about the missing package by name and fail. In that case, find the required package on another disk and install it first, or just install over FTP.

### Installing via FTP

Frequently, a package doesn't exist on the CD because the FreeBSD Project has limited space on its CD-ROM sets and can't possibly fit all 6,000-plus packages onto 4 disks! Also, software on CD is built for a particular release of FreeBSD. Having a CD-ROM of packages for version 4.4 won't help you if you're running FreeBSD 4.6.

Too, if you're tracking -stable, the packages on the CD are slightly out of date, and you should grab the latest package from ftp.FreeBSD.org. (You must have a live Internet connection to do this!)

If you know the full package name and version number, you can get the latest package from the FreeBSD FTP site automatically, like so:

```
# pkg_add -r xearth
Fetching ftp://ftp.FreeBSD.org/pub/FreeBSD/ports/i386/packages-4.4-
release/Latest/xearth.tgz... Done.
#
```

The advantage of this is that the system will automatically find the proper FTP location, download the proper version of the package and all dependencies, and install them all. The downside is, you have to have a live Internet connection.

This method is also less secure than installing from CD. While the packages on the CD set have all been inspected and verified to be what they claim to be, the packages on the FTP server could have been tampered with by a malicious hacker. You could be installing Trojan horses, or worse. (This has never happened, mind you, but it is theoretically possible.)

You can also manually download packages from an FTP site of your choice. (We discussed finding a convenient FTP server in Chapter 1.) To do so, find a convenient FTP site and log in to that server. Then, if you're running a -release, go to pub/FreeBSD/release and into the directory for your version of -release. If you're tracking -stable or -current, go to pub/FreeBSD/ports and choose the directory for your -stable or -release.

Once in the appropriate directory, you'll see a directory tree much like that under /usr/ports. Now, just find your package and download it, then install it via the command line:

```
# pkg_add openuniverse-1.0.b3.tgz
#
```

**NOTE** *This method will not automatically install dependencies. It's most useful for times when you're behind a firewall and must jump through some hoops to download files from the Internet.*

### What Does a Package Install?

Now that your software is installed, how do you find it on your system? There's no Start menu, after all! Not to worry.

For a complete list of what a piece of software has installed, see /var/db/pkg. This directory contains a complete list of every port or package you have installed on the system, and what each set of software contains.

For example, our /var/db/pkg now contains a directory called openuniverse-1.0.b3. If you look in that directory, you'll see the following:

```
# ls /var/db/pkg/openuniverse-1.0.b3/
+COMMENT        +CONTENTS      +DESC
#
```

The +COMMENT file is a brief description of the package; +DESC contains a longer description of the package. The interesting file is +CONTENTS, which lists every file installed by the package. This file is quite long, but we'll look at the start of it.

```
# more /var/db/pkg/openuniverse-1.0.3b/+CONTENTS
❶ @name openuniverse-1.0.b3
@cwd ❷ /usr/X11R6
❸ @pkgdep jpeg-6b
@pkgdep Mesa-3.4.1
@comment ❹ ORIGIN:astro/openuniverse
❺ bin/openuniverse
@comment MD5:2a4775c079a589e78cf54be5444316cb
share/openuniverse/data/stars.dat
```

```
@comment MD5:eee6bb0caf1ae32bc2ff043e7baee17a
share/openuniverse/data/messier.dat
@comment MD5:acd357ee82d95121fbf42ba9982f1dd8
```

The first line (❶) is, of course, the name. Following that is the directory tree where the package was installed (❷) after the cwd keyword. You can see that ope-nuniverse is installed under /usr/X11R6. The pkgdep keywords (❸) are other packages that this package depends on. The ORIGIN comment (❹) is the category in the ports tree where this package was created.

Finally you have the list of files (❺). Each file installed by this program is listed here, along with its MD5 checksum. (The various package-handling tools use the MD5 checksum to verify that a file is still good and that it hasn't been damaged during transit or by operator error.)

Each file is listed relative to the directory tree given in the packing list. For example, the file bin/openuniverse was actually installed under /usr/X11R6, giving us /usr/X11R6/bin/openuniverse. Similarly, various files are listed as being in share/openuniverse, which is under /usr/X11R6, giving us the real directory of /usr/X11R6/share/openuniverse. Most files installed in a share directory are either documentation or program data. You can read the documentation, or just run openuniverse and see what happens.

(Much of this information on files and directories is also available through pkg_info(1), but it's frequently easier to just look for yourself.)

### Uninstalling Packages

Use pkg_delete(1) to uninstall packages:

```
# pkg_delete openuniverse-1.0.b3
#
```

If you want to uninstall a package required by other packages, only do so when you know exactly what you're doing, and why. (For example, you might want to upgrade a dependency package to a newer version.) Don't expect software that requires this package to work once you've uninstalled it, however!

You can use pkg_delete -f to force an uninstall. Pkg_delete will warn you, but will do it anyway.

### Package Information

Uninstalling works well when you remember the exact version number of every package you've installed. If you can do that, I commend you. If you're like me, though, you're lucky to remember that you have a piece of software installed on a system, let alone which version it is!

FreeBSD includes pkg_info, a tool to examine installed packages in a more convenient manner than manually scanning /var/db/pkg. Pkg_info(1) uses the contents of /var/db/pkg to do its work, but automatically handles a lot of boring manual searching and sorting for you.

When it is run without any options, pkg_info lists each package installed on your system, along with a brief description of each:

```
# pkg_info
Hermes-1.3.2          Fast pixel formats conversion library
JX-1.5.3_1            A C++ application framework and widget library for X11
Mesa-3.4.2_1          A graphics library similar to SGI's OpenGL
ORBit-0.5.8_1         High-performance CORBA ORB with support for the C language
XFree86-aoutlibs-3.3.3 XFree86 a.out compatibility libraries
...
```

As you can see, this output will give you the name and version of each package you've installed, so you can uninstall it easily.

### Package Info Arguments

You can use various arguments with pkg_info to gather other information about the packages on your system. When you start using arguments, pkg_info requires either a package name to investigate or the -a flag, which means "for all packages."

For example, to learn which packages on your system require other packages, you would use this option:

```
# pkg_info -aR
Information for Hermes-1.3.2:

Required by:
windowmaker-0.65.0_1
wmakerconf-2.8.1
Information for JX-1.5.3_1:
Required by:
libjtree-1.1.7_1
libjtoolbar-0.5.4_1
code_crusader-2.1.4_1
...
```

To find out the space needed by the files within a package, use pkg_info -s packagename. (Note that this only includes files installed by the package; files *created by* the package are another matter entirely. After all, do you count your text files and email messages as part of your office suite?)

Another common question is which package a file came from. You might be browsing through /usr/local/bin and come across a file that you don't recognize, haven't used, and have no idea why it's there. Use the -W flag to pkg_info to perform a sort of "reverse lookup" on files to see which package they came from:

```
# pkg_info -W /usr/local/bin/xwe
/usr/local/bin/xwe was installed by package xwpe-1.5.22a
#
```

### Controlling Pkg_add

You can use shell-environment variables to control how package-handling tools behave.

#### PKG_TMPDIR

The `PKG_TMPDIR` environment variable controls where pkg_add will unpack its temporary files.

A package is a tarball with some added instructions on how to install things. To install a package, you have to untar it. If you're short on space in the standard directories that pkg_add tries to use, the untar will not finish and the install will fail. By default, pkg_add tries to use the directory given by the environment variable TMPDIR. If that variable doesn't exist, pkg_add checks for room in /tmp, /var/tmp, and /usr/tmp, in that order.

You can set `PKG_TMPDIR` to make pkg_add use a different directory, where you do have room:

```
# setenv PKG_TMPDIR /usr/home/mwlucas/garbage
#
```

(You can add this line to your .cshrc to have it set every time you log in.)

#### PACKAGEROOT

The `PACKAGEROOT` environment variable controls the FTP server used by pkg_add's automatic package fetching. By default, `pkg_add -r` tries to download everything from ftp.FreeBSD.org, the default server. However, you can frequently get better performance by manually choosing a closer, less heavily used mirror.

Set this `PACKAGEROOT` with a particular server name and protocol as a URL. For example, to download from ftp3.FreeBSD.org, enter this:

```
# setenv PACKAGEROOT ftp://ftp3.FreeBSD.org
#
```

## PACKAGESITE

PACKAGESITE, another popular environment variable, gives an exact path to check for a package repository. You might choose to use this if you want to use packages from a particular release, or if you have a local package repository. (We'll discuss setting up a local package repository in the "Building Packages" section, later in the chapter.)

Set the PACKAGESITE variable as an absolute URL:

```
# setenv PACKAGESITE ftp://ftp4.FreeBSD.org/pub/FreeBSD/releases/4.4-
STABLE/packages/All
#
```

## Package Problems

The package scheme seems like a great system, right? Well, sort of. There are a few problems, specifically lags in the software-porting process and the software-synchronization requirements.

The overwhelming majority of packages is software produced by third parties, folks who release their software on a schedule completely independent of FreeBSD. When they release an updated version of their software, the FreeBSD package is updated. There is a delay between the release of an original software package and the port to FreeBSD. A popular port might be updated in hours, while large or less frequently used ports can languish at an older version for days or weeks.

Also, packages are interdependent, and many rely upon others in order to function properly. When the FreeBSD ports team changes a package, that change cascades through all the dependent packages. That's why you'll see packages with names like windowmaker-0.65.0_1. The _1 shows that a program the package depends on has changed, and so this version of WindowMaker is slightly different than the previous version. These bumped version numbers might also indicate that the port itself was slightly changed; for example, the build process for the FreeBSD port of WindowMaker 0.65.0 has been updated once. (Often these changes are purely internal, and don't affect the software's behavior or performance.)

If you're running a FreeBSD release and only installing software from the CD or the version released with your release, this interdependency isn't much of an issue. After all, the packages built for a release do not change. You might be running an older version of FreeBSD, but want a program that was just released. You might be continually upgrading your system, and have older versions of software.

For example, the package wmakerconf-2.8.1 requires windowmaker-0.65.0_1. That's fine if you have the right package installed, but if you have installed windowmaker-0.65.0 or windowmaker-0.65.0_2, pkg_add will think that you don't have the proper required package installed and will go grab the appropriate WindowMaker. This takes up disk space at best, and overwrites existing software at worst.

One way around this problem is always to use packages from the same date or time. (If you set the PACKAGESITE environment variable to the packages directory for a particular FreeBSD release, you'll always have matching packages.) This is perfectly acceptable in many cases, since you don't always need the latest version of a piece of software when a version just a month or two older will work just fine. In other cases, this practice isn't acceptable because an older version might have security problems or performance issues. In that case, I recommend you use ports instead. Rather than checking for installed programs by the name of the package, ports check for the existence of the program itself. To continue our earlier example, the port for wmakerconf won't check for WindowMaker version 0.65.0_2, it will just look for a program called "windowmaker." This makes ports much more flexible.

### Forcing an Install

There will be times when you want to use a package where a dependency has changed, and you don't want to upgrade the dependency or use an older package. Don't do it. Programs can crash, badly, if you do.

Still, it is possible to force an install if you want to—after all, dependency changes are frequently minor and do not affect program behavior. The hard part is verifying that your programs will be okay.

**NOTE** *Before you read further, let me say that you should not be doing this. If you're in this situation, use a port instead. It will take longer, but things will almost certainly work correctly. If this isn't possible, read on.*

Should you consider forcing an install? Well, as a very general rule of thumb, if the package name has changed by either adding a trailing underscore and a number, or if this trailing number has been incremented, the package may work. This is no guarantee, mind you, and if things start breaking, you'll have to uninstall the package and do things correctly.

To force an install, first, manually grab the package you want to use. (Be sure you don't have a packages CD-ROM mounted—you don't want the system to go looking for matching dependencies and install them, overwriting your existing software and causing problems.)

Once you've grabbed your package, run pkg_add -f:

```
# pkg_add -f packagename.tgz
```

You'll see a warning that a dependency was not found, but that the install is proceeding anyway. If the software works, great! If not, uninstall it and start working with ports.

## Using Ports

It takes longer to build software using ports than it does when using packages, and the ports system requires a live Internet connection. Still, the ports system can produce better results than packages.

Let's take a look at a port. We're going to pick on one of my favorite security tools, SKIP.[4]

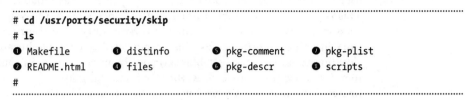

```
# cd /usr/ports/security/skip
# ls
❶ Makefile        ❸ distinfo       ❺ pkg-comment      ❼ pkg-plist
❷ README.html     ❹ files          ❻ pkg-descr        ❽ scripts
#
```

The Makefile in the preceding list (❶) contains the basic instructions for building this port. If you were to take a look at this file, you'd quickly notice that there isn't much in it. The Makefiles for individual ports don't contain much beyond some basic information about the port; they don't have information about how to build FreeBSD software in general. (Most of the FreeBSD ports Makefile system is contained in the directory /usr/ports/Mk; editing these files is a very advanced topic, and you really don't want to go there until you're very comfortable with Makefiles.)

The README.html file (❷) gives a brief description of the port. If you're using a Web browser to skim the ports collection, you'll be directed to this file when you ask for information on this port.

The distinfo file (❸) contains integrity-checking information (or checksums) for the files required to build this program.

The files directory (❹) contains any add-on files required to build this port. Our particular example requires 87 patches, but many ports don't even have a files directory, and build cleanly without patching.

The pkg-comment file (❺) contains a one-line description of the port. Similarly, pkg-descr (❻) contains a longer, more detailed description and (usually) a URL for more information on the program.

The pkg-plist file (❼) holds a list of all the files installed by the port (the "packing list"). If a file is not listed here, it will not be installed.

Finally, the scripts directory (❽) holds a variety of scripts to be run at various stages of the port-building process. This directory might or might not exist—if the port builds without any special tweaking, it won't have any additional scripts. These scripts perform any pre- or post-processing that the port needs, for example, changing permissions on a downloaded distfile so that patch(1) can run properly.

Combined, these files create the tools and instructions needed to build the software.

---

[4] SKIP is Sun's Secure Connectionless Internet Protocol (the acronym stands for Simple Key-management for Internet Protocols). It is a wonderful virtual private network (VPN) protocol that has unfortunately fallen into disfavor in the face of IPSec. This is yet another example of the market bludgeoning cool technology into the grave.

### Installing a Port

If you're familiar with source code, you'll quickly notice that there is no actual source code in the port. Sure, there's patches to apply to source code, and scripts to run on source code, but no actual source code! You might rightly ask just how this is supposed to work without the source code.

When you activate a port, your system automatically downloads the appropriate source code from an approved Internet site. It then checks the downloaded code for integrity errors, extracts the code to a working directory, patches it, builds it, installs everything, and records the installation under /var/db/pkg. If the port has dependencies, and those dependencies aren't installed, it will interrupt the make process to build those dependencies, and then finish its own. To trigger all this, you just have to go to a port directory and type this command:

```
# make install
```

When you do, you'll see lots of text scroll down your terminal window, ending with a "recording installation" message.

This all-in-one installation process handles any changes in dependencies. If a port requires another program, the port will simply gloss over minor changes in that program. For example, perhaps you have a version of Apache that's a few months old. A package would demand that you install the newer version, while a port will just check to see if Apache is installed.

As you grow more experienced with building source code, however, you'll find that this all-in-one approach isn't appropriate for every occasion. Not to worry; the ports system gives you the opportunity to take the port-building process exactly as far as you like, because make install is actually not one but a series of commands.

### Using Make Install

The make install process starts with make fetch. During this stage of the process, make checks to see whether the source code is in /usr/ports/distfiles. If it's not, your system goes to get it.

**Make Fetch**   The make fetch process first checks for the source code in the MAS-TER_SITE listed in the Makefile, then checks a list of backup sites provided by the ports system itself. If it finds the source code, it downloads it, and that downloaded source code is called a *distfile*.

**Make Checksum**   Next, make checksum confirms that the distfile's digital signature matches the one that the port has in the distinfo file. This is a security measure; if the FTP server was broken into by a malicious hacker and the source code replaced by a Trojan horse, or if the download was corrupted, this step will detect it and stop the build with a warning about a checksum mismatch. If the distfile has been deliberately changed, make checksum stops compilation.

*Software authors sometimes make minor changes to their code, but give the source file the same name as when they first made it available for download. The FreeBSD port might or might not work after this change. If you're sure that the distfile has not been compromised or corrupted, and want to use it despite this warning, you can override this with* make NO_CHECKSUM=YES. *I highly recommend that you check with your vendor to see if this is a legitimate change.*

**Make Depends**   The make depends stage checks to see if the port is dependent on any other software, and, if so, whether that software is installed. (For example, an X window manager requires an X server.) If the software on which the port depends is not found, this stage recurses through the various dependencies and completely builds them all.

**Make Extract**   Once you have the port distfiles, you have to uncompress and extract them. This is done under a work directory in the port. To create this directory and uncompress the distfiles under it, use make extract.

**Make Patch**   The make patch stage applies any FreeBSD-specific patches listed in the Makefile to the port.

**Make Configure**   Next, make configure checks to see if the program needs a configure script. If it does, it runs it. If not, the port build proceeds silently to the next step.

**Make Build**   The make build stage compiles the checked, extracted, and patched software.

**Make Install**   Finally, make install installs the software and records its presence under /var/db/pkg.

**Make Target Dependencies**   Each make target depends on the make targets before it. You cannot patch source code that you have not yet fetched, for example. Whenever you use any make target, make runs all previous stages that have not yet been run. For example, make extract performs a make fetch, make checksum, and make extract.

How might you use these make stages in practice? Say that you want to apply some patches to a program before you compile it—patches that address stability or security problems. You want to apply the patch to your source code after you've extracted it and applied the FreeBSD-specific patches. To do so, you could run make patch, apply the new patches to the software under the work directory according to the vendor's instructions, and then return to the port directory and type make install.

### Built-In Port Features

Ports allow you to do a great deal of customization, which you can read about in the port's Makefile. Since the port's Makefile includes specific instructions for building this particular piece of software, it's where options for that software are most likely to be found.

Many ports announce additional features when you first type `make install`, though not all will work (especially some older ones). Whether a feature will work depends on the port maintainer's skills, time, and inclination—remember, this is a volunteer project!

You can always get information about a port's additional features from the Makefile, but let's look at an announcement and see how to use it first. For example, when you try to install /usr/ports/security/snort you'll see a notice:

```
Set WITH_FLEXRESP, WITH_MYSQL, WITH_ODBC or WITH_POSTGRES
to get additional support.
```

A bit of Web searching would show you that mysql, odbc, and postgresql are database packages, and this message tells you that you could build Snort with support for these databases. A similar search would show that flexresp is part of the libnet software package.

If you get an announcement, and you want to use one of these options, press **CONTROL-C** to abort the port build. You can then set these options on the install command line like this:

```
# make WITH_ODBC=YES install
```

This command changes the way the port will be built and will build your version of Snort with support for ODBC database connections. With this feature built into Snort, you would then be able to log data across the network to any database that supports ODBC, such as Microsoft SQL Server or an Oracle database.

Here's one area where ports shine over packages. You couldn't do this customization with a package, unless you had multiple versions of the same package. And sorting through snort-odbc-1.9.tgz, snort-mysql-1.9.tgz, snort-postgres-mysql-libnet-1.9.tgz, and so on would be utterly hideous, waste space on the CD, and be mostly unused.

The Makefile itself will tell you the build options for a port. At the top of the Makefile, you'll see a lot of stuff that describes the port, like this:

```
❶ PORTNAME=      snort
❷ PORTVERSION=   1.8
❸ CATEGORIES=    security
❹ MASTER_SITES=  http://www.snort.org/Files/ \
                 http://www.physik.TU-Berlin.DE/~ibex/ports/distfiles/
❺ DISTNAME=      ${PORTNAME}-${PORTVERSION}-RELEASE
```

*(continued on next page)*

```
❻ MAINTAINER=        dirk@FreeBSD.org

❼ GNU_CONFIGURE=  yes
❽ CONFIGURE_ARGS= --with-mysql=no --with-odbc=no --with-postgresql=no
❾ MAN8=              snort.8
```

Much of this is obvious to people who habitually build software from source. If you're not at that point yet, don't worry. You'll get there with practice. Let's consider this particular example. Not all of these entries are mandatory, and there are many other possible entries in port Makefiles, but these are fairly common.

The PORTNAME (❶) is the name the software uses in FreeBSD's ports system. This is not necessarily the same as the software name, as we saw earlier in our search for Midnight Commander. The PORTVERSION (❷) is the version number of the software, as given by the software's author.

CATEGORIES (❸) lists all the ports directories where the port can be found. For example, this port is under /usr/ports/security.

MASTER_SITES (❹) contains a list of Internet sites where the software can be found. This is where the ports system tries to get the software from. If one site is unreachable, it tries the next.

The DISTNAME (❺) is the name of the original file of software source code. The ports system tries to grab this file from the MASTER_SITES given earlier.

The MAINTAINER (❻) is the person responsible for maintaining the FreeBSD port. This person doesn't actually write the software, but just makes sure that it installs on FreeBSD.

GNU_CONFIGURE (❼) tells the ports system if the software needs to use the classic GNU program autoconf. In a related entry, CONFIGURE_ARGS (❽) lists arguments to be given to autoconf.

There is usually a list of man pages that the program installs (❾). You can check these pages with man(1) to see how to use the program. You might then see a bunch of "if defined" statements like this one:

```
.if defined ❶ (WITH_FLEXRESP)
BUILD_DEPENDS ❷ += ${LOCALBASE}/lib/libnet.a:$ ? {PORTSDIR}/net/libnet
CONFIGURE_ARGS +=--enable-flexresp
CONFIGURE_ENV += CPPFLAGS="-I${LOCALBASE}/include"
LDFLAGS+=       "-L${LOCALBASE}/lib"
.endif
```

This is a build option for the port. The first line in this example is the variable (❶) you need to set—in this case, WITH_FLEXRESP. The second line shows that this adds a dependency (❷) for the port, /usr/ports/net/libnet. The remainder is a bunch of software-building commands that are altered by setting this variable.

You set this variable on the command line. To set `WITH_FLEXRESP`, you would type

```
# make install WITH_FLEXRESP=YES
```

You don't need to understand the balance of this listing right now, but notice the little question mark (?) and plus and equal (+=) symbols scattered throughout it. These mean that you're adding commands to the build process, literally changing how the software is built just by setting this variable! Setting variables on the command line is much simpler than figuring out how to add these commands to the build process on your own.

If you use several make commands to build the port (for example, `make patch` and then `make install clean`), you must include any options you want with every make command. Otherwise, the port might not build correctly. For example, if you wanted to use the flexresp option in Snort, but had your own custom patch to apply, you would need to run the following:

```
# make patch WITH_FLEXRESP=YES
```

Then you would apply your patch and run this:

```
# make install WITH_FLEXRESP=YES
```

Otherwise, you would patch your system with the customization option `WITH_FLEXRESP`, but you wouldn't give it the correct instructions when compiling the software. Your program would be internally inconsistent, and quite possibly would fail.

The hardest part of customizing the way your software builds is deciding which options you'd like. Unfortunately, there is no easy answer to this question, so it's best to check the software manual or Web site to help you decide. More than once I've installed a piece of software, read the documentation, and turned right around to uninstall and reinstall with the options I needed.

### Uninstalling and Reinstalling

One nice thing about installing ports is that, once installed, the port is treated just like a package. You can uninstall a port with pkg_delete, and learn about it with pkg_info. Since the port's installation is recorded under /var/db/pkg, you can also go through the contents file and investigate every file the port includes.

You also can uninstall a port from the port directory. For example, suppose FreeBSD includes several different versions of one port, like the Apache Web server. You might want to build several different versions of the port, evaluate each, and pick one to install for long-term use. Then, once you've evaluated one version of the program, and want to uninstall it, you can run `make deinstall` in the port directory to erase the program from the main system.

*Once you've run* make install, *the compiled program and source files still live under the work subdirectory in the port. You can run* make reinstall *to reinstall an uninstalled program. You can uninstall and reinstall a program as many times as you like.*

At some point, you may find that you want to reinstall a port you've removed with pkg_delete and that when you run make reinstall it fails, complaining that the port is already installed. Why? Well, do a "long list" of the problem port's work directory:

```
# cd /usr/ports/www/apache13/work
# ls -a
total 21
969094 drwxr-xr-x  3 root   wheel     512 Jul 22 21:24 .
778196 drwxr-xr-x  4 root   wheel     512 Jul 27 20:42 ..
969343 -rw-r--r--  1 root   wheel   17163 Jul 22 21:24 .PLIST.mktmp
969344 -rw-r--r--  1 root   wheel       0 Jul 22 21:24 .PLIST.setuid
969345 -rw-r--r--  1 root   wheel      19 Jul 22 21:24 .PLIST.startup
969341 -rw-r--r--  1 root   wheel       0 Jul 22 21:23 .build_done
969115 -rw-r--r--  1 root   wheel       0 Jul 22 21:22 .configure_done
969112 -rw-r--r--  1 root   wheel       0 Jul 22 21:21 .extract_done
969342 -rw-r--r--  1 root   wheel       0 Jul 22 21:24 .install_done
969113 -rw-r--r--  1 root   wheel       0 Jul 22 21:21 .patch_done
318289 drwxr-xr-x  8 root   wheel     512 Jul 22 21:23 apache_1.3.20
#
```

So what does this tell us? Well, all files whose names begin with a period (which is most of the files listed here, except for apache_1.3.20) are "hidden" files that don't show up on a normal directory listing. The ports system and the make process uses these files to keep track of what stage the build process is in. Every port uses these files. See the hidden file .install_done? If that file exists, the port believes that it's already installed, and it refuses to overwrite itself. So there's our problem.

Remove that file, and the make reinstall will succeed.

### Cleaning Up with Make Clean

Ports can take up a lot of room. Some, such as XFree86, can soak up a couple hundred megs of disk once they're extracted and built. Most of this disk usage is from the original source code, which you will no longer need. The ports system includes a method to remove excess source code.

Once you have your program installed and configured the way you like it, you don't really need the copy of the source code in the ports directory any more. You can remove it with make clean. (This blows away the work directory, so be sure that you're happy with your program before you do it!) You can also clean a new port immediately on install by running make install clean when you install it.

You might also clean the port's original distfiles, which are stored in /usr/ports/distfiles. (Check this directory now and then, because it can fill up quickly if you build a lot of ports.) Removing unneeded distfiles frees considerable disk space.

To clean the entire ports tree, run `make clean` directly under /usr/ports. This takes some time, though, and, while there are faster and more efficient ways to remove every work directory in the ports tree, this one is directly supported by the FreeBSD Project.

### Building Packages

If you're using ports, you can build your own packages to install on other FreeBSD machines, which can save you a lot of time and ensure that you have identical software on every machine. If you have several machines running Snort, for example, and you want them all to have the same features, you can build Snort once and then make a package out of it to install on all the other machines.

The command to create a package is `make package`. This will install the program on the local machine and create a package in that port's directory. Simply copy this package to other systems and run pkg_add to install it.

You can even set up an anonymous FTP server (see Chapter 12) and have a local master package repository. Remember the `PACKAGESITE` environment variable? Set that to a path on your anonymous FTP server and put your custom packages there. You can then use `pkg_add -r` on your other machines, and they will automatically grab the customized packages.

### Changing the Install Path

If you have dozens, or even hundreds, of FreeBSD systems, all with mostly identical configurations, you might find the default port or package installation path of /usr/local problematic. In many large server farms, /usr/local is reserved for programs that are unique to the individual machine, and other software packages that are used by every system in the server farm are expected to be installed elsewhere.

A common alternative to /usr/local is /usr/pkg, which you can set for your system with the `PREFIX` variable:

```
# make PREFIX=/usr/pkg install clean
```

When the port is installed, it will go into your chosen location.

### Setting Make Options Permanently

If you get sick and tired of typing the same options repeatedly when building ports, you can list your options in make.conf to have them automatically used whenever you install a port. See the section on make.conf in Chapter 9 for details.

**NOTE** *While we're at it, /etc/make.conf is scanned any time you run make. This means that any options you set there are applied to ports. While features like CPUTYPE might not make a difference for you, it's possible that they will. In any event, it's a possible source of confusion, and you should at least be aware that it exists.*

# Upgrading Ports and Packages

The software-upgrade process can be very simple or a complete nightmare, but with a bit of preparation you can avoid many common pitfalls. The following list of suggestions assumes that you're upgrading an Internet server and that you have actual users depending on it. (If you're upgrading your laptop, you can consider your user notified before you start.)

1.  The first thing to do when upgrading is to be sure that you have a package of the older version of the software available. If things go wrong on a production system, you'll want to be able to fall back to the older version very quickly. If you've installed the software from CD-ROM, check that you still have that disk; if you installed via FTP, download the same package and keep it handy.

2.  If at all possible, test the upgraded software on a nonproduction system. Production server upgrades can give even seasoned administrators white hair and worse tempers. Successfully upgrading once makes further upgrades much easier and faster.

3.  Make sure you have a system backup. See Chapter 3 for details on how to do this with either a tape or a filesystem.

4.  Get your upgraded software, preferably via a package you have built on your test machine. (That way, you know that the port actually builds and installs.) Otherwise, build the software from a port using `make build`. Don't do the actual `make install`, just `make build` to confirm that you can actually compile the program cleanly.

5.  Notify your users that you will be upgrading the service at such-and-such a time, and that the program or machine will be unavailable.

6.  At the scheduled time, do a `make deinstall` or `pkg_delete` on the old package, then a `make install` on the new port. Be ready to fall back to the older version if this doesn't work!

The most frequent problem people have when upgrading is determining which software on their system needs upgrading. My general rule is that things that work should not be upgraded just because a newer version is available. This holds true especially for large, complicated software packages, such as some of the newer desktop window managers.

Still, you may find that even though everything is working just fine, a newer version of a piece of software addresses a problem you have or provides needed functionality. You can make your life easier by upgrading your ports tree to allow you to easily install that newer piece of software.

### Upgrading the Ports Collection

The FreeBSD upgrade process also handles upgrading your ports tree. You can use CVSup and the ports-supfile configuration to upgrade your ports to the latest version—or, indeed, to any version you choose.

To begin, you'll need to install CVSup as described in Chapter 6, and edit the ports-supfile to use a particular CVSup mirror. When you're done, run it with this command:

```
# cvsup ports-supfile
```

CVSup will crawl over your ports tree, comparing each file with the version on the CVSup mirror you've chosen, and make changes in your files as needed. When it finishes, you'll have the latest version of the ports tree.

Once you've finished upgrading your ports collection, you should upgrade your index and your readme files. To do so, go to /usr/ports and type this:

```
# make index && make readmes
```

**NOTE**   *Both of these commands (*make index *and* make readmes*) take quite some time to complete. By using the* &&*, you tie them together; when the first command completes successfully, the second command will run. This saves you the trouble of going back in half an hour and typing the second command.*

The ports collection upgrade doesn't remove old work directories. If you have installed ports and haven't run make clean, the work directories and older source code will still be around, together with the status-tracking hidden files. If you run make in these ports, the hidden files will show that the port is built and will refuse to run, and you'll need to run make clean to build these ports.

### Ports Collection Upgrade Issues

The problem with upgrading the ports collection is that any collection of software is intended to be used as a cohesive whole. If you have an older version of a commonly used tool that your new software requires, you might have to upgrade it as well as programs that depend upon it. The danger is that a simple upgrade can quickly become a cascading series.

Of course, FreeBSD is not the only operating system that suffers from this problem. Every software package on every operating system platform has it. (In Windows you frequently see this manifest as DLL conflicts, unexplained program crashes, or any other weird and unpleasant behavior.) Excellent software design can minimize but not eliminate this problem. Unfortunately, excellent software design is rare.

### Checking Software Versions

On a single-purpose machine, the daisy-chain upgrade isn't that difficult; after all, a Web server doesn't generally have hundreds of software packages installed. However, a workstation does, and even my laptop usually has over 200 entries in /var/db/pkg! (You know, I should really go through and uninstall what I don't use anymore; do I really need that little daemon that follows my mouse?) So what do you do if your system has complex software dependencies?

FreeBSD has a software-version-checking tool called pkg_version(1). Pkg_version compares the version of the software you have installed with the version number in /usr/ports/INDEX and, if your INDEX file is up to date, you're all set. (You did follow my advice in the last section and update your index and readmes, didn't you? Of course you did. You're not the type of person that would go drop some hard-earned cash on a computer book and then ignore it, are you? Of course not.)

A basic version check might look like this:

```
# pkg_version -v
apache-1.3.20                    =    up-to-date with port
autoconf-2.13_1                  =    up-to-date with port
bzip2-1.0.1                      =    up-to-date with port
cvsup-bin-16.1                   ?    orphaned: net/cvsup-bin
emacs-20.7                       =    up-to-date with port
gettext-0.10.35                  =    up-to-date with port
gmake-3.79.1                     =    up-to-date with port
ispell-3.1.20c_2                 <    needs updating (port has 3.2.04_1)
jade-1.2.1_1                     =    up-to-date with port
libtool-1.3.4_2                  =    up-to-date with port
links-0.96pre7                   <    needs updating (port has 0.96,1)
m4-1.4                           =    up-to-date with port
mutt-1.2.5                       =    up-to-date with port
rrdtool-1.0.33                   =    up-to-date with port
sftp-0.9.6_1                     =    up-to-date with port
sudo-1.6.3.7                     <    needs updating (port has 1.6.3.7_1)
ucd-snmp-4.2.1                   =    up-to-date with port
unzip-5.42                       =    up-to-date with port
uulib-0.5.13                     =    up-to-date with port
xsysinfo-1.4a                    =    up-to-date with port
zip-2.3                          =    up-to-date with port
```

Reading down the list of comments next to each piece of software, it's easy to see that most of the software on this system is the latest version. But take a look at the entry for ispell-1.2.10. The message shows that the port is out of date, and at some point you might want to update that program. You need to decide on your own if the package is important enough for you to spend the time needed to upgrade it.

Now, since I personally installed every piece of software on this system, I'm familiar with it, and I know how important everything is. I know that ispell is a spell-checker and that its importance in the grand scheme of Web serving is minimal at best. I'm not going to worry about it. On the other hand, the sudo-1.6.3.7 package is a security tool used to control user privileges; correct operation of this program is absolutely vital. If a newer version is available I *must* investigate and probably upgrade.

The entry for cvsup-bin-16.1 with the message of "orphaned: net/cvsup-bin" tells us that there is no entry for this piece of software in /usr/ports/INDEX, and hence no port for this package. I installed this port from a package; no port is available.

### Automatically Checking Software Versions

You can add an automated software-version check to your weekly status email. Just add the following line to /etc/periodic.conf:

```
weekly_status_pkg_enable="NO"
```

Create /etc/periodic.conf if you don't have one. For full details on /etc/periodic.conf, see Chapter 9.

### *Hints for Upgrading*

Most of the software-maintenance process is based upon knowing what your server is supposed to do. If you are the only administrator of a machine, things are very simple. Once you start having multiple administrators, however, you'll find that keeping track of this information becomes very difficult. I cannot stress highly enough the importance of keeping a server log for every system on your network! Even a text file, /etc/changes, where you jot down things like "mwlucas, 5-15-01: Installed sftp for client bufar@absolutebsd.com" can save you hours of pain later as you try to figure out why some trivial change is causing things to go haywire. It can also keep another administrator from calling you up at 3 AM and asking why the heck the system doesn't work with the default settings.

When you decide to upgrade on a production system, map out your changes. You can use pkg_info -aR to see which packages require other packages.

The general rule of thumb is to upgrade your dependencies first. Those packages that are required by other packages should be the first to be upgraded and tested. After all, if something's wrong with lower-level software, everything that depends on it will fail.

You can use pkg_delete -f to remove dependencies, and then install the newer versions from ports or packages. Then follow the chain upward, upgrading newer versions as required. Again, you can try to run a software package with a newer version of a dependency, but it might not work.

The /usr/ports/sysutils/portupgrade tool is worth considering, because it can handle some of these tasks automatically. Still, you need to understand and be able to deal with conflicts and dependencies yourself.

# 11

## ADVANCED SOFTWARE MANAGEMENT

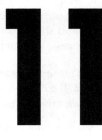

This chapter covers several things you need to know about running software on FreeBSD.

FreeBSD can run a wide variety of software packages, most of which are available as source code so they can be built as native FreeBSD software. And, thanks to some clever design, FreeBSD can also run software from many foreign operating systems. We'll look at how to do this, focusing on the popular Linux compatibility package that allows FreeBSD to run unmodified Linux software.

Also, for your programs to start at boot, and stop cleanly when the system shuts down, you must be able to edit and write proper startup and shutdown scripts. While some programs stop just fine when you kill the operating system they're running on, others (like databases) demand a gentler shutdown process. While you can get by with a variety of ugly hacks, starting and stopping network services cleanly is an excellent habit to get into and enforce. We'll examine how to properly implement and manage these systems in FreeBSD.

And, while under normal circumstances you'll never need to know how FreeBSD's linking and shared library support works, we'll discuss how shared libraries work and how to manage and configure them. Why? Because normal circumstances are, oddly, quite rare in the computer business.

Finally, we'll look at how systems with multiple processors work, and how they interact with software. While multiple processors can greatly increase system power, they won't help you if your software isn't properly configured.

## Startup and Shutdown Scripts

While FreeBSD's main system software is started by /etc/rc, add-on software is started by separate scripts. The ports and packages system installs these scripts for you. If you install your own software, however, you'll need to create a script that handles this startup and shutdown process. Plus, to change an existing add-on package's startup process, you must understand how the startup scripts function.

**NOTE** *This section assumes that you have some basic understanding of shell scripts. If you've never seen or used a shell script before, read the examples here very carefully. Shell scripting is not hard, and the best way to learn is to read examples.*

The /etc/rc shell scripts (see Chapter 9) handle the main system startup process. During boot up, the FreeBSD startup script checks several directories for additional shell scripts. The most popular directory for startup and shutdown scripts is /usr/local/etc/rc.d, though /usr/X11R6/etc/rc.d is another default location. These directories are specified in /etc/defaults/rc.conf, and can be overridden in /etc/rc.conf. (You can add additional script directories with the local_startup rc.conf variable.)

The shell script locator just checks in those directories for any files ending in ".sh". If it finds such a file, it assumes that the file is a shell script and executes it with an argument of start. During shutdown, FreeBSD runs these same scripts with an argument of stop. The scripts are expected to read those arguments and take appropriate action.

### Typical Startup Script

Let's look at a typical startup script, snmpd.sh, which is part of the net-snmp package that we'll install a little later. All you need to know at this point is that it starts the SNMP server daemon at boot, and stops that same daemon on shutdown. Here's the script:

```
❶ #!/bin/sh

❷ if ! PREFIX=$(expr $0 : "\(/.*\)/etc/rc\.d/$(basename $0)\$"); then
    echo "$0: Cannot determine the PREFIX" >&2
    exit 1
fi

❸ case "$1" in
start)
    [ -x ${PREFIX}/sbin/snmpd ] && ${PREFIX}/sbin/snmpd && echo -n ' snmpd'
    ;;
stop)
    killall snmpd && echo -n ' snmpd'
    ;;
*)
    echo "Usage: `basename $0` {start|stop}" >&2
```

```
            ;;
esac

exit 0
```

The `#!/bin/sh` line (❶) indicates that this is a shell script. The remainder of the file (which is similar to a Windows batch file) contains commands that are run by the script.

The first section, set off by `if` (❷) and `fi`, determines the path to the programs, and tells the rest of the script whether it was started in /usr/local, /usr/X11R6, or some other directory. The rest of the script (❸) needs to know this, so it can find its commands.

The `case "$1"` in line (❸) is where the script actually makes a decision. This part of the script reads the first argument that the script is called with. For example, if your script is run as `snmpd.sh start`, `start` is your first argument. If you run it as `snmpd.sh stop`, the `stop` is your first argument. The script has several smaller sections: Everything between the `start)` and the double semicolon (`;;`) are steps that are taken if the first argument is `start`. Everything between the `stop)` and the next double semicolon are actions that are taken if the first argument is `stop`. The last option, the `*)`, is a wildcard for all other arguments that might be typed in.

For example, if you run this script as `snmpd.sh start`, the script runs the following command:

```
[ -x ${PREFIX}/sbin/snmpd ] && ${PREFIX}/sbin/snmpd && echo -n ' snmpd'
```

These are standard UNIX shell commands. This command first checks to see if the snmpd program exists. If it does, it runs it and prints out its name. Similarly, if you call the script with a `stop` argument, it unceremoniously kills all snmpd processes.

To change the way a package behaves at startup, edit its startup script. For example, to start snmpd with an argument of `-D` you would edit the `start` line. Pick out the portion of the command where snmpd is actually started, and insert your change there:

```
[ -x ${PREFIX}/sbin/snmpd ] && ${PREFIX}/sbin/snmpd -D && echo -n ' snmpd'
```

### Using Scripts to Manage Running Programs

You can also use these scripts when the system is running. For example, to restart snmpd to make it reread its configuration file, you could run this command:

```
# /usr/local/etc/rc.d/snmpd.sh stop && /usr/local/etc/rc.d/snmpd.sh start
```

*It's not entirely necessary to use the scripts to manage a running program. If you've read the snmpd.sh shell script, you know that to stop the program the script runs the command* killall snmpd, *and that it starts the program by running* snmpd. *You could just enter these commands at the command line, and it would have the exact same effect as running the previous script twice. You either have to remember what each script does for its particular program or you have to type the full path to the startup scripts. If you're in doubt, use the scripts!*

## Managing Shared Libraries

The basic idea behind a shared library is quite straightforward: It's a chunk of compiled code that provides services and functions to other chunks of compiled code. Shared libraries provide popular functions for all programs to use, and they are designed to be reused by as many different programs as possible.

For example, many programs must hash (or one-way encrypt) data as part of their function. But if every program had to include hashing code, each would be larger, harder to write, and more unpleasant to maintain. What's more, programs would have interoperability problems if they implemented hashes differently. By using a shared library (in this example, libcrypt), a program that needs hashing has access to the functions while eliminating problems of maintenance and interoperability. Similarly, other shared libraries provide common functions to support other software. This reduces the average size of programs, freeing up a reasonably large amount of system memory.

FreeBSD builds a cache of available shared libraries at boottime. Programs don't have to scan the whole disk looking for shared libraries; they just ask the cache for the functions they want. In fact, the ability to manage the library cache is one thing that separates a newbie from a professional.

While FreeBSD provides quite a few sensible defaults for the cache, we'll discuss the tools you need to properly configure and manage your cache in all sorts of odd circumstances. Shared libraries are complex beasts. With ldconfig, ldd, and a little bit of thought, you can start to tame them.

### Ldconfig

The main tool for managing shared libraries is ldconfig(8). (You'll probably hear all sorts of references to it, in one place or another.) We'll discuss a few different ldconfig-related commands: rtld(1), ldd(1), and ldconfig itself.

#### Binary Types: Aout and ELF

First we have the issue of binary types: *aout* and *ELF*. While as an administrator you don't need to know the details of aout and ELF, you should know that aout is the old standard, ELF is the new standard, and programs compiled as one type cannot use shared libraries of the other type. ELF programs cannot use aout-shared libraries. (The FreeBSD Netscape binary is in aout format, which is why you must install XFree86's aout compatibility libraries to use it.) While aout binaries are slowly vanishing, FreeBSD will need to support both types indefinitely.

When you execute an ELF binary that needs shared libraries, the system calls rtld(1), the "run-time linker." Rtld examines binaries as they're loaded, determines which shared libraries they need, and loads those libraries. There's a separate runtime linker for aout binaries called ld(aout).

Rather than searching the entire system for anything that looks like a shared library everytime anything is executed, rtld pulls the shared libraries from a library cache. The cache lives on your system in two separate files: /var/run/ld.so.hints (aout) and /var/run/ld-elf.so.hints (ELF). A misconfigured cache is the most likely cause of shared library problems.

### What Libraries Do You Have?

To see the list of libraries you already have, run ldconfig with the -r flag:

```
# ldconfig -r
/var/run/ld-elf.so.hints:
        search directories:
/usr/lib:/usr/lib/compat:/usr/X11R6/lib:/usr/local/lib:/usr/local/lib/mysql:/usr/loc
al/pilot/lib
        0:-lcom_err.2 => /usr/lib/libcom_err.so.2
        1:-lscrypt.2 => /usr/lib/libscrypt.so.2
        2:-lcrypt.2 => /usr/lib/libcrypt.so.2
...
```

ldconfig -r examines the shared library cache and lists every shared library it finds. On my system, this list runs to 229 shared libraries.

**NOTE** *If a program complains that it can't find a library, check* ldconfig -r. *If the library isn't there, your cache is either misconfigured or incomplete, or the library really isn't on your system.*

### Building the Cache

The cache is built during the system boot process, using ldconfig. For ELF binaries, it's done like this:

```
# ldconfig -elf /list/of /path/names/here
```

Similarly, aout uses this:

```
# ldconfig -aout /other/list /of/paths
```

**NOTE** *The list of path names is set in /etc/rc.conf as ldconfig_paths and ldconfig_paths_aout.*

If you're trying to use shared libraries that you've just installed, they won't be in the cache, and programs may fail. In that case, you need to rebuild the cache, and it's fairly easy to do. Just run ldconfig without any arguments, and ldconfig will rescan the directories listed in ldconfig -r and rebuild the cache.

### Finding a Library

If the library isn't in one of the directories previously scanned, you need to find it. Generally speaking, if you cut the initial "lib" off the library name and use locate or find / -name libname -print, you should be able to find the file. In the worst case, you'll have to dig through a long list of results to find the library you want.

### Adding Libraries

You might find, after you install a piece of software, that you have a new directory of shared libraries. (You'll sometimes find these in a private subdirectory; my PalmPilot software uses /usr/local/pilot/lib, for example.)

It's easy enough to merge a new directory of shared libraries into the existing cache with the -m option. Some ports even use the -m option to configure shared libraries at boot, which eliminates any tedious mucking about in /etc/rc.conf. To merge my Palm library into my existing cache, I would enter this command:

```
# ldconfig -m /usr/local/pilot/lib
```

### LD_LIBRARY_PATH

While the -m option works very well if you're the systems administrator, it won't work if you're just a lowly user without root access.[1] Also, if you have your personal set of shared libraries, your sysadmin won't want to make them globally available, and root must own the shared library directory so that regular users can't just dump things in there willy-nilly. Sysadmins probably won't even want to take the slightest chance of system programs linking against your personal libraries.

Here's where the LD_LIBRARY_PATH environment variable appears. Rather than create a cache, LD_LIBRARY_PATH tells the system to check the directories it lists for new shared libraries.

**NOTE** *This isn't at all secure; if you set LD_LIBRARY_PATH to an overly accessible location, your program can link against whatever's there. LD_LIBRARY_PATH also overrides the cache, so be careful what you put in there!*

You can specify any number of directories in LD_LIBRARY_PATH, separated with colons. For example, I might want to put the directories /home/mwlucas/lib and /compat/linux/usr/lib/local into my LD_LIBRARY_PATH to complete a software install. I would do this like so:

```
# setenv LD_LIBRARY_PATH /home/mwlucas/lib:/compat/linux/usr/lib/local
```

[1] If you're reading this book, you're probably the systems administrator. But you'll need this as a solution for your users.

For example, I generally install StarOffice manually rather than via the port. When I do, the install routine extracts a variety of libraries in /tmp/sv001.tmp and expects to be able to find them when it starts the graphical installer. To make sure that it can find these libraries, I start setup using the LD_LIBRARY_PATH variable to point to the /tmp/sv001.tmp directory, like this:

```
#setenv LD_LIBRARY_PATH /tmp/sv001.tmp
#./setup
```

When the graphical StarOffice installer starts, it then checks that directory for extracted libraries. The result is that I don't have to reconfigure my entire FreeBSD system just to use this program.

**NOTE** *Remember, you can set an environment variable automatically at login by entering it in your .cshrc or .profile file.*

### What Libraries Do My Programs Need?

Lastly, there's the question of what libraries a program expects to have available. You can get this information with ldd(1). For example, to find out what Emacs needs, enter this command:

```
# ldd /usr/local/bin/emacs
/usr/local/bin/emacs:
        libXaw.so.6 => /usr/X11R6/lib/libXaw.so.6 (0x28159000)
        libXmu.so.6 => /usr/X11R6/lib/libXmu.so.6 (0x2818e000)
        libXt.so.6 => /usr/X11R6/lib/libXt.so.6 (0x2819f000)
        libSM.so.6 => /usr/X11R6/lib/libSM.so.6 (0x281e2000)
        libICE.so.6 => /usr/X11R6/lib/libICE.so.6 (0x281ea000)
        libXext.so.6 => /usr/X11R6/lib/libXext.so.6 (0x281fe000)
        libX11.so.6 => /usr/X11R6/lib/libX11.so.6 (0x28209000)
        libutil.so.3 => /usr/lib/libutil.so.3 (0x282a2000)
        libm.so.2 => /usr/lib/libm.so.2 (0x282ab000)
        libc.so.4 => /usr/lib/libc.so.4 (0x282c6000)
        libXThrStub.so.6 => /usr/X11R6/lib/libXThrStub.so.6 (0x28361000)
#
```

This output tells us the names of the shared libraries Emacs requires, and the locations of the files that contain those libraries. You can check this list of required libraries against the output of ldconfig -r to confirm that your program has what it needs. Or you can use this as a shopping list and then go out and get the needed libraries.

# Running Software from the Wrong OS

Traditionally, operating systems have had to have software written for them, and a piece of software would only run on the platform it was designed for. That said, many people have built a healthy business by changing software for one platform so it will run on another system, a process called *porting*.

As an administrator, you can use software written for a platform other than FreeBSD in a few different ways. The most effective way is to recompile the source code to run natively on FreeBSD. Alternatively, and barring your recompiling a program, you can also run non-native software under an emulator, or by re-implementing the application binary interface (ABI) of the native platform.

### Recompilation

Many pieces of software in the ports collection are actually native recompiles of software originally designed for other platforms, such as KDE and Emacs. In fact, software written for Linux, Solaris, or other UNIX variants can frequently be built (recompiled) from source code with little or no modification to run without a hitch on FreeBSD. By simply taking the source code and building it on a FreeBSD machine, you can run foreign software natively on FreeBSD.

Recompiling works best when the platforms are similar. For example, FreeBSD and Linux provide many identical system functions: both are built on the standard C functions, as defined by POSIX, and both use similar building tools and have mostly identical system calls.

However, over the years, the various UNIX platforms have diverged. Each version of UNIX has implemented new features that require new libraries and functions, and if a piece of software requires those functions, it won't build on other platforms.

The POSIX standard was introduced, in part, to alleviate this problem. POSIX is a standard that defines minimal acceptable UNIX and UNIX-like operating systems. Software written using only POSIX-compliant system calls and libraries should be immediately portable to any other operating system that implements POSIX, and most UNIX vendors comply with POSIX.

The problem is ensuring that developers comply with POSIX. Many open-source developers care only about having their software run on their preferred platform. For example, there's a lot of software out there that is Linux-specific, but not POSIX-compliant. And POSIX-only code does not take advantage of any special features offered by the operating system.

For example, FreeBSD has the hyper-efficient data-reading system call kqueue(2). Other systems use select(2) and poll(2) instead. The question developers need to ask themselves is whether they should use kqueue, which would make their software blindingly fast on FreeBSD and unable to work on anything else, or whether they should they use select and poll, allowing their software to run more slowly but on more platforms. The developer can invest more time in setting up the software to use different functions on different platforms; but while this would make users happy, it rather sucks from the developer's point of view. Whatever the developer's choice, someone will complain.

The FreeBSD Project takes a middle road. If a piece of software can be compiled and run properly on FreeBSD, the ports team generally makes it happen. If the software needs minor patches, the ports team includes the patches with the port and sends the patches back to the software's developer. Most software developers gladly accept patches that allow them to support another operating system. Even though they might not have that OS available to test on, or they might not be familiar with the OS, if a decent-looking patch arrives from a reputable source, they probably won't turn it down.

## Emulation

If software would require extensive redesign to support FreeBSD, or if source code is simply not available, we need to turn to another option: *emulation*. The concept of an emulator is simple. An emulator program translates system calls for one operating system to the system calls used by the local operating system, and programs running under the emulator think they're running on their native system. Translating these system calls does create additional system overhead, though, which takes its toll on the speed with which programs run under the emulator.

FreeBSD supports a wide variety of emulators, most of which are in the ports collection under /usr/ports/emulators. In most cases, emulators are useful for education or entertainment. If you have an old Commodore 64 game that you've had an insatiable desire to play again, you can install /usr/ports/emulators/frodo. (You can also learn more about disks than you ever wanted to know by trying to get that C64 floppy to work with UNIX, but that's a separate matter.) To see what classic UNIX hardware looks like, you can install the PDP-11 emulator under /usr/ports/emulators/sim. (For a complete list, see /usr/ports/emulators/README.html.)

However, since these emulators are not really useful for server operations, we won't cover them in depth. You should know that they're available, though, and where to find them.

## ABI Implementation

In addition to recompiling and emulating, the final option for running foreign programs is the one FreeBSD is best known for: *ABI (application binary interface) implementation*. The ABI is the part of the kernel that provides services to programs, including everything from sound-card access to reading files to printing on the screen to starting other programs—all the things a program needs to run. As far as programs are concerned, the ABI is the operating system. By completely implementing the ABI from a different operating system on your operating system, you can run non-native programs as if they were on the native platform.

While ABI implementation is frequently referred to as "emulation," it isn't really. When implementing ABIs, FreeBSD is not emulating the system calls, but providing them natively. By the same token, it would be incorrect to say that "FreeBSD implements Linux" or "FreeBSD implements Solaris." The fact is, when this technique was created, there was no one word to describe what the BSD team was doing. (Even today, there's no one word to describe it. How's *that* for bleeding-edge work?) You'll most often hear it referred to as a *mode*, such as "Linux mode" or "osf1 mode."

The problem with emulating the ABI is overlap. Most operating systems include system calls with generic names such as read, write, and so on. The read system call on a FreeBSD system behaves very differently from the read found on a Windows system. If you re-implement every single foreign system call in your OS, you've just made your operating system a re-implementation of the foreign OS. When a program calls read, how would it know if it was getting the native or foreign version? You can give your system calls different names, but then you're violating POSIX. Or you can provide multiple ABIs and control which ABI a program uses. This is what FreeBSD does.

### Binary Branding

Operating systems generally have a straightforward system function that executes programs: Whenever the kernel sends a program to the execution engine, the execution engine runs the program.

At some point, however, the UNIX program execution system was hacked to include a special check for programs that began with #!/bin/sh, and to run them with the system shell instead of the execution engine. BSD took this idea to the logical extreme, and its execution engine includes a list of different binary types. Each program's binary type directs it to the correct ABI. Thus, a BSD system can have multiple ABIs, and can support programs from a variety of different operating systems.

The nifty thing about this system of redirects is that there's no overhead: Since the system decides how to run the program anyway, why not have it decide which ABI to use? After all, binaries for different operating systems all have slightly different characteristics, which are used to identify them; this system simply makes the process transparent to the end user.

As a result of this ABI redirection, FreeBSD can run Linux, OSF/1, System V, and SCO binaries as if they were compiled natively, thus vastly expanding the range of software available for use on FreeBSD.

**NOTE** *FreeBSD supports this range of ABIs for two reasons. First, someone with the skill to implement it needed it. Second, the documentation was available. The implemented ABIs are all very similar to FreeBSDs; only a few system calls require extensive development.*

### Which ABIs Are Supported?

This scheme makes it entirely possible to implement extremely foreign ABIs. For example, someone could take Windows ABI information from Microsoft and write a Windows ABI module for FreeBSD, which would allow FreeBSD to run Windows programs natively. While this would be pretty darn cool, it would also be a fiendish amount of work to implement in a stable and reliable manner. It hasn't been done, and isn't likely to happen. The three modes that are most supported are SVR4, OSF/1, and Linux.

*SVR4*, or System V Release 4, was the last major release of UNIX from AT&T. It appears in early versions of Solaris and SCO UNIX. Some SCO software is reported to perform more quickly and reliably in FreeBSD's SVR4 mode than it does on actual SCO UNIX.

*OSF/1*, or Digital UNIX, was designed for the Alpha processor. Digital first built the Alpha CPU and created Digital OSF/1 to run on it. Because OSF/1 used a Mach kernel, and FreeBSD doesn't include the various non-POSIX system calls that were part of Mach, FreeBSD's OSF/1 mode is incomplete. In any event, it won't run on Intel-compatible hardware. (Implementing a foreign ABI is difficult enough without providing 64-bit instructions on 32-bit hardware!) Now, chances are, you don't have an Alpha, so we aren't going to discuss it in any depth.[2]

Finally, *Linux* mode allows FreeBSD to run Linux software. This ABI has been the most thoroughly tested because the source code for Linux is available and its ABI is well documented. In fact, the Linux mode works so well that many programs in the ports collection rely upon it. (Chunks of this book were written on StarOffice 5.2 under Linux mode, and I've used Linux Netscape and even Linux WordPerfect without problem.)

### Foreign Software Libraries

While the kernel portion of the ABI solves one major issue, the other portions of the system are another problem because every operating system has its own requirements in addition to the kernel. The biggest issue is shared libraries. If the kernel starts a program, and the program can't find its shared libraries, it won't work correctly. No matter which ABI you use, you must have a copy of the shared libraries for that platform.

### SVR4 and SCO

For example, to use the SVR4 and SCO ABIs, you need access to the appropriate system. While a Sun Solaris 2.6 CD will suffice for the SVR4 module, you need to grab the shared libraries from an actual SCO UNIX machine to use the SCO ABI, which means you need a SCO or Solaris license. This isn't an insurmountable problem, of course, but it does make using this module slightly more difficult—and definitely more expensive.

### OSF/1

A minimal set of OSF/1 shared libraries are available under /usr/ports/emulators/osf1_base. These libraries have a restrictive license and can only be used in fairly narrow circumstances, but you can get a more complete set of shared libraries from an actual OSF/1 system, if you wish. If you have an actual OSF/1 license, you can pretty much do whatever you like with the libraries.

---

[2] If you have a spare Alpha lying around (other than the Multia model known for Random Heat Death), feel free to ship it to me in care of No Starch Press; I'll be delighted to include a discussion of OSF/1 mode in the next edition of *Absolute BSD*.

**Linux**

The shared libraries for the Linux mode are the most freely available of any mode. Since the barrier to entry is so low, we'll discuss Linux compatibility in some detail. Once you have a thorough understanding of how it works, you can apply this knowledge to any other ABI compatibility you need to implement.

## Installing and Enabling Linux Mode

The simplest way to install and enable Linux mode is with /usr/ports/emulators/linux_base, which downloads and installs a large subset of a typical Linux environment into /usr/compat/linux. (It also adds LINUX_ENABLE="YES" to /etc/rc.conf, so that the Linux ABI kernel module will be started when the system boots.)

Depending on what software you've installed, you might already have Linux mode enabled on your system. It runs transparently enough that the ports collection might have installed it without your even knowing! To find out, check /var/db/pkg to see if linux_base is installed. Then use kldstat(8) to see if the Linux ABI kernel module is loaded:

```
# kldstat
Id Refs Address    Size    Name
 1    3 0xc0100000 236ff8  kernel
 2    1 0xc0337000 54f8    vesa.ko
 3    1 0xc119b000 12000   linux.ko
#
```

As you can see, the last module in the preceding list is the Linux ABI module, linux.ko. If the Linux module is not loaded, it won't appear in the list.

If the module is not loaded, you can load it with kldload(8), as discussed in Chapter 4:

```
# kldload linux
#
```

To automatically load the Linux module at boot, add this line /etc/rc.conf:

```
LINUX_ENABLE="YES"
```

You should now be able to run Linux programs without any further configuration.

### Identifying Programs

Modern UNIX binaries are in ELF format, which includes space for a comment, or *brand*. A binary will be executed by the ABI for the brand. If a binary has no brand, it is assumed to be a FreeBSD binary. FreeBSD recognizes four different brands: FreeBSD, Linux, Solaris, and SVR4.

While you cannot directly view the brand on a binary, you can examine and manipulate branding with brandelf(1). To check the branding on a binary, just run brandelf on it:

```
# brandelf /bin/sh
File '/bin/sh' is of brand 'FreeBSD' (9).
#
```

Here you see that this program is branded with FreeBSD, so it will be executed under the FreeBSD ABI.

If you have a foreign program that will not run, check its brand. If it isn't branded, you've probably discovered your problem: FreeBSD is trying to run the program under its native ABI. Change this by setting the brand manually with brandelf -t. For example, to brand a program with Linux, do this:

```
# brandelf -t Linux /usr/local/bin/program
#
```

The next time you try to run the program, it will attempt to run under the Linux ABI. If it's a Linux program, it should give you better results.

### What Is Linux_base?

The Linux kernel module handles the kernel support for Linux compatibility, and if you decide to use the ABI for another UNIX, you'll need to implement much of this on your own. As such, it's a good idea to understand how Linux mode works, to help you troubleshoot problems with other compatibility modes.

One piece of the puzzle is to use the linux_base package. This package extracts a subsection of a Red Hat Linux install under /usr/compat/linux. If you take a look there, you'll see something like the following:

```
#ls
bin    boot    etc    lib    mnt    opt    proc    sbin    usr    var
#
```

Looks a lot like the contents of your root directory, doesn't it? Well, if you poke around a bit, you'll find that, generally speaking, the contents of /usr/compat/linux are comparable to that of the main FreeBSD install. You'll find many of the same programs that you do on a base FreeBSD install.

**NOTE**   *One thing Linux devotees notice immediately is that the contents of linux_base are rather minimal compared to what a Linux user is used to. You can add Linux programs to linux_base as you like; we'll look at doing this later.*

The Linux ABI tries to stay under /usr/compat/linux whenever possible. (It's somewhat like a weak jail.) When you execute a Linux binary that calls other programs, the Linux ABI first checks for the program under /usr/compat/linux. If it doesn't find the program there, it checks in the main FreeBSD system.

For example, suppose you have a Linux binary that calls ping(8). The ABI will first check under /usr/compat/linux for the ping program. When it finds that it's not there, the ABI will then check the main FreeBSD system and will use /sbin/ping.

Alternatively, suppose a Linux binary wants to call sh(1). The Linux ABI will first check under /usr/compat/linux and find bin/sh. When it finds sh there, it will execute that program instead of the FreeBSD native /bin/sh.

### Adding to Linux_base

As I mentioned earlier, the Linux install in linux_base is rather minimal, and some Linux programs expect a broader range of shared libraries to be available. FreeBSD tries to keep ports as small as possible, but compromises by making these additional Linux libraries available as additional ports. The ports collection includes several ports that augment linux_base, most of which are shared libraries. These increase the range of programs that FreeBSD's Linux mode can support. These ports include the following:

- devel/linux-libglade is a graphic interface library required by various programs.
- devel/linux_devel is a collection of tools for developing Linux programs on FreeBSD.
- devel/linux_kdump is a Linux binary debugging tool.
- graphics/linux-jpeg contains shared libraries to handle JPEG image files.
- graphic/linux-png installs shared libraries to handle PNG image files.
- graphic/linux-tiff includes shared libraries to handle TIFF image files.

Installing these ports will round out 99 percent of the functionality you might want to provide to a Linux program.

You may need a shared library or program that is not available in linux_base or a port. If so, the simplest thing to do is to find a Linux system of the appropriate version, copy the files, and install them in the appropriate locations under /usr/compat/linux. If you've created a new directory to contain shared libraries, you'll need to tweak /usr/compat/linux/etc/ld.so.conf.

### Configuring Linux Shared Libraries

FreeBSD's method for configuring shared libraries is very different from Linux's. Linux creates a cache file from a plain-text configuration file, like the one found at /usr/compat/linux/etc/ld.so.conf:

```
# cat ld.so.conf
/usr/i486-linux-libc5/lib
/usr/X11R6/lib
#
```

The initial slashes in these paths are misleading. Why? Remember, the Linux
ABI looks for files under /usr/compat/linux first, and if it finds the files, it
uses them. These directories are actually /usr/compat/linux/usr/i486-linux-
libc5/lib and /usr/compat/linux/usr/X11R6/lib. If you look in these directories, you'll find the Linux shared libraries installed by linux_base. The Linux
ABI kernel module runs Linux ldconfig(8) to read this file, scan the directories
listed, and create or update /usr/compat/linux/etc/ld.so.cache.

When you add shared libraries to your Linux installation, you need to
update this cache. You can do this by unloading and reloading the Linux kernel
module, but this might interrupt service. Instead, you can run the cache-
updating program:

```
# /usr/compat/linux/sbin/ldconfig
#
```

You won't get any output back, but you can check the date on ld.so.cache to be
sure that the cache has been updated. If the date is current, the cache has been
updated.

To help keep things organized, if you add shared libraries to your system
you can put them in a separate directory. For example, I frequently create
/usr/compat/linux/usr/local/lib for whatever random crud I want to add to
that system. To use those libraries, however, I must add the path to ld.so.conf.
(Remember to strip off the initial /usr/compat/linux, however!)

### Installing Extra Linux Packages as RPMs

When a Linux program complains that it cannot find a necessary program, you
may need to add that program under /usr/compat/linux. Since FreeBSD's
Linux mode is based on Red Hat Linux, you can easily grab the appropriate
components of Red Hat Linux and install them in your Linux subsystem.

Red Hat Linux is distributed in RPM (Red Hat Package Manager) format.
(You can find a good selection of Red Hat Linux RPMs at FTP mirror sites
around the world; see www.redhat.com for the latest mirror list.) RPM files are
like FreeBSD's binary packages; they're just compressed files containing everything needed to run a program, and they are designed to be installed and uninstalled as a unit. Although people argue about the merits of RPM versus
pkg_add versus the many other package-management systems used by open-
source software, since FreeBSD's Linux compatibility package is based on Red
Hat Linux, we use Red Hat tools.

When using RPMs, be certain to install the software under /compat/linux. If you just blindly run RPM as described in the rpm(8) man page, you'll wind up overwriting part of your FreeBSD system. This would be bad; while FreeBSD can run Linux binaries, you cannot combine a FreeBSD and Linux userland arbitrarily and expect anything to work. Trying this is a good way to become familiar with the emergency repair process described in Chapter 3.

To safely install an RPM, do this:

```
# rpm -i --ignoreos --dbpath /var/lib/rpm --root /compat/linux packagename
```

NOTE     *Of course, RPM packages are completely separate from FreeBSD's usual package system. You cannot pkg_delete these; you must use RPM to handle them.*

# Using Multiple Processors—SMP

Computers with multiple CPUs have been around for decades, but they are just now becoming popular in the Intel-compatible world. FreeBSD has supported the use of multiple CPUs since version 3, but hardware is just now becoming affordable enough for small companies and hobbyists to implement it.

### What Is SMP?

Symmetric multiprocessing (SMP) describes a system with multiple (more than one) identical processors. Before you ask: Yes, there are other variants on multiple-processor handling that might be used some day. Some computer scientists insist that asymmetrical multiprocessing will be more efficient. You can't buy that hardware, however, so it's moot at the moment.

SMP has quite a few advantages over single processors, and it's not the obvious "more power!" If you think about it on the microscopic level, a CPU can only do one thing at a time. Every process on the computer competes for processor time. If the CPU is performing a database query, it isn't accepting the packet that the Ethernet card is trying to deliver. Every fraction of a second, the CPU does a *context switch* and works on some other process assigned by the kernel. This happens often enough and quickly enough that it appears to be doing many things at once, much as a television picture appears to move by showing individual frames very quickly. With multiple processors, your computer can do multiple things simultaneously. This can be a wonderful thing, but it increases system complexity dramatically.

Since one CPU can only do one thing at a time, many programs have been written to work around this limitation. In fact, many programs that you would expect to be only one process aren't. The Apache Web server, for example, actually starts quite a few processes to serve up Web pages, allowing it to work well on multiple-processor systems.

SMP has long been a feature in commercial UNIX. Sun Microsystems just announced a 102-CPU SPARC system. Even Windows 2000 supports multiple CPUs, in a somewhat goofy way. I had an opportunity to take home a four-processor Intel 486 system at one point, and while I never would have used it, part of me regrets dragging it to the curb. Today a variety of manufacturers provide X86 SMP motherboards, including big-name dealers such as Dell and Compaq.

### Kernel Assumptions

To understand SMP and the problems associated with it, we have to delve into the kernel. All operating systems face the same problems when supporting SMP, and the theory here is applicable across a variety of platforms. FreeBSD is somewhat different from other operating systems, though, because it has 30 years of UNIX heritage to deal with, and its development model doesn't allow work to stop for a month at a time.

Now, that said, let me say that *what follows is a gross simplification*. Kernel design is a tricky subject, and it's almost impossible to do it justice when describing it at a level for nonprogrammers. But here's an explanation of how it all works, in its most basic form.

Your computer appears to be doing many things simultaneously: For example, I have WindowMaker running, Netscape merrily soaking up the cable modem, and assorted port builds going on. Network interrupts are arriving, the screen is displaying new text, the Apache Web server is sending out pages, and so on. Actually, all this only looks simultaneous. Your average CPU can only do one thing at a time.[3]

FreeBSD divides CPU utilization into time slices; a *slice* is the length of time the CPU spends doing one task. One process can use the CPU for either a full time slice or until there are no more tasks for it to do, at which point the next process may run. The kernel uses a priority-based system to allocate time slices and to determine which programs can run in which time slices. If a process is running, but a higher-priority process presents itself, the kernel allows the first process to be interrupted, or *preempted*. This is commonly referred to as preemptive multitasking.

Now, although the kernel is running, it isn't a process; processes are run by the kernel. A process has certain sorts of data structures set up by the kernel, and the kernel manipulates them as it sees fit. You can consider the kernel a special sort of process, one that is handled very differently from regular processes. It cannot be interrupted by other programs—you cannot type killall kernel and reboot the system. And traditionally the kernel doesn't show up in top and similar tools.

Older UNIX and FreeBSD kernels get around some of the SMP problems by declaring that the kernel is nonpreemptive and cannot be interrupted. This simplifies kernel management issues because it makes everything quite deterministic: When a part of the kernel allocates memory, it can count on that chunk of memory being there when it executes the next instruction. No other part of the kernel will grab that particular chunk of memory.

This situation changed (for the better) after version 2.2.

---

[3] Some CPUs (the Alpha) can do multiple things at once. These dual-issue and quad-issue processors are slowly becoming more common. This is one reason why the Alpha was such wonderful technology, and why it's bad for us all that the Alpha is no more.

### FreeBSD 3.0 SMP

The first implementation of FreeBSD SMP was pretty straightforward: Processes were scattered between the CPUs (achieving a rough load balance), and there was a "lock" on the kernel. The CPU had to hold this lock to run the kernel, and before a CPU would try to run the kernel, it checked to see if the lock was available. If the lock was available, it took the lock and ran the kernel. If the lock was unavailable, the CPU knew that the kernel was being run elsewhere and went on to handle something else. This lock was called the *Big Giant Lock* (BGL). Under this system, the kernel could know that data would not change from under it. Essentially, it guaranteed that the kernel would only run on one CPU, just as it always had.

This strategy worked well enough for two CPUs: You could run a medium-level database and Web server on a twin-CPU machine, and feel confident that the CPU wouldn't be your bottleneck. If one CPU was busy serving up Web pages, the other would be free to answer database calls. But if you wanted to run an eight-CPU machine, you were in trouble; the system would spend a lot of time just waiting for the Big Giant Lock to become available! The kernel still knew that it was only doing one thing at a time, and if a kernel instruction changed some internal value, it would still be that way when it returned.

There are many problems with this system, but fundamentally it's simplistic, and neither efficient nor scalable. In fact, the standard textbooks on SMP rarely mention this method of handling the kernel because it's so clunky. Still, it beats some other operating systems' methods of handling SMP. For example, a twin-processor Windows 2000 system's default setup dedicates one processor to the user interface and uses the other processor for everything else. While the interface is snappy and the mouse doesn't drag when you load the system, I would hope that most people don't purchase SMP hardware to address graphical interface problems.

With the growth of system hardware, multiple-CPU systems will become very common in just a few years. For FreeBSD to continue to be a quality operating system, this problem must be addressed.

### FreeBSD 5 SMP

One of the benefits of the BSDi/Walnut Creek merger was the release of the BSD/OS 5.0 code base to the FreeBSD development community. BSD/OS contains a great deal of proprietary information, so the source code cannot be released to the general public. Still, FreeBSD developers were able to read portions of the code. The most interesting part of this code was that multiple CPUs could be in the kernel at once—something that will be heavily implemented in version 5, and which will mark one of the big differences between FreeBSD version 4 and version 5.

To prevent information corruption, the new FreeBSD SMP system combines the Big Giant Lock with a smaller lock called a *mutex*. When a piece of the kernel wants to work on a chunk of data, it slaps a mutex over it. When another part of the kernel tries to access this mutex-locked data, it says, "Oh, I can't touch that," and either waits for the resource to become available or tries to allocate some other resource. The goal is to eliminate the Big Giant Lock, and to have all kernel operations only mutex-lock the small bits of data that they need. As the kernel's smaller systems are rewritten to take advantage of mutexes, their need to hold the BGL will be eliminated. According to Greg Lehey, a major FreeBSD developer and member of the SMP project, this method is expected to scale to beyond 32 processors.

**NOTE** *The BGL could have been ripped out entirely and replaced with mutexes everywhere in one massive frenzy of hacking (as commercial OS vendors do), completing the process in only a couple of months, so why not do so? Because doing so would have meant that FreeBSD-current would have been utterly unusable for several months, and 5.0-release would have been poorly debugged. Too, the volunteer developers working on other parts of the system would have had nothing to do. (Telling volunteer developers that they can't do anything is an excellent way to lose them.)*

This should give you enough understanding of how SMP works that you can administer it reasonably well. Now, let's look at the details of handling an SMP system.

### Using SMP

When using SMP, remember that multiple processors don't necessarily make things go faster. One processor can handle a certain number of operations per second; a second processor just means that the computer can handle twice that many operations per second, but those operations are not necessarily faster.

Think of the CPU count as lanes on a road.[4] If you have one lane, you can move one car at a time past any one spot. If you have four lanes, you can move four cars past that spot. Although the four-lane road won't necessarily allow those cars to reach their destination more quickly, there'll be a lot more of them arriving at any one time. If you think this doesn't make a difference, contemplate what would happen if someone replaced your local freeway with a one-lane road. CPU bandwidth is important.

Most user processes don't have to worry about when to use SMP; a process just requests some CPU time and the kernel allocates it. The program doesn't worry about where this CPU time is coming from.

The problem with SMP occurs when you want to have one process use multiple CPUs. The short answer is, you can't do that unless the program is threaded. Threaded programs are written specifically to run on multiple processors. (Check the program documentation to see if the program is threaded.) Programs such as Apache, which run multiple processes to serve requests, are not threaded but might as well be. Taken as a whole, Apache takes excellent advantage of multiple CPUs.

---

[4] This example assumes that everyone drives the speed limit, taking turns and not cutting each other off, and in general not acting like real drivers in any American city.

### SMP and Upgrades

The most common "problem" people encounter with SMP is when performing the default torture test, an upgrade from source. It appears that no matter what, the system never seems to use more than one CPU at a time. The "top" program will show that the system is 50 percent idle, no matter what.

Trust your eyes. If the system appears to be half idle, you're only using one of your CPUs. The make program that handles building software issues a command, waits for a response, then issues another command. Each of these subtasks might be assigned to a different CPU, but the actual make command won't try to do anything until that original process comes back successful. It only does one thing at a time.

You can get around this problem with make's -j flag, which tells make to run multiple processes simultaneously. The -j flag takes its own argument, the number of make processes to run:

```
# make -j4 buildworld
```

This line tells make to run four processes, and hopefully it will complete more quickly. This doesn't mean that your make will be completed in one-fourth the time, however; you still have other issues to contend with (see Chapter 14).

**NOTE**    *Not all programs can handle being built with the -j flag. At times, even buildworld fails. (There is some discussion of disabling support for* make -j *in buildworld, as it causes many problems.) It's worth trying, but if things go badly, you need to fall back to plain old serial make.*

Multiple processors are not the be-all and end-all of high-performance computing. Your application must be written to take advantage of them. If it isn't, extra CPUs will not help.

# 12

# FINDING HOSTS WITH DNS

The Domain Name Service (DNS) is one of those quiet, behind-the-scenes programs that doesn't get half the attention it deserves. Although most users have never heard of it, DNS is what makes the Internet, as we know it, work. DNS, or *nameservice* as it's also called, provides a map between hostnames and IP addresses. Without DNS, your Web browser or email programs wouldn't use convenient names like www.cnn.com; instead, you'd have to type in IP addresses. This would greatly reduce the Internet's popularity.

Any Internet service you implement will require DNS. We'll discuss how DNS works, how to check DNS, how to configure your FreeBSD system to use DNS, and how to build your own DNS server.

## How DNS Works

DNS simply maps IP addresses to hostnames, and hostnames to IP addresses. For example, a user doesn't want to know that www.AbsoluteBSD.com is actually 209.69.178.25; she just wants to type the URL into her Web browser and go. DNS does the translation. As the system administrator you must be able to install, inspect, and verify DNS information, and you must understand how your system will perform those same operations.

DNS information can be available in any number of places: on the local system, on a local DNS server, on a remote nameserver. UNIX systems use a *resolver* to provide this information, a program that knows about all these information sources and interfaces with them. When a program wants to know the IP address of a host or the hostname for an IP address, it asks the resolver, which consults the appropriate information sources and returns the information to the program that needs it.. We'll look at how to configure the resolver later in this chapter.

Most commonly, a resolver will direct a DNS query from a program to a nameserver, a computer running a program designed to gather DNS information from other computers on the Internet. Once a DNS request hits a nameserver, the nameserver checks its local cache to see if it has looked up that information recently. (Nameservers receive many identical DNS requests; for example, the nameserver at one Internet service provider I worked for received several hundred requests an hour for the IP address for www.cnn.com. Multiply that by all the Yahoo!, eBay, and MSN requests out there, and that cache quickly becomes quite effective.)

If the designated nameserver doesn't have the information, it asks a *root server*, which keeps a list of the nameservers responsible for every domain on the Net. In a process called a *recursive query*, the root server tells the nameserver to go ask the appropriate nameservers, which may in turn refer the query to still other nameservers. Eventually, it is referred to the authoritative nameserver for that domain and the original nameserver gets its answer.

**NOTE**   *When you register a domain, you must list two nameservers. Hosts expect to be able to get information for that domain from those nameservers. If one nameserver fails, the other should pick up the load, and if all the nameservers for a domain fail, the domain vanishes from the Internet. If that happens, the next time someone browses to www.yourdomain.com, they will get a "domain not found" error. Mail will bounce. The world will believe that you don't exist. Even big companies, such as Microsoft, do this on occasion. Your manager or customer will notice you, and not in a good way. Pay attention to your nameservice!*

# Basic DNS Tools

FreeBSD includes several tools for inspecting DNS information. Since most DNS runs over the User Datagram Protocol (UDP), you cannot use telnet to manually query a server as we will do with email and Web services later. Your only access to live DNS information is through host(1) and dig(1).

## The Host Command

To quickly check the IP address of a host, use the host(1) command. For example, to check my publisher's Web page, I would do the following:

```
# host www.nostarch.com
www.nostarch.com is a nickname for nostarch.com
nostarch.com has address 66.80.60.21
nostarch.com mail is handled (pri=20) bysmtp.lax.megapath.net
nostarch.com mail is handled (pri=10) by mail.nostarch.com
#
```

This is somewhat interesting because it shows us that under DNS, one host can have multiple names and multiple Web pages on one IP address. This output tells us that the main No Starch Press Web page is actually a nickname for another hostname, nostarch.com; one IP address can have any number of names. This is much like the phone system in a typical family household, in which several people share one telephone. The people are like hostnames, while the phone number is like an IP address. The host does have a single, canonical name, much as a phone is registered to a single person.

**NOTE** *Many server programs require much more than an IP address to function. For example, if you enter http://66.80.60.21 in your Web browser, you'll actually pull up the page for No Starch Press's hosting provider, not the page for No Starch Press. We'll look at how popular Web servers multiplex multiple Web sites onto a single IP address in Chapter 15, but it's something you should keep in the back of your mind for future reference.*

## Getting Detailed Information with Dig

While the host command is quite helpful, it's certainly not detailed. Also, you don't know where this information came from—whether it was taken straight from the cache or whether the nameserver dug it up from the domain's nameserver. The standard program for finding detailed DNS information is dig(1). (Another tool, nslookup(1), was popular for many years but has since fallen out of favor.) Dig has a variety of options that allow you to debug a wide range of nameservice problems, though I'll cover only the most basic ones here.

In its most basic form, a dig command is simply dig and a hostname. For example, to dig up information on my publisher, I would enter this command:

```
# dig www.nostarch.com
❶ ; <<>> DiG 8.3 <<>> www.nostarch.com
❷ ;; res options: init recurs defnam dnsrch
❸ ;; got answer:
;; ->>HEADER<<- opcode: QUERY, status: ❹ NOERROR, id: 4
;; flags: qr rd ra; QUERY: 1, ANSWER: 2, AUTHORITY: 2, ADDITIONAL: 2
❺ ;; QUERY SECTION:
```

*(continued on next page)*

```
;;        www.nostarch.com, type = A, class = IN
❻ ;; ANSWER SECTION:
www.nostarch.com.        2h13m2s IN CNAME  nostarch.com.
nostarch.com.            2h13m2s IN A     66.80.60.21
❼ ;; AUTHORITY SECTION:
nostarch.com.            7h48m45s IN NS  NS1.MEGAPATH.NET.
nostarch.com.            7h48m45s IN NS  NS2.MEGAPATH.NET.
❽;; ADDITIONAL SECTION:
NS1.MEGAPATH.NET.        7h48m35s IN A    216.200.176.4
NS2.MEGAPATH.NET.        7h48m35s IN A    216.34.237.2
;; Total query time: 11 msec
;; FROM: blackhelicopters.org to SERVER: default -- 127.0.0.1
;; WHEN: Sun Apr  7 12:24:17 2002
;; MSG SIZE  sent: 34  rcvd: 144
```

Wow, talk about a lot of information! (When you're using dig, you're probably trying to debug something. It's better to have too much information than not enough.)

So what have we learned? To start with, anything beginning with semicolons is a comment that either lists the options used by dig or divides the answers into sections.

The first line (❶) lists the version of dig you're using, and the command-line options you used. The second line (❷) lists the options that dig is using. (Since we didn't specify any options on the command line, these are the default options; we'll discuss some useful options later.)

The third line (❸) tells us whether dig got an answer (it did). The next line (❹) contains an important word, NOERROR, which tells us that dig found an answer that appears to be good. If you don't get a NOERROR, you have a problem. (Common errors are NXDOMAIN, meaning that the domain doesn't exist, or SERV-FAIL, meaning that the domain is misconfigured on that server.)

The next couple of lines contain codes that really aren't of use unless you're heavily into debugging DNS or doing some weird things. So let's jump to the four sections that follow: the query, answer, authority, and additional sections.

### The Query Section

In the query section (❺), we see how dig is treating the query. In our sample we see the following:

```
;;        www.nostarch.com, type = A, class = IN
```

Let's start with the easy bit, the class. While DNS can manage many different naming systems, the one we're concerned with is the Internet system, or IN. Internet domains should always have the class IN.

The type is the type of record we're looking for. By default, dig looks for an A (address) record, which means that we have the name, but want the IP address. A PTR (pointer) record request means that we have an IP address and want the associated name.

## The Answer Section

Next we have the answer section (❻). The first thing it contains is the host we're looking for (www.nostarch.com). The next figure (2h13m2s IN CNAME) is the time to live for this information—the amount of time your local nameserver may cache it. The 2h13m2s indicates that this data expires in 2 hours, 13 minutes, and 2 seconds. The IN, again, indicates that this is Internet data. Finally, CNAME means that what follows is a *canonical name* for the server, which tells us that what we're looking for is actually an alias for something else. The dig output confirms that www.nostarch.com is actually an alias for nostarch.com.

The second line of the answer section is almost identical to the first, except it has an A instead of a CNAME. This tells us that what follows is an IP address.

## The Authority Section

To get the IP address of www.nostarch.com, we have to follow the chain of authoritative nameservers. The authority section (❼) lists the servers responsible for the domain, their time to live, and the sort of data and servers that they are. In this case, the nameservers are ns1.megapath.net and ns2.megapath.net. Data for www.nostarch.com is to be cached for 7 hours, 48 minutes, and 45 seconds, and these are (again) Internet (IN) records. The NS means that these are nameservers.

## The Additional Section

Finally, under the additional section (❽), dig lists the IP addresses of all the hosts listed with the host we want. Our example lists the nameservers for www.nostarch.com: ns1.megapath.net and ns2.megapath.net. The interesting thing here is that the time to live is 7 hours, 48 minutes, and 35 seconds. In this case, the time to live isn't the value for how long the local nameserver should keep the information on the hosts, it's how long the data on the nameservers for nostarch.com should be kept. Once this time passes, your nameserver will discard the information and go fetch the nameserver list from one of the Internet's root nameservers. This isn't necessarily good or bad, but if you're trying to solve a problem, it's good to know.

Do a dig on a couple of domains and become familiar with how the output should look.

### Looking Up Hostnames with Dig

Suppose you have an IP address and want to identify the associated hostname; for example, you might want to learn who owns a phone number. This is a common problem on the Internet—you might see an IP address hitting your Web site every five seconds, and wonder who they are and what they're trying to do.

To look up the name, use *reverse lookup* with dig's -x option. Since much of the result is completely identical to what you see in the forward lookup, we'll only look at the section that's different: the answer.

```
# dig -x 66.80.60.21
;; ANSWER SECTION:
21.60.80.66.in-addr.arpa.   2h24m IN PTR   www.megapathdsl.net....
#
```

Although we know that at least www.nostarch.com and nostarch.com live on this IP address, this reverse lookup shows us the most correct name for the host. Both of those machine names live on a machine that is actually called www.mega-pathdsl.net.

The PTR entry in the middle of the answer indicates that this is a *pointer* record. It is a specific sort of entry used to mark IP-address-to-hostname records. When you set up DNS, every host with an IP address will need both a PTR and an A record in your nameservice system.

### More Dig Options

The dig program takes a wide variety of command-line options to control how it checks for information. Check dig(1) for a complete list of these options. We'll only discuss the servername and norecurse options here, because they're the ones most commonly used.

#### Server Name

The first option is the server name. By default, dig queries the first nameserver listed in /etc/resolv.conf. If you're trying to debug a problem, however, you want to ask different nameservers. You can do this on the command line by using the @ option. For example, to ask dns1.yahoo.com what it knows about AbsoluteBSD.com enter this:

```
# dig @dns1.yahoo.com AbsoluteBSD.com
```

The output from this command will look much like the sample output shown earlier, except that you'll see references to Yahoo!'s nameserver. If you're debugging a problem, you should compare this information carefully with that given by your local nameserver. If information from two different nameservers conflicts, you may well have found your problem. (DNS information should only change when you add hosts, rename hosts, or renumber hosts.) You can use some of dig's other options to see exactly where the problem occurs.

#### Controlling How Dig Queries

Dig has two other sorts of options: those that control how dig itself runs, and those that control how dig makes queries. The options that control how dig runs are prefaced with a minus sign (-); those that control how dig makes its queries are prefaced by a plus sign (+). While dig can do a lot of really nifty tricks, they're beyond the scope of this chapter. Controlling how it makes the queries is quite useful, however.

By default, a nameserver will recurse queries to return an answer. While this is helpful if you're asking the nameserver about a domain, you don't want the nameserver to dig up the answer for you when you're debugging; instead, you want to check each nameserver in turn. You can do this with the norecurse option.

```
# dig AbsoluteBSD.com +norecurse
```

Try this one now, with a domain that you're pretty certain your local name-server has never looked at. My favorite DNS server test site is www.moo.com, simply because it's cool, obscure, cute, mostly harmless, and nobody ever looks at it. You're almost guaranteed that nobody on your nameserver has looked at moo.com lately.

If your nameserver doesn't have this information cached, or if this information has expired from the cache, your first section will look much like that of our previous example. The authority section, however, will look quite different:

```
;; AUTHORITY SECTION:
com.                    18h9m59s IN NS   A.GTLD-SERVERS.NET.
com.                    18h9m59s IN NS   G.GTLD-SERVERS.NET.
com.                    18h9m59s IN NS   H.GTLD-SERVERS.NET.
com.                    18h9m59s IN NS   C.GTLD-SERVERS.NET.
com.                    18h9m59s IN NS   I.GTLD-SERVERS.NET.
com.                    18h9m59s IN NS   B.GTLD-SERVERS.NET.
com.                    18h9m59s IN NS   D.GTLD-SERVERS.NET.
com.                    18h9m59s IN NS   L.GTLD-SERVERS.NET.
com.                    18h9m59s IN NS   F.GTLD-SERVERS.NET.
com.                    18h9m59s IN NS   J.GTLD-SERVERS.NET.
com.                    18h9m59s IN NS   K.GTLD-SERVERS.NET.
com.                    18h9m59s IN NS   E.GTLD-SERVERS.NET.
com.                    18h9m59s IN NS   M.GTLD-SERVERS.NET.
```

The nameservers under GTLD-SERVERS.NET are the root servers. They contain the master lists of which nameservers control which domains. By giving you this output, your local nameserver is saying, "I don't know, I'll have to go ask someone else, but you told me to not recurse so I'm stopping here."

To query a root nameserver, combine the norecurse option and server name dig commands and try your query again:

```
# dig @a.gtld-servers.net +norecurse www.moo.com
```

Follow the chain of information for a site or two, and you'll start to really understand how DNS works.

## Configuring a DNS Client: The Resolver

Before you can have your system use a DNS server, you must tell the computer which nameserver to use, and how it should be used. Even a DNS server needs to have the client portion of nameservice set up, because the computer won't know it has a nameserver running unless you tell it! Just about anything you do on a network will require a working nameservice client. Use keywords in /etc/resolv.conf to tell your system's resolver where to look for information.

### Domain or Search Keywords

When you're working on machines on your own network, you don't want to have to type the whole hostname. (If you have 30 Web servers, typing ssh www19.mycompany.com gets old.) To tell the resolver which domains to check by default, use either a domain or a search keyword in /etc/resolv.conf.

#### Specifying the Local Domain

The domain keyword tells the resolver which local domain name to check, by default, for hosts. For example, to specify AbsoluteBSD.com as the local domain, enter this:

```
domain      AbsoluteBSD.com
```

Once the local domain is specified, any command that would ordinarily require a domain name will be assumed to be pointing to AbsoluteBSD.com. Were I to ping www, the resolver would append the name AbsoluteBSD.com to that and tell ping to try www.AbsoluteBSD.com.

#### Specifying a List of Domains with Search

Alternatively, I can use the search keyword to specify a list of domains to try. Perhaps my company has several domain names in use in different parts of the network—I could enter the following:

```
search AbsoluteBSD.com blackhelicopters.org stenchmaster.org
```

In this case, the resolver will check these three domain names in the order written, until it finds a match.

For example, if I enter ping petulance, it will try to find petulance.AbsoluteBSD.com. If that fails, it will check for petulance.blackhelicopters.org, the next domain in order. Finally, it will check for petulance.stenchmaster.com. If no such host exists in any of these domains, the command will eventually fail.

**NOTE** *If you don't list either a domain or a search keyword, the resolver will use the local machine's domain name.*

### The Nameserver List

Now that your resolver knows which domains to try by default, you can tell it which nameservers to use. List each nameserver on a single line, in the order of preference. The nameservers will be tried in order. It would look something like this:

```
nameserver 127.0.0.1
nameserver 209.168.70.3
nameserver 192.168.87.3
```

Note that the first entry in this list is the "loopback" IP address 127.0.0.1. You'll need this entry if the machine is a nameserver because it tells the resolver to check the local host's nameserver. While in some rare instances you might not want to use the local nameserver, you don't have to, but in most cases it's a waste of network bandwidth not to.

With nameserver entries and either `domain` or `search` keywords, your /etc/resolv.conf is complete.

# DNS Information Sources

To truly manage Internet services, you must be able to control your own domain naming service. While many ISPs will provide this service for you, you don't want to have to coordinate with their staff to make a vital change in your infrastructure.

Now that you know how to look at DNS data, and how the chain of DNS authority works, you can start building your own nameserver. FreeBSD includes all the software you need to run a DNS server; all you have to do is configure it and turn it on. We'll do so by building the two possible sources of hostname and IP address information: the *hosts file* and the *named daemon*. Each is configured separately.

### The Hosts File

The /etc/hosts file matches Internet addresses to hostnames for a single host. However, while the hosts file is very simple, its contents are only effective on a single machine. One system cannot use the hosts file from another system, without some unpleasant tricks.

Dynamic nameserver programs have largely superseded /etc/hosts, but the hosts file is still useful on small networks or behind a Network Address Translation (NAT) device. For example, the hosts file is just fine if you have one or two servers and if someone else is responsible for managing your public nameservice. If you have multiple servers that would each have to be maintained separately, you should investigate using a full-fledged nameserver.

Each line in /etc/hosts represents one host. The first entry on each line is an IP address, and the second is the fully qualified domain name of the host, such as mail.mycompany.com. Following these two entries you can list an arbitrary number of aliases for that host.

For example, a small company might have a single server that handles mail, FTP, Web services, DNS, and a variety of other functions. A desktop on that network might have a hosts entry something like this:

```
192.168.1.2    mail.mycompany.com    mail ftp www dns dns
```

Using this /etc/hosts entry, the desktop could find that host (mail.mycompany.com) with either the full domain name or any of the brief aliases listed (such as ftp.mycompany.com, www.mycompany.com, and so on).

If you find that you need more than two or three hosts entries, or that maintaining hosts files is becoming a problem, it's a sign that you need to build a nameserver to handle your hosts data. A nameserver is far more scalable than a hosts file on each machine, and it's much simpler to maintain once you set it up.

### The Named Daemon

The most popular DNS server software is BIND (Berkeley Internet Name Daemon). (The actual server program is called named(8).) BIND is actually a suite of tools that includes named and supporting programs such as dig.

BIND is maintained by the Internet Software Consortium (www.isc.org) and is released under a BSD-style license. While there are competitors, such as djbdns (/usr/ports/net/djbdns), BIND is considered the nameservice reference implementation, so we'll focus on it. The concepts used in BIND are generally applicable to any nameserver programs.

Because BIND has been the target of malicious hackers over the last several years, its most recent version was completely rewritten with a focus on security. It includes some very powerful security features and extremely defensive programming.

#### Masters and Slaves

No matter what nameserver daemon you use, you'll keep running into the terms *masters* and *slaves*. Every domain needs at least two nameservers, but only one can be the master; the rest are slaves.

A master nameserver is the final authority on a domain. When you make changes to a domain, you make the changes on the master nameserver. The slaves take their information from the master nameserver for that domain.

One nameserver can be both a master for some domains and a slave for others. For example, AbsoluteBSD.com has two nameservers, blackhelicopters.org and ralph.glblnet.com; blackhelicopters.org holds the original reference files for this domain, and any changes are to be made on that system. That makes blackhelicopters.org the master nameserver. Every so often, ralph.glblnet.com updates its records for this domain from blackhelicopters.org, making it the slave. If the blackhelicopters.org system is abducted by aliens, ralph.glblnet.com would continue to serve DNS information for AbsoluteBSD.com.

On the other hand, ralph.glblnet.com holds the master records for many other domains, and other nameservers update their records for these domains from ralph.glblnet.com. Therefore, ralph.glblnet.com is both a master and a slave nameserver, but for different domains.

#### Forward and Reverse DNS

You may have heard of or otherwise encountered the concepts of *forward* and *reverse DNS*. Forward DNS is what you do when you have a hostname and you look up an IP address. You saw examples of forward DNS in the A records in our dig examples:

```
nostarch.com.        2h13m2s IN A    66.80.60.21
```

The A means that this is an address record, or forward DNS. This is known as an "A record" or an "address record."

Reverse DNS is what you do when you have an IP address and want a hostname. For example, suppose your system logs show that someone keeps trying to connect to your SSH server from the IP address 66.80.60.21, and you want to know the name of that host. You can look up IP addresses using dig's -x option. Much of the output will look the same as a forward lookup, but the answer is considerably different:

```
# dig -x 66.80.60.21
...
;; ANSWER SECTION:
21.60.80.66.in-addr.arpa.  2h24m IN PTR www.megapathdsl.net.
...
#
```

Examining this output we see that, for historical reasons we won't delve into, IP addresses are displayed in reverse order and as part of the domain in-addr.arpa when you're doing a reverse lookup. Next we have the usual time-to-live data and the IN for Internet data.

The interesting part is the PTR or *pointer record*, which tells us that an IP address "points to" a name. Basically, this is the canonical, most correct hostname for an IP address. This is much like a phone system; again, while many people can share a phone number, it's only registered to one person.

Forward and reverse DNS are generally expected to match, but since many hosts can share one IP address, an A record does not necessarily need a matching PTR record. For example, we saw earlier that nostarch.com has an IP of 66.80.60.21, but the hostname associated with that IP address is www.megapathdsl.net. The part that must match is the A record for www.megapathdsl.net. If the hostname given by a reverse lookup does not have a matching forward record, DNS is not correctly configured, and the tools that rely upon DNS checking, such as certain configurations of TCP wrappers, will reject connections from this system. Fortunately, automated tools exist to check forward and reverse DNS matches.

### In-addr.arpa

There's one major difficulty with PTR records: Often, when they appear, they're listed backwards.

You see, DNS checks hosts from left to right. When you check for the host www.AbsoluteBSD.com, the nameserver first looks for a nameserver for .com. It then checks under .com for AbsoluteBSD.com, then under AbsoluteBSD.com for www.AbsoluteBSD.com. The biggest units are on the left, but in an IP address, the biggest unit is on the right. To check the IP address, we have to reverse it. For example, we turn 66.80.60.21 into 21.60.80.66.

It's very easy to confuse a forward IP address with a reversed IP address, so DNS uses a special marker to indicate that an IP address is reversed. Reversed IP addresses have the string "in-addr.arpa" on the end of them. (The reasons for this date back several years and are quite boring, so we won't go into them.) The bottom line is that our 66.80.60.21 becomes 21.60.80.66.in-addr.arpa.

So why not just leave the IP address forward, and use the in-addr.arpa to indicate it's a reverse DNS check? Glad you asked. The preceding address is a simple one, and if you ran dig, it would check a very limited space. If you're running a large network, you might need to run a DNS query of a much larger range of IP addresses, like 118.168.192.in-addr.arpa, which would translate to everything under 192.168.118. You might even need to run 168.192.in-addr.arpa, or even 192.in-addr.arpa. Each is a check of an increasingly large space—much like doing dig .com. (You'll probably never need to run dig .com, but Internet backbone engineers do, and backbone engineers are the ones who write this sort of program. One of the problems with using professional-strength tools is that they're geared toward, well, professionals.)

**NOTE** *If you're looking for quick-and-dirty answers, host(1) does this reversal for you. Dig also does this for you, if you use the -x option. Don't be confused when you see in-addr.arpa, however.*

### Configuring Named

Before you can start named, you need to set it up. The directory /etc/namedb contains the basic named configuration files.

### named.root

One file that must be present, but that doesn't need editing, is named.root, which lists the *root nameservers*. If a nameserver receives a query for a site it doesn't have in its cache, it asks these nameservers. (This file changes rarely—the last update was in August 1997.) You may need to edit this file if your system is not on the Internet and if you have a private root server.

### named.conf

The other important file is named.conf, named's central file. If your named.conf file is broken, your nameserver is hosed.

The syntax of named.conf resembles C code. If you don't know C, though, don't worry, because the rules are very simple, and the examples demonstrate everything you need to know. Any line beginning with two slashes (//) is a comment. Similarly, any text contained within old-fashioned C comment marks (/* and */) is a multi-line comment.

There are two types of entries in named.conf: *options* and *zones*. Everything in your configuration file should be either an option, a zone, or a comment. A *zone* is a fancy name for a domain (while they aren't, strictly speaking, identical, they're close enough for our purposes). Options control how BIND operates.

## Options

If you ignore the comments in the default named.conf, the file opens with a list of options, most of which are obscure and are commented out by default. You use options by putting them in the options section of the file, which contains the word options and a set of curly brackets. The actual options go between the brackets and are separated from one another by semicolons. Here's a very simple options section from a named.conf file:

```
options {
        directory "/var/named";        listen-on {127.0.0.1; 209.69.178.18; };
};
```

In this example, the option directory has the value "/var/named", and the listen-on option lists two IP addresses.

Let's first look at the directory option, which specifies the directory where named.conf will look for and store DNS files. Beginning here will make setting up your server more straightforward.

The default directory (/etc/namedb) should be fine if all you want to do is provide a nameservice for a couple of domains. However, if you are providing DNS for dozens or hundreds of clients, this directory will quickly become painfully full and will be unable to live on the root partition.

The standard alternative to /etc/namedb is /var/named, which is the location for nameservice files on larger servers. I generally use /var/named even when I have just a few domains to serve, as these files tend to accumulate.

The listen-on option controls which IP addresses named will accept connections on. If you have dozens of IP addresses on a single network card, you might want to confine your named to attaching to only one of those addresses. (This is particularly valuable if you have jails on your system.)

BIND supports many more options, but these are perhaps the most popular. You can check the full BIND Operators' Guide (at http://www.isc.org) for the complete list of options and their usage.

## Zones

The default named.conf defines three zones, or domains, that the nameserver handles by default: the *root zone*, the *IPv4 localhost*, and the *IPv6 localhost*. Each of these zones has an entry in named.conf, beneath the options list. You shouldn't need to tweak the default zones—in fact, if you're thinking of changing them, you're almost certainly doing something wrong. But we'll discuss what these zones are for and what they do.

### The Root Zone

The nameserver uses the root zone when it has no information on a requested domain or host. These queries are recursed to a root nameserver. Here's the named.conf entry for the root zone:

```
zone ❶ "." {
        ❷ type hint;
        ❸ file "named.root";
};
```

The first entry (❶) tells which domain this entry is for. The dot, in quotes, indicates that this is for the entire Internet.

The type (❷) is an indicator that says what sort of domain this is. The root zone is special, and it is the only one with the type of hint.

Finally, the file keyword (❸) tells named which file contains the information for this domain. Named will look in the directory specified in the directory option for a file of this name, and will assign its contents to this zone. We'll look at these files later.

### Localhost Zones

The localhost zones (IPv4 and IPv6) are used for the local host; they provide DNS services for the loopback IP address, 127.0.0.1. Without them, each system call that tried to look up the hostname for the local host would have to wait to time out, slowing the system immeasurably. Each looks much like the root zone, with a different filename.

Here's the configuration for the IPv4 localhost zone. You'll find it in named.conf, just under the root zone:

```
zone ❶ "0.0.127.IN-ADDR.ARPA" {
        ❷ type master;
        ❸ file "localhost.rev";
};
```

Looks pretty similar to the options statement and the root zone in the previous section, doesn't it?

The zone name (❶) appears in quotes after the word zone. Because this zone is used for reverse DNS, we see IN-ADDR.ARPA. (If you reverse the IP address, you'll see it's actually for the 127.0.0 group of IP addresses.)

The type (❷) indicates whether this nameserver is a master or a slave for this domain. Every nameserver is a master for the localhost zones.

Finally, the file keyword (❸) tells the nameserver where the file of information on this domain can be found. The information on this zone is contained in the file localhost.rev, found in the directory specified in the directory option.

### Setting Up a Slave

Perhaps the easiest task in DNS is to set up a slave domain. The entry will look much like the entries for the root zone and the localhost zone. You need to know the name of the domain you want to slave, and the IP address of the master nameserver.

To set up a slave domain, copy the localhost zone entry and change it slightly. The configuration for the slave server for AbsoluteBSD.com, for example, looks like the following, which closely resembles the root and localhost zones.

```
❶ zone "AbsoluteBSD.com" {        ❷ type slave;           ❸ file
"AbsoluteBSD.com.db";             ❹ masters {209.69.178.18;};
}
```

We have the domain name (❶), a label for the type of zone it is (❷), and a file-name (❸). The filename is where the information for the domain is kept. It's traditional in DNS to give these files the same name as the domain, with a ".db" extension. (Despite what the extension might imply, these files are in no way databases.) This file will be created when the slave downloads the domain data from the master.

We then have the IP address of the master server (❹). The slave will request the domain's DNS information from the master at regular intervals. (We'll see what sort of intervals later.) The master nameserver must be listed by IP address; after all, the DNS server must be able to bootstrap its records before it knows the IP of anything!

### Setting Up a Master

The named.conf configuration you need when you want a server to be a master is even simpler than the setup for a slave zone:

```
❶ zone "AbsoluteBSD.com" {        ❷ type master;          ❸ file
"AbsoluteBSD.com.db";
}
```

Once more there's the domain name (❶), a label for the type of zone it is (❷), and a filename (❸). Unlike a slave domain, you'll have to create this file. We'll look at how to create that file in the "Zone Files" section.

### Setting Up Multiple Zones

If you're managing high-end Internet nameservers, you may be responsible for thousands of domains. If you screw up, you will have a lot of people very angry with you. Therefore, before you set up hundreds of zones, think about how you're going to arrange them.

One thing that can make your life easier when setting up multiple zones is to divide a server's zone files between those that the server is the master for and those that the server just backs up. I usually do this with two directories, *master* and *slave*. Files in the master directory are sacred, and must be preserved. Files in the slave zone aren't exactly garbage, but their loss is no big deal.

If you expect to serve thousands of domains, you might want to divide your master zone files still further. I use a set of 36 directories under the master directory, one for each letter and number. Of course, you can create any arrangement of directories that fits your needs. Just remember that you're going to either live with this arrangement or go through some annoyance changing it.

Taking this to the logical extreme, your zone entry could look like the following:

```
zone "AbsoluteBSD.com" {
        type master;
        file "master/clients/a/absolutebsd.com";
};
```

Most people do not need this number of subdirectories, but you could do it if you needed to.

### Zone Files

At this point we have a configuration file that tells named what domains it's responsible for, and where the files that contain the information on those domains live. But we still need to make those files!

Zone files have a rather obscure syntax because, much like sendmail, BIND was assembled by programmers who were more interested in efficiency than ease of use. Unlike sendmail, zone file configuration is not blatantly user-hostile, though some parts of zone files appear inconsistent.

To learn how to work with zone files, follow the given examples and you should be all right. And any time you find yourself scratching your head and wondering why they did something a certain way, just remember that you're digging through the primordial ooze of the Internet. (If DNS were invented today, zone files would probably look very different.)

Here's a simple example of configuring a zone file. FreeBSD includes a shell script to create the localhost file, `make-localhost`. To create the localhost file, all you have to do is go to /etc/namedb and type this:

```
# sh make-localhost
```

And poof! The file localhost.rev appears. We'll dissect this file as our first example.

```
;       From: @(#)localhost.rev 5.1 (Berkeley) 6/30/90
; $FreeBSD: src/etc/namedb/PROTO.localhost.rev,v 1.6 2000/01/10 15:31:40 peter Exp $
;
; This file is automatically edited by the `make-localhost' script in
; the /etc/namedb directory.
;
```

```
❶ $TTL    3600
❷ @      ❸ IN     ❹ SOA    ❺ satariel.blackhelicopters.org.
❻ root.satariel.blackhelicopters.org. (
                        ❼ 20010601        ; Serial
                        ❽ 3600     ; Refresh
                        ❾ 900      ; Retry
                        ❿ 3600000 ; Expire
                        ⓫ 3600 )  ; Minimum
        IN     NS      satariel.blackhelicopters.org.
1       IN     PTR     localhost.blackhelicopters.org.
```

First of all, remember that anything that begins with a semicolon is a comment. (Comment your zone files liberally; it'll help you figure out later what the heck you were doing.)

### $TTL: Time to Live

We'll skip on through this file to the first line of real interest, the $TTL statement (❶). This statement is the zone's default time to live, in seconds (3,600 seconds, in this case), and it dictates how long other servers will cache information from this zone. You can give data in the zone any time to live you choose. This is actually a fairly short time; a good average is 10,800, or 3 hours. Choosing a TTL is something of a black art; stick with the default, and you'll be fine for most purposes.

### Start of Authority

Next is the Start of Authority (SOA) record. This is a brief description of the zone, and of how its characters and servers should treat it. Every zone has exactly one SOA record. The SOA does not include information about what is in the domain, merely information about how long this information lasts.

**The @ sign**   The at symbol (@), which begins the SOA record (❷), is a special character that's shorthand for "whatever named.conf says this file is for," and in this case, named.conf says that this file holds data for the zone 0.0.127.in-addr.arpa. When named reads named.conf and loads this file into memory, it makes this substitution. Using the actual domain name would be less confusing for new users, but you'll see this in most nameservers and will need to be familiar with it. You could use the full domain name in this file instead of the @ symbol if you wished, but almost nobody does that.

**The Data Type and Label**   The IN represents the type of data (❸), Internet data in this case, and SOA means that this is a Start of Authority record (❹). Both elements will appear in every DNS record you create.

**Machine Name**   The next part is the name of the machine where the master file lives (❺). (This file was created on satariel.blackhelicopters.org.)

**Responsible Party**   Then we have the email address of the person responsible for this zone (❻). Since the make-localhost script defaults to root@hostname, the email address lacks the @ sign, because the @ sign had already been assigned to mean the zone name from named.conf.[1] (Were we to put the @ in, the email address would become root0.0.127.in-addr.arpa.satariel.blackhelicopters.org. That would be worse than root.satariel.blackhelicopters.org, wouldn't it?) This is important when you create your own zone files for your domains. Replace the @ in the email address with a period.

In many cases, the nameserver doesn't have a mail server on it. To follow best current practices on the Internet, replace the email address with hostmaster. and your domain name. Every domain is expected to have a "hostmaster" email address to respond to DNS issues.

**Parentheses**   While technically the SOA record should be on a single line, if it were, it would be difficult to read. Instead, standard zone files have this broken up into several lines, with the first opening parenthesis (or round bracket) indicating the line break. Each of the next five lines is part of the SOA record, with the record ending with the closing parenthesis.

**Serial Number**   The first piece is the serial number, which indicates the zone file's version (❼). While the serial number can be whatever you choose, it's most convenient to use the date. You'll usually see the date in YYYYMMDD format with two extra digits at the end. This serial number, 20010601, represents June 1, 2001. The extra two numbers in the serial number represent the number of times the file has changed in a day. For example, there have been times that I've had to update one domain a dozen times in one day, with each change requiring a serial number bump. Here's how this works: Say I create the zone file on May 9, 2002, with the first serial number 2002050901. If I change the zone file on June 8, the serial number changes to 2002060801. If I then change the zone file a second time on that same day, the serial number changes to 2002060802. This system allows up to 100 changes in a day, or roughly one change every 15 minutes. If this isn't enough for you, you need to rethink your work processes.

The serial number is important, because every so often a slave server will contact the master server to see if the zone has updated. It determines whether there's been an update by comparing the serial number of its cached copy to the master zone file's serial number. If the master zone file's serial number is greater than the one on the slave, the slave server determines that the zone file has been updated and downloads the latest domain information.

**NOTE**   *If your secondary nameservers haven't updated their zone files from the master nameserver, it's probably a serial number problem. Even if you swear up and down that you incremented the serial number, increment the serial number again and try once more. It'll probably work.*

---

[1] DNS was created before the @ sign became popular in email addresses. This overlap is email's fault, not BIND's.

**Refresh**  The next number is the refresh value, in seconds (❽). This number determines how frequently slave servers will contact the master server to check for an updated master file. In the localhost.rev file, a secondary nameserver would update every 3,600 seconds, or 60 minutes.

If the slave cannot check its data against the master in a refresh attempt, it keeps giving answers with its current record—that's what a backup nameserver is for, after all! We'll see exactly how this works in the "Refresh, Retry, and Expire in Practice" section.

**Retry**  The next number is the retry value, also in seconds (❾). If the slave cannot reach the master nameserver, it will retry at this interval. Our sample file has a 900 second (15 minute) retry. If the secondary nameserver cannot update at the 1 hour mark, it will keep trying every 15 minutes until the master nameserver answers. Again, we'll see exactly how this works in the "Refresh, Retry, and Expire in Practice" section.

**Expire**  Next we have the expire value, in seconds (❿). If a slave nameserver cannot update its records for this many seconds, it stops giving out its cached information. It's at this point that the administrator thinks bad information is worse than no information. In our example we have 3,600,000 seconds (1,000 hours, or a little over 41 days).

**Minimum TTL**  The last number is the minimum time to live (⓫). In older implementations of BIND, this was used for the time to live for absolutely everything. Today, it's only used for the TTL for negative answers. (Nameservers can cache negative answers.) For example, if you look up givememymoneyback. AbsoluteBSD.com, your nameserver will learn that there's no such host. In localhost.rev, negative answers will be cached for 3,600 seconds (1 hour).

**NOTE**  *Be sure you have a closing parenthesis after the minimum time to live! Otherwise, named will assume that the remainder of the file is also part of the SOA record and get confused.*

**Recycling SOAs**  Now that you understand all the painful details of the SOA record, here's the good news. Once you set up an SOA the way you like, you can recycle that same SOA, with only minimal changes, across multiple domains. I've set up thousands of domains from a template SOA.

### Domain Information

Now that you have a complete SOA record, you can list actual information for the domain. Domain information immediately follows the SOA record.

In the following example, the two lines contain the zone's actual host information:

```
        IN    NS    satariel.blackhelicopters.org.
1       IN    PTR   localhost.blackhelicopters.org.
```

Each of these lines has four parts: a hostname or number, the data type, the server type, and the actual data. The first field contains either a hostname (such as www) or a number (such as 12). The name of the zone is automatically attached to this entry, either at the beginning or at the end, depending on whether the file is for reverse or forward DNS. Since our example is for reverse DNS, the 1 is appended onto 127.0.0 giving us the IP address 127.0.0.1. (If there is nothing in the first field, named will append the zone name anyway, giving us a reasonable default.) The data type is always IN (Internet).

The third field, the type of server we have, is actually interesting. An NS entry (shown in the first line above) represents a nameserver, and in this example, the only nameserver for this domain is satariel.blackhelicopters.org. If you're distributing localhost.rev among several nameservers, you should add additional NS lines for them.

**NOTE** *Because there is no first field in our NS example here, BIND assumes that this is for the 0.0.127.in-addr.arpa zone, or the network beginning with 127.0.0, the domain specified for this file in named.conf.*

A PTR entry (as shown in the second line of the preceding example) represents IP-address-to-hostname mapping. This zone is for the 127.0.0 network. On the second line of our example, we have a .1. This represents the .1 in the network, or 127.0.0.1, the standard loopback IP address. This record points to the local host, in this case localhost.blackhelicopters.org.

### Refresh, Retry, and Expire in Practice

While I've mentioned what the refresh, retry, and expire times mean, that's still a ways from understanding how they work. Here's an example of these times in operation.

Suppose we have a domain with a refresh time of 4 hours, a retry time of 1 hour, and an expire time of 48 hours. This means that the slave nameserver will contact the master every hour to check for updates. Every so often, you edit records on the master nameserver, and they propagate to the slave within an hour.

So far, so good. Now assume that the master nameserver explodes, scattering your hard disk across three counties. What will happen to the slave server? The next time the slave tries to check to see if its records are out of date, it will be unable to reach the master. At that point, it changes how often it checks for updates. Instead of using the refresh time of four hours, it will use the retry time of one hour. Once it can successfully check the status of its records, it will go back to using the refresh time instead of the retry time.

If the slave cannot confirm its data for a length of time equal to the expire time, the domain data is considered too old to be useful and the slave nameserver will discard the data and return an error when anyone asks about the domain. The domain will disappear from the Net.

If your master nameserver really does fail in a horrible way, you have an amount of time equal to the expire plus the retry times to replace it or to reconfigure your slave as a master.

# A Real Sample Zone

The localhost zone file is a somewhat contrived example; it represents only one machine, and has only the one IP address in it. But it's convenient, it's found on every nameserver, and all the data types given are either commonly used or flat-out required.

Now let's consider a zone file that's more representative of the domains you'll be serving. We'll look at the relevant snippets from named.conf and the zone file for AbsoluteBSD.com.

### named.conf

Here's a snippet from named.conf:

```
zone "AbsoluteBSD.com" {
        type master;
        file "master/AbsoluteBSD.com";
};
```

In this example, we're telling named that it is responsible for the domain AbsoluteBSD.com, and that it's the master nameserver. We're also giving it the filename where the information on the domain can be found. If our directory option is set to /var/named, this file would be found in /var/named/master/AbsoluteBSD.com. Without further ado, let's check out that file.

### /var/named/master/absolutebsd.com

```
❶ $TTL 345600

❷ @       IN      SOA     blackhelicopters.org. root.blackhelicopters.org.  (
                                2001101501      ; Serial
                                86400   ; Refresh -- 24 hours
                                7200    ; Retry -- 2 hours
                                2592000 ; Expire -- 30 days
                                345600) ; Minimum -- 4 days

          ❸ IN      NS      blackhelicopters.org.
            IN      NS      ralph.glblnet.com.

          ❹ IN      MX      10      blackhelicopters.org.

            IN      MX      20      ralph.glblnet.com.

❺         IN      CNAME   www.AbsoluteBSD.com.
www       IN      A       209.69.178.30
```

This file looks almost the same as the localhost file we looked at earlier, but it's an actual zone file from a real live Internet domain. Let's see what we've got. First we have the time to live (❶), equal to four days, which means that when a nameserver grabs the IP information for this domain, it'll hang on to it for four days. The SOA record (❷) lists the contact information and a variety of times for refresh, retry, and expire, as well as a serial number.

The zone file lists two nameservers (❸): blackhelicopters.org and ralph.glblnet.com. According to the times in the zone file, ralph.glblnet.com will compare its records to blackhelicopters.org every 24 hours. If it cannot compare its records successfully, it'll keep trying every 2 hours. If ralph.glblnet.com cannot check its records against the master nameserver for 30 days straight, it will stop giving any answer for AbsoluteBSD.com. Finally, remote nameservers will cache no-such-host responses for four days.

**The Mail Exchanger**

We then have a new record type, MX, the domain's *mail exchanger* (❹). While a domain has only one primary mail host, it can have multiple backup mail servers. Nevertheless, the mail must ultimately reach the main mail host. Here's where you indicate which is the preferred mail server and which are backups. (We will discuss this in some detail in Chapter 14.)

**Preference Numbers**

The one additional entry in the MX record (the numbers 10 and 20) is a *preference*. Servers with lower preference numbers are more preferred. In this case, the server blackhelicopters.org, with preference 10, is the preferred mail server for AbsoluteBSD.com. If blackhelicopters.org cannot be reached, ralph.glblnet.com is the backup.

Since you may someday want to add another mail server between the two, or change to a completely different preferred server, leave some space between your preference numbers. If you don't, and you number them 1, 2, 3, and so on, you won't have much flexibility later. For example, on the day when AbsoluteBSD.com has thousands of clients receiving mail, I might have a set of MX records that look like this:

```
        IN      MX      10      mail.AbsoluteBSD.com
        IN      MX      20      mail2.AbsoluteBSD.com
        IN      MX      30      mail.someothercompany.com
```

**Host Records**

Lastly, we have the actual host records (❺), the meat of the zone file. We're concerned with two types of host records: CNAME and A records. As we saw in the dig example, a CNAME is a reference to a *canonical name*, an *alias*. An A record points a name to an IP address. Our example shows that AbsoluteBSD.com is an alias for www.AbsoluteBSD.com. (Remember, when there's no name explicitly given for an entry, it defaults to the domain the file represents!) The host www.AbsoluteBSD.com has an Internet address of 209.69.178.30.

### Periods, Termination, and Zone Files

You've already seen (in the section on "Zones Files" describing the SOA record) that periods can be substituted for the @ sign in email addresses when you're creating zone files. Periods are further overloaded, however, into termination symbols for hostnames. When using the @ symbol in this way, named assumes that all hostnames are part of the zone the file is for. There's no need for you to write out "www.AbsoluteBSD.com"; named knows that you're talking about AbsoluteBSD.com, and just saying "www" suffices. (Every hostname has the zone name appended to it.)

This system works well, except when the host isn't part of the domain in question. For example, since the nameservers for AbsoluteBSD.com are not in that domain, we don't want them showing up as blackhelicopters.org.AbsoluteBSD.com, now do we?

This is where a period comes in. If you put a period after a hostname, named assumes that you've listed the complete hostname, including domain name. As you can see in the preceding examples, every complete hostname after the SOA record has a period after it. Even the CNAME entry pointing to www.AbsoluteBSD.com has a period; if it didn't, it would direct us to www.AbsoluteBSD.com.AbsoluteBSD.com. When you typed **www.AbsoluteBSD.com** into your Web browser, the browser wouldn't be able to find the page. Instead, you would have to type **www. AbsoluteBSD.com.AbsoluteBSD.com**. Now that wouldn't be very helpful, would it?[2]

## Making Changes Work

So, you have your nameserver configured and your zone files are all set up. We're looking pretty good. But the nameserver won't make the changes until you tell named to reread its configuration files.

To apply your changes, use the name daemon controller, ndc(8). Ndc can handle all named management functions, which will vary with how your named is compiled. For a complete list of all functions, run ndc help as root:

```
# ndc help
(builtin) start - start the server
(builtin) restart - stop server if any, start a new one
getpid
status
stop
exec
reload [zone] ...
reconfig [-noexpired] (just sees new/gone zones)
```

*(continued on next page)*

[2] Actually, now that I think of it, having that as an actual hostname would be something that DNS geeks would find funny. Remember that before becoming a DNS geek.

```
dumpdb
stats [clear]
trace [level]
notrace
querylog
qrylog
help
quit
#
```

To learn about all of these options, get one of the big books on DNS. Our important options are stop, start, restart, and reload; ndc stop shuts down the nameserver, ndc start fires it up, and ndc restart stops and starts it. Restarting the nameserver will make it reread every zone file to bring itself up to date and will also flush its cache of third-party DNS information. (That's okay if your nameserver only serves information and doesn't provide lookups for end users.) If you want named to check all its zone files for updated information, but not dump its third-party cache, use ndc reload instead.

## Starting Named at Boottime

If you're running a nameserver, you usually want it to start automatically at boot-time. You can start named at boot with the rc.conf option named_enable:

```
named_enable="YES"
```

If you want to start it manually, use ndc(8), as discussed in the previous section.

## Checking DNS

Once you've created your first zone, get a complete printout of the domain to check your work. (The axfr keyword for dig requests a list of all hosts in the domain.)

```
# dig @primarynameserver domainname axfr
```

Now read the results. Are all the names as you expected? Do you have hosts with double domain names, such as AbsoluteBSD.com.AbsoluteBSD.com? If so, you forgot a period. Are all your mail servers and nameservers showing up? If not, fix them.

You can use dnswalk(1) (/usr/ports/net/dnswalk) to double-check your work. This tool will catch a wide variety of standard configuration problems, though it won't catch conceptual problems. If you have a host using a CNAME, but the canonical name is a CNAME back to the first hostname (a loop), dnswalk will point it out. However, if you set your preferred mail exchanger to mail.whitehouse.gov, it'll let that pass.

To use dnswalk on a domain, use it like this:

```
# dnswalk AbsoluteBSD.com.
```

### Named Configuration Errors

DNS configuration errors appear in /var/log/messages and appear as error messages when you start, restart, or reload named. If your nameserver is not serving information on a domain, check this log file. The log messages are generally fairly explicit and state which line number an error might appear on.

# Named Security

Named is a popular target for hackers because it provides a lot of information about your network and because it defaults to running as root. If someone breaks into named, he owns your machine. We'll tackle both of these problems separately.

The dig example I just gave, in which we snagged a complete list of hosts in a domain, is called a *zone transfer*. A prospective intruder would be very interested in this information, especially if your hosts have descriptive names. ("Oh, ceo.AbsoluteBSD.com must be the company president's machine! That would be neat to hack.")

Because the purpose of a nameserver is to serve names, we can't entirely cut out the bad guy's access. However, we can make sure that named will only give answers to specific queries rather than spilling its guts upon request. Thus, if someone asks for a particular hostname, the nameserver will answer, but if someone asks for a list, nameserver will deny their request.

To restrict zone transfers to only being performed by specific hosts, use the `allow-transfer` option:

```
options {
        directory "/var/named";
        allow-transfer {
                192.168.87.3; 10.115.4.3 ;
                };
};
```

In this example, the hosts 192.168.87.3 and 10.115.4.3 are the only systems permitted to perform a zone transfer. Replace those IP addresses with those of your slave nameservers and your workstation, and you've concealed a lot of information about your network. You might also add the network staff's desktop machines to this list, so that they can perform zone transfers to debug DNS issues.

**NOTE** *You can define much tighter access lists than this. See the bind documentation in /usr/src/contrib/bind/doc for more details.*

How about hackers attacking named itself? We can do two things about this. First, run named in a jail (see Chapter 8) to ensure that a successful intruder won't be able to access anything else on your network. Second, run named as a user other than root. Just make sure the following is set in /etc/rc.conf or /etc/defaults/rc.conf. (This might be the default by the time this book comes out, so be sure to check if it's already done.)

```
named_flags="-u bind -g bind"
```

Once this is set, to gain root access the intruder would have to break into named, then break into root as a regular user on the jail, and then break out of the jail into the main system. You should notice something wrong well before anyone completes all of these steps.

## Controlling Information Order

The order in which the hosts file and a nameserver are checked can greatly affect how a program or system behaves. Firewalls, for example, frequently need customized host entries that other hosts don't need, and they must check the local hosts before consulting the global DNS table. The /etc/host.conf file allows you to control the order in which information services are used, and it has only two possible entries: hosts and bind. Each entry appears on its own line. Host IP information sources are checked in the order that they appear in this file.

For example, if you want your hosts file to be checked before your nameservice, this file would contain the following:

```
hosts
bind
```

If, on the other hand, you wanted your nameserver to be checked before the hosts file, you would use this:

```
bind
hosts
```

**NOTE** *The second information source is only checked if the first one fails. If a machine has conflicting entries in /etc/hosts and DNS, the first one checked wins.*

## More About BIND

As your network grows, you'll need more information on BIND. While one good source is the documentation in /usr/src/contrib/bind/doc, that documentation can be difficult. The standard book on BIND is *DNS and BIND* by Paul Albitz and Cricket Liu (O'Reilly and Associates). This book is very readable and highly recommended—it's the only book that I automatically order each new edition of, sight unseen.

# 13

## MANAGING SMALL
## NETWORK SERVICES

Even a server with a very narrow, specific purpose (like a Web
server) needs a variety of smaller, helper services, like basic administration tools. In this chapter, we'll consider some smaller Internet
servers, such as the time server, SSH, and inetd, and discuss the tools
that FreeBSD makes available for them. We'll also discuss some basic tools
that you'll use when managing larger servers, such as bandwidth management
and secure certificates.

**NOTE** *You'll see clearly marked references throughout this chapter to topics that we won't cover.
When possible, I refer you to authoritative references for further information. (If you're
running a high-volume Internet server—say, handling a million or more email messages
an hour—you'll probably want to get your hands on a reference with something more than
the few pages you'll find here!)*

## Bandwidth Control

Today's computing hardware is relatively inexpensive, and software is cheap, but
the cost of Internet bandwidth is high. If your company offers "unlimited bandwidth" Web service to clients, you'll soon find yourself with a flooded Internet
circuit and no corresponding income. As such, it can be vital to restrict the
bandwidth any one site can consume, as well as the amount of bandwidth used

by any one service. That's where *dummynet* comes in. Luigi Rizzo invented dummynet to simulate poor or lossy links so he could test network protocols under such adverse conditions. Dummynet is quite flexible; you'll even find an example on Rizzo's Web page (http://www.iet.unipi.it/~luigi/ip_dummynet/) simulating an ADSL link to the Moon! (Dummynet is part of IPFW, which we touched on in Chapter 8.)

Although designed to test network protocols, dummynet has since been used to throttle the amount of bandwidth used by any one network service—bandwidth control is simply one side result of this sort of experimentation. And, because dummynet works on specified ports, IP addresses, and protocols, you can use it to restrict the bandwidth usage of IPSec tunnels, sendmail, and such.

You must have IPFW compiled into your kernel to use dummynet. If you followed our example in Chapter 4, you should be all set, but to double-check, run `kldstat -v | grep ipfw` to list all IPFW modules. If you find that your kernel lacks IPFW support, add the following to your kernel configuration, rebuild, and reboot.

```
options        IPFIREWALL
options        IPFIREWALL_VERBOSE
options        DUMMYNET
options        IPFIREWALL_DEFAULT_TO_ACCEPT
```

**NOTE** *Since we're using IPFW for bandwidth control instead of packet filtering, we set things to the default accept mode. If you're doing packet filtering with IPFW instead of IPF, leave out the "default to accept" option entirely.*

### Configuring IPFW

The IPFW packet filtering works by comparing each packet against a rule, in order. Rules say either that a packet is accepted, rejected, or dumped into some other function, such as divert(4) or dummynet.

Because we're using IPFilter for packet filtering, all we have to worry about is the subset of IPFW that handles traffic shaping. Dummynet requires two rules within this subset: an IPFW rule to redirect a packet to dummynet and a dummynet rule describing the bandwidth permitted. We'll see examples of both shortly.

We'll use ipfw(8) to configure IPFW, while logged in as root. But first, since (like many other programs) `ipfw` acts differently depending on its arguments, first check your initial rules with `ipfw list`.

```
# ipfw list
65535 allow ip from any to any
#
```

As you can see in the preceding example, rules are listed first with a rule number, followed by the name of the rule. IPFW rules are numbered from 1 to 65535. Simple enough, it seems. Since we used the "default to accept" kernel option, the last possible rule (rule number 65535) passes all traffic. If we hadn't used that, the last possible rule would have been to deny all traffic.

To tell IPFW to send packets through dummynet, you must create an IPFW rule to direct that particular type of network traffic to a dummynet rule. The syntax for an IPFW-to-dummynet rule must include the following:

- An IPFW rule number
- A statement that this rule will redirect traffic to some other sort of rule (a dummynet rule)
- A number for this other sort of rule
- A traffic description

```
number pipe pipenumber ip from sourceaddr sourceport to destaddr destport
```

In the preceding statement, `number` is the IPFW rule number, and `pipenumber` is the number of the pipe that handles this bandwidth rule. (A *pipe* is an add-on IPFW rule that performs special handling, such as dummynet.) The `sourceaddr` and `sourceport` entries define the IP address and port number where the traffic is coming from, while `destaddr` and `destport` specify where the traffic is going to. The port numbers are optional; if no port is specified, all traffic to or from that IP address is affected. (Both the source and destination can use the special keyword `any` to match any possible address.)

Here's a simple IPFW-to-dummynet rule:

```
100 pipe 1 ip from 192.168.99.100 80 to any
```

In this example, 100 is the IPFW rule. `pipe` is the marker that indicates that this rule is going to redirect traffic through another set of rules. The pipe rule number is 1, and the remainder of the rule is the traffic description.

### Traffic Descriptions

The description of the traffic you want to pump through dummynet is very important. Describing the traffic incorrectly will result in programs having either too much bandwidth or too little.

The basic format for a traffic description is as follows:

```
protocol from address port to address port
```

On the Internet, the protocol is almost always `ip`. The `from` and `to` are labels, indicating where the traffic is coming from and where it is going to. The address labels are IP addresses, and the ports are port numbers. If you want to specify all IP addresses and ports possible, you can use the `any` keyword.

For example, let's say our Web server has an IP address of 192.168.99.100. We want to describe all traffic coming from the Web server and going to any address anywhere on the Internet. A description of this traffic would look like this:

```
ip from 192.168.99.100 80 to any
```

### Creating IPFW Rules

Say we want to filter the amount of bandwidth for our Web server at IP address 192.168.99.100, running on port 80. We've already written a description of this traffic in the previous section. Now we want to include that, and add the necessary information to redirect this sort of traffic into a dummynet rule.

To create the IPFW rule, we need an IPFW rule number and a pipe rule number. IPFW rules are processed in numerical order, but you can create any numbering scheme you like. Since we aren't using IPFW to filter packets, but just to direct packets to dummynet, the order isn't that important. I usually number rules in even increments of 100 to leave room for modifications between existing rules. Order in pipe rules is not important, so I number them consecutively. In keeping with this, I'll number the IPFW rule 100 and the pipe rule 1.

This would give us an IPFW rule like this:

```
100 pipe 1 ip from 192.168.99.100 80 to any
```

### Adding IPFW Rules

Now that you know what you want your IPFW rule to say, you need to add it to IPFW. Use `ipfw add` for this:

```
# ipfw add 100 pipe 1 ip from 192.168.99.100 80 to any
```

This rule tells IPFW to take any traffic coming from port 80 on 192.168.99.100, and redirect it through the pipe rule numbered 1.

### *Creating Pipe Rules*

So, IPFW is directing traffic of a certain description to a dummynet (or pipe) rule. It would help if that pipe rule existed, now wouldn't it? Dummynet rules use the following syntax:

```
pipe pipenumber config bw bandwidth
```

The leading `pipe` in the preceding statement indicates that this is a pipe rule. For `pipenumber` we use the same number we used in the IPFW rule: 1. For bandwidth we specify this connection's permitted bandwidth. For our example, let's say that we want 128 kilobits per second (Kbps) of traffic.

Install this rule into IPFW with `ipfw add`:

```
ipfw add pipe 1 config bw 128Kbit/s
```

So, now all traffic from the Web site on that IP address is redirected through this dummynet rule, which limits total traffic to 128Kbps.

### Reviewing IPFW Rules

To see your IPFW rules, run `ipfw list`:

```
# ipfw list
00100 pipe 1 ip from 192.168.99.100 80 to any
65535 allow ip from any to any
#
```

This listing shows our IPFW rule directing traffic to our dummynet rule. It doesn't show the dummynet rule, however. Pipes are stored in a separate list.

To view the pipes, run `ipfw pipe list`:

```
# ipfw pipe list
❶ 00001: ❷ 128.000 Kbit/s    0 ms   50 sl. 1 queues (1 buckets) droptail
    mask: 0x00 0x00000000/0x0000 -> 0x00000000/0x0000
BKT Prot ___Source IP/port____ ____Dest. IP/port____ Tot_pkt/bytes Pkt/Byte Drp
  0 tcp  ❸ 192.168.99.100/80    ❹ 163.62.168.2/2415  128050681 35518324182  0    0 50486587
#
```

**NOTE**   *The output from* `ipfw pipe list` *is far wider than 80 characters. If possible, use a terminal emulator and make your window very, very wide.*

These four lines describe both our dummynet rule and the associated IPFW rule. Much of this is in-depth information that we don't need to understand—it simply displays dummynet's heritage as a traffic-problem simulation tool. The first entry (❶) is the dummynet rule number, followed by the rule on how dummynet permits traffic (❷). The next interesting item is the source IP address (❸)—in this case, our Web server. At the moment I took this snapshot, one particular destination IP address (❹) is having traffic to it throttled.

### Dummynet Queues

Dummynet works by putting packets in a queue, and then handling these queued packets in order. If you're trying to throttle a high-traffic site, this queue can fill up, so if your Web server starts occasionally locking up for a few seconds after you implement dummynet, you're probably overflowing the packet queue.

To fix this problem, modify your pipe rule to include a queue size, and increase it to the largest possible queue size of 1000KB:

```
ipfw add pipe 1 config bw 128Kbit/s queue 1000Kbytes
```

This larger queue uses kernel memory, however, so don't go slapping it in willy-nilly.

### Directional Traffic Shaping

One thing to remember is that you cannot throttle incoming traffic. If someone posts a bootleg copy of the next Star Wars movie on your Web server, you're going to have a truly ridiculous number of incoming requests a second. No amount of configuration can prevent 30 million people clicking on a link to request pages from your server. The best you can do is restrict how you respond to these requests. This means that all you can do is limit your responses by throttling your outbound connections. In most cases this is okay, since, after all, you're the one serving Web pages or sending mail!

If you use a dummynet rule that tries to control incoming traffic, you'll slow down connections without really affecting incoming traffic at all. As a result, you'll build up connection queues on your server, and only hurt yourself. If you're being flooded with traffic, either refuse this sort of traffic entirely (see Chapter 8), find the demanded content and remove it, or contact your ISP for help.

## Public-Key Encryption

Many security features in server daemons rely upon public-key encryption to ensure confidentiality, integrity, and authenticity. Many different Internet services also use public-key encryption. You need to have a basic grasp of public-key encryption to be able to run services like secure Web pages (https) and secure POP3 mail (pop3ssl).

**NOTE** *If you're already familiar with public-key encryption, you can probably skip this section.*

Encryption systems use a key to transform messages from readable versions (cleartext) to and from encoded versions (ciphertext). Although the words cleartext and ciphertext include the word text, they aren't restricted to text; they also include graphics files, binaries, and any other data you might send. All cryptosystems have three main purposes: to maintain integrity and confidentiality and to ensure nonrepudiation. *Integrity* means that the message has not been tampered with. *Confidentiality* means that the message can only be read by the intended audience. And *nonrepudiation* means that the author cannot later claim that he or she didn't write that message.

Older ciphers relied on a single key, and if you had the key, you could both encrypt and decrypt messages. (You might have had to jump through a lot of hoops to transform the message, as with the Enigma engine that drove the Allies nuts during World War Two, but the key made it possible.) A typical example is any code that requires a key or a password. The one-time message pads popularized in spy movies are archetypal single-key ciphers.

Unlike single-key ciphers, public-key (or asymmetric) encryption systems use two keys: both a private and a public one. Messages are encrypted with one key and decrypted with the other. (The mathematics to explain this are really quite hairy, but it does work—the system is based upon the behavior of really, really, really large numbers.) Generally, the key owner keeps the private key secret, but the public key is handed out to the world at large, for anyone's use. The key owner uses the private key, while everyone else uses the public key. The key owner can encrypt messages that anyone can open, while anyone in the public can send a message that only the key owner can read.

Public-key cryptography fills our need for integrity, confidentiality, and non-repudiation nicely. If an author wants anyone to be able to read his message, while ensuring that it isn't tampered with, he can encrypt the message with his private key, and anyone with the public key can decrypt and read the message. (Tampering with the encoded message would render it illegible.)

Encrypting messages this way also guarantees that the author has the private key. If an author wants to send a message that can only be read by its intended reader, she can encrypt it with the reader's public key, but only the person with the matching private key can read it.

This system works well as long as the private key is kept private. Once that private key is stolen, lost, or made public, it's useless. A careless person who has his private key stolen could even find others signing documents for him. Be careful with your keys, unless you want to learn that someone used your certificate to order half a million dollars' worth of high-end graphics workstations and have them overnighted to an abandoned-house maildrop on the other side of the country![1]

**NOTE** *Absolute BSD is not an in-depth guide to cryptography. Much of what's in here is a generalization. If you're really, really interested in crypto, check out Bruce Schneier's* Applied Cryptography *(John Wiley & Sons). Bring a calculator, and a spare brain to use when yours fills up.*

### Certificates

One interesting note about public-key encryption is that the author and the audience don't have to be people—they can be programs. SSH, the Secure Sockets Layer (SSL) portion of Apache, which is the secure POP3 service, uses public-key encryption, as do many other programs. Public-key cryptography is a major component of the *signed certificates* used by secure Web sites. When you open Netscape to buy something online, you might not realize that the browser is frantically encrypting and decrypting Web pages behind the scenes. This is why your computer might complain about "invalid certificates"; someone's public key has either expired or has gone bad. (We'll learn more about how to use certificates in Chapters 14 and 15.)

Many companies, such as VeriSign, provide a public-key signing service. These companies are called Certificate Authorities (CAs). Other companies that need a certificate signed provide proof of their identity (such as corporate papers and business records), and these public-key signing companies use their certificate to sign the company's certificate. By signing the certificate, the Certificate Authority says, "I have inspected this person's credentials, and he (or she, or it) is who he claims he is." But they're not guaranteeing anything else: The person can use the certificate to build a Web site that sells fraudulent or

[1] This is a true story. Guard your private keys!

dangerous products, or could even use it to encrypt a ransom note. Signed certificates guarantee certain types of technical security, not personal integrity or even unilateral technical security. If someone breaks into the server, you're still in trouble.

Web browsers and other certificate-using software include certificates for the major CAs. When the browser receives a certificate signed by a Certificate Authority, it accepts the certificate. Essentially, the Web browser says, "I trust the Certificate Authority, and the Certificate Authority trusts this company, so I will trust this company." So long as you trust the certificate authority, the process works.

### Create a Request

To get a certificate to secure one of your server programs, you need to generate a certificate request. You then submit this request to a central Certificate Authority for signing. The request itself is fairly simple. While the command line is long, you just need to answer a few questions. (Since you will use these commands only once, we won't dissect them; see openssl(1) for more details, if you're interested).

**NOTE** *Your certificate request must be treated as secret because a hacker can use this as a stepping-stone into your network. Be sure that the file can only be read by root!*

Let's walk through a certificate request. Enter this verbatim:

```
# openssl req -new -nodes -out req.pem -keyout cert.pem
```

In response you should see this:

```
Using configuration from /etc/ssl/openssl.cnf
Generating a 1024 bit RSA private key
.................++++++
...++++++
writing new private key to 'cert.pem'
-----
You are about to be asked to enter information that will be incorporated
into your certificate request.
What you are about to enter is what is called a Distinguished Name or a DN.
There are quite a few fields but you can leave some blank
For some fields there will be a default value,
If you enter '.', the field will be left blank.
-----
Country Name (2 letter code) [AU]:US
State or Province Name (full name) [Some-State]:MI
```

Enter the two-letter code for the country and state or province you live in (US and MI, respectively, in this example), as shown in bold here. If you don't know the two-letter codes, ask someone who leaves the server room on occasion. (They are also defined in the ISO 3166 standard, so a quick Web search will find it.)

```
Locality Name (eg, city) []:Detroit
```

A simple city name is sufficient for the Locality. If you're in a branch office, you might want to use the city where your headquarters is located.

```
Organization Name (eg, company) [Internet Widgits Pty Ltd]:BlackHelicopters
Foundation
Organizational Unit Name (eg, section) []:Network Support
```

The preceding requests are for your company name and the department you're from. If you don't have a company (I don't), just make something up.

```
Common Name (eg, YOUR name) []:magpire.blackhelicopters.org
```

The preceding line is the part that trips up most administrators. The "YOUR" in the text means the server's name, not the admin's name. If you don't put a server name here, the request will be useless.

```
Email Address []:mwlucas@blackhelicopters.org
```

Since this is a personal certificate for my own Web server, I don't need to worry about the email address. If this request is for a company, put a generic corporate address here, like webmaster@AbsoluteBSD.com.

```
Please enter the following 'extra' attributes
to be sent with your certificate request
A challenge password []:RodentsRule
```

This challenge password is also known as a *passphrase*. Again, this needs to be a secret, because anyone with your passphrase can masquerade as you! The passphrase here isn't a very good one; it doesn't have any non-alphanumeric characters, such as dashes, commas, or exclamation points, and it doesn't even have any numbers mixed in with it. For your real certificate requests (or anything on your network), please use a password that sucks less than this.

```
An optional company name []:
```

By this time you've filled in quite enough company names, I'm sure, so just press **ENTER**. After doing so, you'll find a file req.pem in your current directory. It should look something like this:

```
-----BEGIN CERTIFICATE REQUEST-----
MIICIDCCAYkCAQAwgcAxCzAJBgNVBAYTAlVTMQswCQYDVQQIEwJNSTEQMA4GA1UE
BxMHRGVOcm9pdDEkMCIGA1UEChMbQmxhY2tIZWxpcY29wdGVycyBGb3VuZGF0aW9u
MRgwFgYDVQQLEw9OZXR3b3JrIFN1cHBvcnQxJTAjBgNVBAMTHG1hZ3BpcmUuYmxh
Y2toZWxpY29wdGVycy5vcmcxKzApBgkqhkiG9w0BCQEWHG13bHVjYXNNAYmxhY2to
ZWxpY29wdGVycy5vcmcwgZ8wDQYJKoZIhvcNAQEBBQADgY0AMIGJAoGBANCjXfOh
WX/n1Kb5Sc9m7Nofvc3Nck5j7XzNnd5OUIc93Jj+Egw/KnlrniptpNicvqzQJ6zs
7jOk1uMUMbHfllxUOUtRGfLthCvfstB4OZzdMYUAfAT1r15i7fnaCRagshekelOh
deadbeefTCk6mC7OYcsGuqrVuQkEcA/kPDxdAgMBAAGgHzAdBgkqhkiG9w0BCQcx
EBMOR2VyYmlsc0FyZUNvbwwDQYJKoZIhvcNAQEBBQADgYEAwC7lNqZbHFKaOjiw
h35gU6TAC8NEODRLuEulLWClEIPsTK6HHV7KU4uOq42HEunf61dpPaPkGO3htoeu
yOc5Rjk9F11cvRbBjpajv+TllxTBGveuhatsn43d9Epi3glrcpueisd87LMxtnht
OBf9nz6GaH+2o2BsGxwH3yws5oO=
-----END CERTIFICATE REQUEST-----
```

You'll also find a cert.pem file that looks much like this:

```
-----BEGIN RSA PRIVATE KEY-----
MIICXAIBAAKBgQDQo139IVl/55Sm+UnPZuzaH73NzXJOY+18zZ3edFCHPdyY/hIM
Pyp5a54qbaTYnL6sOCes7O4zpNbjFDGx35ZcVNFLURny7YQr37LQeNGc3TGFAHwE
9a9eYu352gkdSbY5YlPr+7K63bRkskwpOpguzmHLBrqq1bkJBHAP5Dw8XQIDAQAB
AoGAO8olXC4bdOELo5IbCdmoFJY2EW1HzZkrbLGMBTz1+tvKhPmCeIn9hRBHIkeL
jxvUNLfuNssrNBeQEUEvQJcfgk+QW8zq5UV6xin7Rb1JYu+1TzyBt1QMAx99cDEq
WWOoqvYIz1IzQq6FA5/J93Kj3yJ7I6NOCs8c9BxYvnjd6WECQQDOARUKZhwLD7gQ
HM3aIMXV7hOnzqj1Ygz2Rw/GEj+eWiam9NDlxIjqCuXAp34rDcyp++ZFX8flOJQ+
yHOt7625AkEA2uUvUhobOvTAFBofrFHigRQRD8YFDbXIPLtrXxqAmuD1SyABBgBy
yGpsmXwdBP/1xR1xu4n+Mu2KVPiNZpZ1xQJASlNGEHvYEPqBy86qWcZf3PGCSgzm
ZJCweBhfUqteW6MEYRjzxPmf5wLYx119zimO7TyBASLS5hzc817l9daraQJBAJ6B
8YdRcq6LHwAvfpoI3aO8u7IhYY1xAiPAT9sZVOFSXy3cagFP1867ChMGxfjV2Suo
y6/TGCkGy/IF3lbYQOUCQGABvzCfcw3/xVY7co6k8kSu1Mf1dj/MYZhOoI7qrbUN
O+Cez+e2UvoiahCW3IWlmBFBZ8HJUoGzkCO+wVmZzZO=
-----END RSA PRIVATE KEY-----
```

If these files don't exist, or don't look basically like this, you didn't run openssl properly. Go back and try it again or mail req.pem to your Certificate Authority, who should send you back a file that looks much like one of the preceding files. Save that response to a file named signature.pem and run this command:

```
# cat signature.pem >> cert.pem
```

This will copy the signature onto the end of the certificate and create a complete signed certificate. This certificate is good for anything on the host it's for; you can use it for a Web page, for a pop3ssl connection, or anything else that requires a certificate.

## Being Your Own CA

When you're first learning, you probably won't want to go through the trouble and expense of having a Certificate Authority sign every certificate you create. Chances are, too, that you'll want a couple of certificates just to learn with. Signing a certificate is a simple mathematical process, and perfectly easy to do yourself.

> **NOTE** *If you sign your own certificates, client software will generate warnings that the "certificate signer is unknown." This is expected–after all, people outside my office have no idea who Michael Lucas is, or why he's signing Web site certificates! VeriSign and other CAs are trusted. I'm trusted by the people who know me,[2] but not trusted to verify the identity of other people.*

To sign your own certificates, first create a directory readable only by root and do all your CA work here:

```
# mkdir ca
# chown root.wheel ca
# chmod 700 ca
```

Then run the following openssl command to create a certificate authority key:

```
# openssl genrsa -des3 -out ca.key 1024
```

Enter a passphrase when prompted, and be sure to remember it, or the key you've just created is worthless. (You cannot use the certificate without the passphrase!) Finally, use the key you've just created to create a certificate for your CA:

```
# openssl req -new -x509 -days 365 -key ca.key -out ca.crt
```

Enter your passphrase when prompted (if you've forgotten it already, the only thing you can do is create a new key), and you'll enter a series of questions and answers identical to the one you saw when you created your certificate request. You now have a CA key (ca.key) and a CA certificate (ca.crt) that you can use to sign the request you created earlier. The preceding command, while long, never varies, so we won't go over it in any detail. Just trust me.

---

[2] Well, most of them, anyway. Many of them. A few, at least. Oh, never mind.

You'll be asked for your passphrase again. Once you type it, the actual signing process is very quick, and you should see a file named signature.pem, the signature file that a CA would send back to you. Just append it to your public key as discussed in the previous section, and you have a complete certificate!

# SSH

One of UNIX's great strengths is its remote administration ability. Whether the server is in front of you or in the basement of a locked laboratory in a maximum-security military installation surrounded by savage guard dogs and rabid weasels, if you have network access, a username, and a password, you can control it.

For many years, telnet(1) was the standard way to access a remote server. Telnet is nifty. You can use it to connect to an arbitrary TCP port on a host and manually talk to servers across the network. (We'll use it later in this chapter to test various services.) However, as a remote administration protocol, telnet has one crushing problem: Everything you send over most versions of telnet is unencrypted. Anyone sitting anywhere along your connection with a packet sniffer can grab your password, and not even the best password-selection scheme in the world will protect you against a packet sniffer. I've seen packet sniffers on Internet backbones and on small local networks. The only defense against a packet sniffer is to handle connections in such a way that intruders will get no useful information from them.

That's where SSH, or secure shell, comes in. SSH behaves much like telnet in that it gives you a highly configurable terminal window on a remote host. But unlike telnet, everything you send across the network is encrypted. SSH ensures not only that your passwords can't be sniffed, but also that the various commands you type (and their output) are scrambled. While telnet does have a few advantages over SSH (it requires less CPU time, and it's simpler to configure), its advantages are heavily outweighed by SSH's security advantages.

If you're looking for more information, *SSH, The Secure Shell*, by Daniel Barrett and Richard Silverman (O'Reilly & Associates), is perhaps the best book about SSH on the market today.

### Testing SSH

Unlike some of the other protocols we're going to look at, SSH is difficult to test by hand. One thing you can do is confirm that the SSH daemon is running by using telnet to connect to the TCP port that SSH is supposedly running on:

```
# telnet localhost 22
Trying ::1...
Trying 127.0.0.1...
Connected to localhost.
Escape character is '^]'.
SSH-1.99-OpenSSH_2.3.0 FreeBSD localisations 20010713
```

The last line of this output tells us that SSH is running and accepting connections.

Now, unless you're capable of encrypting packets by hand, on the fly, this is about as far as we can go. Hit the escape character (**CONTROL-]**) to close the connection, and you'll return to the local command prompt.

### Enabling SSH

If your system isn't already configured to enable SSH at boottime, just add the following to /etc/rc.conf:

```
sshd_enable="YES"
```

On your next reboot, SSH will be enabled. If you don't want to reboot now, just type **sshd** as root to run SSH.

### Basics of SSH

SSH uses public-key cryptography. The SSH daemon offers the public key to clients and keeps the private key to itself. Each chunk of data you send over the connection is handled as a message, which your local system encrypts with the public key; the server then decrypts the data with the private key. Since both public and private keys are necessary to complete this transaction, your data is secure; even if someone captures your SSH traffic, all she'll see is garbage.

#### Creating Keys

If your system lacks /etc/ssh/ssh_host_key or /etc/ssh/ssh_host_dsa_key, you can create them like this:

```
# /usr/bin/ssh-keygen -N "" -f /etc/ssh/ssh_host_key
# /usr/bin/ssh-keygen -d -N "" -f /etc/ssh/ssh_host_dsa_key
```

*The SSH protocol is several years old, and is beginning to show its age. While it's still secure, people need more flexibility than it provides. For that reason, the Secure Shell 2 standard is becoming more common. Unless specified, you can assume that everything that follows applies to both versions of SSH. If a feature is found only in original SSH1 or in SSH2, it will be noted. Some files differ depending on the version of SSH being used, and those are noted as well.*

### Confirming SSH Identity

The whole process of public-key cryptography goes south if you get an incorrect public key for a host, which can happen either through user error or malice. The most accurate way to check host identification is to compare the public key on the server with the public key available over the network. Your public key defaults to /etc/ssh/ssh_host_key.pub for version 1; the version 2 default is /etc/ssh/ssh_host_dsa_key.pub. Since the two versions of SSH have different protocol requirements, they need different keys.

While you could copy both the SSH version 1 and SSH version 2 public keys to every host you want to connect from, and manually compare keys before connecting, host keys can be hundreds of characters long. This is not merely a pain, it's enough of a pain to prevent anyone from actually performing the check. Fortunately, SSH allows you to generate a *key fingerprint*, which is a much shorter version of a key. You cannot use the fingerprint to encrypt traffic or negotiate connections, but the chances of two unrelated keys having the same fingerprint are astronomical. To generate a fingerprint for a SSH version 1 key enter this command:

```
# ssh-keygen -lf /etc/ssh/ssh_host_key.pub
1024 7c:07:0f:1e:74:1a:42:11:b9:08:41:e4:f3:c9:05:a7
root@petulance.blackhelicopters.org
```

The response to this command is the key fingerprint. The first number, 1024, is the number of bits in the key (1024 is standard nowadays). The hexadecimal string starting with "7c" and ending with "a7" is the public-key fingerprint. You should copy this key fingerprint from the original server to a place where you can access it from your clients, either on a Web page or on a list. You'll need to use it the first time you connect.

You can use the same command on an SSH2 key, if you substitute the file that holds the SSHv2 key on the command line.

*If your server provides both SSH1 and SSH2, as FreeBSD does by default, it's a good idea to prepare fingerprints for both public keys. You have no way to tell which version a user will use to connect.*

### SSH Clients

Your main problem with SSH will be finding a client that works on your preferred desktop system. If you use a BSD desktop, SSH comes with your system, and other UNIX operating systems usually have SSH packages available. If possible, use OpenSSH (http://www.openssh.com)—it's developed by the OpenBSD team, and is quickly becoming the most popular implementation of SSH.

If you're running a Microsoft operating system, I recommend MindTerm (though I've also had strong recommendations for Putty and Terraterm). MindTerm is free for noncommercial use, supports both SSH1 and SSH2, and is written in Java, which means that it will run on any platform that has a Java virtual machine (JVM). (Most Web browsers include a JVM.) The MindTerm documentation will have you running with an SSH client in just a few minutes. A quick Web search will lead you to any of the three, and any one will almost certainly fit your needs.

### Connecting via SSH

To connect to another host with FreeBSD's ssh client, type **ssh hostname**. In response, you should see something like this:

```
# ssh moneysink.blackhelicopters.org
The authenticity of host 'moneysink' can't be established.
RSA key fingerprint is 7c:07:0f:1e:74:1a:42:11:b9:08:41:e4:f3:c9:05:a7.
Are you sure you want to continue connecting (yes/no)? yes
```

Your client does two things immediately. One, it retrieves the public key from the remote host. Two, it checks its own list of SSH keys for a key for that host. If the client has the host key in its list, and the host key retrieved from the remote host matches it, the client assumes you're actually talking to the correct host. If the client doesn't have the host key in its list of known hosts, it presents the key fingerprint for your approval.

You can decide whether to accept or reject the connection upon seeing the key; the fingerprint you see should be identical to the fingerprint you created on the remote host. If the fingerprint isn't identical, you're either talking to the wrong host or you have a fingerprint for the wrong version of SSH. Compare the fingerprint we created to the fingerprint the remote host is offering—if it matches, this is the same host. Once you accept the key, it is saved in your ~/.ssh/known-hosts (for SSH1) or ~/.ssh/known-hosts2 (for SSH2) file.

It's not always worth the time to manually compare keys. If you're building a new server on your local network for your use only, perhaps you don't have to. (You should still copy the fingerprint, however, since you'll eventually want to connect from some remote location and will need to be able to verify the key.) If many people will be connecting to this server, it's generally okay to put the fingerprints on a Web page somewhere. Whatever the case may be, you'll need to decide how much secrecy you'll need.

### Configuring SSH

All of the files for systemwide configuration of SSH are kept in /etc/ssh, and we'll consider them one at a time.

*Because the defaults for SSH change slowly over time, as the Internet's general security stance tightens, I won't give the defaults for each setting. See the appropriate files on your system to see how it is configured.*

#### /etc/ssh/ssh_config

The /etc/ssh/ssh_config file controls the default operation of the ssh client. While users can override the settings in this file with either their own private ~/.ssh/config files or command-line options, this gives the administrator the opportunity to provide reasonable defaults.

*Anything you set as the client can be overridden by the server. For example, though you might request X11 forwarding, if the server doesn't offer that feature, you cannot use it.*

**ForwardX11 yes**   X applications can display on any machine, not just the one they're running on. If you want to run X applications on a remote machine and have the display forwarded back to your workstation, set this to yes.

**RhostsAuthentication yes**   If the user's account on the remote server has a .rhosts file listing the local machine, trust it. This is almost always disabled by the server, for good reason; in fact, I cannot think of a single good reason to use this setting.

**FallBackToRsh no**   If an ssh connection attempt fails, the ssh client will attempt to open an rsh connection instead, which is insecure. If you can't connect safely, don't connect at all—there's probably a good reason why you can't connect! If you set FallBackToRsh to no, the rsh attempt will not be made.

**CheckHostIP yes**   With this option enabled, the ssh client will automatically compare the IP address of the server with the IP address given in the .ssh/known_hosts file. This helps detect IP spoofing and changed IP addresses. Set this to no to disable this check.

**StrictHostKeyChecking no**   This option is for the particularly paranoid. If set to no, the ssh client will refuse to connect to a host whose key is not in ~/.ssh/known_hosts. It will also refuse to add new hosts to the known_hosts file; you will have to add them manually.

**Port 22**   This is the default port to connect to on the remote host. You can change this to provide some security through obscurity, but it's generally not worth it.

**Protocol 2,1**   This option specifies the order in which the SSH protocols are offered to a client. You can disable a protocol by not including it on the list.

**Cipher blowfish**   SSH can use either the 3DES or Blowfish protocols. While Blowfish is faster, it's also newer, and in the cryptography world newer does not automatically mean better! Still, Blowfish has resisted cryptanalysis so far, and has a promising future. The default is 3DES.

### /etc/ssh/ssh_host_key and /etc/ssh/ssh_host_dsa_key
These files contain the system's private SSH cryptographic keys and are readable only by root. The DSA file is for SSH2, the other is for SSH1.

### /etc/ssh/ssh_host_key.pub and /etc/ssh/ssh_host_dsa_key.pub
These are the world-readable cryptographic keys for this system. Public-key cryptographic systems will combine this public key with the private key and generate a unique numerical fingerprint. Again, the DSA file is for SSH2, the other is for SSH1.

### /etc/ssh/sshd_config
The /etc/ssh/sshd_config file describes the services your SSH daemon offers to other hosts. While a client can request any protocol or service that they like, the server has the final word. This allows the system administrator to permit actions he doesn't care about while rejecting the unacceptable.

The following sections describe the keywords the file contains.

**AllowGroups**   By default, anyone with a legitimate shell can log in to the server, but with this option set, only users in the specified groups can log in. Groups are created in /etc/group (see Chapter 9). To specify groups, list each on a single line, separated by spaces. (While you can use an asterisk (*) as a wildcard, you cannot use numerical GIDs.) The group listed must be the user's primary group—the group shown in /etc/passwd.

**AllowTcpForwarding**   Users with SSH access can encrypt any traffic between any two hosts. Set this to no to prevent this. If a user has shell access, however, she could install her own TCP port forwarder and get around this.

**AllowUsers**   This option allows you to explicitly list users who are allowed to use this SSH server. By default, any user can log in.

**Ciphers**   If you're cryptographically literate, you can choose the order in which cryptographic algorithms are tried. List them all on a single line, separated by commas. If you know little or nothing about cryptography, use the defaults.

**DenyGroups**   This is the opposite of the AllowGroups option explained earlier; users in this system group cannot log in. The listed group must be their primary group, meaning it must be listed in /etc/passwd and not just /etc/group.

**IgnoreRhosts yes**   The .rhosts files are left over from the days when rlogin and rsh were accepted UNIX standards. While they might be useful during a migration from rsh to ssh, they're generally obsolete and dangerous. To allow the use of .rhosts files, set this to no.

**KeepAlive**   OpenSSH checks the status of idle connections every so often. If the other end cannot be reached, the session is disconnected and cleaned up. This check is called a "keepalive." A transient network problem can cause an SSH session to disconnect if you're using keepalives. To keep your SSH session open if at all possible, set this to no. Without keepalives, though, you can leave orphaned SSH sessions lying around for weeks on end—your end of the connection may never realize that the computer on the other end has been rebooted or has even burst into flame. Using keepalives is generally recommended.

**PasswordAuthentication**   This option controls how users are allowed to use passwords to log in. It's more secure to use RSA or DSA cryptographic authentication, but most people aren't set up to do that. (Yet.) For now, set this to yes. We won't discuss RSA and DSA authentication here.

**PermitEmptyPasswords no**   This is almost exactly as bad as it sounds. Don't set it to yes. Really. Trust me on this one.

**PermitRootLogin no**   This option controls whether someone can directly log in as root via SSH. It's far wiser to have people SSH in as themselves, and use su(8) to become root. That way, when your system is cracked, you have a fighting chance to identify whose account was used, and at least have someone to blame. It won't help the problem, but it might make you feel better.

**UseLogin**   If you set this to yes, then sshd will interoperate with the login(1) program. This permits the use of login.conf and all the other nifty login tweaks described in Chapter 9.

**X11Forwarding**   This option controls whether or not clients can forward the graphics from X programs to their client workstations. Since X has had such a long history of security issues, many admins disable this without a second thought. Third-party X11 forwarders are available, however, and could be installed by anyone with shell access. Also, denying X11 forwarding doesn't stop someone from manually forwarding X over unencrypted TCP/IP. While this option defaults to no, if you have shell users you might as well turn it on.

## System Time

Your users will expect the computer to know what time it is. If a database starts entering dates three hours behind, or if emails arrive from tomorrow, you'll hear about it pretty quickly. You have three tools for managing system time: the time zone, tzsetup(8); the network time protocol tools, ntpdate(8); and ntpd(8). Set your time zone before you do anything else.

## Setting the Time Zone

The time zone is simple to set with tzsetup(8), a menu-driven program that will make the appropriate changes on your system. Large companies might use a default of Greenwich Mean Time on their systems, while others use their own local time. Follow the geographic prompts and choose the appropriate time zone for your situation.

## Network Time Protocol

When using network time protocol (NTP), each system states its system time on request. Clients can accept this time and match it, or they can use times from several different systems to compute an average time. The average time is the best for long-term use.

Network time protocol requires the use of time servers, and many Internet servers provide a time service accessible to the public. The servers are roughly lumped into two types, Tier 1 and Tier 2.

### Time Server Tiers

Tier 1 clocks are directly connected to some highly accurate time-keeping device, such as an atomic clock. They are designed to be absurdly accurate. If you need this sort of accuracy, then what you really need is your own atomic clock. Prices have dropped quite a bit in the recent past; a reasonably good atomic clock can be had for only thousands of dollars. You can also use other systems, such as a radio clock, if the time lag caused by the speed-of-light delay is acceptable. If you don't need this accuracy in your timekeeping, look at the Tier 2 servers.

Tier 2 NTP servers feed off of the Tier 1 servers, providing their time service as a public service. This service is accurate to within a fraction of a second, and is more than good enough for almost all applications. Some digging will even lead you to Tier 3 time servers, which feed off of Tier 2 servers. While you should use the lowest tier number you can, any Internet server will be perfectly happy getting its time from either a Tier 2 or 3 server.

If you do a Web search for NTP servers, you'll quickly find an up-to-date list of public NTP servers. For each of your servers, pick two nearby NTP servers, and write down their names and IP addresses. We'll use them to set up ntpdate and ntpd.

## Ntpdate

Ntpdate(8) connects to a single NTP server, grabs the correct date, sets the system clock correctly, and exits. While you would normally run ntpdate only once, usually at system boot, you can run it easily at the command line, giving ntpdate the name or IP address of an NTP server:

```
# ntpdate kerberos.digex.net
30 Sep 17:30:44 ntpdate[616]: step time server 204.91.99.129 offset -35.707691 sec
#
```

As you can see here, the system time was off by about 35 seconds, but it is now synchronized with the NTP server kerberos.digex.net.

### Ntpdate at Boot

You can run ntpdate at boottime with the following flags, giving the name of the time server you want:

```
ntpdate_enable="YES"
ntpdate_flags="timeserver.AbsoluteBSD.com"
```

**NOTE** *Do not do this on a busy server with time-sensitive programs, such as database servers! If all of your times suddenly jump by an hour or two, your database administrator or clients will be most annoyed.*

### Ntpdate Flaws

Ntpdate checks the time once, and never again. If your system has hardware problems, the system time can slowly fall out of sync. While this isn't a concern on desktop operating systems, it is a problem for machines that are expected to be up for months or years. On long-living systems, you want to either run ntpdate on a regular basis or use ntpd.

### Ntpd

Ntpd(8) intermittently checks the system time against a list of time servers. It takes a reasonable average of those times, and slowly adjusts the system time to match the average. If any of those time servers is badly off from the others, it discards that value. This gives you the most accurate system time possible, without demanding too much from any one server, and it helps keep errant hardware in check.

### Ntpd Versions

The original time protocol daemon was called ntpd; the improved version found in FreeBSD is technically known as xntpd. Since the original has long since faded into obscurity, everywhere you look on the system xntpd is known as ntpd. Don't be confused by this.

### Configuring Ntpd

Ntpd requires a configuration file, /etc/ntpd.conf. Here's a sample:

```
driftfile /etc/ntp/drift
server 203.94.99.229
server 192.37.16.177
```

Let's do the easy thing first. The ntpd program needs a temporary file; in the preceding example, it's /etc/ntp/drift. While ntpd will create this file itself, it won't create any directories, so we have to create the /etc/ntp directory. We then list two chosen Tier 2 servers by IP address for the servers to communicate with. That's it!

Your servers can be set up to broadcast time updates across the local Ethernet, sharing time information with any other local servers running ntpd. This sounds good, but it is not a good idea on a server exposed to the public Internet.

### Starting Ntpd

Once you have /etc/ntp.conf, just type **ntpd** to start ntpd. To start ntpd at boot, add the following entry in /etc/rc.conf.

```
xntpd_enable="YES"
```

# Inetd

The inetd daemon handles connections for less frequently used daemons. For example, since most systems don't have a steady stream of incoming FTP requests, there's no need for the additional overhead of an FTP daemon listening, when it's going to be idle 99.9 percent of the time. Instead, inetd listens on the FTP port. When an FTP request comes in, inetd starts up the FTP daemon and hands off the request.

Inetd also handles functions that are so small and rarely used that they're easier to implement within inetd, rather than route them through a separate program. This includes things such as discard (which dumps any data it receives into the black hole of /dev/null), chargen (which pours out a stream of characters), and so on. These are disabled by default, but are available if needed. The standard inetd configuration includes information for many standard UNIX services, including telnet, ftp, and pop3. It also includes information for quite a few obscure protocols.

## /etc/inetd.conf

Take a look at /etc/inetd.conf. Most daemons have separate IP and IPv6 configurations, so if you're not running IPv6, you can ignore all IPv6 entries. Let's look at one line from this file, the ftp configuration:

```
❶ ftp   ❷ stream ❸ tcp   ❹ nowait ❺ root   ❻ /usr/libexec/ftpd ❼ ftpd -l
```

The first field (❶) is the service name, which must match a name in /etc/services. Inetd relies upon the service name to determine which TCP or UDP port to open.

The second field (❷) is the socket type. All TCP connections are type stream, while UDP connections are type dgram. There are other possible values, but if you're considering using them you're either (a) reading documentation for a particular program, or (b) almost certainly wrong.

The third field (❸) is the protocol, which can be tcp, udp, tcp6, or udp6 (udp6 and tcp6 protocols are for IPv6 connections). As IPv6 grows more accepted and integrated with server programs, you'll start to see protocol labels of udp46 and tcp46. This means that the daemon can accept either sort of connection.

The next field (❹) indicates whether inetd should wait for the particular service to accept the connection, or just start the program and go away. As a general rule, TCP programs use nowait while UDP programs need wait. If a service uses nowait, you can control the maximum number of connections per second the service will allow by adding a slash and a number directly after the nowait, like this: nowait/5. If you don't do this, and you receive a flood of connections, inetd will start as many copies of the program as it needs to service those requests. (This is a simple way to knock a server off the Internet.)

The next field (❺) says who the daemon runs as. Some daemons can run as special, dedicated users. We'll see specific examples of that in the next two chapters.

The sixth field (❻) is the full path to the program that inetd runs when it receives a connection request. If it's a service included in inetd, it appears as internal.

The last field (❼) gives the command to start an external program and any command-line options needed.

### Configuring Programs in Inetd

/etc/inetd.conf seems to need a lot of information, but if you want to add a program, you can probably copy an existing line and use it with minor modifications. For example, let's consider implementing a very trivial network service, the Quote of the Day (QotD) service. When you connect to the QotD port, a QotD server sends back a random quote and disconnects. FreeBSD includes a random-quote generator in its games collection, fortune(1). This random quote generator is all we need to use to implement an inetd-based network program. We'll use the fortune program to generate our random quotes.

### Port Number

If you search /etc/services for "qotd", you'll find that it's listed as port 17. QotD runs on port 17.

### Network Protocol

Since the QotD service requires that you connect to a network port, and get something back, it's going to be a TCP-based service. (The alternative, UDP, would not work, because UDP connections don't expect anything to come back.) We have to specify TCP in our inetd configuration. Using any TCP service requires you to specify "nowait" in the fourth field of inetd.conf.

### User

We'll run our quote-generating command as root. In an ideal world, we would create a separate user just for this service, but I'm not going to bother for this example.

### Path

Fortune lives in /usr/games/fortune.

### Running the Command

We don't need any command-line options for fortune. (You could use -o if you want, but that's probably not a good idea on a publicly available server.)

### Sample inetd.conf Configuration

Putting this all together, our line in /etc/inetd.conf looks like this:

```
qotd    stream  tcp     nowait  root    /usr/games/fortune      fortune
```

While this example is trivial, other alterations to /etc/inetd.conf are no more difficult.

## Inetd Security

Newer sysadmins tend to think of inetd as a single service with a monolithic security state. Nothing could be further from the truth. Inetd itself is fairly secure, but it unfairly takes a certain amount of blame for problems in the programs it forwards requests to. Some of the programs provide insecure protocols (such as telnet and ftp), while others have a history of abuse.

Still, many people categorically disable inetd. Others make sure that all the services are disabled except enable inetd itself, because several ports provide services via inetd, and having it enabled makes installing these programs slightly easier. I recommend disabling inetd unless you have specific services that you want to provide, and then enabling only those services.

## Starting Inetd

You can start inetd at the command line by just typing **inetd** as root. Alternatively, you can set it to start automatically at boot by changing /etc/rc.conf:

```
inetd_enable="YES"
```

### Changing Inetd's Behavior

You can set flags in /etc/rc.conf, in the variable inetd_flags, to alter inetd's startup behavior. The default inetd flags turn on TCP Wrappers, as per /etc/hosts.allow (see Chapter 8). Here are some other useful flags:

| Flag | Description |
|------|-------------|
| -l | Logs every successful connection. |
| -c | Sets a maximum number of connections per second that can be made to any service. The default is unlimited. Note that unlimited is not the same as "infinite"—your hardware will only handle so many connections. |
| -C | Sets a maximum number of times a single remote IP address can connect to a service. The default is unlimited. |
| -R | Sets the maximum number of times any one service can be started in one minute. The default is 256. If you set this to 0, you allow an unlimited number of connections. |
| -a | Sets the IP address to bind to. Inetd usually listens on all available IP addresses. |
| -w | Uses TCP Wrappers for external services as per hosts.allow (see Chapter 8) |
| -W | Uses TCP Wrappers for internal services as per hosts.allow (see Chapter 8) |

As an extreme example, if you wanted to use TCP Wrappers, allow only two connections per second from one host, and allow an unlimited number of connections per minute, you would set this as follows:

```
inetd_flags="-Ww -C 2 -R 0"
```

# 14

## EMAIL SERVICES

One of the basic tasks of an Internet server is to relay and receive email. FreeBSD is a quite powerful mail server, and can handle millions of emails a day. This chapter discusses how to handle email flow in the server-to-server case, the client-to-server case, and the server-to-client case. When a server communicates with a server, or a client sends mail to a server, it uses the standard SMTP email protocol. When a client downloads its mail from a server, it uses the POP3 protocol.

## Email Overview

Most email is generated by a user at a desktop computer. This is most often a Windows PC or a Mac with Outlook, Eudora, Netscape, or one of their cousins, but you can send mail with almost any operating system. My preferred FreeBSD client is Mutt (/usr/ports/mail/mutt).

The client sends the email to an email server. Almost every company or ISP has at least one dedicated email system. The email server performs some basic sanity-checking on the email sent by the client, and it then tries to find a server that claims responsibility for this message (see "Finding the Correct Mail Host" later in the chapter). The email server transmits the email message to another mail server.

When the recipient checks his email, the client software goes to the mail server, asks for all the messages, and downloads them to the desktop. If the recipient replies, the whole process is reversed.

### Where FreeBSD Fits In

The server section is where FreeBSD excels. A properly configured FreeBSD system can process thousands of messages an hour. If you buy good hardware, a FreeBSD system can receive and transmit over 40,000 pieces of email an hour. That's an average of over 11 messages a second, complete with whatever rambling text, monstrous graphics, and overblown HTML the messages include.

### The Email Protocol

To many people, email seems like magic; you hit *send* and the message is transmitted across the ether to the recipient. However, it's actually pretty easy to send email by hand, without using a client. The ability to do this is yet another trick that can be used to debug difficult problems or impress your friends. (If your friends are impressed by nerdy tricks, that is.)

#### Testing Connectivity

You can determine whether a host can receive mail by using telnet and specifying that you want to connect to a server's SMTP port (25).

```
# telnet hostname 25
```

You can use this technique, first and foremost, to determine whether a mail server is running on a particular system. Let's connect to the local system[1] and check out the mail system:

```
# telnet localhost 25
Trying ::1...
Trying 127.0.0.1...
telnet: connect to address 127.0.0.1: Connection refused
telnet: Unable to connect to remote host
#
```

Okay, my laptop isn't running a mail server. Let's try something we'll actually get a response out of:

```
# telnet AbsoluteBSD.com 25
Trying 209.69.178.18...
Connected to AbsoluteBSD.com.
Escape character is '^]'.
220 AbsoluteBSD.com ESMTP Sendmail 8.9.3/8.9.3; Sun, 10 Jun 2001 17:23:15 -0400
(EDT)
```

Voila! We're speaking directly to the mail server. We now know that a mail program is running. This server even tells us that it uses sendmail as a mail-transfer agent, and gives the local date and time.

---

[1] Remember from Chapter 5 that 127.0.0.1 is always the local host.

The most mysterious part of this is the first part of the response. In this case, it's 220. The email protocol says that each response from the server should include both a numerical code and a human-readable response. The sending program only has to look at the leading number; the longer response is there for the convenience of your poor little organic brain.

**Talking to an Email Server**

Now let's start a conversation with the program. You open negotiations with the helo command and the hostname you're connecting from:

```
helo turtledawn.AbsoluteBSD.com
```

The server responds with something like this:

```
250 AbsoluteBSD.com Hello pedicular.AbsoluteBSD.com [192.168.1.200], pleased to meet you
```

The response includes the response code (250) and the hostname you're talking to (AbsoluteBSD.com). The "hello" means that the server is willing to talk to you, and it gives the host name of the machine you are connecting from. In this case, the DNS on the server indicates that 192.168.1.200 is actually called pedicular.AbsoluteBSD.com.

You then tell the mail server who your message is from:

```
mail from: mwlucas@AbsoluteBSD.com
```

The server should tell you that you're allowed to send mail:

```
250 mwlucas@AbsoluteBSD.com... Sender ok
```

If the server is not accepting mail from your address or your location, it will tell you here. If everything's all right, you name the recipient with the rcpt to: command:

```
rcpt to: mwlucas@AbsoluteBSD.com
250 mwlucas@AbsoluteBSD.com... Recipient ok
```

At this point, the mail server you're talking to knows both the sender and the recipient. (This is the most common place where email transmission is rejected. See the "Relay Control" section that follows.) Now you're ready to send your email. Issue the data command:

```
data
354 Enter mail, end with "." on a line by itself
```

You can type whatever message you like here. Just like the message says, when you're done enter a single period on a line by itself. The following example sends the words "Test message":

```
Test message
.
```

After you type your lone period, the mail server will give you an okay message:

```
250 RAA03288 Message accepted for delivery
```

Type **quit** to exit:

```
quit
221 AbsoluteBSD.com closing connection
Connection closed by foreign host.
#
```

This technique can be used for both good and evil. As an administrator, you can test your email configuration without mucking with a client that might obscure test results.[2] However, it's also trivial to forge email, simply by creating your own `mail from:` statement.

### Who Uses the Email Protocol?

The email protocol is used when one email server transmits messages to another. It is also used when a desktop email client wants to send a message to its server.

### Relay Control

Generally speaking, an email server will either accept mail destined for its local domains or mail being sent from its local domains. Let's continue with the AbsoluteBSD.com mail server example. If that server receives an email for an address at AbsoluteBSD.com, it will accept the message. If the server receives an email from an address at AbsoluteBSD.com but to another domain, and if other access controls are met, the server will accept the message. If someone completely unrelated to AbsoluteBSD.com tries to use that mail server as a relay for mail to a third party, the server will reject it.

People who send unsolicited commercial email (aka *spam*) search constantly for email servers that allow anyone to transmit email through them. If your server allows this sort of relaying, you are a potential source of junk email.

---

[2] In some circles, forging email to a friend is a rite of passage. That doesn't mean that you should do it, mind you. A competent systems administrator can also recognize forged email at a glance, just by checking the email's full headers.

**NOTE** *You really, really must control email access through your system. If you allow unrestricted relay through your servers, you will be blacklisted by various groups. You can expect to lose connectivity to about 30 to 40 percent of the Internet until you control relay access.*

So, what are these "other access controls"? One of the most common is restricting the IP addresses that can send mail to any address through your system. By only allowing people on your local or corporate network to send email through your servers, you instantly eliminate outsiders' ability to use your server to transmit junk mail.

If you provide dial-up service to users, you can also configure your mail server to allow relay from those IP addresses. It's possible that someone could buy a dial-up package from you and use your server to send out junk mail. It's best to make sure that your terms of service not only preclude this behavior, but also list very high punitive damages to compensate you for the masses of complaints you will receive.

### Junk Mail Blacklists

"How do you use the blacklist of junk email servers?" you ask. Using one of these blacklist services is a very effective way to cut down on received junk mail, but it can also block legitimate traffic, so you need to at least be aware of whether you're using such a service. These services are generally subscription-only, and they require a service contract.

The biggest junk-mail blocking service is the Realtime Blackhole List, or RBL (http://mail-abuse.org). Most mail server programs include hooks to check sites against the RBL. Consult the blacklist's Web site to see how to integrate their features into your mail server.

## Email Programs

For many years now, UNIX has included the sendmail email server. This program is huge, obscure, obtuse, and downright intimidating to new administrators. Many experienced UNIX administrators also find it huge, obscure, obtuse, and downright intimidating. Take a look in /etc/mail/sendmail.cf for an example of a very basic sendmail configuration file.

Been there? Okay, you can get off the ceiling now. FreeBSD supports alternatives that are not only simpler to configure than sendmail, but also more efficient and more secure, as well. Unless you have to use or provide some older styles of mail service, you don't need to use sendmail.

### Who Needs Sendmail?

An ancient (for the Internet) adage holds that "Sendmail is complicated because the real world is complicated." That's true. Sendmail is also well tested, and FreeBSD's sendmail maintainer is also a sendmail developer. Sendmail is needed if you relay mail via BITNET, UUCP, or some other obscure protocols. Almost nobody in North America today uses any of those services. They are used in other parts of the world, where bandwidth is dear and hardware even dearer.

Sendmail even breaks one of the cardinal rules of UNIX, that of having many small tools that can be combined at will. Sendmail is huge and monolithic. The replacements are smaller, and made of several individual programs.

If your email services run entirely over the Internet, like the majority of the mail servers I've seen, you don't need sendmail. If you provide services to a wide variety of clients, at some point you will run into one of those edge cases where sendmail is the only solution. You can build a sendmail solution for that one special client, and leave the rest of the world running on a simpler, easier-to-manage email platform.

Personally, I like sendmail. I'm rather proud of being able to hand-edit /etc/mail/sendmail.cf. I also know a guy who is proud of being able to crush full beer cans against his forehead. Neither is something you really want to brag about, however.

### Replacing Sendmail

The two most popular non-sendmail mail servers are qmail and postfix. Both are smaller and easier to secure than sendmail. Both are easier to configure. Postfix has a more BSD-style license, however, while qmail has restrictions on its use, modification, and redistribution. All else being equal, the license makes the difference; we'll use postfix. Since postfix can handle up to a million different email messages a day on commodity hardware, it'll certainly meet your needs.

### Installing Postfix

You can install postfix just like any other piece of software, via port or package. Postfix has a couple of extra steps, however, that vary with the version of FreeBSD you are using. I recommend installing it from a port, and following the instructions given by the port.

### Pieces of Postfix

Unlike sendmail, postfix has many smaller parts. One part handles receiving mail from the network. Another part handles delivering mail to individual mailboxes. Yet another transmits queued email. To run postfix well, you must be at least vaguely familiar with the main components. Don't worry if you don't understand what all of these things do yet; we'll cover that as we go.

**Master**   The master daemon supervises all the other parts of postfix. It tells other programs when to run and how much they should do. If something isn't running, you should check the configuration of the master daemon.

**Smtpd**   The smtpd program receives email from the network. It does some basic checking to be sure that this is a real piece of email and not an attack of some sort.

**Sendmail**   The program called sendmail handles mail generated locally. Many UNIX programs expect to be able to dump their output into something called "sendmail" and have it mailed. To minimize breakage, postfix includes a program that behaves just like sendmail, but instead delivers the mail to the postfix system (in a maildrop directory, which we'll discuss later).

**Pickup**   The pickup program takes messages from sendmail's maildrop directory, does some basic error checking, and hands the message off to the innards of postfix.

**Cleanup**   The cleanup program receives messages from all other sources. It adds things like the From: header if needed, transforms the mail headers as appropriate, and sends the message to the incoming queue.

**Queue Manager (qmgr)**   Both incoming and outgoing mail sits in queues. The queue manager (qmgr) examines each message, decides where it should go, and hands it off to the appropriate delivery agent.

**Trivial-rewrite**   The trivial-rewrite daemon resolves addresses, determining whether they're local or remote, and rewrites the headers appropriately.

**Local**   The local delivery agent puts mail in local user mailboxes. If you're replacing sendmail and have users using .forward files or procmail to handle their mail, use this delivery agent.

**Virtual**   The virtual delivery agent handles delivery to local user mailboxes, but it doesn't handle .forward files or procmail. It does handle virtual domains, however. If you're running a typical Internet server, where clients download their mail to a personal computer, this is your best choice.

**Smtp Client**   The smtp client program accepts mail from the queue manager and tries to deliver it to remote hosts (other domains).

### Configuring Postfix

Postfix's configuration files are stored in /usr/local/etc/postfix. You'll find a whole mess of sample files here, but they're generally just plain-text versions of man pages. The files you need to be primarily concerned with are main.cf and master.cf.

Master.cf tells postfix's master program how to handle the other daemons it's responsible for. While it's possible that you'll need to tweak this file, you almost certainly won't. Postfix is fast and efficient enough that the defaults probably exceed your needs.

Main.cf controls mail handling. It tells postfix where to send different types of mail, what sorts of mail to accept, and how to behave in general. This is the file you'll need to configure.

We won't cover all the options: Some you should never touch unless you're a very experienced mail administrator, others are obvious (such as the path to particular programs). In general, options are variables. For example, the following line in main.cf would define the variable $myhostname:

```
myhostname = mail.AbsoluteBSD.com
```

In later configuration statements, you can set other variables to $myhostname. That way, when you change one variable, the change will propagate properly throughout the system. The port sets most of these to sensible defaults, but you'll almost certainly need to tweak something.

So, without further ado, here are the config statements you need in order to get basic email working.

```
myhostname = mail.AbsoluteBSD.com
```

The myhostname variable is the default hostname, originally taken directly from the operating system. It's used for all sorts of things. You probably don't want to change this, but it is an option if you're doing something funky—for example, if you have a machine that's part of your network but dedicated to a particular client with another domain name. You might also change myhostname if you're inside a firewall and want to conceal your host's real name.

```
mydomain = AbsoluteBSD.com
```

The mydomain variable is similar to myhostname—mydomain is the domain name of the host. It's created by taking the hostname and lopping off the first word. You might need to set this manually if you have an unusual hostname.

```
myorigin = $mydomain
```

The myorigin variable's setting is where outbound mail appears to be coming from. It defaults to $myhostname. On your central mail server, you probably want to set this to $mydomain. You'd like your email address to appear as "username@domain.com", not "username@mail.domain.com", after all.

On other machines that send mail, the default is fine. You'll probably want all these remote machines to send their automated reports to you, and changing the apparent source will just confuse you.

```
mydestination = $myhostname, localhost.$mydomain
```

The mydestination variable specifies the domains and hostnames that the machine thinks it should receive. The default is to accept mail for the system's hostname and for localhost. For example, mail.AbsoluteBSD.com would accept mail for mail.AbsoluteBSD.com and localhost.AbsoluteBSD.com.

The mydestination default is fine for a standalone machine, but if this is the corporate mail server, you would want to add a few additional hosts. The example given with postfix is a good place to start:

```
mydestination = $myhostname, localhost.$mydomain, $mydomain,
          mail.$mydomain, www.$mydomain, ftp.$mydomain
```

You might want to add other important machines in your network, such as nameservers, to this list.

These settings should get you up and running.

### Restricting Mail Relay

The simplest way to control mail relaying in postfix is with IP address restrictions. The mynetworks statement in main.cf controls which clients can transmit email through the server:

```
mynetworks = subnet
```

The default setting will work for a small office, but you need to add some things if you're providing email service for an Internet network. The subnet keyword tells postfix to allow anything on the same subnet as the server to send email. Take a look at ifconfig -a for your current subnet address. To specify additional networks by IP address, just list them. Separate different subnets by commas.

```
mynetworks = 192.168.141.128/28, 127.0.0.0/8
```

If you cannot relay email from a client system, check to confirm that its IP address is in $mynetworks.

```
relaydomains = $mydestination
```

You can also use the domain name to control relaying, by using the relaydomains setting in main.cf. In this example, if mail is to or from a host in the $mydestination list, postfix will relay it.

If you're using virtual domains (see the "Virtual Domains" section later in the chapter), postfix will also relay for those domains.

### Central Relaying

If you want all your machines to relay their mail through a central mail server, you can use the relayhost keyword. You might have a dozen servers that send mail on rare occasions, but want your central mail server to handle all the communication with the outside Internet. (This is a very common configuration.) Set relayhost to the name or IP address of your mail server:

```
relayhost = mail.AbsoluteBSD.com
```

## Email Aliases

The /etc/mail/aliases file contains redirections for mail sent to specific accounts. Although the aliases file originated with sendmail, many different mail programs understand it. Each line starts with an alias name, followed by a colon and a list of real users to forward the mail to.

### Forwarding Email from One Account to Another

Many people prefer to have mail that is sent to "root" actually redirected to their email account. The following example forwards all email sent to root to another user:

```
root:      mwlucas@absolutebsd.com
```

### Forwarding Email from Nonexistent Accounts

Many email addresses don't have accounts associated with them. For example, Internet standards require any system that sends email to have a "postmaster" email address. Nobody wants to set up a separate account just for this. Instead, you can forward email from these addresses to a real account:

```
postmaster:    root
```

The aliases file already contains a wide variety of standard aliases for addresses that are generally expected to be available at a server. Scan this file and update it for your systems.

### Aliased Mailing Lists

You can also list multiple users to create small local mailing lists. This doesn't scale well when you have many users, but it's great for quick and simple problems.

```
sales:     mwlucas, bpollock, sales@nostarch.com
```

### Forwarding Email to Files

Among the alias file's more interesting features is the ability to redirect mail to something other than a mail account. If you list a filename, it appends the message to that file. You could maintain a permanent log of a user's mail with something like this:

```
username:    /var/log/username-log, username
```

### Forwarding Email to Programs

You can also send email to a program for automated handling. List the program name, preceded by the pipe (|) symbol. If you've written a script that processes incoming mail, for example, you can use this line to redirect the mail:

```
orders:          |/usr/local/bin/process-orders.pl
```

### Lists in Alias Files

Finally, you can include other files in the aliases file. This allows a user to modify an alias on her own.

```
clientlist:     include:/usr/home/salesdude/clientaddresslist
```

In this example, the /usr/home/salesdude/clientaddresslist file is just a list of email addresses, one per line. This will allow your salesperson to maintain a list of clients, without bothering you each time a new contact needs to be added.

### Activating Alias Changes

The only caveat with this simple system is that /etc/mail/aliases is not actually processed each time a message is received. Rather, the aliases file is used to build a small database file (/etc/mail/aliases.db) that postfix uses to route mail. Accessing a binary database is much faster than scanning a text configuration file, which becomes important on systems with scant processor power, or ones that handle high volumes of mail.

Any time you edit the aliases file, or any file that the alias file includes, you need to run newaliases to rebuild this database. You can safely run newaliases through cron; users maintaining include files won't see their changes until the cron job runs, but most users accept this if they know what to expect.

### *Email Logging*

Almost all mail programs place log messages in /var/log/maillog. If you want to know what your server is doing, check that file. Remember, you can use `tail -f /var/log/maillog` to watch what's happening on your server as it occurs. The type of messages that show up in your log file vary with the mail server program you're using.

### *Virtual Domains*

One of the main reasons FreeBSD is so popular is because it can support many, many domains on one server. Most people who want Internet service for a domain name have very simple needs: a Web page and email addresses. One FreeBSD machine can handle hundreds and hundreds of simple Web and email sites through the magic of virtual domains.

The idea behind a virtual domain is simple: It's an additional name for a server. The server is configured to handle Web requests or email for that domain. We'll visit the Web part when we discuss the Apache Web server in Chapter 15. For now, let's look at email.

To use the virtual domain feature, add the following line to main.cf:

```
virtual_maps = /usr/local/etc/postfix/virtual
```

This tells postfix where to look for virtual-domain information. Virtual-domain information is kept in a "map" that matches virtual users to real system users. By default, email is delivered to the user whose username matches the email name. For example, the mwlucas account on AbsoluteBSD.com has the email address mwlucas@AbsoluteBSD.com. If I wanted to give the address mwlucas@van-hornefabrication.com to a customer, and put mail handling for that domain on the same server, by default his email would be deposited in my account. This is bad. The virtual domain email map tells postfix to drop email for that address into a different account.

### Virtual Domain Maps

The format for the virtual file is very simple:

```
domainname.com
postmaster@domainname.com      system-user1
user2@domainname.com           system-user2
user4@domainname.com           system-user3
```

First, you need the name of the domain you want to provide service to. Then you list valid email addresses and the user accounts or email addresses they are redirected to. For example, to provide a virtual domain for AbsoluteBSD.com we might have a virtual file like this:

```
AbsoluteBSD.com
postmaster@AbsoluteBSD.com     mwlucas
sales@AbsoluteBSD.com          sales@nostarch.com
questions@AbsoluteBSD.com      mwlucas
refunds@AbsoluteBSD.com        /dev/null
```

Messages for postmaster@AbsoluteBSD.com are redirected to the mwlucas account. The sales@AbsoluteBSD.com account is directed to an entirely different domain. The questions@AbsoluteBSD.com address is also directed to mwlucas, while refunds@AbsoluteBSD.com is copied to the system file /dev/null.

Like many other UNIX configuration files, the virtual domains table is actually kept in a small database file. When you edit the file, you need to update this database with postmap(8).

```
# postmap /usr/local/etc/postfix/virtual
```

Changes will take a moment or two to become visible, unless you forcibly reload the postfix configuration files. And that takes us nicely to our next topic.

### Postfix Commands

Postfix includes several commands to simplify managing your email server. We'll look at the basics here.

**postconf** This program lists your entire postfix configuration setup, including the values of all variables.

**postfix check** This command examines your postfix configuration, and points out any particularly bad problems.

**postfix start** This command starts the postfix system.

**postfix stop** This (wait for it...) shuts down postfix.

**postfix reload** This command forces postfix to reexamine all its configuration files for changes. Postfix checks for changes every few minutes anyway; this is useful if you're in a hurry.

### Finding the Correct Mail Host

So, we know how to transmit and receive email from server to server and from client to server. How does the email server know which remote server to send a piece of mail to?

When a mail server has a piece of email for a remote domain, it does a DNS check. The DNS record for a domain lists the mail servers for that domain as "MX" records (see Chapter 12). The mail server tries to deliver the mail to the email server with the lowest preference number first. If the preferred email server cannot be reached, the server tries the server with the second-lowest preference number. It tries successively less preferred servers until it either delivers the mail or it cannot deliver it anywhere.

### Undeliverable Mail

If a message is undeliverable, the server places it in a queue. Every so often, it tries to transmit the message again. If the message cannot be delivered in five days, the message is returned to the sender as "undeliverable."

## POP3

POP3 is the protocol used by desktop email clients to fetch mail from a server. Clients transmit mail to their server via SMTP, just like servers transmitting to other servers.

### Installing POP3

The most popular POP3 daemon is qpopper (/usr/ports/mail/qpopper). This program has its roots in BSD, and has been supported by Eudora for some time now. You can install it from package or port.

Qpopper runs out of inetd. Both the port and package will display a message explaining how to edit /etc/inetd.conf to support it. The example is an adequate default; we'll fine-tune that configuration later.

### Testing POP3

POP3 can work in both unencrypted and encrypted modes. It's difficult to test encrypted POP3 by hand, unless you can compute cryptographic transactions in your head on the fly. You can easily test unencrypted POP3, though, and testing qpopper can help you determine whether a problem exists on the server or on the client.

To begin, telnet to port 110 on the server.

```
# telnet magpire.AbsoluteBSD.com 110
Trying 192.168.1.222...
Connected to magpire.AbsoluteBSD.com.
Escape character is '^]'.
+OK Qpopper (version 4.0.3) at magpire.AbsoluteBSD.com starting.
<3915.992459999@magpire.AbsoluteBSD.com>
```

This is roughly what you should see when you connect.

### Authenticate to POP3

Once you are connected by telnet, identify yourself to the POP3 server with the "user" command:

```
user mwlucas
+OK Password required for mwlucas.
```

Now, use the pass command to give your password. Your password will be displayed on the screen in clear text. Be sure nobody's looking over your shoulder while you do this!

```
pass YourPasswordHere
+OK mwlucas has 1 visible message (0 hidden) in 500 octets.
```

### Viewing Mail

I have one message! That's odd; I don't receive mail on this particular system. To view that message, use the retr command and the message number.

```
retr 1
+OK 500 octets
Return-Path: <mlucas@gltg.com>
Delivered-To: mwlucas@magpire.AbsoluteBSD.com
Received: from turtledawn (turtledawn [192.168.1.200])
        by magpire.AbsoluteBSD.com (postfix) with SMTP id D51998041C
        for <mwlucas@magpire.AbsoluteBSD.com>; Fri,  8 Jun 2001 14:48:59 -0400 (EDT)
Message-Id: <20010608184859.D51998041C@magpire.AbsoluteBSD.com>
Date: Fri,  8 Jun 2001 14:48:59 -0400 (EDT)
From: mlucas@AbsoluteBSD.com
To: undisclosed-recipients:;
X-UIDL: $ld"!9>2"!P?)"!J1U"!
test
```

Oh, right. I did this when I demonstrated testing mail servers.

With these tests, you can be sure that POP3 works. If your installation doesn't behave like this, you need to investigate further.

### POP3 Logging

When you start qpopper with the -s option, it logs all activity to syslog, using the local0 facility and the notice priority (see Chapter 19). This defaults to putting the log in /var/log/messages, but you can arrange it any way you like.

### POP3 Modes

You can use POP3 in three different ways: default, APOP, and SSL (pop3ssl).

#### Default POP3

We saw an example of default POP3 earlier. It works, but isn't very secure. Anyone with a packet sniffer can grab your username and password just as if she were looking over your shoulder. This is a common protocol in the Internet service provider world.

#### APOP

APOP provides secure authentication, but requires additional overhead. Both the client and the server compute a "shared secret" based on the password and various other bits of information, such as the current time. The client sends that shared secret to the server. If it matches what the server computed, access is granted.

This might be a good choice for your server: APOP is a little older than pop3ssl, and many clients support it. While the authentication information is secure, the email itself isn't.

#### Pop3ssl

Pop3ssl is the newest version of the POP3 protocol, and tunnels both the authentication and data parts of the transmission over SSL. This is the most secure type of POP3 service you can have today.

We'll consider each type of POP3 in turn. In order to use either APOP or pop3ssl, you need to have a basic POP3 setup anyway.

### Qpopper Preconfiguration Questions

Before you configure qpopper, you need to settle two questions: What kind of users will you have and will you be using local mail readers?

#### User Types

If you're providing corporate mail services via qpopper, you are ultimately responsible for setting up the clients (or, at best, working with the people who have to set up the clients). You can insist upon things like "All users must type their usernames in lowercase" and "Mail must remain on the server." You can also insist that they use APOP or pop3ssl instead of default POP3.

If you're providing services for hundreds or thousands of people, you need a configuration that allows more user mistakes and handles a wider variety of email clients. You won't keep your users long if you insist that they use one of your approved email readers instead of the mail program that they've used for years!

### Local Mail Readers

Some users read email locally on the server, using a UNIX-based email client, such as mutt(1) or pine(1). These clients change the users' mail file directly on the server.

If qpopper can safely assume that the mail spool will not change out from underneath it, it can make several optimizations that will greatly improve performance. This isn't a big deal for systems administrators—many sysadmins don't use POP3, relying instead on ssh and a local mail reader. Some power users might want to use both, however. If you don't allow the combination of local mail readers and POP3, you can optimize qpopper.

### Default Qpopper Configuration

A raw install of qpopper will give you basic POP3 functionality, as demonstrated earlier. Users will be able to connect and download their mail. You can do various things to improve performance, however, and you can enhance your setup rather easily.

Earlier versions of qpopper were configured entirely by options on the command line in /etc/inetd.conf. This worked well when qpopper was a simple program that only supported default POP3. As APOP and pop3ssl became more common, however, command-line configuration became less and less practical. Once the command-line arguments start to wrap around the screen two or three times, you really need to convert your program to use a configuration file.

While a vanilla POP3 qpopper install doesn't need a config file, we're going to use one.

### Config Files and Inetd

The obvious place on a FreeBSD system to put the qpopper configuration file is under /usr/local/etc/qpopper. By default, only root can access the qpopper directory. More advanced qpopper implementations will also store user databases and security certificates in this directory.

To tell qpopper to take its settings from a file in this directory, use the -f flag. You can make all your other changes in the configuration file, and never have to touch /etc/inetd.conf again. This would make your inetd.conf entry look like this (and despite the page width, this is all on one line):

```
pop3 stream tcp nowait root /usr/local/libexec/qpopper qpopper -s -f
/usr/local/etc/qpopper/qpopper.conf
```

### Qpopper.conf

Now that you've told your system how to run qpopper, you need to create the configuration file. Each configuration statement in qpopper.conf appears on its own line, preceded by the word set. Any of these options can be combined with APOP and pop3ssl.

### Qpopper Mode

The most important option you have is how qpopper is going to work. The following setting controls whether qpopper will accept clear-text passwords, as used in the manual test earlier.

```
set clear-text-password = default
```

You have a few different options here. We're going to look at the most common.

By default, qpopper checks to see if the user is set up for APOP. If so, then clear-text passwords are not allowed. If the user is not set up for APOP, then clear-text passwords are permitted. Use this for standard services.

Specifying always as the setting means that qpopper will accept clear-text passwords, even if the user is set up for APOP. You might need to use this in an ISP environment; while you'd like the user to use APOP, some users have email clients that simply cannot handle it.

Specifying never means that clear-text passwords will not work, even if you're using pop3ssl. You must use APOP to get your mail.

Specifying tls means that clear-text passwords are acceptable if you're running over an encrypted connection (such as SSL). After all, the entire connection is encrypted!

We'll discuss APOP and POP3 over SSL later (in "APOP Setup" and "Configuring Pop3ssl," respectively.)

### Username Case

If you have a variety of users, some of them will type their username in all capital letters. That's how usernames appear in the movies, after all! By putting the following line in your configuration, usernames received from clients are transformed into all lowercase before qpopper attempts to authenticate them.

```
set downcase-user        = true
```

This can reduce your technical support calls.

### Mail Spool Handling

A POP3 client can choose to either copy all messages from the server, download and delete all messages from the server, or delete some messages from the server while leaving the rest. The first two choices (leave everything and delete everything) are typical of core mail-server functionality. The third, a mix of saving and deleting, is a lot of work, and it is set with the following line:

```
set server-mode          = false
```

Server mode assumes that the client will either save all its mail or delete all its mail. This makes qpopper much faster, and reduces server disk I/O. If you enable server mode, you greatly increase qpopper's efficiency.

You also make some promises to qpopper when you enable server mode, however. Qpopper will assume that mail is only delivered to clients by qpopper. This is where the "mixing local mail readers and POP3" problem appears. If you use a local mail reader to check mail on an account, and someone pops that account's mail while you're reading it, you can damage users' mail. You don't want to do that. If you don't combine POP3 and local mail clients, and don't read your users' mail, setting this to true is perfectly safe and will improve performance.

### Reducing Disk Activity

If you set the following option, you will decrease your disk activity by a third:

```
set fast-update          = false
```

This setting doesn't mix with local mail readers, however. You will also break UNIX programs that notify you of new mail on the UNIX system. This is perfectly safe on a POP-only mail server.

## APOP Setup

APOP uses a challenge-response system. When a user connects to the POP3 server, the server takes the user's known password and computes a challenge based upon it. This challenge is sent to the client. The client takes the challenge, combines it with the password, computes a response, and sends it back to the server. The server, meanwhile, has performed the same calculation and it compares the client's response to its own result. If they match, the client has proven that it has the password. Mail download is permitted.

Why go to all this trouble? Well, the password itself has never passed over the network. This eliminates any chance for password theft via qpopper requests. Web browsing, telnet, and so on, all give other opportunities for password theft.

### APOP Password Database

Since APOP computes a shared secret based on the user's password, qpopper must have access to the user's password. In UNIX, password encryption is a one-way trip; even given the /etc/master.passwd file, you cannot extract the password.[3] APOP therefore requires a separate username and password database. This APOP user database is kept in /usr/local/etc/qpopper/pop.auth.db, and it should only be readable by root.

You administer the APOP user database with qpopauth(8). Before you can do anything, you must initialize the database:

```
# qpopauth -init
```

Once you have a database, you can use qpopauth to manage users.

---

[3] You can do something called a "brute force attack," where you try to find a text string that has a cryptographic collision with the password. This takes a lot of CPU time, and a lot of time, and is utterly inappropriate for a server protocol.

### Adding Users

This command adds a user to the database:

```
# qpopauth -user username
```

You'll be prompted for a password. If the user does not exist on the main system, qpopauth will not let you add the user.

### Deleting Users

The following command deletes the specified user from the database:

```
# qpopauth -delete username
```

### Listing Users

If a user runs the following command, it tells him whether he is in the APOP user database. If root runs this as qpopauth -list ALL, it lists every APOP user:

```
# qpopauth -list
```

### Enabling APOP

When you set up APOP, you need to decide whether plain-text POP3 will still be permitted. If you want to allow people to use either plain POP3 or APOP, you need to change the clear-text-password option. (The default lets people use plain-text passwords only if they are not set up as APOP users.)

Use the set clear-text-password option in your qpopper configuration file to require the use of APOP.

```
set clear-text-password = always
```

### Supporting APOP

Allowing both APOP and plain POP3 can cause password confusion because the APOP user database and /etc/master.passwd are not synchronized by anything except administrator intervention. When a user calls and says that she can't get her mail, you'll have to find out if she's using APOP or POP3. The user probably won't know, so you'll have to walk her through her mail client to find out, or just change both passwords to a known value. APOP is a better idea all around.

A better idea still is pop3ssl.

### *Configuring Pop3ssl*

The POP3-over-SSL process is similar to the default POP3 protocol. Instead of sending a username, however, the client sends a request for SSL. If your server can grant it, the remaining steps of the process are all encrypted.

All of the performance options are set as if you're running standard POP3. You need to set several configuration options to use pop3ssl, however, as follows.

```
set clear-text-password = tls
```

With this `clear-text-password` option, you can use clear-text passwords if you're using SSL encryption. A user could use APOP or pop3ssl, but not vanilla POP3.

```
set tls-cipher-list = bf,des,des3
```

These `tls-cipher-list` settings are the cryptographic ciphers that your system will support. You can get a complete list of ciphers your system supports by running `openssl list-cipher-commands`. The preceding example supports most email clients.

```
set tls-server-cert-file    = /usr/local/etc/qpopper/server.cert
```

This `tls-server-cert-file` setting specifies the location of your signed certificate file. We created a signed server certificate in the previous chapter.

After setting these options, you should be all set to provide pop3ssl services. This is by far the most preferable method, and easy enough to do.

### Qpopper Security

Qpopper has a questionable security record, but it has undergone an extensive code audit and is now as secure as any POP3 server daemon. You still need to keep up on security advisories, however, just as you would for any program that transmits user data across the network. Since qpopper runs out of inetd, you can use TCP Wrappers to help secure it.

# 15

## WEB AND FTP SERVICES

Although the Internet started back in the 1970s, it wasn't until the advent of Web pages in the mid-1990s that the Internet became a household name. The Netscape Corporation took the open-source Web browser Mosaic and turned it into a commercial product. The result was an information and communication revolution that is still going on. While many dot-com companies have crashed and burned, an age of person-to-person communication began with the Netscape Web browser. Technologies such as peer-to-peer are expanding the Internet even further, but the Web is still what comes to mind when people think of the Internet.

FreeBSD's Web server performance is legendary. For many years, some Microsoft subsidiaries even used FreeBSD in preference to their own Windows NT platform. (The very day I write this, the *Wall Street Journal* announced that Microsoft is still using FreeBSD internally, despite corporate protestations to the contrary.) This has led to Microsoft releasing a shared-source ".NET for FreeBSD" toolkit. Yahoo! runs FreeBSD, as do a wide variety of other high-demand Web server farms. The Apache Web server, the most popular Web server in the world, is developed on FreeBSD.

This chapter will discuss building your own high-performance Web and FTP server with FreeBSD.

## How a Web Server Works

A basic Web server is fairly straightforward: A Web browser requests a page and a Web server spits it out then closes the connection. That's the easy part. Things get considerably more complicated when you start to use modules, dynamic pages, and so on, but we'll discuss the basics in this chapter.

The Web uses Hypertext Transfer Protocol, or HTTP, a very simple protocol like POP3. Over the last few years, functions have been added to HTTP to make it more complicated, but basic HTTP operations are simple enough to be performed by hand. Let's try it: We'll telnet(1) to connect to port 80 on a server, and type **GET /**.

```
# telnet blackhelicopters.org 80
Trying 209.69.178.18...
Connected to blackhelicopters.org.
Escape character is '^]'.
GET /
<font color=white> Nothing to see here.

This is not the site you're looking for.
Connection closed by foreign host.
#
```

If you've ever looked at any HTML, the output from this command should look very familiar to you. If not, you might check the "view source" option on your Web browser the next time you call up a Web page. You'll see that this is the actual HTML that generates the pretty picture in your browser. (If you can't get this much from your Web server, it probably isn't working. Check your error logs.)

FreeBSD includes several Web servers, but the most popular on the Internet, by far, is Apache.

## The Apache Web Server

If you look under /usr/ports/www, you'll see several different ports with "apache" in their names. Most of these are slightly different versions of the Apache Web server, and before installing anything, you'll need to pick a version. Here's a brief look at your options.

| | |
|---|---|
| **apache-jserv** | This is an Apache server with a Java servlet engine. You can use this to handle JavaServer Pages. |
| **apache13** | This is probably the version you'll want: Apache version 1.3 without any advanced features. Still, some Apache setups require massive or far-reaching changes in Apache itself. Check the other Apache ports to see if one of them will better fit your needs. |
| **apache13+ipv6** | This is Apache patched to support IPv6 connections. Use this if you're using IPv6. |

| | |
|---|---|
| **apache13-fp** | Microsoft FrontPage Server Extensions are a popular Web development platform, but installing FrontPage Extensions can be a pain. Use this port if you want to support FrontPage. |
| **apache13-modssl** | This port includes modular Secure Sockets Layer (SSL) support, for secure Web sites. The secure connection component, mod_ssl, is based upon OpenSSL. Use this to support secure connections. |
| **apache13-ssl** | This includes integrated (nonmodular) SSL support, which is considered obsolete; use mod_ssl instead. |
| **apache2** | This isn't merely a cutting edge Web server, it's bleeding edge. This version of Apache may well scalp you. Apache 2 is well worth installing just to keep up on the technology, but you probably don't want it in production use yet. Also, many Apache modules have not yet been ported to apache2. If you want a bland, basic Web server with a bleeding-edge back end, this will make you happy. |

To build the programs in the most efficient manner possible, you can choose to build Apache from ports. This takes longer to build, but results in a stronger, better, faster Web server. To enable this option, set APACHE_PERF_TUNING=YES when building your chosen port:

```
# make APACHE_PERF_TUNING=YES all install
```

## Apache Configuration Files

You'll find Apache's main configuration files in /usr/local/etc/apache. There are five main files: access.conf, httpd.conf, magic, mime.types, and srm.conf. Originally, Apache used all five files extensively, but these days httpd.conf, magic, and mime.types are the ones most often used. (The functions in access.conf and srm.conf have been rolled into httpd.conf; the original files remain mostly for us older admins who expect to find them.)

To properly administer Apache, you need to understand what each of these files is for and how to manage them.

### Mime.types

The mime.types file contains a list of all standard file types and their identifying characteristics. All Web servers must identify the type of file they are transmitting to the client, so that the client can take appropriate actions. For example, most Web browsers open up a PDF reader when they download a PDF. The mappings contained in mime.types give Apache the information it needs to support this functionality. You should almost never have to touch this file, unless you are specifically told to in a program's documentation.

### Magic

This file contains identifying characteristics for a variety of unusual file types that the mime.types file cannot cope with. Because the mime.types file can't deal with all of the file types in the world, Apache's built-in mime_magic module uses the magic file to try to identify unknown files. You should never have to touch the magic file, unless a program's installation documentation explicitly tells you to.

### Httpd.conf

The httpd.conf file controls the Web server's behavior, and it's where the interesting things happen. This file is well commented (any line beginning with pound sign (#) is a comment), so we won't discuss it in much detail; we'll leave the discussion of every possible Apache configuration for much bigger books. Most of Apache's configuration takes place in this file, however, so we can't escape it entirely.

## Configuring Apache

The best way to create an Apache configuration file is to edit and use the sample primary configuration file (httpd.conf). But whatever you do, don't touch what you don't understand. Unlike your DNS server, you don't want to create an Apache configuration from scratch! The default httpd.conf contains large sections that control things like character-set handling, and unless you really want your Web server's handling of the Chinese language to be completely different from any other Web server on the planet, your best bet is to leave these settings alone.

**NOTE** *The arrangement of the default httpd.conf file is a bit irregular. While it probably makes sense to the authors, the rest of us are left scratching our heads if we try to just sit down and read it. (It doesn't help that the default file is over 1,000 lines long!) That said, we'll discuss the configuration options in a more sensible order.*

### Server-Wide Settings

The following configuration options define general server behavior.

### Server Root Path

The ServerRoot setting specifies the path to the main Web site files.

```
ServerRoot "/usr/local"
```

If your server handles a single large site, you might want to point this at a different location on a partition dedicated to Web files.

**NOTE** *When you reference another file in httpd.conf, Apache prepends the ServerRoot to it unless you begin the filename with a slash (/). For example, if your ServerRoot is /usr/local, "docs/cgi-bin" would become "/usr/local/docs/cgi-bin", while "/usr/local/etc/apache/vhost.conf" would remain unchanged.*

### Document Root Path

```
DocumentRoot "/usr/local/www/data"
```

The HTML documents for the main Web site go in the DocumentRoot directory.

### Httpd Servers

```
MinSpareServers 5
MaxSpareServers 10
StartServers 5
```

If you do a `ps -ax` on your server, you'll see a number of httpd processes because each request to the Web server is handled by a separate process. When a dozen people all type in your Web server's URL and hit ENTER simultaneously, a separate process handles each request. This is part of how Apache can handle such a high load.

When Apache first starts, it fires up a number of httpd processes equal to the `StartServers` value. Every so often, it checks to see how many httpd processes are running, and how many are actually serving content. In order to guarantee that there are enough httpd processes to handle additional requests, Apache keeps `MinSpareServers` and `MaxSpareServers` around.

If your Web server suffers from sudden floods of traffic, you might want to increase the `MinSpareServers` and `MaxSpareServers` values. The `StartServers` value shouldn't need to be increased, though, because even if you were to shut down and restart Apache, it can handle several hundred httpd processes in just a few seconds.

### Maximum Number of Clients

```
MaxClients 150
```

`MaxClients` specifies the maximum number of httpd processes that Apache is allowed to run at one time, and when this limit is reached, the Web server might appear to be unavailable. This limit is designed for older systems, and can easily be increased on more modern computers. Experiment to see how many httpd processes your system needs.

**NOTE** *You can see how many httpd processes are running at any given time by running* `ps -ax | grep httpd | wc -l`*.*

### Maximum Httpd Requests

Each httpd process that starts answers requests and then hangs around waiting for the next request. If you have a fancy Web program that leaks memory, making each httpd process use more and more memory, you'll see the size of each httpd process increase when you run top.

If you have this memory usage problem, you can set `MaxRequestsPerChild` to shut down a process after it handles a set number of requests. Setting this to 0 means that each process can handle an unlimited number of requests:

```
MaxRequestsPerChild 0
```

Most FreeBSD systems run just fine with this set to 0, but you can change this option if you find that you have many httpd processes using a lot of memory. If that's the case, the problem is usually due to some Web application.

### Listen

```
Listen 80
```

The `Listen` option controls which TCP ports or IP addresses Apache will bind to. You can specify individual IP addresses like this:

```
Listen 192.168.8.44
```

Then combine this with a port number to run Apache on an unusual port:

```
Listen 192.168.8.44:88
```

Or, you can listen on all the IP addresses on the system, on an unusual port:

```
Listen 88
```

You can use multiple `Listen` statements to make Apache available on any port or IP address on your system.

### BindAddress

```
BindAddress *
```

Much like the `Listen` statement, `BindAddress` controls which IP address Apache attaches to. By default, Apache attaches to every port on the system, but you can restrict it to a single IP address with this option. `BindAddress` is basically identical to `Listen`.

### Modules

```
LoadModule
AddModule
```

You can add functions to Apache with these modules. The modules listed in the base configuration provide basic Apache functionality, so don't alter the existing `LoadModule` and `AddModule` statements unless you know exactly what you're doing. (We'll discuss Apache modules in more detail in the "Apache Modules" section later in the chapter.)

### Port

```
Port 80
```

This is the TCP port that Apache listens on. You can use multiple `Port` statements.

### User and Group

```
User www
Group www
```

These options specify the UNIX user and group that Apache runs as. Just as you can log into your FreeBSD system and start a program that runs with your permissions, the Apache Web server expects to be started by a particular user and use that user's permissions.

Recent FreeBSD systems ship with the user www and group www, generic accounts with no privileges that are intended for use by the Web server. (You can't log in as www.) While you'll sometimes see a document that suggests running Apache as root, don't run the Web server as root, whatever you do; if an intruder breaks into your Web server, they'll get root on your system as a side benefit!

### Administrator Email Address

```
ServerAdmin webmaster@AbsoluteBSD.com
```

This setting specifies the email address of the person who runs the server. If someone notices a problem with your server, this is where he will be told to send email.

### Server Name

```
ServerName www.AbsoluteBSD.com
```

This is a name of the Web site. It must be a real hostname, and whatever name you give must have a DNS entry or Apache won't start. For testing purposes, though, you can use an entry in /etc/hosts instead of an actual DNS entry.

### Directory Index

The DirectoryIndex statement gives the name of the default document in a directory. When a client calls up a directory, rather than a filename, Apache checks for files with this name, in order.

```
DirectoryIndex index.php index.html
```

Here, if a Web browser calls up http://www.AbsoluteBSD.com/refunds/, Apache checks for index.php and then index.html, and returns the first it finds.

The default httpd.conf file has a fairly complicated set of rules for determining the DirectoryIndex setting. This is an excellent example of a conditional setting that is based on the modules loaded. You can strip out all that and replace it with a simple one-line entry, if you're not using any of these advanced modules.

### Hostname Lookup for Logs

```
HostnameLookups Off
```

This setting controls whether Apache saves IP addresses or hostnames to its logs. Enabling this makes your logs look nicer, with computer names instead of IP addresses, but you should leave it off as a general rule. Turning it on will simply add load to your server, and most log-file analysis programs can do this lookup on their own.

### Error Log Location

```
ErrorLog /var/log/httpd-error.log
```

This is the location of the error log.

### Logging Level

```
LogLevel warn
```

The LogLevel statement controls the amount of data logged. Valid labels are debug, info, notice, warn, error, crit, alert, and emerg. The system logger uses these labels to determine the amount of data logged. The warn setting is a good, median level.

### Log Format

```
LogFormat "%h %l %u %t \"%r\" %>s %b \"%{Referer}i\" \"%{User-Agent}i\"" combined
```

The LogFormat statement controls the data logged by the server. There are several different default LogFormat settings established for your convenience:

- The "common" format logs the IP address of the client, the time of the request, the file requested, and a few other basic things.
- The "referrer" format logs the site that referred the client—meaning, another Web page with a link to yours.
- The "agent" format records the Web browser used.
- The "combined" format logs all of the above. (This can generate very large logs, so be sure you have lots of disk space.)

**NOTE** *If you dig through the Apache documentation, you can write your own LogFormat statements easily enough. The formats mentioned here are understood by all the popular Web log analysis programs, however, so don't change them arbitrarily.*

### Custom Logs

```
CustomLog /var/log/httpd-access.log combined
```

The CustomLog statement controls the name of the log file and the format used. In the preceding example, the main Web site logs to /var/log/httpd-access.log in the "combined" format.

You can have several CustomLog statements for different purposes. For example, if you're using an Apache module that provides special functionality that you want logged, but you don't want to break the WebTrends product being used by your clients, you can use multiple CustomLog statements to write to two separate log files.

### Aliases

```
Alias /icons/ "/usr/local/www/icons/"
```

Use the Alias statement to provide aliases for directories on your Web site, much like a symlink. In the preceding example, someone looking at http://www.AbsoluteBSD.com/icons/ would actually be pulling files from the directory /usr/local/www/icons/.

*Error Document*

```
ErrorDocument 404 /missing.html
```

When a browser requests a document that's not on the server, the server returns an error. You can create a custom error page with the `ErrorDocument` directive.

*Include*

```
Include /usr/local/etc/apache/vhosts.conf
```

The httpd.conf file can include other files, a feature that can be useful when you have several subsystems maintained by different people. This can also be useful if you want to make your configuration easier to digest.

For example, many add-on Apache modules have their own bits of configuration code. It's simpler to give each model its own configuration file and include it than to pile it on the main httpd.conf file. Similarly, if you have a person whose job it is to maintain virtual hosts, you can create a virtual hosts file with permissions that allow that person (or group of people) to maintain it (see Chapter 8).

### Directory Configuration

Apache has many nifty features, but it's not a good idea to enable everything everywhere—a bit of sloppy programming can result in your giving out too much information from your Web site, or even letting someone break in.

Permissions to access Apache functions are set on a directory-by-directory basis. The configuration looks much like XML: You have a `Directory` label in angle brackets, a list of permissions and settings, and then a closing directory entry with a backslash. Any options or settings between the opening and closing `Directory` statements affect that directory. Here's the basic format:

```
<Directory /path/to/files>

...options and settings here

</Directory>
```

By default, Apache uses very restrictive permissions and settings. For example, you'll see the following entry right at the top of the directory listings in httpd.conf:

```
<Directory />
    Options FollowSymLinks
    AllowOverride None
</Directory>
```

Apache allows users to upload their own configuration files to change the server's behavior—in short, to let users specify their own options, password protection, MIME types, and so on. The `AllowOverride None` line shown in the preceding example means that users can't set these options on a directory unless we say so.

And yes, that slash (/) represents the ServerRoot directory, as specified in the systemwide options. Unless specified otherwise, every directory on the server has these permissions, though you can override these settings on particular directories. (We'll briefly discuss the various permission options in "Directory Configuration," later in this chapter; for now, just realize that nobody does diddly without our say-so.) To loosen permissions on a directory-by-directory basis, have a look at the default httpd.conf, where you'll find a set of looser permissions set on various directories.

### Directory Features

Now that we've disallowed every feature Apache offers, we can explicitly enable the features we'd like to have. They will allow your Web designers to do many different things, but as an administrator you need to know what each one does. Here are some of the features you might set on a directory.

### *Controlling Access with IP Addresses and Netblocks*

The `Allow` and `Deny` options control which IP addresses and hostnames are permitted to access content in a directory. Browser clients are compared against the "allow" and "deny" lists in the order given in the `Order` statement. Apache then permits or rejects access depending on the results. When `Order` is `deny,allow`, the default is to allow access unless prohibited by a `Deny` statement. When `Order` is `allow,deny`, the default is to deny access unless permitted by an `Allow` statement.

You allow and deny hosts by IP address and hostnames. Every attempted connection is compared against these descriptions, and is treated appropriately. Every attempted connection is part of a special group, *All*. Much like with TCP Wrappers, you can use the All group and more specific client identification to allow and exclude particular hosts.

Confused? Let's walk through a sample.

```
Order allow,deny
Allow from all
Deny from *.AbsoluteBSD.com
```

I'm browsing to a site from an AbsoluteBSD.com machine. Apache first checks the `Order` list (because this is the first statement it encounters), and is told to look at the `Allow` list and then the `Deny` list. Since AbsoluteBSD.com is part of `all`, I'm allowed in at first. But then Apache checks the deny list and, whoops, I'm cut off.

Note that Apache gets the hostnames from reverse DNS. Because, in many cases, it's trivial for an administrator to change the reverse DNS hostname, you're safer using IP addresses, or even blocks of IP addresses, to control access.

All of the following are legitimate types of IP address and IP address block arguments for an `Allow` or `Deny` statement.

```
192.168.0.1,192.168.0.2,192.168.0.3
192.168
192.168.0.0/16
192.168.0.0/255.255.0.0
```

The first line here controls a series of three IP addresses. The last three lines mean exactly the same thing as each other, and are simply three different ways of expressing all IP addresses beginning with 192.168.

You can easily restrict access to your internal Web site to only company IP addresses by doing something like this:

```
Order allow,deny
Allow from 192.168.1/24
Deny from all
```

(This, of course, assumes that your company firewall is configured to block spoofed traffic.)

### Httpd.conf Options

Options are general server features that can be enabled and disabled on a directory-by-directory basis. They allow a Web developer to do all sorts of nifty tricks, such as execute programs on the server, enable and disable password protection on directories, and change language handling. These options give the Web developer a lot of power, and they can also generate a lot of support calls, so you need to know what each is and how it works.

You specify options inside a directory with the `Options` keyword. For example, to enable the ExecCGI option for the directory /usr/local/www/data/catalog, you would use the following configuration:

```
<directory /usr/local/www/data/catalog>
    Options ExecCGI
</directory /usr/local/www/data/catalog>
```

You can also specify multiple options on a single line:

```
<directory /usr/local/www/data/catalog>
    Options ExecCGI,MultiViews
</directory /usr/local/www/data/catalog>
```

Now, let's examine the standard options.

**All**   The `All` option is the Apache server's built-in default. If you have an empty httpd.conf, the Apache server lets almost any Apache function work in the directory. If a user uploads a password-protection script to keep people out of the directory, it will work. If a user uploads a CGI script that exploits a local system flaw to start a root shell on a high-numbered TCP port, giving anyone in the world a backdoor into your system, it will work too. The `All` option allows every single Apache option except MultiViews (described shortly).

The sample httpd.conf file shipped with Apache specifically sets `Options None` in the ServerRoot directory, which means that the Apache program's built-in permissive default is turned off by the sample configuration. If you're using the sample httpd.conf as a base (as you should), the `All` option is explicitly shut off, and you will need to specifically enable options in any directory in which you wish to use them.

**ExecCGI**   CGI scripts that are in a directory with this option set can run.

**FollowSymLinks**   You can use symlinks (or symbolic links, or aliases, as discussed in ln(1)) to point to other files on the server. A user could symlink to just about any file on the server, and that file would be visible (if the file permissions allow it, of course).

**Includes**   Server-side includes (SSI—HTML files that include shell commands) and CGI scripts will work in a directory with this option set, but both can be a security risk unless defensively programmed. After all, you're allowing anyone who can call up your Web site to run the command you use in your HTML page. With a bit of conniving, many intruders can make a command do things the Web designer never intended. (Search the Web on server-side includes and security, and you'll find many different security problems described.) If you don't know how to use SSI safely, don't enable this!

**IncludesNOEXEC**   This allows server-side includes, but disables the #exec SSI feature and the include function of CGI scripts. Without the #exec feature, HTML code cannot run just any command, and SSI commands must be written within a carefully restricted range. Basically, this allows simple server-side includes and CGI scripts, while eliminating the most common security holes. Again, check Google for many different descriptions of the thousands of security issues caused by sloppy server-side includes.

**Indexes**   If a directory doesn't contain an index document (such as Directory Index), the server will return a prettily formatted list of the directory contents. You might consider this a security problem, depending on the contents of your directory. For example, if someone browses the directory of my personal Web page, I don't care, but if they browse a directory that contains private code, I care a great deal.

MultiViews   The server can handle documents that are written to be viewed in multiple languages. For example, a Web developer could write a single HTML document that contains text in English, Chinese, and Spanish. With MultiViews enabled, Apache will send the client the page in the language the Web browser uses.

None   No options are allowed. Every one of the nifty features discussed here will not work.

SymLinksIfOwnerMatch   The server will use symlinks if the owner of the symlink is the owner of the file that the symlink points to. This means, in English, that a user can use symlinks to point to her own documents.

AllowOverride   If you allow override, users can alter the options permitted in a directory. When you allow override, Apache checks each directory for a file called .htaccess, and processes the contents as additional server configuration info. This allows Web developers to both handle much routine configuration themselves and to install insecure CGI scripts in random locations.

You'll need to decide whether to permit the use of .htaccess overrides. If you're running a corporate Web server, and your Web developer pretty much gets what he wants anyway, there's no reason not to allow whatever override he desires. If, on the other hand, you're running a public or ISP Web server, and you don't allow a certain group of clients to use CGI scripts, you should be sure to disallow certain overrides.

These are the valid AllowOverride statements; all allow the user to override anything with an .htaccess entry.

- AuthConfig allows you to password-protect directories. This is a pretty safe option, and it is generally expected on server farms where any idiot with a credit card can get an account.

- FileInfo allows users to insert their own MIME information for a directory. While it's generally better to add this sort of information to the server's mime.types file, there will be occasions where people need this—for example, when they upload a file that's used only within their company, and they need to tell the browsers what to expect.

- Indexes allows the user to control how indexing is handled, including setting a new default document, controlling how icons appear in server-generated indexes, and so on.

- Limit allows the user to use the Allow, Deny, and Order keywords. This option is also quite safe.

- None means that the user can make no changes. This is a good option to use as a default, but it's a little too restrictive for most applications.

- Options allows the user to set any of the options described here. This is good if you know and trust the Web developers, or if you don't care if someone uploads an insecure program and the server is compromised.

With the foregoing in mind, a reasonable set of user defaults is

```
AllowOverride Limit, AuthConfig, Indexes, FileInfo
```

**Controlling HTTP Requests**

An HTTP method is a command sent by a browser to a server. You've probably heard of the HTTP methods GET and POST. These tell the server to transmit a particular page and to process a list of uploaded information, respectively. There's a whole list of methods, however, each with a separate purpose. You can use the Limit directive to restrict the methods your server accepts.

The Limit and LimitExcept directives control which HTTP methods can be used in a directory. In most cases, you won't have to worry about which methods are used within a particular Web page—that'll be the Web developer's problem. You do need to know how to enable and disable them, however. (If you're a Web developer reading this book to learn about how the server works, good for you! Now go look up the various methods in your HTTP book.)

The Limit directive explicitly lists methods that can be used in a directory, along with rules for their usage, in an "allow" and "deny" format. We considered Limit when restricting access to a directory by particular IP addresses, in the previous section, "Httpd.conf Options."

The LimitExcept directive is similar to Limit, except that the rules you create only apply to the unlisted methods. Like the Directory directive, both the Limit and LimitExcept statements use angle brackets (< and >) to show when they begin and end.

For example, to prevent all users from uploading files to your server, you could use the following configuration:

```
<Directory />
  <Limit GET POST OPTIONS PROPFIND>
    Order allow,deny
    Allow from all
  </Limit>
  <LimitExcept GET POST OPTIONS PROPFIND>
    Order deny,allow
    Deny from all
  </LimitExcept>
</Directory>
```

In the first part of this code, beginning with Limit, we use the Limit statement to create a list of specific HTTP methods—GET, POST, OPTIONS, and PROPFIND—that we want to control. The Order and Allow statements, as discussed earlier, let every method in this list go through. We end this section with /Limit.

In the LimitExcept section that follows, we're creating a list of everything *not* in the Limit list. (This is the same list we saw in the first section.) We don't want to block what we specified in the previous list, but we do want to block what is *not* in that list. That's why we use LimitExcept. Here, the Order and Deny statements prevent any method not on the list from working.

If you add an HTTP method (say, from an Apache module), the LimitExcept module will automatically include it.

There are quite a few other uses for Limit and LimitExcept, but if you're really interested, you'll want to get one of the many big books on Apache.

### Password-Protecting Directories

How about creating a password-protected directory on a Web site? While there's a quick-and-easy way to do this with a plain-text file containing usernames and encrypted passwords, like many other quick-and-easy methods, this one is quite slow. Since we're building high-performance Web servers here, we're not going to do it the easiest way.[1] Instead, we'll look at a way that's very slightly more trouble to deal with but will perform much better.

Much as system usernames and passwords are stored in a database for efficient access, Apache can use a database to store usernames and passwords. You can use the FreeBSD system's user database (/etc/passwd and friends) to authenticate Web users, but this is a bad idea. If you do, you'll allow hackers to break in more easily, you may increase system load, and you can cause all sorts of bad things that you'd go nuts trying to track down. In fact, this is such a massively bad idea that I'm not going to tell you how to do it. Go hunt down the Apache FAQ if you want to know how to do this.[2]

### *Directory Setup*

To use the Apache database, you'll first need to set up your directory to require a database file. To do so, create a file named .htaccess, in the directory in question, that looks something like this:

```
AuthName "Private Directory"
AuthType Basic
AuthDBMUserFile /usr/local/etc/apache/userdb
require valid-user
```

AuthName is the text that will appear in the password box, and you can change the text between quotes to anything you want. AuthType tells Apache what sort of authentication to use. For standard usernames and passwords, use an AuthType of "basic."

---

[1] Every time I've implemented the quick-and-dirty method, I've had to go back months or years later and convert it to the more correct method. Start off right; you won't regret it.

[2] They won't tell you how to do it, either; they'll just berate you for considering it.

The `AuthDBMUserFile` directive tells Apache where the user database is kept. Do not put this file in a directory in the Web site itself, or users could then download it and try to break it—and with enough time, anything breaks. Instead, put it in a location on the server completely outside of the ServerRoot directory. If you have user accounts on the system, and each manages a Web site, put it in the user's home directory.

### Web Users Database

Now that you know where you're going to put the database file, you'll use dbm-manage(1) to create it. Dbmmanage takes at least two arguments: the name of the database file and a command to execute on that file.

To create the database, just add a user to it; dbmmanage will notice that the file doesn't exist, and will create it. Specify the username you want to create on the command line, and dbmmanage will prompt you for a password:

```
# dbmmanage /usr/local/etc/apache/userdbm adduser username
```

View, update, and delete are three other useful dbmmanage options. Use view to see all the users in the database, and their encrypted passwords. In the following example, we see the contents of a very small username database, with only one user:

```
# dbmmanage /usr/local/etc/apache/userdbm view
mwlucas:jvvAuD7bpZwY2
#
```

Use update to change a user's password. To remove a user, use the delete option. (See dbmmanage(1) for a discussion of several other options.)

Once you have a user database and your directory is set up to require passwords, any visitor to that Web directory will be asked for a username and a password to access the site.

### Apache and SSL

Many online shopping malls and password-protected areas use what they call "secure Web sites." What they normally mean is that they use SSL to encrypt traffic between the server and the client. While these sites aren't as secure as the name implies, SSL functionality is a vital part of almost any Web server, and Apache has an add-on module to handle SSL connections. To use it, install the apache13-modssl port.

All SSL servers require a certificate. (We discussed generating a public-key certificate request in Chapter 13.) You can either create a legitimate certificate or generate your own test certificate, though if you use a test certificate with an SSL Web server, your clients will get warnings when they attempt to view pages over SSL.

The completed certificate has two parts: a certificate file (server.crt) and a private key (server.key). Place both of these files on the Web server, in a location outside of the ServerRoot, to protect your private key from being downloaded. Then make the private-key file only readable by the Web server with chmod and chown.

```
# chmod 600 server.key
# chown www server.key
#
```

Now that you have the certificate on the computer, you need to tell Apache about it. Take a look at the httpd.conf file installed by the apache13-ssl port and you'll see that most of it looks exactly like the configuration file installed by the standard Apache port, though you'll see a few additional IfDefined SSL statements to load the SSL modules. Near the bottom of httpd.conf, however, you'll find some entries to define the certificate file and the key file:

```
SSLCertificateFile /usr/local/etc/apache/ssl.crt/server.crt
```

This is the path to your certificate file. It needs to begin with a slash (/); remember, any path in httpd.conf that doesn't begin with a slash is assumed to be under the DocumentRoot! Give the full path to your certificate file here; the default works, but you can change it if you're using virtual hosts.

Similarly, there's an httpd.conf option to tell Apache where your server key lives:

```
SSLCertificateKeyFile /usr/local/etc/apache/ssl.key/server.key
```

The default httpd.conf in the apache13-ssl port includes some "glue" to tell the system to listen for SSL connections on port 443, the standard TCP port for secure connections. By telling Apache where the certificate and key files live, Apache knows to accept SSL connections.

That's it! Your default Web site is now up and offers secure Net connections through SSL. (To set up additional secure sites with virtual hosts, see the "Virtual Hosting" section later in the chapter.)

**NOTE**  *It's best to avoid the term "secure Web server" when you mean SSL. While the encryption on traffic between the server and the client prevents packet sniffing, attackers could still break into either the server or the client. A secure Web server requires good Web page design, server maintenance, and educated users and administrators.*

### Controlling Apache

Apache is a complicated program that can be managed in several different ways. As with every other program, FreeBSD includes startup and shutdown scripts in /usr/local/etc/rc.d (see Chapter 11). Apache includes its own custom program to manage the Web server.

You can also manipulate the Web server program directly. For example, you can use the system startup/shutdown script manually to start or stop the Web server, as discussed in Chapter 11.

```
# /usr/local/etc/rc.d/apache.sh start
# /usr/local/etc/rc.d/apache.sh stop
```

This works, but is very limited. For more careful control of Apache, use the apachectl(8) command.

### Controlling Apache with Apachectl

You can start, stop, and check Apache with Apache's special-handling command, apachectl(8). While most of apachectl's options are related to starting and stopping the Web server daemon, you can also use it to check your configuration or see how well your Apache server is running. These options are configtest, status, fullstatus, start, startssl, graceful, and stop.

This starts Apache:

```
# apachectl start
```

The following command starts Apache with SSL support:

```
# apachectl startssl
```

You must have SSL support in your Apache setup for this to work.

This next command stops Apache, terminating all open connections immediately:

```
# apachectl stop
```

To do a "graceful restart," allowing existing HTTP connections to complete and then restart Apache, use this command:

```
# apachectl graceful
```

It can take a long time to complete, however.

This next command gives you a status screen, full of detailed information about your server's current condition:

```
# apachectl fullstatus
```

It requires lynx(1) (available in /usr/ports/www/lynx).

The next command gives you a quick-and-dirty status report, also in lynx:

```
# apachectl status
```

This next command runs `apachectl configtest`.

```
# apachectl restart
```

If the configuration is acceptable, it kills all httpd processes immediately and then restarts Apache.

The next command checks your Apache configuration and will tell you if there's something wrong with httpd.conf or one of its related files:

```
# apachectl configtest
```

Many other apachectl subcommands call configtest before acting, just to be sure that Apache will successfully restart.

### Other Ways to Control Httpd

The apachectl program doesn't work well when you are running a heavily customized Apache instance. For example, if you combine FrontPage with SSL, Apache expects to be started with arguments for both. While you could use apachectl configtest, stop, restart, and graceful, you would have to specify all the various flags for these add-on modules in a way that apachectl accepts, which can be a pain. Using the httpd command directly is much simpler in these cases.

While httpd has many command-line options, the one that concerns us most is -D, which *defines* behavior for the server. For example, to tell Apache to start with SSL support, you would use the following command:

```
# httpd -DSSL
```

To start Apache with FrontPage support, use -Dfp:

```
# httpd -Dfp
```

As you might guess, you can combine these:

```
# httpd -DSSL -Dfp
```

The exact define you need will be described in the Apache module's documentation.

**NOTE**    *I've seen some heavily moduled servers that require nine or ten -D statements to start properly. If your server starts picking up modules, edit /usr/local/etc/rc.d/apache.sh to manage Apache properly, and use that to control the server, rather than using apachectl.*

### Apache Modules

Apache is a modular server, which means that you can add and remove pieces of server code. Apache can handle such diverse things as Microsoft FrontPage Extensions, scripting languages such as PHP, and embedded Perl. There are also such things as Apache modules to compress each page before you send it, vastly decreasing bandwidth. Each module is a port under /usr/ports/www. Module port names begin with "mod_", such as mod_gzip.

*In most cases, a module requires its own configuration information. To simplify your life, you can put the configuration in a separate file and have httpd.conf pull it in with* Include *statements. This way, when you alter a module, you know where everything is.*

Here are some of the popular Apache modules. Each is available on FreeBSD as a port of the same name, under /usr/ports/www. For example mod_gzip can be found in /usr/ports/www/mod_gzip.

| | |
|---|---|
| mod_dav | Provides DAV (Distributed Authoring and Versioning) services. |
| mod_dtcl | Integrates a Tcl (Tool Command Language) interpreter with Apache, allowing rapid processing of Tcl CGI scripts. |
| mod_gzip | Compresses data before it's sent, if the browser supports it. This is well worth installing. |
| mod_mp3 | Turns Apache into an MP3 streaming server. |
| mod_perl | Embeds Perl into your Apache server, allowing rapid handling of Perl CGI scripts. |
| mod_php3 | Provides support for the PHP scripting language, version 3. |
| mod_php4 | Provides support for the PHP scripting language, version 4. |
| mod_python | Embeds Python into your Apache server, for rapid handling of Python CGIs. |
| mod_ruby | Embeds Ruby into Apache, permitting rapid handling of Ruby CGIs. |

There are many other modules, but these are my favorites.

### FrontPage and SSL

Microsoft's FrontPage poses a particular problem because, unfortunately, Microsoft's support for FrontPage Extensions on platforms other than its own is spotty at best. If you're interested in supporting FrontPage, install Microsoft's FrontPage Extensions module, apache13-fp port. It's very difficult to add this module later. Similarly, the Secure Sockets Layer (or SSL) module has a large footprint in Apache. (Not nearly as bad as FrontPage, mind you!) If you want SSL, aka *https* or *secure Web pages*), install the apache13-modssl port.

You might note that this leaves out the possibility of combining SSL and FrontPage, and you'd be right. Combining these at once is not for the faint of heart or for the inexperienced. Don't combine them until you're comfortable with both systems separately.

When the time comes for you to combine FrontPage with SSL, grab the latest version of the FrontPage Extensions from ftp://ftp.microsoft.com/products/frontpage. Extract the tarball and follow the instructions. If you run into problems, check the FreeBSD-isp mailing list archives. They're the people who are most likely to have experience with the latest versions.

# Virtual Hosting

Virtual hosting is having one server handle multiple Web sites. The server is configured to handle Web requests for each of these domains, and it returns the appropriate page for the domain. Many companies need a very small Web site, containing just a few pages of information and perhaps a CGI script or two to process requests for information. This is an excellent application for virtual hosts. I've had FreeBSD boxes handle thousands of these small domains without breaking a sweat or putting the system load up over 0.2. When each of those sites pays $9.95 a month to handle a couple dozen hits a day, you're quickly looking at real money on inexpensive hardware.

One common stumbling block to understanding virtual hosts is the belief that the "www" in a URL is some sort of magic incantation that points to a Web site. This is a common, but incorrect, idea. When you type a URL, such as http://www.AbsoluteBSD.com, you're telling your Web browser to go look for a machine named www.AbsoluteBSD.com, connect to port 80, and see what it has to offer. You could type in http://mail.AbsoluteBSD.com, and the client would look for a machine with that name.

The trick underlying a virtual host is very simple: Many hostnames point to one machine. The problem on the server side is to differentiate between the requests for multiple domains, and then to serve up the appropriate pages. This leads to two different styles of virtual hosts: name-based and IP-based.

### Name-Based Virtual Hosts

Modern Web browsers, such as Netscape 3 and Internet Explorer 4 and later, include the name of the Web site that they're trying to reach when they request a Web page from a server. This makes it possible for the server to differentiate between requests for the various Web sites it serves. If you are fairly sure that your clients are not using Netscape 2 or Internet Explorer 3, you can tell your server to use these names to identify virtual hosts. Name-based virtual hosts are the standard almost everywhere, and should be your standard unless you have a good reason otherwise.

Place your virtual host configuration at the end of the httpd.conf file, or even in a separate file (using the httpd.conf keyword Include to pull that file in). Do not mix your virtual host configurations with your main server configuration, or you will get quite confused when you have to sort it out.

To configure name-based virtual hosts, first tell Apache which IP address to use for them with the NameVirtualHost httpd.conf directive. While multiple name-based virtual hosts can live on one IP address, Apache must know which IP address to bind these to:

```
NameVirtualHost 192.168.33.254
```

Once this is set, any requests that come in to that IP address will be treated as a named virtual-host request. Now you have to tell Apache where to get information on each virtual host. At the very least, each virtual host needs the name of the Web site and the directory where the HTML documents for that Web site can be found. Here's an example of a basic virtual host that only needs these two items:

```
<VirtualHost 192.168.33.254>
  ServerName www.absolutebsd.com
  DocumentRoot /home/mwlucas/www
</VirtualHost>
```

The `<VirtualHost>` and `</VirtualHost>` labels tell Apache that the information between them is for a single virtual host, and they include the IP address of the virtual host.

The `ServerName` directive tells Apache the name of this virtual host. The server uses this entry to handle requests for www.AbsoluteBSD.com.

Finally, the `DocumentRoot` entry tells Apache where to find the HTML documents that make up this site.

It works this way: When a browser sends a Web request to the virtual host IP address of 192.168.33.254 and asks for www.AbsoluteBSD.com, Apache pulls the documents out of the directory /home/mwlucas/www and returns them to the client.

### IP-Based Virtual Hosts

Not all browsers send the site name along with the Web request. In fact, this was the standard in the earlier days of the Internet (Netscape 2 and Internet Explorer 3), when IP addresses were so plentiful it seemed they could never run out. Browser clients assumed that they could just make a connection to the Web server on port 80, and the only thing that would be on that port was that particular site.

You might think that that time vanished with the Apple II and Betamax, but no. In 2001 I came across a corporate network that had 12,000 desktops running a Mosaic-based Web browser on Windows for Workgroups. This browser is so old that it expected every Web site to have a unique IP address and did not transmit the site name with the Web request. And the company's intranet Web server had to support these clients. While you'll probably never have to worry about these sorts of clients on the public Internet, you should still know how to configure them in case you encounter this sort of situation.

Additionally, sites that use SSL expect to have a single hostname for a single IP. To combine SSL with virtual hosts, you must use IP-based virtual hosts.

To use IP-based virtual hosts, specify the IP address in the `VirtualHost` space, much like you do for name-based virtual hosts. This looks exactly like the `VirtualHost` setup used by name-based virtual hosts, except that the IP address in the `VirtualHost` space is unique. The only difference between setting up an IP-based virtual host and a name-based virtual host is that IP-based virtual hosts don't need the `NameVirtualHost` directive.

Here's a minimal setup of an IP-based virtual host:

```
<VirtualHost 209.69.178.18>
ServerName www.blackhelicopters.org
DocumentRoot /home/mwlucas/www2
</VirtualHost>
```

Any request that arrives at port 80 on the IP address 209.69.178.18 will receive the HTML in /home/mwlucas/www2.

### Tweaking Virtual Hosts

Once you have the minimal virtual hosts (described in the previous sections) working, you can add additional touches to them. Here we'll discuss various virtual-host options that will work with both IP-based and name-based virtual hosts, and how they can be used.

#### Port Numbers

Different documents can be served on different ports. (You've probably seen this before, when a hostname in a URL has a colon followed by a number.) If Apache is listening on ports 80 and 81, for example, you could have a different virtual host on each port, as long as you add the port number after the IP address in the VirtualHost directive.

For example, here's a configuration that creates two different sites (http://www.AbsoluteBSD.com and http://data.AbsoluteBSD.com:8080) using two similar virtual hosts on different ports. Both sites are on the same IP address, but on different ports.

```
<VirtualHost 209.69.178.18:80>
ServerName www.AbsoluteBSD.com
DocumentRoot /home/mwlucas/www
</VirtualHost>
<VirtualHost 209.69.178.18:8080>
ServerName data.AbsoluteBSD.com
DocumentRoot /home/mwlucas/data
</VirtualHost>
```

#### Virtual Host Logs

By default, virtual hosts write their logs to the default Apache log, but you might want to split the logs out by virtual host. (This is common when you're running a commercial Web server and want each customer to get their own logs.) Do so with the `ErrorLog` and `TransferLog` directives, both of which take the name of the log file as an argument:

```
<VirtualHost 209.69.178.18:80>
ServerName www.AbsoluteBSD.com
DocumentRoot /home/mwlucas/www
ErrorLog /home/mwlucas/absolutebsd.com-error-log
TransferLog /home/mwlucas/absolutebsd.com-access-log
</VirtualHost>
```

The TransferLog directive can also take the type of information to be logged as a second argument. We saw the standard log styles in the discussion of the `LogFormat` directive (in the "Log Format" section) earlier in this chapter.

### Options and AllowOverride

By default, virtual hosts inherit the `Options` and `AllowOverride` settings of the root directory. As a reminder, here's a sample configuration for the root directory:

```
<Directory />
    Options AuthConfig Limit
    AllowOverride none
</Directory>
```

All Web sites and all directories on this server have default `Options` of `AuthConfig` and `Limit`, and do not permit any of the `AllowOverride` settings. To override these for a virtual host, use the `Options` and `AllowOverride` statements within the virtual host description. (You can use any option that is valid in the main server configuration on a virtual host.)

By overriding these options, you can set server access on a client-by-client basis; for example, you could allow server-side includes on one virtual host, but not on others. The following virtual host has its own `Options` settings that override the server's default settings:

```
<VirtualHost 209.69.178.18>
ServerName data.AbsoluteBSD.com
DocumentRoot /home/mwlucas/data
Options Limit IncludesNOEXEC
</VirtualHost>
```

Now that you can configure virtual hosts for clients, they'll want to upload files (typically via FTP).

# .NET on FreeBSD

.NET is a technology that is expected to be popular for writing Web-based programs. (Technically, Microsoft's official .NET platform is .NET Server.)

.NET is an implementation of the ECMA Common Language Infrastructure (CLI), a standard created and promoted by Microsoft. Microsoft has released a separate implementation of the CLI that runs on both FreeBSD and Windows 2000, called the Shared Source Common Language Infrastructure (SSCLI), and code-named *Rotor*. Presumably, the Microsoft .NET Server version integrates more tightly with the Microsoft world than this shared-source version does.

As this book is being published, Rotor is available in a beta release. I expect it to be updated regularly. This section discusses the basics of installing the SSCLI on FreeBSD.

### Installing the SSCLI

The SSCLI is available in /usr/ports/lang/cli. At this time, the port only builds properly if you are using /bin/sh as your shell. If you're using another shell, change to /bin/sh to install this port. Then run these commands:

```
# cd /usr/ports/lang/cli
# exec /bin/sh
# export SHELL=/bin/sh
# make install
```

This will download and compile the software, but it won't install because Microsoft allows use of this software only under its license terms. When the software finishes compiling, it will warn you that you must read the license agreement, which you'll find in /usr/ports/lang/cli/work/sscli/license.txt. Read it, and be sure you understand it. Microsoft habitually licenses its software under terms that may be uncomfortable for people accustomed to FreeBSD, and changes those terms as it sees fit.

Once you have read the license, run this command:

```
# make -DI_AGREE_TO_LICENSE_TERMS install
```

**NOTE** *I recommend not running* make clean *as part of the install. The Rotor toolkit includes a lot of source code, documentation, and examples, which you might well need in order to use this experimental software. A* make clean *would remove most of it.*

The preceding command will install the SSCLI under /usr/local, in a subdirectory that will depend on the version of Rotor you are installing. (The first beta version installed in /usr/local/cli-20020326.) Add this directory to your $PATH, and you're ready to run Rotor programs.

FTP, the file transfer protocol, is the classic protocol for moving files from one computer to another over the Internet, and most of your users will want to use it to transfer files to or from servers. Like many other older protocols, FTP has not aged well. You'll find a wide variety of issues with it, and over the years, fixes for these problems have been bolted onto the protocol. While FreeBSD makes handling FTP as easy as possible, you'll still need to do some work with it to keep it chugging along.

### FTP Security

Because FTP transmits passwords and usernames in clear text, anyone with a packet sniffer on the local network will be able to capture FTP usernames and passwords. Nobody except the network administrator should have a packet sniffer on your network, so you're probably all right for regular users. Your users will probably insist on having FTP access, however.

Do not transmit sysadmin passwords over the network in clear text, however. Instead, use scp(1) to upload and download files to and from your account. (We'll look at scp at the end of this chapter.) Scp isn't too popular (yet), and the encryption it uses can overload a server if you have a great number of connections open.

### The FTP Client

FTP is a fairly complex protocol, and, unlike POP3 or SMTP, can't be easily tested. You must use an FTP client to use FTP, and FreeBSD includes one. To connect to a host, just type **ftp** and the hostname.

```
# ftp magpire.blackhelicopters.org
Connected to magpire.blackhelicopters.org.
220 magpire.blackhelicopters.org FTP server (Version 6.00LS) ready.
Name (magpire:mwlucas):
```

The client sends your local username as a default, but you can enter a different username if you need to. It will then ask you for your password:

```
331 Password required for mwlucas.
Password:
230 User mwlucas logged in, access restrictions apply.
Remote system type is UNIX.
Using binary mode to transfer files.
ftp>
```

If everything goes as planned, you should now be logged into the remote server in a shell almost like a command shell. You cannot execute commands, but you can move around and view files using standard UNIX commands, such as ls and cd.

### Downloading with FTP

Use the get command to copy a file from the remote server to your local server, like so:

```
ftp> get .cshrc
local: .cshrc remote: .cshrc
150 Opening BINARY mode data connection for '.cshrc' (767 bytes).
100% |*************************************************|   767        00:00 ETA
226 Transfer complete.
767 bytes received in 0.00 seconds (173.42 KB/s)
ftp>
```

As you watch, your FTP client will open a connection to move the file over. You'll see a line of asterisks move across your screen as the file is moved, and an ETA line that will update with the length of time remaining in the download. When the file transfer is finished, you'll get a notification, the size of the file moved, and an FTP prompt.

### Uploading with FTP

Use the put command to copy a file from your local system to the remote system. Its output looks much like the example above, so I won't repeat that here.

### Moving Multiple Files

Use the mget and mput commands to move multiple files at once. For example, here's how you'd move all of the files with .txt extensions in your current directory:

```
ftp> mget *.txt
```

### Disabling the Prompts

By default, ftp will prompt you to confirm that you really want to move each file. But if you're pulling down a directory with dozens or hundreds of files, you almost certainly don't want to be asked to confirm each one. You can turn the verification on and off with the prompt command.

```
ftp> prompt
Interactive mode off.
ftp> mget *
```

In this example, we are downloading all the files in the current directory without asking for verification for each one.

### Binary and ASCII Transfers

The difference between binary and ASCII transfers is one big source of confusion, resulting from the different handling of the return and newline characters. DOS systems and UNIX systems have long disagreed on how to mark the end of a line, as you may have seen when moving files between the two. If you do an Internet search, you'll find many documents describing the issue in all its painful detail, and many articles from one side denouncing the other for being Just Plain Wrong. All you need to know is how to live with the problems they cause.

UNIX systems default to using binary transfers, while Windows-based systems default to using ASCII. You can tell an FTP server to use binary transfers with the `bin` command, and ASCII with the `a` command.

Basically, you can successfully transfer both binary and ASCII files in binary mode. You can transfer ASCII files with ASCII mode, but binary files transferred in ASCII mode will be corrupted. Binary mode works for everything, so use it.

### Viewing Files

Finally, we have the question of looking at files. The `less` command displays the contents of a file, one page at a time, which allows you to scan things, such as index and readme files to learn exactly what you need to download.

## The FTP Server

Now that you know how to do basic file transfer with FTP, let's look at how to provide basic FTP services.

By default, FreeBSD runs the FTP daemon from inetd. Most systems don't get many FTP requests, and inetd can easily handle the few requests that do arrive. If you won't be supporting more than a few simultaneous FTP sessions, the default settings will work well.

However, if you're running a high-capacity FTP server and will be servicing dozens, hundreds, or even thousands of simultaneous connections, running FTP from inetd will just add additional system overhead. You'll run into inetd's bottlenecks and rate-limiting, and find that your users are unhappy.

To solve these problems, you need to pull ftpd out of inetd. Set up ftpd to run in *standalone* mode, where it is permanently listening to the network and handling requests itself.

### Setting Up Standalone Ftpd

To run ftpd in standalone mode, first disable inetd's ftpd by commenting out the appropriate line in /etc/inetd.conf. We do this because only one program can run on a TCP port at one time. Since inetd starts before any local programs, it would tie up the FTP TCP ports; your standalone ftpd would not be able to run.

Next, you need to tell ftpd it is running in standalone mode, by using the -D flag. You can do so by starting ftpd automatically at boot with a script in /usr/local/etc/rc.d, just like other standalone or add-on programs. A sample script would look like this:

```
#!/bin/sh

/usr/libexec/ftpd -D
```

Users can then make FTP connections to transfer files. That's really it! Everything else is tweaking your FTP server.

### Logging Ftpd Usage

The ftp daemon has a variety of logging functions. If you specify -l once (the default in /etc/inetd.conf), ftpd will log all successful and unsuccessful login attempts. If you specify it twice, ftpd will log all FTP activities: downloads, uploads, directory creation and removal, and any other file alterations.

Add these options to the end of the ftpd command line in your startup script. If you wanted ftpd to run in standalone mode, and to log all FTP activity, your script would include the following line:

```
/usr/libexec/ftpd -D -ll
```

### Disabling Server Changes

You might want to prevent users from uploading files or changing the server's filesystem in any way. This is good for a server that only provides downloads, such as a corporate document server or a mirror site. To do so, use the -r flag.

### Caging Users

One common concern with FTP is that it can allow users to download arbitrary files on the system, and that FTP passwords can be sniffed. You don't want your system compromised because some doofus user handed out his password!

To prevent users from digging around on your system, you can *cage* (or *chroot*) them into their home directories. When caged, a user can FTP into the system and upload, download, or change files in his home directory (or its sub-directories) only. If the user tries to visit a directory outside of the home directory, however, the system will not allow it. This is much like a small jail, which we discussed in Chapter 8.

Chroot is useful for Web servers that have multiple clients on one machine. After all, the users only need to see their own directory, not anyone else's.

#### Chrooting Users

To cage a user, add the username(s) to the file /etc/ftpchroot. Each time a user logs in with ftp, the user's account is checked against the contents of /etc/ftpchroot. If the username appears there, the user is locked into her home directory. Caged users have complete control in their home directory, and can create how-ever many subdirectories and store as many files as their disk space allows; they simply cannot leave their home directory and go exploring the system.

#### Chrooting Groups of Users

Users who are members of a group listed in /etc/ftpchroot are caged as well. (Group names have an at sign (@) in front of them.) You can list a group in /etc/login.access and disallow SSH logins, and all users in that group will be pretty tightly chained.

For example, suppose we have a system with two junior system administrators, Phil and Chris. These administrators should be loading files only into their home directories. Similarly, we have a group of clients who maintain their own Web sites. These clients are all in the webclients group, listed in /etc/group. To chroot all of these users, set up /etc/ftpchroot like this:

```
phil
chris
@webclients
```

### Disallowing FTP Access

The name of the /etc/ftpusers file is rather deceptive; rather than containing a list of allowed users, it contains a list of users who are *not* allowed to log in with FTP. FreeBSD's default /etc/ftpusers lists a variety of system accounts, such as root and nobody.

You can list groups in this file by prefacing them with the @ symbol. For example, you could disallow members of the wheel group from using FTP. (People who can use the root password should not be transmitting their passwords in clear text!)

### Connection Messages

When a client first makes an FTP connection, the contents of /etc/ftpwelcome are displayed. You can put legal warnings, capacity statements, obscenities, and threats, or whatever else you like in here, and users will see it before they even get a login prompt. This is an excellent place to put an "unauthorized use disallowed" message, which is actually admissible in court if someone hijacks your services for illegal purposes.

### Welcome Messages

Once a user has logged in, the /etc/ftpmotd file is displayed. Terms of usage are commonly displayed here.

### Setting Up Anonymous FTP Servers

Anonymous FTP sites are a popular way to provide files and documents to the Internet at large. Anonymous FTP sites are frequently hacked, however. While FreeBSD's ftpd is quite robust and secure, you should still take some basic precautions and set your server up properly to avoid problems. Here are some recommendations:

1.  If at all possible, set ftpd to run read-only by starting it with the -r flag.
2.  Use ftpd's -S flag to log all anonymous FTP activity to the file /var/log/ftpd. The file must exist before ftpd will start the log, so you need to run touch /var/log/ftpd to create it.
3.  Create a user called ftp. This user's home directory will be the root of the anonymous FTP directory, and all files must be placed in this directory.

4. Create the directory /home/ftp/pub for the traditional pub folder in an FTP server. If you want users to be able to upload files, make this directory mode 777 (chmod 777 pub). If it's read-only, make this directory mode 444. This will give you basic anonymous FTP.

### A Warning on Anonymous FTP

Allowing just anyone to upload files to your server may seem like a friendly activity. You might have bandwidth to spare, and you might desire to provide a public service. In an ideal world, this would be lovely.

If you allow anyone to store data on your system, however, people can use your FTP server to store illegal software, child porn, or terrorist data. To make it harder for you to find, they can create hidden directories or disguise the data. Even if you go looking through all the crud people will upload, if you see a file labeled FreeBSD FTPd configuration.txt, you're probably going to ignore it; you can't be expected to check every single file. It's not your fault that that file is actually an MPEG of the Gerbil Liberation Front training for their secret mission to cram the president into a wheel and make him run for his life.

NOTE    *FreeBSD includes a variety of FTP servers in /usr/ports/ftp, many of which have nifty features, good-looking Web sites, and devoted user communities. Check the freebsd-security mailing list archives for a discussion of a server before you install it, however, because many popular FTP servers have a history of bad security holes. For example, one popular FTP server has the unofficial tagline of "providing remote root since 1994." Look around, and be choosy.*

# 16

# FILESYSTEMS AND DISKS

The importance of managing filesystems and disks cannot be over-stressed. Disk flexibility and reliability are paramount to the operating system because your disks contain your data. FreeBSD has a variety of filesystems and different ways to handle them. In this chapter, we'll look at the most common things a systems administrator deals with.

## Device Nodes

Device nodes are special files that represent a piece of hardware on the system. They're used as logical interfaces between user programs and either a device driver or the physical device. By using a command on a device node, sending information to a device node, or reading data from a device node, you're telling the operating system to perform an action upon a physical device. These actions can be very different for different devices—after all, writing data to a disk generates very different results than writing data to a sound card! These device nodes can be found in the /dev directory.

Before you can do any work with a disk or disk partitions, you need to know its device name, or the name of the file on the disk that represents it. Device node names are frequently cryptic, and are generally based upon the name of the device driver for that piece of hardware; device driver names are, in turn, usually based upon the chipset used in the device, not upon what the device appears to be. See /dev for examples of many different device nodes.

There are man pages covering most device nodes. The device nodes we're most interested in are those for disk devices of one sort or another. The following list shows the most common device nodes you'll encounter. (See the man page for each if you want the gory details.)

| Device Node | Description |
| --- | --- |
| /dev/fd* | Floppy disks |
| /dev/acd* | IDE CD-ROMs |
| /dev/ad* | IDE hard disks and partitions |
| /dev/cd* | SCSI CD-ROMs |
| /dev/da* | SCSI hard disks and partitions |

### Hard Disks and Partitions

Let's look at IDE disks first. Our first IDE disk is called /dev/ad0. Subsequent disks would be /dev/ad1, /dev/ad2, and so on, and subdivisions of each disk all start with this name[1] and then add something on the end, like /dev/ad0s1b. While you might expect a disk to start off as a monolithic whole, you will see lots of subdivisions if you look in /dev for everything that begins with /dev/ad0:

```
#ls /dev/ad*
/dev/ad0       /dev/ad0s1b    /dev/ad0s1f    /dev/ad0s1h
/dev/ad0s1a    /dev/ad0s1e    /dev/ad0s1g
#
```

So, what are all these subdivisions? Think back to when you allocated disk space for FreeBSD. If you followed the recommendations in this book, you used the whole disk for FreeBSD. You could have created a second chunk of disk for another operating system, or even cut the disk into two FreeBSD sections. These sections are called *partitions* in the Microsoft and Linux world, and *slices* in FreeBSD land. The "s1" in the preceding /dev/ad* listing represents these large partitions, or slices. The drive referenced there has one slice, with further subdivisions marked by letters.

In FreeBSD, a *partition* is a further subdivision inside a slice, and as part of the install, you created partitions inside the slice. Each partition has a unique device node created by adding a unique letter to the slice device node. For example, partitions inside the slice /dev/ad0s1 show up as /dev/ad0s1a, /dev/ad0s1b, /dev/ad0s1e, and so on. Each of the partitions you created during the install—/usr, /var, and so on—is assigned to one of these partition device nodes.

[1] As is very common in computers, the first disk is device number 0, the second disk is device number 1, and so on.

Partition device nodes can be assigned almost arbitrarily, with some exceptions. Traditionally the node ending in "a" (in our example, /dev/ad0s1a) is the root partition, and the node ending in "b" (/dev/ad0s1b) is the swap space. The "c" label indicates the entire slice, from beginning to end, though you can assign "d" through "h" to any partition you like. You can only have eight partitions in one slice, and you can have up to four slices per drive.

For example, the device node /dev/ad0s1a is disk number 0, slice 1, partition 1, and is probably the root filesystem. The device node /dev/ad1s2b is on disk 2, and is probably a swap slice.

SCSI drives have slices and partitions just like IDE drives, but their device nodes are slightly different. Instead of beginning with /dev/ad, SCSI hard drives have names beginning with /dev/sd. For example, the second slice on your third SCSI hard drive is /dev/sd2s2.

**NOTE** *Here and there you'll see the word traditional. This means that it's the way things are usually done. Whenever possible, it's a good idea to stick with the tradition. You don't want some junior systems administrator tripping over your nontraditional disk layout and telling the system to swap on your data partition, now do you?*

## The /etc/fstab File

The filesystem table lists every filesystem on your computer's hard drives, showing where each filesystem is mounted and any special options that mount(8) uses. Each filesystem appears on a separate line in /etc/fstab, as shown in the following sample:

```
#more /etc/fstab
# Device            Mountpoint    FStype   Options      Dump    Pass#
/dev/ad0s1b         none          swap     sw           0       0
/dev/ad0s1a         /             ufs      rw           1       1
/dev/ad0s1f         /test1        ufs      rw           2       2
/dev/ad0s1g         /test2        ufs      rw           2       2
/dev/ad0s1h         /usr          ufs      rw           2       2
/dev/ad0s1e         /var          ufs      rw           2       2
/dev/acd0c          /cdrw         cd9660   ro,noauto    0       0
/dev/acd1c          /cdrom        cd9660   ro,noauto    0       0
proc                /proc         procfs   rw           0       0
#
```

The first field in the preceding listing gives the device name, which was discussed earlier.

The second field lists the mount point (the directory where this filesystem is found). This is usually something like /usr, /var, and so on, though some special partitions, such as swap spaces, have a mount point of none.

Next is the filesystem type. The standard FreeBSD partition uses type FFS, the UNIX Fast File System (ufs). Other options include, but aren't limited to, msdos (FAT partitions), mfs (Memory File System), and cd9660 (CD-ROM). Before you can mount a filesystem, you must know how it's formatted. (As you might guess, trying to mount a DOS floppy as a UNIX filesystem will not give satisfactory results.)

The fourth field shows the mount options used on this filesystem. The mount options describe special ways you want the kernel to treat the filesystem. We'll discuss mount options in more detail later in this chapter, but here are a few special mount options used only by /etc/fstab:

ro      The filesystem is mounted as read-only. Not even root can write to it.

rw      The filesystem is mounted as read-write. This is the standard noasync mount. (Noasync is explained shortly, in the "FFS Mount Types" section.)

noauto  The boot process will not automatically mount the partition at boot, or when mount -a is run. This option is used for CD-ROM and floppy-disk drives, which might not have media in them.

The dumpfield tells the dump(8) program whether or not this filesystem needs dumping. If this field equals 0, dump won't back up the filesystem. Otherwise, the number given is the minimum dump level needed to back up the filesystem. (See Chapter 3 for details.)

The last field, Pass#, tells the system when to mount the filesystem during the boot process. Filesystems with a Pass# of 0 will not be mounted automatically at boot. Only the root filesystem has a Pass# of 1, and it is mounted first; all other filesystems have a Pass# of 2, which means that they should be mounted after the root filesystem is mounted.

In the previous example, /dev/ad0s1b is a swap partition, and /dev/ad0s1e is mounted as /var. You might notice that there are two CD-ROM drives: /dev/acd0c and /dev/acd1c (one is actually a CD-ROM burner). You will need to know which partition is on which device node to manipulate disk partitions.

## Disk Basics

All filesystems have certain things in common, not least of which is the disk drive, that rectangular thing with connectors at one end.

The disk drive is basically a little magic box. If you treat it badly, you can hear the magic screech and grind. When you mistreat it enough, you might even let the magic smoke out, and the drive will never run again. To really understand filesystems, you need to know a little bit about the incantations going on inside that magic box, so let's have a look. (If you have a dusty old disk drive that you no longer have respect for, feel free to crack the case and follow along.)

**NOTE** *The following is a generalization, of course, and many of you probably already know far more than this.*

When you open the hard drive's case you'll find a stack of round disks, commonly called *platters*. When the disk drive is on, these platters (commonly made of glass or plastic) spin at thousands of revolutions per minute (RPM). The RPM count on hard drives is a measure of platter rotation speed.

The platters are covered with a layer of magnetic material, which itself is usually covered in iron oxide.[2] This magnetic material is arranged in thousands of circular rings, called *tracks*, that extend from the platter's inner core to its outer edge, much like growth rings in a tree. These tracks hold data as strings of zeros and ones. Each track is subdivided into *sectors*, and each sector on the outer tracks holds more data than that same sector on an inner track, and it takes less time to read the same amount of data on an outer track than on an inner track because any point on an outer track is moving faster.

Heads sit over each platter, and all data written to or read from the platters passes through those heads. As a rule, these heads can read and write data quickly, but they have to wait for the disk to move into the proper position under them so that the data can be transferred. Drive performance basically boils down to how quickly those rusty platters can move under the drive heads, which is why RPM is so important.

Each track holds blocks of data, the size and placement of which restricts how efficiently the filesystem works and what sorts of files it can best handle. Each filesystem uses its own particular index to record the placement of data on the platters, and one operating system can't necessarily read another's index. (DOS used a single File Allocation Table (FAT), later expanded to FAT12, FAT16, FAT32, and so on.) The UNIX Fast File System (FFS) uses many scattered index nodes, or *inodes*, instead.

## The Fast File System

FreeBSD's filesystem, the Fast File System (FFS) is a direct descendant of the filesystem shipped with BSD4.4. (In fact, as of this writing, one of the original filesystem authors is still developing the FreeBSD filesystem, adding a lot of the nifty features we'll discuss shortly.) FFS is sometimes called UFS for UNIX File System, and many system utilities still call FFS partitions UFS.

NOTE   *FFS has moved from BSD into several other vendors. If a UNIX vendor doesn't specifically tout their "improved, advanced" filesystem, they're almost certainly running the BSD filesystem.*

FFS is designed to be fast and reliable, and to handle the most common (and uncommon) situations as effectively as possible. FreeBSD ships FFS configured to be as widely useful as possible on relatively modern hardware, but you can choose to optimize it for trillions of small files or a half-dozen 30GB files, if you choose. You don't have to know a huge amount about FFS's internals, but you should know a few basics. To begin with, it helps to know that FFS divides the disk into inodes and blocks.

---

[2] Yes, iron oxide is rust. Please do not add rust to your platters to make them hold more data; I proved it doesn't work many years ago.

**Inodes**  Inodes contain very basic information about files, including permissions, size, and so on, as well as a list of the blocks in the file. Collectively, the data in an inode is known as *metadata*, which is simply data about data.

**Blocks**  Blocks contain the file's actual data.

While inodes contain lots of different information, all you need to know is that they're the *index* of the file on the disk. They are what allows the operating system to find the information it's attempting to retrieve.

### Vnodes

Inodes and blocks worked wonderfully back in the early days of UNIX. As years passed, however, it became normal to swap disks between different machines and even different operating systems. CD-ROMs, with their unique layout, became popular; floppy disks slowly converged on FAT32 as a standard; and other UNIXes developed their own variant filesystems. Because BSD needed to speak to all these different systems, another layer of abstraction was needed.

That abstraction was the virtual node, or *vnode*. You never manipulate vnodes directly, but you'll see references to them throughout the system documentation, so it's important to know what they are. The vnode is a translator between the kernel and whatever sort of filesystem you've mounted. When you write a file to an FFS filesystem, the vnode talks to an inode. When you write a file to a Microsoft-style FAT filesystem, the vnode talks to the file allocation table. (Vnodes are actually used for far more than talking to the filesystem, but we won't get into that here.)

Every tool that reads and writes to disks actually does so through vnodes, which map the data to the appropriate filesystem for the underlying media. You'll see references to inodes only when dealing with FFS filesystems, but you'll see vnodes when you deal with any filesystem.

### FFS Mount Types

Unlike Windows or Macintosh filesystems, FFS partitions can be treated in several different ways depending on how they're mounted. The manner in which a partition is mounted is called the *mount type*. Remember that, as discussed in "Device Nodes," earlier in this chapter, you must know a filesystem's physical device name in order to mount it. And an unmounted filesystem cannot be accessed. You cannot read it, write to it, or see it in any way. You're stuck.

To change the boottime mount options on a partition, add the options to the appropriate line in /etc/fstab in the "options" column.

#### Read-Only Mounts

If you only want to look at the contents of a disk, and not write to it, you can mount the partition as read-only (or rdonly). This is unquestionably the safest way to mount a disk, and one of the most useless ways to mount a disk for many server uses, because you cannot alter the data or write new data.

Many systems administrators mount the root partition, and perhaps even /usr, as read-only to minimize any potential system damage from a loss of power. Even if you lose the physical hard drive due to a power surge or some other hardware failure, the data on the platters remains intact. That's the advantage of read-only mounts; the disadvantage is that it makes maintenance far more difficult because you can't write to read-only mounted disks!

### Synchronous Mounts

Synchronous (or sync) is the old-fashioned way of mounting a filesystem. When a disk is synchronously mounted, you can read from it much as you would expect, but when you write to it, the kernel waits to see whether the write is actually completed before telling the program that the write is completed. If it isn't completed, the program can choose to act appropriately.

Synchronous mounting provides the greatest data integrity in the case of a crash, but it is also slow. ("Slow" is a relative term these days, when even a cheap disk can outperform what was the top end several years ago.) Consider using synchronous mounting when you wish to be truly pedantic on data integrity, but in most cases it's truly overkill.

### Asynchronous Mounts

For faster access at a higher risk of data loss, mount your partitions asynchronously (async). When a disk is asynchronously mounted, the kernel writes data to the disk, and tells the program that the write was successful without waiting for the disk to confirm that the data was actually written. Asynchronous is fine on disposable machines, but don't use it with important data.

### Noasync Mounts

Finally, we have a method that combines sync and async, called noasync; this is FreeBSD's default. When using noasync, data that affects inodes is written to disk synchronously, while the actual data is handled asynchronously. Noasync is used in combination with soft updates (see the "Soft Updates" section later in the chapter) to create a truly robust filesystem.

## FFS Mount Options

FreeBSD supports several *mount options* in addition to the mount types. While you don't need to know the details of all of the mount options, you should at least know that they exist, should you encounter a circumstance that requires one.

noatime    Every file on FFS includes an access-time stamp, called the *atime*, which records when the file was last accessed. If you have a large number of files and don't need this data, you can mount the disk noatime and not have this time-stamp updated.

noexec    The noexec mount option prevents any binaries from being executed on this partition. Mounting /home noexec can help to prevent users from installing and running their own programs, but for it to be effective, be sure to also noexec mount /tmp, /var/tmp, and any other places that they can write files.

**nosuid**   The nosuid option prevents setuid programs from running on your system. Setuid programs allow users to run programs as if they're another user. For example, some programs (such as login(1)) must be run by root, but if you make login setuid, anyone can run it and it will work.

Setuid programs obviously must be carefully written so that they can't be exploited and used to get unauthorized access to your system. As such, many administrators habitually disable all unneeded setuid programs. You can use nosuid to do so, but it will be useless if you have a script wrapper that allows you to run scripts as setuid, such as suidperl, on the system.

**nosymfollow**   The nosymfollow option disables symlinks, or aliases, to files. (Symlinks are mainly used to create aliases to files that reside on other partitions, anyway.) To create an alias to another file on the same partition mounted nosymfollow, use a regular ln(1)-style link.

**nodev**   Finally, the nodev option disallows using any device nodes on the filesystem, which can help prevent mistakes if you're accessing a drive used by another UNIX. Disallowing device nodes on filesystems that shouldn't have them cannot hurt. In most cases, the only partition that should have device nodes is root (/).

If you've mounted a hard drive native to another UNIX, be sure to mount it as nodev. Accidentally accessing a device node native to another operating system will almost certainly crash or damage your system!

You cannot use jails on a partition mounted as nodev; remember, jails have their own minimal set of device nodes.

## What's Mounted Now?

How do you determine what you have mounted on your system? Well, you can start by running mount(8) without any options. This gives you a list of all mounted filesystems:

```
# mount
/dev/ad0s1a on / (ufs, local, soft-updates)

/dev/ad0s1f on /test1 (ufs, local, soft-updates)
/dev/ad0s1g on /test2 (ufs, local, soft-updates)
/dev/ad0s1h on /usr (ufs, local, soft-updates)
/dev/ad0s1e on /var (ufs, local, soft-updates)
procfs on /proc (procfs, local)
#
```

Here we see that our filesystems are almost all standard FFS partitions that are all mounted locally with soft updates enabled. (We'll look at soft updates later in the chapter.) If you're using features such as SMB (see Chapter 21) or the Network File System to mount partitions, they'll show up here. This is another quick way to get the device names for each of your partitions.

You can also do more interesting tasks with mount, as we'll see later. First, though, let's look at what can go wrong with your partitions.

# Dirty Disks

No, disks don't get muddy through use (although dust on a platter will quickly damage it, and adding water certainly won't help). A dirty disk partition is one that's in a kind of limbo: The operating system has asked for information to be written to it, but the data is yet to be written completely. Part of the data block may have been written, the inode might have been edited but the data not written out, or any combination of the two.

If the power goes out while you're writing to disk, the system will come back up with "unclean disks."

## Fsck

FreeBSD includes a very powerful filesystem checking tool, fsck(8). When a rebooting system finds a dirty disk, it automatically checks the disk and tries to clean everything up. You will lose any data that was not written to the disk, but fsck will do its best to clean what you have. If successful, everything should be right where you left it—except for that unwritten data.

### Failed Automatic Fscks

Occasionally the reboot will fail, and you'll be left staring at a single-user prompt asking you to run fsck manually. At this point, you have a few choices. If you enter fsck, fsck will check every block and inode on the disk. It will probably find any number of blocks that have become disassociated from their inodes, and will make a good guess as to how they fit together and how they should be attached. It won't be able to tell which directory these files belong in, however.

Fsck will ask if you want to perform this reattachment. If you answer "n", it deletes the damaged files. If you answer "y", it will add the disassociated file to a lost-and-found directory (such as /usr/lost+found) on the partition on which they were found, with a number as a filename. Use grep in that directory to search your missing files by content or, if there are only a few files, have a look at them with a tool such as more(1) to identify them.

### Turning Off the Fsck Prompt

If your disk was in the middle of a very busy operation when it became dirty, you could end up with many, many disassociated files. Rather than spend an hour typing "y" over and over again to tell fsck to attempt to place these files, run fsck -y at the single-user prompt. This tells fsck that you're answering "y" to every question, and it's much easier than sitting there typing "y" repeatedly.

> **NOTE** *At times when running experimental filesystems on -current, I've had the entire contents of a disk migrate to /usr/lost+found and /var/lost+found thanks to* fsck -y. *Recovery becomes difficult at that point. Having said that, in a production system running FreeBSD-stable, I've never had a problem with an automatic disk repair.*

You can set your system to automatically try a fsck -y on boot. I don't recommend this, though, because if there's the faintest chance of my filesystem winding up in digital heaven, I want to know about it. I want to type the offending command myself and feel the trepidation of watching the fsck run. Besides, it's always unpleasant to find that your system is trashed, without having the faintest clue of what happened. But if you must try it, set the following /etc/rc.conf option:

```
fsck_y_enable="YES"
```

### Avoiding fsck -y

What options do you have if you don't want to use fsck -y? Well, fsdb(8) and clri(8) allow you to debug the filesystem and redirect files to their proper locations. You can restore files to their correct directories and names. This is difficult, though,[3] and is recommended only for Secret Ninja Filesystem Masters.

## Mounting and Unmounting Disks

Mount(8) mounts disk devices onto your filesystem. (Go ahead and boot your FreeBSD machine into single-user mode [see Chapter 3] and follow along.)

On boot, the system mounts the root partition, which gives it enough information to do basic setup and get core systems running before mounting the rest of the filesystems. To do anything interesting in single-user mode, though, you'll need to mount your other filesystems.

### Mounting Standard Filesystems

To mount a filesystem that is listed in /etc/fstab, such as /usr or /var, enter a command like this:

```
# mount /usr
#
```

This mounts /usr as read-write.

### Mounting with Options

To use a separate option, such as read-only, you can use the options flag -o. These options include async, noasync, sync, rdonly, nodev, and noexec, as discussed in the "FFS Mount Types" section earlier. For example, to mount /usr as read-only, enter this:

```
# mount -o rdonly /usr
#
```

[3] I'm using "difficult" much like this: "Climbing Mount Everest wearing sandals and shorts is difficult."

A read-only mount is a great choice for a damaged filesystem. In the past, I've had filesystems that were so badly damaged that they wouldn't fsck. (These were Usenet news servers with hundreds of thousands of articles, and I generally did something to damage them badly. Hey, everybody has to learn somehow.) If you just want to pull some information off the disk without risking further damage to data, you can mount the partition as read-only and copy to your heart's content. (This isn't true in the case of physical disk damage, mind you; if one of the platters is coming apart, you're basically doomed.)

### Forcing Read-Write Mounts

If a partition is marked dirty, you will need to fsck it before mounting it as read-write. While this generally isn't a problem, you may not want to fsck it for various reasons. If so, you can try using the -f flag to force it to mount, though forcing a mount has a good chance of crashing your system, again.

```
# mount -f /usr
#
```

### Mounting All Standard Filesystems

To mount all the filesystems listed in /etc/fstab, use the -a option. (The filesystems will use whatever options are given in /etc/fstab.)

```
# mount -a
#
```

### Mounting at Nonstandard Locations

To mount filesystems at arbitrary locations, specify them by device name and mount point. You might use this option when installing a new disk, such as mounting the old disk partitions as /old/var, /old/home, and so on, so you can copy their contents at your leisure.

```
# mount /dev/fd0 /home/mwlucas/floppy
#
```

### Unmounting

When you have finished with a piece of removable media, eject it with umount(8). Enter the directory where the media is mounted (/home/mwlucas/floppy in the following example) as an argument.

```
# umount /home/mwlucas/floppy
#
```

If you cannot unmount a drive, you're probably accessing it in some way. For example, you cannot unmount a drive while you have a command prompt in a directory on it or while you're reading from or writing to it.

# Soft Updates

Soft updates is the biggest innovation to hit FFS in years. Soft updates organize and arrange disk writes so that the filesystem metadata on the disk remains consistent and it comes close to giving the performance of an async mount with the reliability of a sync mount. While that doesn't mean that the data will all be written to disk—a power failure at the wrong moment will still corrupt data—a soft update will prevent a lot of problems.

### Enabling Soft Updates

If you followed the suggestions in Chapter 1, you installed your system with soft updates enabled. (Running mount without arguments will tell you whether soft updates are turned on.) However, if you didn't turn on soft updates, they're fairly easy to enable—or disable—with the filesystem tuning program tunefs(8). (Tunefs has many other functions, but most of them require in-depth knowledge of the filesystem.)

To enable soft updates, boot your system into single-user mode, unmount the filesystems you want to change, and use tunefs to enable soft updates:

```
# umount /usr
# tunefs -n enable /usr
# mount /usr
```

Now boot into multi-user mode, and you'll have soft updates! Having done this once, the filesystem remembers that it is running soft updates across reboots.

To disable soft updates on a partition, replace the enable in the previous example with disable.

### IDE Write Caching and Soft Updates

Like all filesystems, soft updates works best with SCSI hard drives, due to the robustness of the SCSI architecture. Still, soft updates works as well as the IDE architecture allows, with one critical exception: Many modern IDE drives support *write caching*.

Write-caching IDE drives have a small onboard chip that records data that needs to be written to the drive. This can be tricky for soft updates, because soft updates expects the hard drive to be honest—when the hard drive reports that data is written to disk, it expects that data to be on that platter. But IDE write caching reports when the data is safely stored in the drive's cache, not when it has been written, and it may be a second or more until that data is actually on the disk.

While this differential wouldn't pose a big risk if this only happened on occasion, it occurs continuously on a server. As such, if you care about your data, you should disable write caching by adding the following line to /boot/loader.conf:

```
hw.ata.wc=0
```

While disabling write caching will slow down the IDE drive somewhat, your data will be safe. I safely run with write caching enabled on desktop and laptop machines, where data is not being written to disk continually, but on servers it's a very bad idea to leave IDE write caching on. [4]

## Virtual Memory Directory Caching

When you examine a directory (such as when you run ls), the system needs to build a list of files in the directory—a fairly performance-intensive operation. If you're doing this a lot, you can improve performance by caching the contents of the directory with the sysctl vfs.vmiodirenable.

This option may be on by default in later versions of FreeBSD, but if not, you can set it automatically at boot in /etc/sysctl.conf:

```
vfs.vmiodirenable=1
```

## Mounting Foreign Filesystems

For our purposes, any disk that isn't an FFS partition is a foreign filesystem. Fortunately, FreeBSD includes extensive support for these foreign filesystems, with the caveat that only those functions supported by the filesystem will work. (FAT doesn't support filesystem permissions, for example. You can set filesystem-level security flags on a FAT filesystem all you want, and they won't do a thing.)

Each filesystem has its own unique mount program that handles the vagaries of that filesystem, and each filesystem needs support in the kernel. To make your life a little easier, the mount programs automatically load the appropriate kernel modules as needed.

### Using Foreign Mounts

To mount any foreign filesystems, you need the same information you would need when mounting an FFS filesystem: a device name and a mount point. You also need the name of the command to mount that type of filesystem. (We'll consider the various foreign filesystems and the commands to mount them in the next section.)

For example, to mount a CD-ROM, include a /cdrom mount point and the device name. We'll use the default for the first IDE CD-ROM here, /dev/acd0c.

---

[4] It's just generally a bad idea to use IDE disks in servers, but I think you have the point by now.

```
# mount_cd9660 /dev/acd0c /cdrom
#
```

Once the CD-ROM is mounted, you can read what's on it. Simple enough, eh?

If you try to mount a disk using the wrong mount for its filesystem, you'll get an error. I'm quite used to seeing this when mounting unfamiliar floppies:

```
# mount /dev/fd0 /mnt
mount: /dev/fd0 on /mnt: incorrect super block
#
```

This floppy is MS-DOS-formatted. It works just fine if I use mount_msdos though.

No matter what sort of filesystem you are mounting, you can unmount it with umount(8):

```
# umount /cdrom
#
```

### Foreign Filesystem Types

Here are some of the most commonly used foreign filesystems, along with a brief description of each and the appropriate mount command.

#### MS-DOS

FreeBSD includes extensive support for FAT filesystems, the DOS/Windows 9x File Allocation Table filesystem, commonly used in dual-boot systems and on floppy disks. You can format a floppy disk in FFS, however, so you cannot assume that all floppy disks are MS-DOS formatted. If you try to mount a floppy disk and it won't work as an MS-DOS disk, try to mount it as an FFS disk. (Personally, my only use for floppy disks is to transfer files to and from a Windows machine that I don't control—for example, for taking files to the print shop. I make it my personal standard to always format floppy disks as MS-DOS format.)

The mount command is mount_msdos(8).

If you mount a lot of MS-DOS devices, investigate /usr/ports/tools/mtools, a collection of programs for working with MS-DOS that offers better performance than the default FreeBSD tools.

#### NTFS

The Windows NT/2000/XP standard filesystem, NTFS, is tightly integrated with Microsoft's kernel. To write to an NTFS partition, you must have extensive knowledge of how the filesystem works. Unfortunately, since that information is not available from Microsoft, you can read NTFS partitions but writing may corrupt the partition. The mount command is mount_ntfs(8).

**NOTE** *Since Microsoft holds its filesystem interface so dear, and changes it regularly, don't count on this for frequent use. Using mount_ntfs can damage the filesystem.*

### ISO-9660

ISO-9660 is the standard data CD-ROM filesystem. FreeBSD allows you to read CD-ROMs and to write them if you have a CD-ROM burner. Just about every CD-ROM you will encounter has the ISO-9660 format. The mount command is mount_cd9660(8).

### Ext2fs

The standard Linux filesystem, ext2fs, supports many of the same features as the FreeBSD filesystem, and can be safely written to and read from without any problems. Like the NTFS mounts, ext2fs mounts are quite useful in disaster situations. If an NT or Linux Web server explodes one day, you can slam the hard drive into your working FreeBSD box and copy the data from it. While transferring a physical hard drive isn't exactly the simplest way to transfer data, if a machine is badly damaged, it might be the fastest. Use mount_ext2fs(8) to mount an ext2fs filesystem.

### *Mount Options and Foreign Filesystems*

Rather than using special mount commands for each different filesystem, you can give the type of filesystem as an option to mount(8). To do so, specify the type of filesystem with the -t option. There's no particular advantage or disadvantage to mounting filesystems this way, but it does work.

```
# mount -t cd9660 /dev/acd0c /cdrom
```

## Filesystem Permissions

The method you use to mount a filesystem, and the person who mounts it, control the permissions of the mounted filesystem. For example, both FFS and ext2fs store permissions in the filesystem, mapping them to user IDs (UIDs). Since ext2fs normally behaves much like FFS, and all the permissions information it needs is available within the filesystem, FreeBSD respects its permissions.

NTFS has its own permissions system, however. Since that system bears only coincidental resemblance to that used by UNIX, NTFS permissions are discarded when mounted on a FreeBSD system, and it's treated much like a DOS floppy or CD-ROM.

By default, only root can mount filesystems, and root owns all non-UNIX filesystems. If that's not your preference, you can use the -u and -g flags to control the user ID and group ID of the owner on a file when you're mounting MS-DOS, NTFS, or ISO-9660 filesystems. For example, if you're mounting an MS-DOS floppy for the user "cstrzelc", and want her to be able to edit the contents, you could use this command:

```
# mount_msdos -u cstrzelc -g cstrzelc /dev/fd0 /mnt
#
```

The cstrzelc user now owns the files on the floppy.

*To let a user mount filesystems, set the sysctl* vfs.usermount *to 1 and be sure that the user owns the mount point.*

## Removable Media and /etc/fstab

CD-ROMs are traditionally mounted on /cdrom, and floppy disks are usually mounted on /mnt. To make your life a little easier when mounting media, set up /etc/fstab to reflect this. If a removable filesystem has an entry in /etc/fstab, you can drop the device name when mounting it. This means that you don't have to remember the device name or the exact command to mount that particular filesystem.

```
# mount /mnt
#
```

That would be easier than typing mount_msdos /dev/fd0 /mnt every time, wouldn't it?

When listing removable media in /etc/fstab, be sure to include the noauto flag, or your boot will stop in single-user mode, because there's nothing in the floppy drive or CD-ROM tray!

## Creating a Floppy

What most Windows users think of as "formatting a floppy" is actually a multi-stage process that usually includes formatting the disk, as well as giving it a disk label and a filesystem. You need to perform all of these operations to create a floppy in FreeBSD.

*For our purposes, we'll assume that you have a standard 1.44MB floppy disk, which has been the standard on x86 hardware for over a decade. If you have an 800KB disk, or some other unusual size, you'll have to modify this process somewhat, but the general steps are the same.*

### Low-Level Formatting

To begin formatting your disk, low-level format it with fdformat(1). This program only requires two arguments: the floppy's size and the device name.

```
# fdformat -f 1440 /dev/fd0
Format 1440K floppy `/dev/fd0.1440'? (y/n): y
```

When you type **y**, fdformat will start running a low-level format to prepare the disk to receive a filesystem; it won't create one. Low-level formatting is the slowest part of making a floppy usable.

### Creating an FFS Filesystem

If you're creating an FFS floppy, label the disk with disklabel(8). This writes basic identification information to the floppy, sets partition information, and can even mark a disk as bootable. Marking a disk as bootable doesn't actually put any of the programs that you would need on it, mind you; it simply puts a marker on the disk so that the system BIOS can tell that this disk is bootable.

Making a FreeBSD boot floppy is annoying, and if you need one you should just grab one from the installation media. Here, we'll install a plain disk label without any special characteristics:

```
# disklabel -r -w /dev/fd0 fd1440
#
```

The -r option in this example tells disklabel to access the raw disk, which is necessary because there is no filesystem yet. The -w option tells it to write to the disk: We're writing to /dev/fd0, and installing a standard 1.44MB floppy disk label. (You can find a full list of the floppy disk labels in /etc/disktab, as well as labels for many other types of drive.)

Finally, create a filesystem with newfs(8).

```
# newfs /dev/fd0
Warning: Block size restricts cylinders per group to 6.
Warning: 1216 sector(s) in last cylinder unallocated
/dev/fd0:       2880 sectors in 1 cylinders of 1 tracks, 4096 sectors
        1.4MB in 1 cyl groups (6 c/g, 12.00MB/g, 736 i/g)
super-block backups (for fsck -b #) at:
 32
#
```

### Creating an MS-DOS Filesystem

To swap data between a Windows machine and your FreeBSD box, MS-DOS format your floppy. While you will still need to run fdformat(8), as discussed earlier, you won't need to disklabel your floppy.

```
# newfs_msdos /dev/fd0
/dev/fd0: 2840 sectors in 355 FAT12 clusters (4096 bytes/cluster)
bps=512 spc=8 res=1 nft=2 rde=512 sec=2880 mid=0xf0 spf=2 spt=18 hds=2 hid=0
#
```

**NOTE** *The FFS newfs output looks much more interesting, doesn't it? That's because FFS is a more complex and interesting filesystem than MS-DOS. MS-DOS is easier to use in multiple machines, however. You need to decide what best fits your needs. You can use all sorts of options when creating filesystems; see newfs(8) or newfs_msdos(8) for details.*

# The Basics of SCSI

Throughout this book, I've said repeatedly that SCSI disks are better than IDE. And it's true: SCSI disks are faster, more reliable, and more expensive than IDE or EIDE drives. SCSI disks are also considered more difficult to manage, but much of this difficulty probably comes down to being unfamiliar with the technology. SCSI disks can also do far more than IDE disks, however, which makes them more tricky.

Many new junior sysadmins aren't familiar with handling SCSI systems, so I'm going to spend a little time discussing what you really, really have to know to handle SCSI well.

**NOTE** *If you are seriously interested in SCSI, check out* The Book of SCSI *by Gary Field (No Starch Press).*

## SCSI Types

There are several different types of SCSI: SCSI-1, SCSI-2, Wide, Ultra, LVD, and so on. While the SCSI devices look similar, one look at their connectors will show the difference.

SCSI-1 devices use a 50-pin connector that resembles an IDE cable. More modern SCSI-2 systems use a 68-pin connector that has very small pins and a trapezoidal connection housing. You'll also see external SCSI systems that use other sorts of cables, such as Centronics cables that resemble those on older parallel printers. (If someone hands you a SCSI cable with 25 pins, do not use it, even with an adapter. It will destroy system performance, data integrity, and your peace of mind.)

## SCSI Adapters

To use SCSI, you need a host adapter. This is a plug-in card just like a video card or any other peripheral. Many servers have SCSI adapters installed on the motherboard, much as desktops today have IDE adapters built in, which makes things a bit easier.

The SCSI host adapter is one of the most likely bottlenecks in your system. If you have a slow adapter and fast disks, the adapter wins.

## SCSI Buses

Many parts of your computer have a *bus*, and SCSI is no exception. In simplest terms, a bus is where you plug things in. One of your IDE buses has two ports (the plugs on the IDE cable), and the PCI bus has several (the slots on your motherboard). An old SCSI bus has 8 ports, including one used by the SCSI adapter itself. These ports are the plugs that can be attached to the SCSI cable, and you can plug up to 7 devices into an old SCSI system. A newer SCSI bus has 16 ports (still including the card), and if your system has the space and the power, you can plug 15 devices into it.

Some SCSI cards have attachment spaces for two cables because they have two buses. In these configurations, each bus is treated individually and has a unique number. (If you only have one bus, it still has a unique number, which is 0.)

### Termination and Cabling

SCSI signals travel along the length of the cable. In many electrical systems, including SCSI, a signal that reaches the end of a wire will reflect back along the wire, which is not a good thing in the case of SCSI. As such, you terminate the SCSI bus with a terminator (a small piece of hardware, almost like a cap) that tells the signal to stop without reflecting back along the cable.

SCSI buses must be terminated at each end. Some SCSI devices include an option for "internal termination," which can make things tricky. Since your SCSI bus stops at the first terminator it sees, if you have an internally terminating device in the middle of your bus, you won't see some of your components because the signal will stop.

While it may seem like a pain to find and use external terminators, do so if possible. External termination will save you trouble later when you have to replace a drive.

**NOTE** *Don't put SCSI devices along the cable in a "Y" format. The bus must be in a straight line. Some cables look like they allow you to do this, but these cables are deceptive and should not be used in this way.*

### SCSI IDs and LUNs

A SCSI ID is an address the bus uses to tell signals within the computer where to go. Each device has a unique SCSI ID that identifies it along the bus. On a raw physical level, the bus tags each piece of data with the SCSI ID of its destination. Each SCSI ID must be unique in most systems, and if you have identical ones along the chain, the first device to boot will grab the ID.

Each possible port on the bus has a unique ID. Since this is a computer system, those ID numbers begin with 0 and end at either 7 or 15, depending on the bus. The adapter is typically SCSI ID 7.

Some SCSI systems also support Logical Unit Numbers, or LUNs. This is a clever trick to make it possible to have multiple devices share one SCSI ID. If every component in your SCSI system supports LUNs, you can use them, but every device that shares a SCSI ID must have a unique LUN.

Managing your SCSI system is like sending mail. The bus number is like the city. Your SCSI ID is the street address. If multiple buildings share the same street address, the delivery man will drop his package at the first one he sees. Similarly, the LUN is like an apartment number. (You don't want your packages dropped in the lobby.) If every device on your system has a unique SCSI address, you'll be fine. If it doesn't, stop everything and make sure it does.

# FreeBSD and SCSI

To use SCSI properly with FreeBSD, you'll need to make some kernel changes (see Chapter 4). There are two basic kernel tasks you need to handle: the boot-time SCSI delay and wiring down devices.

### Boot-Time Delay

A SCSI system includes all sorts of intelligent chips to handle data flow along the bus, which can take longer to power up and enable than IDE hardware. As such, FreeBSD includes a delay in the boot process to allow this to happen, and this is controlled by the SCSI_DELAY option:

```
options          SCSI_DELAY=8000
```

The time given, in milliseconds, is set by default to 15000 (or 15 seconds). The amount of time your system requires will depend on your hardware. A delay of 15 seconds is a generous estimate for older hardware. If you have newer SCSI equipment, you can probably reduce this to 5 seconds or so. If you have problems, of course, turn it back up. Using a 15-second delay doesn't hurt anything, and it doesn't indicate problems.

### Wiring Down Devices

The other annoyance is that the FreeBSD kernel numbers the SCSI devices based on the order in which they're found. (Every operating system has to deal with SCSI booting behavior in some way, and this is simply BSD's way.) As such, if you change the devices on your SCSI bus, you could change the order in which they are probed: What was disk 0 when you installed BSD could become disk 1 after you add a new tape drive. This change would cause partitions to be mounted on the wrong mount points.

You can have similar problems with SCSI buses—if you add another SCSI card, your buses can be renumbered! As you might imagine, unmitigated chaos results from either of these problems.

To prevent this problem, you can hard-code this information into the kernel to prevent future confusion, a process called *wiring down* the SCSI devices. To wire down the device, you need the SCSI ID, SCSI bus number, and LUN (if used) of each device on your SCSI chain, available at /var/run/dmesg.boot.

For example, on a test system, I have the following dmesg entries for my SCSI adapter:

```
ahc0: <Adaptec aic7880 Ultra SCSI adapter> port 0xac00-0xacff mem 0xd9000000-
0xd9000fff irq 11 at device 10.0 on pci0
aic7880: Ultra Wide Channel A, SCSI Id=7, 16/255 SCBs
```

The first line of this output shows us that the main SCSI card is an "Adaptec aic7880 Ultra" adapter. The second line gives us more information about the adapter on this card. This is really only one physical card. (You learn a lot about what's actually inside your computer hardware by examining dmesg, don't you?) The host adapter is using SCSI ID 7, and no LUN. By opening the case and looking at the physical card, I can verify that there's only one SCSI bus.

A little later in the dmesg file, I have these entries for my disks:

```
...
❶ da0 at ❷ ahc0 ❸ bus 0 ❹ target 2 ❺ lun 0
...
❻ da1 at ahc0 bus 0 target 8 lun 0
...
```

This tells us that the disk da0 (❶) is on the SCSI card ahc0 (❷). We also know that it is on bus 0 (❸). The "target" is the SCSI ID 2 (❹). Finally, the LUN of this drive is 0 (❺). The second SCSI disk (❻) is on the same SCSI card, on the same bus, and has the same LUN. Its SCSI ID is 8, however.

To wire down a drive, tell the kernel exactly where each disk lives so that the kernel doesn't have to guess how a SCSI device should be numbered:

```
device        da0 at scbus0 target 2 unit 0
device        da1 at scbus0 target 8 unit 0
```

Similarly, you can wire a particular SCSI bus to a particular card, and even to a particular slot on a card. For example, we know that SCSI bus 0 is on ahc0. While this system only has one SCSI card, we don't want a new SCSI card to subvert SCSI bus 0. We can wire this SCSI bus to this particular slot on this card with the following kernel configuration:

```
device        scbus0 at ahc0 bus 0
```

Once you've entered these settings, rebuild your kernel with the proper information, and reboot. You'll see these devices coming up in this configuration, which isn't at all exciting, of course, because that's where you started.

To prove that you've wired your devices to something in the kernel, play with this configuration a little. You might, say, go into your kernel configuration and change all the instances of da0 to da7. After a recompile and a reboot, you'll see a /dev/da1 and a /dev/da7 in your boot messages. (This little test might make it difficult for your system to boot. Don't capriciously change the names of the disk your root and /usr filesystems live on!)

## Adding New Hard Disks

Handling new disks can be something of a pain because you have to format them, give them a filesystem, mount them somewhere, and move your data. You have a couple of different options here to make the first few steps easier. You can use sysinstall(8), which is simple and fast and makes life simpler, or you can do it the ugly command-line way. Being always in a hurry, you'll almost certainly want to use sysinstall.

Sysinstall occasionally has problems with some older disks (usually about 300MB or less). If you're using older disks, you might have no choice but to use the command-line method. In that case, check the FreeBSD Handbook for assistance.

We'll assume that you are adding disks to an existing system, and that your eventual goal is to move some of your current data to this disk. We'll cover two examples: creating a new /usr/obj on this disk and moving /home to a new disk.

**NOTE** *Before doing anything with disks, be sure that you have a complete backup. A single dumb fat-finger mistake in this process can destroy your system! You do not want to accidentally reformat your root filesystem, for example.*

### Creating Slices

Your first step in working with a new hard disk will be to partition it. Follow these steps:

1. Become root, and start sysinstall. We'll want to do post-install configuration, so choose Configure and start with Fdisk.

2. This menu should look somewhat familiar; you used it when you installed FreeBSD. (You can see screenshots in Figure 1.4 in Chapter 1.) You'll see your existing FreeBSD disk and your new disk. Choose the new disk.

3. If this disk is recycled from another server, you might find that it has a filesystem on it. Decide whether you want to keep what's on the disk, or erase it and start over. It's usually simplest to just remove the existing partitions and filesystems. Use the arrow keys to move to the existing partition, and press **d** to delete it.

4. You can either create a new slice by pressing **c**, or just use the whole disk by pressing **a**. In a server, you almost certainly want to use the entire disk. When you've chosen your slices, make the changes effective immediately by pressing **w**. You'll see a warning like this:

```
WARNING:  This should only be used when modifying an EXISTING installation.  If you
are installing FreeBSD for the first time then you should simply type Q when you're
finished here and your changes will be committed in one batch automatically at the
end of these questions.  If you're adding a disk, you should NOT write from this
screen, you should do it from the label editor.
Are you absolutely sure you want to do this now?
```

5.   Yes, you're absolutely sure. Tab over to "Yes" and hit enter.

6.   You'll then be asked if you want to install a boot manager on this disk. You don't need a boot manager on an additional disk, so arrow down to Standard and press the spacebar. Then arrow down to OK and press **ENTER**. The sysinstall program should tell you that it has written out the FDISK information. We now have a FreeBSD slice on the disk. Leave the fdisk part of sysinstall, and head on to create partitions in the slice.

### Creating Partitions

To create partitions on your disk, follow these steps:

1.   Choose the Label option of sysinstall. Here you can create a new partition with the **c** command, specifying its size in either megabytes, gigabytes, disk blocks, or disk cylinders. (You'll probably want megabytes or gigabytes.) You can also decide if each new partition will be a filesystem or a swap space.

**NOTE**   *When creating partitions, be sure that your new disk name is at the top of the screen. You don't want to relabel your current disk!*

2.   Enable soft updates, if they aren't enabled by default.

3.   When you're satisfied with the way partitions on your new disk are labeled, press **w** again to write the label changes to the disk. You now have a partition table. (Take note of the partition names (such as da7s1e); you'll need them later.)

4.   Finally, press **w** to commit the changes. You should see a text box about newfs pop up. (This may take several minutes—formatting a 100GB hard drive is no simple task!)

5.   When this finishes, exit sysinstall.

### Configuring /etc/fstab

If you've added swap space, you should configure /etc/fstab to recognize it. (You did write down the partition names for your new partitions, right?) Your swap space is probably something like da7s1b (substituting your disk's name for da7). There's already an entry for your existing swap space in /etc/fstab, which you can use as a model when adding this new space.

For example, suppose a test server has a swap line that looks like this:

```
/dev/da0s1b          none          swap     sw          0          0
```

If your new disk is /dev/da7, and you've created a swap partition on /dev/da7s1b, add a line like this:

```
/dev/da7s1b          none          swap     sw          0          0
```

At your next boot, FreeBSD will find this entry and turn it into a swap space.

You should also add a similar entry for your new data partition(s). Here is an /etc/fstab entry to mount a new /dev/da7s1e partition on /crud, a new mount point created just for this drive:

```
/dev/da7s1e              /crud          ufs      rw            0       0
```

### Installing Existing Files onto New Disks

Chances are that you will want your new disk to replace an existing FreeBSD partition or to subdivide an existing partition. To do so, make your new partition available on the system on a temporary mount point. Move files from the old location to the new location. Then remount the partition at the desired location.

### Temporary Mounts

Suppose you have a new partition /dev/da7s1e that you want to use for /usr/src, and you want to move the files from the existing /usr/src to the new partition. To talk to the new partition, however, you need to mount it at some different location temporarily.

The temporary location can be any directory on your system. The /mnt directory is traditionally used as a temporary mount point for partitions.

```
# mount /dev/da7s1e /mnt
#
```

### Moving Files

Now you need to move files from their current location to the new partition without changing their permissions or otherwise affecting them. This is fairly simple to do with tar(1). (We use tar to preserve our filesystem permissions.)

You can simply tar up your existing data to a tape or a file, and untar it in the new location, but that's kind of clumsy. You can concatenate tar commands to avoid that middle step, however:

```
(cd /old/directory && tar cf - .) | (cd /newplace && tar xpf -)
```

If you don't speak UNIX at parties, this line looks fairly stunning. Let's dismantle it. First, you're going to the old directory and tarring up everything you find there with (cd /old/directory && tar cf - .). Next, the output is piped to the new directory, where it is untarred with | (cd /newplace && tar xpf -). Wait a few minutes, and you'll be all set.

For example, to move /usr/src onto a new partition temporarily mounted on /mnt, you would do this:

```
# ( cd /usr/src && tar cf - . ) | ( cd /mnt && tar xpf - )
```

This isn't simple, but it's not incomprehensible. Of course, if it makes you feel more comfortable, you can create a tarball in one location and uncompress it elsewhere. All you need is the disk space to do so.

*This does not delete the files from the original location. When you're sure that they're copied correctly, use* rm -rf *to remove them.*

### Moving Live Files

You cannot safely move files that are being changed. For example, if you're moving your mail spool to a new partition, shut down your mail services. Otherwise, the files will change as you're trying to copy them.

### *Stackable Mounts*

Suppose you don't care about your old data; you simply want to split an existing disk to get more space, and you plan to recover your data from backup. Fair enough.

All BSD filesystems are *stackable*. This is an advanced idea, and not very useful in day-to-day administration. However, it can bite you when you try to split up one partition between two disks.

Suppose, for example, that you have data in /usr/src. (If you followed the installation advice, or you've upgraded your system, you should.) Do an ls, and confirm that the data is still there. Now mount your new partition over /usr/src:

```
# mount /dev/da7s1e /usr/src
#
```

If you look in /usr/src now, you'll see that the directory is empty.

But here's the problem: The new partition is mounted "above" the old disk, and the old disk still has all that data on it. If you unmount the new partition and check that directory again, you'll see your data miraculously restored! The new partition obscured the lower partition.

Although you can't see it, the data on the old disk still takes up space. (You can view how much disk space you're using with df(1) and du(1).) If you're splitting a disk to gain space, and you just mount a new disk over part of the old, you won't gain any disk space on the original disk.

The moral is: Even if you are restoring your data from backup, make sure you remove that data from your original disk to recover the disk space.

# 17

## RAID

One of the big features of SCSI systems is their ability to use RAID, or Redundant Array of Independent Disks.[1] The "I" in the definition used to mean "Inexpensive," but that's kind of relative. A one-terabyte RAID array costs far less than a single one-terabyte disk, but it is still very expensive.

A RAID system splits data between the drives to improve performance or reliability. RAID works either in hardware or software.

## Hardware vs. Software RAID

FreeBSD supports both hardware and software RAID. Hardware RAID is managed by the SCSI controller, and host adapters that can handle RAID are called *RAID controllers*. When you run RAID in hardware, the controller handles all the computations of how to arrange data on the hard drives, thus reducing the load on your system. Most hardware RAID system are very stable, and a hardware controller is unquestionably the best way to handle RAID.

---

[1] You can also have IDE RAID systems, but they suffer from all the disadvantages of IDE. If you want a recap, we discussed those disadvantages at great length in Chapter 1.

Software RAID is managed by the operating system, and the OS is left to figure out how to arrange data on the disks. This method increases system load but uses less expensive equipment than hardware RAID.

It's much simpler to use hardware RAID than it is to use software RAID because, typically, all you need to do is follow the manual. There's usually a simple menu-driven RAID BIOS that allows you to set partition sizes and restore damaged disks, and that's all you need to know. Software RAID, on the other hand, demands that sysadmins actually know what they're doing. We'll discuss software RAID in detail in this chapter. Hardware RAID has the same theory, but there's really not much to discuss beyond the theory and which menu option to select.

## RAID Levels

RAID comes in a variety of types. RAID-0, RAID-1, and RAID-5 are the most popular.

RAID-0 is more commonly called *striping*, and technically isn't RAID at all. It requires at least two disks, and data is shared between the disks in a way that increases throughput and disk size, but without redundancy. You could use RAID-0 to combine several 100GB drives to create one massive virtual disk, for example, but a hard drive failure will destroy data on the one drive, and any striped system that requires that drive will become useless when that one drive fails. You'd need to restore from backup in order to access any information. RAID-0 is useful if you need a single filesystem that's really, really large, but it provides no reliability benefits.

RAID-1 is called *mirroring*, where the content of one disk is duplicated on another. (You need disks in multiples of two.) This is a good method to use for low-cost reliability.

In RAID-5, data is partially duplicated across all the drives and arranged in such a manner that the loss of any one drive will not destroy any data. In "hot-swappable" systems, the damaged drive can even be replaced and rebuilt while the system is running. Again, you need two disks or more.

Finally you have RAID-10 (also known as RAID-0+1), which combines striping and mirroring. You want at least four disks for this, in multiples of two, divided into two sets. Each set of disks is striped together, and each set of stripes mirrors the other. If you can afford this setup, use it.

Given the choice, you should use hardware RAID because it simplifies maintenance and takes considerably less skill to run. Run RAID-10 if you have enough disks, and if not, RAID-5 or RAID-1, in that order. (I've used RAID-0 on my home system, but I don't recommend it for serious application.)

## Software RAID

We'll focus on software RAID because it's much more complicated, much more annoying, and far more difficult to run than hardware RAID. Users under tight budgetary constraints frequently have to resort to software RAID, after all. If you're using hardware RAID, read this chapter for the concepts, but check your hardware manual to see which buttons to pick.

FreeBSD includes two software RAID managers: ccd and Vinum. Ccd is far older and only handles RAID-1. Vinum is newer, faster, stronger, handles RAID-0, 1, 5, and 10, and is able to leap taller buildings in fewer bounds. We'll therefore discuss Vinum.

*No operating system's software RAID is for the faint of heart or those who are not willing to dig into problems. This includes FreeBSD's.*

## Vinum Disk Components

Vinum divides disks into three separate pieces: volumes, drives, and subdisks.

### Volumes

Vinum creates virtual disks, or *volumes*. One Vinum volume looks like a standard disk partition that you can read, write, format, and so on. Our users and programs will actually see this volume instead of a disk partition. You cannot mix Vinum data and standard filesystems on a single partition.

### Drives

Partitions dedicated to Vinum are called *drives*. One Vinum volume can include as many drives as you like. (You could use just a single disk for Vinum, but you'd simply be absorbing the overhead of software RAID and not getting any benefits.)

You can dedicate entire disks to Vinum drives if you want, but you don't have to. I frequently use the outer section of a hard drive for swap space, and dedicate the remainder to a Vinum drive.

### Subdisks

Vinum drives hold *subdisks*, which are simply spaces set aside for Vinum on a particular Vinum drive. (Remember, in Vinum a drive is just a partition; this is space set aside for Vinum data in a partition assigned to Vinum.) If you wanted, you could even create two subdisks on the same physical disk just by putting them in different partitions. (There isn't much use for this, other than to demonstrate just how badly software RAID performs if it's set up quite badly.)

To put it all together, a volume is made up of drives. Drives contain subdisks.

## Vinum Plex Types

A *plex* is a single copy of the data in a volume. As long as you have one complete plex, all your data is available. Mirroring works by having more than one plex in a volume. Vinum supports up to eight plexes per volume, so you can make your data very redundant. The way you arrange your plexes determines the sort of RAID you're using.

### Concatenated Plex

To make one big volume, create a *concatenated plex*, which is simply all the subdisks available, in order. This gives you only one plex, or one copy of your data.

A concatenated plex is the least efficient way to use disk resources. Oh, it's good enough if you have two IDE disks on one controller, but it's simply a waste of system resources if you use SCSI. And it isn't even RAID; it's just a big virtual disk. You can use two concatenated plexes to provide mirroring, however, and you can also easily expand volumes built from concatenated plexes by adding more disks.

### Striped Plex

The *striped plex* provides RAID-0, where data is arranged across the disks in a manner to enhance performance. The subdisks in a striped plex must all be the same size, and you must have at least two of them.

With a single striped plex, you again have no redundancy of your data. You could build two striped plexes on four disks, however, and create a redundant RAID-0 setup. If you're considering this, you really ought to look at RAID-5 instead.

### Mirrored Plex

The *mirrored plex* copies data across multiple plexes. Again, the subdisks in a mirrored plex must all be the same size. A mirror requires at least two plexes, however, so you do get actual data redundancy. This is RAID-1.

### RAID-5 Plex

A *RAID-5 plex* stripes and mirrors data across multiple subdisks. This includes multiple copies of your data on multiple disks, and is quite redundant. You must have at least three subdisks of the same size to run RAID-5.

**NOTE**   *We won't discuss Vinum RAID-5 in any depth. For examples and discussion of RAID-5 or RAID-10, check the Vinum Web site at http://www.vinumvm.org. You must understand the basics presented in this section before even attempting either of these.*

### *Preparing Vinum Drives*

We're going to go through the steps of setting up a concatenated plex, a striped plex, and a mirrored plex on a sample system. In all cases, we will need to do the following:

- Choose partitions to become drives.
- Create subdisks on those drives.
- Configure Vinum to create appropriate plexes for those drives.

We'll do everything on the same sample system, which starts off with the following disks and partitions:

```
# df
Filesystem   1K-blocks      Used     Avail Capacity  Mounted on
/dev/ad4s1a     248111     73649    154614     32%   /
devfs                1         1         0    100%   /dev
/dev/ad4s1f    2032839    133492   1736720      7%   /test1
/dev/ad4s1g    2032839   1266476    603736     68%   /test2
/dev/ad4s1h   29497862   3975801  23162233     15%   /usr
/dev/ad4s1e    3048830    241823   2563101      9%   /var
procfs               4         4         0    100%   /proc
```

```
/dev/da0s1e    3525041        1  3243037    0%    /crud
/dev/da1s1e    3758456        1  3457779    0%    /crud2
#
```

Df(1) shows how much disk space you're using and where your partitions are mounted. As you can see from the preceding output, we have two empty partitions on SCSI disks, /crud and /crud2. (You can tell that they're SCSI disks because of the device names at the beginning of the lines, and you can tell that they're empty because the Capacity column reads 0% for both.) We're going to use those partitions for a striped virtual disk. I've already backed up all the data on those partitions, which is necessary, because the Vinum setup process completely overwrites the drive!

To prepare your Vinum drives, first unmount the partitions:

```
# umount /crud
# umount /crud2
#
```

Another check with df should show that the drives are no longer visible. Remove the entries for these partitions from /etc/fstab, so FreeBSD doesn't try to put them back on boot. Once you've done that, you're ready to go.

### Dedicating Partitions to Vinum

Now that we have the partitions idle and unmounted, we have to tell the partitions that they are now dedicated to Vinum—we do this with disklabel(8). This will convert a standard partition to a Vinum drive. Disklabel reads and writes "labels" on the disk, giving basic information about where partitions start and end, how they're formatted, and their physical characteristics. Just running disklabel diskname will print out the existing disklabel. One of our Vinum disks is /dev/da1, so let's look at it:

```
# disklabel da1
# /dev/da1c:
type: SCSI
disk: da1s1
...
8 partitions:
#        size    offset    fstype   [fsize bsize bps/cpg]
  b:  1048576         0    swap                            # (Cyl.    0 - 65*)
  c:  8803557         0    unused        0     0           # (Cyl.    0 - 547*)
  e:  7754981   1048576    4.2BSD     1024  8192   22       # (Cyl.   65*- 547*)
#
```

Disklabel produces a lot of output, including information about many things you cannot change, such as disk speed, the number of cylinders, and so on. I'll trim out a lot of these things in these examples, but you might want to run disklabel on your disks to see exactly what information is available.

What we need to see right now is the information at the end of the disklabel, where the partitions are laid out.[2] Df showed us that /crud was actually /dev/da0s1e. The preceding disklabel is for da1s1. The "e" line in the partition table represents the partition we want to dedicate to Vinum:

```
 e:  7754981  1048576     4.2BSD    1024 8192    22  # (Cyl.   65*- 547*)
```

Running disklabel -e will bring up a copy of the disklabel in a text editor. You want to change the fstype column in the entry for slice e from 4.2BSD to vinum. When you save and exit, the changed disklabel will be written to the disk. When you're finished, run disklabel da0 again to check your work. The partition table should look like this:

```
#      size   offset    fstype   [fsize bsize bps/cpg]
 b:  1048576       0      swap                          # (Cyl.   0 -  65*)
 c:  8803557       0    unused      0    0              # (Cyl.   0 - 547*)
 e:  7754981  1048576     vinum                         # (Cyl.  65*- 547*)
```

Edit the disklabel of the Vinum partition on the other disk in the same way. The disk partitions are now dedicated to Vinum.

### Configuring Vinum

Now that you have disk space to put Vinum on, you can configure it. Basic setup is simple if you use the built-in tools.

Vinum includes a program, vinum(8), for communicating with the Vinum kernel module. You control Vinum only through this program. If you type **vinum** at a command prompt, you drop into an interactive Vinum shell where you can adjust the configuration, view the setup, and perform any other Vinum operations. Alternatively, you can just give the proper command-line arguments and vinum will perform a single action and exit. We'll use both the command-line method and the interactive mode.

**NOTE** *The program name being the same as the feature name can confuse people. When talking about the whole Vinum system, the V is capitalized. The program always appears in the manual section (vinum(8)).*

### Vinum.conf

Vinum stores its actual configuration in a database on the disk, and you cannot read it without using vinum(8). You can create a vinum(8) configuration file,

---

[2] You might notice that disklabel claims that there are eight partitions, but we only see three. The slice can hold up to eight partitions, but five aren't actually in use.

however, which is useful when initially configuring Vinum. You can check your initial setup work more easily when you have a configuration file, and you can change and rebuild your configuration without too much trouble when you track everything in a configuration file.

Once Vinum is configured, however, the configuration file is irrelevant; the actual configuration is stored in the on-disk database. You can make changes directly to the Vinum system without touching the configuration file. Do not look at the configuration file for current configuration information; remember to consult vinum(8) for the current setup.

**NOTE** *In this chapter, I'll be using /etc/vinum.conf as a configuration file. If you come across this file on a system, just remember that it might not mean anything at all.*

### Concatenated Plex

We'll start by setting up a single concatenated volume to give us the biggest possible disk size. We'll use a single plex, or only one copy of the data. There is no redundancy in this model, but it will create a larger disk.

Here's an /etc/vinum.conf file for a concatenated plex:

```
drive alpha device /dev/da0s1e
drive beta device /dev/da1s1e
volume test
      plex org concat
      sd length 3243037k drive alpha
      sd length 3457779k drive beta
```

Have a look at the first two lines in this listing. The first thing we do is identify the drive partitions with the drive keyword. The two drives in this example are /dev/da0s1e and /dev/da1s1e. (Remember, in Vinum terms, partitions dedicated to Vinum are *drives*.) Each drive needs a unique name, and I've named them *alpha* and *beta*.

We then need to name our volume, or virtual partition, with the volume keyword. In this case, on the third line of the listing, I've named it *test*. Next, on the fourth line, we say how we're organizing our plex with the plex org keyword. We use concat to specify concatenation.

Finally, on the fifth and sixth lines, we tell Vinum the size of our subdisks on this drive. Remember, our original check with df showed us that /dev/da0s1e had 3243037KB available and /dev/da1s1e had 3457779KB available. We want to use all available space on these partitions for Vinum.

**NOTE** *You can go into great detail about exactly how you want your volume set up, what sort of disk block and stripe size you want to use, and so on, but Vinum doesn't require that level of detail. It defaults to sensible values.*

**Creating the Volume**

Now we create the volume with `vinum create` and the filename to tell Vinum to read your configuration and create everything:

```
# vinum create /etc/vinum.conf
❶ 2 drives:
D alpha              State: up      /dev/da0s1e    A: 384/3551 MB (10%)
D beta               State: up      /dev/da1s1e    A: 409/3786 MB (10%)

❷ 1 volumes:
V test               State: up      Plexes:      1 Size:       6543 MB

❸ 1 plexes:
P test.p0      C State: up          Subdisks:    2 Size:       6543 MB

❹ 2 subdisks:
S test.p0.s0         State: up      D: alpha       Size:       3167 MB
S test.p0.s1         State: up      D: beta        Size:       3376 MB
#
```

Read your vinum(8) output carefully to see if the result matches your understanding of your configuration file. Our most important indicator of success is that every entry has the state of up, which indicates that the operation was successful.

Let's have a look at this output. First we see our two drives, alpha and beta, both of which are up (❶). We also see the device names and the space usage.

Then we have a list of volumes (❷). Our one volume appears, named test, with a total size of 6543MB. Similarly, we have one plex, with two subdisks (❸). The plex is named after the volume name, with a trailing ".p0".

Finally, we see our subdisks and the drives that they were created on (❹). Each subdisk is named after its volume, the plex it is assigned to, and an arbitrary subdisk number, such as test.p0.s1.

Our Vinum partition is now available. It will have a device name under /dev/vinum, named after the volume name. For example, our "test" volume is available as /dev/vinum/test.

**Initializing Vinum Partitions**

Before we can use our Vinum volume, it needs a filesystem. Since sysinstall doesn't recognize Vinum (yet!), you need to do this with newfs(8). If you're an experienced systems administrator, you can use any newfs flags you like to choose block sizes, and so on. The defaults work fine for most people:

```
# newfs -v /dev/vinum/test
```

You'll see newfs output scroll by, listing every superblock on the drive.

Once you have a filesystem, mount the drive and see what happens.

```
#mount /dev/vinum/test /mnt
#df
Filesystem        1K-blocks      Used     Avail Capacity  Mounted on
/dev/ad4s1a          248111     55829    172434     24%    /
devfs                     1         1         0    100%    /dev
/dev/ad4s1f         2032839    133492   1736720      7%    /test1
/dev/ad4s1g         2032839   1266476    603736     68%    /test2
/dev/ad4s1h        29497862   3974853  23163181     15%    /usr
/dev/ad4s1e         3048830      6757   2798167      0%    /var
procfs                    4         4         0    100%    /proc
/dev/vinum/test     7282594         1   6699986      0%    /mnt
#
```

On the last line of the preceding df output, we see that our Vinum volume is ready and available for use, and that it's roughly the combined size of the two smaller disks we used to create the volume! (If you want more human-readable output, try df -h to see disk space in a more friendly manner.)

```
/dev/vinum/test     7282594         1   6699986      0%     /mnt
```

As you can see, concatenating disks is useful for combining several small disks into one large one, giving new life to older or smaller disks. While this doesn't give us any reliability, it does help make older and smaller disks useful again. Other uses of Vinum are more interesting, such as striping. Let's see how that works by turning these two disks into a striped system.

### Removing Vinum Configuration

Vinum uses an *accumulative* configuration process. If you don't destroy your old configuration, any new configuration is simply added to it. Accumulative configuration works well when you're adding disks to a RAID system or restoring a damaged volume. It works poorly when you just want to start over. This is reasonable—after all, most people in a production system alter a configuration more frequently than they erase it and start over!

To start from scratch, you must erase the existing configuration from the on-disk database. You cannot just edit the configuration file, because it has no real relationship to Vinum's internal operations.

To get rid of our existing Vinum configuration and the mounted partitions, we must first unmount the existing Vinum partition. (It is always a poor idea to destroy anything while the operating system is using it.)

Once the Vinum partition is safely unmounted, we can destroy the existing configuration. In the following example, we'll use vinum's interactive mode. Type **vinum** at the command line to drop into a vinum shell.

```
# vinum
vinum ->
```

Here you can enter vinum(8) commands and interact more directly with the system. You can start over with the resetconfig command:

```
vinum -> resetconfig
 WARNING!  This command will completely wipe out your vinum configuration.
 All data will be lost. If you really want to do this, enter the text

 NO FUTURE
 Enter text ->
```

Yes, that's NO FUTURE in all caps. It's Vinum's subtle way of reminding you that you're about to absolutely destroy any data on that partition, as well as your configuration. If you're not certain, just hit **ENTER** to go back to the main vinum prompt. If you're sure, enter **NO FUTURE** and hit **ENTER**.

```
Enter text -> NO FUTURE
Vinum configuration obliterated
vinum ->
```

Press **CONTROL-D** to leave vinum. You now have no Vinum configuration and are ready to build a new one.

### Striped Volumes

The vinum.conf file that follows shows a striped volume. (Remember, a striped volume spreads its data between two disks.)

```
drive alpha device /dev/da0s1e
drive beta device /dev/da1s1e
volume test
plex org striped 279k
        sd length 3243037k drive alpha
        sd length 3243037k drive beta
```

This looks quite similar to the concatenated setup, with some minor changes. We still have our alpha and beta drives, and the volume name is still test.

The plex org keyword has changed to striped and a number. The number at the end of the plex setup line indicates the stripe size; the amount of data that will be written to one drive before switching to the other drive. The 279KB (279k) shown here is a reasonable default.

**NOTE**  *Why use such a weird size for the stripe? Well, Vinum and the filesystem have certain interactions. If you use an even number you might very well find that you have all of your inodes on one drive. You might even have all of your data on only one drive! This would utterly eradicate any advantages of striping. You want to be absolutely certain that Vinum will use all of your drives, and this number works.*

The subdisk labels in our output look slightly different than in the earlier example, however. Since we're striping, we need to have subdisks of identical size. If one disk is larger than the other, that space will be useless because both disks will use the amount of space available on the smaller drive, wasting whatever space remains on the larger drive. If you intend to use Vinum striping, plan your drive partitions accordingly.

Once you have your new vinum.conf set up, run vinum create. The output of vinum create will look almost exactly like our previous example, but it will say "striped" instead of "concat." Again, examine it carefully to be sure it says what you want it to! Then run newfs and mount the new volume, and see what you have.

```
# mount /dev/vinum/test /mnt
# df
Filesystem        1K-blocks       Used     Avail Capacity  Mounted on
/dev/ad4s1a          248111      65146    163117      29%  /
devfs                     1          1         0     100%  /dev
/dev/ad4s1f         2032839     133492   1736720       7%  /test1
/dev/ad4s1g         2032839    1266476    603736      68%  /test2
/dev/ad4s1h        29497862    4193767  22944267      15%  /usr
/dev/ad4s1e         3048830     123222   2681702       4%  /var
procfs                    4          4         0     100%  /proc
/dev/vinum/test     6286319          1   5783413       0%  /mnt
#
```

This new /mnt partition is smaller than the concatenated volume, since we lost the extra space on one drive, but accesses will be faster since we're sharing the load across multiple disks. The faster access speed will be especially obvious with multiple processes writing to the volume simultaneously.

### Mirrored Volumes

Finally, let's mirror our drives. To begin, first unmount the partition, eliminate your old Vinum configuration with vinum destroy, and create a new /etc/vinum.conf.

```
drive alpha device /dev/da0s1e
drive beta device /dev/da1s1e
volume mirrortest setupstate
plex org concat
        sd length 3243037k drive alpha
plex org concat
        sd length 3243037k drive beta
```

This configuration is a bit different from our previous ones. Our drives are the same, but everything else looks a little different. For one, our volume has a different name, *mirrortest*. The setupstate keyword tells vinum(8) to assume that the existing contents of the disks are identical—we're lying to Vinum. Lying to your computer is not good. The computer will usually catch on quite quickly and panic. (This leads directly to Chapter 20.) Before we use the volume, however, we will newfs it and overwrite everything, so Vinum will never have an opportunity to catch on.[3]

This time we have two plexes, each of the concatenated type. Each plex is concatenated, but has only one subdisk, each of which lives on a separate disk. Our first plex has one subdisk on drive alpha, while the other has one subdisk on drive beta. Again, they are the same size.

We know that a plex is one copy of the data. Since we have two plexes, each on a separate disk, we know that the data is mirrored across the disks. Now that you have a configuration, use the vinum command to implement it on the actual hard drives.

```
#vinum create vinum.conf
2 drives:
D alpha              State: up       /dev/da0s1e    A: 384/3551 MB (10%)
D beta               State: up       /dev/da1s1e    A: 619/3786 MB (16%)

1 volumes:
V mirrortest         State: up       Plexes:     2 Size:       3167 MB

2 plexes:
P mirrortest.p0    C State: up       Subdisks:   1 Size:       3167 MB
P mirrortest.p1    C State: up       Subdisks:   1 Size:       3167 MB

2 subdisks:
S mirrortest.p0.s0   State: up       D: alpha       Size:      3167 MB
S mirrortest.p1.s0   State: up       D: beta        Size:      3167 MB
#
```

You have a mirrored volume, as you can see by the two plexes listed. Newfs, mount, and you're ready to go!

### Starting Vinum at Boot

To start the Vinum system at boot, edit /etc/rc.conf and /etc/fstab. The rc.conf option is quite simple:

```
start_vinum="YES"
```

---

[3] This is the computing equivalent of writing your rent check on the night before payday.

We looked at /etc/fstab in Chapter 16. Follow the examples already in that file, and add a line something like this to the filesystem table:

```
/dev/vinum/mailvol   /var/mail     ufs   rw   2  2
```

### Other Vinum Commands

The vinum(8) program includes a variety of simple commands to allow you to view its condition.

### Status Check

The simplest thing of all is to ask Vinum how it's doing. The vinum ls command shows each plex you have, its size, the name of its drive, and its state:

```
# vinum ls
S mirrortest.p0.s0     State: I 43%    D: alpha      Size:        3167 MB
S mirrortest.p1.s0     State: I 41%    D: beta       Size:        3167 MB
#
```

Everything should all be in an "I" state. If it isn't, check vinum(8) and the Vinum Web site (http://www.vinumvm.org) and see what your error means. If you want more information, you can do vinum list -r. This will print out detailed status information on every volume, plex, and subdisk in your system.

### Configuration Check

To double-check your Vinum system configuration, use vinum printconfig. This shows us the drive names, followed by the volume name, and then the plexes and subdisks.

```
#vinum printconfig
# Vinum configuration of magpire.blackhelicopters.org, saved at Fri Aug 17 19:24:43
2001
drive alpha device /dev/da0s1e
drive beta device /dev/da1s1e
volume mirrortest
plex name mirrortest.p0 org concat vol mirrortest
plex name mirrortest.p1 org concat vol mirrortest
sd name mirrortest.p0.s0 drive alpha plex mirrortest.p0 len 6486074s driveoffset
265s plexoffset 0s
sd name mirrortest.p1.s0 drive beta plex mirrortest.p1 len 6486074s driveoffset 265s
plexoffset 0s
#
```

### Replacing a Failed Mirrored Plex

The purpose of a mirror is redundancy in case of a drive failure. So, if a drive fails, how do you replace it?[4]

First, if at all possible, be sure you have a good backup. You'll be working directly on the Vinum device, and any mistake can destroy your data. If you don't have a current backup, take a backup before proceeding. Your remaining plex(es) should still be up and serving data, after all!

Next, you need to replace the failed hard drive, which can be difficult. For one thing, you've got to identify the failed drive. A vinum list will tell you which of your drives has failed, identifying the drive by device number. You can then compare the device name to those listed in /var/run/dmesg.boot and get the SCSI ID, LUN, and bus number. Once you identify the failed drive, then shut down the computer, find the matching hard drive, replace it with a drive with the same settings, and boot up again.

Once you reboot, then check to be certain that the new drive came up with the same drive device name as the old one. (This will make later configuration simpler.)

Now, ask Vinum how it's doing:

```
# vinum list
1 drives:
D alpha                State: up        /dev/da0s1e     A: 384/3551 MB (10%)
D beta                 State: referenced                A: 0/0 MB

1 volumes:
V mirrortest           State: up        Plexes:      2 Size:      3167 MB

2 plexes:
P mirrortest.p0    C State: up          Subdisks:    1 Size:      3167 MB
P mirrortest.p1    C State: faulty      Subdisks:    1 Size:      3167 MB

2 subdisks:
S mirrortest.p0.s0     State: up        D: alpha        Size:      3167 MB
S mirrortest.p1.s0     State: stale     D: beta         Size:      3167 MB
#
```

[4] As I was writing this chapter, I noticed a high-pitched noise coming from my computer. Upon investigation, one of my two SCSI hard drives was warm enough to make me jerk my hand back quickly. Since the computer room is kept at about 65 degrees Fahrenheit, it seemed to be time to replace the drive. Sometimes, Fate works with technical folks. Other times, it just picks a decent time to abuse us.

The beta drive that was on /dev/da1s1 shows up as "referenced," which means that it's included in the configuration but isn't working correctly. In a cascading chain of errors, the plex on this particular drive is "faulty" because the drive isn't working. The underlying subdisk is "stale," as the data on it does not match the mirror.

None of this is good, but it's all to be expected. As a virgin replacement, the disk partition we've called "beta" has nothing whatsoever on it. If you see any of these errors on an existing Vinum volume, however, it means that the drive in question is having trouble and should be replaced.

### Preparing the Replacement Drive

Before we can use the new drive, we need to partition and label it. You did that earlier in this chapter with sysinstall(8), and this will be almost exactly the same. To begin, start sysinstall with the fdisk menu option. Next, delete any disk partitions shown, and dedicate the whole drive to FreeBSD. Then go into the Label editor.

From our previous setup in /etc/vinum.conf, we know that our Vinum partition was 3243037KB. We have a slightly more convenient measurement in the earlier vinum ls, where we can see that one subdisk is 3167MB. We must leave at least that much space for our Vinum partition on our new drive. (I recommend that you allocate a couple extra meg, just in case, if possible.) Now, write your changes to the disk, as if you were adding a disk to your system, and then run disklabel to change the slice type of your Vinum partition, as if you were first setting up Vinum.

**NOTE** *At the rate disk drive size grows these days, it's quite likely that a replacement disk will be much larger than the original, and probably even faster. Feel free to allocate the remainder of the disk. When I have extra space left over, I frequently move a little-used chunk of data–say, /usr/src or /usr/ports/distfiles–onto a large new partition. It's accessed infrequently enough that it won't inflict a great performance hit upon my Vinum system, and yet frees disk space elsewhere. Move data that doesn't need the resilience and speed that Vinum provides, and that is easily recoverable.*

### Plex Recovery

Finally, you're ready to recover your volume. First off, you need to tell Vinum that it has a new disk. Remember, Vinum's configuration is cumulative. If you just recreate the whole volume, you'll add the old information to itself. This will confuse Vinum and make you lose your data. For example, our vinum.conf shows drives named alpha and beta. Vinum already knows about those drives. If I were to use that same vinum.conf and run vinum create a second time, we would be telling Vinum that it had two alpha drives and two beta drives, both on the same physical device! This would be vastly confusing to us, let alone a poor, dumb machine. Similarly, you don't want to obliterate the entire configuration, and make it forget about the drives it already has. All you want to do is change a bit of the existing setup.

In this example, we want to recover drive beta. Since we don't care about what's on the shiny new replacement drive beta, we can overwrite that part of Vinum's configuration. To do so, create a Vinum configuration file, /etc/vinum.conf.recover. List only the one drive in there, without any additional information on plexes or subdisks.

```
drive beta device /dev/da1s1e
```

That's the drive name and the partition it's on. Now, we add this information to the existing Vinum configuration by running vinum create:

```
# vinum create /etc/vinum.conf.recover
2 drives:
D alpha               State: up      /dev/da0s1e    A: 384/3551 MB (10%)
D beta                State: up      /dev/da1s1e    A: 2/3170 MB (0%)

1 volumes:
V mirrortest          State: up      Plexes:        2 Size:       3167 MB

2 plexes:
P mirrortest.p0    C State: up        Subdisks:     1 Size:       3167 MB
P mirrortest.p1    C State: faulty    Subdisks:     1 Size:       3167 MB

2 subdisks:
S mirrortest.p0.s0    State: up      D: alpha       Size:        3167 MB
S mirrortest.p1.s0    State: stale   D: beta        Size:        3167 MB
#
```

Notice that the state on our beta drive is now "up," instead of "referenced." The plex is still "faulty," mind you, but we're making progress.

Now that you have a drive, you can actually tell Vinum to recover the disk. Vinum is fairly smart; it doesn't start drives it cannot talk to. All you have to do is tell Vinum to start the replaced plex, and it will recover it for you:

```
#vinum start mirrortest.p1
Reviving mirrortest.p1.s0 in the background
# vinum[685]: reviving mirrortest.p1.s0
#
```

You can watch its progress with `vinum list`:

```
# vinum list
2 drives:
D alpha              State: up        /dev/da0s1e      A: 384/3551 MB (10%)
D beta               State: up        /dev/da1s1e      A: 2/3170 MB (0%)

1 volumes:
V mirrortest         State: up        Plexes:      2 Size:       3167 MB

2 plexes:
P mirrortest.p0   C State: up        Subdisks:    1 Size:       3167 MB
P mirrortest.p1   C State: faulty    Subdisks:    1 Size:       3167 MB

2 subdisks:
S mirrortest.p0.s0   State: up        D: alpha        Size:       3167 MB
S mirrortest.p1.s0   State: R 11%     D: beta         Size:       3167 MB
#
```

Note the last line: `mirrortest.p1.s0`. Our replacement disk is 11 percent recovered. If your mirror is under heavy load, this will take a while. Eventually, however, it will recover, and you'll be back in business with fully mirrored disks.

Pretty cool, huh?

# 18

## SYSTEM PERFORMANCE

"It's slow." That's one of the most dreaded phrases a systems administrator can hear. The user doesn't know why the system is slow—it just "feels" that way. Usually there's no test case, no set of reproducible steps, and nothing particularly wrong. These two words can cause the systems administrator hours of work, digging through the system trying to figure out what's going on.

One phrase is still more dreadful, especially after you've invested those hours debugging the problem: "It's still slow." For an inexperienced systems administrator, slow systems are easy to accelerate: Buy faster hardware. This generally fixes speed problems. It also costs a lot of money and simply conceals whatever's wrong, without really using the equipment you have.

FreeBSD includes many tools designed to help you examine system performance, and to give you the information you need to actually find out what's slowing things down. That will tell you what you need to do to fix the problem. You might very well need faster hardware, but you can quite possibly shift the load around within a system and improve overall performance. The first step is to understand what your problem really is.

# Computer Resources

Speed problems are generally caused by running more on a computer than the computer can handle. That seems obvious, but think about it a moment. What does that mean?

A computer has four basic resources: disk input/output,[1] the network bandwidth, memory, and CPU. If any one of these is filled to capacity, the others cannot be used to their maximum effect. For example, your CPU might very well be waiting for a disk to deliver data or for memory to finish paging. A faster CPU won't increase system performance in this case.

Simply upgrading hardware when the system slows down does fix speed problems, but not in the way that you might think. If you have a program that fills up the system memory, buying a new system with a faster CPU will probably fix the problem. A new system probably has more memory than the old one, after all!

By identifying what the system is running short on, and addressing only that need, you can stretch your existing hardware much further. After all, why buy a whole new system when a couple hundred dollars of memory will fix the problem? (Of course, if your goal is to rotate this "slow" system into place as your new desktop, that's another matter.)

Perhaps you can reschedule work; one common cause of system slowdowns is running multiple large programs simultaneously. For example, I once scheduled a massive database log rotation that moved and compressed gigabytes of files at the same time as the system's automated daily checks. Since the job required shutting down the main database, and hence created system downtime, speed was crucial. Performance on both processes slowed unbearably. Rescheduling the log job greatly reduced downtime.

We're going to examine several FreeBSD tools for examining what a system is doing. Armed with that information, we'll consider how to fix some performance issues. We have separate tools to examine each of the potential bottlenecks.

FreeBSD changes continually, and later systems might have new tuning and performance features. Take a look at tuning(7) on your system to find any new performance tips. We'll cover tuning information that is useful on any FreeBSD (and almost any UNIX) system.

> **NOTE** *One word you're going to keep stumbling across in this chapter is "abnormal." As the systems administrator, you're supposed to know what is normal for your system. It's somewhat like art: You might not be able to define normal, but you need to recognize it when you see it. It's a good idea for you to use these tools to check your systems regularly when they're behaving correctly, so you will have a good idea of what is out of whack when the system slows down. We'll also look at some long-term monitoring tools, so you can gauge system performance over months or years.*

[1] Technically, network bandwidth is part of input/output. However, it's special enough that we'll treat it separately.

## Disk Input/Output

We looked at disk operations in some detail in Chapter 16. When it comes to performance, disk speed is usually a big bottleneck. If programs are waiting for disk activity to complete before proceeding, they will slow your system down. (This is commonly called "blocking on disk," meaning that the disk is blocking program activity.) The only real solution for this is to use a faster disk or a RAID array, or to split your disk activity between two disks.

How do you know if your disk is actually blocking program activity? We'll look at that in "Using Vmstat," later in the chapter.

## Network Bandwidth

If your system performance slowdown is due to network problems, you need more bandwidth. In short: You can only push as much bandwidth as you have. If your T1 is full, you need more bandwidth. If your system cannot fill the existing bandwidth, use the tools discussed in Chapter 5 to increase system capacity.

To check for this problem, begin by monitoring how much bandwidth your system is using. Chapter 15 discusses how to generate long-term graphs of bandwidth usage. We also discussed networking in Chapter 5. Consult netstat -m, and increase your kernel's NMBCLUSTERS, as described in Chapter 4. That's really all there is to it.

Other system conditions are more complicated.

## CPU and Memory

The top(1) tool is a good place to start if you're examining a system that seems to be running slowly. It provides a good overview of system status, but it only shows information about the CPU and memory usage; input/output and bandwidth are not touched.

### Using Top

To read a top display, you must understand a great deal about how the system works, so we'll spend a good chunk of time on this. To run top, just type **top**. To display kernel processes as well as user programs, use top -S. You'll see a display much like the following, and it will refresh every few seconds.

```
# top -S
❶ last pid:   436; ❷ load averages:  0.14,  0.08,  0.07   ❸ up 0+01:06:16 08:12:26
❹ 46 processes:  3 running, 43 sleeping
❺ CPU states:  1.2% user,  0.0% nice,  0.8% system,  0.0% interrupt, 98.1% idle
❻ Mem: 70M Active, 102M Inact, 26M Wired, 6016K Cache, 41M Buf, 107M Free
❼ Swap: 200M Total, 200M Free
❽
  PID USERNAME PRI NICE  SIZE   RES STATE   TIME  WCPU    CPU COMMAND
  287 mwlucas    2   5 2892K 2136K select  0:13  0.10%  0.10% xsysinfo
```

*(continued on next page)*

```
378 mwlucas    2   0  101M  64920K RUN     0:08  0.10%  0.10% soffice.bin
376 mwlucas    2   0 35372K 32736K RUN     0:13  0.05%  0.05% mozilla-bin
274 mwlucas    2   0 28208K 26304K select  1:01  0.00%  0.00% XFree86
170 root       2   0   912K   508K select  0:08  0.00%  0.00% moused
277 mwlucas    2   0  3888K  3116K select  0:03  0.00%  0.00% wmaker
  5 root      18   0    0K     0K syncer   0:00  0.00%  0.00% syncer
430 mwlucas   28   0  1912K  1160K RUN     0:00  0.00%  0.00% top
399 mwlucas    2   0  4500K  4000K select  0:00  0.00%  0.00% Eterm
...
```

Very tightly packed, isn't it? Top tries to cram as much data as possible into a standard 80-character by 25-character terminal window. The display updates every two seconds, so you have a fairly accurate, close to real-time, view of your system. We'll take this a piece at a time and explain what every entry means.

### PID Values

Every process on a UNIX machine has a unique process ID or PID. Whenever a new process is started, it is assigned a PID one greater than the previous process. The last pid value is the last process ID used in the system. In the previous example, the last pid is 436 (❶). The next process to be created will be 437, then 438, and so on. You can watch this increment to see if an abnormal number of processes is being created. Hopefully, you've looked at your system to see how quickly this number rises when things are running well. If the last pid value keeps climbing rapidly, programs are being started and stopped very quickly. This might indicate some daemon that keeps crashing, or a user trying to start too many programs.[2]

### Load Average

The load average (❷) is a somewhat vague number that's intended to give a rough impression of the amount of load on the system.[2] The load average equals the average number of processes waiting for CPU time, plus the average number of jobs that are waiting for access to the disk. An acceptable load average depends on the system; if the numbers are abnormally high, you should investigate. Many 486s feel bogged down at a load average of 3, while some modern systems feel snappy at a load average of 10.

Top lists three load averages. The first (0.14 in our example) is the load average over the last minute, the second (0.08) is for the last 5 minutes, while the last (0.07) is for the previous 15 minutes. If your 15-minute load average is high, but the 1-minute load is low, you had a major spike in activity that has passed. How well did your system hold up? On the other hand, if the 15-minute value is low, but the 1-minute average is high, something happened within the last 60 seconds and may still be going on now. If all of the load averages are high, the condition has persisted for the whole 15 minutes.

---

[2] Some users actually try to use up system resources by starting programs. This is called a *forkbomb*. These users are like script kiddies, but not as educated.

## Uptime

The last entry on the first line is the *uptime* (❸), or how long the system has been running. The system in our example has been up for one hour and six minutes, and the current time is 08:12:26. I'll leave it up to you to figure out when the system booted.

## Process Counts

On the second line you'll find information about processes that are currently running on the system (❹). Running processes are actually doing work; they're answering user requests, handling mail, or whatever else is going on. Sleeping processes are waiting for input from one source or another, and are just fine. Processes in other states are usually waiting for a resource to become available, or are hung in some way. Large numbers of nonsleeping, nonrunnable processes can be a hint of trouble. Investigate further to find out which processes those are.

## Process Types

The CPU states line (❺) indicates what percentage of available time the CPU spends handling different types of processes and other duties. It shows five different process types: user, nice, system, interrupt, and idle.

*User processes* are average everyday programs; they could be daemons run by root, commands run by regular users, or whatever. If it shows up on the list of system processes (that is, on ps -ax), it's a user process.

*Nice processes* are those whose priority has been deliberately manipulated by the user. We'll look at this in some detail in "Reprioritizing with Niceness."

*System processes* are in the kernel, and they include things such as virtual memory handlers, running networking, writing to the disk, and so on.

The *interrupt* category shows how much time the system spends handling interrupt requests (IRQs).

Lastly, the *idle process* shows how much time the system spends doing absolutely nothing. If your system CPU regularly has a very low idle time, you might want to start thinking about rescheduling some jobs or getting a faster processor.

**NOTE** *When you're working on a multi-CPU system, keep in mind that top displays the average usage among all the processors. You might have one processor completely tied up compiling something, but if the other processor is idle, top will show only 50 percent usage.*

## Memory

Then we have the Mem line, representing actual physical RAM (❻). Unlike Windows, which simply divides memory into "used" and "unused" categories, FreeBSD uses memory in several different ways.

*Active* memory is the total amount of memory in use at the moment for running user programs and their data. When a program ends, the program information is put into *inactive* memory and the data pulled from the disk is put in the *cache* memory.

Similarly, the *Buf* entry shows the size of the memory buffer. The memory buffer contains data recently called from disk.

*Free* memory is unused.

*Wired* memory is memory used for in-kernel data structures, as well as for particular system calls that must have a particular piece of memory immediately available. Wired memory is never swapped out.

## Swap

Then we have the Swap line, (❼), which simply represents the total swap available and how much is in use. *Swapping* is when the system uses the disk drive as additional memory. We'll look at swap in more detail later in the chapter.

## Process List

Finally, we have a list of the processes on the system and their basic characteristics (❽). The table format is designed to present as much information as possible in as little space as possible. Every process is on its own line. Let's look at each column in the following sections.

**PID**    First we have the process ID number, or PID. Every process running on the system has a unique PID. When you issue kill commands, you use the PID to identify the process you want to affect.

**Username**    Next is the username of the person running the process. If multiple processes consume large chunks of CPU or memory, and they are all owned by the same user ID, you know who to talk to.

**Priority and Nice**    The PRI (priority) and NICE columns are interrelated, and indicate how much precedence the system gives these processes. We'll talk about priority and niceness a little later in the chapter.

**Size**    Size is the amount of memory that the system has set aside for this process.

**Resident Memory**    The RES column shows how much of the program is actually in memory, or resident, at the moment. A program might have a huge amount of memory reserved for it, but only be using a small fraction of it.

**State**    The STATE column shows what the process is doing at the moment. Processes can be in a variety of states at any given time: waiting for input, sleeping until something wakes them, actively running, and so on.

**Time**    The TIME column gives the total length of time that the process has been running.

**CPU Usage**    The WCPU column gives a weighted CPU usage that shows the percentage of CPU time that the process is using, as adjusted for the process's priority and niceness. The CPU column shows what percentage of CPU time the program is actually using.

**Command Name**    Finally, in the COMMAND column, we have the program name.

### Memory Usage

If your system is running slowly, check its memory and CPU usage first. While they're no more likely to be running amok than any other part of the system, they're the easiest to measure. Let's discuss memory first.

FreeBSD errs on the side of caching recently accessed data because a surprising amount of information is read from disk time and time again. If this information can be cached in physical memory, it can be accessed very quickly. If the system needs more memory, it dumps the oldest cached chunks in favor of new data.

For example, the example top output we're discussing is from my laptop, which is using a lot of buffer and inactive memory. Part of that is due to my Web browser. I started Mozilla when I booted the system yesterday morning so I could check my morning comics.[3] For a couple of moments, the disk light stayed solidly lit while the system read the program off the disk. I then shut the browser down so I could do some work.

Since this Web browser was accessed, it sat in the system buffer cache. When I started the browser again this morning, it only had to be called out of cache rather than from disk, so it started much more quickly. Had I started some other large process, it would have dumped that Web browser from the cache to read in more data.

If your system is operating well, you will have at least a few megs of free memory. If you have more than a few megs free, your system is not being used to nearly its full potential. In the example earlier, I could get rid of 128MB of RAM and not affect system performance much at all.

If you have a good chunk of memory in cache or buffer, you don't have a memory shortage. You might make good use of more memory, but it isn't strictly necessary. Similarly, if you have a lot of free memory, you probably don't have a memory shortage. If active and wired memory is consuming most of your available memory, more RAM wouldn't hurt.

When you're out of free space, and have little or no memory in cache or buffer, you should investigate your memory use further. You may well have a memory shortage. Take a look at the "Using Vmstat" section later in the chapter to check.

### Swap Space Usage

Virtual memory, or *swap* helps cover brief RAM shortages. For example, if you're untarring a huge file, you might easily fill up all your physical memory and have to start using virtual memory. It's not worth buying more RAM for this occasional use when swap suffices.

Like memory cache, swap caches data that it has handled recently, and once you've touched swap, it never returns to being free. For example, I have a server that has been up for 772 days at this writing. At one point, I used about a hundred megs of swap to handle a massive compile. My top display still shows that I'm using that 100MB of swap, while I have over 200MB of memory free.

---

[3] Sluggy Freelance (www.sluggy.com) and Help Desk (www.ubersoft.net), if anyone cares.

Using swap space is not a bad thing, especially since a program will typically spend 80 percent of its time running 20 percent of its code. Since much of the rest of that time spent running is startup, shutdown, and error code, you can safely let those bits go to swap space and have minimal impact.

So don't worry if you find that you're using a bit of swap space on occasion. But, if you're constantly using swap, you probably need more memory.

## CPU Usage

A processor can do only so many things a second, and if you want to do more than your CPU can handle, the requests will start to queue up. You'll develop a processor backlog, and the system will slow down. That's CPU usage in a nutshell.

If top shows your CPU hovering around 100 percent all the time, you must take action. While new hardware is certainly an option, you do have other choices. For one, investigate the processes running on your system to see whether they're all necessary. Did some junior administrator install the SETI@Home client (/usr/ports/astro/setiathome) to hunt for aliens with spare CPU cycles? Are there things running that were important at one time, but are now unnecessary? Find and kill those unnecessary processes and make sure that they won't start the next time the system boots.

Once that's done, evaluate your system performance again. If you still have a problem, try rescheduling or reprioritizing.

### Rescheduling

Rescheduling is easier than reprioritizing, and it is a relatively simple way to balance system processes so that they don't load up on CPU time. As discussed in Chapter 9, you can use cron(1) to schedule system tasks for various times, but users can use it too. If you have users who are running massive compile jobs or doing huge database queries, you might consider using cron to schedule them to run at night. Frequently, jobs such as the monthly billing database search can be run between 6 PM and 6 AM, and nobody will care. Similarly, you could schedule your `make buildworld && make buildkernel` to start at 1 AM.

### Reprioritizing with Niceness

If rescheduling won't work, you're left with reprioritizing, which is a bit trickier. When reprioritizing, you tell UNIX to change the importance of a given process.

For example, if you want a software install to run, but only when nothing more important is running, you reprioritize it with "niceness," which is simply a relative measure of how much CPU time a process demands. The nicer a process is, the less CPU time it demands. The default niceness is 0, but niceness runs from 20 (very nice) to -20 (not nice at all). (This might seem backwards; you could argue that a higher number should mean a higher priority. That leads to a language problem, though, as calling this factor "crankiness" or "greed" didn't seem like a good idea at the time.)[4]

---

[4] This might be one of the few circumstances where common sense won out in naming UNIX commands.

In the top display seen earlier (in the "Using Top" section) you saw a PRI column for process priority. FreeBSD calculates a process priority by combining a variety of factors, including niceness, and runs high-priority processes first whenever possible. Niceness affects priority, but you cannot directly edit priority.

If you know that your system is running low on CPU capacity, you can choose to start a command with nice(1) to assign the command a priority. Specify the desired niceness level by putting a single dash in front of the command. For example, to start a make buildworld at nice 15, you would run this command:

```
# cd /usr/src
# nice -15 make buildworld
```

Only root can assign a negative niceness to a program. To run a program with negative niceness, use a double dash (nice --5). For example, if you have a critical kernel patch that must be applied as soon as possible, and you want the compile to finish as quickly as possible, use a negative niceness like so:

```
# cd /sys/i386/compile/MYKERNEL
# nice --20 make depend && nice --20 make all install
```

Usually, you won't have the luxury of telling a command to start off nicely, but will instead need to change a process's niceness on the fly (generally, when you find out that it's soaking up all your CPU). You can do so with renice(8), which will reprioritize by process ID or owner. To change the niceness of a process ID, you run renice with the new niceness and the process ID.

For example, one of my systems has a FreeBSD CVSup mirror. If I find that the mirror is taking up so much CPU time that it's getting in the way of things I have to do, I can change its niceness to 20. The maximum niceness we can use is 20, which basically tells the system to run this command only if nothing else at all wants CPU time. To renice a running process, I first need to know its process ID. I know the process is named cvsupd because I've looked at this system's top output over the last several months. I then look at all the processes running on the system, and pull out the one for cvsupd with the following command:

```
# ps -ax | grep cvsupd
  322  ??  Is     0:00.01 /usr/local/sbin/cvsupd -C 5 -b /test2 -s sup
#
```

The first column in the preceding ps output is the process ID, PID 322. Now to renice it, I would enter the following:

```
# renice 20 322
322: old priority 0, new priority 20
#
```

Boom! The cvsupd daemon will now only run when nothing else requiring system time is running. This will greatly annoy users of the service, of course, but I presumably have a good reason for doing so. (Since this is a private mirror, not a public one, I feel no particular need to be kind to my users.)

To renice every process owned by a user, use the -u flag. For example, to make my processes more important than anyone else's, I could enter this command:

```
# renice -5 -u mwlucas
1000: old priority 0, new priority -5
#
```

The 1000 is my user ID number on this system. Again, presumably I have a very good reason for doing this besides a need for personal power.[5]

> **NOTE** *Renicing, rescheduling, and process management don't create additional CPU time, they simply rearrange the CPU time you do have. If you cannot reschedule processes, and you cannot satisfactorily renice things to tune the way the system behaves, you really do need faster or additional hardware. Some systems have an extra motherboard slot for an additional CPU, which is a quick and inexpensive way to boost performance when the system is CPU-bound. If you have multiple CPUs, definitely take a look at the discussion of SMP in Chapter 11.*

## When Swap Goes Bad

I said earlier that using swap space isn't bad in and of itself because swap space is used as virtual memory. (In other words, memory space on the hard drive is being used in the same way as RAM.) Swap space is much slower than chip memory, but it does work in a pinch, and many programs don't need to have everything in RAM in order for them to run. If programs spend 80 percent of their time in 20 percent of their code, then 80 percent of their bulk can be put into swap space without seriously impacting performance.

Many sysadmins use the term swapping generically, lumping two different activities (paging and swapping) together without understanding the crucial difference between them.

### Paging

When you read about virtual memory, you'll see references to *pages*. A page is simply a section of memory, 4KB on x86 hardware under FreeBSD. (Different platforms have different page sizes.)

Data moves between real and virtual memory in units of pages. *Paging* happens when a portion of a running program is moved onto swap. This process can actually improve performance on a heavily loaded system because unused bits can be stored on disk until they're needed.

---

[5] Being a selfish person doesn't qualify as a good reason. Or so I've been told.

## Swapping

*Swapping* describes what happens when an entire runnable process is moved into swap. If the computer doesn't have enough physical memory to store a process that isn't being run at that particular microsecond, the system can move the entire process to swap. Then, the next time the CPU runs that process, the process's memory is moved from swap into physical memory, and some other process is probably consigned to swap.

The problem with swapping is that disk usage goes through the roof and performance drops drastically. Since requests take longer to handle, there are more requests of the system at any one time. And logging in to check the problem only makes the situation worse, because logging runs an extra system process. This performance hit is sometimes called the *death spiral*.

Memory shortages will hurt system performance more than anything else. If you're frequently swapping, you *must* get more memory or resign yourself to lousy[6] performance.

> **NOTE**  *Every system has bottlenecks, or places where performance is limited. If you eliminate one bottleneck, performance will increase until another bottleneck is hit. The system's performance is limited, or "bounded," by the slowest component in the computer. For example, a Web server is frequently network-bound because the slowest part of the system is the Internet connection. If you upgrade the Internet connection, the system will hand out Web pages as fast as either its CPU or disk allows.*

### Are You Swapping or Paging?

FreeBSD includes several programs for examining system performance. Among those are vmstat(8), iostat(8), and systat(1). We'll discuss vmstat because I find it to be the most helpful. Iostat is similar to vmstat, and systat provides similar information in a more graphic format.

### Using Vmstat

Vmstat(8) shows virtual memory statistics at the current time. While its output takes some getting used to, it is very good at showing large amounts of data in a very small space. Type **vmstat** at the command prompt, and follow along.

```
# vmstat
 procs      memory      page                    disks     faults      cpu
 r b w     avm   fre   flt  re  pi  po  fr  sr ad4 da0   in   sy  cs us sy id
 0 0 0    7096 479140    21   0   0   0   9   0   0   0  331  102 437  0  1 99
#
```

The display is divided into six sections: process (procs), memory, paging (page), disks, faults, and cpu. We'll look at each then quickly and then dive into detail on the bits that are most important for investigating your performance issues.

---

[6] I would use a better word than "lousy," but my editor frowns upon the flavorful language I learned from an ex-sailor co-worker.

### Processes

There are three columns under the procs heading.

r      Lists the number of processes that are waiting to run on the CPU. These are processes that are ready to run, but which simply cannot get access to the CPU to execute. If this number is high, your CPU is bottlenecking your system.

b      Gives the number of processes that are blocked waiting for system input or output—generally, waiting for disk access. These processes will run as soon as they get their input. If this number is high, your disk is the bottleneck.

w      Shows processes that are runnable but are entirely swapped out. If you start having processes swapped out on a regular basis, your memory is inadequate for the work you are doing on the system.

### Memory

The memory section has two columns.

avm    Shows the average number of pages of virtual memory that are in use. If this value is abnormally high or increasing, your system is using up virtual memory.

fre    Shows the number of pages that remain available for use. If this value is abnormally low, you have a memory problem.

### Paging

The paging section shows how hard the virtual memory system is working.

flt       Shows the number of page faults, where the information needed is not in memory and needs to be fetched from the disk.

re        Shows how many pages have been reclaimed or reused from cache.

pi        Short for *pages in*, it shows how many pages are moving from physical memory to swap.

po        Short for *pages out*, it shows how many pages are moving from swap to real memory.

fr and sr   Show how many pages are freed and scanned per second, respectively. You don't have to worry about these too often, unless your system is under very heavy memory load.

### Disks

The disks section shows each of your disks by device name. The number shown is the number of disk operations per second. You should divide your disk operations between different disks whenever possible, and arrange them on different buses (as discussed in Chapters 1 and 13). If one disk is obviously busier than the others, and the system has operations waiting for disk access, consider moving some frequently used files from one disk to another.

### Faults

The faults section shows system faults. Faults, in this case, aren't bad, they're just received system traps and interrupts.

in    Shows the number of system interrupts (IRQ requests) the system received in the last five seconds.

sy    Shows the number of system calls in the last five seconds.

cs    Gives the number of *context switches*, or times the CPU changed from doing one thing to doing another.

### CPU

Finally, the CPU section shows how much time the system spent doing user tasks (us), and system tasks (sy), and how much time it was idle (id). This is the same information presented by top.

#### Making Use of vmstat Information

So, how do you use this information? First, check the first three columns to see what the system is waiting for when it's slow. If you're waiting for CPU access (the r column), then you're short on CPU horsepower. If you're waiting for disk activity (the b column), then your disks are your bottleneck. If you're swapping (the w column), then you're short on memory. Simple enough, eh?

If you're having problems with memory, you can expect the page section to have very high values. (The details of virtual memory management are an arcane science that I won't cover in depth here.) They key is to know what your system normally looks like, and hence what would be abnormal.

#### Monitoring Multiple Disks

Vmstat shows what's happening on your disks and where data is being written. The number of disk operations per second is a valuable clue to how well your disks are handling their load.

However, if you have a lot of disks, you may notice that they don't all appear on the vmstat display. Vmstat is biased toward fitting into an 80-column display, and hence cannot list every possible disk on the system. If you don't mind overflowing 80 columns, you can use vmstat's -n flag to set the number of drives you want to display. The 80-column limit is important on a system console, but it can easily be overcome when you're using SSH from a workstation.

### Continuous Vmstat

When using vmstat, you're probably more interested in what's happening over a period of time than in taking a brief snapshot. Use vmstat with the -w flag to run it as a continuously updating display and to specify the number of seconds between updates. Many internal system counters are recalculated every five seconds, so five seconds is the minimum recommended time between updates.

```
# vmstat -w 5
 procs      memory        page                    disks     faults      cpu
 r b w     avm    fre   flt  re  pi  po   fr   sr ad0 md0   in   sy  cs us sy id
 1 0 0  165208  51408   431   0   0   0  408    4   0   0  243 2656 255 13  3 83
 0 0 0  165208  51408     8   0   0   0    0    0   0   0  267  829 232  0  2 97
 1 0 0  172480  51408     9   0   0   0    2    0   0   0  277  986 279  2  1 97
 1 0 0  174584  51108    44   0   0   0   21    0   0   0  262 3694 269  1  3 96
...
```

Press **CONTROL-C** when you're done, and just sit and watch your system do its work, and see how it reacts when scheduled jobs kick off. In the preceding example, we have the occasional moment where processes are waiting on CPU time (as shown by the intermittent 1 in the r column), but the disk and memory all seem to be behaving well. An occasional wait for some resource doesn't mean that you need to upgrade that system component; if performance is acceptable, don't worry about it.

# Real-World Performance Tuning

All this theoretical stuff is nice, but how do you troubleshoot performance in real life? At this point, I hope you've actually read the previous chapters of this book, as we're going to be referring to information brought up in all sorts of different places. We'll use a real-world test on a real-world system to demonstrate how performance troubleshooting works.

The standard FreeBSD torture test is the make world process run during an upgrade from source. It pounds on the CPU and the disk, and absorbs all the memory it can get its greedy hands on. We'll focus on the make buildkernel stage of this process because it's shorter than the make buildworld stage, which makes for a better test. Let's see how we can use the techniques and information presented here to reduce the total time needed to run the build.

The system I'll be using for the test has two 1 GHz Pentium CPUs, a new 60GB IDE drive, two somewhat elderly 4.5GB SCSI-2 drives, and 512MB of RAM. It's running a few smaller programs as well, but there is no X server, window manager, or Web server. Initially, the system is installed on the one IDE disk; the SCSI disks are completely idle. The install is fairly default, with soft updates (see Chapter 16) set on the /usr partition.

### Fairness in Benchmarking

Benchmarking is a difficult task. We're not officially benchmarking here, but we'll still do some things to make sure that each run of our test is as fair as possible. I'll reboot the system between tests to eliminate anything that might be lurking in the buffer cache. In this case, we want to improve performance ourselves, not use FreeBSD's buffering and caching to do it for us. Similarly, I'll remove /usr/obj (where the buildkernel creates its files) between runs.

**NOTE**  *While* make buildkernel *is a fairly standard sort of test, don't assume that it is the be-all and end-all of FreeBSD performance. I'm using it here because it's a standard process, and everyone has access to it. Test performance on your systems using programs and commands that you actually use, not arbitrary benchmarks.*

### The Initial Test

To begin, we'll record datestamps from the beginning and end of each run. This will give us an absolute measurement of how any changes affect performance:

```
# date >> timestamps && make buildkernel && date >> timestamps
```

This command records the start and stop times in a file called timestamps, and runs make buildkernel.

Now start the build and look at top, the first few lines of which are shown here:

```
last pid:  6262;  load averages:  0.87,  0.37,  0.15    up 0+01:00:43  12:14:17
46 processes:  2 running, 44 sleeping
CPU states: 21.2% user,  0.0% nice, 29.4% system,  0.6% interrupt, ❶ 48.8% idle
Mem: 16M Active, 38M Inact, 36M Wired, 2240K Cache, 61M Buf, ❷ 407M Free
Swap: 2048M Total, 2048M Free

  PID USERNAME PRI NICE   SIZE    RES STATE   C    TIME  WCPU    CPU COMMAND
  529 root      96    0  2420K  1956K ect     0    0:01 0.10%  0.10% sshd
  275 root      96    0  1020K   588K ect     0    0:08 0.00%  0.00% moused
  354 root      96    0  2420K  1956K ect     1    0:00 0.00%  0.00% sshd
  223 root       8    0  1084K   688K slp     0    0:00 0.00%  0.00% diskcheckd
  252 root      96    0  2364K  1676K ect     1    0:00 0.00%  0.00% sshd
...
```

You can see right away that the system is not short on memory; with 407MB free (❷) it should be good for quite some time. The CPU is 48.8 percent idle (❶), so a lack of processor time does not appear to be the bottleneck.

Let's look at a snippet of vmstat output, updated every five seconds:

```
# vmstat 5
 procs      memory       page                    disks     faults      cpu
 r b w     avm    fre   flt  re  pi  po   fr  sr ad4 da0   in    sy   cs us sy id
 0 2 0   17952 396524   173   0   0   0  199   0   0   0  354   385  630  2  2 96
 2 1 0   18872 394908  2260   0   0   0 2281   0  31   0  369  2682 2342 37 16 47
 2 2 0   19268 394384  1801   0   0   0 1856   0   2   0  336  2107 1687 40 12 48
 0 2 0   19164 393768  2074   0   0   0 2143   0  15   0  353  2617 2162 32 14 53
 2 2 0   21680 389032  2045   0   0   0 1892   0   1   0 ·337  2349 1908 40 12 47
 0 2 0   16096 393452  1916   0   0   0 2242   0   1   0  338  2281 2240 39 14 47
 2 2 0   17888 390616  2260   0   0   0 2236   0   1   0  342  2830 2844 35 17 47
 1 2 0   18880 389728  2260   0   0   0 2337   0  30   0  370  2804 2909 35 19 46
 0 2 0   16484 391684  2031   0   0   0 2234   0   1   0  338  2477 2183 37 16 47
 1 2 0   18416 389052  2230   0   0   0 2219   0  11   0 ·352  2886 2876 33 18 49
...
```

Okay, something is definitely not correct here. The r column shows how many processes can be run but that can't get CPU time. Our system is almost 50 percent idle, yet some processes cannot get CPU time! What's going on?

Well, this is a multiple-processor system. Remember, a CPU does only one thing at a time. What we see here is that one CPU at a time is actually full, while the other isn't doing anything at all. The solution is to split the load between our CPUs. We can do this in a make with the -j flag, as discussed in Chapter 6. That'll be our next test.

When the make buildkernel finishes, take a look at the times to set our benchmark:

```
#more timestamps
Sun Aug 19 12:11:47 EDT 2001
Sun Aug 19 12:23:43 EDT 2001
#
```

Just 4 seconds under 14 minutes, or 716 seconds. That's our benchmark; can we beat it?

### Using Both CPUs

Let's try using *both* our processors to see what happens to the time.

```
# date >> timestamps && make -j2 buildkernel && date >> timestamps
```

We could use numbers over 2 for -j, but 2 is a good place to start. In theory, this should use much more of our CPU.

Let's see how theory compares to reality:

```
last pid:  3855;  load averages:  1.08,  0.36,  0.16    up 0+00:07:18 12:36:45
51 processes:  1 running, 47 sleeping, 1 zombie, 2 mutex
CPU states: 23.0% user,  0.0% nice, 41.2% system,  0.0% interrupt, ❶ 35.8% idle
Mem: 16M Active, 14M Inact, 29M Wired, 8K Cache, 51M Buf, 442M Free
Swap: 2048M Total, 2048M Free

  PID USERNAME PRI NICE   SIZE    RES STATE  C   TIME  WCPU   CPU COMMAND
 2016 root       8    0   612K   512K t      1   0:01 1.46% 1.22% cc
  282 root      96    0  1020K   588K ect    1   0:01 0.00% 0.00% moused
 1653 root      96    0  1756K  1632K ect    1   0:01 0.00% 0.00% make
  351 root      96    0  2420K  1952K ect    1   0:01 0.00% 0.00% sshd
...
```

Only 35.8 percent idle is a lot better (❶); both processors are working now. Let's check vmstat:

```
procs     memory       page                    disks    faults       cpu
r b w   avm    fre    flt re  pi  po   fr  sr ad4 da0   in   sy   cs us sy id
0 4 0 19236 385696 2521  0   0   0 3021   0   8   0  350 3691 5099 52 27 21
0 5 0 29304 374976 2768  0   0   0 2381   0  14   0  357 3929 5403 56 28 16
0 2 0 20992 381444 3140  0   0   0 3634   0  25   0  364 4143 6585 52 32 16
0 1 0 19348 378600 2925  0   0   0 3064   0  39   0  386 4542 8170 39 34 27
0 6 0 25296 372936 3464  0   0   0 3356   0   7   0  349 4734 9110 47 37 16
0 2 0 20456 374884 2584  0   0   0 2860   0  44   0  383 3683 5209 52 27 21
0 6 0 27140 367312 2828  0   0   0 2660   0  10   0  352 4081 6572 52 32 16
...
```

Well, this is better on the CPU front. If you watch long enough, you'll see an occasional bubble of CPU shortage, but it's much better than it was before. (Momentary shortages are perfectly natural—you only need to worry when they keep recurring.) But the contents of the b column, which lists processes that cannot run because they're waiting for the disk, is alarming. It is never 0, which tells us that our process has become disk-bound.

Still, let's look at our current timestamps:

```
Sun Aug 19 12:35:25 EDT 2001
Sun Aug 19 12:46:46 EDT 2001
```

It's 11 minutes, 21 seconds, or 681 seconds. Using both CPUs chopped about 30 seconds off the process. While that's only about a 5 percent increase in speed, we got that increase without spending a dime on additional hardware. Our next problem is to reduce the I/O bottleneck.

### Directory Caching

The least intrusive way to reduce disk input/output is to enable directory caching with the vfs.vmiodirenable sysctl (Chapter 16). We could do this without rebooting the system with sysctl(8) (Chapter 4). (You might already have this enabled, depending on your version of FreeBSD, but you should check it.)

```
# sysctl vfs.vmiodirenable=1
vfs.vmiodirenable: 0 -> 1
#
```

Since our test says we need to reboot the system anyway, though, let's set this sysctl in /etc/sysctl.conf, delete /usr/obj, and reboot. Next, we'll run the make buildworld with the same command. Our top output looks almost identical to the last run, so I won't bother showing it here again, and when we run vmstat, it also looks very similar. Here are the timestamps:

```
Sun Aug 19 13:21:58 EDT 2001
Sun Aug 19 13:33:15 EDT 2001
```

The total is 677 seconds. We've saved 4 whole seconds by caching directory lists. Why so little?

Well, the purpose of caching something is so it can be reused later. When you build a piece of software, the build process visits each directory just once. If you never return to the same spot and actually use the cache, it's pointless. We've seen a minor savings from the rare occasions when make buildkernel visits a directory repeatedly, but that's all. You'd see better improvements on processes such as a Web server, which accesses the same files over and over again.

So, our disk is still the bottleneck. It's time for some major surgery.

### Moving /usr/obj

The make buildkernel process reads files under /usr/src and writes them under /usr/obj. Let's take one of our ancient SCSI disks and mount it on /usr/obj, leaving /usr/src on the new IDE disk. For our first test, we'll use a default mount without soft updates, just to illustrate a point. Our system disks now look like this:

```
# df
Filesystem   1K-blocks     Used    Avail Capacity  Mounted on
/dev/ad4s1a     248111    74081   154182     32%   /
/dev/ad4s1f    2032839   133492  1736720      7%   /test1
/dev/ad4s1g    2032839  1266476   603736     68%   /test2
/dev/ad4s1h   29497862  3842891 23295143     14%   /usr
/dev/ad4s1e    3048830   977220  1827704     35%   /var
procfs               4        4        0    100%   /proc
/dev/da0s1e    3525041        1  3243037      0%   /usr/obj
#
```

In theory, input and output will be spread between different disks. Our top output is similar, but vmstat looks different:

```
 procs      memory      page                    disks   faults      cpu
 r b w    avm    fre  flt  re  pi  po   fr  sr ad4 da0   in   sy   cs us sy id
 0 4 0  29200 329436 2433   0   0   0 2109   0   2  12  367 3390 3220 58 24 18
 0 0 0  15388 338376 2298   0   0   0 2939   0   1  23  390 3315 4487 49 24 26
 0 0 0  19124 336604 2453   0   0   0 2559   0   3  30  413 3672 5333 39 29 32
 0 3 0  23680 330252 2000   0   0   0 1818   0  14  65  489 2979 4874 29 24 46
 0 4 0  22832 329136 2628   0   0   0 2768   0   1  16  374 3783 5158 50 28 23
 0 5 0  23404 326976 2624   0   0   0 2702   0   0  15  373 3815 5550 52 29 20
...
```

We're still blocking, waiting for disk throughput, but take a look at the ad4 (IDE disk) and da0 (SCSI disk) columns. Load is now split between the two. When we're done, our timestamps look like this:

```
Sun Aug 19 13:59:54 EDT 2001
Sun Aug 19 14:11:41 EDT 2001
```

Seven hundred and seven seconds! That's just as bad as when we started! Ouch. A thing to remember, however, is that this decrepit SCSI drive, without soft updates, performed just as well as a modern IDE drive. Buying a modern SCSI drive would definitely enhance performance. Let's enable soft updates on our new /usr/obj and see what happens:

```
# umount /usr/obj
# tunefs -n enable /usr/obj
tunefs: soft updates set
# mount /usr/obj
#
```

Now delete everything in /usr/obj, reboot, and try again. A check of vmstat shows that disk throughput is unquestionably our bottleneck, again. With soft updates, our time goes down to 670 seconds. Soft updates gave us a total 6 percent improvement. While this certainly isn't great, the time savings add up over the course of a day or a long build.

You should now have a very good idea of how to tune your system. Play with it some more. Perhaps /usr/obj as a mirrored Vinum partition, with soft updates—this pulls the time down to 663 seconds, or a 7 percent improvement. That's about as good as it gets. Throughout it all, vmstat shows that disk throughput is the bottleneck.

## Lessons Learned

In the preceding process we learned that disk speed is inarguably the bottle-neck. This particular four-year-old SCSI disk handles data just as quickly as a modern IDE disk, but if we want faster performance we need a faster disk. Faster disks are much less expensive than a whole new machine, even if that new machine includes a faster disk.

Best of all, you can now go to your manager and say, "This is bad. We need a faster disk. Our vendor, AbsoluteBSD.com, has them for $400," and be certain of your facts. That's much better than saying, "This is bad; we need a new server."

Of course, programs other than `make buildkernel` have completely different requirements and must be evaluated separately. While a 5 to 10 percent increase isn't a huge performance boost, it can make the difference between doing maintenance during the normal maintenance window and pulling a desperate triple shift to get the new equipment slammed into place so that people can do their work the next morning.

# 19

## NOW WHAT'S IT DOING?

Every systems administrator must be able to answer this basic
question at the drop of a hat: "How is the server doing?" You must
know what your systems are doing to be able to make good planning
and capacity decisions. Your manager will want nice reports on how
things are running, and even if you haven't been asked for these reports yet,
you will be. Your best bet is to have this information ready before it's needed.

FreeBSD supports report generation, pretty graphs, daily status checks, and
more. Let's take a look.

### Status Mails

If you look in /etc/crontab, under the command periodic(8), you'll see that
FreeBSD systems run maintenance jobs every day, week, and month. These jobs
perform some basic system checks and notify the administrators of changes,
items requiring attention, and potential security issues. The output of the scheduled jobs is emailed daily to the root account on the local system. The simplest
way to find out what your system is doing is to read these mails; many very busy
systems administrators, like you, have collaborated to make these messages useful and necessary.

The configuration of the daily, weekly, and monthly reports is controlled in
/etc/periodic.conf, /etc/defaults/periodic.conf, and /etc/periodic. See
Chapter 9 for details, or just jump straight to the scripts in /etc/periodic.

### Forwarding Reports

Because you probably don't want to log in as root to all of your servers every day, send your mail to a centralized mailbox by editing /etc/mail/aliases (see Chapter 14) to point mail to some other account. If you have many servers, you may end up with a lot of mail, but with experience you'll quickly learn how to skim the reports looking only for critical or unusual changes.

# Logging with Syslogd

UNIX's logging system is one of its most delightful features. Unlike some operating systems that force you to use a small range of limited logs, UNIX allows you to log almost anything, at almost any level of detail. While you'll find system logging hooks for the most common UNIX resources, administrators can choose a logging configuration that meets their needs. Almost all programs integrate with the logging system, syslogd(8).

Syslogd handles messages according to their facility and level, both of which are included in messages to syslogd. You'll need to understand both facility and level to manage your system logs, so they are described next.

### Facilities

A *facility* is a log-entry source (a program) that sends messages to syslogd. This is an arbitrary label—it is essentially just a text string that's used to sort out one program from another. In most cases, each program that needs a unique log needs a unique facility. Many sorts of programs or protocols have facilities dedicated to them—for example, FTP is such a common protocol that syslogd has a special facility just for it. Syslogd also supports a variety of generic facilities that can be used by any program. Programs can lie about their facility, but you'll be able to track them down by finding their name with their message.

The standard facilities and the type of information they provide are listed here.

| | |
|---|---|
| auth | Publicly accessible information pertaining to user authorization, such as login and su. |
| authpriv | Private information pertaining to user authorization, accessible only by root and other selected users. |
| console | Messages normally printed to the system console can be captured with the console facility. |
| cron | Messages from the system scheduler go through the cron facility. |
| daemon | A catch-all for all system daemons without other explicit handlers, either in syslogd or in their program. |
| ftp | FTP daemons will automatically log to this facility. (See Chapter 15.) |
| kern | Messages from the kernel. |
| lpr | Catches messages from the printing system. |
| mail | Catches messages from the mail system. |

| mark | Not an actual log from a system; instead, the mark facility puts an entry in your log every 20 minutes. This is useful when combined with some other log. |
|---|---|
| news | Catches messages from the Internet News daemons. |
| ntp | Collects messages from Network Time Protocol. |
| security | Includes messages from various security programs, such as ipf(8) and ipfw(8). |
| syslog | The log service can log to itself. Just don't log when you log logs from syslogd, or you'll make yourself dizzy. |
| user | The catch-all message facility. If you don't specify a logging facility for user programs, they'll use this. |
| uucp | Logs from the UNIX-to-UNIX Copy Protocol. (This is a piece of pre-Internet UNIX history you'll probably never encounter.) |
| local0 through local7 | These are reserved for administrator use. Many programs have an option to set a logging facility; choose one of these if at all possible. For example, you might tell your customer service system to log to local0. |

### Levels

A log message's *level* represents its relative importance. While programs send all their logging data to syslogd, most systems only record the important stuff that syslogd receives and discard the trivial messages. Of course, one person's trivia is another's vital data, and that's where the levels come in.

FreeBSD offers eight levels of syslogd importance. You can use these levels to tell syslogd what to record and what to discard. The levels follow, in order from most to least important.

| emerg | System panic. Messages are flashed on every terminal. The system is basically hosed. You don't even have to reboot—the system is doing it for you.[1] |
|---|---|
| alert | This is bad, but not as bad as the emerg level. The system can continue to operate, but this error should be attended to immediately. |
| crit | These are critical errors, such as hardware problems (like bad blocks or a failing SCSI cable) or serious software issues. You can continue running, if you're brave. |
| err | Miscellaneous errors. These are bad and should be fixed, but they won't destroy the system. |
| warning | Miscellaneous warnings. |
| notice | General information that should be logged, in case you need it, but that probably doesn't really require action on your part. |

[1] You might think this is funny now, but you won't if it ever happens to you.

info | General program information, such as individual transactions in a mail server.

debug | This level is usually only of use to programmers, and occasionally to sysadmins who are trying to figure out just why some program behaves the way it does. Debugging logs can contain whatever information the programmer felt necessary to debug the code, which may include information that will violate user privacy.

none | This means "don't log anything from this facility here." It's most commonly used when excluding information from wildcard entries, as we'll see later.

### Syslog.conf

The /etc/syslog.conf file has two columns. The first describes the information to be logged, by facility and level. The second tells the action to be taken when a log message matches the description. Syslogd compares each submission to the entries in /etc/syslog.conf and, when it finds a matching entry, processes the log entry in the manner described.

Information sources include both a facility and a level, separated by a period. When you specify a level, the system defaults to recording messages of that level or greater. For example, look at this entry from /etc/syslog.conf:

```
mail.info               /var/log/maillog
```

This tells the system to log messages from the mail system to /var/log/maillog if they have a severity level equal to or above "info".

### Wildcards

You can also use wildcards in your information source. For example, use this line to log absolutely all messages from the mail system:

```
mail.*                  /var/log/maillog
```

To log everything from everywhere, uncomment the all.log entry:

```
*.*                     /var/log/all.log
```

This works, but it's got too much information to be of any real use; if you use it you'll find yourself building complex grep commands just to find what you want. Also, this would include all sorts of private information, thanks to the debug level.

### Excluding Information

Use the authpriv facility and the none level to exclude authentication information. The semicolon allows you to combine entries on a single line:

```
*.*;authpriv.none       /var/log/all.log
```

## Comparison

The comparison operators < (less than), = (equals), and > (greater than) can also be used in /etc/syslog.conf. You can use these with levels to log data above a certain level in one file and data below a certain level in another. While syslogd defaults to recording all messages of the specified level or above, you might want to include only a range of information.

For example, suppose you want one log for mail traffic and another for mail debugging information:

```
mail.info          /var/log/maillog
mail.=debug        /var/log/maillog.debug
```

The preceding `mail.info` entry captures all log messages sent to the mail facility of `info` level and above. The second line only captures messages that have a level no higher than `debug`. You can't use a message source of `mail.debug`, or the debugging log will contain everything in the previous log! This way you don't have to sort through debugging information to learn what your mail server thinks it's doing, and you don't have to sort through mail-transmission information to get to your mail server's debugging output.

## Local Facilities

Many programs expect to be able to use syslogd to handle their logging. Most of these can be set to use a facility of your choice. The various `local` facilities are reserved for these programs.

For example, you might tell a program to log to the facility `local3`. Just how you set the facility varies from program to program. Once you get the program to mark messages with a facility and send them to syslogd, you have to tell syslogd to catch those messages and to do something with them.

```
local3.*           /var/log/programname
```

In general, if a program supports logging to a facility, use a local facility.

## Logging by Program Name

If you're out of facilities, or if your program simply doesn't support syslogd, you can use the program's name to handle logging. An entry for a name requires at least two lines: the program name with a leading exclamation point and then a line with the logging information.

For example, to log ppp, you could do this:

```
!ppp
*.*                /var/log/ppp.log
```

This entry first specifies the program name, and then uses wildcards to tell syslogd to append absolutely everything to a file. (You can't be certain that a random third-party program will have reasonable log levels available, so it's safest to record everything until you know otherwise.)

### Logging Host

My networks habitually have a single logging host that handles not only the FreeBSD boxes, but also Cisco routers, 3Com switches, every other UNIX box, and any other syslogd-speaking systems. Since you have only one host whose logs need handling, this saves a lot of maintenance.

Use the at symbol (@) to can send log messages to another host. For example, the following line would dump everything your syslogd receives to the logging host on my network:[2]

```
*.*                 @loghost.absolutebsd.com
```

The /etc/syslog.conf on the log host determines the final destination for the messages it receives. Fortunately, each log message includes the hostname.

### Logging to User Sessions

To log user sessions, list usernames separated by commas. Then, if those users are logged in when the log message arrives, the system will write the message on their terminal.

To write the messages to all users' terminals, use an asterisk (*) for the destination. For example, the default syslog.conf includes this line:

```
*.emerg               *
```

This says that any message of emergency level will appear on all users' terminals.

### Sending Log Messages to Programs

Finally, to have another program handle the logs, use a pipe symbol ( | ) to redirect the messages to that program:

```
mail.*              |/usr/local/bin/mailstats.pl
```

NOTE    *Traditionally, UNIX demands tabs between the columns in /etc/syslog.conf, but FreeBSD permits you to use spaces. Be sure to use tabs only if you share one syslog.conf between different UNIXes.*

## Rotating Logs with Newsyslog.conf

Log files grow and you must control their growth. The standard way to do so is with *log rotation*. When using log rotation, the oldest logs are deleted, each old log is renamed to the next oldest name, the current log is moved, and a new log file is created.

---

[2] Don't blindly follow this example, or I'll look for anything interesting in your logs and post it in some prominent public location. Do not log to someone else's logging host!

FreeBSD includes a basic log-file handler, newsyslog(8), which will also compress files, restart daemons, and in general handle all the routine tasks of shuffling files. Cron runs newsyslog once an hour.

Newsyslog reads /etc/newsyslog.conf and checks each log file listed there. If the conditions listed for rotating the log file are met, the log is rotated and other actions are taken as appropriate.

The /etc/newsyslog.conf file uses one line per log file, and each line has seven fields. For example:

```
/var/log/slip.log     root:network    640  3    100  *    Z
```

We'll examine each field in turn.

### Log File Path

The first entry on each line is the full path to the log file to be processed (/var/log/slip.log in our example).

### Owner and Group

The second entry (root:network in our example) lists the rotated file's owner and group, separated by a colon (such as root:wheel). This field is optional, and is not present in many of the standard entries.

Newsyslog can change the owner and group of old log files. By default, log files are owned by root and are in the wheel group. While it's not common to change the owner, you might have to use this ability on multi-user machines.

You can choose to only change the owner, or only change the group. In these cases you must use a colon, even though nothing appears on the other side of it. For example, :www will change the group to www, while user827: will change the owner to user827.

### Permissions

The third field (640 in our example) is the permissions mode, in standard UNIX three-digit notation. (See Chapter 7 for details.)

### Count

Next is the *count* field (having a value of 3 in our example), which represents the number of old log files that newsyslog will keep—kind of. Newsyslog starts counting archived log files at 0. Many computer systems start numbering at 0, but newsyslog includes 0 as well as the count number. With the default count setting of 5 for /var/log/messages, /var/log includes the following files:

```
messages
messages.0.gz
messages.1.gz
messages.2.gz
messages.3.gz
messages.4.gz
messages.5.gz
```

Those of you who can count will recognize that this is six backups, not five, plus the current log file! While, as a rule, it's better to have too many logs than not enough, if you're tight on disk space, deleting an extra log file or two might buy you some time. Some Web servers can have hundreds of sites on a single server; removing one or two files times 100 sites can create a lot of disk space.

**Size**

The fifth field (100 in our example) is the file size. When newsyslog runs, it compares the size listed here with the size of the file. If the file is larger than the given size in kilobytes, it is rotated. If the file size doesn't affect when you want it rotated, put an asterisk (*) here.

**Time**

So far, this seems easy, right? Well, the sixth field, time (* in our example), can make new administrators cry.

The time field has four possible values: an asterisk (*), a number, and two different date formats. If you don't want to rotate a log at a particular time, put an asterisk (*) here. If you use a plain naked number, newsyslog rotates the log after that many hours have passed. For example, if you want a log to rotate every 24 hours, but don't care exactly when this rotation happens, put 24 here.

The date formats are a little more complicated.

### ISO8601 Time Format

Any entry beginning with an at symbol (@) is in ISO 8601 restricted time format. This is a standard used by newsyslog on most UNIX systems, and was the time format originally used in MIT's primordial newsyslog program. Unfortunately, this standard is not at all clear, but since it's a standard, FreeBSD supports it.

A full date in ISO 8601 format is 16 digits with a T in the middle. The first four digits are the year; the next two are the month; the next two are the date. The T is inserted after the date as a sort of decimal point, separating whole days from fractions of one. An ISO 8601 date must include the T.

The next two digits are hours; the next two are minutes; the next two are seconds. For example, the date and time February 2, 2002, 9:15 and 8 seconds PM is expressed in ISO 8601 as

```
20020202T211508
```

While complete dates in ISO 8601 are mostly straightforward, confusion arises when you don't list the entire date. For example, you can choose to specify only fields near the T, leaving fields farther away blank, which will be read as wildcards. For example, T23 matches the twenty-third hour of every day of the year. With a newsyslog time of @T23, the log rotates every day at 11 PM, and 4T00 matches midnight of the fourth day of every month.

As with crontab, you must specify hours. A date like @7T will run once an hour, every hour, on the seventh of the month. After all, it matches all day long! This can be useful for debugging, but isn't generally desirable.

### FreeBSD-Specific Time

One problem with the ISO 8601 time system is that it doesn't allow you to easily designate weekly jobs (it's not uncommon to want to rotate a log on Mondays, for example), and it's impossible to specify the last day of the month. That's where the final time format comes in. Any time with a leading dollar sign ($) is written in the FreeBSD-specific month-week-day format.

This format works much like cron, allowing you to set particular days of the week to run a job on, and uses three identifiers: M (day of month), W (day of week), and H (hour of day). Each identifier is followed by a number indicating the particular time it should be run. Hours range from 0 to 23, while weekdays range from 0 (Sunday) to 6 (Saturday). M starts with 1, and goes up to the number of days in that particular month. For example, to rotate a log every Sunday at 8 AM you could use a time of $W0H8. To rotate the log on the fifth of each month at noon, you could use $M5H12.

One interesting feature of this system is that it lets you automatically schedule a job for the last day of the month by using L to represent the last day of the month. Without this, it's very difficult to do an end-of-month job without writing a script that knows how many days are in each month, compares the current date to the scheduled date, and decides if it will start the program. (That gets ugly quickly.) For example, to start your month-end log-file accounting two hours before the end of the month, use a time of $MLH22.

**NOTE** *You can rotate logs at a given time, or when they reach a certain size, or both. If you use both, the log will rotate whenever either condition is met. If you're only rotating on one condition (meaning you want to rotate every day, no matter how large the file gets), use an asterisk (\*) in the other field.*

### Flags

Now that you know how to express the exact time that you want your log to run, we encounter the flags field (Z in our example), which offers two options for handling your log files. Some programs log their data in plain text, while others use a binary format; each sort of log needs to be treated differently.

Binary files can only be written to in a very specific manner. Newsyslog starts each new log file with a "log-file turned over" message, but adding this to a binary file will damage it. The B flag tells newsyslog that this is a binary file, and that the message should not be written. On the other hand, many log files are plain ASCII text, and compressing them can save a huge amount of space. The Z flag tells newsyslog to compress the rotated log files with gzip.

You can use only one of these flags; after all, compressing binaries doesn't save much room, and only text logs can use a "turned over" message.

### Pidfile Path

The next field is the *pidfile* path (not shown in our example). A pidfile is a simple way to record a program's process ID (PID) so that other programs can easily view it. Not all programs have pidfiles; the ones that do store their pidfiles under /var/run (take a look and see what's on your system).

If you list the full path to a pidfile in /var/run, newsyslog will send a kill-style signal to that program when it rotates the log. For example, the Apache Web server needs to be notified when you rotate its logs. By listing its pidfile here, you can have newsyslog send a kill -1 to Apache so it will handle its part of log-file rotation.

Most programs will handle log-file rotation on a kill -1, or SIGHUP, but some programs need a specific signal when a log file is rotated. If you have one of these programs, you can list its exact signal number in the last field.

### Example newsyslog.conf Entry

Let's slap this all together in a worst-case, you-have-*got*-to-be-kidding example. Assume you have a database log file that you want to rotate at 11 PM on the last day of every month. The database documentation says that you need to send the program an interrupt signal (SIGINT, or signal number 2) upon rotation. You want the archived logs to be owned by the user dbadmin, and only viewable by that user, and you need six months of logs. What's more, the logs are binary files. Your newsyslog.conf line would look like this:

```
/var/log/database   dbadmin:  600  6    *    $MLH23 B /var/run/db.pid  2
```

This is an extreme example; in most cases, you just slap in the filename and rotation condition and you're done. But I thought I'd make you twitch.

## Reporting with SNMP

The report emails are good, but they're very general, and logs are difficult to read for long-term trends. To learn more about how your server is doing, either now or in the long term, use the Simple Network Management Protocol (SNMP) reporting tool. SNMP is an industry-standard way to gather information from hosts across a network. Many different vendors support SNMP, and you can use the techniques we discuss here to monitor any SNMP-speaking device.

You can use free tools to tell SNMP to generate nice, pretty pictures of how well your system is working. To use those tools effectively, however, you must have some basic understanding of what SNMP is and how it works. Once you understand that, we'll consider the most popular set of SNMP tools for FreeBSD.

### Basics of SNMP

SNMP works on a standard client/server model. The SNMP client, or agent, sends a request across the network to an SNMP server running on a computer. The SNMP server, snmpd, then gathers information from the local system and returns it to the client.

An SNMP agent can also send a request to make changes to the SNMP server. If your system is properly (or improperly, depending on your point of view) configured, you can issue commands via SNMP. This "write" configuration is most commonly used in routers, switches, and other network devices.

UNIX has its own configuration system, and doesn't usually let you issue instructions via SNMP. (Some daemons might allow you to configure them via SNMP, and you can write shell scripts to be called by setting an SNMP value, but those are special cases.) For our purposes, we don't want to be able to write configurations at all. Writing system configurations or instructions via SNMP requires careful setup and raises all sorts of security issues; it's an excellent topic for an entire book.

### MIBs

SNMP manages its information via a Management Information Base, or MIB. (We saw an example of a MIB tree in Chapter 4, when discussing sysctls.)

Each SNMP server has a list of information it can extract from the local computer. The server arranges these bits of information into a hierarchical system, or Management Information Base tree. Each SNMP MIB tree has a very general main category, network, physical system, programs, and so on, with more specific subdivisions. Think of these trees as well-organized directories, where subdirectories contain more specific information. Similarly, the uppermost MIB contains a variety of MIBs beneath it.

MIBs are referred to by name or by number. For example, here's a MIB pulled off a sample system:

```
interfaces.ifTable.ifEntry.ifOutErrors.1
```

The first term in this MIB, `interfaces`, shows us that we're looking at the network interfaces on the system (network cards, parallel ports, and so on). If there were no interfaces on this particular system, this first category would not even exist. The `ifTable` is the *interface table*, or a list of all the interfaces on the system. `ifEntry` shows one particular interface, and `ifOutErrors` means that we're looking at the outbound errors on this particular interface. Finally, the trailing 1 means that we're interested in interface number 1.

MIBs can also be expressed as numbers, and most SNMP tools prefer numerical MIBs. Unfortunately (or not) our feeble brains prefer words, but your poor brain must be capable[3] of working with either. (We'll learn exactly how to do this translation with a particular piece of software in the section "Translating Between Numbers and Names"; for now, just trust me.) The preceding example can be translated to this:

```
.1.3.6.1.2.1.2.2.1.20.1
```

Expressed as words, the MIB has five terms separated by periods. Expressed as numbers, the MIB has 11. That doesn't look right if they're supposed to be the same. What gives?

[3] *Enjoyment* is not a requirement, merely capability.

The numerical MIB is longer because it includes the default `.1.3.6.1.2.1`, which means `.iso.org.dod.internet.mgmt.mib-2`. This is the standard subset of MIBs used on the Internet (SNMP could also be used to manage non-Internet devices). Almost every MIB you encounter will have this leading string, which is why almost nobody bothers writing it down anymore.

If you're in one of those kinky moods, you can even mix words and numbers:

```
.1.org.6.1.mgmt.1.interfaces.ifTable.1.ifOutErrors.1
```

These MIBs look useful, but how do you find out what each one means? SNMP MIBs can vary from device to device and with the server used. Check the documentation for your SNMP agent, or your device, to see which MIBs are available.

When you make an SNMP query, you'll use the MIB to extract exactly the information you want. Since most networked devices shouldn't give out information to just anyone, let's look at how SNMP provides basic security with communities.

### Net-snmp

Net-snmp (http://net-snmp.sourceforge.net) is the best set of SNMP programs that runs on FreeBSD. It's small, extensible, and efficient, and it's included as a FreeBSD port (/usr/ports/net/net-snmp4). This is a popular package, and the port is generally quite up to date because the net-snmp folks are actively interested in FreeBSD and are quite responsive to useful problem reports, requests for help, or (better still) patches.

**NOTE** *Just to make things slightly difficult, net-snmp was previously called ucd-snmp. The University of California at Davis is no longer quite so involved in the project, hence the name change. You'll see references to both net-snmp and ucd-snmp.*

When you install net-snmp from ports, the build process will ask you several different questions. Go ahead and accept the defaults; you can override them later with the configuration file we'll create.

The net-snmp port includes an SNMP client, an SNMP server, and a translation tool. We'll consider each in turn.

### Snmpwalk

The net-snmp port includes a generic tool, snmpwalk(1), that you can use to examine the SNMP tree on other hosts. Snmpwalk works well on any sort of server: I use my FreeBSD system to snmpwalk Cisco routers, assorted switches, other BSD machines, and even Windows-based systems. To use snmpwalk, give it the name of the host you want to check and the SNMP community name:

```
# snmpwalk hostname community
```

Try snmpwalk on a system running an SNMP daemon, using the default community of "public":

```
# snmpwalk localhost public > snmpwalk.out
#
```

The snmpwalk command generates a lot of output, so in this example we've redirected it to a file. Look at the output. You may be surprised at the amount of information a system offers via SNMP.

### Specific Snmpwalk Queries

You can also make very specific queries via SNMP simply by specifying the portion of the tree you're interested in. For example, suppose you want to know the value of the MIB .1.3.6.1.4.1.2021.11.9.0. (This is the percentage of CPU time spent on user programs when running the net-snmp server. The next section tells us how to get that information.) You can add this MIB to the end of your snmpwalk query to just ask about that MIB.

```
#snmpwalk localhost public .1.3.6.1.4.1.2021.11.9.0
enterprises.ucdavis.systemStats.ssCpuUser.0 = 1
#
```

This tells me that 1 percent of my system CPU time is being spent running user programs. Nifty, eh?

You can use snmpwalk to get information from any device that speaks SNMP. For example, the Windows NT documentation tells us that the MIB 1.3.6.1.4.1.311.1.1.3.1.1.1.1 represents "available memory." How about using snmpwalk from your FreeBSD system to check this value without bothering to log on to the NT system? Try this:

```
# snmpwalk windowsserver public .1.3.6.1.4.1.311.1.1.3.1.1.1.1.0
enterprises.311.1.1.3.1.1.1.1.0 = 154447872
#
```

It can be much simpler to use specific queries like this than it would be to log into a system to run top; and these queries work on any system with SNMP tools. Later, we'll automatically query servers by MIB and use the results to generate our pretty graphs of server status.

Commercial solutions for checking SNMP servers run to hundreds or thousands of dollars. Using these free SNMP tools is an excellent way to begin using FreeBSD on any network.

### Translating Between Numbers and Names

So you want to know how to translate between the numbers and the words? And you wonder what MIBs are available on your system and perhaps even what they mean? Well, that's not *entirely* unreasonable. The net-snmp port includes the translation tool snmptranslate(1).

First, choose a MIB that you want to translate. You have the output of an snmpwalk run on your system saved, right? Well, let's pluck a bit of output from it and see what we have. I'll pick the following line from my local system:

```
enterprises.ucdavis.memory.memAvailSwap.0 = 204672
```

This looks important, doesn't it? Available swap would be handy to know.

To begin with, you need to know that snmpwalk gives only the last section of the MIB. You have to know that the enterprises tree is always prefaced by .1.3.6.1.4. (This is common knowledge in the SNMP world.) Now, armed with that esoteric knowledge, give this full MIB, and the -Td switch, to snmptranslate:

```
# snmptranslate -Td .1.3.6.1.4.enterprises.ucdavis.memory.memAvailSwap.0
.1.3.6.1.4.1.2021.4.4.0
memAvailSwap OBJECT-TYPE
  -- FROM       UCD-SNMP-MIB
  SYNTAX        INTEGER
  MAX-ACCESS    read-only
  STATUS        current
  DESCRIPTION   "Available Swap Space on the host."
::= { iso(1) org(3) dod(6) internet(1) private(4) enterprises(1) ucdavis(2021)
memory(4) memAvailSwap(4) 0 }
#
```

This gives you a heap of useful information about the MIB, including its numerical equivalent (.1.3.6.1.4.1.2021.4.4.0) and its description ("Available Swap Space on the host."). Note the numerical MIB; we'll need it soon. The last tidbit is the name of each part of the MIB and its matching number.

**NOTE** *You can also run this command in reverse: give it a numerical MIB and it will spell out the whole named MIB.*

### Setting Up Snmpd

Before you can use SNMP to monitor your system, you need to set up the snmp daemon. Rather than installing a default configuration file, the net-snmp port installs a default configuration file in /usr/local/share/examples/ucd-snmp/ EXAMPLE.conf. In addition to having default communities of "public" and "private," this default configuration includes a variety of possible security holes.

Fortunately, net-snmp includes a program to create an SNMP daemon configuration file, snmpconf(1). To use snmpconf to create a standard configuration for your system, run this command:

```
# snmpconf -i -g basic_setup
```

This command will take you through a basic snmpd configuration, which will install the file in the proper place. (Since we'll be using snmpconf only once, we won't go over each part of this command.) The configuration is fairly straightforward, but we'll walk through it to be sure you've set everything properly. (While this program lets you set all sorts of advanced stuff, we'll only configure what we need in order to perform basic monitoring.)

Snmpconf will ask many "yes" or "no" questions. You should first see something like this:

```
************************************************
*** Beginning basic system information setup ***
************************************************
Do you want to configure the information returned in the system MIB group
(contact info, etc)? (default = y):
```

You do want to provide some basic system information, so type **y**.

```
Configuring: syslocation
Description:
  The [typically physical] location of the system.
    arguments:  location_string

The location of the system:
```

Enter a system location here, like "server room" or "server room A-30", or whatever works. This designation can be helpful if you have multiple servers in multiple locations, but if you have only one server it's almost moot. But beware: Whatever you enter will show up in monitoring software, so be sure to not put anything offensive or irrelevant here.

The script will then ask you for a "syscontact", the person responsible for the system. If you have multiple server administrators, this is an excellent place to put the email address of the person who should be contacted regarding problems or issues. You might also put in an alias that forwards to multiple people, so that you don't have to reconfigure snmpd when your contact person leaves or is reassigned.

```
Do you want to properly set the value of the sysServices.0 OID? (default =
y):
```

Yes, you do. This section describes extremely basic properties of the system, but not ones that accept a "y" or "n" answer. Because you'll be filling in actual values to be used in the SNMP configuration, you'll enter **0** for "no" and **1** for "yes."

```
Configuring: sysservices
Description:
  The proper value for the sysServices object.
    arguments:  sysservices_number

does this host offer physical services (eg, like a repeater) [answer 0 or 1]:
```

Some people have telco cards for FreeBSD that allow them to hook a standard x86 PC into a telephone switch to handle phone-company-level operations. If you're not one of them, enter **0** for the preceding question.

```
does this host offer datalink/subnetwork services (eg, like a bridge):
```

FreeBSD can be configured as a bridge, but if you haven't done so, answer **0**.

```
does this host offer internet services (eg, supports IP): 1
does this host offer end-to-end services (eg, supports TCP): 1
does this host offer application services (eg, supports SMTP): 1
```

Answer **1** to all of the three preceding questions. A FreeBSD Internet server supports them all.

```
**************************************
*** BEGINNING ACCESS CONTROL SETUP ***
**************************************
Do you want to configure the agent's access control? (default = y):
```

You don't want just anyone to be able to access your system, so answer **y**.

```
Do you want to allow SNMPv3 read-write user based access (default = y):
Do you want to allow SNMPv3 read-only user based access (default = y):
Do you want to allow SNMPv1/v2c read-write community access (default = y):
```

SNMP version 3 is fairly advanced stuff, and far beyond what we need for basic monitoring. Also, we are not using read-write SNMP; we want our monitor to only be able to read information, not issue commands on the system! Answer **n** to all of the above. You'll get your read-only access by answering **y** to the next option.

```
Do you want to allow SNMPv1/v2c read-only community access (default = y): y
Configuring: rocommunity
Description:
  a SNMPv1/SNMPv2c read-only access community name
    arguments:  community [default|hostname|network/bits] [oid]

The community name to add read-only access for:
```

Those of you experienced with SNMP are familiar with the default communities of "public" and "private", but don't use them: they're the first thing an intruder will look for. Choose community names like you would a good password; don't use ones that are easily guessed, and don't use common words; do mix letters and other characters, and so on. If you don't intend to allow anyone to write SNMP commands on your system, then you probably only need one community name.

```
The hostname or network address to accept this community name from [RETURN for all]:
```

Enter the IP address of your network monitoring system as the answer to the preceding question. If you're monitoring only this machine, from itself, put the loopback IP address (127.0.0.1). You can list an entire network in the standard slash format discussed in Chapter 5 (for example, 192.168.0.0/16). Finally, if you put "0.0.0.0/0", anyone on the Internet can read SNMP values from your system if they have (or guess) the correct community name.

```
The OID that this community should be restricted to [RETURN for no-restriction]:
```

You can restrict different SNMP communities to subportions of the MIB tree. Though you don't need to bother doing so for our purposes, you might choose to restrict communities in more complex setups than this one.

```
Finished Output: rocommunity  public 127.0.0.1
Do another rocommunity line? (default = y):
```

If you're doing only the monitoring we discuss in this chapter, you only need one SNMP community. Answer **n** to the preceding question.

```
**************************************
*** Beginning trap destination setup ***
**************************************
Do you want to configure where and if the agent will send traps? (default = y):
```

A *trap* is where the system will send a notice to another system when a MIB is set or unset. We aren't using them. Answer **n**.

```
******************************************
*** Beginning monitoring setup ***
******************************************
Do you want to configure the agent's ability to monitor various aspects of your
system? (default = y):
```

We aren't using process monitoring right now, but we will monitor disk space.
Answer **y** to both the preceding question and the following one.

```
Do you want to configure the agents ability to monitor disk space? (default = y):
Configuring: disk
Description:
  Check for disk space usage of a partition.
    The agent can check the amount of available disk space, and make
    sure it is above a set limit.

    disk PATH [MIN=100000]

    PATH:  mount path to the disk in question.
    MIN:   Disks with space below this value will have the Mib's errorFlag set.
           Can be a raw byte value or a percentage followed by the %
           symbol.  Default value = 100000.

    The results are reported in the dskTable section of the UCD-SNMP-MIB tree

Enter the mount point for the disk partion to be checked on: /usr
Enter the minimum amount of space that should be available on /usr: 10%
Finished Output: disk  /usr 10%
```

Enter each partition you have on your system above. If you're unsure, check
/etc/fstab or df(1). Generally speaking, it's a good idea to warn the user if the
system has less than 10 percent free space on any one partition.

```
Do you want to configure the agents ability to monitor load average? (default = y):
n
Do you want to configure the agents ability to monitor file sizes? (default = y): n
```

We aren't monitoring load average or file size, so answer **n** to the previous two
questions. You can set this up later when you understand more about SNMP
and monitoring.

```
The following files were created:

  snmpd.conf installed in /usr/local/share/snmp
#


      Stop and start snmpd to read the new configuration.


# killall snmpd && snmpd
#
```

Congratulations! You now have a complete SNMP configuration. Break out snmpwalk and see what sort of information you can read from your system.

### Index Numbers

Now let's look at something that frequently confuses new SNMP users. Take the following snippet of snmpwalk output describing the disks on our system. Remember: snmpwalk reads the SNMP information available from a server; this is a small chunk of output from the complete listing of information available from snmpd.

```
enterprises.ucdavis.dskTable.dskEntry.dskIndex.1 = 1
enterprises.ucdavis.dskTable.dskEntry.dskIndex.2 = 2
enterprises.ucdavis.dskTable.dskEntry.dskIndex.3 = 3
enterprises.ucdavis.dskTable.dskEntry.dskPath.1 = /usr
enterprises.ucdavis.dskTable.dskEntry.dskPath.2 = /
enterprises.ucdavis.dskTable.dskEntry.dskPath.3 = /var
enterprises.ucdavis.dskTable.dskEntry.dskDevice.1 = /dev/ad0s1f
enterprises.ucdavis.dskTable.dskEntry.dskDevice.2 = /dev/ad0s1a
enterprises.ucdavis.dskTable.dskEntry.dskDevice.3 = /dev/ad0s1e
```

All the partitions listed in snmpd.conf appear here. In the first three lines of the preceding example, we see that the dksIndex is a number from 1 to 3. Using snmptranslate, we learn that these are the reference numbers for the disk partitions we're monitoring; each partition has been assigned a unique index number.

In the next three rows, dskPath, we map the index 1 to /usr, index 2 to /, and index 3 to /var.

Then, in our next three entries, dskDevice, we see that there are three entries yet again. How do we use these disparate entries? By working backwards. For example, we see that dskDevice.1 is /dev/ad0s1f. We know that entry 1 is /usr, which tells us that /usr is on this physical device.

Because MIB trees are based on the information you want to pull, not the device that you want to access, a partition's information appears on nonconsecutive lines, making things slightly more difficult to read. But with a little patience, you'll be able to put it all together.

You'll see index numbers in anything SNMP reports that comes in multiple units. While disk partitions are the first one everyone stumbles across, you'll find that you'll get indexes for just about anything. Just look around for a key to these indexes; it'll be at the top of the section.

# Long-Term Monitoring with MRTG

For long-term monitoring, we'll use a program that will query SNMP at specific intervals and record the answers it gathers. The most popular programs for this purpose are cricket and MRTG. Both are included in the FreeBSD ports collection and install cleanly on FreeBSD. We'll discuss MRTG (/usr/ports/net/mrtg) here.

MRTG, the Multi-Router Traffic Grapher, uses SNMP data to automatically generate reports on a Web page with nicely labeled graphs. MRTG can run as a daemon, but is traditionally a cron job run every five minutes. You will need a Web server on the machine running MRTG.

You can use MRTG to give supervisors, managers, and co-workers convenient access to performance data without giving them server access. And, because MRTG keeps records over the course of a year, you can get a good idea of real-life trends. MRTG is also quite useful for justifying hardware and software expenditures, since you can point to exactly how much CPU time a machine is using, and how its performance has changed as you've added software.

### Configuring MRTG

You can use the included cfgmaker(1) tool to generate a default MRTG configuration that measures network throughput on interfaces, like so:

```
# cfgmaker communityname@machine > mrtg.cfg
```

For example, if I wanted to run MRTG on my local machine, using the community name "GetLostLoser", I could run this command:

```
# cfgmaker GetLostLoser@localhost > mrtg.cfg
```

Cfgmaker makes SNMP queries of the specified device and generates a basic configuration file, which we dumped into the file mrtg.cfg in the preceding example. By default, MRTG monitors only network traffic.

Before you can use this configuration file, you need to add a WorkDir directive to the top of it to tell MRTG where to store its logs, graphics, working files, and HTML. I generally put the WorkDir somewhere under my Web server root directory, like this:

```
WorkDir: /usr/local/share/apache/htdocs/mrtg
```

You'll probably want to password-protect this directory, too, if the Web server is on the public Internet or otherwise exposed to the world at large. (See Chapter 15.)

## Sample mrtg.cfg Entry

The generated mrtg.cfg has a lot of information, including some unnecessary HTML. If you look through the created file, you'll see that cfgmaker has generated a configuration for every single interface on the machine, which is proper because it measures network throughput by default. The loopback interface, and any down interfaces, are commented out; the remaining uncommented parts are a series of entries much like this:

```
❶ Target ❷ [localhost.3]: 3:GetLostLoser@localhost
❸ MaxBytes[localhost.3]: 1250000
❹ Title[localhost.3]: petulance.blackhelicopters.org: xl0
❺ PageTop[localhost.3]: <H1>Traffic Analysis for xl0
  </H1>
  <TABLE>
    <TR><TD>System:</TD><TD>petulance.blackhelicopters.org in Basement Server
Room</TD></TR>
    <TR><TD>Maintainer:</TD><TD>mwlucas@blackhelicopters.org</TD></TR>
    <TR><TD>Interface:</TD><TD>xl0 (3)</TD></TR>
    <TR><TD>IP:</TD><TD>petulance.blackhelicopters.org  (192.168.1.100)</TD></TR>
    <TR><TD>Max Speed:</TD>
        <TD>1250.0 kBytes/s (ethernetCsmacd)</TD></TR>
  </TABLE>
```

### Labels

The string inside the square brackets ([])(❷) is an arbitrary label that indicates a unique subsystem being monitored. In this example, the label is localhost.3. This might be a network interface, the disk space on a partition, CPU usage, or anything. All files generated by MRTG for this monitored subsystem will have a name starting with this label.

To monitor any number of items, you must give each a unique label of any length. I usually create labels like "webserver1.EthernetTraffic" or "webserver9.AvailableSwap". Labels with names similar to the MIB you want to monitor are most useful, but they can become quite long, so strike a balance that you feel comfortable with.

### Target

The Target keyword (❶) tells MRTG which machine to query and which interface on that machine this configuration is for. (The actual target appears after the colon.) If you change the community name or IP address of your system, you can edit it directly here. In this case, the target is 3:GetLostLoser@localhost: an interface number, a SNMP community, and a hostname.

We spoke about indexes in MIBs earlier in "Index Numbers"; if you were to snmpwalk the MIB tree, you would find that this interface has the index number 3. You can dig through the snmpwalk output to find out which interface has this index number. Each interface has a unique IP address, however, and it's generally easier to use that to identify the interface. MRTG kindly includes the IP address a little later in the configuration.

### MaxBytes

MaxBytes (❸) is the maximum value allowed for this item. Since this is a network interface, MaxBytes is the maximum number of bytes this network card can handle (a 10BaseT card). MRTG has enough brains to figure out the MaxBytes values for most common network types.

You should never have to change this value if you're measuring throughput. You will have to change it to monitor other things, such as CPU or memory utilization.

### Title and PageTop

Title (❹) and PageTop (❺) are arbitrary HTML. You can put almost any HTML in these spaces to display it on the generated MRTG Web page.

### Edited Configuration File

Once I finish editing the basic MRTG config to my taste to monitor a network interface, it generally looks like this:

```
WorkDir: /usr/local/share/apache/htdocs/mrtg
Target[webserver1.EthernetTraffic]: 3:GetLostLoser@localhost
MaxBytes[webserver1.EthernetTraffic]: 1250000
Title[webserver1.EthernetTraffic]: Ethernet Interface
PageTop[webserver1.EthernetTraffic]: <H1>Traffic Throughput for Ethernet
Interface</H1>
<P>Call the Helpdesk if you have any questions
```

You'll notice that, first of all, the label has been changed to something meaningful. Also, the HTML under PageTop has been trimmed considerably, because I know perfectly well where the system is, after all, and who to talk to about it. If these pages are intended for management, I might add a couple of lines of HTML after PageTop describing what the machine does or how to interpret the data.

You can list any number of machines or interfaces in one configuration file. Set up things appropriately for your system.

### Testing MRTG

When you have a configuration you like, test it by running MRTG by hand a few times:

```
# mrtg mrtg.cfg
```

MRTG will warn you that it can't find log files the first two times, after which it should run silently. This alone is not a problem. However, if you get an error that MRTG cannot reach a target, the Target entry is misconfigured, and either the community name, hostname, or MIB is wrong. Check those, correct the problem, and try again. Once MRTG runs silently, add it to root's cron to run every five minutes. (You can also set up a specific user to run MRTG, but there's no real need for this.)

MRTG will send its output to the directory you specify in `WorkDir` in the configuration file. If you followed the previous example, when you look at http://<hostname>/mrtg/webserver1.EthernetTraffic.html, you'll see a pretty graph of your network traffic since you started running MRTG. There are two different lines on the graph: one for inbound traffic, the other for outbound. MRTG measures things in pairs. You can see a sample MRTG graph in Figure 19-1.

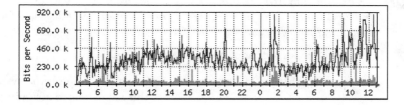

*Figure 19-1: Sample MRTG graph*

Get MRTG measuring traffic on one of your machines, and then we'll measure some other interesting things by choosing our SNMP MIBs.

### Tracking Other System Values

By default, MRTG measures network traffic, but you can use it to measure any information available via SNMP. All you need are the MIBs for the information you want to measure. To make MRTG monitor these MIBs instead of network traffic, add them to the `Target` entry like so:

```
Target[label]:mibnumber1&mibnumber2:GetLostLoser@localhost
```

For example, to measure system CPU time (MIB `.1.3.6.1.4.1.2021.11.9.0`) and user CPU time (MIB `.1.3.6.1.4.1.2021.11.10.0`), use this line:

```
Target[cpu]:1.3.6.1.4.1.2021.11.9.0&1.3.6.1.4.1.2021.11.10.0.:GetLostLoser@localhost
```

Remember, MRTG charts MIBs in pairs, so pick values to monitor accordingly. Sensible choices are things like "available swap and total swap" or "system CPU usage and user CPU usage." Measuring combinations such as available swap versus the percentage of disk available would give you difficult-to-understand charts.

How do we know which MIBs to use? Well, digging through the snmpwalk output, and translating the system and user CPU times (`enterprises.ucdavis.systemStats.ssCpuUser.0` and `enterprises.ucdavis.systemStats.ssCpuSystem.0`, respectively), we find that they translate to `.1.3.6.1.4.1.2021.11.9.0` and `.1.3.6.1.4.1.2021.11.10.0`. You don't want to go digging through the MIB tree to find this sort of thing, however, so I'll make it a little easier for you.

### Useful Net-snmp MIBs

Here are some net-snmp MIBs worth monitoring by name, with their corresponding numerical values in parentheses. All of these can be found under .1.3.6.1.4.1.2021. For example, the `Memory.MemTotalSwap` MIB can be determined by querying `1.3.6.1.4.1.2021.Memory.MemTotalSwap`.

**NOTE**  *Before using any MIB, be sure to test it at snmpwalk. Each query should return a single line. If it returns multiple lines, there's probably an index on the end of it that you should include before entering that MIB in MRTG.*

Without further ado, here are some useful MIBs:

| | |
|---|---|
| `memory.memTotalSwap (4.3)` | The total swap on the system. Check this value before assigning limits involving swap in other MRTG graphs. |
| `memory.memAvailSwap (4.4)` | The amount of swap remaining. |
| `memory.memTotalReal (4.5)` | The total memory actually available on the system. While you don't need to monitor this value (after all, the RAM in a system rarely changes), you should check it before setting limits in MRTG. |
| `memory.memAvailReal (4.6)` | The amount of unused real memory. |
| `memory.memBuffer (4.14)` | The amount of memory in the system buffer. |
| `memory.memCached (4.15)` | The amount of memory in the system cache. |
| `dskTable.dskEntry.dskTotal (9.1.6)` | The total size of a partition. Like the other totals, this is just for reference. This MIB will almost certainly have indexes. |
| `dskTable.dskEntry.dskAvail (9.1.7)` | The amount of space remaining on the disk, in blocks. |
| `dskTable.dskEntry.dskPercent (9.1.9)` | The percentage of the disk in use. |
| `systemStats.ssCpuUser (11.9)` | The percentage of the CPU time spent in non-kernel programs. |
| `systemStats.ssCpuSystem (11.10)` | The percentage of CPU time spent running the kernel. |

There are many, many more MIBs you could monitor, and entire books have been written about SNMP and monitoring. Still, these select few should cover the basic system services, and give you those important pretty pictures for your staff meeting.

### Monitoring a Single MIB

Although MRTG is designed to monitor things in pairs, you can monitor a single MIB by listing it twice:

```
Target[localhost.memAvail]:.1.3.6.1.4.1.2021.4.6.0&.1.3.6.1.4.1.2021.4.6.0:GetLostLo
ser@localhost
```

This will work just fine to show only one MIB on the MRTG graph.

*Be sure to pick a separate label for the target, and use it for all configuration statements for that target. If you don't, MRTG will either complain or overwrite the log files from other targets.*

### Customizing MRTG

Once you have a working MRTG setup, be careful testing new configurations. I generally test a new MRTG configuration in a separate WorkDir, so that any misconfigurations won't damage existing log files or production status pages.

The mrtg.cfg file contains a wide variety of options that allows you to customize almost every aspect of MRTG's appearance and functionality. Here you'll find some of the most useful MRTG configuration options, and how they can be used in production environments.

#### WithPeak[label]: wmy

MRTG's log format condenses older entries into average values, which tends to decrease values over time. The WithPeak option forces MRTG to keep and graph the maximum values over time. While your graphs will be more complex as a result, they will contain more useful information. This option can be set for the weekly, monthly, and yearly graphs, or a combination.

#### MaxBytes[label]: number

This is the maximum value that a MIB can reach. (The label is misleading if the MIB doesn't measure bytes.) MRTG uses this value to decide if it got a sensible answer from the device.

Both MIBs being measured use MaxBytes, so be sure you're measuring sensible pairs! If you're doing something particularly weird and need different MaxBytes variables, use MaxBytes1 and MaxBytes2.

#### YLegend[label]: text

MRTG will put this text along the side of the graph. Put whatever you're measuring here, such as "% CPU Time".

### LegendI[label] & LegendO[label]: text

MRTG always measures two MIBs. The first MIB is the traditional "In" value, and the second the "Out". You can put short descriptions of what you're measuring here to have them appear beneath the graph.

### Legend1[label] & Legend2[label]: text

Legend1 is the label for the first MIB you measure; Legend2, the second. Both will appear at the bottom of your chart, in the key.

### Legend3[label] & Legend4[label]: text

These labels will be used if you're recording maximums (with the WithPeak option). If you're not recording maximums, these labels will have no effect.

### Directory[label]: directoryname

Large MRTG setups can generate a lot of files. The directory keyword allows you to put the files for a particular label in a subdirectory of the WorkDir.

### Options[label]: option-names

Options allow you to handle special cases. All options are specified on one line, after the target. Some good examples follow:

| | |
|---|---|
| growright | By default, MRTG draws graphs from right to left. Use this option to make it draw graphs from left to right. |
| bits | This changes the graphs from measuring bytes to bits. Bits are not only more impressive, but they may also be more accurate, depending on what you're measuring. For example, many people measure bandwidth in bits, not kilobytes. |
| gauge | SNMP generally retains information in counter form. MRTG subtracts the previous reading from the current reading to get the change in the last five minutes. Use the gauge option for SNMP MIBs that don't change, such as disk capacity. |
| unknaszero | When a target is not reachable for any reason (including power failure or network problems), the system will assume the last known value for the charts. Whether or not this is more accurate is a matter of some controversy. This option causes MRTG to assume a value of zero when it cannot reach a target. |

### MRTG Index Page

The last bit of configuration we'll need to do is to create a single HTML index page for our MRTG setup. MRTG includes an indexmaker tool that automagically does this for us. Just run this:

```
# indexmaker mrtg.cfg > index.html
```

You'll probably want to edit this, but it's a nice starting place.

### Sample MRTG Configurations

This section contains some sample MRTG configurations. To use them, insert the correct hostname and community name. Also, note that the Target statements are supposed to be all on one line; the printed page simply isn't wide enough to handle this at a type size you can see without a magnifying glass. In each example, you will need to edit the Target statement to give the proper hostname and community name, and you'll probably want to edit the PageTop setting so your graph displays the correct information for your host.

#### User and System CPU Usage

This first sample compares user CPU usage with system CPU usage as percentages. (Note that we use the gauge option.)

```
Title[myhost.AbsoluteBSD.com.cpu]: myhost.AbsoluteBSD.com CPU usage
YLegend[myhost.AbsoluteBSD.com.cpu]: CPU usage
WithPeak[myhost.AbsoluteBSD.com.cpu]: wmy
MaxBytes[myhost.AbsoluteBSD.com.cpu]: 100
Target[myhost.AbsoluteBSD.com.cpu]:.1.3.6.1.4.1.2021.11.9.0&.1.3.6.1.4.1.2021.11.10.
0:public@myhost.AbsoluteBSD.com
ShortLegend[myhost.AbsoluteBSD.com.cpu]: CPU
LegendI[myhost.AbsoluteBSD.com.cpu]: User CPU
LegendO[myhost.AbsoluteBSD.com.cpu]: System CPU
Legend1[myhost.AbsoluteBSD.com.cpu]: User Processor Usage
Legend2[myhost.AbsoluteBSD.com.cpu]: System Processor Usage
Legend3[myhost.AbsoluteBSD.com.cpu]: Maximal 5 Minute User Processor Usage
Legend4[myhost.AbsoluteBSD.com.cpu]: Maximal 5 Minute System Processor Usage
Options[myhost.AbsoluteBSD.com.cpu]: growright, gauge
PageTop[myhost.AbsoluteBSD.com.cpu]: <H1>CPU usage for myhost.AbsoluteBSD.com </H1>
```

#### Swap Usage

Before you can measure swap space, you'll need to know how much swap your system has. You can get that information by doing an snmpwalk to get the total swap available, or `snmpwalk hostname community .1.3.6.1.4.1.2021.4.3`. Put that value in the MaxBytes space, and under the PageTop, so it will show up on your graph.

```
Title[myhost.AbsoluteBSD.com.swap]: myhost.AbsoluteBSD.com Available Swap
YLegend[myhost.AbsoluteBSD.com.swap]: swap
WithPeak[myhost.AbsoluteBSD.com.swap]: wmy
MaxBytes[myhost.AbsoluteBSD.com.swap]: 128000
Target[myhost.AbsoluteBSD.com.swap]:
.1.3.6.1.4.1.2021.4.4.0&.1.3.6.1.4.1.2021.4.4.0:public@myhost.AbsoluteBSD.com
ShortLegend[myhost.AbsoluteBSD.com.swap]: Swap
LegendI[myhost.AbsoluteBSD.com.swap]: Available Swap
LegendO[myhost.AbsoluteBSD.com.swap]: Available Swap
Legend1[myhost.AbsoluteBSD.com.swap]: Available Swap
Legend2[myhost.AbsoluteBSD.com.swap]: Available Swap
Legend3[myhost.AbsoluteBSD.com.swap]: Maximal 5 Minute Available Swap
Legend4[myhost.AbsoluteBSD.com.swap]: Maximal 5 Minute Available Swap
Options[myhost.AbsoluteBSD.com.swap]: growright, gauge
PageTop[myhost.AbsoluteBSD.com.swap]: <H1>Available Swap (out of 128M) for
myhost.AbsoluteBSD.com </H1>
```

### Disk Partition

Measuring the amount of space used on a disk partition is similarly easy, though
you'll need to know the MIB index for the disk partition first. (See the examples
in "Index Numbers" earlier in this chapter.) Be sure to give the correct size in
the PageTop space.

```
Target[myhost.AbsoluteBSD.com.root]:.1.3.6.1.4.1.2021.9.1.9.1&.1.3.6.1.4.1.2021.9.1.
9.1:public@myhost.AbsoluteBSD.com
Title[myhost.AbsoluteBSD.com.root]:  Myhost.AbsoluteBSD.com Root partition % used
MaxBytes[myhost.AbsoluteBSD.com.root]: 100
WithPeak[myhost.AbsoluteBSD.com.root]: wmy
Suppress[myhost.AbsoluteBSD.com.root]: y
LegendI[myhost.AbsoluteBSD.com.root]:  % used
Legend1[myhost.AbsoluteBSD.com.root]:  % used
YLegend[myhost.AbsoluteBSD.com.root]: percent used
ShortLegend[myhost.AbsoluteBSD.com.root]: used
Options[myhost.AbsoluteBSD.com.root]: gauge, growright
PageTop[myhost.AbsoluteBSD.com.root]: <H1>myhost Root partition (% of 128M) used
</H1>
```

### Network Traffic

Just for completeness, let's look at a sample of how to measure network traffic.
This assumes a 10Mbps network connection; if you're using 100BaseT, multiply
MaxBytes by 10.

```
Title[myhost.AbsoluteBSD.com.traffic]: myhost.AbsoluteBSD.com network traffic
MaxBytes[myhost.AbsoluteBSD.com.traffic]: 125000
WithPeak[myhost.AbsoluteBSD.com.traffic]: wmy
Target[myhost.AbsoluteBSD.com.traffic]: public@myhost.AbsoluteBSD.com
Options[myhost.AbsoluteBSD.com.traffic]: growright, bits
PageTop[myhost.AbsoluteBSD.com.traffic]: <H1>Network traffic on
myhost.AbsoluteBSD.com </H1>
```

### Monitoring Non-BSD Systems

MRTG can monitor any system that uses SNMP; it is a standard spoken by almost
every network-equipment and operating-system vendor. To do so, all you need is
the list of MIBs that the product supports and what they mean. Tables of MIB
interpretations—simple text files containing tables of how to read the vendor's MIB
tree—are generally available from vendors. Each file starts something like this:

```
IPV6-MIB DEFINITIONS ::= BEGIN

IMPORTS
    MODULE-IDENTITY, OBJECT-TYPE, NOTIFICATION-TYPE,
    mib-2, Counter32, Unsigned32, Integer32,
    Gauge32                         FROM SNMPv2-SMI
    DisplayString, PhysAddress, TruthValue, TimeStamp,
    VariablePointer, RowPointer     FROM SNMPv2-TC
    MODULE-COMPLIANCE, OBJECT-GROUP,
    NOTIFICATION-GROUP              FROM SNMPv2-CONF
    Ipv6IfIndex, Ipv6Address, Ipv6AddressPrefix,
    Ipv6AddressIfIdentifier,
    Ipv6IfIndexOrZero              FROM IPV6-TC;
```

Copy these definition files to a directory on your system. Next, set the environment variable MIBDIRS to point to that directory, and snmptranslate will recognize them.

You can even install SNMP on your NT systems; this makes them easy to
monitor, at a fraction of the cost of commercial systems. The only difference
between MRTG and a commercial system is that you must know what you're
doing to use MRTG. I highly recommend Garth Williams' "SNMP for the Public
Community" site (http://www.wtcs.org/snmp4tpc/) for SNMP on other platforms. Be warned in advance: To call Microsoft's implementation of SNMP
"skeletal" would leave you without an adequate description of its error messages.
Windows 2000 and XP are better than NT, but not by a huge amount.

# 20

## SYSTEM CRASHES AND PANICS

One of the nice things about FreeBSD is its stability; the only Blue Screen of Death is a screensaver. In fact, it was almost a year before I realized that a FreeBSD machine could crash for reasons other than bad hardware.

FreeBSD can crash, or *panic*, but it allows you to recover from a panic fairly easily, so don't, er, panic. You can even connect to the console remotely when the system is completely locked up and nonresponsive, and force a reboot. FreeBSD provides the tools you need to discover exactly what happened, and gives you extensive debugging information about the panic. (Even if you don't know what to do with this information, you can submit a problem report and discuss the issue with the FreeBSD development team.)

## What Causes Panics?

When does a system panic? Well, panicking is a choice that the kernel makes. If the system reaches a condition that it doesn't know how to handle, or if it fails its own internal consistency checks, it will panic.

If you're using FreeBSD as a desktop, you can panic it by doing a variety of things, most of which are hardware related. For example, in older FreeBSDs, you could panic a laptop by pulling out certain PCMCIA cards without shutting the card down first. (That is fortunately no longer the case.) Now, to panic a system, you pretty much have to do something wrong while logged in as root (or be running -current).

It's much more difficult to panic a server. Panics generally occur only if you have configured your kernel improperly, if you exhaust your system resources, or if you've tickled a previously unknown FreeBSD bug. The first two are pretty straightforward to fix, and are discussed in Chapters 4 and 18. The last is the most disturbing.

FreeBSD is complex, and not even its royal-blood lineage or open-source development process can protect it from bugs. (Some people argue that no software is bug-free.) Fortunately, that heritage and development process give you the information to debug FreeBSD yourself, and the tools to provide the information necessary for other people to debug it. You might begin with a cryptic error code, but you'll quickly learn that it means something to someone.

**NOTE** *If you're not a programmer, don't worry. By preparing your system to debug panics, you'll help someone else to fix the problem. Hopefully, you'll never need to debug your system, but if you do, you'll be glad you have it set up properly!*

### What Does a Panic Look Like?

When a system panics, it stops running all programs. Instead of the usual console messages, the console displays a message much like this one:

```
Fatal trap 12: page fault while in kernel mode
fault virtual address   =       0x80c0153a
fault code / supervisor write, page not present
instruction pointer = 0x8:0xc015aa84
stack pointer =         0x10:0xc7377e7c
frame pointer =         0x10:0xc7377e80
code segment =          base 0x0, limit 0xfffff, type 0x1b
             =          DPL 0, pres 1, def32 1, gran 1
processor eflags =      interrupt enabled, resume, IOPL=0
current process =       5 (syncer)
interrupt mask =        bio
trap number =           12
panic: page fault
```

If you're an inexperienced sysadmin, messages like this can turn your blood cold, but don't fret yet. FreeBSD sometimes gives somewhat friendly messages that describe what's wrong, which give you a specific place to start looking, or at least a term to Google. I've seen panics that give very specific instructions on kernel options that should be set to prevent their recurrence. Other panic messages, like this one, are much more puzzling.

The only word that looks even vaguely familiar in this panic message is the fourth line from the bottom, where we see that the current process is something called "syncer". Most people don't know what the syncer is, and most of those who recognize it know better than to try to fix it. The "mysterious panic" is among the worst situations you can have in FreeBSD.

## Responding to a Panic

If you get a system panic, the first thing to do is get a copy of the panic message. Since FreeBSD is no longer running at this point, the standard UNIX commands will not work—the system won't let you SSH in or out, and even simple commands like script(1) will not work. The console might be utterly locked up, or it could be in a debugger. In either event, you need the error message.

The first time I received an error message like the preceding one, I scrambled for paper and pen. Eventually I found an old envelope and a broken stub of pencil, and crawled between the server rack and the rough brick wall. I balanced the six-inch black-and-white monitor that I'd dragged back there in one hand, while with my other hand I held the old envelope against the wall. Apparently I had a third hand to copy the panic message to the envelope, because it somehow got there. Finally, scraped and cramped, I slithered back out of the rack and victoriously typed the whole mess into an email. Surely the crack FreeBSD developers would be able to look at this garbage and tell me exactly what had happened.

After all of this struggle, the initial response was quite frustrating: "Can you send a backtrace?"

I've seen many, many messages to a FreeBSD mailing list reporting problems like this, and they always get this same response. Most of the people who send these messages are never heard from again, and I understand exactly how they feel. When you've been dealing with a server that crashes, or (worse) keeps crashing, the last thing you want to do is reconfigure it.

The problem with the panic message on my envelope was that it only gave a tiny scrap of the story. It was so vague, in fact, that it was like describing a stolen car as "red, with a scratch on the fender." If you don't give the car's make, model, and VIN number or license plate, you cannot expect the police to make much headway. Similarly, without more information from your crashing kernel, the FreeBSD developers can't catch the criminal code.

There's a simple way around this problem, however: Set up your server to handle a panic before the panic happens. Set it up when you install the server. That way, you'll get a backtrace automatically if it ever crashes. This might seem like a novel idea, and it certainly isn't emphasized in the FreeBSD documentation, but it makes sense to be ready for disaster. If it never happens, well, you don't have anything to complain about. If you get a panic, you're ready and you'll be able to present the FreeBSD folks with a complete debugging dump the second a problem appears.

### Prerequisites

To prepare for a kernel panic, you need to have the system source code installed. You'll also need one (or more) swap partitions that is at least 1MB larger than your physical memory, and preferably twice as large as your RAM. If you have 512MB of RAM, for example, you need a swap partition that is 513MB or larger, with 1024MB being preferable. (On a server, you should certainly have multiple swap partitions on multiple drives!) If your swap partition isn't large enough, you'll have to either add another hard drive with an adequate swap partition, or reinstall. (While having a /var partition with at least that much disk space free is helpful, it isn't necessary.)

If you followed the installation suggestions in the beginning of the book, you're all set.

### Crash Dump Process

The kernel crash-capturing process works somewhat like this. If a properly configured system crashes, it will save a core dump of the system memory. You can't save it to a file, because the crashed kernel doesn't know about files; it only knows about partitions. The simplest place to write this dump is to the swap partition, and the dump is placed as close to the end of the swap partition as possible. Once the crashing system saves the core to swap, it reboots the computer.

During the reboot, /etc/rc enables the swap partition. It then (probably) runs fsck on the crashed disks. It has to enable swapping before running fsck, because fsck might need to use swap space. Hopefully, you have enough swap space that fsck can get everything it needs without overwriting the dump file lurking in your swap partition.

Once the system has a place where it can save a core dump, it checks the swap partition for a dump. Upon finding a core dump, savecore copies the dump from swap to the proper file, clears the dump from swap, and lets the reboot proceed. You now have a kernel core file, and can use that to get a backtrace.

### The Debugging Kernel

The standard FreeBSD kernel install removes all the debugging information from the kernel before installing it, including *symbols*, which provide a map between the machine code and the source code. Such a map can be larger than the actual program, and nobody wants to run a kernel that's three times larger than it has to be! However, we need this map, and other debugging information, to diagnose what went wrong in the crash.

This map also includes a complete list of source-code line numbers, so the developer can learn exactly where a problem occurred. Without this information, the developer is stuck trying to map a kernel core to the source code by hand, which is somewhat like trying to assemble a million-piece puzzle without a picture, or even knowing that you have all the pieces. Overall, this is an ugly job. It's even uglier when you consider that the developer who needs to do the work is a volunteer. That's why your debugging kernel should include its symbols.

To keep the symbols, add these lines to your kernel configuration:

```
options         DDB
makeoptions     DEBUG=-g
```

The DDB option installs the DDB kernel debugger. (This isn't strictly necessary, but it can be helpful and it doesn't take up that much room.) The makeoptions you set here tell the system to build a debugging kernel.

### Post-Panic Behavior

When configuring your system, you'll need to decide how you want the system to behave after a panic. Do you want the computer to reboot automatically, or do you want it to stay at the panic screen until you manually trigger a reboot? If the system is at a remote location, you'll almost certainly want the computer to reboot automatically, but if you're at the console debugging kernel changes, you might want it to wait for you to tell it to reboot.

To reboot automatically, include the kernel option DDB_UNATTENDED:

```
options DDB_UNATTENDED
```

If you don't include this option, the system will wait for you to tell it to reboot.

### kernel.debug

Once you have the kernel configured the way you want, do the usual dance (described in Chapter 4) to configure and install it.

Once you've installed your new kernel, you'll find a file in the kernel compile directory called kernel.debug. This is your kernel with symbols; save it somewhere. The next time you upgrade your system or customize the kernel, this debugging kernel will be overwritten by a new debugging kernel. If you've built a kernel just for testing, you want to be sure that you have your known-to-be-good debugging kernel available.

One of the frequent causes of a failed debugging process is losing the debugging kernel and trying to debug a crashed kernel with a different kernel.debug. This won't work. I generally copy kernel.debug to /var/crash/kernel.debug.date, so I can tell when a particular debug kernel was built. This lets me date-match the current kernel to a debugging kernel, and also tells me when a kernel.debug is old enough that I can delete it.

With any luck, you'll never need these debugging kernels, though personally, I've found my luck to be unreliable. Debugging kernels take little disk space and provide quick answers when trouble hits, so I strongly suggest using them.

### Dumpon

Now it's time to tell the system where to write the core dump—this location is the *dumpdev*. FreeBSD uses the swap partition as the dump device, which is why it has to be slightly larger than your physical memory. (You can use a UFS partition, but after the crash it won't be a usable UFS partition any more!)

You can get the device name from /etc/fstab. Look for a line with a FSType entry of swap; the first entry in that line is the physical device name. For example, on my laptop, my swap field in /etc/fstab looks like this:

```
/dev/ad0s4b          none         swap    sw          0        0
```

Tell the system to use a dump device with dumpon(8), which must be set each time the system boots. Of course, as you might guess, there's an rc.conf switch for this. My swap partition is /dev/ad0s4b, so I specify this as the dump device in /etc/rc.conf:

```
dumpdev="/dev/ad0s4b"
```

### Savecore

Next, tell your system where to save the dump after the reboot using savecore(8). You can change the default, /var/crash, with rc.conf's `dumpdir` setting. (This directory must exist; savecore will not create it!)

As you become more experienced in saving panics, you may find that you need to adjust the core-saving behavior. Read savecore(8), and set any appropriate options in `savecore_flags` in /etc/rc. One popular flag is `-z`, which compresses the core file and can save some disk space. Savecore is now smart enough to automatically eliminate unused memory from the dump, which can save a lot of room.

### Upon a Crash

If you're in front of your computer when it crashes, you'll see the panic message. If the system is set to reboot automatically, numbers will start to flow by, counting the megs of memory being dumped. Finally, the computer will reboot, fsck will run, and you can watch savecore copy the memory dump from swap to a file.

If your system doesn't reboot automatically, you'll need to enter two commands after the panic, at the debugger prompt: **panic** to sync the disks and **continue** to start the reboot process. (FreeBSD supports many other debugging options, but you have to know how to use the kernel debugger to make use of them.)

### Dumps and Bad Kernels

Some kernels just crash and die during boot, or won't stay up long enough to fix a problem. In that case, you need to boot with a different kernel.

The problem here is that savecore needs to use a kernel file to build the dump image. By default, savecore uses the booting kernel. If you are booting off a different kernel after a panic, you must run savecore manually to tell it where to find the proper kernel file. Interrupt the boot during the initial countdown, and boot into single-user mode with this command:

```
ok boot -s
```

When the system gives you a command prompt, fsck your system first. After a panic, the disks are almost always dirty:

```
# fsck -p
```

(This can take several minutes on a modern (huge) disk.)

Once fsck finishes, mount the filesystem where you keep your kernel core files:

```
# mount /var
```

Finally, save your kernel core using the proper kernel file, telling savecore which kernel file to use with the -N flag. If your panicked kernel is /kernel.bad, use something like this:

```
# savecore -N /kernel.bad /var/crash
```

You can, of course, use additional savecore options like -v and -z in a manual core dump.

## Using the Dump

If you're a kernel developer, this is where you stop listening to me and rely upon your own debugging experience. If you're a new systems administrator, though, you probably don't know enough about C and kernel internals to have any real hope of debugging a complicated kernel issue. As such, we'll focus on extracting enough information to give a developer a good shot at identifying the problem.

If you look at /var/crash after a dumped panic, you'll see the files kernel.0 and vmcore.0. (Each subsequent crash dump will get a consecutively higher number, such as kernel.1 and vmcore.1.) The vmcore.0 file is the actual memory dump, while the kernel.0 file is a copy of the crashed kernel. The kernel.0 file isn't useful for what we're doing, but keep it just in case. The vmcore.0 file is vital.

Once you actually have a crash, you might copy your debugging kernel to /var/crash/kernel.debug.0 to keep dumps in sync with their kernels.

**NOTE** *The rest of this process is an excellent opportunity to use script(1).*

Now start the gdb debugger. Gdb takes three arguments: a -k to configure the debugger appropriately for kernel work, the name of a file containing the kernel with symbols, and the name of the memory dump:

```
# gdb -k kernel.debug.0 vmcore.0
```

Once you do that, gdb will spit out its copyright information, the panic message, and a copy of the memory-dumping process. We've seen an example of a panic earlier, so I won't repeat it now; what's new is the debugger prompt you get back at the end of all this:

```
(kgdb)
```

You've now gotten further than any number of people who have system panics. Pat yourself on the back. To find out exactly where the panic happened, type **where** and hit **ENTER**.

```
(kgdb) where
#0  dumpsys () at ../../../kern/kern_shutdown.c:505
#1  0xc0143119 in db_fncall (dummy1=0, dummy2=0, dummy3=0,
    dummy4=0xe0b749a4 " \0048\200%") at ../../../ddb/db_command.c:551
#2  0xc0142f33 in db_command (last_cmdp=0xc0313724, cmd_table=0xc0313544,
    aux_cmd_tablep=0xc030df2c, aux_cmd_tablep_end=0xc030df30)
    at ../../../ddb/db_command.c:348
#3  0xc0142fff in db_command_loop () at ../../../ddb/db_command.c:474
#4  0xc0145393 in db_trap (type=12, code=0) at ../../../ddb/db_trap.c:72
#5  0xc02ad0f6 in kdb_trap (type=12, code=0, regs=0xe0b74af4)
    at ../../../i386/i386/db_interface.c:161
#6  0xc02ba004 in trap_fatal (frame=0xe0b74af4, eva=40)
    at ../../../i386/i386/trap.c:846
#7  0xc02b9d71 in trap_pfault (frame=0xe0b74af4, usermode=0, eva=40)
    at ../../../i386/i386/trap.c:765
#8  0xc02b9907 in trap (frame={tf_fs = 24, tf_es = 16, tf_ds = 16, tf_edi = 0,
    tf_esi = 0, tf_ebp = -524858548, tf_isp = -524858592,
    tf_ebx = -525288192, tf_edx = 0, tf_ecx = 1000000000, tf_eax = 0,
    tf_trapno = 12, tf_err = 0, tf_eip = -1071645917, tf_cs = 8,
    tf_eflags = 66182, tf_esp = -1070136512, tf_ss = 0})
    at ../../../i386/i386/trap.c:433
#9  0xc01ffb23 in vcount (vp=0xe0b0bd00) at ../../../kern/vfs_subr.c:2301
#10 0xc01a5e58 in spec_close (ap=0xe0b74b94)
    at ../../../fs/specfs/spec_vnops.c:591
#11 0xc01a55f1 in spec_vnoperate (ap=0xe0b74b94)
    at ../../../fs/specfs/spec_vnops.c:121
#12 0xc0207454 in vn_close (vp=0xe0b0bd00, flags=3, cred=0xc32cce00,
    td=0xe0a8d360) at vnode_if.h:183
#13 0xc0207fab in vn_closefile (fp=0xc3369080, td=0xe0a8d360)
    at ../../../kern/vfs_vnops.c:757
#14 0xc01b1d50 in fdrop_locked (fp=0xc3369080, td=0xe0a8d360)
    at ../../../sys/file.h:230
#15 0xc01b155a in fdrop (fp=0xc3369080, td=0xe0a8d360)
    at ../../../kern/kern_descrip.c:1538
#16 0xc01b152d in closef (fp=0xc3369080, td=0xe0a8d360)
    at ../../../kern/kern_descrip.c:1524
#17 0xc01b114e in fdfree (td=0xe0a8d360) at ../../../kern/kern_descrip.c:1345
#18 0xc01b5173 in exit1 (td=0xe0a8d360, rv=256)
    at ../../../kern/kern_exit.c:199
#19 0xc01b4ec2 in sys_exit (td=0xe0a8d360, uap=0xe0b74d20)
    at ../../../kern/kern_exit.c:109
#20 0xc02ba2b7 in syscall (frame={tf_fs = 47, tf_es = 47, tf_ds = 47,
    tf_edi = 135227560, tf_esi = 0, tf_ebp = -1077941020,
    tf_isp = -524857996, tf_ebx = -1, tf_edx = 135044144,
    tf_ecx = -1077942116, tf_eax = 1, tf_trapno = 12, tf_err = 2,
    tf_eip = 134865696, tf_cs = 31, tf_eflags = 663, tf_esp = -1077941064,
    tf_ss = 47}) at ../../../i386/i386/trap.c:1049
```

```
#21 0xc02ae06d in syscall_with_err_pushed ()
#22 0x80503a5 in ?? ()
#23 0x807024a in ?? ()
#24 0xbfbfffb4 in ?? ()
#25 0x807daaf in ?? ()
#26 0x807d6eb in ?? ()
#27 0x80630c1 in ?? ()
#28 0x8062fed in ?? ()
#29 0x805ea4c in ?? ()
#30 0x8065949 in ?? ()
#31 0x806544d in ?? ()
#32 0x806dc17 in ?? ()
#33 0x80616b7 in ?? ()
#34 0x80613f0 in ?? ()
#35 0x8048135 in ?? ()
(kgdb)
```

Whoa! This is some pretty intense stuff. If you copied this and the output of
uname -a into an email and sent it to hackers@FreeBSD.org, various developers
would take note and help you out. They'd probably write you back and tell you
other things to type at the kgdb prompt, but you'd definitely get developer attention. You'd be well on your way to getting the problem solved, and helping the
FreeBSD folks squash a bug.

### Advanced Kernel Debugging

If you're not familiar with programming, nobody would blame you if you
stopped here, but dig we must. So, without further ado, let's see what we can
learn from the debug message, and try to figure out some things to include in
that first email. Without being intimate with the kernel, you can't solve the
problem yourself, but you might be able to help narrow things down a little.

By gathering the information you can before sending an email, you short-
circuit a round or two of email. (If you've used email support in a crisis, you
know just how valuable this is!) Without being a kernel hacker, you can't know
which tidbit of knowledge is most important, so you need to include everything
you can glean from the output.

The first thing to realize is that the debugger backtrace contains actual
instructions carried out by the kernel, in reverse order. Line #1 is the last thing
the kernel did before dumping the system entirely in line 0. (When someone
says "before" or "after," they're almost certainly talking about chronological
order and not the order things appear in the debugger.)

In a panic, the kernel will call either a function called *trap* or (if you have
INVARIANTS in your kernel) one called *panic*. You'll see variants on trap and
panic, such as db_trap, but you just want the plain, old unadorned trap or
panic. Look through your gdb output for either of these functions. In the previous example, there's a trap in line #8. We see other types of trap on lines 4–7,

but no plain, straightforward trap statements. These other traps are helper functions called by trap to try to figure out exactly what happened and what to do about it.

Whatever happened right before line #8 chose to panic. In line #9, we see:

```
#9  0xc01ffb23 in vcount (vp=0xe0b0bd00) at ../../../kern/vfs_subr.c:2301
```

The hex numbers don't mean much, but we see in this panic something called vcount. If you try man vcount, you'll see that vcount(9) is a standard system call. The panic occurred while executing code that was compiled from line 2301 of the file /usr/src/sys/kern/vfs_subr.c. (All paths in these dumps should be under the kernel source directory, usually /usr/src/sys.) This gives a developer a very good idea of where to look for this problem.

### Examining Lines

Let's look at line #9 in more detail. Use the up command and the number of lines you want to move:

```
(kgdb) up 9
#9  0xc01ffb23 in vcount (vp=0xe0b0bd00) at ../../../kern/vfs_subr.c:2301
2301            SLIST_FOREACH(vq, &vp->v_rdev->si_hlist, v_specnext)
(kgdb)
```

Here we see the actual line of vfs_subr.c that was compiled into the panicking code. You don't need to know what SLIST_FOREACH is (it's a macro, by the way). Getting this far is pretty good, but there's still a little more information you can squeeze out of this dump without knowing exactly how the kernel works.

### Examining Variables

If you have some minor programming experience, you'd probably suspect that the terms in the parentheses after SLIST_FOREACH are variables, and you'd be right. Each of those variables has a range of acceptable values, and someone familiar with the code would recognize the legitimate ones. By printing out the contents of each variable, we can jump-start the debugging process. (Tell gdb to print a variable's contents with the p command, giving the variable name as an argument.)

Let's look at the middle variable, vp:

```
(kgdb) p vp
$2 = (struct vnode *) 0xe0b0bd00
(kgdb)
```

The (struct vnode *) bit tells us that this is a pointer to a data structure. You can show its contents by putting an asterisk in front of the variable name, like so:

```
(kgdb) p *vp
$3 = {v_flag = 8, v_usecount = 2, v_writecount = 1, v_holdcnt = 0,
  v_id = 6985, v_mount = 0x0, v_op = 0xc2d52a00, v_freelist = {tqe_next = 0x0,
    tqe_prev = 0xe083de1c}, v_nmntvnodes = {tqe_next = 0xe0b0b700,
    tqe_prev = 0xe0b0c024}, v_cleanblkhd = {tqh_first = 0x0,
    tqh_last = 0xe0b0bd2c}, v_dirtyblkhd = {tqh_first = 0x0,
    tqh_last = 0xe0b0bd34}, v_synclist = {le_next = 0x0, le_prev = 0x0},
  v_numoutput = 0, v_type = VBAD, v_un = {vu_mountedhere = 0x0,
    vu_socket = 0x0, vu_spec = {vu_specinfo = 0x0, vu_specnext = {
        sle_next = 0x0}}, vu_fifoinfo = 0x0}, v_lastw = 0, v_cstart = 0,
  v_lasta = 0, v_clen = 0, v_object = 0x0, v_interlock = {mtx_object = {
      lo_class = 0xc0335c60, lo_name = 0xc02ef5c1 "vnode interlock",
      lo_flags = 196608, lo_list = {stqe_next = 0x0}, lo_witness = 0x0},
    mtx_lock = 4, mtx_recurse = 0, mtx_blocked = {tqh_first = 0x0,
      tqh_last = 0xe0b0bd84}, mtx_contested = {le_next = 0x0, le_prev = 0x0},
    tsp = {tv_sec = 3584, tv_nsec = 101067509},
    file = 0xc02ef50a "../../../kern/vfs_subr.c", line = 1726,
    has_trace_time = 0}, v_lock = {lk_interlock = 0xc036e320,
    lk_flags = 16777216, lk_sharecount = 0, lk_waitcount = 0,
    lk_exclusivecount = 0, lk_prio = 80, lk_wmesg = 0xc02ef5d1 "vnlock",
    lk_timo = 6, lk_lockholder = -1}, v_vnlock = 0x0, v_tag = VT_NON,
  v_data = 0x0, v_cache_src = {lh_first = 0x0}, v_cache_dst = {
    tqh_first = 0x0, tqh_last = 0xe0b0bdd8}, v_dd = 0xe0b0bd00, v_ddid = 0,
  v_pollinfo = 0x0, v_vxproc = 0x0}
(kgdb)
```

**NOTE**  *For those of you who are learning C, this is an excellent example of how it's easier to hand around a pointer than the object it references.*

An interested developer can dig through this to see what's going on. Let's look at the first variable, vq, and try to get similar information from it:

```
(kgdb) p vq
$4 = (struct vnode *) 0x0
(kgdb)
```

This isn't exactly a problem, but we're stuck. A pointer equal to 0x0 is a null pointer. There are many legitimate reasons for having a null pointer, but there isn't anything in it for us to view. Feel free to try, however; you really can't hurt the dump any further by using gdb.

```
(kgdb) p *vq
Cannot access memory at address 0x0.
(kgdb)
```

You've probably heard the words "null pointer" in close proximity to the word "panic." Without digging into the kernel code, you can't assume that this particular null pointer caused the panic. In fact, in this particular panic, the null pointer is perfectly legitimate; the kernel panicked trying to decide what value to assign to this newly allocated pointer.[1]

### Apparent Gdb Weirdness

You could try digging a little further into the data to see what's going on. The second variable in our panic (vp->v_rdev->si_hlist) actually goes on a bit; let's take a look a little deeper into it:

```
(kgdb) p vp->v_rdev
There is no member named v_rdev.
(kgdb)
```

Normally, this would work, and if you've used gdb before, you might think that gdb is wrong, but in this case it's correct. Here, v_rdev is a convenience macro, though only people who have read the kernel source code would know that. Actually, v_rdev expands to v_un.vu_spec.vu_specinfo. You couldn't be expected to know that, but don't be surprised if a developer asks you to type something different than what actually appears in the trace.

To view vp->v_rdev, enter this command:

```
(kgdb) p vp->v_un.vu_spec.vu_specinfo
$5 = (struct specinfo *) 0x0
(kgdb)
```

If you've gotten this far, you should be able to recognize the null pointer here, but that's about it.

### Results

In this particular case, your extra digging would produce the answer for a developer very quickly. The tidbit in the contents of the vp structure identifies the problem almost immediately.

```
v_type = VBAD
```

This is a vnode that isn't currently used, and shouldn't even be in this part of the system. A developer would jump directly on that, and try to learn why the system is trying to set a new vnode to a bogus value.

---

[1] How did I know this? I exchanged several emails with a kernel developer about this dump, that's how.

I got this particular kernel dump from a kernel developer, who commented that while he "could fix vcount() to return 0 for invalid vnodes—it wouldn't, strictly speaking, be incorrect—but the *real* bug is somewhere else, and 'fixing' vcount() would just hide it." This is the correct attitude to have on this sort of problem—BSD users expect bugs to be found, not painted over. This means, however, that you can expect your developer to come back to you with requests for further information, and probably more things to type into gdb. He might even ask you to send the kernel.debug and vmcore file.

### Vmcore and Security

The vmcore file contains everything in your system's memory at the time of the panic, which may include all sorts of security-impacting information. Someone could conceivably use this information to break into your system. A developer might write you and request a copy of the file for all sorts of legitimate reasons: It makes debugging easier and can save countless rounds of email. Still, consider the potential consequences of someone having this information very carefully. If you don't recognize the person who asks, or if you don't trust her, there's no way you should send the file!

If the panic is reproducible, however, you can cold-boot the system to single-user mode and trigger the panic immediately. That way, if the system never starts any programs that contain confidential information, and nobody types any passwords into the system, the dump cannot contain that information. Reproducing a panic in single-user mode hence generates a "clean" core file.

To prepare a clean core file, enter **boot -s** at the loader prompt to bring the system to a command prompt, then do the minimal setup necessary to prepare a dump and panic the system:

```
# dumpon /dev/ad0s4b
# mount -art ufs
# /usr/local/bin/command_that_panics_the_system
```

The first line tells the system where to put its dump (put your correct swap partition name here). The second line mounts the filesystems as read-only, so you won't have to fsck after your panic. (Since you know the crash is coming, why make yourself fsck?) Finally, you run the command that triggers the panic. You may need some additional commands, depending on your local setup, but this should get you up and running in most cases.

### Symbols vs. No Symbols

As a final treat, here's a debugging session from the same panic and the same kernel, but without debugging symbols. Compare it to the initial output from where, discussed earlier in the chapter.

```
(kgdb) where
#0   0xc01c5982 in dumpsys ()
#1   0xc0143119 in db_fncall ()
#2   0xc0142f33 in db_command ()
#3   0xc0142fff in db_command_loop ()
#4   0xc0145393 in db_trap ()
#5   0xc02ad0f6 in kdb_trap ()
#6   0xc02ba004 in trap_fatal ()
#7   0xc02b9d71 in trap_pfault ()
#8   0xc02b9907 in trap ()
#9   0xc01ffb23 in vcount ()
#10  0xc01a5e58 in spec_close ()
#11  0xc01a55f1 in spec_vnoperate ()
#12  0xc0207454 in vn_close ()
#13  0xc0207fab in vn_closefile ()
#14  0xc01b1d50 in fdrop_locked ()
#15  0xc01b155a in fdrop ()
#16  0xc01b152d in closef ()
#17  0xc01b114e in fdfree ()
#18  0xc01b5173 in exit1 ()
#19  0xc01b4ec2 in sys_exit ()
#20  0xc02ba2b7 in syscall ()
#21  0xc02ae06d in syscall_with_err_pushed ()
#22  0x80503a5 in ?? ()
#23  0x807024a in ?? ()
#24  0xbfbfffb4 in ?? ()
#25  0x807daaf in ?? ()
#26  0x807d6eb in ?? ()
#27  0x80630c1 in ?? ()
#28  0x8062fed in ?? ()
#29  0x805ea4c in ?? ()
#30  0x8065949 in ?? ()
#31  0x806544d in ?? ()
#32  0x806dc17 in ?? ()
#33  0x80616b7 in ?? ()
#34  0x80613f0 in ?? ()
#35  0x8048135 in ?? ()
```

That's it. There are no hints here about where the panic happened, just the
function names that happened. An extraordinarily experienced hacker might
happen to recognize a place in the kernel where the exact system calls take

place, in exactly this order. If the kernel developer is really, *really* interested in the problem, he could get some information out of it like this:

```
(kgdb) p vcount
$1 = {<text variable, no debug info>} 0xc01ffb00 <vcount>
(kgdb) up 9
#9  0xc01ffb23 in vcount ()
(kgdb) p/x 0xc01ffb23 - 0xc01ffb00
$2 = 0x23
(kgdb)
```

The p/x command means "print in hexadecimal." Here, we've learned roughly how far into vcount() the problem happened. If the developer has a similar kernel built with similar source code, he can do this:

```
(kgdb) l *(vcount + 0x23)
0xc01fb913 is in vcount (../../../kern/vfs_subr.c:2301).
2296            struct vnode *vq;
2297            int count;
2298
2299            count = 0;
2300            mtx_lock(&spechash_mtx);
2301            SLIST_FOREACH(vq, &vp->v_rdev->si_hlist, v_specnext)
2302                    count += vq->v_usecount;
2303            mtx_unlock(&spechash_mtx);
2304            return (count);
2305    }
(kgdb)
```

That's it. There's no way to get the bad vnode information out. The developer is left on his own, poking through the code to see if he can figure out the problem via sheer dogged determination. And in any event, it's very unlikely that any developer capable of working on a problem will have the exact setup that you have on a panicking system. While many of them would be happy to set up such a system in exchange for lavish amounts of hard currency, it's a bit much to expect for free.

## Serial Consoles

Being able to gather debugging information is nice, but what if you need to do so remotely? Or what if you need to reset the machine remotely when it isn't responding to the network? This is best done with a serial console. If I had had a serial console on my first panicking system, I wouldn't have been juggling pen, paper, and monitor.

Real UNIX hardware (such as Alpha and SPARC) has a hardware serial console capability. On these systems, you can attach a serial cable to the serial console port and have unfettered access to the BIOS, boot messages, and startup controls. (Most x86 hardware does not allow this; you must be at the console to look at the BIOS or to press the space bar to interrupt the boot. A very few Intel motherboards, such as the L440GX, do have this functionality, but this is a special feature you must hunt for.)

This can be a problem when your FreeBSD system is in a colocation facility on the other side of the country. You have a couple of options here: a hardware serial console or FreeBSD's built-in software serial console. Either console requires an accessible serial device nearby. If you have two FreeBSD boxes in one location, you can plug them into each other. If you have a huge array of FreeBSD boxes, companies such as Lucent make network-accessible "terminal servers" that do nothing but handle gobs of serial connections.

### Hardware Serial Console

Nothing any operating system can do will give you access to the PC-compatible BIOS messages across a serial port. This stuff happens before the operating system starts and before the hard drive is read.

Some hardware solutions do exist to work around this. The best I've seen is the PC Weasel (http://www.realweasel.com). It's a video board with a serial port instead of a video port. By connecting a serial cable to the Weasel, you can manipulate the BIOS remotely, interrupt the boot to come up in single-user mode, and generally do whatever you like with the system as if you were at the console. (There are other manufacturers of similar devices, but they either require proprietary client software or are far more expensive.)

### Software Serial Console

FreeBSD includes a software serial console. As FreeBSD boots, it decides where to put its console—on the monitor and keyboard by default. With a few tweaks, though, you can have the console come up on a serial port, but your system must have a serial port. (Some hardware is increasingly arriving "legacy-free," which means that it lacks serial ports and ISA slots; you may need to buy a PCI serial card.)

This serial console has a couple of disadvantages: It does not kick in until FreeBSD's boot loader starts and you will not see BIOS messages, though you will get a chance to interact with the boot process. Still, it's good enough for most uses.

#### Software Serial Console Physical Setup

You must have a null modem cable to use a serial console (available at any computer store or from online vendors—check pricewathc.com). Get the best cable you can find; if you have an emergency and need to use the serial console, you're probably not in the mood to deal with line noise.

Plug one end of the null modem cable into the serial console port on your FreeBSD server—by default the first serial port (COM1 or sio0, depending on what operating system you're used to). You can change this with a kernel recompile, but it's generally simpler to just use the default on a server.

Plug the other end of your null modem cable into an open serial port on another system. I recommend either another FreeBSD or other UNIX system, or a terminal server. You can use a Windows system, but that won't give you any remote-control functionality. (Yes, you can use VNC or PC Anywhere on the Windows system, but you're starting to look at a complicated setup when a simple FreeBSD box would suffice.)

If you have two FreeBSD machines at a remote location, and want to use serial consoles for both of them, simply attach the console cable to the second serial port on the other server. If you have three machines, you can daisy-chain them into a loop. By combining twos and threes, you should be able to get serial consoles on any number of FreeBSD systems. (I've worked in areas with 30 or 40 FreeBSD machines in one room, where installing monitors was simply not practical, and serial consoles were used to great effect.)

**NOTE** *If tracking which machine is attached to which port becomes a problem, invest in a terminal server.*

### Configuring the Software Serial Console

If you're using the serial console exclusively, tell the system to use it by adding an entry in /boot/loader.conf:

```
console="comconsole"
```

To switch back to the default video console, remove the line or comment it out. You could also set this explicitly in /boot/loader.conf with this line:

```
console="vidconsole"
```

### *Changing the Configuration*

If you're in a server-room situation, you may find that you want to switch back and forth from a standard console to a serial console. I generally manage large arrays of FreeBSD boxes via the serial console. If one particular machine is exceptionally troublesome, I might go and put a real console on it; I don't want to reconfigure /boot/loader.conf to make the physical console work—I want it to "just happen." You can do this easily with FreeBSD.

One of the first things any x86 system does upon boot is check for the presence of a keyboard. You can set up your FreeBSD system so that it will use a regular console if it detects a keyboard, and a serial console if it doesn't. (It's the best solution we have with inflexible x86 hardware.) To make this work, edit the file /boot.config by putting only this in it:

```
-h
```

This is the argument passed to the system boot, much as if you interrupted the boot and typed boot -h. (Of course, to really do that, you would need to have a keyboard plugged in, so that would render the whole thing kind of moot!)

If you have -h in /boot.config, and you don't have a keyboard, the system will use the serial console. If there is a keyboard, the system will use the video console. This method of doing the check is rather kludgy, but it's good enough if you know the rules.

### Using a Serial Console

You can access the serial console in a variety of ways, all of which require a second computer. If your second computer is running a Microsoft operating system, the Hyperterm program gives you access to your serial ports (just set your terminal preferences to 9600 baud, 8 bits, no parity, and 1 stop bit). To use a handheld with a serial port (I frequently use a Handspring Visor with a serial cradle), run one of the several free vt100 terminal programs on it. If your second computer also runs FreeBSD (as it should if you want the maximum bang for your buck), you can use FreeBSD's terminal program. Since this is a FreeBSD book, this is the solution we'll discuss.

FreeBSD accesses serial lines with tip(1), a program that allows you to connect to a remote system in a manner similar to telnet. To run tip, do this:

```
# tip portname
```

A port name is shorthand for specifying the number and speed to be used on a serial port. The file /etc/remote contains a list of port names. Most of the entries in this file are relics of the day when UUCP was *the* major data-transfer protocol and serial terminals were the norm instead of the exception. At the end of this file, however, you'll see a few entries like this:

```
# Hardwired line
cuaa0b|cuaa0b:dv=/dev/cuaa0:br#2400:pa=none:
cuaa0c|cuaa0c:dv=/dev/cuaa0:br#9600:pa=none:

# Finger friendly shortcuts
com1:dv=/dev/cuaa0:br#9600:pa=none:
com2:dv=/dev/cuaa1:br#9600:pa=none:
com3:dv=/dev/cuaa2:br#9600:pa=none:
com4:dv=/dev/cuaa3:br#9600:pa=none:
```

Older UNIX hands will recognize cuaa0b and cuaa0c. (The "com" entries were added for the convenience of people who have grown up with Windows.) Assume that you have two FreeBSD boxes wired back-to-back, with each one's serial port 1 null-modemed into serial port 2. You'll want to connect to your local serial port 2 to talk to the other system's serial console:

```
# tip com2
connected
```

And you won't see anything else, no matter what you type.

If you log into the other system and reboot it, you'll abruptly see action in your tip window:

```
boot() called on cpu#1
Waiting (max 60 seconds) for system process `bufdaemon' to stop...stopped
Waiting (max 60 seconds) for system process `syncer' to stop...stopped

syncing disks... 8 8 2 2
done
Uptime: 21m20s
Rebooting...
cpu_reset called on cpu#1
cpu_reset: Stopping other CPUs
cpu_reset: Restarting BSP
cpu_reset_proxy: Stopped CPU 1
```

There will be a long pause while the system boots. If you're near the system, you'll see the standard BIOS messages flash by. Eventually, you'll see something like this:

```
Console: serial port
BIOS drive A: is disk0
BIOS drive C: is disk1
BIOS 639kB/523200kB available memory

FreeBSD/i386 bootstrap loader, Revision 1.0
(mwlucas@magpire.blackhelicopters.org, Sat Jul  7 18:40:47 EDT 2001)
Loading /boot/defaults/loader.conf
/boot/kernel/kernel text=0x1d7b58 data=0x3b28c+0x5132c
syms=[0x4+0x30420+0x4+0x3a852]
/
Hit [Enter] to boot immediately, or any other key for command prompt.
Booting [/boot/kernel/kernel] in 10 seconds...
```

Hit the space bar to interrupt the boot.

At this point, it's just like you're at the keyboard. It doesn't matter if the system is 1,000 miles away; you can change your booting kernel, get a verbose boot, bring it up in single-user mode and manually fsck the hard drive, whatever. The serial console can't save you from a BIOS or hardware failure, but it will make other things much simpler to diagnose.

Type **boot** to continue loading the kernel. Eventually you'll see this:

```
Additional TCP options:.
Starting background filesystem checks

Tue Jul 10 19:40:21 EDT 2001
```

This is almost exactly like being at the console, except you get no logon prompt.

### Serial Login

By default, serial ports are not treated as logon devices. Many people use their serial ports for serial mice or modems, not for console connections, and if you put mouse movements into a logon prompt, the system will be confused at best. You can use a serial port as a mouse port, a modem port, or a console port, but not all at the same time. People who want to get a logon prompt over a serial line are generally assumed to know how to activate the terminal on that port.

To activate the terminal, first check the /etc/ttys file for a list of all the terminals and pseudo-terminals on the system. The serial port is just another terminal. In terminal-speak, sio0/com1 is known as ttyd0, for "tty dialup 0".[2] Find the line for ttyd0:

```
ttyd0   "/usr/libexec/getty std.9600"   dialup  off secure
```

The fourth field in this line says that this terminal is off. Change that "off" to "on", and then it's time to restart the daemon init, or process ID 1, that provides terminal services. You don't need to check ps output to get the process ID of init; init always has the process ID 1. If init is not running, the system is not running, and you can restart it gracefully with the -1 signal.

```
# kill -1 1
```

Once you do this, you'll abruptly see activity on your serial console.

```
Tue Jul 10 19:50:02 EDT 2001
FreeBSD/i386 (magpire.blackhelicopters.org) (ttyd0)

login:
```

### Emergency Logon Setup

In some very bad situations, a FreeBSD system might stop talking to the network. Perhaps the network card has gone bad, or the system panics when some program starts. I was once in a situation where a server on the other side of the country panicked upon boot because the database program crashed the whole system as soon as it started. The system would reboot, check its disks, start up its programs, and crash. I needed to add one command-line option to the database program's startup script for the crashes to stop.

The problem, though, was that the system wouldn't be up long enough for me to SSH in, become root, and shut down the database. While I had a serial console, it wasn't configured to allow logins. I could sit there on the serial

---

[2] The astute among you might wonder what "tty" stands for. It's "teletype." Yes, UNIX is that old.

console and watch the panic message appear over and over again, all the while thinking, "You know, if I could just log in over this serial port, I could fix that startup script." Here's how to do exactly that. While you might never need this, if you do, you'll be grateful you know it.

Because FreeBSD does not restrict console access until the system reaches multi-user mode, you can interrupt the boot process, boot to single-user mode, and make your changes. To do so, open your serial-console connection, and then get someone on the other end to power-cycle the machine. (This isn't good for your computer, but neither is repeated crashing!) Now boot into single-user mode, and at a command prompt, do the following:

```
# fsck -p
```

This will clean up any damage done by the power cycle. Now run this:

```
# mount -a
```

You can now access your local filesystems. Now, edit the /etc/ttys file to enable the serial port logon as described in the previous section. Here you can also edit the startup script that's causing the system to crash.

Exit the shell to complete the boot, and you'll be able to log in via the serial console.

### Disconnecting the Serial Console

The tip(1) program uses the tilde (~) as a control character. To disconnect the serial console, enter the disconnect sequence "tilde-period" at any time:

```
~.
```

You'll be gracefully disconnected, but not logged out (serial is a very loose protocol). If you go back in and type **tip com2** again, you'll be back at your login session. If server1 has a cable plugged into the console port of server2, it might look like this:

```
server1#tip com1
connected

server2#
```

This might not worry you, but a break-in on server1 would immediately compromise server2. Make it an unbreakable habit to log out when you're connected via serial!

## Submitting a Problem Report

You could argue that this should have been included in Chapter 2 on "Getting More Help." "Problem Report" (PR) sounds impressive, doesn't it? Submitting a PR requires a certain minimum level of information, however, that you wouldn't have until after reading this chapter.

### Problem Report System

FreeBSD uses GNATS, a popular bug-tracking database, to track problem reports. The main FreeBSD GNATS database is available under http://www.FreeBSD.org/support.html. For a problem report to be entered into GNATS, it must be submitted in an appropriate format in one of two ways.

First, you can submit your PR on the Web. This might mean a lot of cutting and pasting, but it's certainly possible. The PR form can be found online at http://www.FreeBSD.org/send-pr.html.

If you have a FreeBSD system on the Net, however, you'll find that the simpler way to do this is with send-pr(1). This generates a template for you to fill out with the proper information, and formats the message specifically for use in GNATS. Patches, suggestions, and bug reports submitted via send-pr are recorded permanently.

### What's in a PR?

The Problem Report process isn't for problems like "my network card doesn't work." You need to troubleshoot your own problems, with the help of a mailing list or list archive, if appropriate. Send-pr is for patches and debugging information.

A good PR contains enough information to fix the problem, and hopefully even a suggested solution. If you have time to spare, go take a look through some of the open PRs; you might find it illuminating. As I write this, there are 1,918 open PRs. Many contain good, solid debugging information. Others are, to put it kindly, less useful.

The FreeBSD FAQ contains a joke by Dag-Erling C. Smørgrav: "How many -current users does it take to change a light bulb?" Part of the answer is: "Three to submit PRs about it, one of which is misfiled under doc and consists only of 'it's dark.'" Remember this when filing a PR; include debugging output, or better still a patch to fix the problem. Before you open a PR, you need to carefully evaluate what sort of problem you have. If the problem amounts to "it's dark," you need to dig a little more.

### Using Send-pr

The send-pr command brings up a text template in whatever editor you have in $EDITOR. Once you've completed the template, send-pr mails it to GNATS for you. It's assumed that your system has basic email functionality. If that isn't the case for you, use the Web interface (http://www.FreeBSD.org/send-pr.html) to submit your PR. Here's a sample of the template:

```
To: FreeBSD-gnats-submit@freebsd.org
From: Michael Lucas <mwlucas>
Reply-To: Michael Lucas <mwlucas>
Cc:
X-send-pr-version: 3.113
X-GNATS-Notify:


>Submitter-Id:    current-users
>Originator:      Michael Lucas
>Organization:    <organization of PR author (multiple lines)>
>Confidential:    no <FreeBSD PRs are public data>
>Synopsis:   <synopsis of the problem (one line)>
>Severity:   <[ non-critical | serious | critical ] (one line)>
>Priority:   <[ low | medium | high ] (one line)>
>Category:   <choose from the list of categories above (one line)>
>Class:           <[ sw-bug | doc-bug | change-request | update | maintainer-update
] (one line)>
>Release:    FreeBSD 5.0-CURRENT i386
>Environment:
System: FreeBSD pedicular.blackhelicopters.org 5.0-CURRENT FreeBSD 5.0-CURRENT #5:
Wed Apr 24 07:27:19 EDT 2002
mwlucas@pedicular.blackhelicopters.org:/shared/usr/currentobj/usr/src/sys/BLEEDING
i386
     <machine, os, target, libraries (multiple lines)>
>Description:
     <precise description of the problem (multiple lines)>
>How-To-Repeat:
     <code/input/activities to reproduce the problem (multiple lines)>
>Fix:
     <how to correct or work around the problem, if known (multiple lines)>
```

### Filling Out the Form

No matter which method you use, the problem lies in filling out the form. Let's go over it one line at a time.

| | |
|---|---|
| **To, Subject, Submitter-Id** | These lines can be left alone. GNATS will take care of this for you. |
| **From** | Make sure that the From line contains a valid email address; this is where GNATS or a developer will try to contact you. |

| | |
|---|---|
| **Originator** | This is your name, generally pulled from your system environment. While some folks use handles on the Internet, this is a good place to put your real name. It's difficult to treat a serious problem with the attention it deserves if your name shows up as "Doctor Web." |
| **Organization** | You can either fill in your organization or leave it blank. |
| **Confidential** | This defaults to "no". GNATS is a public database. If you're putting confidential information in a PR, you're doing something wrong. (If you believe that you have discovered a bug with security implications, you can contact security-office@FreeBSD.org. Don't do this just because the debugging information includes your root password, however.) |
| **Synopsis** | This line is probably the most critical. Give a brief, one-line description of the problem, because developers frequently use this to decide which PRs to take a look at. A synopsis like "My system sucks!" will get closed with a terse comment about useless PRs, while something like "kernel panic under heavy CPU load, dump debug attached" has a better chance of attracting skilled attention. If you have a patch to fix the problem, put the word "PATCH" in the synopsis, which will almost guarantee a reasonably quick response. |
| **Severity** | This field gives you three choices; pick a reasonable one. If you get a reputation for listing minor bugs as "critical," you'll find yourself ignored fairly quickly. (This all works on the honor system, and reputation counts for more than you might think.) |
| **Priority** | The Priority field is a bit of a misnomer. This issue might be high priority for you, but developers tend to ignore this field. Still, you get the option to set it. A good synopsis line will get a better response than a priority of "high," but entering a priority of high here might relieve your stress. |
| **Category** | This field has several options, many of which are obsolete or pointless. For example, if you have a problem with a piece of contributed code, filing a PR in the GNU category will probably get you a response of "talk to the authors." For kernel panics, use the "kern" category. |
| **Class** | This field contains a general description of your PR. The choices are mostly self-explanatory. If you can crash a program or the system, it's an "sw-bug." |

| | |
|---|---|
| **Release** | Your system type is automatically entered in the Release field. If you're filling out a PR on a different system than the one exhibiting the problem, you'll want to correct this. |
| **System** | Lastly, put the output of `uname -a` in the System field. You can add additional information to this field to describe other relevant parts of your environment. For example, if the machine is a heavily loaded news server, mention that. If you have a snippet of a configuration file that reproduces the panic, put it here. |
| **Description** | The Description field is a free-form, plain-text section for you to go into detail about the issue. Don't rant or rave; just describe what happens. Include any error messages, if you have them. This is where you put your debugger output. If you don't have debugger output for a kernel panic, do not send a PR. Also include your kernel configuration and the contents of /var/run/dmesg.boot. |
| **How-To-Repeat** | In this field use either a snippet of code, a series of instructions, or a text description of how to reproduce the problem. For some PRs, this can be very short—"read FreeBSD-questions for a week and see how often this is asked" is a perfectly legitimate How-To-Repeat for doc changes. More technical problems require more information. |
| **Fix** | The most important part of the PR goes under Fix. If you have a patch that fixes the problem, put it here. If you have a workaround, put it here. Anything you've discovered about how to solve the problem goes here. Sometimes the most unusual fix or condition provides the vital clue for the solution.[3]

A good PR always has something in the Fix field. Your solution might not be the one implemented, but it demonstrates that you've put some thought into the matter. The incredible support FreeBSD offers through the mailing lists and Web sites sometimes obscures the fact that when you're up against the wall, the ultimate responsibility for solving problems rests on you. |

[3] If you're using the Web interface, do not cut and paste patches into the Fix field. The Web submission form transforms all tabs into spaces, and destroys patch formatting.

When you save and exit your editor, send-pr will ask if you want to submit the problem report. If you think that your PR includes enough information to fix the problem, say "yes". Your system will mail it in.

No matter which method you use to submit a PR, you'll receive a confirmation email. The subject includes the PR number, usually something like "kern/22459", and your synopsis. Any mail sent to FreeBSD-gnats-submit@ FreeBSD.org with that subject line will be attached to that PR. You can submit patches and responses from any computer with a working mail system.

Similarly, any response sent to your patch will be tracked with the PR. You can check the status of your PR at http://www.FreeBSD.org/cgi/query-pr.cgi.

**NOTE** *Now that your suggestion is in the FreeBSD system, it'll be tracked forever. That is not a guarantee that your suggestion will be taken, or that your problem will be solved; it'll simply be recorded, publicly, forever.*

### PR Results

A properly filled-out PR will generally be quickly snatched up and closed. As of this date, I've submitted 59 PRs. Most have been solved or committed, and closed. The odd ones out were trivial goofs on documentation that lives under /usr/src/contrib, an area where the Project specifically disavows responsibility for minor fixes. If I can get over 90 percent of my PRs successfully closed, anyone can.

If you happen to hit an area of the system that nobody is particularly familiar with, your PR might languish for some time. If it seems that your PR has been forgotten, drop a friendly note to the appropriate mailing list with your PR number and a brief explanation of what it is and why it's important. Since FreeBSD is a volunteer effort, it's quite possible that something happened to the person who would normally handle your type of PR. While many FreeBSD developers are professional programmers, for many of them this is still a hobby that must take a backseat to sick kids or the big deadline. If nothing else, you can contact one of the commercial support companies listed on the FreeBSD Web site.

A surprising number of difficult PRs are closed quickly, given the proper information. Just remember that the FreeBSD folks are doing this out of love for their work, not because they have to. They want to produce quality code, which is a stronger motivation than a paycheck. If you can help them produce a quality product, they'll be delighted to work with you.

Congratulations! You're now as prepared for a crash as any non-kernel developer can be. Proper preparation can make your life easier, and preparing for the worst is one of the best ways to sleep uninterrupted at night.

# 21

## DESKTOP FREEBSD

Why use FreeBSD on the desktop? Well, why not? FreeBSD makes as good a desktop as it does a server. While FreeBSD's development focus has generally been on the server side, that same crash-resistance and stability makes it a wonderful desktop.

Your FreeBSD desktop will allow you to access your local Windows NT network, share your files, browse the Web, read email, and compose letters, all without crashing even once. Plus, using FreeBSD as a desktop is a wonderful way to learn UNIX and build your confidence as a sysadmin.

**NOTE**  *At one time, "workstation" meant "UNIX computer." The UNIX in question was SunOS, a direct descendant of BSD4.2. If people could use BSD as a workstation that long ago, it'll certainly work for you now.*

This chapter will not discuss in great detail exactly how to turn FreeBSD into a comfortable desktop, because that would be another book in itself! We'll go into some detail when discussing FreeBSD software that offers SMB support (Server Message Block, or SMB, is discussed in the next section), but otherwise we'll mostly provide pointers to useful programs that are documented elsewhere. With the understanding of FreeBSD you have acquired by reading this book, and the help of the mailing list archives, you should be able to make these tools work with just a bit of guidance.

## Accessing File Shares

If you're on a typical office network, the standard network file-sharing protocol is Microsoft's Common Internet File Sharing, or CIFS. (CIFS was once known as Server Message Block, or SMB.) This is the typical "Network Neighborhood" that Windows users can access. While originally provided only by Microsoft Windows systems, this protocol has become something of a standard.

Thankfully, today there's an open-source CIFS file-sharing server, called Samba. Plus, many other commercial products, such as LanManager and NetApp, provide services via this protocol. FreeBSD itself includes programs to access CIFS shares, which exist in two parts: a kernel module and several user-land programs.

### Prerequisites

Before you start, gather some basic information about your Windows network:

- The workgroup or Windows domain name
- A valid username and password
- The IP address of the WINS server, or the DNS hostnames of all the hosts you want to access. (You can get the WINS server IP by running `ipconfig /all` on a Windows system.)

### Character Sets

The first problem you have when attempting to access Windows shares is supporting the multiple character sets so common in Windows. (It's very easy for a Windows user to use characters not found in the standard English alphabet, and you don't want such a character to confuse your kernel.)

The FreeBSD kernel does not include the libraries to support multiple character sets, so you'll need to add them. Install the libiconv port from /usr/ports/converters/libiconv before you attempt to add CIFS support to your kernel.

### Kernel Support for CIFS

Now recompile your kernel to handle CIFS by adding the following options to your kernel:

```
options         NETSMB
options         NETSMBCRYPTO
options         LIBMCHAIN
options         LIBICONV
options         SMBFS
```

The SMBFS kernel functions are also available as a module, but since you have to rebuild your kernel anyway to include SMB networking support, you may as well compile it statically.

### SMB Tools

Once you've built the kernel, install the SMB tools from /usr/ports/net/smbfs.[1] These tools must be exactly synchronized with your kernel, which makes packages mostly useless, unless you have several identical machines, and if you upgrade your FreeBSD install, you must upgrade the port. To make life still more difficult, the master SMBFS source-code repository lurks behind a very overloaded link in Kazakhstan. As such, I recommend that you store the distfile somewhere on your network, so you can easily rebuild the tools without having to refetch the source from the other side of the world (well, depending on where you're located).

### Configuring CIFS

The SMB tools use a configuration file—either $HOME/.nsmbrc or /usr/local/ etc/nsmb.conf. All settings in nsmb.conf override settings in user home directories.

The configuration file is divided into sections by labels in square brackets. For example, settings that apply to every SMB connection are kept in the [default] section. You can create your own sections by specifying servers, users, and shares, in one of the following formats:

```
[servername]
[servername:username]
[servername:username:sharename]
```

For example, information that applies to an entire server goes in a section named after the server. Information that applies to a specific user is kept in a username section, and information that only applies to a single share is kept in a label that includes the share name. You can lump the information for all the shares under a [servername] entry if you don't have more specific information per share or per user.

**NOTE** *Nsmb.conf uses CIFS values—for example, my Windows username is mlucas, but my UNIX username is mwlucas, so I use mlucas in nsmb.conf.*

#### nsmb.conf Keywords

You use keywords, some of which can only be used in particular sections, to assign a configuration to a section. For example, servers have IP addresses and users don't, so you wouldn't add the IP address keywords to a user section.

To use a keyword, assign a value with an equal sign, as in keyword=value. Here are the keywords.

---

[1] In FreeBSD 4.4 and later, these tools are included in the base operating system.

```
workgroup=string
```

The workgroup keyword specifies the name of the NT domain or Windows Workgroup you want to access.

```
addr=a.b.c.d
```

The addr keyword sets the IP (or IPX) address of an SMB server with this Windows hostname. This keyword can only appear under a plain [servername] label.

```
nbns=a.b.c.d
```

The nbns keyword sets the IP address of the NetBIOS (WINS) nameserver. You can put this line in the [default] section or under a particular [servername].

```
nbscope=string
```

The nbscope keyword sets the NetBIOS scope. If you don't know what NetBIOS scope is, you probably don't need to set it.

```
retry_count
```

The retry_count keyword specifies the number of times the SMB client will try to contact a server before assuming that the connection has broken. The default is probably fine.

```
timeout
```

The timeout setting is the length of time the system will wait for a response to an SMB request before trying again. Again, the default is probably fine.

```
password=string
```

The password keyword sets a *clear-text* password for a user or a share. If you must store passwords in nsmb.conf, be sure that only root can read the file. Storing a password in $HOME/.nsmbrc is a bad idea on a multi-user system.

You can scramble this password by running smbutil -crypt, and the scrambled password will have double dollar signs ($$) in front of it. However, while this will help prevent someone accidentally seeing the password, it can be easily unscrambled by a malicious user.

### Minimum Configuration: Name Resolution

So let's build a basic nsmb.conf file. At an absolute bare minimum, we first need to be able to find hosts for which we need a workgroup and a NetBIOS name-server. I also have a user set up on the Windows-based servers to share files, so I'm going to put that username in the [default] section:

```
[default]
workgroup=EXAMPLE
nbns=192.168.2.80
username=unix
```

Armed with this information, you should be able to perform basic SMB name queries. Use smbutil(1) to test this:

```
# smbutil lookup fileserv4
Got response from 192.168.2.80
IP address of fileserv4: 192.168.1.202
#
```

If this works, you have basic SMB functionality.

### Other smbutil Functions

Before you can mount a filesystem from a Windows host, you must log in to it. (Only root can use these smbutil functions.)

```
# smbutil login //unix@fileserv4
Password:
Connected to UNIX
#
```

So our password is correct. Let's see what resources this server offers with smbutil's view command:

```
# smbutil view //unix@fileserv4
Password:
Share       Type      Comment
-------------------------------
jsmith$     disk
gdonner$    disk
mlucas$     disk
...
```

You'll get a list of every shared resource on the SMB server.

Now, assuming you're finished, log out of the server:

```
# smbutil logout //mlucas@fileserv4
Password:
Connection unmarked as permanent and will be closed when possible
#
```

### Mounting a Share

Now that you've finished investigating, let's actually mount a share with mount_smbfs(8). The syntax is as follows:

```
mount_smbfs //username@servername/share /mount/point
```

I have a share on the fileserver called mlucas. To mount my personal fileserver share on my FreeBSD box as /home/mwlucas/smbmount, I would do this:

```
# mount_smbfs //mlucas@fileserv4/mlucas /home/mwlucas/smbmount
```

Check your work with df(1).

```
# df
Filesystem              1K-blocks     Used    Avail Capacity  Mounted on
/dev/ad0s1a                 99183    49105    42144     54%   /
/dev/ad0s1f               5186362  3091500  1679954     65%   /usr
/dev/ad0s1e                198399    22816   159712     12%   /var
procfs                          4        4        0    100%   /proc
//MLUCAS@FILESERV4/MLUCAS   128000    54320    73680     42%
/usr/home/mwlucas/smbmount
#
```

I can now do basic file operations, including using Emacs and StarOffice on the documents in this shared drive. Life just got a little better.

### Other mount_smbfs Options

Mount_smbfs includes several options to control how the system behaves. Use mount_smbfs's -f option to choose a different file permission mode, and the -d option to choose a different directory permission mode. For example, to set a mount so that only I can access the contents of this directory, I would use mount_smbfs -d 700. (This would make the UNIX permissions far more stringent than the Windows ones, but that's not my concern at the moment.) I can even change the owner with the -u option, and the group with the -g option.

The -I option tells mount_smbfs to skip the NetBIOS name resolution, and to only use the hostname or IP address provided on the command line instead.

The -N option tells mount_smbfs to read the password from the configuration file, and not to prompt for one. This means that you need to have your clear-text password in nsmb.conf, as discussed earlier.

The -W flag specifies a new workgroup. It overrides any settings in nsmb.conf.

The Windows filesystem, and hence SMB, uses case-insensitive filenames, but UNIX is case sensitive. SMBFS defaults to leaving the case as it finds it, but that may not be what you want. Use the -c flag to tell mount_smbfs to change the case on files on SMB filesystems: -c l changes everything to lowercase, while -c u changes everything to uppercase.

When working with mount_smbfs, I've found it flexible enough to handle almost any situation on a Windows network, thus allowing you to use your FreeBSD system seamlessly with the rest of the office.

### Sample nsmb.conf Entries

You can customize the nsmb.conf file to use different usernames to access different shares or to bypass NetBIOS name resolution for particular hosts. Here are some more complicated examples, using the configuration entries we defined earlier.

All of our advanced samples here assume that they're part of the configuration that includes this bare-minimum entry:

```
[default]
workgroup=EXAMPLE
nbns=192.168.2.80
username=mlucas
```

### Unique Password on a Standalone System

You would use something like the following if you had a machine named "desktop" with a password-protected share. Many Windows 9x systems have this sort of password-protection feature.

```
#I have a share on my desktop with a separate password
[desktop:mlucas]
password=$$1725a5038393e12ee
```

### Accessing a Second Domain

In this example, we're trying to access a separate domain, named "development." This domain has a separate username and password than our default:

```
#development is in a different NT domain, with a shared username
[development]
workgroup=EXAMPLE2
username=support
```

### CIFS File Ownership

Ownership of files between UNIX and Windows systems can be problematic. For one thing, your UNIX usernames probably won't map to Windows usernames, and UNIX has a different permissions scheme than Windows.

Since you're using a single Windows username to access the share, you have whatever access that account has to the Windows resources, but you should assign the proper UNIX permissions for that share. By default, mount_smbfs assigns the new share the same permissions as the mount point used. The directory /home/mwlucas/smbmount in our example is owned by mwlucas, in the group mwlucas, and has mode 755. These permissions say that I can edit what's in this directory, but no other user can.

## Serving Windows File Shares

Just as FreeBSD can access CIFS shares, it can also serve them to CIFS clients (such as Windows) with Samba. You can find Samba in /usr/ports/net/samba. You'll find the Samba Web site at http://www.samba.org, and a useful tutorial at http://www.linux.org/docs/ldp/howto/HOWTO-INDEX/howtos.html. There are entire books written about Samba, and I cannot possibly do it justice in just a few paragraphs, so we'll end our Samba discussion here.

## Accessing Print Servers

UNIX printing is an arcane matter, mainly because of the vast array of hardware support. The UNIX printing system was originally designed to work on a teletype, which imposed very specific requirements. It has been expanded to handle dot-matrix, character, inkjet, laser, and every other sort of printer, but it suffers from that legacy. If we could start over with the UNIX printing system and only support laser and inkjet printers, life would be much simpler. Unfortunately, we can't.

### Lpd

If you are lucky enough to work in a place with a UNIX-based print server, setting up a printer should be very simple. If, on the other hand, you are using a Microsoft print server, things are a little more complicated. To make your life a bit easier, ask your Windows administrator to install Microsoft's Print Services for UNIX package (NT, 2000, and XP).[2]

---

[2] Unfortunately, installing Print Services for UNIX means several hours of work for the Windows administrator as she installs the service, reinstalls the latest Microsoft service pack, and then reapplies all the patches that need to be installed on top of that. Don't be too hard on her when she refuses. It will take much less time for you to work around her problems than for her to make your life easier.

The standard UNIX print server protocol, lpd (line printer daemon) runs on TCP port 515. (There is also a line printer daemon program, lpd(8).) To see whether a system offers lpd, telnet to the print server on port 515, just as we tested mail and Web servers in earlier chapters. If you can connect, the system is running the line printer daemon. (Don't expect to see anything while making the connection—the line printer protocol is a pain to speak by hand.)

### /etc/printcap

Once you know you have an lpd-based print server available, it's time to configure your system to talk to it. The key lies in the file /etc/printcap. Basic printcap information appears in Chapter 9, but let's look at it in a bit more detail here. Here's a sample printcap file:

```
❶ lp|SalesPS|ThirdFloorPrinter:\
    ❷ :rp=SalesPS:\
    ❸ :rm=printserver:\
    ❹ :sd=/var/spool/output/lpd:\
    ❺ :lf=/var/log/lpd-errs:
```

The first line in this file gives us the printer's name, SalesPS|ThirdFloorPrinter (❶). UNIX printers are traditionally called "lp", "lp1", "lp2", and so on; lp is your default printer; thus the SalesPS printer is our default. In this example, the pipe symbol (|) separated other names for the same printer from each other.

The rp entry, SalesPS (❷), is the desired printer's name. You'll need to get a list of printer names from your network administrator. If it's a Microsoft print server, you might check the printers that the print server has shared out, which are the available printers. Be sure to choose a printer that supports PostScript, the generic printing protocol. All modern printers use PostScript, and some also support proprietary printing systems. Fortunately, most FreeBSD programs send either PostScript or plain text to printers.

**NOTE** *Microsoft servers frequently share one printer under several names and use the name to differentiate how the printing is handled. If you find this to be the case, be sure to choose the PostScript version!*

If you don't know the name of the remote printer, try lp1, AUTO, or PORT1. (Case is important!) While lp1 and PORT1 are generally PostScript, AUTO will try to detect the sort of print job you're sending.

The rm entry (❸) is the name of the server. You must be able to ping this server by the name you give here.

The sd entry (❹) is where your local printer daemon will store output it is trying to print.

Finally, the lf entry (❺) is the printer log file. If you're having trouble printing, check the permissions on the spool directory. It should be owned by root and the daemon group, and have a permissions mode of 755 (see Chapter 7).

If you substitute correct entries for your print server and your printer name, you should be able to use this entry unmodified. You might want to correct the different names, but it's not strictly necessary. (Not doing so might confuse you later, though, when you see a reference to "ThirdFloorPrinter" somewhere!)

### Running a Local Lpd

Once you have a decent-looking printcap entry, you should be able to start your local line printer daemon, lpd(8). This local printer daemon catches print requests made on your local system and sends requests to the remote printer daemon. You can start this at boottime by enabling it in rc.conf.

```
lpd_enable="YES"
```

Alternatively, you could just run lpd as root.

### Printer Testing

Test your printer setup with the command lpq(1), which will display your printer setup. If everything works, you should see something like this:

```
# lpq
no entries
#
```

If your printer is actually printing something at the moment, it'll look more like this:

```
# lpq
lp is ready and printing
Rank    Owner    Job  Files                        Total Size
1st     mwlucas   4   (standard input)             93151 bytes
#
```

To fine-tune your printer setup, see the /etc/printcap information in Chapter 9.

## Local Printers

If your print server doesn't provide ldp services, or if it's directly attached to the parallel port, there's another process to follow. It's friendly looking, it's script-driven, and it requires you to install a whole bunch more software. Take a look at /usr/ports/print/apsfilter.

The good news is that apsfilter will help you speak CIFS to a remote print server. It will help you configure a local printer, either a fancy laser one or one of those El Cheapo $59 inkjet USB models. You might wind up going through the configuration script several times trying to get it right, unless you know exactly what sort of equipment you have, but it will work quite well once you get it set up.

# X: A Graphic Interface

The GUI you sometimes see on a UNIX system is called the X Window System, or X for short. X has some advantages and disadvantages over other windowing systems, but once you get used to it, X can be quite useful.

One of my favorite features of X is that a program can display output on a different machine than it's running on. I frequently run a program on one server and have the user interface appear on my desktop. For example, I only have StarOffice installed on my laptop. When I'm working on one of the servers in my basement[3] and need to whip up a printed complaint letter to a software vendor about their lousy product, I connect to the laptop sitting in the upstairs library and start StarOffice. Although the program is running on the laptop, the interface displays on my local terminal. At times this can actually be more convenient than working on the laptop, as I keep the printer, envelopes, and stamps near the server room.

### X Prerequisites

Before you can set up X, you need to know some basic things about your system. Break out the manual for your monitor and try to find the values for "horizontal sync" and "vertical refresh." Also get the manual for your video card and find out its exact model name and number.

### X Versions

FreeBSD supports a version of X known as XFree86, which is based upon X version 11, release 6, or X11R6. At the time I write this, two different versions of XFree86 are in use: Version 3.3 is the older, stable standard, while version 4 is the new, up-and-coming standard. The version you have will depend on the default in FreeBSD when you installed.

If you have one version but want the other one, you can uninstall all ports that use X, remove the entire /usr/X11R6 directory tree, and install the port of the correct version from under /usr/ports/x11. (This will take a long time and use a lot of disk space.) You then get to reinstall all your X-dependent ports. Enjoy.

### Configuring X

To configure X, you can use the text-based tool xf86cfg, or the graphic tools xf86config (version 4) or xf86Setup (version 3). But beware: Unlike just about anything else you can do with a computer, improper use of XFree86 can actually physically damage both your monitor and your video card. If you test your XFree86 configuration and see your screen flare, strobe, or look like it's having any sort of trouble, leave X immediately. (You can force X to shut down with the key sequence CTRL-ALT-BACKSPACE.)

---

[3] Before you get too impressed at my having a server room in my house, know that my wife calls the basement server room "the junkyard" and the machines that lurk therein "Frankensteins." I don't see what's wrong with using a 166 MHz Digital Alpha to heat the teapot, but she has other ideas.

### Making X Look Decent

The default X setup is ugly. Really, really ugly. It's ugly because X only handles basic screen drawing. While that's not a problem when it comes to drawing terminal windows, menus, and whatnot, X just won't make very pretty pictures. To make X realistically usable, you'll need some sort of desktop environment or window manager.

The subject of window managers is yet another topic of debate among UNIX users. You can find people who believe that the best window manager in the world is the one that ships with X: twm(1). I have to admit that it's not bad, in a bare-bones, back-to-nature, tree-bark-eating sort of way. If I had a system with only 4MB of RAM, twm would be my choice.

Since any computer I work on these days has more than 4MB of RAM, however, I tend to use window managers with a few more features. If you look under /usr/ports/x11-wm, you'll see quite a few window managers. Feel free to experiment with them. I'll mention four specifically, just because of their popularity and my experiences with them.

### Popular X Desktops

My personal favorite window manager is WindowMaker (/usr/ports/x11-wm/windowmaker). It's fast, light, highly customizable, supports themes, and looks darn good on just about any size monitor.

The fvwm2 (/usr/ports/x11-wm/fvwm2) window manager is an old classic that's still in heavy use today. It's very flexible, and all configuration is handled by a text file. It is stable, has a small footprint, and is very reliable. It's also boring.

The most popular desktop environments among many newer UNIX users are Gnome (/usr/ports/x11/gnome) and KDE (/usr/ports/x11/kde2). Both try to be all things to all people. Both include system configuration tools, Web browsers, and office suites. In my opinion, both are painfully bloated and obtuse, much like the proprietary systems they hope to replace. If you prefer a Windows- or Mac-style interface, though, you might be happy with either one of these.[4]

The choice of windowing environment is highly personal. I think it would be interesting to do a psychological study of UNIX users, classifying them by window manager choice. (Useful, no. But interesting.) Play with several, and you'll soon find one that fits your working style.

## Desktop Applications

Once you've selected a window manager, you're ready to get some desktop applications. The standard UNIX desktop application is still the command line. There's a special type of terminal window used for X windows, called an xterm. Some window managers include their own terminal application, and several different types of X terminal program have been written. But you'll find an xterm wherever you go.

---

[4] Gnome and KDE fans would say that my preferred environment lacks vital features. It's all a matter of what you expect on your desktop.

You probably didn't install X just to use a terminal window, however. Let's look at some of the basic applications you might need.

### Web Browsers

You won't find Internet Explorer for FreeBSD coming out any time soon, and that's probably a good thing. FreeBSD includes several different Web browsers, however, the most well known of which is Netscape.

#### Netscape

You'll find several different versions of Netscape under /usr/ports/www. The "communicator" versions include an email client, a news reader, and a Web-page authoring tool; the "navigator" versions include only the Web browser.

The FreeBSD and BSDi versions of Netscape include security holes that Netscape has not bothered to address. If you want to use Netscape, use the Linux versions. The Linux versions can use Linux plug-ins, which are more common than FreeBSD plug-ins, but require that you install the Linux compatibility module (see Chapter 11). Using the Linux version of the browser also allows you to use the Linux RealPlayer and Shockwave plug-ins.

#### Mozilla

If you want a newer browser than Netscape, take a look at Mozilla (/usr/ports/www/mozilla), the code that Netscape 6 is based on. Mozilla is fairly solid and reliable, and is getting better all the time. It also supports Java and Flash, and is my preferred browser. The Linux port of Opera (/usr/ports/www/linux-opera) is growing in popularity, and many people compare it favorably to Netscape. Still another popular choice is konqueror, the file manager included in the KDE window manager that handles both local file viewing and Web page rendering. You get it by installing KDE.

#### Text Browsers

If you don't have X installed, you can surf the Web using a text-mode browser. This is the original way the Web was used, way back in the early 1990s. I frequently use a text-mode browser when I'm in a hurry and just need to get some information without worrying about the graphics or other pretty features. The three most popular text-mode browsers are Lynx (/usr/ports/www/lynx-ssl), w3m (/usr/ports/www/w3m), and links (/usr/ports/www/links). Using one of these browsers can also be an enlightening experience; for example, many blind people use one of these tools to access the Internet.

### Email Readers

FreeBSD supports many different mail readers (see /usr/ports/mail for a complete list). Again, because people have very different tastes in mail clients, try several and pick one you like. Still, here's look at some popular ones.

### GUI Mail Readers

If you're coming from a Windows or Mac background, you'll probably find that Arrow (/usr/ports/mail/arrow) or Evolution (/usr/ports/mail/evolution) will be comfortably familiar. Evolution resembles Microsoft Outlook, but it requires huge chunks of the Gnome desktop environment. You can also use the email client found in Netscape (/usr/ports/www/linux-netscape47-communicator) or Mozilla (/usr/ports/www/mozilla). These are simple and intuitive for most users coming from a GUI environment.

### Mutt

If you're looking for a more UNIX-like mail reader, you might try Mutt (/usr/ports/mail/mutt). Mutt is the end result of 15 years of mail-reader evolution. Every old UNIX hand I know who has tried Mutt has liked it.[5] Mutt is highly configurable and allows the reader to process information very quickly.

One of Mutt's nicest features is that it's threaded; thus, messages that are part of a single discussion are grouped together, in order. I receive a truly monstrous amount of email, at times over 2,000 messages a day. Each must be read and evaluated. Only a fraction of these require my personal attention, and perhaps two dozen need an answer. (There are usually several more that I should answer, but never get around to.) If I had to use a mail program like Microsoft Outlook, I would be utterly lost. Mutt allows me to manage this tsunami in an almost reasonable manner.

### Pine

Another popular UNIX mail reader is Pine. This looks more friendly than Mutt and it's menu-driven. While it's not as configurable as Mutt, it's a good choice for someone who isn't as technical or who doesn't process obscene amounts of email. My wife quite happily reads her email in Pine.

### *Office Suites*

If you're working on a desktop, you'll want things like a word processor, spreadsheet, drawing program, and so on. FreeBSD includes three, though you'll need X installed to run all of them.

### StarOffice

StarOffice (/usr/ports/editors/staroffice60) is a full office suite with a lot of features. (This is actually a Linux version running under Linux mode.) StarOffice is fairly effective; this book was written using it. This version of StarOffice costs a nominal fee.

---

[5] At this point, I will of course be deluged with mail from people saying that their gray beard is far longer than mine, and they've tried Mutt and didn't like it. Oh, well.

### OpenOffice

The company that produced StarOffice was bought out by Sun Microsystems, who decided to release the source code of the program. This meant that they had to rip out a whole bunch of stuff that had been licensed from other companies, and replace it. The result is OpenOffice (/usr/ports/editors/openoffice). OpenOffice is expected to run natively on FreeBSD. It might be some time before all the features of StarOffice are fully available, however. I highly recommend OpenOffice, version 1.0 or later, for average use.

### Koffice

Another popular choice is koffice (/usr/ports/editors/koffice). It's built with KDE, however, so you might find its system requirements rather high.

## *Music*

Everyone who works at a computer for any length of time winds up playing CDs. While a computer's speaker system isn't up to audiophile standards, it's good enough for work.

FreeBSD includes a variety of CD players, all under /usr/ports/audio. Gnome and KDE include their own CD-playing programs. There are a couple of utilities designed for use with WindowMaker, of which /usr/ports/audio/wmcdplay is my favorite. Many people like xmms and gkrellm as well.

Browse through the directory and you'll find any number of CD, MP3, MIDI, and MPEG players.

## *Graphics*

Today's computing world uses a variety of graphic formats. It can be very frustrating to try to view a file in an unfamiliar format. Here we'll mention some of the most common graphic formats, and what programs you need to use to see them.

### Viewing Common Graphics

Most of the common graphic formats can be viewed with xv (/usr/ports/graphics/xv). The xv program handles file formats including (but not limited to) GIF, JPEG, TIFF, PBM, PGM, PPM, X11 bitmap, BMP, XPM, PCX, IRIS RGB, and PNG.

Another common format is PostScript or Encapsulated PostScript. You can view these files with ghostview (/usr/ports/print/ghostview).

When you encounter an unfamiliar graphics format, chances are there's a small program that will open it in /usr/ports/graphics/README.html.

### Viewing Video

To view video, try xanim (/usr/ports/graphics/xanim) or xmps. The avifile port can play MPEG4/DIVX videos.

### Creating Graphics

To create your own graphics, check out the Gimp (/usr/ports/graphic/gimp). This toolkit has been favorably compared to Adobe Photoshop.

### Desk Utilities

These days, people are used to putting all sorts of things on a computer screen, from sticky notes to calculators. I prefer using real sticky notes myself—you can pull them off the edge of your monitor and hand them to someone else—but if you want this functionality, FreeBSD includes it. For a complete list, shuffle through /usr/ports/deskutils. We'll just cover the highlights here.

### GnuCash

One of free software's killer applications is GnuCash, a personal money manager much like Quicken. You can find it in /usr/ports/deskutils/gnucash. While it requires that you have Gnome installed, you can use it while running any other window manager. GnuCash cannot yet interoperate with bank financial systems in the same way Quicken can, but it should be able to about the time this book comes out.

### Palm

Similarly, personal digital assistants are quite common these days. WinCE devices are too tightly tied to Microsoft's operating environment to work well with FreeBSD. However, Palm-based devices, including Handsprings, do work well with FreeBSD. You'll find an entire category of Palm software under /usr/ports/palm.

## Games

Now the important stuff! FreeBSD includes a variety of nifty games, all under /usr/ports/games. If you're running KDE or Gnome, you already have a few simple games installed. If you want to snag these packages without the accompanying window managers, they're available as /usr/ports/games/kdegames2 and /usr/ports/games/gnomegames. The ports will automatically install the bare-minimum underlying libraries to use them. Many of us are stuck doing that anyway, because some other piece of software requires them.

### Xevil

For straightforward mayhem, network play, and fast action, check out xevil. It's an old-fashioned 2-D shooter, with ladders and robots and all sorts of things that need to be shot, burned, and exploded. It's not for the easily offended, but you can easily lose days with this simple toy. Best of all, it's lightweight; you don't need Gnome or KDE or qt or xview or any other graphics toolkit to run it.

### Heretic, Doom, and Quake

If you're into fancier graphics or three dimensions, there's native FreeBSD ports of Heretic, Doom, and Quake (/usr/ports/games/quakeforge). These are classic games produced by Id Software: Run around, get bigger weapons, find evil monsters, and feed them the rockets they so richly deserve. The one problem with Doom is that it only runs on 8-bit X terminals.

You can start up a Doom-compliant X session with this command:

```
# startx -bpp 8
```

This means you have to exit and restart X to play these games, but that's not too bad. After all, try running Doom on a modern Windows system and see if you like what you see.

### Nethack and Angband

If xevil and Doom are simply too graphically intense, you can step back into the 1980s with Nethack, Angband, and their variants. Both are simple games that run on block maps. You are a character in a dungeon, trying to reach the lowest level and take out whatever horrible beast lives in that version of the game.

Nethack runs without X, and is addictive nonetheless. Angband runs on X, but can use richer graphics than Nethack. Both have forked time and time again, so you can pick and choose among the variants. My personal favorite is vanilla Angband, but I've lost several hours to Nethack as well.

### Civilization

If violence isn't your thing, proceed directly to Freeciv (/usr/ports/games/freeciv). Freeciv is a Civilization clone. You start with a tribe of settlers, and try to build a worldwide empire. You compete with other players across the network, or just play solo. Of all the things that made me risk missing the deadline for this book, Freeciv was by far the most insidious and most dangerous.

If you prefer original software to a clone, you can also run a demo version of Civilization 2. Check under /usr/ports/games/civ2demo.

### Minesweeper, Pac Man, Mahjongg, etc.

Other games are fun to have around, just in general. When I started in technical support, I would play Minesweeper to kill time while on hold or letting a user drone on about the problem of the week. There are several Minesweeper clones, such as freesweep, wmtimebomb, and yamsweeper. You can find a Pac Man clone under xchomp. Mahjongg lives as xmahjongg or xvmahjongg. There's chess, and Go, and just about every classic game that has kept humanity occupied for the last thousand years.

# AFTERWORD

If you've made it this far, you now know how to manage and use FreeBSD as a platform for just about any server task. You might have to learn how a new program works, but you know enough about the operating system to make it work as you need to.

Congratulations! FreeBSD is a wonderful, flexible platform, and is capable of assuming just about any role in your network. To wrap things up, I'd like to talk briefly about some other aspects of FreeBSD.

FreeBSD is two things. In this book we've focused on the programs and software that constitutes the operating system. The other half is the community that creates those bits.

## The Community

The FreeBSD community is composed of computer scientists, programmers, users, systems administrators, documentation writers, and just about anyone who is interested in the system. They come from all walks of life, all education levels, and all over the world. I personally have had dealings with FreeBSD users and developers from all over the United States, Canada, Mexico, the United Kingdom, Russia, Kazakhstan, Denmark, Poland, Australia, and Japan. Some of the people I've worked with are from still other countries, but nationality simply isn't important in this community. I'm sure people are from a wide variety of races and creeds, but it simply doesn't matter online. Some are doctors. Some are computer scientists. Some work in video rental shops. At one point I worked closely with a brilliant developer who turned out to be a teenager. Since most of the community's interaction is online, the only things that represent you are your words and your work.

While members have conflicts, especially over the future direction of the software portion of FreeBSD, on the whole it's less fractious than you could expect from any group of thousands of people from such widely varying backgrounds.

These are the people who improve FreeBSD, drive it forward, and make it more than a collection of ones and zeros.

Each person does it for his own reasons. A tiny portion are developers who are paid to improve the code, either by corporations dependent on FreeBSD or government agencies such as DARPA. Most actual developers work on FreeBSD as a hobby, so they can program things more correctly than they are allowed to do at their day job. The deadlines FreeBSD has are announced months or years in advance, and developers set their own work habits and their own level of contribution.

Many of us are not developers, but work on some other part of FreeBSD instead. Since I started this book, I became a member of the Documentation Project, the group responsible for writing the instructions. While code is nice, if nobody can learn how to use it, the system is pretty much useless! Other people answer questions on the mailing lists, or run support sites. We do it for satisfaction and enjoyment, or to give back some of what we've been given.

You're free to simply take what FreeBSD offers, and do as you will with it. After a while, many of us found that we wanted to return something to the group. This is how the community grows, and a growing community means that FreeBSD will continue.

## What Can You Do?

If you're interested in helping out, for whatever reason, there's a lot you can do. You don't have to be able to write a lick of code to contribute to FreeBSD. Every so often, someone posts on a mailing list, "I'd like to help, but I can't code." This lament has appeared repeatedly on the FreeBSD mailing lists since I started reading them in 1996, and probably far earlier. The standard response to these messages is silence. After all, if you've already decided you can't help there's really nothing for anyone to say.

No one's denying that the programmers are the spotlight heroes of FreeBSD. Many of these people have impressive skills, and most of us could never even dream of being the next Bruce Evans. Matt Dillon rightfully collected copious kudos for his stunning response to a bug report from Apple Computer. Each BSD team has its own tales of coding heroism. If you can't program your way out of a wet paper bag, however, you can still help. The basic question is, "What can you do?" Not "What does the project need?", not "Wouldn't it be cool if my favorite OS did such-and-such?", not "What feature do you want?"; what skills do you have right now? Chances are those skills can be valuable to any BSD project, or to any other free-software project.

For example, I've worked for years in computer support. I've spent a few years trying to master programming, mainly to get out of the support arena. While I've moved up, and am perilously close to management these days, I'm still deeply interested in computer internals. Mastery of operating system internals comes from reading the code. For years, I believed that I couldn't contribute to FreeBSD until I learned to code as well as some of the Secret Kernel Masters.

I also do a truly unhealthy amount of writing. I'm good at it. One day I decided to try to write a FreeBSD technical article, and it was snapped up by a magazine. Since then I've published hundreds of pages about FreeBSD. People know my name. I'm a respected contributor, and I've never written a line of code.

What do you do well? Leverage that skill. It will be appreciated.

### If Nothing Else . . .

If you truly have no useful skills, and you have no other ideas, just reread this book and the FreeBSD FAQ, subscribe to FreeBSD-questions@FreeBSD.org, and help other users. I started this way. If you elect to do this, I encourage you to politely guide people to existing information resources. When someone asks a question that is in the FAQ, give them a URL to the FAQ's main page. If the question has been asked before, suggest that they search the mailing list archives. If you can teach people to help themselves, we can reduce mailing list traffic. (As someone subscribed to 13 different FreeBSD lists, I have to say that reducing mailing list traffic is good.) As the old saying goes, teach them to fish and we'll sell them fishhooks. After answering mailing list questions for a while, you'll start to see things that the Project needs. One of those needs will match your skills.

When you see a problem that you think you can solve, stop for a moment and ponder it. If necessary, make a note of it and come back to it the next day. Is this really something you can do? It doesn't matter how dumb or small it is; can you actually sit down with your professional tools and do it?

## Getting Things Done

Here's the big secret of getting things done in FreeBSD. Everything that it contains is there because somebody saw a need that he or she could fill, and did something about it. NetBSD and FreeBSD started when a bunch of 386BSD patch kit users got sick of waiting for the next release. Mike Smith is hammering ACPI (Advanced Configuration and Power Interface) support into FreeBSD 5.0 because he thinks it's important. I didn't ask permission from the FreeBSD project before starting to write articles about it. You don't ask before answering mailing list messages, and you don't have to ask before starting on a FreeBSD project. If your idea is large enough that you feel you'd like an outside opinion before starting work, use a mailing list.

First, search the mailing list archives for your idea. Read any previous discussion about it. Many projects are suggested, but never implemented. Chances are, someone else has had your inspiration before and abandoned it. If someone's previously brought up your idea, and it's been discussed and approved of, you can assume that you'd get the same reaction. If the discussion is old enough that it appears the project died stillborn, start working.

For example, every so often someone sends email to the FreeBSD-hackers mailing list suggesting that IBM's JFS (journaled file system) be ported to FreeBSD. This is generally considered to be a Good Thing. The person goes away and is never heard from again. Now, porting a filesystem is a lot of work and requires a very particular skill set. It's not surprising that a lot of people have given it a try, and failed. But you don't need to send yet another message asking if it's a good idea. If you have the skills to do it, go for it! You'd meet nothing but delight if you posted a message on FreeBSD-hackers saying, "At such-and-such URL, you can find my initial patches for porting JFS to FreeBSD. I can mount a drive, create files, but upon creating a directory weird things happen. This may destroy your data, fry your kernel, and upset your pets. I would appreciate any comments."

### Second Opinions

If nobody's previously beaten your idea into the ground, and you still want a second opinion, ask on a mailing list. If you really want their attention, you need to be very brief and to-the-point. Most truly useful ideas can be summarized in a single sentence, or two at the most; anything after that is implementation details. Remember, some people get over two thousand pieces of email a day. A simple post saying, "Hey, would people find this useful?" is a great way to tell the difference between a boneheaded waste of time and a serious need.

Avoid suggestions that boil down to, "Why doesn't someone else do the work for this?" Most of these suggestions fall into three categories: obvious ("Hey, wouldn't it be cool if we supported the CPU in my automobile?"), foolish ("Why don't we have a kernel option READMYMINDANDDOWHATI-WANT?"), or both ("Why not support my Sinclair ZX80?"). In either case, the person asking is almost always completely unqualified to actually do anything about the matter, and doesn't even offer to buy a drink for those who can. You can generally rest assured that the people who are qualified to do the work have considered these ideas, and are either doing something about it or are working on more important tasks.

You can't expect a thousand people to respond with, "It's a great idea." The mailing lists are public discussion boards. If everyone agrees with a message, they won't all post "me too!" But if you get a few people agreeing with you, and nobody says, "Your concept is so awful that it simultaneously sucks and blows," you can generally assume that it's a decent idea. This is the closest thing FreeBSD has to "management buy-in." You can consider this full-blown approval.

Occasionally, someone might write you back saying, "I think Fred's working on that; why don't you drop him a line?" You might find that you can join an existing effort. Other people will want to discuss the implementation with you. You can take this as approval; they wouldn't bother discussing the fine details if they didn't like the idea.

The same sort of thing applies to every portion of the project. Can you translate the documentation into Sanskrit? Yep. Can you start a users' group in Topeka? Absolutely. If no such project exists, go do it.

## Do It!

This is perhaps the most vital part. Once you have buy-in, shut up and do it. We can talk all day about your project, but it's wasted keystrokes unless something comes out of it. Most of the ideas I've seen on the FreeBSD lists die on the vine. There is a huge amount of basic grunt work that can be done. Nobody bothers to do it, so it doesn't happen. All of the BSDs—indeed, all open-source projects—suffer from this to some extent. Non-programmers can help greatly by simply picking some little hole and doing the work to fill it. Some people set up independent Web sites, such as Dan Langille's excellent FreeBSD Diary (http://www.FreeBSDDiary.org). The committers and contributors directly enhance the bits that the Project produces. Others are just known as "that dude who hangs out on the mailing list and helps people with ppp." All are absolutely vital. Your help will make FreeBSD prosper and grow.

I look forward to seeing you on the mailing lists.

# APPENDIX:
# SOME USEFUL SYSCTL MIBS

This appendix is a dictionary of some useful sysctl MIBs. The tools for manipulating MIBs are discussed in Chapter 4. (When a MIB is detailed elsewhere in this book, reference is made to the appropriate chapter.) Your system certainly has many more sysctls than these, but the ones described here are the ones I frequently trip over in day-to-day work.

**WARNING** *Thoughtless use of sysctls can easily damage or destroy a working system. For example, if you set a limit on resources below the amount being used, you can crash the system in a fairly spectacular manner. Be sure you understand the implications of what you're doing before setting sysctls.*

When writing this appendix, I was tempted to only describe sysctls that are safe for new administrators, but doing so would have limited the utility of this section. Instead, I'm asking you to please take the dangers of sysctl fiddling to heart. If you don't understand what a sysctl does, don't play with it!

For example, some sysctls allow you to adjust vnode operations. Attempts to fine-tune vnodes will most probably harm system performance, but there are situations where you will want to do exactly that. Similarly, don't go rummaging through the virtual memory system unless you understand virtual memory! Search the man pages and mailing list archives for further details on individual sysctls before playing with them.

*Some sysctls are described as "toggles." In this case, a value of 1 means that the sysctl provides the service described. A setting of 0 means that the service is disabled.*

Without further ado, here are the sysctls, each followed by a typical value and an explanation of what it does.

```
kern.maxvnodes: 20973
set at: /boot/loader.conf
```

The maximum number of *vnodes* (virtual filesystem nodes) the system can have open simultaneously.

```
kern.maxproc: 1044
set at: /boot/loader.conf
```

The maximum number of processes that the system can be running at any one time.

```
kern.maxfiles: 2088
set at: runtime
```

The maximum number of files that the system can have open at any one time.

```
kern.argmax: 65536
set at: read-only
```

The maximum number of bytes you can use in an argument to execve(2). Basically, this is the maximum number of characters you can use in a single command line. You might run up against this in some unusual circumstances. If you do, please see xargs(1).

```
kern.securelevel: -1
set at: runtime or /etc/rc.conf
```

The current kernel security level. See Chapter 7.

```
kern.maxfilesperproc: 2088
set at: runtime
```

The maximum number of files any one process can open.

```
kern.maxprocperuid: 1043
set at: runtime
```

The maximum number of processes one user ID can run.

```
kern.dumpdev: /dev/ad0s1b
set at: /etc/rc.conf
```

The name of the swap device where a kernel panic will be dumped, as set by
dumpon(8) during the boot process. The swap partition must be larger than or
equal to the system's physical memory. We discuss dumping and panics in some
detail in Chapter 20.

```
kern.ipc.somaxconn: 128
set at: runtime
```

The maximum number of new connections the system can accept at any one
time. The default is 128. If you're running a heavily loaded server, kick this up
to 512 or even 1024.

```
kern.ipc.maxsockets: 2088
set at: /boot/loader.conf
```

The total number of sockets available on the system.

```
kern.logsigexit: 1
set at:  runtime
```

When a program exits abnormally, it usually sends a signal. When this toggle is
set, the name of the program and the exiting signal are logged to /var/log/
messages.

```
kern.init_path: /sbin/init:/sbin/oinit:/sbin/init.bak:/stand/sysinstall
set at: /boot/loader.conf
```

Init(8) is the process that actually starts the system. If you've damaged your system (say, during a source upgrade gone very bad), you can use this sysctl to
offer another path to an init program. If you're doing this, however, you're
probably in very bad shape.

```
kern.module_path: /;/boot/;/modules/
set at: runtime
```

The path where kldload(8) checks for kernel modules.

```
kern.timecounter.method: 0
set at: runtime
```

FreeBSD has two different methods to determine the time since the system
booted. One is extremely accurate, but takes more system resources to use. The
other is faster, but not as accurate. The difference between the two is measured in
milliseconds, but if you're using an application that requires extremely precise tim-
ing, those milliseconds can make a difference. Set this sysctl to 1 to use the slow,
hyper-accurate method. The default is good enough for almost all applications.

```
kern.coredump: 1
set at: runtime
```

This toggle controls kernel core dumps. When set to 1, the kernel will dump the core on a panic. See Chapter 20 to find out what to do with it.

```
kern.quantum: 100000
set at: runtime
```

The maximum number of microseconds a process can run for if other processes are waiting for CPU time. If you're considering changing this, you are probably doing something wrong.

```
kern.filedelay: 30
set at: runtime
```

Controls how often the system synchronizes file data between the vnode buffer cache and the disk. This one is for experienced systems administrators only!

```
kern.dirdelay: 29
set at: runtime
```

Controls how often the system synchronizes directory data from the vnode buffer cache to the disk. Again, for experienced systems admins only!

```
kern.metadelay: 28
set at: runtime
```

Controls how often the system synchronizes filesystem metadata from the vnode buffer cache and the disk. Again, this is for experienced systems administrators only!

```
vm.v_free_min: 582
set at: runtime
```

The minimum number of pages of cache and free memory that must be available before a process waiting on memory will be awakened.

```
vm.v_free_target: 2513
set at: runtime
```

The total number of pages of free and cache memory that the virtual memory manager tries to keep or exceed.

```
vm.v_free_reserved: 185
set at: runtime
```

If the number of pages of free memory falls below this reserved value, running a process will tell the virtual memory manager to start swapping out memory.

```
vm.v_inactive_target: 3769
set at: runtime
```

The number of pages of memory that the virtual memory system will try to free up when it kicks in.

```
vm.v_cache_min: 2513
set at: runtime
```

The minimum desired size of the virtual memory cache queue.

```
vm.v_cache_max: 5026
set at: runtime
```

The maximum desired size of the virtual memory cache queue.

```
vm.swap_enabled: 1
set at: /boot/loader.conf
```

This controls the use of swap space. If set to 0, your system will not swap. If your swap disk is damaged, or if you're running -current and someone broke swapping, you might want to try this.

```
vm.swap_idle_enabled: 0
vm.swap_idle_threshold1: 2
vm.swap_idle_threshold2: 10
set at: runtime
```

If you're constantly swapping on a large system, setting the swap_idle_enabled sysctl tells the virtual memory manager to pull idle processes into virtual memory more quickly than other processes. The threshold sysctls tell the system how many seconds to wait before considering different sorts of processes idle. The defaults are probably fine; just enabling vm.swap_idle_enabled should do the trick. Do not enable this unless you're having heavy virtual memory use!

```
vfs.vmiodirenable: 1
set at: runtime
```

Allows FFS to use the virtual memory system to cache directory lookups, increasing disk performance. Combined with the directory hashing code and soft updates, this increases disk access by as much as 6000 percent.

```
vfs.usermount: 0
set at: runtime
```

If set, users may mount filesystems. This allows people to use floppy disks and CD-ROMs. The user must own the mount point.

```
net.inet.ip.forwarding: 0
set at: runtime
```

Controls the kernel's ability to forward packets. If you have multiple network cards, you might want your FreeBSD system to act as a gateway, router, or firewall. When set, the system will forward packets internally. You can turn forwarding on and off at will.

```
net.inet.ip.redirect: 1
set at: runtime
```

Toggles the ability to send ICMP redirect packets if the system is providing routing services. It has no effect if the system is not performing routing.

```
net.inet.ip.ttl: 64
set at: runtime
```

The maximum number of hops any non-ICMP protocol can take across the network.

```
net.inet.ip.sourceroute: 0
set at: runtime
```

Toggles forwarding of source-routed packets.

```
net.inet.ip.accept_sourceroute: 0
set at: runtime
```

If set to 1, the system will accept source-routed packets aimed at it. If you don't know what source-routing is, just accept my word that this is not usually a good idea.

```
net.inet.ip.fastforwarding: 0
set at: runtime
```

If you're providing routing services, this sysctl greatly accelerates packet throughput. It does so by eliminating most of the sanity checks performed on packets and by completely bypassing any packet-filtering rules.

```
net.inet.icmp.drop_redirect: 0
set at: runtime
```

If set to 1, your system will ignore ICMP redirect packets. These are not commonly used on the public Internet, and only rarely used inside private networks.

```
net.inet.icmp.log_redirect: 0
set at: runtime
```

In normal circumstances, your system should never see an ICMP redirect. While they have legitimate administrative uses, if they're in use you'll know. Enabling this sysctl makes the system log any ICMP redirects it receives.

```
net.inet.icmp.bmcastecho: 1
set at: runtime
```

When set, the system will respond to ICMP requests to the broadcast address of a network—the highest-numbered address in the block of IP addresses. This is required for standards compliance, but was such a source of trouble that it's disabled by default now.

```
net.inet.tcp.rfc1323: 1
set at: runtime
```

Enables the window-scaling algorithms described in RFC 1323.

```
net.inet.tcp.rfc1644: 0
set at: runtime
```

Enables Transactional TCP, as described in RFC 1644.

```
net.inet.tcp.sendspace: 16384
net.inet.tcp.recvspace: 16384
set at: runtime
```

The number of bits reserved for send and receive buffers. Whenever a connection is opened, the system sets aside a send and a receive buffer for use by that connection. These values both default to 16384, or 16KB. If you have a small number of high-bandwidth connections, you can increase these sysctl values. 32768 is a decent value in this case. Do not alter this sysctl if you have a large number of connections—you'll increase system load dramatically and kill your performance. These values are vital parts of the NMBCLUSTERS kernel memory calculation; if you increase them, you increase the amount of kernel memory set aside for mbufs. Crank these up too high, and you can panic your kernel during boot.

```
net.inet.tcp.log_in_vain: 0
set at: runtime
```

Logs attempts to connect to any TCP port where no program is listening.

```
net.inet.tcp.blackhole: 0
set at: runtime
```

By default, TCP/IP returns an error code when you attempt to connect to a closed port. This shows up as a "connection reset by peer" error. If you set this to 1, attempts to connect to a closed TCP port are dropped, but no error is sent. This slows down ports scans, and can add some semblance of security to your system. It is not a replacement for packet filtering, however!

```
net.inet.tcp.delayed_ack: 1
set at: runtime
```

Tells the system to try to include the TCP connection teardown information on a data packet, rather than sending additional packets to signal the end of the connection.

```
net.inet.tcp.path_mtu_discovery: 1
set at: runtime
```

Enables Path MTU discovery.

```
net.inet.tcp.slowstart_flightsize: 1
set at: runtime
```

Specifies the number of packets that can be sent during the slow-start portion of a TCP transaction across a wide area network.

```
net.inet.tcp.local_slowstart_flightsize: 65535
set at: runtime
```

This is the number of packets that can be sent during the slow-start portion of a TCP transaction across a local network.

```
net.inet.tcp.newreno: 1
set at: runtime
```

Toggles RFC2582 connection recovery, also known as the TCP NewReno Algorithm.

```
net.inet.tcp.do_tcpdrain: 1
set at: runtime
```

Tells the system to flush packets from the reassembly queue when it is low on mbufs.

```
net.inet.tcp.always_keepalive: 1
set at: runtime
```

If you set this to 1, old dead connections will eventually be found and killed. It increases the amount of network traffic by a smidgeon, but will clean up many situations that come from having a server up for 30 months straight. If set to 0, connections will remain alive even on unreliable connections. This is a trade-off between long-term stability and short-term convenience.

```
net.inet.udp.log_in_vain: 0
set at: runtime
```

Logs attempts to connect to any UDP port where no program is listening.

```
net.inet.udp.blackhole: 0
set at: runtime
```

By default, TCP/IP returns an error code when you attempt to connect to a closed port. This shows up as a "connection reset by peer" error. If you set this to 1, attempts to connect to a closed UDP port are dropped, but no error is sent. This slows down ports scans, and can add some semblance of security to your system. It is not a replacement for packet filtering, however!

```
hw.ata.ata_dma
set at: /boot/loader.conf
```

Controls use of DMA in IDE devices. This is the modern standard. Set this to 0 if your hardware uses PIO instead of DMA. (If you have PIO hardware, you probably know it.)

```
hw.ata.wc
set at: /boot/loader.conf
```

Controls the use of write-caching in IDE drives. Setting it to 1 will improve performance at the cost of data integrity in the case of a system crash.

```
hw.ata.tags: 0
set at: /boot/loader.conf
```

Enables tagged queuing. Only certain IBM hard drives support this. If you have it, it will be clearly marked on the packaging.

```
hw.ata.atapi_dma: 0
set at: /boot/loader.conf
```

Controls the use of the DMA access model in ATAPI devices. Check your hardware manual to see if your hardware supports DMA. ATAPI can have problems with DMA, so this defaults to "off". You can try it, but it might very well hang your system.

```
jail.set_hostname_allowed: 1
set at: runtime
```

Controls whether jail owners can change the hostname of their jails. See Chapter 8.

```
jail.socket_unixiproute_only: 1
set at: runtime
```

Controls whether jail owners can use protocols other than TCP/IP. See Chapter 8.

```
jail.sysvipc_allowed: 0
```

Controls whether jail owners can use System V IPC calls. See Chapter 8.

```
compat.linux
set at: read-only
```

These sysctls provide information for the Linux compatibility kernel module. See Chapter 11.

# INDEX

*NOTE: Italicized page numbers refer to illustrations or tables.*

## Symbols

## A

apache13+ipv6 option, 348
apache13-modssl option, 349
apache13 option, 348
apache13-ssl option, 349
apache2 option, 349
apachectl command, 365–66
apache-jserv option, 348
Apache Web server, 348–67
    configuration files, 349–50
    controlling, 364–67
    controlling HTTP requests,
        361–62
    directory configuration, 356–57
    directory features, 357–61
    password-protecting directories,
        362–63
    server-wide settings, 350–56
    and SSL, 363–64
APOP, 341, 344–45
application binary interface (ABI),
    264, 265–67
application layer, 92
*Applied Cryptograph* (Schneier), 309
apropos command, 29
archives, 48–49
A record, 287
ARP (Address Resolution Protocol),
    91, 96
arp command, 96
Arrow (email reader), 512
ASCII transfers, 375
"ast" devices, 38
asynchronous mounts, 385
Asynchronous Transfer Mode
    (ATM), 91, 216
ATA_STATIC_ID option, 73
atime, 385
ATM (Asynchronous Transfer
    Mode), 91, 216
atomic clocks, 321
AuthConfig statement, 360
AuthDBMUserFile directive, 363
authentication, 130–32, 340
auth facility, 444
AuthName, 362
authority section, of dig, 281
authpriv facility, 444, 446

"available swap and total swap"
    option, 465
avm column, 434
axfr keyword, 300

## B

backup and recovery, 37–60
    backup programs, 42–48
        dump/restore, 45–48
        tar, 42–45
    fixit disk, 59–60
    recording what happened, 51
    restoring from an archive, 48–51
    revision control, 51–57
        getting older versions, 54
        ident and ident strings, 56–57
        reviewing file's revision
            history, 56
        viewing log messages, 55–56
    single-user mode, 57–59
    system backups, 38
    tape devices, 38–41
backup kernel, 72
bandwidth, 303–8, 425
Barrett, Daniel, 314
base 2, 94
bash, 23
b column, 434
benchmarking, 437
Berkley Packet Filter, 80
B flag, 451
BGL (Big Giant Lock), 274–75
Big Giant Lock (BGL), 274–75
binary branding, 266
binary math, 94
binary transfers, 375
binary types, 260–61
binary values, 65
/bin command, 59
/bin/csh, 206
BIND (Berkeley Internet Name
    Daemon), 286–92
    configuring named, 288–92
    forward and reverse DNS,
        286–87

## G

## H

# K

k5 (CPU Type), *204*

k6 (CPU Type), *204*

k6-2 (CPU Type), *204*

k7 (CPU Type), *204*

KDE (desktop environment), 510

KeepAlive option, 320

keep state option, 169

kern.flp file, 4

kern.hostname, 63

kern_securelevel="-1" option, 224

kern_securelevel_enable="NO" option, 224

KERNCONF variable, 122

kernel, 61–87

   *See also* system panics and crashes

   access to memory, 139

   adding to, 84–85

   automatic building of, preventing, 206

   bad, 478

   booting an alternate kernel, 83–84

   building, 80–83, 207

   configuring, 63–69

      with Loader.conf, 66–68

      manually configuring loader, 68–69

      sysctl program, 63–66

   current security level, 524

   customizing, 71–80

      backup kernel, 72

      device entries, 78–80

      editing kernel files, 72–77

      multiple processors, 77–78

      preparation, 71–72

      USB devices, 80

   debugging, 476–77, 481–82

   loading and unloading modules in multi-user mode, 70

   packet forwarding ability, 528

   replacement, preventing, 146

   saving images, 223

   securelevels, 146–49

   sharing, 87

   support for CIFS, 500

   and symmetric multiprocessing, 273

   tweaking performance, 85–87

   updating, 122

   what it is, 62

kernel.debug file, 477

kern facility, 444

kern root, *64*

keyboard, options for, 222

key fingerprint, 316

keymap="NO" option, 222

key option, 233–34

keywords

   client, 158–59

   and configurations, 168–69

   finding software by, 233–34

kill -15 -1 command, 182

killall snmpd command, 260

killstyle signal, 452

kldload tool, 70, 80, 525

kldstat command, 70

kldunload command, 70

kmem group, 139

knobs, 217

KNOWN keyword, 158

koffice (office suite), 513

KTRACE option, 77

# L

L2 cache, 84

Label option, 401

Langille, Dan, 520

language choice, 30

LAST_ACK,FIN_WAIT_1 state, 105

layers, network, 89–92

ld(aout) run-time linker, 261

ld_library_path, 262–63

ldconfig_paths="/usr/lib/compat /usr/X11R6/lib /usr/local/lib" option, 224

ldconfig tool, 260–63

lease requests, 192

legal restrictions, software, 234–35

less command, 375

# U

with short statement, 168
-w option, 395
Word, Microsoft (word processor
     software), 235n3
WorkDir directive, 462
workgroup keyword, 502
write caching, 67–68, 390–91
write-caching, 531
write permission, 140, 141, 142, 143
-Ww flag, 156
www-supfile, 117

# X

-x (extract all files from an archive)
     mode, 43–44
X11 forwarding, 318, 320
X11R6 (graphic interface), 509
Xevil (software game), 514
xf86cfg tool, 509
xf86config tool, 509
xf86Setup tool, 509
XFree86 (graphic interface), 22,
     509
-x option, 287, 288
xterm (terminal window), 510
X Window System, 15, 208

# Y

-y flag, 44

# Z

-z (gzip) flag, 44
-Z flag, 451
-z flag, 478
zones, of named.conf, 289–90
    setting up multiple, 291–92
    zone files, 292–95
zone transfer, 301

# THE BOOK OF VMWARE
## The Complete Guide to the VMware Workstation

*by* BRIAN WARD

This comprehensive guide to installing and running VMware includes sections on device emulation; configuring the guest operating system; networking and file transfers; and troubleshooting common questions and answers.

2002, 264 PP., $39.95 ($55.95 CDN)
ISBN 1-886411-72-7

# THE BOOK OF SCSI
## 2nd Edition
## I/O for the New Millennium

*by* GARY FIELD, PETER M. RIDGE, ET AL.

This thoroughly updated second edition offers down-to-earth instructions for installing, implementing, utilizing, and maintaining SCSI on a PC.

2000, 428 PP. W/CD-ROM, $49.95 ($77.50 CDN)
ISBN 1-886411-10-7

# THE LINUX COOKBOOK
## Tips and Techniques for Everyday Use

*by* MICHAEL STUTZ

This is a complete reference to all of the free software that comes with Linux, with sections on printing, converting and managing files, editing and formatting text; working with digital audio; creating and manipulating graphics, and connecting to the Internet.

2001, 396 PP., $29.95 ($44.95 CDN)
ISBN 1-886411-48-4

# THE LINUX PROBLEM SOLVER

## Hands-on Solutions for Systems Administrators

*by* BRIAN WARD

This book is a must-have for solving technical problems related to printing, networking, back-up, crash recovery, and copiling or upgrading a kernel. The cd-rom supports the book with configuration files and numerous programs not included in many Linux distributions.

2000, 283 PP. W/CD-ROM, $34.95 ($53.95 CDN)
ISBN 1-886411-35-2

# THE BOOK OF WEBMIN

## . . . Or How I Learned to Stop Worrying and Love Unix

*by* JOE COOPER

This comprehensive guide shows you how to use Webmin's unique features, including integrating the most popular services (like Apache, BIND, Sendmail, and more) as well as the standard system features (such as network configuration, disk configuration, users and groups, etc.). Tutorials show how to accomplish common tasks with each service.

NOVEMBER 2002, 320 PP. $34.95 ($52.95 CDN)
ISBN 1-886411-92-1

**Phone:**

1 (800) 420-7240 OR
(415) 863-9900
MONDAY THROUGH FRIDAY,
9 A.M. TO 5 P.M. (PST)

**Fax:**

(415) 863-9950
24 HOURS A DAY,
7 DAYS A WEEK

**Email:**

SALES@NOSTARCH.COM

**Web:**

HTTP://WWW.NOSTARCH.COM

**Mail:**

NO STARCH PRESS
555 DE HARO STREET, SUITE 250
SAN FRANCISCO, CA 94107
USA

Distributed in the U.S. by Publishers Group West